UNION STEAMSHIPS
Remembered
1920 - 1958

Union Steamships

Remembered
1920 - 1958

by
ARTHUR M. TWIGG

"It was a darned good service."
Walter Sovde

Copyright © 1997

All rights reserved. No part of this book may be reproduced in
any form without permission in writing from the publisher,
except by a reviewer who may quote brief passages in a review
to be printed in newspapers or magazines.

Front cover painting by
Michael Dean
Typesetting and layout by
Jean Robinson
Printed and bound in Canada by
Friesens

Canadian Cataloguing in Publication Data

Twigg, Art, 1923-
Union Steamships remembered, 1920 - 1958

Includes index.
ISBN 1-55056-516-8

1. Union Steamship Company of British Columbia--History.
2. Union Steamship Company of British Columbia--Biography.
3. Union Steamships Limited--History. 4. Union Steamships
Limited--Biography. 5. Steamboats--British Columbia--Pacific
Coast--History. I. Title.
HE945.U5T94 1997   387.5'06'5711   C97-910132-8

Published by
A.M. Twigg
4113A Twigg Road
Campbell River, B.C. V9H 1E9
250-923-6704

DEDICATION

to all mariners who have sailed the B.C. coast over the years,
especially those who served aboard the Union Steamships
both ashore and afloat, many of whom helped the Company
to be rightfully known as "The Lifeline of the Coast"

and

to members of my family who stood by me over the past seven years,
offering me encouragement and help along the way:
my mother, Mrs. R.O. Twigg
my wife, Gloria Twigg, who unfortunately died in April 1996
my two sons, John Twigg and Alan Twigg, successful writers in their own right

Freight wagon at Union Wharf 1922

ACKNOWLEDGEMENTS

After seven years of work, the time has come for me to express my gratitude to the many people who so willingly helped me to complete my book about the Union Steamship Company and its personnel. The enthusiasm that I received at every turn was simply amazing.

Following, listed alphabetically, are the names of people and organizations who assisted me in this project:

John Allan, for his drawing and technical information; Marilynn Ames, for typing assistance; Mike Benson, ex U.S.S. Purser, the second person I interviewed, who loaned me his collection of U.S.S. newsletters; Lorrie Belveal of Sointula who has a great collection of U.S.S. memorabilia; Clinton H. Betz in Washington state who gave me some beautiful photographs of Union ships; Bob Blackmore of Tex Guard Heritage Video for research on the *Cheslakee* sinking;

the staff of the Campbell River Museum, especially Irene Ross, as well as Sandra Parish and Linda Hogarth; Mike Clements of Gibsons for his photographs and photography work; Bas Collins of West Vancouver who loaned me a collection of early newspaper clippings; and Computor Smith who transcribed my old Commodore disks onto compatible I.B.M. format;

Michael Dean of Ladysmith for his artwork and cover painting, as well as his enthusiastic support from start to finish; Bill Etchell who kept supplying me with newspaper clippings about U.S.S. as he came across them at the Vancouver Maritime Museum;

Wayne Grey for his indispensable help with my computer and related problems; Lorne Groner who helped keep my old Commodore computer going in the early days; Mr. & Mrs. K. Gumley for accommodation over a five year period on my trips to Vancouver;

Bob Hackett, whose father was the Union agent at Sechelt for years, for all his historical background and cassette tapes; Patrick Hind for his early help with photographs; Captain Charlie Lewis for his expert advice and proof-reading; Sam Johnson, who was Curator of Elphinstone Museum when I called in to do research;

John and Patricia Horne for proof-reading, pictures and historical facts; Russell Kelly, editor of B.C. Bookworld, a successful writer himself, for editing and typing; Bob and Faye Logan for computer help and pictures.

Ken McPhearson of Port Hope, Ontario, who provided wartime details on the three corvettes which the U.S.S. Co. converted to passenger-freight ships, namely the *Coquitlam, Camosun* and *Chilcotin;* Mr. and Mrs. Callum McLeod for lodging and sustenance while doing research in Vancouver;

David Nuttall, successful lawyer and author, for advice and exceptional moral support when I needed it most; Ed Roach, son of well-known U.S.S. Captain Harry Roach, for his proof-reading, corrections, pictures and news clippings;

Jean Robinson and Earl Schmidt of Friesens for their assistance with the design, typesetting and printing;

Denis Shaw, former Purser in the fleet, the first person I interviewed, whose knowledge and collection of pictures, news clippings, etc. was invaluable to my effort; Ben Smith, former engineer with the U.S.S. Co., whose humour, engineering background and research became indispensable in writing about the engineering department aboard the ships and proof-reading;

Captain John Smith, who became a good friend. After interviewing him early in my research, he, above anyone, became my greatest source of general and technical information. He was a tireless researcher and his background knowledge of the personnel and ships was second-to-none. His grandfather and uncle were both Masters in the Union fleet. Unfortunately he died May 26, 1995;

Walter Sovde, my friend, who said "Art, you ought to write a book"; Alan Twigg for his literary expertise; and John Twigg for rewriting and editing;

Of all the people who helped me so willingly, I don't think I could have completed the book without the marvellous photography work done for me by Mrs. Trudy Vince, wife of Gordon Vince, a former Engineer with the U.S.S. Co. Trudy set up her own studio in their home at Fanny Bay and commenced to turn out over a thousand photographs for me;

Cecil Woods, member of the World Ship Society, who gave me enthusiastic personal support as well as picture research at the Maritime Museum;

Once I started on the book, one of my first stops was at the Vancouver Maritime Museum where I met the Curator, Leonard McCann. His cooperation and immediate support for my work was invaluable and at the same time very heart warming. In time a new Director for the Museum was appointed, Jim Delgado, and his support, both personally and on behalf of the Museum, in the end was the icing on the cake. I also wish to thank the Maritime Museum in Vancouver for their permission to use ships' specifications and also the origins of Native place names used on many Union ships.

> This work is intended as a reference book. It is a detailed compilation of ships and personnel involved with the U.S.S. Co. from 1920 to 1958. As such, some of the stories relate to both ships and personnel and I have deliberately included them in both parts of the book.

FOREWORD

by Norman Hacking

It all started in a humble way when Vancouver was a small sawmilling community dependent on the waterfront for its existence. A group of local sea captains formed the Burrard's Inlet Towing Co. to provide a primitive ferry service between the sawmills on the south and the sawmills on the north shores of the inlet and provide towage for the occasional windjammer which arrived to load lumber for foreign ports, most of which was harvested on the present shores of Vancouver city and North Vancouver.

With the coming of the Canadian Pacific Railway in 1887 the village of Gastown became the international boom town of Vancouver. A year later a service to Australasia was inaugurated by the Union Steamship Co. of New Zealand. With the close cooperation of the New Zealand company, the Burrard's Inlet Towing Co. became the Union Steamship Company of British Columbia Ltd. in 1890. Money was raised from British shareholders, who optimistically bought the little passenger steamer *Cutch* and ordered three small freighters in Scotland, built in sections, which were reassembled on the shores of False Creek. They were completed with the same distinctive funnel colours and livery of the New Zealand company of the same name.

Prior to the arrival of the Union Company of British Columbia the logging camps and small outports north of Vancouver were entirely dependent upon the port of Victoria. Creation of the new company made all the difference in the world, and the Union became the principal lifeline between the far remote north and the terminus of the C.P.R.

The Company acquired the admiration and respect of all B.C. coast dwellers until it ceased to exist in 1959. Loggers and fishermen relied on its ships for their very existence. Officers and crew were known for their friendship and reliability as they called at remote ports as far north as Alaska.

And so the Union Steamship Co. of B.C., like its prototype in New Zealand, came to an end and is now remembered with affection by every old-timer on the coast. Their number is dwindling, and Art Twigg, an old Union hand, has done his level best to recall the colourful memories of the past.

Norman Hacking of North Vancouver, British Columbia's foremost maritime journalist, has written several books, including The Princess Story: A Century and a Half of West Coast Shipping, *with W.K. Lamb.*

CONTENTS

PART I
SHIPS OF THE UNION STEAMSHIPS FLEET
1920 - 1958

S.S. *Coquitlam I*	3	M.V. *Comox II*	55
S.S. *Cassiar I*	5	S.S. *Cardena*	57
S.S. *Camosun I*	8	S.S. *Lady Alexandra*	70
S.S. *Cowichan*	13	S.S. *Catala*	78
S.S. *Cheslakee*	17	S.S. *Lady Cecilia*	88
S.S. *Cheakamus*	22	S.S. *Lady Cynthia*	95
S.S. *Chelohsin*	26	M.V. *Lady Rose*	100
S.S. *Venture*	32	S.S. *Camosun II*	107
S.S. *Chasina*	37	S.S. *Cassiar II*	110
S.S. *Chilco*	39	The White Boats Era	113
S.S. *Lady Pam*	41	S.S. *Coquitlam II*	118
S.S. *Capilano II*	46	S.S. *Camosun III*	123
S.S. *Cheam*	50	S.S. *Chilcotin*	127
S.S. *Lady Evelyn*	52		

PART II
SEAGOING PERSONNEL
1920 - 1958

1 Masters and Mates	134
2 Engineers	273
3 Pursers, Assistant Pursers and Freight Clerks	305
4 Chief Stewards, Waiters/Stewards	353
5 Deck Crews	373

THE END OF AN ERA 418

ENDNOTES	420
INDEX OF SHIPS	422
INDEX OF PERSONNEL	424
MAP	427

Chilcotin and *Lady Cynthia* at Gillies Bay
August 1950

(Ashmore Collection)

PART I

SHIPS OF THE UNION STEAMSHIP FLEET
Operating from 1920 to 1958

S.S. *Coquitlam 1*	1892 - 1923	M.V. *Comox II*	1924 - 1943
S.S. *Cassiar 1*	1901 - 1923	S.S. *Cardena*	1923 - 1958
S.S. *Camosun 1*	1905 - 1935	S.S. *Lady Alexandra*	1924 - 1953
S.S. *Cowichan*	1908 - 1925	S.S. *Catala*	1925 - 1953
S.S. *Cheslakee*	1910 - 1913 #1	S.S. *Lady Cecilia*	1925 - 1951
S.S. *Cheakamus*	1913 - 1942	S.S. *Lady Cynthia*	1925 - 1957
S.S. *Chelohsin*	1911 - 1949	S.S. *Lady Sylvia*	1937 #3
S.S. *Venture*	1911 - 1946	M.V. *Lady Rose*	1937 - 1951
S.S. *Chasina*	1917 - 1923	S.S. *Camosun II*	1940 - 1945
S.S. *Chilco*	1913 - 1935 #2	S.S. *Cassiar II*	1940 - 1951
S.S. *Lady Pam*	1935 - 1946	S.S. *Coquitlam II*	1946 - 1957
S.S. *Capilano II*	1920 - 1949	S.S. *Camosun III*	1945 - 1958
S.S. *Cheam*	1920 - 1921	S.S. *Chilcotin*	1947 - 1958
S.S. *Lady Evelyn*	1923 - 1936		

All but two of the above listed ships were steamships. The *Comox II* and the *Lady Rose* were diesel fueled motor vessels.
1. The *Cheslakee* sank at Van Anda in 1913; she was raised, lengthened and renamed the *Cheakamus*.
2. The *Chilco* was formerly operated by the All Red Line. Her name was the *Santa Maria*. Union Steamships bought out this company in 1917 and renamed her the *Chilco*. She was remodeled in 1935 and renamed the *Lady Pam*.
3. This ship was launched and named the *Lady Sylvia*, but it was found that there was another ship using this name, so it was renamed the *Lady Rose*.

Ship Colours

1800 - 1913   Green hull, white super structure with red and black funnel patterned after U.S.S. Co. of New Zealand.

1913 - 1958   Black hull, white super structure with red and black funnel.

1945 - 1947   Three new ships were delivered being the *Coquitlam II*, *Camosun III* and the *Chilcotin*. They were painted all white and were referred to as the "white boats." After being in service for a while, the white was found to be impractical so their hulls were painted black.

1956   An efficiency expert was hired by the company and one of his first experiments was to paint the three converted corvettes or "white boats" in three different colour tones using streaks and diagonal stripes.

1957   These three ships were then changed back to black hulls, white superstructure, with the familiar black and red funnels.

S.S. Coquitlam I

Coquitlam means "a small red salmon" after a fish that once teemed in the Coquitlam River but is now extinct. It was also the name of a Salish tribe from the north arm of the Fraser who spoke the Cowichan dialect. It is one of the few native names in the lower Fraser Valley still used as place names: Coquitlam and Port Coquitlam municipalities, the Coquitlam River and Mt. Coquitlam (1,766 m.).

In Union service 1892-1923; later as the Bervin 1939-50 Official No. 100205
Type: Steel screw freighter-passenger vessel. Hull prefabricated in sections by J. McArthur & Co., Glasgow. Launched from Union shipyard in Vancouver's Coal Harbour in 1892. Assembled by Henry Darling
Dimensions: Length 120.0', breadth 22.0', depth 9.6'. Gross tons 256
Engines: Bow McLachlan & Co., Paisley, Scotland. Compound 28 RHP. speed 10 knots maximum, 9 average
Capacities: Passenger licence 24 (deck); rebuilt for Alaskan service in 1897 to provide 93 berths with licence 157. Cargo capacity 300 tons

S.S. *Coquitlam*
(Vancouver Maritime Museum)

The *Coquitlam* was the last and largest of three ships whose hulls were prefabricated by J. McArthur & Co. and Bow McLachlan Co. in Glasgow. All three were prefabricated in sections brought over to Vancouver, B.C. on the S.S. *Grandholm* in 1891. She was assembled and launched in Vancouver's Coal Harbour in April 1892, all under the direction of Henry Darling. She was very economical to run and had a speed of nine knots.

Shortly after completing her sea trials, under the command of Captain E. McLellan, the *Coquitlam* was chartered by the Union Co. to a fishing company as a tender for the sealing fleet in the Gulf of Alaska. Despite warnings, the *Coquitlam* loaded sealskins in disputed waters. On June 22, 1892 she was seized by United States Customs with 6,000 sealskins aboard. She was escorted to Sitka, Alaska where charges were laid and a verdict of guilty was pronounced. The *Coquitlam* was towed to Port Townsend, Wash.

The case went on for 30 years and cost Union Steamships thousands of dollars, which the fledgling company could ill afford. The Company posted a large bond and the *Coquitlam* was released. Years later the Union Steamship Co. and the United States government agreed to a settlement of $48,000, a far cry from the $104,700 claimed by the ship's owners.

Upon returning to service under the Union flag in 1894, the *Coquitlam* was again chartered to a halibut fishing firm, carrying freight and passengers to northern ports. In 1897 her passenger accommodation was increased to 50. She then began a regular run to canneries on Rivers Inlet and the Skeena River. Then came the Gold Rush in the Klondike, and her passenger space was enlarged again, allowing her to carry 157 people. When the gold fever slackened she was returned to her old regular cannery service, alternating every 10 days with the *Capilano*. [1]

On May 26, 1909, the *Coquitlam* caught fire off Cape Roger Curtis Point, Bowen Island. The fire was aft and the crew finally got the best of the stubborn blaze. Although the woodwork and cabins were burned, she was able to proceed to her northern route.

The *Coquitlam* soon had the reputation of being the workhorse of the fleet. In 1917, she ran into some trouble while making a landing with supplies and coal for a new mine. The tide caught her and she was taken into a rock cliff, puncturing her side. She started to take on water and Captain Neil Gray quickly decided to make a run for a safe spot to beach her, but it was three miles away. Chief Engineer Freddie Smith kept the pumps going and they reached their destination, beached the ship, and were able to put a temporary patch inside her hull. She was refloated and even completed her run, delivering her freight and then returning to her home port, Vancouver. [2]

In 1918, in the middle of Queen Charlotte Sound, she lost her propeller. With no means of propulsion and no means of contacting anyone, the ship drifted. By chance the *Venture* came along, and towed her down to Alert Bay. They stranded her on the beach and under the able direction of Freddie Smith working in his bathing suit, a new propeller, which had been sent up from Vancouver, was installed. Again, once her new prop was on, she proceeded north to complete her freight run. [3]

It is interesting to note that in all three of these mishaps the *Coquitlam* carried on without going back to her home port. A workhorse indeed!

In August 1923, the Union Steamship Co. decided to sell the old *Coquitlam* to a new firm owned by Captain A. Berquist and C.D. Vincent. She was renamed the *Bervin,* a name derived from the first three letters of the new owners' last names. The *Bervin* was operated by the new owners very successfully, which became a thorn in the Union Company's side for the next 15 years. Captain Berquist dropped out of the partnership in 1926.

However, in 1939 the Union Steamship Co. acquired the Frank Waterhouse Company and as the *Bervin* was then part of their fleet, she once more was operated by the Union fleet until 1950, when she was sold to the Canadian Fishing Co. and converted into a fish barge. She had been operating on the B.C. coast for 58 years, which must be some sort of a record!

She was beached in 1959 as a breakwater in Trinity Bay on the north side of Malcolm Island. One old-timer remarked, "She's gone home to die, she's one of the last of the iron hulled ships in these parts. If she had been steel, she never would have lasted this long!"

S.S. Cassiar I

Cassiar is a corruption of casha or caska, "a creek." The district from which the name is taken contains many streams and extends along and north of the Stikine River between the Coast Range and the Rocky Mountains. The name Cassiar originated with the Caska Indians, a division of the Nahane people, and is said to have been corrupted from Caska by the French-Canadian explorer Thibert. Cassiar, the most famous of the Union fleet's names, was borne by three ships.

In Union service: 1901-23
Official No.: 103472
Type: Wooden passenger-freight vessel. Built 1901 at Wallace Shipbuilding Co., False Creek, Vancouver, using hull of J.R. McDonald, a schooner launched at Ballard, Wash. in 1890
Dimensions: Length 120.6', breadth 29.0', depth 6.9'. Gross tons 597
Engines: Bow McLachlan direct acting, inverted surface condensing, one multi-tubular boiler, single-ended amidships. Speed 9 knots. Coal burner, fuel consumption 17.5 miles/ton
Services: B.C. logging camp routes
Capacities: Passenger licence 144, cabin berths 42, also a loggers' saloon with open berths. Cargo 110 tons.

S.S. *Cassiar* at Campbell River circa 1901
(Elphinstone Museum)

Her hull was of wood and was formerly the *J.R. McDonald*, launched in Washington state in 1890. She had been severely wracked by a fire in her hold. When the Union Steamship Co. purchased her in 1901 she was rigged as a schooner. She was then

S.S. *Cassiar* as the *J.R. McDonald* 1890

converted into a 120-foot steamer at Wallace's Shipyards in Vancouver's Coal Harbour.

She was given the name *Cassiar* and was launched on Sept. 28, 1901. She proceeded to make this name famous up and down the coast. She was put into service immediately on the "logging camp" run and soon became known as the "loggers' palace."

On her maiden voyage the skipper was Captain Charles Moody, the Pilot George Gaisford, the Chief Engineer A.S. de Gruchy, and her first Purser was Percy Chick. Mr. Chick was later drowned. He was aboard the *Chehalis* when she was run down and capsized off Brockton Point.

In the early days of logging on the coast, served principally by the *Cassiar*, "the blood and thunder of battle roared along her deck." Arthur Jervis, an Irishman and a trained boxer known as the "Black Mate," was called upon to quiet many a logger. In later years Bill Hodgson, a short man with red hair, known as the "Red Mate" took over the difficult task. [4] One reason for all the commotion was that the *Cassiar* had a bar on board that quite often had to be closed because the rowdy crowd of loggers would become unruly from sitting at the bar far too long.

"The *Cassiar* used to come into the bay on a Sunday and in those days these boats had a bar and they could sell liquor, but they could only do so while the boat was underway. In this bay, they had two floats so men who wanted liquor would be on the float when the boat would come alongside. They'd climb on board, the ship would cast off its moorings and move to the other float which was 400-500 feet away, but it would take half an hour to get there. During that time the bar was open, so Sunday night in that camp there was a lot of liquor around." [5]

In 1907, the *Cassiar* was called upon to pick up the passengers from the *Comox*, which had run aground in fog on a reef at Cortes Island. She took the passengers to Heriot Bay and then they transferred to the *Coquitlam*, which took them on to their destinations.

"The Union Steamships' *Cassiar* has struck a rock in Surge Narrows during a heavy snowstorm," reported a Vancouver newspaper in a "Remember When" column dated 1960 about the *Cassiar* going aground on Jan. 12, 1910. "Lifeboats were swung ready to prepare to abandon ship but two hours later she was refloated and was able to continue her run to Vancouver."

It was said the *Cassiar I* was a lucky ship. Because her hull was made of wood, it was very resilient so she survived many a bump, but she did have strange behaviour at times. When approaching a dock to make a landing, sometimes her valves would stick and instead of slowing down, she would plough right ahead, perhaps into the wharf or go up on the beach.

She had only one serious mishap. She struck a rock at Trivett Island near Simoom

S.S. *Cassiar* aground at Trivett Island 1917 *(Farina Collection)*

Sound on Aug. 16, 1917 at 2:30 a.m. Records are at odds as to who was in charge of her when she went aground. In one place it reports Captain Robert Wilson was on the bridge and another says it was the pilot Jack Robinson. The second mate at the time was Lorne Godfrey. The chief engineer was Paddy Farina. The *Cassiar* was so badly damaged that the passengers had to be taken off in the lifeboats and rowed over to Simoom Sound, nearby. One of the ships' officers gave the following story to the *Vancouver World* newspaper published on Aug. 30, 1917:

"The vessel was proceeding as usual when suddenly she was brought up with a crash which quickly told us what had taken place. There was no panic at any stage. We had one woman on board going to Charles Creek Cannery. The officer said that after the boats were lowered, while the *Cassiar* was fast sinking and with perfect discipline, everyone held back until Mrs. Johnstone stepped into a lifeboat. Then the loggers piled into the boats. We rowed away reaching shore in a few minutes. How long it took for the vessel to find bottom I don't know. We couldn't see very well in the darkness and I don't know whether she was completely submerged when she settled. A good many of the passengers were able to save their valuables but others lost most of their baggage. Most of the crew lost everything."

The passengers who were landed at Simoom Sound were well cared for by the Postmaster J.W. Dunseith, with the help of the *Cassiar*'s cook. Some of the passengers made their way out on small boats from the area, but those who were still behind at Simoom Sound were picked up three days later by the *Cowichan*. The Purser aboard at the time of this sinking was Clarence Williams, who later became Assistant Wharf Agent on the Vancouver dock. He received commendation for his work in retrieving the ship's valuables and papers.

When daylight came the *Cassiar* was found to be badly damaged and at high tide only the tip of her bow was visible. The salvagers pulled her off into deep water so she submerged completely, they turned her around and pulled her gradually up on the beach, patching the holes as they appeared, and then pumped her out. She was then towed to Vancouver by the salvage tug *Salvor*. Her arrival was the talk of the day along the waterfront. She was taken to Wallace Shipyards where she was refurbished and largely rebuilt." [6]

Paddy Farina, the Chief Engineer, stayed aboard her during this tow back to Vancouver, keeping the pumps going. He said, "For a while during the tow, I had to walk over dozens of drowned rats that were aboard her when she sank."

She resumed sailing and ran for another six years before being retired in 1923.

In 1925 she was sold to a U.S. fishing company in Puget Sound which gave her back the original name she had before the Union Co. had purchased her, the *J.R. McDonald*.

Six years later she was sold to another American interest and was tied up on Lake Washington as a floating dance hall. It is said she was used for some scenes in the famous Charlie Chaplin movie *The Gold Rush*.

Captain Boden Sr., one of her former masters, credits the *Cassiar* with charting the lower coast. Another well-known Union personality who was her skipper at times was Jock Muir. He started on her in 1913, as a quartermaster.

The *Cassiar* showing repairs to bow before being towed to Vancouver circa 1929 *(Farina Collection)*

S.S. Camosun I

Camosun was taken from the Native name for the bay where Victoria stands. The original settlement was called Camosack or Camosun, meaning "a deep narrow gorge" or "swift running water." Three Union ships carried this name.

In Union service: 1905-36
Official No.: 121204 (was still registered in Glasgow until 1908)
Type: Steel passenger-freight vessel. Built 1905 by Bow McLachlan & Co., Paisley, Scotland
Dimensions: Length 192.7', breadth 35.2', depth 17.9'. Gross tons 1369
Engines: Triple-expansion 224 NHP; two boilers cylindrical multi-tubular. Speed 14 knots maximum
Services: The first large ship operated by the Union Co. on regular service to Prince Rupert and northern B.C. ports.
Capacities: Passenger licence 199, berths 68, deck accommodations 120. Cargo 300 tons

S.S. *Camosun*
(Betz Collection)

In 1904 the Union Steamship Co. ordered its first combination freight and passenger ship to be built specifically to order, from Bow McLachlan & Co. in Paisley, Scotland. She was a very powerful steel vessel and given the name *Camosun*, the first of three ships with that name in the company's history, and by all accounts the most famous of the three.

The *Camosun* was an extremely powerful vessel. A South American republic had offered $300,000 for her during World

War I to use as a tug. [7]

She was launched in December 1904 and sailed from Troon, Scotland on Feb. 19, 1905 under Captain B.L. Johnson. Andrew Beattie came out with her as Chief Engineer. (He stayed with the company from that day on and died aboard the *Catala*, dockside at Prince Rupert.) Captain Johnson handed the command over to Captain C.B. Smith in Jamaica, who brought her around through the Straits of Magellan to the Pacific and up to San Francisco where she put in for repairs. A newspaper report of 1908 quoted a Lloyds of London survey which found her decks were sprung and she needed repairs to her steering gear and boiler mountings. This cost the Union Steamship Co. $19,000. Litigation between the company and the builders started in 1907 and ended in 1911 with the Union Company getting only a very small settlement.

Accompanying this story is a picture of John H. Browne, later Captain Browne, with a life buoy ring marked with the ship's name, *Camosun*, Glasgow. Why was a Union Steamship working in B.C. waters still registered in Glasgow, one would ask? Due to the dispute between the builders of the *Camosun* as described above, the Union Steamship Co. probably refused to take over actual ownership until the matter was settled one way or the other. John Browne was serving as Pilot on the *Camosun* when this picture was taken.

The *Camosun* arrived in Vancouver on June 20, 1905 and berthed at the foot of Abbot Street, close to the Union Company's wharf. A large crowd was on hand to greet her and thronged on board to admire her beautiful decor and passenger facilities.

She sailed on her maiden voyage on July 4, 1905 to Port Simpson via Bella Coola. In 1906 she dropped anchor into the uncharted harbour off Tuck's Inlet, which was to become the city of Prince Rupert, as the wharf was not built until 1907. [8]

On another trip to this uncharted harbour in 1906, even with a government surveyor on the bridge, she ran over Lima Reef. However she stayed afloat due to having a double bottom and was out of service only one month. [9]

In 1907 the Gold Rush started and the Grand Trunk Pacific Railroad was being extended, so the *Camosun* was kept busy with all this feverish activity. In May of 1907 the *Camosun* had a Marconi Wireless Telegraph installed, making her the first ship on the Pacific Coast to be so equipped. However, this claim to fame was a little premature, for a newspaper story from June 16, 1908 states, "*Camosun* Wireless Apparatus Removed." The story goes on to explain that because the Marconi Company forbade its operators to communicate with any other system and there were no other vessels or station on the coast with Marconi equipment, the *Camosun*'s radio equipment had never been used.

The *Camosun* also was featured in an unusual race-related labour dispute in 1907, which was described this way by Company historian Jessie M. Van der Burg:

"In October 1907, a battle royal took place aboard the *Camosun* between five Chinese cooks and eight Japanese firemen.

John H. Browne
(J. Smith Collection)

The Japanese were not satisfied with the food prepared by the Chinese cooks, and a general fight took place in which salt, bottles, plates, spoons and dishes of all kinds flew through the air. The engineer and crew separated the Orientals and when the boat docked the Chinese cooks all left. Their places were filled by Japanese cooks when the ship sailed the following night. As a result Chinese cooks on other boats went on strike. There was such a heavy demand for cooks on the coastal steamers that the *Camosun* sailed on one trip without a cook. One of the stewards filled in and he recalled the huge mound of potatoes that had to be peeled." [10]

The *Camosun* established herself as the favourite ship on the coast. She was fast and kept to her schedule in fair or foul weather. It was said you could set your watch time by her.

A newspaper report of Feb. 27, 1908 says she broke her own record of 48 hours sailing time from Prince Rupert to Vancouver with a new time of 46 hours. Two months later she sailed the same distance in 43 hours, 46 minutes, breaking her own record again.

The citizens of Prince Rupert secured the mail contact for the Company as a result of petitioning the government in 1908 to give the contract to the Union Steamship Co. because it was so much more reliable than any other steamship line calling into Prince Rupert in those days.

Irene Howard wrote in her book *History of Bowen Island* the following which illustrates clearly how coastal people felt about the Union ships and the *Camosun* in particular: "The Union Company in its seven decades built up a tremendous amount of goodwill, inspiring genuine emotion, as reflected in this letter to the editor: 'We in the north living in isolation and wilderness of snow appreciate and bless this ship [*Camosun*] and its Master. Old and young live, wait and listen for that ship's shrill whistle which means it's our food supplies, mail, miners, trappers, familiar faces returning back to their north abode. On boat days our children are restless at school, coaxing their teacher to let them go down to the wharf to watch the ship come sliding in." [11]

In 1908 the *Camosun* under Captain Saunders broke her propeller in Grenville Channel. She was in no danger, but when the CPR steamer *Princess May* came by all the passengers aboard the *Camosun* were transferred to the *Princess May* and taken to Vancouver. The *Camosun* was able to make it to Port Essington, where repairs were effected. She then proceeded on to Vancouver and resumed her regular sailing schedule.

In October 1909 she had another honour bestowed on her, and that was she loaded 160 bales of pulp from the new pulp mill at Swanson Bay to be trans-shipped in Vancouver and loaded onto the *Empress of India*, destined for Kobe, Japan, according to a report in the *Vancouver World* newspaper.

Freight of every description was part and parcel of Union business in those busy years for the quest of gold and railway construction. In October 1907 the *Camosun* carried a record load of 50 tons of frozen fish and 6,000 cases of salmon. Cattle also were a common cargo, as Jessie Van der Burg noted: "Beef on the hoof was frequently part of the freight, and many were the lurid and incredible scenes that took place when the wild range cattle were being loaded. Many a time the crew took to upper reaches of the masts when a drove of wild cattle took possession of the deck. Every now and then the cattle would rush aboard and rush right across the ship, through the railing, and plunge into the waters of the Inlet. Then they would swim for dear life while the crew tried to round them up with rowboats. Some cattle would make it ashore further down the Inlet and be rounded up by interested spectators, others would get ashore and roam through the city for days before they were rounded up again." [12]

In 1910 Captain A.E. Dickson took over the *Camosun* from Captain Batchelor. By this time the *Camosun* was regarded as the Company's flagship. In 1912 she was converted to oil, along with the *Chelohsin* and the *Cowichan*.

Tex Lyon, the wharfinger at Port Hardy for years, said this about Captain Dickson: "Oh yes, I remember him very well. He was responsible for knocking many, many posts out of the docks along the B.C. coast. Yeah, the old *Camosun*, if she stopped on dead centre, look out, because it took a little time to bar her over to get her in gear again."

When the *Cheslakee* sank at Van Anda on Jan. 7, 1913, the *Camosun* stood by and picked up her passengers and took them to Vancouver. In the spring of that year she was running a weekly service to Rivers Inlet.

The war broke out in 1914 and the *Camosun*'s captain, A.E. Dickson, by this time Commodore of the fleet, left for war service overseas. He returned after 18 months' war service and rejoined the *Camosun*.

At 2 a.m. on March 7, 1916 - during a snowstorm - the *Camosun* ran aground on a reef two miles north of Lima Point, Digby Island at the entrance to Prince Rupert Harbour. There were 17 passengers aboard and they were taken off by launches into Prince Rupert. At first it was expected she would be refloated quickly, but tides were not high enough until March 22 and even then the task was very risky because a storm came up and heavy swells made the job hazardous. Captain Logan of the B.C. Salvage Co. successfully refloated the *Camosun* and was given high praise. The repair bill was $18,669, and the job took 23 days. [13]

An inquiry into the grounding cleared the crew of any blame. "Camosun Hit Reef by No Fault of Officers" reported the *News Advertiser* on March 19, 1916. It said the ship grounded "with a strong northerly set of the current under thick weather conditions." As the inquiry adjourned, Captain MacPherson handed certificates back to Captain Dickson and the watch officers.

In the spring of 1918 the *Coquitlam* hit a deadhead in the middle of Queen Charlotte Sound and lost her propeller. She was towed to Alert Bay by the *Venture* and stranded on the beach. The *Camosun* brought her up a new propeller from the Vancouver wharf.

The *Camosun* was in a serious collision on Jan. 23, 1923, which was described by Jessie Van der Burg: "The *Camosun* south bound out of Prince Rupert in Grenville Channel under Captain Dickson was in collision with the *Princess Beatrice*. The *Camosun* was damaged from her boat deck to the water line. However she was able to proceed to Vancouver with all her passengers on board. There was a long lawsuit over this collision, the initial judgment was appealed, and the final decision settled the blame on the *Princess Beatrice*. The *Camosun* had to go into drydock and she was the first ship to be put into the new Wallace Drydock." [14]

The *Camosun* ashore on Digby Island 1916 *(F. Rogers Collection)*

That same winter, the *Camosun*, under the able navigation of Captain Edward Georgeson, had run in dense fog all the way from Bella Coola but then had the misfortune, within minutes of a safe docking at the Union dock, to go aground near Brockton Point. There was no damage to the ship but the passengers were removed from the ship in a most unusual fashion. The Vancouver Fire Department was summoned and brought their big ladder truck into Stanley Park and the passengers were

*Camosun I
circa 1920
(J. Smith Collection,
Vancouver Maritime
Museum)*

disembarked using this long ladder. [15]

On March 22, 1930, the *Camosun* ran ashore on Calvert Island. She refloated herself after being aground for six hours and proceeded to Namu, where the *Cardena* took off most of her passengers. She then went back up to Prince Rupert where she was repaired, much to the satisfaction of the people in this northern community. [16]

In 1925, after operating on the Company's main northern route for 20 years, the *Camosun* was transferred to the Ocean Falls - Bella Coola route, where again she proved very popular.

The last days of the *Camosun* were well-described by Jessie Van der Burg: "She was retired in 1935 after 30 years of marvellous service on this coast. In 1936 she was towed to Bedwell Bay, the final resting place for discarded ships. She was then sold to Japanese scrap iron merchants. The crew and customers alike regretted her loss, particularly as her seaworthiness in foul weather was outstanding." [17]

S.S. Cowichan

Cowichan comes from the Halkomelem word Q(a)w-(a)can meaning "warm mountains" - an apparent reference to sheltered uplands at the head of the Cowichan River. The Cowichan tribe lived in the area of southeast Vancouver Island, hence the place name Cowichan Bay.

In Union service: 1908-25
Official No.: 126210
Type: Steel passenger-freight vessel. Built 1908 by Ailsa Shipbuilding Co., Troon, Scotland. Launched as Cariboo, but name changed when registry duplication discovered after arrival on the Pacific coast.
Dimensions: Length 156.1', breadth 32.0', depth 13.5'. Gross tons 961
Engines: Twin triple-expansion, 116 NHP, built by MacColl & Co. Two multi-tubular boilers, build by D. Rowan & Co. Speed 11 knots
Services: Union's main logging camp routes
Capacities: Passenger licence 165, cabin berths 53. Cargo 125 tons

The *Cowichan* (Betz Collection)

The *Cowichan* had been especially designed for servicing logging camps and trade which was springing up among the scattered inlets and bays of the B.C. coast. With her 157-foot length and being twin screw she was easy to manoeuvre in narrow inlets, tight corners and rocky bays.

She left the shipyards at Ayer on the Clyde and went to Barry to coal up, leaving there on April 13, 1908. She stopped at

Buenos Aires, then San Francisco on June 30, and arrived in Vancouver at 6 a.m. on July 21, 1908 after 89 days at sea under Captain Polkinghorne. George H. Foster was the Chief Engineer.

"This new steamer is more than has been modestly claimed for her by the owners," stated *The Province* (Vancouver) in a glowing article on the new vessel.

"The expense of her interior must have been enormous for a vessel of her size and purpose. The woodwork is of the most uniform grain English white oak and in that respect eclipses any other ships coming here.

"One good feature is the separation of the different classes. A First Class passenger gets what he pays for, including spaciousness and exclusiveness. There is little chance for annoyance by loud talking and the provision made for ladies in the after music room is excellent.

"The loggers have quarters all to themselves. They are good and commodious and they get full value for the lower fare.

"There is a special cabin for Indians and Klooches, another for Chinese and another for Japanese.

"The dining room is first class and the kitchen is superior in character and equipment." [18]

Her name was to be the *Cariboo* but this had to be quickly changed when she arrived because it was discovered that another ship operating on the Great Lakes bore that name. After being in service for awhile the local people nicknamed her the "Cow."

Jim Spilsbury says, "You could tell it was the *Cowichan* by her peculiar whistle. When they first pulled the whistle cord it would fill up with condensation from hot steam hitting the cold whistle and instead of a steady blow you would hear a low sound which graduated up to a steady pitch."

On her maiden voyage she was under the command of Captain Charles Moody. She sailed to Van Anda and Campbell River, sort of an excursion trip to break her in and as well to show her off to local people.

Her first service run was to relieve on the Prince Rupert route, but soon she was on her logging camp run leaving every Monday and Wednesday. For a while she sailed on Saturday nights to Nanaimo, Denman Island, Union Bay and Comox. She would then bunker coal and return via Nanaimo to Vancouver. Very little has been recorded of the Union Steamships servicing the Comox-Union Bay area. It was a convenient route for the *Cowichan* when she burned coal, but after she converted to oil in 1912 she no longer needed to bunker up at Union Bay.

Excursions were being promoted by the then Manager Ernest Beazley and one of the most popular was a weekend trip on the *Cowichan* to Savary Island, Toba Inlet and Cortes Island, which was described by Company historian Gerald Rushton: "Meals and cabin berth were included in the unbelievable fare of $12 - a 360-mile round trip from Saturday afternoon to Monday morning's breakfast!" [19]

The *Cowichan* and the *Comox I* were servicing Lasqueti Island but not on a regular basis. In 1913 a wharf was built at Tucker Bay on Lasqueti enabling large ships to dock there. A post office followed and soon a regular steamship service was established. However in 1923 the *Cowichan* hit a rock on its approach to Tucker Bay. The Union Steamship Co. surveyed the bay and decided the entrance was too dangerous and their regular service was cancelled. In 1915 a fish cannery was built at False Bay, further up the Island from Tucker Bay. Then a new wharf was built at False Bay. In 1927 the Union Steamships began servicing Lasqueti Island again on a regular basis. [20]

The *Cowichan* went aground in Welcome Pass and completely destroyed her stem below the water line and crumpled her shell plating, according to a *Canadian Merchant Service Guild* magazine in 1923. Damage was estimated at $4,600. Later in the same year it was reported she grounded near Dumaresq's Cannery but was not damaged.

In 1925 two Union ships collided a few miles off Sechelt. The famous *Cowichan* was proceeding south in heavy fog under the command of Robert Wilson, one of the fleet's foremost skippers, when she was rammed on the port side by the *Lady Cynthia*, under the command of a younger master, Jack Boden. Fred Rogers, in his book *Shipwrecks of B.C.* describes this tragedy:

"On Monday evening, December 28, 1925, the Gulf of Georgia and lower coastal waters were locked under a thick blanket of foul smelling fog. Off the Sechelt Peninsula, several vessels were blindly groping their way. Two of them, the Union Steamship's *Cowichan* and the steamer *Lady Cynthia*, were drawing closer. The *Cowichan* was southbound for Vancouver, the *Cynthia* northbound for Powell River.

"On the *Cynthia*, Capt. J. Boden heard what he thought was the whistle of a tug and altered course to pass. Then, to his surprise, another whistle sounded dead ahead. It was from the *Cowichan*. Realizing that she was very close, he ordered slower speed and sounded his whistle. The other ship did likewise. At about 100 yards, the ghostly image of the *Cowichan*'s lights loomed out of the fog. When the *Cynthia* first sighted the *Cowichan* at 9:30 p.m. she was making about five knots. Captain Boden ordered the starboard engine ahead and the port engine astern to effect a glancing blow, but the *Cynthia*'s steel bow sliced into the *Cowichan*'s port side, rolling her and knocking passengers off their feet.

"The vessels collided about four miles southeast of Sechelt light. Fortunately there was a light wind and a calm sea. As water began filling the *Cowichan*'s engine room, the ships were kept locked together to help plug the hole. Capt. R. Wilson then calmly ordered his passengers and crew to transfer to the *Cynthia* by climbing over the forepeak railing. They had already gathered their baggage in preparation for arrival in Vancouver, so there was no panicky rush to save belongings. The *Cynthia* then reversed to free herself and the *Cowichan* sank in 60 fathoms - only 11 minutes after the collision.

The *Cowichan* (Spilsbury Collection)

"The *Cowichan* carried 15 passengers and a crew of 31, none of whom were seriously injured. After the *Cowichan* went down, the *Lady Cynthia* turned about for Vancouver."

Al Newman, a freight clerk aboard the *Cowichan* at the time, told Gerald Rushton this version of events: "It all happened between 9:20 and 9:27 p.m. After helping the last of his crew overside, Capt. Robert Wilson stepped onto the *Lady Cynthia*'s deck and shouted to Boden on the bridge, 'Pull her out now, Cap, or she'll take us down with her!' It seemed only moments after the vessels parted that the *Cowichan* went down by the stern, and her bow shot up out of the water. After the crash the fog suddenly cleared." [21]

In the Marine Inquiry that followed this sinking, both masters were commended for their seamanship. However in my research I have discovered some contradictory reports as to whether Captain Boden decided on his own that he was going to hold the *Cynthia* pinned into the *Cowichan* or whether Captain Wilson had to plead with Boden to keep his engines going slow ahead so as to keep the *Cowichan* afloat until he was able to get all his passengers and crew transferred. Gerald Rushton in *Whistle Up the Inlet* says Boden shouted from the *Cynthia*'s bridge that he was going to hold the *Cynthia* pinned into the *Cowichan* but other sources suggest that was Wilson's idea. [22]

Mrs. Vic Hayman, whose husband was quartermaster on the *Cowichan* at the time although not on watch during the accident, recalls him telling her later that Wilson had to ask Captain Boden to keep the *Cynthia* pinned into the gaping gash of the *Cowichan* to give his passengers and crew time to get across and aboard the *Cynthia*.

Harry Ives, a former Assistant Purser with the Company, also is emphatic that it was Wilson who saved the day. He says that Wilson told Boden what to do, and that Wilson was the last person to cross over to the *Cynthia*, and that once across he just stood there in silence and calmly watched his ship go to the bottom. When she had gone he turned and said, "Guess I'll go down and get a mug-up." He remained calm and confident that he had done all he could at the time. Harry says he heard and gathered all this information from mess table talk and discussions amongst such union men as Jack Halcrow, Harry Roach and Eric Suffield.

I find it strange that Mr. Rushton's version is so contrary to what I found in my research. One source I found was from an actual eye witness on board the *Cowichan* at the time, and the other from mess table talk amongst other officers of the fleet. However, the most marvellous thing overall was that no lives were lost. It could have been a terrible disaster and both skippers should be lauded, as indeed they were, for that fact.

Cowichan coming to dock at Savary Island
(U.B.C. Collection)

S.S. Cheslakee

Cheslakee was the name of the once-populous Native community on the Nimpkish River, off Broughton Strait, visited by Captain Vancouver and recorded in his journal as "Cheslakee's village."

In Union service: 1910-13
Official No.: 130309
Type: Steel passenger-freight vessel. Built in 1910 by Dublin Dockyard Co. and completed at Belfast
Dimensions: Length 126.0', breadth 28.1', depth 10.0'. Gross tons 526
Engines: MacColl & Co., triple-expansion, 58 RHP. Speed 12 knots maximum.
Services: Coast logging camp routes
Capacities: Passenger licence 148, cabin berths 56. Cargo 120 tons

S.S. *Cheslakee* Vancouver, B.C. *(Vancouver Maritime Museum)*

The *Cheslakee*, by dint of her disastrous foundering and sinking at Van Anda on Jan. 7, 1913, made a name for herself in the annals of B.C. coast shipping, albeit not to the ship's credit, so much so that when the ship was raised and reconditioned her name was changed to the *Cheakamus*.

As the *Cheslakee* she had an operational life with the Union Steamship Co. of only three years, but renamed as the *Cheakamus* she ran and served the B.C. coastal communities for 29 years.

The *Cheslakee* was built in 1910 at the Dublin Dockyard but only the hull and main deck with crew's quarters were completed when she was launched. She was then towed to Belfast where her triple-expansion engine was installed by Workman-Clark and Co., giving her a speed of 11 to 12 knots. She left Belfast on June 29, 1910 under the command of Capt. J.W. Starkey. When she arrived in Vancouver without any superstructure she looked more like a tug than a passenger ship. [23]

Cheslakee in Howe Sound circa 1912 *(Elphinstone Museum)*

The first sailing of the *Cheslakee* was a momentous event even in the Belfast shipyards, where the great liners *Titanic* and *Olympic* were being built. As the *Cheslakee* steamed around the harbour and then down the river outward bound for America, every man working on the two big liners left his task to watch the relatively tiny ship steam bravely off on her long journey to the distant coast of pioneer British Columbia. The sailing also had been celebrated so much by the skipper that the hangover reportedly put him out of commission for several days. [24]

An inkling of what it must have been like in 1910 to sail from Europe to the B.C. coast can be seen in the following story collected by Jessie Van der Burg in the 1940s, which tells of the difficult dockside parting of the ship's cook and his wife:

"The cook, a small person of some five feet, provided the onlookers with a rare scene as the ship was preparing to sail. The cook's wife had come down to see her husband off on his long voyage. Both had been celebrating and were very drunk. The cook would go on board, only to come back to shore, over the single plank which represented a gang plank, and take a long and moving farewell, during the farewell an argument would develop, he would take a swing at her and she would retaliate, and the cook would stalk off on board, weaving his way perilously over the plank. In a few minutes the couple would be overcome with remorse and back down the plank would come the cook and the scene would repeat itself.

"On arrival in Vancouver the cook disappeared for several days, reappearing at the Company's office with a sail fish, ready for mounting, remarking that it was a herring to catch a mackerel, meaning a bribe to secure him a job. However, luck was against him and history has it that he returned to his native land." [25]

The *Cheslakee* made the long voyage via St. Vincent, where she took on coal and water and refuelled at Montevideo and sailed down through the Straits of Magellan. She called at Coronel and San Francisco, and arrived in Vancouver on the morning of Sept. 16, 1910, 89 days after her departure. Captain Starkey said of the trip, "Varying kinds of weather were struck but in the worst of the storms the vessel took the seas easily and shipped no water . . . the crew which brought her 'round were all impressed by the seaworthiness of the craft." [26]

A contract for completing the vessel's superstructure, including cabins and general fitting-out, was placed in October with Wallace's Shipyard in North Vancouver. Twenty-three first class cabins were added, providing 56 berths and a small lounge. The *Cheslakee* was granted a B.C. coast licence for 148 passengers. Her dining saloon provided 30 seats and her freight capacity was 120 tons. She entered into service two months later under Captain John Cockle,

Cheslakee float landing at New's Channel *(Vancouver Maritime Museum)*

who had served in the Union fleet since 1896. [27]

Though the *Cheslakee* had made it safely through two oceans and through the perilous Straits of Magellan, it seems that the added superstructure must have changed her balance, because as marine historian Fred Rogers described in *Shipwrecks of British Columbia*, a problem soon arose:

"On her first trip upcoast she rolled and swayed as if top-heavy. While passing through Surge Narrows, she listed on her beam at an alarming angle and threatened to capsize in the whirlpools. The *Cheslakee* was quickly earning a bad reputation. She gave definite signs of being cranky, and many passengers experienced fearful moments in stormy seas. Some mariners even predicted that sooner or later she would flip right over and add to the coastal death toll. This prophecy was soon to be fulfilled.

"On Jan. 6, 1913, the *Cheslakee* steamed out of Vancouver at 20:40 p.m. with 99 passengers. Capt. John Cockle had a pilot [Robert Wilson] who ran direct to Van Anda, at the north end of Texada Island, her first stop. The sea was moderate with SSE winds when the steamer docked at Van Anda at 03:20 a.m. to let off 7 passengers [and several boards of freight]. Ten minutes out from there a heavy gust of wind rolled her over on a dangerous angle, and when she failed to regain an even keel the skipper turned back to the wharf. [Actually Wilson made the decision to turn back, then called Capt. Cockle who agreed, and they made it the dock and began disembarking passengers.]

"From below decks, the engineer reported water in the ash chute, which was now below surface. The pumps were started. Suddenly, with the *Cheslakee* listing farther away from the dock, the gangplank crashed into the water, taking with it several passengers who were [soon] rescued. A longer plank was then put out to enable the remaining passengers to disembark.

"Two loggers were trapped in Cabin 2 when the pressure of the rising water prevented them from opening a door. One was badly cut when he smashed a window to escape; the other was believed to have panicked and drowned. A child and three

Cheslakee wrecked at Van Anda
(Vancouver Maritime Museum)

women who were asleep went down with the ship.

"The worst moments came when the forward lines to the dock broke and the ship heeled over, although the stern lines kept her from drifting away. The last to leave were the purser, a Chinese cook, and two Japanese who jumped overboard. The cook vanished after hitting the water [the plank broke].

"As the *Cheslakee* flooded, she levelled off and sank at the dock with only the stack and the top of her pilothouse showing." [28] (see photo on previous page)

The sinking of the *Cheslakee* was the only accident involving loss of life in a Union passenger ship in the Company's history, which is most remarkable given the many thousands of trips made through the hazardous coast of British Columbia, and a telling comment on the prowess of the Union mariners.

The death toll would have been higher than seven if not for the bravery of Capt. Cockle, who personally rescued three men from the forward smoking room by lowering himself down from the entrance and enabling the men to reach his boots and thus pull themselves up out of the steeply-sloping passageway. Four years later, Cockle lost his own life in World War I. [29]

There are some differences in details between the historical accounts of the event by Rogers above and the inherently sympathetic report of former Union traffic manager Gerald Rushton in his book *Whistle Up The Inlet*, among others, but it is clear that the death toll also might have been lower if some of the passengers hadn't tarried to dress. Whether the ship sank within about five minutes of reaching dock, as some say, or the 10 or 15 minutes others say, it's clear from where and how the bodies were found that at least some of the passengers made fatal mistakes in not promptly abandoning ship. As recounted to me by historian Bob Blackmore, "Mrs. Simpson and Mary Pepper were found in the dining room. Both were wearing life jackets. One was partially dressed, the other had on only underclothing. The baby was found in the dining room while her mother's body was located in cabin 11. One logger was found in a cabin and one logger was found clinging to the ship's rail."

The survivors received shelter and were cared for well in Van Anda's hotel nearby. Most of them were soon taken aboard the *Camosun*, which happened upon the scene en route to Vancouver, while some waited for the next northbound ship.

A marine court of inquiry opened on Jan. 20 and heard testimony from many of the passengers and crew as well as expert witnesses, and concluded the seamanship in the incident was commendable and was "the means of avoiding what might have been a much more serious and lamentable catastrophe." [30]

Though an earlier coroner's inquest attached some blame to a freight clerk who apparently ignored an order from Capt. Cockle to advise all passengers to leave the ship, it appears from my review of dozens of newspaper reports that the marine court blamed the sinking mainly on the fact the *Cheslakee* probably was top heavy due to the superstructure added after she arrived in B.C.

Many accounts and stories have been written about the sinking of the *Cheslakee* over the years. It is interesting to note that the death toll varies in these stories from four to 18 people. A version that appeared in *The Westcoast Mariner* magazine of October 1989 is one of the most controversial of them all, saying that a total of 18 people drowned, including 11 loggers who had been trapped below. The story claims that after the *Cheslakee* was raised and was being towed to Victoria, the bodies of these loggers were flushed out and buried at sea while passing Stillwater. It is strange that no such account of these 11 loggers was ever brought out in either inquiry, yet the man who recounted this story in *The Westcoast Mariner* believed it to be true.

A meticulously-researched account of the event was being prepared on video by

Mr. Bob Blackmore, of TexGuard Heritage Video, which will provide more details. He can be contacted at (604) 486-7834.

The *Cheslakee* was successfully salvaged by the B.C. Salvage Co. She was replanned, sliced in half, and lengthened by 20 feet between the two halves. This was the first time such a method had been used, but nowadays it has become a common practise, especially with B.C. Ferries. Her name was changed and she was given a new life on the coast, returning to service in June 1913 carrying the name *Cheakamus*.

Raising the *Cheslakee*
(F. Rogers Collection)

Raising the *Cheslakee*
(Vancouver Maritime Museum)

S.S. Cheakamus

This ship was named for the Cheakamus River and Cheakamus Canyon north of Howe Sound. It is believed that the original Native name was Chehagamus, meaning "a fish trap." For the first two of her 31 years' Union service she was called the Cheslakee. The name Cheakamus was later transferred to one of the Union's small ferries.

In Union service: 1913-41
Official No.: 130309
Type: Steel passenger-freight vessel (see Cheslakee)
Dimensions: 145.3', breadth 28.1', depth 10.7'. Gross tons 688
Engines: MacColl & Co., triple-expansion 58 RHP. speed 12 knots, 10.5 average
Services: Main logging routes, latterly on local trips
Capacities: Passenger licence 148, berths 56. Cargo 120 tons

S.S. *Cheakamus*
(Betz Collection)

The *Cheakamus* was a ship with a history that must have haunted her for all the 29 years of faithful and reliable service for the Union Steamship Co. In her other life as the *Cheslakee* she made a name for herself by her disastrous sinking at Van Anda and the lives that were lost as a result. Replanned, refurbished and renamed *Cheakamus*, her steady service to B.C. coastal communities seems to have been generally overlooked, for very little has been written about her.

Weeks after she sank, the *Cheslakee* was towed to Esquimalt, where company manager E.H. Beazley had her lengthened by 20 feet. Her name was changed with special sanction from Ottawa to *Cheakamus* and she resumed service in June 1913. [31]

One of Union Steamship Company's long-time employees, Bill Scott, started his career as quartermaster aboard the *Cheakamus* on July 2, 1919.

A good look at what it was like in the early days for settlers to board the *Cheakamus* and other Union ships in Vancouver and travel up the coast to their new homes can be seen in Frances Duncan's and Rene Harding's book *Sayward* (for Kelsey Bay) published in 1979, which describes one family's experiences aboard the *Cheakamus*, which had taken over the route to Sayward from the *Cassiar* in 1917. The following is an excerpt from that book:

"It was a dank evening in March, 1920, when the taxi let us off near the Union Steamship dock at the foot of Carrall Street, Vancouver. We, the J.B. Howes family of Victoria, walked along the dingy wharf, dad leading the way, laden with suitcases, mother carrying her caged canary, I with our dog on a leash, and my brother Ivan following with more baggage.

"A few people were gathered at the gangway of the small coastal steamer *Cheakamus*, which was about to sail for northern ports. We hurried to board her.

"Loud voices and snatches of song heralded the arrival of others. We turned to see three men weaving uncertainly in our direction, duffle bags and blanket rolls impeding their progress. Ivan grinned, remarking that they had been having a last fling before leaving the bright lights.

"Dad attended to the tickets and then led us up to the forward deck, where we were obliged to pick our way through and over men and gear. I had never seen so many rough and rugged individuals before. They were loggers, returning to up-coast camps after the winter layoff.

"The noisy trio on the wharf created amusement as two of them fumbled for tickets. The third man decided to retrace his steps while his companions were busy with the officer on duty; he was away to a fair start before his buddies were alerted. Off they charged after him, amid shouts and laughter from those looking on. The unwilling drunk was lugged back, protesting loudly.

"We followed dad into the crowded space before the purser's office; the air was thick with smoke and fumes. I felt uncomfortable, and kept close to my parents. A steward showed mother and me our cabin while Ivan took our dog down to the freight deck, where the old fellow was made secure for the journey to Salmon River, our destination.

"Mother and I were glad of the privacy of our cabin. The steward told us there were two other ladies on board but we didn't see them. They disembarked during the night, leaving mother and me the only females aboard a ship laden with loggers.

The original *Cheslakee* which sank at Van Anda was refloated, repaired and renamed *Cheakamus* in 1913 *(J. Smith Collection)*

"The next morning, as I came out of our cabin, I nearly fell over a prostrate form lying asleep, hat tilted over unshaven face. The entire passageway was taken up by sleeping men. I stepped gingerly to the ladies' room, and there, too, I found men spread out on benches around the walls. It was embarrassing for a teenager to use the facilities.

"We had breakfast in the little dining salon, then went upstairs to find the revellers of the day before in trouble. Two had sobered up, but the third was in a wild

Cheakamus at wharf at Quadra (Valdes) Island *(Joyce, Lewis and Mary Collection, Campbell River Museum)*

frame of mind, threshing about and trying to shake off the restraining hands of his buddies, while the irate captain laid down the law.

" 'If you don't control that man, I'll put him off at the next stop!' he thundered. The worried men promised to keep their friend quiet, and as we watched they pulled the struggling fellow backward into a cabin and slammed the door shut.

"The *Cheakamus* pulled alongside small wharves and floats where men waited to catch the lines, and one could see by their pleased expressions that boat day was a big event.

"There were logging camps comprising a group of rough buildings, and others just a huddle of shacks. In one little bay the captain brought his ship up to a boom, and a nimble-footed logger ran along a boomstick to receive mail and parcels handed down by an officer. At another spot where no habitation was visible, the boat tooted and came to a standstill, then out from a small inlet there emerged two men in a rowboat. They drew alongside the *Cheakamus* to receive supplies and mail. More people lived along the coast at that time than do now.

"Johnstone Strait presented a dreary scene. A cold wind whipped up waves which beat against rocky shores, and mountains seemed to drop straight down to the sea, their peaks hidden by swirling clouds. My brother and I tried going out on deck but the biting wind drove us in.

"Some time in the afternoon Ivan beckoned mother and me to join him at a front window. He pointed toward dark mountains. 'That's where we get off,' he said, seeming quite pleased. We couldn't make out a thing. 'When we get to the mouth of the river you'll see the flats and the Indian rancherie,' he added.

"Dad came to warn us to be ready as we would be landing soon.

"Mother and I peered from the lounge window and presently a small wharf came into view, standing forlorn and unoccupied, there being no sign of habitation. The only building other than a little shed at the end of the pier, was a dilapidated freight shed, standing on a rise above the beginning of a rock-cut leading into the valley beyond.

"The whistle blew and the *Cheakamus* eased up to the dock. Now a lone pedestrian appeared on the approach. He was a big man, with coat collar turned up against snow which had begun falling. Catching the line thrown from the boat, he made it fast, then looked up, and seeing dad with us, his face creased in a welcoming smile.

" 'That's Nobby Clark, another vet,' dad said.

"The sight of Nobby cheered mother considerably. She admitted later that had our home in Victoria not been sold she would have turned around and gone right back.

"The gangplank was pushed out and we stepped out onto the wharf. This was it. We had arrived.

"Mother and I waited while our settlers' effects were being unloaded. All along the boat's rail men peered down with evident curiosity. Now a horse and wagon clattered on to the pier . . . to take us to our new home." [32]

The *Canadian Merchant Service Guild* year book for 1923 tells of the *Cheakamus* striking the Cortez Reef, causing $6,500 worth of damage to the ship, and then of another accident causing $4,700 in damage, but there were no details of how and what took place with these accidents.

The *Cheakamus*, along with the *Chelohsin*, was taken out of service in 1937 and her passenger accommodation was modernized. In 1941 she was converted to a tow boat and sold to the American Army Transport Service for $75,000. The A.T.S. continued to operate her as the *Cheakamus*, and she carried general cargo and often had jeeps stowed in her hold.

Two ex-Union Steamship men served aboard her in this period, Chief Officer Joe Hackett and seaman Bob McLean. They joined the *Cheakamus* while she was being converted to a tug at the B.C. Marine yards in 1941. McLean thought she didn't operate too well as a tug boat because they cut her down so much in the stern and she was so low in the water that she often was awash.

Cheakamus arriving at Savary Island on one of its twice-weekly visits *(Spilsbury Collection)*

S.S. Chelohsin

This famous ship name means "open to the mouth" i.e. having a navigable entrance, according to the missionary Rev. C.M. Tate. It was an appropriate name for this vessel, which at one time or another entered almost every port or channel on the northern B.C. coast.

In Union service: 1911-49
Official No.: 130805
Type: Steel twin-screw passenger-freight vessel. Built 1911 at Dublin Dockyard Co., Ireland and completed at Belfast
Dimensions: Length 175.5', breadth 35.1', depth 14.0'. Gross tons 1,134
Engines: Twin triple-expansion IHP 1,420 MacColl & Co., Belfast. Two multi-tubular boilers amidships. Speed 14 knots maximum, 12.5 average.
Services: Operated at first to Prince Rupert on the main northern route and later on principal logging route and to Port Hardy
Capacities: Passenger licence 191, cabin berths 66, deck settees 95. Cargo 150 tons

S.S. *Chelohsin*
(Vancouver Maritime Museum)

A new vessel was ordered by manager Gordon Legg from the Dublin Dockyard Co. at the end of 1910. She was to be named the *Chelohsin* and became one of the most famous of all Union Steamships. For many years she served the coastal logging camps and some loggers called her the Charlie Olsen. Others called her the Loggers' Hearse.

The *Chelohsin* cost $140,550, quite a

large sum in those days. She was twin-screw and 1133 gross tons. Her licence allowed for 191 passengers and 38 crew. All four decks were steel plate, and her two 34-foot derricks provided a lift capacity of over four tons. She could carry 150 tons of general cargo. She was taken from the Dublin Yards to Belfast where her twin triple-expansion engines were installed. During sea trials on Sept. 25, 1911 she attained a speed of over 14 knots. Three weeks later she left Belfast under Captain Starkey and arrived in Vancouver 72 days later, on Dec. 28, 1911. [33]

Newspaper reports said the *Chelohsin* was one of the smartest-looking vessels to be seen and her passenger accommodation was the equal of any vessel on the coast. Her staterooms were finished in oak and had sliding windows (in 1937 these were replaced by standard port holes). Some of the rooms had hot and cold running water. The main observation room had large square windows and was forward on the top deck. There was a smoking room forward on the upper deck and the ladies' saloon was aft on the same deck. The dining saloon on the main deck seated 46 passengers.

On her first official trip on Feb. 24, 1912, the *Chelohsin* sailed up Howe Sound carrying a full complement of Vancouver's shipping officials and business leaders. The Captain was John Cowper and Chief Engineer was George Foster. That evening she left on her maiden voyage for the Skeena River, Prince Rupert, Port Simpson and Anyox. Captain Cowper, who had been on local steamers since 1889, was soon succeeded by Captain Jack Edwards. On board at the time as Third Mate was a new man, James Findlay, who in later years became one of the finest skippers in the Union fleet. He already had his Master's ticket in sail and steam but he wanted to start at the bottom with his new employer so he could familiarize himself with navigating on the B.C. coast before he took a command himself. [34]

The *Chelohsin*, along with the *Cowichan* and the *Camosun*, originally were coal burners but in June 1912 the *Chelohsin* was converted to oil at the Wallace Ways in North Vancouver. As well, other repairs were done over a period of several weeks at a cost of $30,000. This was the largest job done on a steel ship in the Port of Vancouver to date. [35]

During this year Captain A.E. Dickson took over as her Master. She was put on a northern route leaving Vancouver every Saturday. Soon after this run began she grounded in the Skeena River, suffering extensive damage. As a result, Union officials protested to the federal government

S.S. *Chelohsin* aground
(Robson Collection)

in Ottawa about the lack of navigational aids in the area. [36]

Gordon Legg, who had managed the company since 1889 and who had ordered the *Chelohsin* to be built, retired on Sept. 22, 1911. He was succeeded by J.H. Welsford, a dynamic London-based cargo shipping magnate whose company earlier had bought a controlling interest in Union Steamships. One of Welsford's first acts was to purchase an additional 30,000 Union shares to in effect pay for the *Chelohsin*, but it was only part of a larger plan to try to take advantage of the opening of the Panama Canal in 1914 by linking his cargo line from Liverpool to Texas and Mexico with a Pacific Coast service. [37]

Chelohsin grounded at Minstrel Island in Chatham Channel 1947 *(Roach Collection)*

In the spring of 1913 the *Chelohsin* serviced logging camps on Johnstone Straits and Kingcome Inlet, along with the *Cowichan* and *Cassiar*. [38]

In early 1914 the *Chelohsin* had a run of bad luck. She ran into and smashed the dock at Salmon River. On her return run to Vancouver she fouled a sunken log in Lewis Channel and damaged her shaft, so she had to go into drydock for repairs. She went back to sea for two days but had to return to drydock to have her boilers cleaned out. The *Chelohsin* was anchored off the Wallace Shipyard in North Vancouver. At 3 p.m. that day she began to heel over. As she was rolling over she began to take in water through a port hole that had been left open. The government dredge *Mastodon* was nearby and her crew attached a steel hawser to the *Chelohsin* and winched her into shore until she was grounded. Their quick response played a major role in keeping the *Chelohsin* from capsizing. [39]

In 1923 while northbound to Prince Rupert the *Chelohsin* hit some logs and damaged her propeller. She returned to drydock and the repairs cost $2,000 - still a tidy sum then.

For the next 23 years the *Chelohsin* gave steady and reliable service all over the B.C. coast, especially to the myriad of logging camps and gyppo loggers scattered around the remote inlets and bays. The *Chelohsin* became the workhorse of the fleet. Thousands of coastal residents and travellers had come to rely on her and it was said you could set your watch by her when she came by.

One stormy night in February 1935 the *Chelohsin* and the CPR ship *Princess Charlotte* collided off Point Atkinson. The *Chelohsin* was outward bound for the upcoast logging camps and the *Princess Charlotte* was inward bound from Seattle. There were no injuries, but both ships were damaged. The *Charlotte* suffered dented plates and superstructure damage. Her forward emergency lifeboat was sheared off by the *Chelohsin*'s bow. The *Chelohsin* came out of the collision with a bent stem and buckled plates. She spent the next three months at Burrard undergoing repairs and a complete engine overhaul. [40]

In 1937 she was finally given a rest and withdrawn from service to be extensively replated, remodelled and modernized at a cost of $81,000. The renovations were done at Wallace's shipyards and took about three months. Staterooms were modernized, hot and cold running water was installed in every stateroom and the original sliding windows in the staterooms were replaced by standard port holes. Her lounge, smoking rooms and dining room were all rebuilt, and her engines were serviced. Her skipper at the time was Captain Bob Wilson, said to be one of the finest skippers ever for the Union Steamship Co.

In 1942 the *Chelohsin* was assigned a

new intermediate route, sailing bi-weekly to Port Hardy and servicing the military establishment at Yorke Island. [41]

When the war ended in 1945 the Union Steamship fleet was in desperate shape. They needed new tonnage. The only ships left were the *Chelohsin*, the *Cardena* and the *Catala*. A loss of any one ship would have been a serious blow to their operations.

In 1947 the *Chelohsin* suffered a serious grounding in the dangerous Chatham Channel. She ran aground at Rocky Point and was holed at 6:45 a.m. on Nov. 12. There were no injuries. Captain Harry Roach was on the bridge and immediately ordered the pumps started. He was able to proceed 10 miles to Minstrel Island, the nearest port, where her 40 passengers were disembarked and all cargo unloaded. Captain Roach then proceeded to ground her prow on the beach as a precaution against her taking on more water. The *Salvage Chieftain* was sent to her aid and after surveying the damage found it wasn't as extensive as first thought. One of her boilers was out of commission, but the crew of 35 was able to remain aboard.

The *Chelohsin* was soon repaired and back in operation. However on Nov. 6, 1949 at 8 p.m. she ran aground at Stanley Park near Siwash Rock. The grounding ended her long career on the B.C. coast. Thousands of people came to Stanley Park to see the stranded ship and the dramatic efforts to refloat her. There were traffic jams in the park and tie-ups on the Lions Gate bridge that morning as motorists slowed to look at the stranded ship. Hundreds of people and amateur photographers scrambled down to the beach from Stanley Park Drive to get a better look. Once the fog lifted, hundreds of pleasure boats circled the famous old ship to watch the salvage efforts during her last gasp at life.

The loss of the *Chelohsin* couldn't have come at a worse time for the Union Steamship Co. They had no replacement for her, and from here on the fortunes of this famous, old reliable company seemed to go downhill.

The Vancouver newspapers were filled for many days with photos and stories about how and why the grounding happened, but the full story of what happened did not come out and now might never be known. However, I was fortunate in recent years to be able to interview a close witness to the event, Mr. Charles Hamer, who was on the *Chelohsin* as Third Mate at the time, though not on duty on the bridge, and his detailed eyewitness account of the trip south from Lund to Vancouver in thick fog and of the grounding at Stanley Park can be found under his name in the Masters and Mates section. It is especially noteworthy insofar as Mr. Hamer indicates that the Company

Chelohsin at Wallace Shipyards, Vancouver *(Vancouver Maritime Museum)*

Last day of the S.S. *Chelohsin* aground at Stanley Park Nov. 6, 1949 *(D. McLeod)*

was negligent because its equipping of the bridge generally was substandard and especially because the Company refused to have the ship's radar repaired in Powell River, the lack of which was a key contributing factor in the accident.

The other deck officers on that trip were Captain Alfred Aspinall, Chief Officer Paddy Hannigan and Second Mate William Nicholson. Captain Aspinall happened to be relieving the *Chelohsin*'s regular master, Captain Harry Roach, who was on holidays. The Quartermaster was Joe Best, a veteran crew member and tops at his job. The Chief Engineer was Lance Jefferson.

Captain Roach's son Ed, who also had worked aboard Union ships, took his dad down to see the *Chelohsin* impaled on the rocks in Stanley Park. The father said, "She handled like a little kettle and when she came out from the Old Country she did 14 knots and she still did 14 knots at the end of her days." After looking at his old ship for a while, Captain Roach turned to his son and said, "You know, none of us has clean hands."

The steering engine of the *Chelohsin* was in the wheelhouse, which made that space very warm in summer but comfortable in winter. This engine was Joe Best's pride and joy: he polished its brass fittings until they sparkled. After the grounding Best said, "It was the only time I had the desire, as well as the opportunity, to walk off the job without notice."

All attempts to refloat the *Chelohsin* failed, so the Union Co. put her up for sale 12 days after the grounding, on an 'as is' basis. On Nov. 24, 1949 she was purchased by Food Dehydrators for $1,600. The firm's identity surprised people in marine circles. The purchaser was Victor David, an amateur salvager and also head of David Neon Ltd.

David hired 12 men to work with him on the site. Waterfront experts said the *Chelohsin* would never be refloated, but he proved them wrong. Two tugs pulled her off the beach and towed her into the Evans Coleman dock, close by the Union Steamship dock. Apparently David planned to convert the *Chelohsin* into a floating fish processing plant.

Some of David's success in refloating the *Chelohsin* could perhaps be attributed to the *Chelohsin*'s Chief Engineer at the time of the grounding, Lance Jefferson. Jefferson's son recalls that David visited his father often, asking questions about the *Chelohsin*'s layout and how she was constructed.

David's plan to convert the ship into a fish processing plant was dashed by government regulations prohibiting such a move. He eventually sold the *Chelohsin* to a San Francisco scrap dealer. She was towed out of Vancouver by a powerful American tug, along with the S.S. *Cassiar*, backwards. A headline at the time read "*Chelohsin* humiliated, towed out of the City backwards."

Don McLeod, Purser aboard the *Chelohsin* at the time of the grounding, photographed the half-submerged vessel the next morning, and published his picture as a post card. He stamped the back of the card with the *Chelohsin*'s official date stamp, dated Nov. 6, 1949, the last day she was in service.

Left: *Chelohsin* at Beaver Creek, Loughborough Inlet

Below: *Chelohsin* at Comox wharf with S.S. *Charmer*. Boat services to Comox began in 1860 and ran until the 1950s.
(Courtenay Museum)

S.S. Venture

In Vancouver's early days there existed a Venture Steamship Co. whose first vessel carried the name Venture. Boscowitz S.S. Co. purchased the Venture Co. but later lost the ship *Venture* to fire. They built another ship and named her Venture. When Union Steamships bought out Boscowitz Co. in 1911 the *Venture* came with the purchase and Union kept her name.

In Union service: 1911-46
Official No.: 129475
Type: Steel twin-screw passenger-freight vessel. Built 1910 by Napier & Miller, Old Kilpatrick, Scotland, for Boscowitz Co. Taken over in September 1911 by Union
Dimensions: Length 180.4', breadth 32.0', depth 17.0'. Gross tons 1,011
Engines: Direct-acting, triple-expansion IHP 1,150, built by Miller & Macfie. Speed 13 knots
Services: Built specifically for northern cannery trade, and continued on Skeena River route seasonally
Capacities: Passenger licence 186, cabin berths 60, deck settees 85. Cargo 550 tons. Equipped with Marconi wireless

S.S. *Venture*
(Betz Collection)

The original *Venture* was owned by the Venture Steamship Co. of Vancouver. She was purchased by the Boscowitz Co. but caught fire while loading cases of salmon at the Inverness Cannery in January 1909. She burned to the waterline and was a total loss. The ship and the canned salmon were covered by insurance.

The Boscowitz Co. ordered a new *Venture* to be built which was put into service in 1910. The Union Steamship Co. bought out the Boscowitz Co. in 1911. At the time they operated two ships, the new S.S. *Venture* and the S.S. *Vadso*, which both came under the Union house flag. The names *Venture* and *Vadso* were kept intact. Their names were anomalies because all other Union ships had names beginning with the letter C, but the acquisitions were instrumental because they enabled Union Steamships to dominate the cannery trade and thus also the smaller port business along the entire mainland coast. [42].

The *Venture*, having been built to order, was exceptionally well-suited for the coastal trade. When Union Steamships decided to build the *Cardena*, it used the *Venture*'s plans and structure as a starting point. The *Venture* and the *Cardena* closely resembled one another, as observers could easily see.

The *Venture* was an excellent sea boat but apparently she had a perpetual list caused by heavier machinery installed on her port side. [43] Her life boats were of the old wood clinker-built type. Her bridge telegraph was mounted in the centre of the bridge, unlike most vessels which had two telegraphs, one on each side of the bridge. Captain Bob Wilson often used to sit on the bridge railing of the *Venture* with the telegraph behind him and make a landing sending signals on the telegraph blindly from behind his back!

John Hogan was Chief Engineer on the *Venture* for many years. Captain John Park commanded the *Venture* on her maiden voyage for Union Steamships, and Captain Harry Roach was in command on her last voyage.

Tex Lyon, the wharfinger at Port Hardy for years, recalls that the *Venture* had no refrigerated hold and thus big sides of meat destined for various camps were hung on hooks on the foredeck between the bow and foremast to keep them cool.

As one historian has noted, "The *Venture*

Venture circa 1935
(Meredith Collection)

Venture docking in Simoom Sound *(Tickner Collection)*

". . . was one of the best ships for stowing freight. Canned salmon was stowed in talls and half-flats and more salmon with less effort could be stowed on her. She carried about 80 first-class passengers and as many as 200 steerage. Each year a great migration took place as the canneries prepared for the months of salmon packing. Chinese labourers were brought up the coast from Vancouver and native people moved from their villages to work in nearby canneries." [44]

On the *Venture*'s first trip with Captain John Park in command, his Chief Officer was John Boden Sr. The *Venture* had just left Port Hardy and Boden was on watch when he received a message that a vessel was aground on rocks in Christie Pass. Crews of the grounded ship had lit fires on the beach. Boden roused Captain Park who took the *Venture* close in and found it was the *Princess Beatrice*. She had 200 passengers aboard, mostly cannery workers returning home after the fishing season. They were taken off in the *Venture*'s lifeboats and as there were no means of looking after them at Hardy Bay they were landed at Alert Bay. [45]

The *Venture* had her first marine accident in January 1917 when she collided with the S.S. *Wakena* while entering First Narrows. It was a minor collision and later in court the *Venture* was cleared of blame. [46]

A year later Captain James Noel, with Edward Georgeson as Pilot and Jock Malcolmson as Mate, took the *Venture* to the aid of the S.S. *Ravalli* which had caught fire in Grenville Channel. The fire began in her coal bunkers in the hold so the captain ran her into Lowe Inlet. Captain W.J. Main - then quartermaster on the *Venture* - took part in the rescue. As Main described in a 1966 letter to marine columnist Charles Defieux, "We didn't know she was on fire until we came into the bay on our way down to the cannery. We had the hoses going before we got our ship alongside. We took the passengers off and boarded her with our hoses but it was too late. Captain Noel decided to beach the *Ravalli* so we pushed her across the bay and she grounded and burned to the waterline on the beach." [47]

On Sept. 16, 1922 the *Venture* had just finished loading salmon at the North Pacific cannery when the wireless operator rushed up to Captain Andy Johnstone with an SOS he had picked up from an American ship, the *Queen*. She was on the rocks at Whitecliff Island, 12 miles away, with a full load of passengers. Captain Johnstone sent a radio message to the stricken ship saying the *Venture* would proceed to her aid right away. There was a heavy fog but when the *Venture* approached, blowing her fog horn, the *Queen* answered with hers, so Johnstone was soon able to bring the *Venture*'s bow right alongside the stern of the *Queen*. Crews extended a gang plank between the ships and all passengers, as well as mail and valuables, were safely taken aboard the *Venture*. The passengers were taken to Prince Rupert to clear Customs. Many of them came back aboard the *Venture* and booked passage down to Vancouver. [48]

The *Venture* was one of the workhorses of the fleet for years. Though she had been built especially for the northern trade, she was able to fill in anywhere in the company's schedule.

During the Second World War she spent a lot of time transporting troops to outposts along the coast and so was camouflaged along with other ships and had her wheelhouse covered with a bullet-proofing material. But as Ed Roach recalls his father Harry Roach explaining, attempts to mount a gun on the *Venture* were quite unsuccessful. "She was taken over to Burrard Drydock and a gun was mounted on her stern. They took her out into English Bay and fired a round off and she shook so hard she just about fell apart. She was just so rickety they abandoned the idea," Ed said.

On July 19, 1940 when the *Venture* was returning from her regular northern route, she joined the Victory Parade of ships in Vancouver harbour staged in aid of the war effort. [49]

On a chilly January night in 1944 the *Venture* under Captain Jack Boden rescued four people from drowning. They were identified only as Mrs. & Mrs. Shaw, their small son, and an unidentified man. The family was being rowed to the floating dock anchored in Shushartie Bay to board the *Venture*. Their rowboat was swamped. The two men were able to get the woman and boy inside the half-submerged boat while they clung to the sides in the icy water. As the *Venture* approached the float, Captain Boden had to use his searchlight and luckily spotted the swamped rowboat. He maneuvered the ship alongside the boat and the four were picked up.

Ben Smith, an oiler fresh out of the Navy, joined the Company on Jan. 4, 1946 and signed on the *Venture*. "She was just about ready to fall apart then," he recalls. "She was probably the only junk shipped from Canada to China. I guess she was the senior ship in the fleet and when I went aboard her and stepped down into the engine room I thought, my God, this is the end. Everything seemed to be leaking and blowing out steam. You felt like you needed an umbrella to walk around the engine room. However, she did the job, but after coming off the navy ships this was a shock."

Smith was aboard the *Venture* on her last coastal voyage for the Union Steamship Co. before she was sold to Chinese interests and he marked the occasion by buying one of the little round plaques with paintings of the various Union ships that were for sale in the newsstands and having many of the crew autograph it. He still has that memento and showed it to me, so herewith is a list of some of the crew who were aboard the *Venture* on her last voyage:

    Harry Roach, Master
    A. McKinnon, Third Mate
    R. Baldry, Chief Engineer
    Reg Emms, Second Engineer
    W. Patterson, Third Engineer
    B. Smith, Oiler
    A. Turner, Winchman
    Charlie Strachan, Winchman
    Rick Renwick, Stevedore
    P.M. Paton, Quartermaster
    Dave Satchwell, Deckhand
    Stan Greus, Deckhand
    Pat Morrissey, Oiler
    M. Maximuk, Oiler
    Pat Meakin, Fireman
    Dick van der Werff, A./Purser
    James Bowie, News Agent.

Smith applied to be one of the crew to sail her to China but was turned down and the position went to Pat Morrissey. That turned out to be a stroke of luck for Ben because the *Venture* - renamed the *Hsin Kong So* - caught fire while docked in Honolulu and some of the crew lost all of their belongings.

I was able to obtain clippings from the Honolulu Star-Bulletin newspaper about the fire, which included the following:

"The *Hsin Kong So* arrived safely in Hawaii tying up at Pier 7 E, after completing the first leg of her journey across the Pacific, over to her new owners in Shanghai.

"Shortly after her arrival she was ravaged by a fire which swept through the ship. Examination of the ship after the fire showed three decks, including the officers, crew and passenger quarters were completely gutted. There were some minor injuries to crew members but all of them got off the ship safely, but some lost all their belongings. One man was left walking around in only a pair of shorts. Fortunately the Red Cross was able to clothe this man and others who were in the same predicament.

"Once the fire was put out, examination revealed that the whole wooden section of the ship would have to be rebuilt, however little water entered the engine room, so her plant was in usable condition. Cost of repairs is estimated to be $33,000. It is expected that the ship will have to stay in Honolulu several months undergoing restoration before she can proceed to her destination in China.

"The crew that sailed her over to Hawaii will be repatriated back to Vancouver, B.C. and a new crew will have to be brought over to sail her on to China." [50]

The *Hsin Kong So* eventually did make it to Hong Kong but again caught fire at dockside and this time was completely destroyed - a sad end for one of B.C.'s most historical ships that had served the coastal communities for 35 years.

After being sold to Chinese interests the old *Venture* was renamed the *Hsin Kong So*. She was ravaged by fire in Honolulu en route to China. *(Ashmore Collection)*

S.S. Chasina

The name Chasina, with which the *Selma* was rechristened in 1917, comes from Chasina Island in the Okis Hollow channel west of Maurelle Island; its meaning is unknown. The Okis Hollow passage, generally restricted to small craft, was used regularly by Union's logging-route ships to enter Johnstone Strait from the Surge Narrows area as an alternative to the main route through Seymour Narrows.

In Union service: 1917-23
Official No.: 85705
Type: Iron passenger-freight vessel. Built 1881 by J. Elder & Co., Glasgow, as steam yacht Santa Cecilia for the Marquis of Anglesea. Renamed Selma under new owners before arrival at Vancouver under Capt. Charles Polkinghorne in 1910, and bought by All Red Line. Renamed Chasina when Union took over their service in 1917
Dimensions: Length 141.8', breadth 22.1' depth 11.6'. Gross tons 258
Engines: Compound 80 RHP. Speed 13.5 knots maximum, 11.5 average
Services: On Vancouver-Powell River route
Capacities: Passenger licence 200 (winter 153). Cargo 40 tons

S. S. *Chasina* (Personality Ships of B.C.)

According to an article in the July 1990 issue of *Nautical Magazine of Glasgow*, the *Chasina* when she was launched "was one of the most magnificent, deep-sea cruising yachts afloat, and with her handsome lines and clipper bow, she caused a sensation wherever she went." That special appearance was fitting, because the many escapades the *Chasina* became involved in were sensational too, including high-society affairs and parties, treasure hunting, rum running and other crimes, and finally a mysterious death-filled disappearance.

"She was born *Santa Cecilia* and was launched on her career from the Fairfield yard of J. Elder & Co., Glasgow, in 1881. ... She was conceived for the Marquis of Anglesea, known as the "Mad Marquis" for his madcap escapades and lavish entertainment. *Chasina* kept company with the elite of European society and many were the crowned heads of Europe including the spirited King Edward VII.

"She cruised many of the famous, international watering places of the Mediterranean and hosted fashionable champagne parties in Venice, Monte Carlo, the Scandinavian fjords, as well as London and Liverpool nearer home.

"The gossip of the time had it that the Marquis of Anglesea was in love with a beautiful lady of London and had *Santa Cecilia* built especially for a projected voyage around the world with a few select guests including his beloved beauty." [51]

It's not clear if that voyage ever took place, but after many years in high society the *Santa Cecilia* fell into hard times and dubious hands. At one point she disappeared for about two years, supposedly purloined from a French port by a banker absconding with a large sum of money and his lover aboard, but eventually she surfaced in Montevideo and was auctioned off to satisfy some heavy debts of her owners.

She was bought by the bearded, piratical-looking one-eyed Captain Charles Polkinghorne, who then was a director of the All Red Line, which operated small coastwise ships out of Sechelt. En route to Vancouver she was used in an unsuccessful search for pirates' treasure around Cocos Island off the coast of South America. She was renamed the *Selma*, probably after Selma Park, a tract of land owned by the All Red Line, and put to work on a daily run between Vancouver and Powell River.

In 1917 the Union Steamship Co. bought the All Red Line operation and with it the *Selma*. She was renamed the *Chasina* after the Company's policy at that time of using West Coast Indian names which began with the letter C. She was soon sailing with the familiar red, black-topped funnel of the Union Steamship Co. in the coastal trade.

Two well-known Union skippers came over to the Union Steamship Co. when the All Red Line was purchased. One was Captain H.E. Lawrey and the other was Harry Roach, who was a seaman at the time and later one of the best-known captains of Union Steamships. [52]

Six years later in 1923 Union Steamships put the *Chasina* up for sale. She was purchased by rum running interests and was in that business until 1928. She was then tied up at B.C. Marine ways, neglected and rusting. In the late 1930s she was purchased by F.C. Eccles and an associate of Vancouver for only $1,700, only a fraction of the $250,000 she was valued at when launched.

She was restored under a Newfoundland flag and according to a newspaper report supposedly was to enter the tomato trade between Vancouver and Mexico, but on May 16, 1931 she left Vancouver and actually went to Shanghai, which she reached after encountering severe storms and almost running out of fuel. From there she sailed to crime-ridden Macao, which she left Sept. 25, 1931 en route to a rendezvous with another vessel 1,000 miles off the U.S. west coast, but she was never seen again, despite a major search by the Canadian Navy, the RCMP and the Royal Navy. It is speculated that she was carrying contraband cargo, possibly drugs and/or illegal immigrants. The Supreme Court of Canada declared her lost - a necessary move for insurance claims for both the ship and its crew. A total of 11 men went to their deaths aboard her.

S.S. *Chasina*
(Vancouver Maritime Museum)

S.S. Chilco

Chilco means "the path or waterway of the Chil" (or Cinl), known today as the Chilcotin River. The original name of the *Chilco*, which operated from 1917 to 1935, was Santa Maria, later changed to Lady Pam.

In Union service: 1917-35 as the Chilco
Official No.: 87034
Type: Steel passenger-freight vessel. Built 1883 by J. Elder & Co., Glasgow, as a clipper-bow steam yacht, Santa Maria, for John A. Rolls. Later owned by Lord Hartswell, and in 1914 was steamed to the Pacific Coast after being purchased by the All Red Line. Renamed Chilco when taken over by Union.
Dimensions: Length 151.0', breadth 22.0', depth 12.6'. Gross tons 305
Engines: direct acting, compound 80 RHP. Speed 13 knots, 11.5 average
Services: On Vancouver-Powell River route as the Chilco, alternating with the Chasina for a period
Capacities: Passenger licence as the Chilco 200 (winter 144)

S.S. *Chilco*
(J. Smith Collection)

The *Chilco*, formerly the *Santa Maria*, was built in 1883 by the J. Elder Co., Glasgow, as a clipper bow steam yacht for John A. Rolls. Later she was bought by Lord Hartswell. The All Red Line, then jointly owned by Captains Polkinghorne and Sam Mortimer, purchased the *Chilco* in 1914 and ran her from Vancouver to Powell

River and way points until 1917, when their company and all its land holdings were taken over by Union Steamships.

She made her first run for the Union Steamship Co. on July 17, 1917 under Captain Bill Mounce. The First Mate was Harry Roach, who was 18 at that time. He had come over from the All Red Line to Union at the time of the purchase.

Fred Corneille, a long time deck officer with Union Steamships, recalls an incident in which the *Chilco*'s bow got stuck under the wharf at Roberts Creek:

"The *Chilco* had an anchor davit up forward. As she approached the dock the tide was low enough that her bow went under the dock and the anchor davit bent but then sprung up again when the bow continued moving forward. There she was, hooked under the wharf unable to back herself out. The mate at the time knew there was a set of fallers aboard going back up to their logging camp. They always carried their saws, axes, wedges and other tools, so he went to them and said 'Hey you guys, how would you like to cut this boat free from the dock?' This was right up their alley and they went to work right away, sawing through the bull rail and heavy planks, enabling the *Chilco* to back out and away."

In 1923, while tied up at the Union dock, the *Chilco* caught fire and damage was estimated at $2,500 - a large sum in those days.

After coming under Union Steamship management, the *Chilco* was operated mainly on the Vancouver - Powell River route, the same as under the previous owners. In 1935 she was withdrawn from service, overhauled, refitted, and had her passenger accommodation extensively remodelled. At the same time her name was changed to the *Lady Pam*.

Under the *Chilco* name this ship was in service with Union Steamships for 18 years, and continued serving the company for another 11 years as the *Lady Pam*.

S.S. *Chilco*
(J. Smith Collection)

S.S. Lady Pam

In Union service: 1935-46, with passenger accommodations rebuilt
Official No.: 87034
Type: Steel passenger-freight vessel. Built 1883 by J. Elder & Co., Glasgow, as a clipper-bow steam, yacht, Santa Maria, for John A. Rolls. Later owned by Lord Hartswell, and in 1914 was steamed to the Pacific coast after being purchased by All-Red Line. Renamed Chilco when taken over by Union.
Dimensions: Length 151.0', breadth 22.0', depth 12.6'. Gross tons 305
Engines: Direct-acting, compound 80 RHP. Speed 13 knots, 11.5 average
Services: On Vancouver-Powell River route as the Chilco, alternating with the Chasina for a period. The Lady Pam was employed generally in West Howe Sound, serving summer camps and local routes
Capacities: Passenger licence as the Chilco 200 (winter 144), but later, as the Lady Pam, 130 all year. Cargo 40 tons

S.S. *Lady Pam* (Mel Thomas Collection, Vancouver Maritime Museum)

The *Lady Pam* was one of the most distinctive-looking ships in the Union fleet because of her yacht-like appearance, her clipper-style bow, and a cloud of black smoke usually emitting from her stack. At a distance people had no trouble recognizing the *Pam*.

Over her 62-year career she sailed under three different names. She was launched in 1883 in Glasgow for owner John H. Rolls and named the *Santa Maria*. Later she was purchased by Lord Hartswell, who sold her to the All Red Line in B.C. She arrived on the West Coast in 1914 and was put on the Vancouver-Powell River route. In 1917 Union Steamships took over All Red Line along with its two ships, the *Selma* and the *Santa Maria*, and renamed them the *Chasina* and the *Chilco* respectively. [53]

Union operated the *Chilco* on the same route but withdrew her from service in 1935 and remodelled her passenger facilities. She then resumed service as the *Lady Pam*. The captain who took her out on her maiden voyage under this name was W.W. "Bill" Mounce and the First Mate was Harry Roach. Roach had worked on her as a deck hand in 1917 when she was still the *Santa Maria*.

Dennis Shaw, a long time Purser with Union, said that the name "Pam" was suggested by Harold Brown, then general manager of the company. His wife's name was Pamela.

Shaw also recalls a time when he was Purser aboard the *Lady Pam* and shared a room with the Mate, Wally Walsh. Shaw had the top bunk and one day he jumped out of the top bunk and crashed right through the floorboards. Amid the splintered wood he saw a burlap bundle. He called Wally and they pulled it out and unwrapped it. Inside was a ship's brass bell with the inscription "Santa Maria." Wally immediately said, "I'm taking this home with me!" and he did. Shaw recently tried to locate any relatives of Wally's but without success. The whereabouts of the bell remains a mystery.

John Allan, who was decking on the *Pam*, said that the crew's quarters were small and restricted and just above the waterline. "One thing," he said, "when the *Pam* sailed through the narrows and passed another ship, you had to make sure your port hole was closed or else the wash would splash into your room."

Don Thompson, who worked as a fireman on the *Pam*, said it was so hot in the engine room in summer that you were paid an extra five dollars per month. "The *Pam* wouldn't hold steam," Thompson recalls, "so you had to come down, even on your day off, to fire her up."

As was typical of such ships of the times, she had a speaking tube between the engine room and the pilot house. John Allan recalls once while he was at the wheel of the *Pam*, Captain Roach had a call from one of the engineers down below on the speaking tube, and upon answering this call, a voice said, "Captain, we've got a nut loose down here in the engine room and we're going to have to stop her." At the time one of the engineers was a somewhat unusual fellow. Captain Roach answered, "Right, Chief," and as he stuffed the bung into the speaking tube he turned to Allan and said, "There sure as hell is a nut loose down there."

When ex-crewmen who served aboard the *Pam* get together they invariably discuss her "Armstrong Steering Wheel." This wheel was about six feet across and when you stood on the floor of the wheelhouse the spoke would be near your neckline. The wheelhouse floor had to be stepped so a man could handle the wheel. Even so, you would have to stand on one side or the other of the wheel to turn it. This step or curved hole in the deck made a convenient waste basket for cigarette butts and other junk. The wheel was so big it took two men to turn it at times. Once the ship was put on course the quartermaster would often jam a stool under one side of the wheel to hold her steady. Sometimes the Mate on watch would help the quartermaster turn the wheel, one would be on one side pulling down and the other would be on the other side pulling up. When you wanted midship the man at the

Lady Pam leaving Keats Island 1944
(G. Wragg painting)

wheel would let the wheel run, but he had to be extremely careful and stay clear because more than one man got injured trying to grab the wheel and stop it spinning. Johnny Smith, who later in his career was a Master on B.C. Ferries, obtained his first seaman's job on the *Pam*. He was hired by Bob McBeath, who was Shore Mate at the time, to replace a fellow who had got jammed by the wheel and had broken his collar bone. Even Captain Yates injured his hand one time while trying to help the quartermaster.

In 1936 the *Pam* came to the rescue of three young girls whose canoe had been swamped just off of Sechelt. Two girls had clung to the foundering canoe while the third attempted to swim to shore for help. Bertram Owen-Jones, a deckhand on the *Pam*, spotted the girl in the water and yelled to the officer on watch, kicked off his shoes, jumped overboard and started swimming towards her. He reached her just in time and managed to keep her head above water until help from the ship arrived. The other two girls were rescued by a life boat sent to them from the *Pam*.

Owen-Jones received a medal for bravery from the Guild for rescuing the girl. He went on to become a deck officer with Union Steamships.

The *Lady Pam* was involved in a few marine mishaps, although written records of them - if they exist at all - are scarce. Frank Skinner was Purser aboard the *Pam* when she went aground at Grace Harbour, Gambier Island, some time in the mid 1930s. There were no injuries and no serious damage to the ship. Skinner was on the top deck getting passengers ready to disembark and it occurred to him they were approaching the dock pretty fast. Joe Hackett was on the bridge. The ship went right past the dock and ran up onto the beach. Apparently the *Pam*'s compound engine, unlike the triple-expansion engine, can be very finicky when trying to get it into reverse. On this occasion it probably stopped dead centre and wouldn't reverse. Skinner says Joe Hackett used his head, because as soon as he realized he wasn't getting the right response he quickly gave three quick blasts on the whistle indicating that he was going astern. He thought the engineer would hear this and might realize something was wrong and correct the situation.

One ex-Union man told me a story about the *Lady Pam* accidentally running down and cutting in two a yacht that was sitting becalmed in the shadows off Point Atkinson, without any running lights on: "We were dead-heading back to Vancouver from Britannia Beach quite late and it was a beautiful evening, and as such there were a lot of shadows cast over the water. As we came around Point Atkinson we collided with this yacht. I was down in the dining room. I felt the crash and then heard this rumble and scraping as this yacht went right under us from stem to stern. There were several men and women aboard the yacht and one had a flashlight. We quickly lowered a lifeboat and were able to find and pick them all up. They had clung to debris and were all hollering for help. It was obvious to us that they had been drinking."

Two men from the yacht took the Union Steamship Co. to court but unfortunately for them drew Judge Sidney Smith, who had a Master's ticket himself. They lost the case mainly because they had had no running lights on. The Master of the *Lady Pam* at the time was Captain A.C. "Big Mac" McLennan.

In 1942 the *Lady Pam*, under the command of Captain Malcolmson, was outward bound from Vancouver on a foggy morning when she collided with the *Princess Elaine,* which was inward bound heading for the First Narrows. In those days there was no radar or radio communications between ships. Probably due to tide and fog the *Elaine* had veered further north than usual and the outward-bound *Pam* hit the *Elaine* on the starboard side, aft, tore out all the railings and swung right around the stern of the *Elaine* and pierced her on the port side. According to Dennis Shaw, who was Purser aboard the *Pam* at the time, the *Pam*'s bowsprit went right into the *Elaine*'s crew quarters aft on the port side. When the *Pam* withdrew, a seaman's duffle bag hung from the broken end of the bowsprit. Part of the bowsprit was left in the *Elaine*. If a seaman had been lying in that bunk he would have been killed. The *Elaine* had to go into drydock, but the *Pam* continued on her way. According to Don Thompson, fireman aboard the *Pam*, the crew had a good laugh about this David and Goliath routine the *Pam* participated in. Another Union hand recalled that Captain Malcolmson never left the wheelhouse but was leaning out of the *Pam*'s wheelhouse shouting invectives at the *Elaine* for cutting him off. It was after this accident that the *Pam*'s bowsprit was cut off and the bow just brought to a point.

The above stories of marine mishaps all were told to me by fellows who were there at the time but nowhere in my research did I find references to them in other journals.

S.S. *Lady Pam* (G. Jones)

The *Pam* took part in the "Win the War Cruises" around Vancouver harbour on July 19, 1941. Her captain on this occasion was Harry McLean.

On VE Day, 1945, the *Lady Pam* was just off Whytecliff Park when word of the surrender came through. Harry Roach was her Captain and he immediately started blowing the *Pam*'s whistle constantly, and as well ordered all the signal flags to be flown as they entered the harbour. Word has it, despite the surrender and everyone being in a happy mood, the *Pam* was challenged by the army signal station under the bridge as she entered the harbour.

On one trip in the mid forties, the *Lady Pam* docked in Vancouver with one more passenger than was listed on the Purser's passenger report. She had left Port Mellon and was heading for Vancouver. Frank Lawrence was the Purser and a young woman, obviously in advanced pregnancy, came up to the Purser's wicket and asked him if there were any staterooms on board because she was experiencing cramps and knew her time was near.

The *Pam* had no staterooms but Frank dashed up to the bridge and spoke to Captain Malcolmson. They arranged for her to use the Captain's cabin. Then Lawrence dashed around the ship asking if there was a doctor or nurse aboard. He found a woman who had been a nurse but her only experience was working in a veterans' hospital.

The baby, a girl, was delivered safely and the mother named her *Pam* after the ship on which she was born. The World Ship Society, B.C. Branch, ran a little story about this incident in its newsletter *The Barnacle* in September 1991 in an effort to locate Baby Pam, but no one came forward.

In 1945, one night after the *Pam* was tied up at the Union dock for the night, the Purser's office was broken into and the thief jimmied the cash drawer. It was the Purser's practice to put all the cash into the ship's safe every night but this night he had neglected to do so. The Purser had no occasion to open his cash drawer until the next day after clearing the harbour. The theft wasn't noticed until someone came up and asked the Purser for some change. When he opened the drawer it was empty. Head office was notified immediately, but of course he had no working cash at all, so he had to borrow some money from a cafe at Gibsons Landing. The police met the ship when it arrived back in Vancouver and questioned all the crew but didn't arrest anyone.

John Allan, who was decking on the *Pam* during the 1940s, recalled that the crew were a happy group. One evening after the ship had tied up for the night they all went into town, had a beer or two, and on their way back to the ship they passed a shop selling orange toques. They trooped in and each bought an orange toque. One of them, Doug Mowat (later a B.C. MLA) bought a long orange scarf.

Next morning when Captain Roach came down to the *Pam* and found his crew all wearing orange toques he was thrilled to see his crew having so much spirit. Unfortunately someone cut Mowat's scarf in half. In 1947 Mowat broke his neck in a swimming accident and was no longer able to work on ships.

Later in 1945 the *Pam* lost her licence to carry passengers and was used as a freight boat. Charlie Lewis, who later became a Master on B.C. Ferries, recalled being aboard the *Pam* during this period and he said he was doing a variety of jobs on her, such as quartermaster, winchman, stevedore, etc. Later that year he sat and wrote for his Mate's ticket which he was successful in obtaining.

In 1946 the *Pam* was taken out of service and was sold to a logging company. They towed her to Oyster Bay, just south of Campbell River, where they blasted a hole in her side and sank her in the sand to form part of a breakwater, along with other old hulks, to protect the booming ground. I recall rowing down to see her after she had been sunk and I boarded her to look around. What a sad experience this was. I went into the Purser's Office and papers were scattered everywhere. It was especially sad for me because my first job as Freight Clerk with the Union Steamships was aboard the *Lady Pam* and the Purser at the time was the well-known Harold Crompton. I took the adjacent photo in 1990. It shows all that is left of this once-beautiful ship. This beach is only about a mile from my home and I find it quite amazing that she should end her days close to where I live and where I sat writing about her.

Remains of *Lady Pam* sunk as part of the breakwater, Oyster Bay, B.C. Sept. 1989 *(Twigg Collection)*

S.S. Capilano II

Capilano is the English translation of the Native family name Ky-Ap-Lan-Huh, meaning "of a great chief". Chief George Capilano (baptized George after embracing Christianity) escorted Captain Vancouver into Burrard Inlet with 40 war canoes on 15 June 1792. Chief Joe Capilano was received by King Edward VII, and Chief Matthias Joe attended the coronation of Queen Elizabeth. Three vessels with this proud name flew the Union flag.

In Union Service: 1920-49
Official No.: 141709
Type: Wooden single-screw passenger and freight vessel. Built 1920 at B.C. Marine, Vancouver
Dimensions: Length 135.0' breadth 26.9', depth 8.2'. Gross tons 374
Engines: Inverted direct-acting, triple-expansion, NHP 51, built in 1914 for the Washington.
Speed: 13.5 knots maximum
Services: Operated first to Selma resort and other gulf points, later generally to Bowen Island and Howe Sound, with PGE railway connections
Capacities: Passenger licence May to September 350 (winter 150). Cargo 50 tons

S.S. *Capilano II*
(J. Smith Collection)

The first *Capilano* was a steel-hulled ship and more of a freighter than a passenger ship. The *Capilano II* was a wooden-hulled vessel and was built to order as a passenger ship but she did have cargo space. Her licence was for 350 passengers and 50 tons of freight.

The Union Steamship Co. signed a

contract with B.C. Marine Ltd. in 1919 to build the *Capilano II* for $70,000. Her hull was built of seasoned Douglas Fir. Her engines were removed from the steamer *Washington* which the company had purchased previously for $45,000. At the time, these engines were rated among the best triple expansion engines on the coast for their size. She had a speed of 13 knots. [54]

The Company's plan was to have her service their new resort being developed at Selma Park, along with regular calls at Roberts Creek and Wilson Creek. On Sundays she made calls at Halfmoon Bay and Buccaneer Bay.

The *Capilano II* was launched on Dec. 20, 1919 and was christened by the wife of the Company's general manager, Thomas Beazley.

At the time of her launching, B.C. Marine Ltd. printed a very interesting little souvenir booklet. Captain Dennis Farina, whose father Paddy was Chief Engineer on the *Capilano II*, kept a copy of this booklet. Page 4 has an extract from a speech given at the launching by Innes Hopkins, the managing director of B.C. Marine Ltd.:

"This is the largest boat so far launched from these Yards, but not the last large boat, as we expect to have others before long." Page 8 has these words: "To-day, effort! To-morrow, prosperity!" Page 9 reads, "The 'coming events' on the horizon of British Columbia's sky line may best be measured by the shadows her hulls cast upon the waters to-day!" Page 10, "We have but hoped this hour so good, Should be by all men Understood: 'That woodman's hands with craftsman's might, Can build a vessel staunch and tight.' "

Following the festive ceremony, the guests, who included many of the city's prominent citizens, returned to the Company's offices for a large tea.

Paddy Farina was Chief Engineer on the *Capilano* for 30 years. He joined her when she was launched and stayed with her until the day she was sold. Gerald Rushton in his book *Whistle Up The Inlet* says "Paddy kept her engine room the best-polished in the fleet." [55]

The *Capilano*'s first run was on May 1, 1920, under Captain George Whalen. Captain Neil Gray who had been Captain on the *Chasina* became the *Capilano*'s regular Captain and remained on her for the following two years.

The *Capilano II* seemed to have had a rather charmed life compared to other ships in the Union fleet. One minor accident is recorded: she grounded on mud flats in McNab Creek and easily freed herself. However a well-known newspaper columnist of the day, Jimmy Butterfield of the *Province*, heard about this and wrote an article in which he described the *Capilano* as a "pot-bellied, fussy little boat." This riled Farina, who later took Butterfield to task (see Paddy Farina's entry in the Engineers chapter, pp.379-80).

In 1934 the *Capilano II* was put on the Bowen Island - Squamish run, along with the *Lady Evelyn*, servicing the PGE Railway.

S.S. *Capilano*
Main Deck Lounge
(Vancouver Maritime Museum)

On July 29, 1940 the ship, commanded by Captain W.L. Yates, took part in a "Win the War Cruise" parade of ships sponsored by the Union Steamship Co.

In 1944 the *Capilano II* was reconditioned and a buffet saloon was added for passengers' convenience.

Although the *Capilano II* didn't have many marine mishaps, she had a persistent problem with her steering chain mechanism slipping and jamming her helm, which was a constant concern. On Feb. 5, 1947 she was

Capilano II in Snug Cove
(Farina Collection)

sailing from New Brighton for Hopkins Landing under the command of Captain Jock Malcolmson when the chain slipped and the helm jammed. "Oh my God!" Malcolmson cried when he discovered this, and at that instant he collapsed at the wheelhouse door. The Mate, Don Campbell, stopped the ship immediately and assumed command. He rushed full speed to Gibsons Landing where a doctor came aboard, examined Malcolmson and pronounced him dead. He was only 55 years old.

The final voyage of the *Capilano II* under the Union Steamships house flag was on Jan. 31, 1949. Her end came suddenly and was a surprise to all. The Captain on her final voyage, which was to be up the Sunshine Coast to Stillwater and back, was Captain Robert Naughty. Following is an eyewitness account of that sailing as told to me by John Smith, who was a member of the crew on that fateful day:

"We were to sail at 9:30 a.m. There was a strong westerly blowing and we started loading the freight at 7 a.m. With such a strong wind blowing, the winchman soon had trouble controlling the cargo boards without someone assisting at the hatchway. The mate in charge of the loading was Robbie Robinson and he took the matter up with Captain Suffield, the Marine Superintendent, who told them to continue working. Captain Naughty soon came into the picture and saw what was happening. He ordered extra longshoremen. There ensued a great battle of words between Captain Naughty and Captain Suffield. This was not a great start to what was to be a very eventful day.

"However, the ship sailed on time with only six passengers aboard. When the *Capilano* reached First Narrows she was digging in deep and the westerly wind was now blowing gale force. Captain Naughty contemplated going into Howe Sound and out Barfleur Channel. It took us more than two hours to reach Cape Roger Curtis, which normally was a one and a half hours run. At that time one of the crew reported that the decking of the fo'c'sle was leaking and working loose. Her seams were splitting open! The Chief Engineer, Paddy Farina, was called to investigate and when he saw what was happening he reported back the alarming news immediately to Captain Naughty.

"Captain Naughty got onto the radio telephone and phoned Captain Suffield and said he was going into Gibsons Landing, but Captain Suffield told him to keep to the schedule. Captain Naughty then gave orders to drop the derricks. The crew was called out and they were able to get one derrick down and secure into its crutch. They went to work on the second derrick but it got away from them and took a swipe at the funnel, but fortunately one of its lines got fouled up and arrested the swing and it stopped only inches away from the funnel. If it had hit the funnel it would have been game over. The ship was rolling and tossing until it got into the lea of Eastbourne and then we headed into Gibsons Landing.

"Captain Naughty went ashore and phoned Captain Suffield. When he returned, all the passengers were discharged and arrangements were made to send them by bus to their destinations, and the *Capilano* was to head back to Vancouver. We arrived back in Vancouver at 7 p.m. where we were met by Captain Suffield, Harry Biles the Shore Mate, and other Company officials."

The insurance underwriters were called down next morning to examine her hull. They could see that her wooden hull was splitting open. She was condemned right on the spot, there and then. She was purchased by Mahood Logging Ltd. from a Victoria scrap dealer and was sunk at Lang Bay to become part of a breakwater protecting a log booming ground. Paddy Farina, whose name was synonymous with the *Capilano II*, had to find a new berth, but before he left he removed the *Capilano*'s whistle and took it with him. He joined the *Lady Cynthia*, and installed the *Capilano*'s whistle on her.

Capilano II at Keats Island, B.C. *(A. Welbourn)*

S.S. Cheam

Cheam: The old *Bowena* was renamed Cheam in 1921. It was the name of a Native village in the outlying Chilliwack district, denoting "a wild strawberry place." It was also given to Cheam Mountain, pronounced See-Am, meaning "The Chief."

In Union service: 1920-23
Official No.: 96995
Type: Wooden twin-screw passenger-freighter. Built 1901 as the City of Nanaimo by McAlpine & Allen at False Creek, Vancouver. Purchased later by Capt. J.A. Cates and renamed Bowena for Terminal Steam Navigation run to Bowen Island and Howe Sound. Taken over by Union with the Bowen resort in December 1920 and renamed Cheam.
Dimensions: Length 159.0', breadth 32.0', depth 9.4'. Gross tons 821
Engines: Compound NHP 51. Speed 10.5 knots
Services: Continued on the Bowen Island excursion run and Britannia-Squamish route
Capacities: Passenger licence summer 500, winter 200. Cargo 200 tons

S.S. *Cheam*
(Logan Collection)

This ship was built in False Creek by McAlpine and Allen at the Lamey & Kyle millsite in 1891. Her first owners were the Mainland and Nanaimo Navigation Co. and she was appropriately named the *City of Nanaimo*. She was constructed of wood, 150 feet long.

The Dunsmuir family foreclosed on the previous owners in 1896 and took over operating the *City of Nanaimo*, running her on the east coast of Vancouver Island and the Gulf Islands as part of the Dunsmuir family's E&N Railway operation.

In 1905 the CPR purchased the ship and she became part of its coastal steamship service, operating mostly on the Victoria-Comox route. In 1912 the CPR sold the ship to Captain Cates, who renamed her the *Bowena* after Bowen Island. He ran her to Bowen Island where he was developing

S.S. *Bowena* circa 1912, later renamed the *Cheam*
(Logan Collection)

property holdings and creating a resort.

At this time the Union Steamship Co. had been operating for almost 30 years and were looking to expand their business, so they bought Cates' Terminal Steam Navigation Co., including the Bowen Island property and two ships, the *Ballena* and the *Bowena*. [56]

However, before the deal closed the *Ballena* caught fire at the Union dock and was a complete loss. The *Bowena* also was damaged but her new owners repaired her at a cost of $15,000 and changed her name to *Cheam*. Under the new name she went into service in May 1921 under Captain F.W. Gilbert, who had transferred to Union Steamship Co. at the time of the sale. [57]

Less than two years later, on April 29, 1923, she again caught fire, this time while docked in North Vancouver. The blaze destroyed the storeroom, which contained the steering gear, control rods, engine telegraph and electric light wires, and badly damaged the main passenger deck. Damages amounted to $3,220. [58]

The *Cheam* ran as an excursion vessel, mainly to Bowen Island, helped by the *Capilano II* running on the East Howe Sound-Squamish route. Traffic was so heavy on weekends that the *Cheam* often had to double back to Vancouver and pick up extra loads of passengers waiting to go to Bowen Island. Her master at this time was the well-known Billy Yates. In one notable adventure with Yates, the *Cheam* in several trips carried a total of about 2,000 school children out to see the HMS *Hood*, anchored in Vancouver harbour on July 2, 1924. [59]

After serving the lower coastal area for 32 years - three of them under the Union Steamship house flag - the *Cheam* was retired, but suffered the ignominy of becoming a floating bunk house. It was said she was treated so badly that her bottom fell out. She was scrapped in 1926.

S.S. Lady Evelyn

In Union service: 1923-36
Official No.: 109680
Type: Steel twin-screw passenger-freighter. Bought by Union from Howe Sound Navigation in 1923
Dimensions: Length 189.0', breadth 26.1', depth 9.5'. Gross tons 588
Engines: Triple-expansion NHP 150, IHP 1,500, two engines. speed 14 knots maximum, 13 average
Services: Generally on West Howe Sound and Georgia Strait routes
Capacities: Passenger licence summer 480, winter 200. Cargo 100 tons

Lady Evelyn (J. Smith Collection)

The *Lady Evelyn*, originally named the *Deerhound*, was built at Birkenhead by J. Jones & Sons for the West Cornwall S.S. Co. in 1901. As the *Deerhound* she plied the St. Lawrence River as a mail packet. She made headlines in 1914 for rescue work in the *Empress of Ireland* disaster which claimed 1,024 lives. [60] She was commissioned in the R.C.N. from 1917 - 1919.

Seven years earlier the *Deerhound* herself had narrowly escaped disaster. A newspaper clipping I have tells of Earl Richards seeing her lying at Penzance in 1907, waiting to sail to Canada. He and his father were offered passage on her, but they thought her too small for the Atlantic and declined. "It was just as well, as she ran out of fuel and water on her way to Quebec and nearly foundered," he said.

The *Deerhound* in WW. I garb (note gun on the stern) (*National Archives of Canada*)

The *Deerhound* was brought to Vancouver in 1922 by Captain Thompson, owner of the Howe Sound Navigation Co. His company was incorporated in 1921 and operated several vessels under what was known as the Marine Express. Thompson operated her over the following year. The Union Steamship Co. was very impressed with her weekend passenger loads so they decided to purchase her. They paid $180,000 in October 1923, but in year-round operation she did not make money for the Company. They tried her on the Pender Harbour run in her first year but in order to make it there and back at a reasonable hour they had to run her at full speed and this simply was not economical. [61]

The *Lady Evelyn* had the distinction of being the first of the 'Lady' ships for Union Steamships, with Evelyn honouring the wife of the then Governor-General. Starting with the *Lady Evelyn* in 1923, this policy of the day boats being prefixed with "Lady" was initiated. She was followed by the *Lady Alexandra*, *Lady Cecilia*, *Lady Cynthia*, *Lady Pam* and the *Lady Rose*. (The *Lady Rose* was originally launched and named the *Lady Sylvia* but this had to be changed because another ship was registered as *Sylvia*.)

The purchase of the *Lady Evelyn* also brought Captain Billy Yates back to the Union Steamship Co. He had been with Union previously but had joined Marine Express in 1913. Captain Yates spent the next 31 years with Union, becoming one of the best-known captains in the fleet.

In 1925 the Union line's *Cowichan* sank and the *Evelyn* was pressed into overnight runs even though she was not suited for this type of service. "We used to bring back lots of livestock, horses, cows, sheep," says Fred Corneille, a deck officer on the *Evelyn*. "We

Lady Evelyn at Sechelt dock circa 1927 (*Hackett*)

would just put them down in the hold and let them run loose. By the time we got to Vancouver, the hold was a mess."

Corneille also says the *Evelyn* had an unusual design feature: "She had a flush deck, that is, the main deck went right through from bow to stern, there was no between deck or upper deck. She was the only ship where the engineer could see what was going on. His controls were on top of the engines and he could see what was happening. Sometimes this could be a hazard, as he could see what the captain was doing and perhaps do the thinking for him."

Freddie Smith, the famous Chief Engineer who worked on all the Union ships in his 44 years with the Company, said the *Lady Evelyn* was his favourite ship in the fleet. Iain Morrison, a former deck officer with Union, had a barometer off the *Lady Evelyn* hanging in his home when I interviewed him in 1989.

The *Lady Evelyn* was retired in 1935 and anchored in Bedwell Bay. She was scrapped the following year.

Lady Evelyn at Roberts Creek (note the old cars on the wharf) *(G. Taylor)*

M.V. Comox II

Comox is an abbreviation of the name in the Euclataw tongue for the Comox district of Vancouver Island. The full name means "plenty" or "riches" - the district being noted for its abundance of berries and game.

In Union service: periodically between 1924 and 1943
Official No.: 152548
Type: Wooden passenger-freight motor vessel. Built 1924 by Wallace Shipbuilding Co., North Vancouver
Dimensions: Length 54.0', breadth 15.5', depth 7.2'. Gross tons 54
Engines: Diesel Atlas Imperial, Oakland, Cal., 3 cylinders, BHP 55. Speed 7 knots
Services: Used as a ferry between Whytecliff and Snug Cove, Bowen Island, 1924-26, and again 1939-42, also for connections from Pender Harbour to Jervis Inlet and Sechelt Inlet, as well as charters
Capacities: Passenger licence 25. Cargo about 15 tons

M.V. *Comox II*
(Vancouver Maritime Museum)

The *Comox II* was a wooden vessel built to order for the Union Steamship Co. by Wallace Shipbuilding in 1926 at a cost of $20,000. Many people believe she was a fish packer originally and converted for Union but this is not so. She was built specifically as a feeder vessel for Howe Sound routes but began by operating from

Pender Harbour to Jervis Inlet supplying logging camps. She was the oddest-looking vessel in the Union fleet.

In the later 1920s the *Comox II* was moved and operated out of Porpoise Bay. Freight was landed at Sechelt and trucked over to Porpoise Bay. She ran the Skookumchuck Rapids to the Egmont and Jervis Inlet areas. She would connect up with the Union ship going south at Pender Harbour and return the following day. From 1924 to 1926 she sailed between Whytecliff Park and Bowen Island. She then returned to the Porpoise Bay run again, staying on it into the 1930s. It was mostly a summer service, for in the winter months she was required for the Howe Sound run. Her captains in this period were Billy Yates and John H. Browne.

In the early 1930s she was operating out of Snug Cove, Bowen Island as a feeder vessel for the West Howe Sound ports, which was her originally intended role. Passengers going from Vancouver to West Howe Sound would be dropped off at Snug Cove, board the *Comox II* and be taken to ports up the Sound. Passengers returning would get off the *Comox II* at Snug Cove and board another ship to Vancouver. The Captain in this period was the famous Billy Yates and other crew included Dennis Farina, who in later years became Captain of the *Malibu Princess*, Slim Holdgate, who became Chief Steward with the Company, and a chap by the name of Bucky Reid.

In 1939 she was put on the Whytecliff-Bowen Island run again. Her Master was J.R. 'Buster' Browne, son of one of her former captains, John H. Browne. On May 24, 1940 Captain Browne sighted an overturned sailboat with three men clinging to the craft. He sped to the scene and rescued the men from the cold waters of Howe Sound.

Bob McLean, son of Captain Harry McLean, a well-known Union Co. skipper, began his sea career on the *Comox II* when Byron Crowell was her Captain. McLean says there was only a three-man crew then. He recalled that his berth was a nice warm spot, right above the galley stove! McLean left Union in 1949 and four years later joined the Vancouver Fire Boat as her Captain, a position he retained for 31 years until he retired in 1984.

Though the *Comox II* was the ugly duckling of the Union fleet, it certainly proved to be a good starting point for several successful seamen on the B.C. coast.

In 1941 the *Comox II* was taken off the Bowen Island run and laid up at the Union dock until she was purchased in 1943 by Canfisco, then converted for use in the fish-processing industry. John Smith, an ex-Union Steamships seaman, saw her in 1981 being used as a diving boat for scuba divers. In April 1992 I visited Bill New, president and general manager of Coast Ferries, and while wandering around his plant I spotted the *Comox II* tied up to a float. One of his employees, Keith Thorp, bought her in 1972 and was living aboard her. As of this writing she is still afloat but does not put out to sea anymore.

M.V. *Comox*
(Vancouver Maritime Museum)

S.S. Cardena

Cardena is one of two Spanish names (the other being Catala) given to early Union ships. It was taken from Cardena Bay on the south shore of Kennedy Island at the mouth of the Skeena River, which appropriately was in the centre of the fishing industry the *Cardena* was designed to serve. Cardena Bay was named after Garcia Lopez de Cardenas, one of Coronados' captains (later an admiral) in his New Mexico expedition. Cardenas is said to have been the first European to see the Grand Canyon.

In Union service: 1923-59
Official No.: 150977
Type: Steel twin-screw passenger and cargo steamer. Built 1923 by Napier & Miller, Old Kilpatrick, Scotland
Dimensions: Length 226.8', breadth 37.1', depth 18.4'. Gross tons 1,559
Engines: Direct-acting, triple-expansion, IHP 2,000. Speed 14 knots maximum, 13 average.
Services: Weekly on northern cannery route to the Skeena River, also in the Bella Coola and logging camp services
Capacities: Passenger licence 150, cabin berths 132, deck settees 60. Cargo 50 tons; refrigeration for 30 tons of boxed fish; carried 11,000 cases of canned salmon

S.S. *Cardena* off West Vancouver
(T. Dougan)

By all accounts, and especially from the seamen who knew her, the *Cardena* was said to have had the most beautiful lines of any ship on the B.C. coast. She was indeed very graceful as she sped over the sea. Along with her fetching appearance she also was renowned for faithful and reliable service to all the settlements along the B.C. coast, which she served for over 30 years. In my research, I found there was probably

Cardena at Stewart Island *(Roach Collection)*

more written about the *Cardena* than any other coastal ship.

The contract to build her was awarded in 1922 to Napier and Miller on the Clyde, in Scotland. She was designed and patterned after the S.S. *Venture*, but was 50 feet longer. The best features of the *Venture* were incorporated into the *Cardena*. As well she had a large observation room forward and something new: four outside rooms with full facilities on the top deck. Clarence Arthur, Chief Engineer on the *Cardena* for years, took one of these rooms for himself. He was the only chief engineer in the whole fleet to have his quarters on the boat deck.

The *Cardena* was built to carry 350 tons of general cargo and had a new feature which was a freezer compartment that could handle 30 tons of boxed frozen fish.

After her sea trials the *Cardena* left Scotland on May 3, 1923 under Captain A.E. Dickson. Billy McCombe, who later became a senior Captain with Union Steamships, was a junior officer on her trip to British Columbia. George Foster, a senior engineer with the Company, had stood by the *Cardena* while she was being built and was her Chief Engineer on her voyage to B.C. She arrived in Vancouver in the afternoon of June 11, 1923. Other ships in the harbour at the time blew their whistles, giving a noisy salute to the Union Company's new flagship.

Shortly after her arrival, Captain Dickson took the *Cardena* out on her maiden trip, taking Company dignitaries and friends up Howe Sound. Reports say they were all suitably impressed with the new ship.

On June 20, 1923 the *Cardena* made her first official trip up north. She replaced the *Chelohsin*, which had serviced the area for more than 10 years. The deck officers on that trip were Captain Dickson, Chief Officer W. Mounce, Second Mate Ernest Sheppard, Third Mate J. Mercer. The Purser was R. Smith and the Chief Steward was Bert Ebden.

The Company's expansion program begun in the early 1920s was paying off. Led by the *Catala* and the *Cardena*, the Company became predominant on the north coast, while their new day boats - *Capilano*, *Lady Evelyn*, *Lady Alexandra*, *Lady Cynthia* and *Lady Cecilia* - took over on the Sunshine Coast. During this period of growth, Company president Richard Welsford and long-time director Sir Arnold Rushton visited from England and boarded some of these ships to see them in action. [62]

Four years after her maiden voyage, the *Cardena* made the headlines in a big way by saving the CNR's *Prince Rupert* from certain disaster on Ripple Rock in treacherous Seymour Narrows. The *Cardena*'s skipper, Andy Johnstone, had just come on watch in the early morning of Aug. 22, 1927 when Chief Officer Jock Muir, whom he was relieving, heard a series of five short blasts from a ship in the area, signalling she was in distress. It was quite foggy so Captain Johnstone headed cautiously in the direction of the whistle blasts. All of sudden looming out of the mist they saw it was the *Prince Rupert*. She was hung up on Ripple Rock!

Ernie Plant, who had been at the wheel during Muir's watch, was heading below when Muir said, "Don't go away now Ernie, we're heading on a rescue mission. The *Rupert* is stuck on Ripple Rock."

Captain Johnstone gave Gerald Rushton the following version of the story: "The

Prince Rupert had passed us farther up the straits on her way south, and there was a strong ebb tide running in Seymour Narrows. Apparently she had struck Ripple Rock head on and passed clear over it. However, with her engines stopped, the force of the ebb tide had swept the *Prince Rupert* astern so that she struck a second time and pinned herself on the rock. The ship's rudder had been driven into and become interlocked with the starboard propeller. Her position, with a capacity passenger load, was extremely hazardous and precariously near the starboard side cliffs. As my ship drew close, I shouted to Mr. Mercer, our first mate, to cast the *Cardena*'s steel towing line aboard from our after reel, which he did and made fast to the *Prince Rupert*'s stern. It was a superb feat of heaving-line throwing by big John Mercer, who was an old-time halibut schooner man with huge hands. The fog was then clearing sufficiently for the *Cardena* to come alongside the *Prince Rupert*'s port side and make fast.

"I looked up and called to her bridge and there was my old chief officer of the *Camosun* when I was second mate, now Captain Dan Donald; but in the excitement he didn't seem to recognize me. Then, working the *Cardena* in the manner of a tug moving a liner, we pulled the vessel off the pinnacle. I could have towed her all the way to Vancouver if we'd been the other side of the Narrows or if her rudder could have been brought amidships. As it was, we first got her into mid-channel and safe from the threatening cliffs, thus preventing a possible major disaster. Then we towed her back to a safe anchorage in Deep Cove, just a mile from the Narrows entrance, towing being difficult owing to the *Rupert*'s rudder being jammed hard a-starboard. The decision to leave her safely anchored in Deep Cove proved a sound one, as two powerful tugs later had plenty of trouble sharing the task of bringing her the 110 miles to the Burrard Dry Dock in Vancouver." [63]

Once the *Cardena* had pulled the *Prince Rupert* into the quiet waters of Deep Cove about a mile from Ripple Rock, the *Cardena* took aboard as many passengers as she possibly could, as well as the mail and other valuables. Luckily the CPR *Princess Beatrice* was going by and she also came alongside the *Rupert* and took the rest of her passengers off and into Vancouver.

Although the *Cardena* proved to be an excellent rescue ship in that instance, from then on her record was mainly one of herself needing to be rescued.

Her first scrape came in 1929 when she ran aground on a sand bar in the Skeena River slough, near the North Pacific Cannery. The S.S. *Salvage Princess* happened to be in Prince Rupert at the time and arrived within an hour. She attempted to pull the *Cardena* off but failed. Captain Findlay then ordered the passengers taken off the next day along with freight and mail. Two days later the *Cardena* floated free with the help of the salvage vessels. She was taken to drydock and the damage was found to be slight. For the next three weeks the *Venture* took over the *Cardena*'s run.

Ill luck followed the *Cardena* on her first trip after being repaired. She was under the command of Captain Andrew Johnstone and went aground on Village Island in the Skeena River. Once again the passengers were taken off the next day and the following day she was refloated and taken back to Vancouver for repairs. The

Ernie Plant proudly points to where he is standing on the *Cardena's* starboard railing when the two ships were side by side in Deep Cove. Plant is above the "C" in *Cardena*. He was later transferred to the *Catala* and was aboard her two months later when she grounded on Sparrowhawk Reef. *(Plant Collection)*

Cardena aground in Skeena River
(Vancouver Maritime Museum)

grounding took place on Dec. 19, 1929. [64] A postcard was put out - not by the Company, you can be sure - showing the *Cardena* high and dry on both groundings.

Though the ships of all steamship lines were quick to come to the aid of each other in distress, at other times there was a fierce rivalry for prestige and commercial success, one instance of which involving the *Cardena* was described this way by Gerald Rushton in *Whistle Up the Inlet*:

"Captain Andy Johnstone recalled with some glee when his favourite ship the *Cardena*, in the fall of 1931, was finishing unloading at the Ocean Falls dock, while the CP's *Princess Joan* was simultaneously completing her discharge at the other side of the dock, both ships being northbound to Prince Rupert. His radio operator handed him a Company message stating that it was essential for the *Cardena* to load northbound cases of salmon at Bella Bella, as the cannery had no storage room left. This did not present any problems, but minutes later (the radio operator) reported that he had intercepted a similar message from the Canadian Pacific to the master of the *Princess Joan*. Now, this was serious because if the CP vessel reached Bella Bella first, which she could easily do with her faster speed, and occupied the single cannery berth, the *Cardena* would have to wait her turn with a delay of seven hours, and miss the tide in the Skeena River. This was because the *Princess Joan* could load only 500 cases an hour, whereas the *Cardena*, which easily handled 1,500 cases an hour, could be in and out of Bella Bella in little more than two hours. So Andy devised his plan of action.

"The *Joan* got away first from Ocean Falls, the *Cardena* tagging behind 15 minutes later. The CP ship was heading for Lama Pass, the normal and rather circuitous route to the Bella Bellas. It was fast getting dark, and before the *Cardena* reached the entrance of Gunboat Passage - a narrow uncharted channel well known to Andy and seldom used by larger vessels - he switched off all lights, even in the main saloon, to disguise his turnoff from the main channel. Then he steamed through Gunboat Passage and had already loaded 1,000 cases of salmon before the *Joan* came in sight. When the Joan drew close, Captain Johnstone, who had a foghorn voice, yelled to his opposite number on the bridge: 'Don't worry, Cap'n, we'll be out of your way in another hour!'" [65]

Captain Johnstone ran a tight but happy ship and his crews stayed with him. Some of them even formed an orchestra which would play aboard ship and entertain passengers. It consisted of Tom Lucas, quartermaster at the time and later a well-known Master in the fleet. He was mainly responsible for forming the orchestra. Others in the band were his brother Ernie, Fred Tite from Prince Rupert, and Johnnie Walker who in later years went longshoring on the Union dock. When they had time they even had a former member of the Boston Symphony Orchestra conduct them in practice sessions.

Port Hardy was one of the *Cardena*'s southbound calls and Captain Johnstone always tried to get there well ahead of time, so the ship could lay over for a few hours to enable the orchestra to play for dances at the local dance hall. On one occasion the *Cardena* had to load 1,500 cases of canned salmon at Goose Bay. Captain Johnstone radioed ahead to Goose Bay to have extra workers available to help load the salmon because he had promised the people of Port Hardy that they would be there in time for a dance party that had been arranged beforehand. Fifteen hundred cases of canned salmon were loaded in 35 minutes, which must have been some sort of record, and Captain Johnstone got the *Cardena* to Port Hardy in time to keep his promise. [66]

The next accident involving the *Cardena* happened at Namu, probably in the early 1930s. It was around Christmas and the *Cardena* was southbound. As she approached the dock at Namu her telegraph signal chain broke. A small B.C. Packers freighter, the *P.W.*, was alongside the dock. The *Cardena* couldn't stop because of the failed telegraph. The *Cardena*'s Master was able to give a series of whistle blasts as a warning that something was wrong and the crew of the *P.W.* scrambled off before the *Cardena* hit her. The *P.W.* was cut in two right at the wharf. She was eventually raised and put back into service. No one was injured, and the *Cardena* wasn't damaged and continued on to Vancouver.

In 1934 Captain Johnstone went to the Pilotage and another famous skipper, Captain Georgeson, took over the *Cardena*. In this same period, Company manager Harold Brown had blueprints drawn up for another *Cardena*, a new and improved version. The plans had been reviewed and approved by other captains in the fleet, but the shareholders felt that the estimated cost - $600,000 - was too high, so the plans never got off the drawing board, though later the Company suffered badly from lack of capacity.

In February 1935 the *Cardena* had a very dangerous and harrowing experience, having to ride out an icy gale in Queen Charlotte Sound. The following is an excerpt from a story by *The Vancouver Sun* reporter Pat Terry, who claimed to have dragged it out of a silent Captain Georgeson after the *Cardena* had arrived 12 hours late:

"The *Cardena* was en route to Prince Rupert when the cold spell hit her. Seas breaking inboard left a deposit of polished ice. Wind flung freezing spindrift in the faces of the men working her. Still she ploughed northward into colder and colder waters that were churned up into tempestuous waves. It was a battle against tremendous cold all the way.

"At Bella Coola it was found that three sailors were frostbitten. She was unable to make her usual call at Port Essington, so bad was the weather.

"On her return journey Capt. Georgeson found conditions even worse. The ship moved southward into the Queen Charlotte Sound in a howling blizzard, whose grim music sang overpoweringly of the trouble ahead of her.

"Entering the [Johnstone] Strait, the captain was faced with making a decision. Both anchors were dropped off the northern tip of Vancouver Island and she rode out the storm safely, but in acute discomfort.

"There was no rest for officers or crew. The situation, one demanding the greatest watchfulness and the highest seamanship, was a delicate one.

"The *Cardena*, riding heavy seas at the southern end of Queen Charlotte Sound, laid in Arctic conditions from 2:40 p.m. on Sunday until 6 a.m. on Monday, the 21st. All that time the captain and his crew were anxiously peering through a raging snowstorm watching for a break." [67]

Finally a break in the weather did come and the *Cardena* was able to proceed to Vancouver and arrived only 12 hours behind schedule, a remarkable achievement given the adverse conditions.

In 1937 the *Cardena* had Canada's Governor General, Lord Tweedsmuir, travel north aboard her from Bella Coola. The ship made headlines again, not only because of her distinguished passenger. As Captain Georgeson steered her toward the Claxton Cannery, the crew noticed flames rising from the building. He ordered full speed ahead and readied the ship's pumps. When the *Cardena* pulled alongside, the cannery's hoses were hooked up to the ship's pumps and for three hours they fought the fire, while the passengers aboard had a grandstand view. [68]

After the war broke out in 1939, the *Cardena* and other ships on the coast were all painted over in wartime gray. There were fears of Japanese submarines operating in coastal waters. Running to schedule at the time was very difficult. Many Air Force and other military bases were established along the coast, which had to be serviced by Union ships. Several, including the *Cardena*, carried engineer trainees for the Canadian Navy.

The Union Steamship Co. tried to do its part in the war effort by sponsoring "Win the War Cruises." On July 29, 1940, six ships of the Union fleet took part in a parade around the harbour. The *Cardena* took part in this parade, with Captain Jack Boden on the bridge.

During these war years all ships including the *Cardena* were operated without any relief and were extended to their limits. On one occasion the *Cardena* was called upon by the military to pick up an RCAF squadron at Sidney on Vancouver Island and ferry them up to Annette Island in Alaska.

In the early part of 1942, at which time all coastal shipping was under blackout regulations, the *Cardena* was rammed one evening by the tug *La Pointe*. Tex Lyon, the wharfinger at Port Hardy, says the *Cardena* was proceeding north up Goletas Channel when the *La Pointe* rammed into her port side, midships, destroying staterooms 15 and 17 on the main deck. Water and steam lines were broken, and live steam sprayed in every direction.

It was a miracle that both staterooms were vacant at the time of the collision, for otherwise there surely would have been fatalities.

The registered occupants of stateroom 15 were Mr. and Mrs. Bob Chase along with Mrs. Rose Rouillard, Helen Chase's mother. They were travelling to Bella Coola. Mr. and Mrs. Chase had gone up on deck to join in a party with some air force men going to Bella Bella. Mrs. Rouillard had decided to stay behind in the stateroom and have a rest rather than join the party.

Cardena at Shushartie Bay after being rammed by the tug *La Pointe* (M. Benson)

Cardena showing damage after being rammed by the tug *La Pointe* (M. Benson)

The air force boys thought that Helen's mother would enjoy the party and insisted that they go down to the stateroom and bring her up. So down they went and as Bob

said, "We grabbed her by both hands and yarded her out of the room." They were only about 10 feet down the ship's corridor when the tug hit the *Cardena* and obliterated the stateroom where Mrs. Rouillard only moments earlier had been lying down. A piece of the *Cardena*'s side plate had been crumpled in and the settee where Mrs. Rouillard had been resting was completely crushed. She would have been killed instantly. As Bob Chase says now, "Here's a case where a drink saved our lives."

Immediately after the impact there was panic aboard the *Cardena* as live steam filled the ship, but once engineers controlled the flow of steam the panic subsided. The

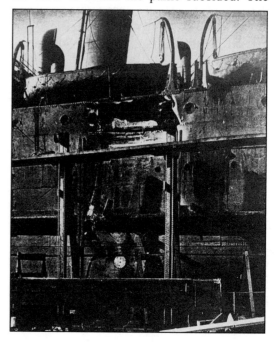

first thought by most people aboard was that they had been torpedoed by a Japanese submarine because it was wartime and rumours of the day had it that Estevan Point had been shelled by the Japanese.

The Chases had high praise for Captain Boden's handling of the situation, and how wonderfully well the crew reacted. The passengers were embarked into lifeboats and were picked up out in the channel by a a very large American yacht passing by, which took them to Port Hardy.

Captain Boden had to make sure that each lifeboat had a ship's officer aboard. The Purser, old Pat Pattison, had put all the ship's papers, money and valuables into large paper bags and was in one of the lifeboats holding these bags on his shoulders as if the tide was going to come up. Captain Boden is reported to have looked at this comical scene and said to Pat, "Well, I guess you'll have to do." Bob Chase said, "Having Pat in the lifeboat was like having a comedian along."

Captain Boden then beached the *Cardena* at Deep Creek across from Christie Pass.

The Union Steamships' *Venture* happened to be in Port Hardy and the passengers off the *Cardena* simply walked across the wharf and boarded her. They were taken back to Vancouver and put up at the Grosvenor Hotel for a week. The *Cardena* was temporarily patched by Second Engineer MacKenzie. The ship then sailed back to Vancouver. Officers aboard the *Cardena* at the time were Captain John Boden, Chief Officer John Mercer, Second Mate Len King, Chief Engineer Clarence Arthur, Second Engineer MacKenzie, Purser Pat Pattison, Assistant Purser Harry Braddick, Freight Clerk Mike Benson and Chief Steward Jack Minnes.

By the end of World War II in 1945, the Union Steamship Co. was badly in need of new ships to replace some of their aging and worn-out vessels. Later that year management decided to purchase three Castle Class corvettes from the War Assets Corporation at $75,000 each. What looked good on paper turned out to be a disaster in service. Their cargo space wasn't adequate and their cost of operating was 50 per cent more than the *Cardena*'s. They looked nice but the Company sometimes was forced to lay them up in winter because they were so expensive to run, so the *Catala* and the *Cardena* still had to shoulder most of the workload, the *Catala* on the Ocean Falls run and *Cardena* on the logging camps run.

In 1947 the Company decided to tie up the three converted corvettes during the winter and were going to have the *Cardena* service Bella Coola then cross over to the Queen Charlotte Islands, but they received such howls of protest over this that they relented and put the *Coquitlam II* on a route directly to the Queen Charlottes.

On Dec. 21, 1947 one of the Company's most famous skippers, Captain Robert Wilson, collapsed on the bridge of the *Cardena* while taking the ship north to bring back a full load of loggers going home for Christmas. Up and down the coast he was known as "Captain Bob." He had served the coastal people for over 35 years and was particularly well-known and liked by the loggers. The ship's Chief Officer, Jack Summerfield, immediately took command and contacted head office asking permission to turn the ship back to Vancouver, but it was not given. Summerfield then rang for full speed ahead and made for Campbell River, where there was a hospital. However, Captain Bob had passed away. He was the last of four Captains in the fleet who died aboard their ships.

The *Cardena* had more bad luck in the early morning hours on July 16, 1948. She went aground at False Bay about 1:30 a.m. Chief Officer "Wee" Angus McNeill was in command at the time. I remember it well because I was on board at the time as Assistant Purser. I was just going to bed and was taking off my jacket when I heard a strange scraping along the hull. My cabin was just above the water line on the port side. When I heard that unusual noise I put my jacket back on and rushed out of the room. A moment later we hit a reef at the

Cardena aground at False Bay circa 1948 *(Forbes Collection)*

entrance to False Bay. The *Cardena* went well aground. There wasn't any panic. Captain W. McCombe, who had gone off watch about an hour before, immediately took over command from Chief Officer McNeill.

At the time of the grounding most passengers were in their beds and there were reports of some passengers being thrown out of bed by the impact. However, I don't recall anybody being hurt. Captain McCombe immediately ordered the lifeboats lowered and the passengers were taken over to the False Bay wharf. One of the ship's fuel tanks had been punctured and a thick oil poured into the bay. This made rowing difficult, and many passengers had their clothes soiled by the oil.

Mr. and Mrs. Charles Williams, who ran the False Bay store, opened up and brewed coffee and helped take care of the passengers for the rest of the night. Women and children were given all the available rooms in the hotel and the others grabbed sleep wherever they could in the hotel lounge and lobby. Sandwiches, and later ice cream, were brought ashore from the ship by crew members. Next morning the *Chelohsin* arrived. She had been sent up by the Company to False Bay to take the tired and sleepy passengers back to Vancouver.

The Captain and crew remained aboard the *Cardena* all night. I recall walking around the deck next morning and running into "Wee" Angus. What could one say to the man who has just run his ship aground? We passed each other without saying a word.

It was fortunate that the *Cardena* did not heel over. Next morning when the tide went out we could see why. Somehow she had grounded between two pinnacles of rock which held the *Cardena* up as though she was in a vice. She had really gone hard aground and only about 15 feet of her was sitting in the water.

Salvage tugs soon arrived on the scene and the first attempt to pull her free failed. Two of her holds had been holed but her double bottom saved her from extensive flooding. Later that day she was pulled free and was able to limp into Vancouver under her own power. The tug *Salvor* escorted her down. She had to have some of her plates replaced but she was soon back in service.

In November 1949 the *Chelohsin* went aground in Stanley Park and was a total loss, so the *Cardena* had to replace her on the logging camp route. The two old stalwarts of the Company, the *Cardena* and the *Catala*, became the workhorses and kept the Company going while their fancy sisters, the converted corvettes, continued to be a problem with their high operating costs.

The *Cardena* went aground again on Nov. 11, 1950, this time picking a nice soft spot on Savary Island. Stan Green, Second Mate on her at the time, gave me this story: "It was low tide and Captain Roach misjudged the tide when he was approaching to make a landing at Savary Island. The ship grounded in the sand and with the falling tide the sand just sucked the hull in and she was held fast. I tried rocking the *Cardena* by swinging a load of boom chains back and forth with the winches but she wouldn't budge, so we just sat there for a few hours until the tide came in and the ship floated free."

Later the same day, trying to make a landing at Surge Narrows, coming around a point, a strong tidal current took the *Cardena* ashore a short distance from the dock. The passengers were taken off in the lifeboats and over to the dock for safety reasons. Lines were run to some trees ashore to make sure that with the falling tide the ship would be held upright. Later with the rising tide the *Cardena* floated free and proceeded on her run. Twice in 24 hours the *Cardena* had gone aground. Could this be a record?

Unfortunately, the saga of the *Cardena*'s troubles did not end there, for such groundings and other accidents kept on happening.

On March 24, 1952 at about 7 a.m. the *Cardena* was approaching the Lions Gate Bridge, inbound from Powell River with 86 passengers aboard. The skipper was Harry Roach. He had tried to clear an outgoing vessel in the narrows and had swung too far over and had grounded on the mud flats at the mouth of the Capilano River, with about six feet of water around her. The passengers were taken off by assisting tugs and over to West Vancouver for a bus trip to Vancouver. No one was injured and the *Cardena* suffered very little damage. Tugs were able to pull her off the mud flats later in the day.

Early in 1953 the *Cardena* went aground again, this time on her way to Sullivan Bay. Just after midnight, entering Patrick Passage en route to Sullivan Bay she struck a rock off a small island in the channel. Neil Campbell, the Chief Officer, was on the bridge. She was badly holed in the forepeak. Captain Harry Roach got the pumps going and managed to keep the flooding under control until they reached Sullivan Bay. With tugs standing by, the *Cardena* was able to return to Vancouver under her own steam. After the accident the Department of Transport installed a light on the island. [69]

On Oct. 23, 1953 she had another accident in First Narrows, this time a serious collision with the CPR's *Princess Elizabeth*, which was outbound in a heavy fog. Both ships were feeling their way blindly but cautiously, yet almost directly beneath the Lions Gate Bridge they collided head-on. A passenger on the *Cardena* said, "She [the *Elizabeth*] loomed out of the fog like a ghost ship." Another passenger who had been standing on the boat deck took off and ran to the stern, scared stiff. Not until he got a life jacket on did he calm down.

The *Elizabeth* had torn a gaping 20-foot hole in the *Cardena*'s bow. Two seamen from the *Cardena* were injured and sent to hospital. However, damage to both vessels was well above the water line so neither was taking on water, but both ships were locked together by bent plates and the *Cardena*'s anchor had become tangled in the *Elizabeth*'s forepeak. Being in the middle of the narrows, both Masters realized they had to get away from the busy shipping lane, so with a little power from the *Elizabeth* the two ships drifted over to the English Bay area.

A cutting torch had to be brought out from B.C. Marine Repairs to cut apart the two ships, though the *Cardena*'s anchor was left embedded in the bow of the *Elizabeth* when they finally were separated. Both ships then proceeded to their respective docks.

Mrs. Elda Mason, author of a book on Lasqueti Island, was aboard the *Cardena* when she crashed with the *Princess Elizabeth* and she wrote me her recollections of the accident: "I well remember that frightening moment when the *Cardena* and the *Princess Elizabeth* were in collision under the Lions Gate Bridge. I thought we had struck a rock but the grinding effect was from the wrenching of the tearing metal as the two ships collided and were locked together. We remained in this position for about four hours. We

Cardena being attended by the *Salvage Queen* after hitting a rock in Surge Narrows in 1950 *(Collinsen Collection)*

passengers were required to wear life jackets the whole time. We wandered about the ship listening to various reports and rumours. We were well fed, courtesy of the Union Steamship Co. As the fog slowly lifted we could look up at the curious passengers of the *Princess Elizabeth* as they looked down from their larger vessel. Reporters came aboard and I have a picture of my two young daughters and myself being interviewed."

We now move ahead to Nov. 30, 1956. The *Cardena* had been accident free for the previous three years, which as the records show was a fair go for her. However on this night at 11 p.m. she climbed up on a rock at Duval Point, near Port Hardy. Captain Ernie Sheppard was her Master on this occasion. The ship had just left the Port Hardy dock and was proceeding north to Bella Coola in a light rain. Tex Lyon, the wharfinger at Port Hardy, gave me this recollection of what took place: "I had worked the ship and it was around 11 o'clock when she left. It was raining and very dark but you could see the blinker on the lighthouse miles away. I watched the *Cardena* leave and noticed that she seemed to be going on an odd course. She must have continued on that course because when she hit the point she was a long way out of her regular route. She went aground hard. I got a call from the D.O.T. telling me that the *Cardena* was ashore. I said, 'She can't be, I just worked on her half an hour ago.' They said, 'Well, she is and might need some assistance.' So I got in a small boat and went out there. The forestry boat was alongside her at the same time. She took the passengers off. The *Cardena* looked rather sad. The bow was right up on the rocks and the stern was down in the water."

Fortunately, most of the passengers had already disembarked at previous stops and the 30 passengers still aboard were able to step directly over the aft rails of the *Cardena* into rescue boats, as the *Cardena*'s stern was quite low in the water. Tugs pulled her free the next morning and since she was not holed or otherwise seriously damaged she again was able to return to Vancouver under her own steam. [70]

In 1956, in the wake of a debilitating strike by the Seamen's International Union in 1955, the old Union Steamships Company of British Columbia Ltd. was wound up and reorganized under the Union Steamships Limited name by the Senator McKeen group of shareholders, who had gained control in 1954. [71] In the fall of 1956 they appointed James Macdonell as executive vice president and general manager. Also that year, the "Daddy Boats," *Lady Cynthia* and *Lady Alexandra*, were taken out of service.

In 1957, with passenger trade dwindling, only one ship, the S.S. *Camosun*, was being operated to serve the northern trade. On alternate weeks she served the Queen Charlotte Islands. The two other converted corvettes were used strictly for the tourist trade. So in 1957 the *Catala* and the *Cardena* were the mainstays of the Company. The *Cardena* was especially active serving the coastal logging industry, while the *Catala* had great success with a six-day Freight Boat or Vagabond tour route running up to Alert Bay, Port Hardy and Bella Coola.

The battle to wrest subsidies from Ottawa escalated late in 1957 as the Company struggled to continue operations. In January 1958 Captain Macdonell threatened to withdraw all passenger boat services unless the subsidy question was settled to the Company's satisfaction, but nothing happened, perhaps because of complications arising from the transition from a Liberal to a Conservative government, so in a political move the passenger services by the Company were

S.S. *Cardena* was a Model Ship! reputed to have the most beautiful lines of any ship on the coast in her day

withdrawn. [72] The *Catala* was drydocked and her dining room was converted to a cafeteria. The bluff didn't work though, and the *Catala* was returned to service in April. By this time the *Cardena* also had been tied up. Captain Macdonnell tried to open the subsidy question again with Ottawa and at the same time said the Company would convert the *Cardena* to diesel and put her back in service if a subsidy was agreed upon. It didn't work either so the *Cardena* lay idle, tied up at the Union dock, rusting for the following three years.

The *Catala* soon joined her in mothballs at the Union dock. On Jan. 14, 1959, it was announced that Union Steamships and all of its ships had been purchased by Northland Navigation Co. It was the end of an era, and the company that had been known as the lifeline of the coast was no more.

On Dec. 2, 1959, the *Catala* and the *Cardena* were put up for sale on an as-is-where-is basis. The *Cardena* was sold first, in February 1961, to the Capital Iron and Metals Co. of Victoria, where she was stripped down to her hull. The hull was then towed to Powell River to become part of a breakwater at the mill town. Later she was towed to Kelsey Bay to form part of a breakwater there which protected the MacMillan Bloedel log-dumping pond. J.D. Moraes, the manager of the Kelsey Bay operation, sent me a picture of the hull of the *Cardena* forming part of this breakwater. The old *Cardena*'s hull is still providing a useful service, day in and day out, as she did in the past, all along the coast for 36 years.

It is interesting to note she has outlasted her successor as the flagship of the fleet, the *Catala*, which had previously been turned into a floating restaurant. She capsized and sank at Ocean Shores, Wash. and had to be cut up for scrap in 1966. The *Cardena*'s hull was still doing a job up at Kelsey Bay, more than 70 years after she was built in Scotland in 1923.

As well, the *Cardena*'s bell was located in a collection of Union Steamships and Northland Navigation memorabilia owned by the late Capt. Terry, and was donated to the Vancouver Maritime Museum in December 1993.

Cardena at Capital Iron wharf in Victoria, B.C. prior to being scrapped in 1961 *(Vancouver Maritime Museum)*

S.S. *Cardena* used as part of booming ground breakwater at Sayward *(McMillan & Bloedel Logging, Kelsey Bay Division)*

pp. 68-69: Drydocking Report
(R.A. Logan)

USED-1. 1M. 3-53. C. & S.

UNION STEAMSHIPS LTD.
FRANK WATERHOUSE & CO. OF CANADA LTD.
DRYDOCKING REPORT

S/S CARDENA

Date and Time of Docking: 17th February 1954, 6.30 a.m. to 19th February 1954, 7.45 a.m.

Port: Vancouver, B.C. Marine

Reasons for Drydocking: Annual Survey

Condition of Hull when docked: Good

Condition of Rudder and Clearance: Good, ¼" clearance

Condition of Propellers and Clearance: Leading edges on port propeller slightly bent; all faired up.

Weardown of Sternbush: Pt. 1/8", Stb. 3/16"   Strut Bearing:

Tail Shaft Drawn: No   Sternbush Rewooded: No   Strut Bearing Rewooded:

If Sterntube Oil—Gland fitted: No   Condition:

New Rubber fitted: —

Condition of Zincs: Good   No.: 6 on each side   Renewed: —

Condition of Eliminators: Good   No.: 1 on each side   Renewed: —

Sea Connections—Opened for Survey: All   Condition: Good. Condenser discharge valve chest taken off, so that doubling plate could be renewed.

Anchor Chains Ranged: Pt. & Stbd.   Condition: Good

Shackles—Port: 6   Starbd.: 6

Docking Plugs—No. Removed: 6   No. Replaced: 6   By: B.C.M. and checked.

PAINTING	ANTI-CORROSIVE	ANTI-FOULING	BOOT TOPPING	OTHER PAINT
Brand Name	#1 International	#2 International		
Quantity Used	26 gals.	26 gals.		
Sprayed or Brushed	Sprayed	Sprayed		
Location of Application	F. 0" – 13'0" A. 0" – 14'6"	F. 0" – 13'0" A. 0" – 14'6"		

Condition of Weather when Painting: Wet & Cold

Time Elapsed after Painting before Floating Ship: 2 days

TANKS

	F.P.	No. 1	No. 2P	No. 2S	No. 3P	No. 3S	No. 4	No. 5P	No. 5S	No.	No.	No.	A.P.
At Time of Docking	Full	Full	1'9"	2'11"	1'8"	1'8"	Full	7'6"	Full				M.T.
At Time of Undocking	M.T.	0'8"	1'9"	2'11"	1'8"	1'8"	M.T.	M.T.	M.T.				M.T.

Draft at Time Prior to Docking   F. 7' – 6"   A. 14' – 0"

Draft when Refloated   F. 6' – 8"   A. 12' – 6"

(SEE REVERSE SIDE)

Other Particulars of Work Done in Drydock: Port and Starb'd. boilers opened up for Survey studs on starb'd. boiler shell for feed water control valve chest renewed. Starb'd. boiler auxiliary steam valve seat removed, skimmed up, valve ground in, studs and nuts for same renewed. Whistle valve renewed. Pressure gauge cock on starb'd. boilers renewed. All other valves ground in. Port boiler mountings valves ground in. Joint between main stop valve and auxiliary stop valve remade. Boiler tubes swept out and cleaned out. All doors rejointed. Port boiler brickwork washed over. Forward corners of starb'd. boiler patched.

Aft. fuel pump opened up, ridge ground off top of cylinder, steam valve ports washed away, steam piston rings renewed.

Fan engines opened up.

Under-water fittings opened up, valves ground in. Storm valves cleaned out.

Domestic tanks; sanitary and fresh water gravity tanks cleaned out, cement washed. Hotwell tank cleaned out and painted with apexior.

Four turns packing put in each stern gland.

Engine room tank top cleaned for testing No.4 tank

Holding down bolts on port engine tested; 7 regrummeted, 2 renewed and 4 holes welded up.

All steam, waterpacking and jointing supplied, except 1 box ¼" Serpent 'A'.

Port engine opened up, H.P. and I.P. piston rods removed, skimmed up, also neck bushes. Gland packing and springs renewed, slide valves and pistons opened up.

Main bearings, bottom ends and thrust block opened up.

Piston rings on circulating pump renewed.

Sprinkler pump opened up, studs on water end cover renewed to 3/4" dia.

Bilge pump, piston and water end rings renewed. Fire pump, piston rings renewed.

Port feed pump, piston and water end rings renewed; steam valve chest faces for above pump scraped up.

No.1 Generator overhauled, H.P. and L.P. piston rings renewed.

Air pump overhauled, foot, bucket and head valves ground in; new steam piston and rings, crosshead block.

Transfer pump cylinder bored out, new piston and rings.

Surveyors in Attendance: Messrs. Sullivan, Squire, Laing.

SUPERINTENDENT ENGINEER

S.S. Lady Alexandra

The origin of the name Lady Alexandra is unknown but may have some connection to the Lady Welsford who christened her in 1924 and whose family were the controlling shareholders at the time.

In Union service: 1924-53
Official No.: 151207
Type: Steel twin-screw passenger and freight vessel. Built 1924 by Coaster Construction Co., Montrose, Scotland
Dimensions: Length 225.4', breadth 40.1', depth 9.7'. Gross tons 1,396
Engines: Reciprocating steam triple-expansion, two engines NHP 270, IHP 2,000; Yarrow water-tube boilers. Speed 14 knots
Services: To Bowen Island resort and on Howe Sound to Squamish. Twice-weekly evening dance cruises, and public excursions during summer season
Capacities: Passenger licence 1,400 (Howe Sound); 1,200 on special excursions, 900 to Victoria or Nanaimo. Six staterooms (12 berths). Dining salon seated 86, convertible for dancing with band podium. Cargo 300 tons

Lady Alexandra arriving in Vancouver 1925 (J. Smith Collection)

The *Lady Alexandra* was her official name but she was more often affectionately called the *Lady Alex* or just plain *Alex*. She was the biggest excursion ship north of San Francisco and was probably known and familiar to more people in B.C. than any other ship on the coast in her day. She was ordered and specially designed for the excursion trade and had a daytime licence to carry 1,400 people. She was mainly used for taking large picnic groups to Bowen Island and for other daytime excursion trips.

As Gerald Rushton described her, "She boasted a magnificent open promenade deck stretching three parts the length of the ship. Below, the finest dining saloon of any coastal steamer, seating 86, and a splendid hardwood dance floor extending the breadth of the ship, complete with orchestra stand, and was convertible for cruise dancing on short notice." [73]

Her moonlight dance cruises were famous and as time went by they became notorious and were soon dubbed the "booze cruises," which they really were. I interviewed many fellows who worked aboard her in those years and when I asked them to tell me on record about what went on they usually just laughed and wouldn't talk, though I did manage to collect a few stories which I will relate.

The *Lady Alexandra* was ordered from the Coaster Construction Co. of Montrose, Scotland late in 1923. Her keel was laid on October 1923 and she was launched on Feb. 21, 1924, with engines from a World War I minesweeper that lasted her throughout her life. The christening was performed by Lady Rushton, then the Lord Mayoress of Liverpool and widow of James H. Welsford, a shipping magnate who had bought control of Union Steamships in 1910 but who died suddenly in 1917 at age 53. (Their son Richard Welsford became managing director of Union Steamships and a resident of Vancouver in 1920.) Gerald Rushton was sent out to Vancouver along with Richard Welsford from the Company's Liverpool office to train as an "office man," and who became the Union Company's long-time traffic manager and eventually the Company's unofficial historian by writing two books about the Company. [74]

The *Lady Alexandra* left Scotland under the command of Captain C.B. Smith on May 7, 1924. (Previously Captain Smith had brought out the *Camosun I* for the Company, having picked her up in Kingston, Jamaica, taking over there from Captain B. Johnstone.) Captain Smith had a quick trip, bringing the *Alex* through the Panama Canal and arriving in Vancouver on June 21, 1924. The Chief Engineer on the trip was George Foster, who had stood by the *Alex* as she was being built.

Four days after her arrival from Scotland the *Alex* was pressed into service to carry 800 passengers to view the giant British battleship HMS *Hood*, anchored in Vancouver harbour. Captain Gaisford was

Lady Alexandra alongside dock in Scotland prior to sailing for Canada in 1924 under the command of Capt. C.B. Smith *(Sound Heritage Book)*

the *Alex*'s first master.

Before the *Alex* began her day trips to Bowen Island and her evening dance cruises, she dumped her ballast of "golden sand" brought over from Scotland specifically to create a pleasant beach below the resort hotel on Bowen. The following year when the *Catala* was brought out she too carried a load of sand ballast which was also dumped on the resort beach.

Although she was principally to be used for day trips and excursions, Union Steamships had planned to use her during the off season for transporting canned salmon from canneries up north, but that was tried only once. She went up to the Skeena River with a load of cans and on her southbound journey she carried a full load of salmon. Coming across the open waters of Queen Charlotte Sound, she listed dangerously, rolling up to 35 degrees. The Company, convinced her design wasn't suitable for such perilous waters, never sent her that far north again. [75]

Frank Skinner, who became a purser for Union Steamships and later was the Company Agent in Prince Rupert, began his career aboard the *Alex* in the mid 1920s. He helped in the newsstand/store aboard the *Alex* during the summer season. This was the fleet's only newsstand owned and operated by the Company itself, all others were operated by the Canadian Railway Association. A fellow named Aubrey Jones was in charge of the store when Skinner worked aboard her, the Captain was Jack Boden Sr. and Stan Hunter was the Purser. Dennis Farina, later a deck officer, also started his career helping in the newsstand on the *Alex*.

Captain Boden, one of the fleet's senior skippers, wanted to work closer to home in the summer so he left his northern run and bumped Captain Billy Yates off the *Alex* for seven consecutive summers in the 1920s. While that was happening, Captain Yates relieved on other day boats and assisted Captain Walker, the Marine Superintendent, but in later years Captain Yates and the *Lady Alexandra* became synonymous: the *Alex* was his ship. [76]

John Smith, a quartermaster on the *Lady Alex* with Captain Boden, remembers Captain Boden as a man you couldn't rattle: "I recall one time aboard the *Lady Alex* when we were backing out of Squamish and the telegraph broke. Jack Summerfield was on the bridge. There was great shouting and consternation. Captain Boden heard all the noise and quickly came up on the bridge. He saw what the problem was and quickly took over command. He calmly stationed members of the crew between the bridge and the engine room fiddley. He would give the order to the closest man, who in turn would pass it along to the next man and so on until it was shouted to an engineer below in the engine room. The ship didn't lose any time and in the meantime an engineer went to work and fixed the telegraph cable."

John Allan, who also served as a quartermaster on the *Alex*, tells a story of Captain Harry McLean deciding one day to try to turn the big *Alex* around in tiny Snug Cove on Bowen Island, though the usual practise was simply to back out. Though it took countless wheel commands and engine commands, he succeeded. "He just wanted to prove it could be done," John said.

With the arrival of the *Alex*, Union Steamships began a vigorous promotion campaign for Bowen Island. Eventually six picnic grounds were opened and they catered to large company picnics for such as Woodward's Stores, the Longshoremen's Union (the Port of Vancouver had to be shut down so all union members could attend), B.C. Telephone Co., Kelly Douglas, White Lunch, David Spencers, B.C. Electric and many others.

In the late 1940s one Longshoremen's picnic resulted in what became known as "the great beer bust." The Longshoremen had ordered 200 cases of beer to be loaded on the *Alex* and taken to Bowen Island for their Sunday picnic. While the beer was being unloaded, the RCMP decided that was far too much beer to be consumed on the island that day, so 120 cases were taken back aboard the ship and kept there until the next morning when the longshoremen returned to work and could unload it. But when Monday morning arrived, only 90 cases were discharged. Since there were no shipping bills and this was a private deal, no one kept count of how many cases were coming and going. One can only speculate where the 30 cases of beer went while stored overnight in the mail locker on the ship!

One gets an idea of the mood of the times from an oft-told story about a swimming race arranged one summer by Captain Boden between Jimmy Watson, a quartermaster on the *Lady Alex* and said to be an excellent swimmer, and the best swimmer the Longshoremen could put up. The contestants were to dive off the *Alex* in Snug Cove (which Boden is said to have done often himself), swim across the bay, touch a boom of logs tied up there and swim back. Watson won and when Boden asked him what he trained on, he said "Beer, Captain, and more beer!"

Along with the picnics, the *Lady Alexandra*'s moonlight dance cruises on Wednesday and Saturday nights also gained great popularity and indeed became notorious and widely known as the Booze Cruises. The ship would leave the Carrall Street wharf at 8 p.m., arrive at Bowen Island before 9 p.m., disembark the passengers who would go to the dancehall, and take the passengers aboard again around midnight for the return trip to Vancouver.

Though alcohol officially was not sold aboard ship, and nor was it sold at the dances, it was common practise for people to take along their own bottles, or perhaps buy it from bootleggers. In any case, it often became mayhem among the inebriated revellers aboard ship. They really were wild at times.

Shortly before midnight the *Alex*'s whistle would signal to passengers on shore that it was time to reboard and return to Vancouver, and the crush of passengers would be staggering as people rushed to get a seat for the return trip, since seats often were in short supply. Sometimes all five gangplanks were used. I recall taking tickets at one such gangplank and the crush was so great that you just grabbed anything thrust at you. When the ship was loaded, we took the tickets to the purser's office and dumped them on the desk. They all had to be counted and sorted. In my lot I discovered that someone had passed off a Chicago Hat Shop stub to me as a ticket. What a laugh we all had over that.

Often there was a dance band on board, which usually had played at the resort's dancehall, and they would go up to the bridge as the ship was leaving and play "Aloha" or "At the End of a Perfect Day." Many people will remember that an expert diver, Percy Dobson, often would do a beautiful swan dive off the bridge rail with the spotlight on him. [77]

Sometimes ordinary passengers would climb over the ship's bow railing as she backed out of the cove and also would dive in, fully clothed, and swim back to the wharf, apparently prefering to stay overnight in a rented room or cabin or even just to sleep in the bushes with a companion on a warm evening.

Once the *Alex* got underway at midnight the revellers got into full swing. One inebriated passenger decided to do a swan dive over the dance floor railing to the dining room below. I'm told he survived.

Another well-known story tells of a couple who loosened the wooden cover from one of the lifeboats, climbed into it and began making love. Then the deck crew

Lady Alexandra en route to Bowen Island with a full load of holidayers

came along and bolted down the cover, so the lovers were stuck in there until the ship docked in Vancouver.

Another time, an intoxicated lady somehow crawled out onto a ledge underneath the ship's bridge and got stuck. She had to be left there until the ship docked because the officers thought it would be too dangerous to try to rescue her while the ship was moving.

The well-known Captain Billy McCombe also did a tour of duty on the *Alex* and one of the first things he did was have two large floodlights mounted on the aft side of the bridge, plus he obtained a bullhorn. When the *Alex* neared the Lions Gate Bridge he would turn on the floodlights and announce through the bullhorn, "Okay folks, time to end all the love making!"

Iain Morrison, a former deck officer, gave me this recollection of the "Booze Cruises": "They would come aboard the ship sober but coming back they couldn't stand up. We would have to carry them off the ship and lay them on a dolly like cordwood and pull them out to the taxi stand on the wharf. The policeman on the wharf would have to look after them. My wife Winnie would often take the trip with me and she was scared stiff. We were often over our passenger limit of 1,400. Sometimes we would have over 2,000 passengers aboard."

An overload of passengers aboard the *Alex* was common, but of course the Company had to be careful about it. On one occasion Wally Walsh, the shore mate at the time, saw two customs officers hovering around the dock waiting for the *Alex* to come in. He knew that the ship had a big load of passengers to disembark so he quickly pulled three gangplanks into place and when the ship docked the passengers as usual streamed down all of them. The customs officers did try to make a count of the passengers but soon realized it was hopeless, as they could watch no more than two planks at a time. [78]

The *Lady Alexandra* thus was a very busy ship during the summer seasons, and so for crew members work days of 12 to 16 hours were common. Their days began at 7 a.m. loading freight and mail for the day's run, and upon her return around 5 p.m. the freight and mail had to be unloaded and the ship cleaned thoroughly, which usually took until 7 or 8 p.m. - making 12-hour days the norm. Then on days when there was a dance cruise or the ship had to meet a train in Squamish the quitting time could be as late as 1 a.m., plus the crew members were expected to maintain order on a ship with up to 2,000 drinking, partying passengers - making a gruelling 18-hour workday! For all that, the deck crews were paid $69 a month - not much even in the 1930s. It's no wonder the Company had trouble keeping a steady crew aboard her.

The only permanent employees amongst the deck crew on the *Alex* were the quartermaster, winchman and dayman, and since there was only one quartermaster aboard at any one time, his job was a killer. The rest of the deck crews usually were students and waterfront drifters. Living quarters for the crew aboard ship were not all that good either, and though the food generally was good, it depended on who was Chief Steward and how well he was able to manage the ship's food budget.

The *Lady Alexandra* also was used for many popular daily excursion and charter voyages. Trips were made to Bowen Island from New Westminster, up the Fraser River, and from White Rock to Victoria. The Surrey Legion, for example, chartered the *Alex* to carry 800 of its members to Victoria and back. [79]

On one of these trips, Chief Steward Harry Audley brought his wife along and during the voyage she slipped and fell and as a result of her injuries was confined to a wheelchair for the rest of her life, but because she was travelling without a ticket, no claim could be made against the Company's insurance.

John Allan, a Quartermaster aboard the *Alex*, recalls one charter trip on which they carried a full load of Registered Nurses. One would think that would have been a seaman's dream, but John said it was a nightmare because they were all so persistent! "Being aboard the *Alex* was always interesting," he said, also recalling a time during the Jubilee year in 1949 when all the stars of *Showboat*, including Betty Phillips, came aboard in their costumes for a special cruise.

The *Lady Alex* also participated in her share of special sailings, such as being one of three Union ships that joined in a parade of ships on May 29, 1939 to salute King George VI and Queen Elizabeth, who were sailing out of Vancouver to Victoria aboard the *Princess Marguerite*.

In 1940, the *Alex* was one of eight Union ships used for "Win the War Cruises," an idea the Company came up with in which people who purchased war savings stamps were given free tickets for cruises. On that occasion the *Alex* was commanded by Captain Eric Suffield. A week later the *Lady Alex* hosted the entire Battalion of the 2nd Irish Fusiliers for a cruise up Howe Sound. [80]

The *Lady Alexandra* operated relatively free of accidents, but she did have one serious grounding. On June 15, 1947, with Chief Officer Owen-Jones on the bridge, she was badly holed when she struck a rock on the east shore of Howe Sound at 11:12 p.m. during a blinding rainstorm. She was returning from a special trip to Britannia Beach and Squamish, but she had not yet been equipped with radar because she operated mainly as a day boat. The pumps were put to work and with a rising tide the ship floated free, though the pumps couldn't keep up with the water coming in. Captain Yates took over command and decided to make a run for Snug Cove, seven miles away, and they made it. There were only eight passengers aboard and they were taken to Vancouver via Horseshoe Bay. Temporary repairs were made to the *Alex* and she was towed back to Vancouver by the tug *Commodore*. [81]

By 1951 the cruise and excursion business was falling off so that year the *Alex* was only put into service for the summer, from May 24 to Labour Day, and in 1952 she was withdrawn altogether. According to marine writer Charlie Defieux, her last voyage was on Sept. 25, 1952. She was then laid up for almost seven years. On Aug. 8, 1956, there was a story in *The Vancouver Sun* by Les Rimes about how the *Lady Alex* was rusting her days away tied up at the Terminal dock. He went on to report rumours that she might be converted to a floating restaurant.

In 1959 the *Lady Alex* was purchased by a group of Vancouver businessmen and converted into a floating restaurant. She was to be moored at the foot of Cardero in Coal Harbour. It was claimed that she would be the largest floating restaurant in the world. The new owners, known as Lady Alexandra Holdings, included R.J. Desbrisay, Ralph Stacey, George Thody, John J. Anderson and Jim Craddock.

The new owners paid only $35,000 to Northland Navigation for the ship, with her machinery intact, and then hired George Knap to remove her engines, boiler, shaft and propeller, which they sold and thereby recouped most of their original investment. They completed her restoration and conversion, keeping the familiar Union Steamship colours, and soon had her operating as a restaurant. Though her days as a steamship were over, the Department of Transport nonetheless ruled that she would still have to go into drydock periodically to have her hull cleaned and serviced.

The Lady Alexandra Restaurant opened in February, 1960, and initially was quite popular, specializing in seafood, but it suffered a serious setback in 1961 when a defective switch on one of the deep fryers led to a fire that caused so much damage the ship had to be towed into drydock for repairs.

In 1967 I attended a dinner meeting aboard the *Alex* organized by former Union Steamship employees. One of the main organizers, Ernie Plant, later gave me a guest list signed by all who attended and there were 60 names on it, including such well-known personalities as Vic Hayman, Don McLeod, Harry Roach, Tom Lucas, Frank Skinner, Gerald Rushton, Bob Naughty, Bob McBeath, Harry Audley, Harold Crompton, Denis Shaw, Don Thompson, Stew Hale and Eddie Enwright.

Lady Alexandra Holdings fell into hard times and in 1970 sold their floating restaurant to new owners, who were known as Princess Louise II. The principals were B. Brynelsen and M. Davis, associated with Brenda Mines, and Vancouver businessman Ted Turton, a major player on the Vancouver Stock Exchange. On Jan. 5, 1970, the *Lady Alexandra* was taken to B.C. Marine Shipbuilders and almost entirely rebuilt. The remodelling was directed by internationally-acclaimed marine artist and yachtsman Ray Wallace of California, who also had been responsible for the conversion of the *Princess Louise*, a former CPR coastal steamer, into a very successful floating restaurant in Los Angeles. [82] The work on the *Lady Alex* was completed at Lynn Terminal in North Vancouver, and it was said the final cost was over $1 million.

Charlie Defieux, writing in *The Vancouver Sun* on June 17, 1970, said there was little left of the old *Alex* after her redesigning: "She won't be recognized for what she was and no doubt many of us will regret we didn't give her first owners more support. They at least retained her as she was." Even her name was changed, to the *Princess Louise II*, reflecting the corporate connection with the first *Princess Louise*.

In August 1970 the refurbished *Princess Louise II* was ready to be towed back to her berth alongside the Bayshore Hotel and 150 guests were invited aboard for the trip, but as Norman Hacking reported in his column in the *The Province* (Vancouver) on Aug. 15, there was a problem: "Copious drinks, fine food and beautiful girls had been provided to mark the occasion. Her new owners have spared nothing to make her unrecognizable as her old self but they forgot one thing. There were no lifeboats or life jackets aboard so the harbour master would not allow any passengers to stay aboard her for the trip across the harbour. All the guests had to be loaded on buses and driven over to the Bayshore to wait for her arrival there."

That blunder by the promoters may have been an omen of problems to come, because the general public and especially those who knew the *Alex* in her previous life certainly didn't like the looks of her after the remodelling.

The *Princess Louise II* apparently wasn't a commercial success in Vancouver either, so in 1972 the owners had her towed to Redondo Beach in California, still to operate as a floating restaurant but again without commercial success. On Feb. 22, 1980, the *Province* reported that she had been converted into a disco named "Dirty Sally's" and also had a gaming room for backgammon.

The final demise of the *Lady Alexandra* came in March 1980 when she was heeled over by huge storm-driven waves that breached a breakwater that had been protecting her. She was scuttled in an attempt to allow the sea itself to protect the vessel but instead of sinking upright and on her keel, the ship landed on rocks which tipped her on her side. Internal damage from water and shock was so extensive that her owners could not salvage her or even tow her to the scrapyards in Long Beach. Reluctantly a decision was made and she was towed well offshore and sunk. [83]

Lady Alexandra as a floating restaurant heading for Redondo Beach, California

The *Lady Alexandra* served on the B.C. coast for 28 years, lay idle for seven years and then was spruced up and operated as a floating restaurant in her old name and colours for another 10 years. In 1970 she was sold to new owners who invested $1 million in her and changed her name and appearance, but they couldn't keep her afloat financially so she was taken down to California and turned into a disco named "Dirty Sally's." It must have been just too undignified for the grand old Lady, so she rolled over and died at age 56.

Left: *Lady Alexandra (Princess Louise II)* - her final hour at Redondo Beach, California

Below: Plaque from lifeboat station removed from *Lady Alexandra* when she was a floating restaurant in Vancouver Harbour. John Allan was Quartermaster. 1951

S.S. Catala

Catala is taken from Catala Island at the entrance of Esperanza Inlet on the west coast of Vancouver Island. It commemorates the pioneer missionary work of Father Magin Catala, who was revered as a holy man for his sanctity and prophetic powers. Father Catala came north to the Spanish settlement of Santa Cruz de Nootka and spent the years 1793-94 on Vancouver Island with native Indians of the area, returning to California in 1795.

In Union service: 1925-59
Official No.: 152822
Type: Steel twin-screw passenger-freighter
Dimensions: Length 218.0', breadth 37.1', depth 18.4'. Gross tons 1,476
Engines: Triple-expansion 200 NHP; Yarrow water-tube boilers. Speed 14 knots
Services: Weekly on northern main route to Prince Rupert and Stewart. Later in regular service to Port Hardy and Bella Coola
Capacities: Passenger licence 267, cabin berths 120, deck 48. Cargo 300 tons; refrigeration for 30 tons of boxed fish

S.S. *Catala*, flagship of the fleet
(F. Rogers Colletion)

The *Catala* was ordered in 1924 from the Coaster Construction Co. of Montrose, Scotland, and was built to specifications befitting the Union Steamship Company's time of greatest growth and expansion. She was launched on Feb. 25, 1925 and christened by the wife of Company president Richard Welsford, who had taken over management of the Company after the death in 1920 of his father J.H. Welsford.

Captain Andy Johnstone stood by the *Catala* as an adviser as she was being built and fitted out but it was Captain James Findlay who brought her over to B.C. from Scotland. Despite encountering a gale, the *Catala* made good time and soon was dumping its ballast of another load of fine white sand for the Company's lovely beach on Bowen Island. Her maiden voyage was on July 25, 1925, sailing to Prince Rupert under the command of Captain Johnstone.

The *Catala* became the flagship of the fleet upon her arrival in B.C., taking over from the *Cardena*. Although her lines were not as graceful as the *Cardena*'s, her spacious decks, excellent accommodations and fine cuisine gave passengers the feel of being on a miniature liner, so she was able to assume her flagship role with assurance.

Though the *Catala* looked beautiful from the exterior, inside she still had her share of quirks, notably what Billy McCombe, who for many years served as Mate and later Master of the *Catala*, described as her having "two left-handed engines." I checked this statement with Ben Smith, a former engineer with Union Steamships, and he explained, "The *Catala* was installed with two right-handed or starboard engines. Needless to say, some modification was required. First of all, the controls on one had to be placed on the opposite side. Then the Stephenson Linkage, reversing gear and valve ports had to be altered as well. Now both engines could be operated from the inboard side by one engineer. She was to run this way for her complete career, with one engine turning the way it was designed, the other running (so to speak) in reverse. This caused no hardships to the engineer nor to the efficiency of the vessel, but indeed it was a bit unusual." Smith also consulted about this with Johnny MacAulay, another Union Steamships engineer. (see sketch)

Left: *Catala* on ways in Scotland
(Mrs. Tosh Collection)

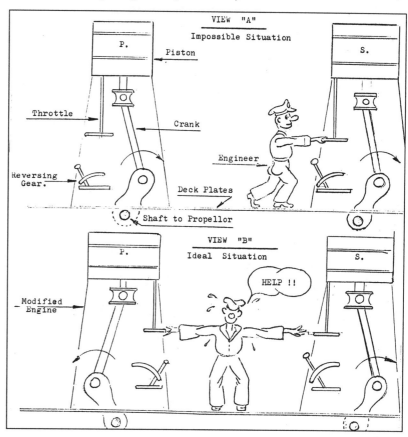

Drawings of *Catala's* engines by Ben Smith

In the following two years the *Catala* and the *Cardena* firmly established the Union Steamship Company's dominance on the northern B.C. coast, though that dominance was almost lost in 1927 when the *Catala* was southbound from Stewart and went hard aground on Sparrowhawk Reef, about 40 miles north of Prince Rupert, and badly damaged her outer hull. (The reef itself was named after HMS *Sparrowhawk* which ran aground there in 1874.)

The accident happened in broad daylight at 1 p.m. on Nov. 8, with chief officer Ernest Sheppard on the bridge in command. There were 44 passengers aboard including the Company's assistant manager, A.L. Clements, who was making a round-trip inspection and was accompanied by his wife.

Captain Dickson immediately ordered

the lifeboats lowered and most of the passengers were soon transferred to a tug boat and taken to nearby Port Simpson. Indian launches from the settlement also came out and helped transfer the passengers. [84]

Mr. Clements took some dramatic photos of the ship hung high up on jagged rocks and teetering at about 45 degrees, and later he gave the photos to Alan Thomas, who became treasurer of the Company and who in turn donated them to the Vancouver Maritime Museum.

Catala aground on Sparrowhawk Reef *(M. Dean)*

Shortly after the accident, though, the Company was not at all keen for photos to get out, as we learn from Ernie Plant, who was quartermaster on the *Cardena* when it dashed up to the scene to pick up the *Catala*'s passengers and crew and bring them back, all as first-class passengers. Plant recalls that one of the deckhands on the *Cardena* had a camera and as he was getting set to take a photo of the *Catala*, one of the mates aboard the *Cardena* knocked the camera from his hands and ordered "No pictures!"

The Company's sensitivity about the *Catala*'s grounding probably was a reflection of the questionable circumstances, in that it happened early in the afternoon on a clear, bright day. Though an inquiry reportedly found that visibility was impaired by glaring light [85], and Sheppard escaped being censured or even criticized, one still has to seriously question how such a bad accident could happen in near-perfect weather conditions.

More recently, two eyewitness accounts of the incident have become available, from Freddy Smith, who was Chief Engineer on the *Catala*, and William McCombe Sr., who was Second Mate, both of which are recorded in the Sound Heritage book *Navigating the Coast*. First, Smith's story:

"We lost the *Catala* when she grounded on Sparrowhawk Ledge, but they bought her back again from the insurance company. I was aboard when she grounded. The chief officer put her on the reef. He went inside the marker, instead of going around it, and of course, she hit. She hit far enough to stay there. If she'd kept on going she'd have ripped the bottom out and kept going, but the tide was going out. We had very few passengers on. The crew took them off and took them to Port Simpson and the engineers stayed on board with the skipper and the chief officer until she listed very badly and then the water started to come in on the starboard side and she took a bad list and the old man called down and told us to abandon ship. She stayed fairly upright, but as the tide went out, the water started coming in through the stoke-hold. She took a bad list. She was pretty well over on her side when we left her. It came right in through the tank tops. She was punctured and the rocks pushed right through the tank tops and the water came in through the stoke-hold first of all. It was all mixed up with fuel oil. It got all over the ship and the woodwork upstairs in the cabins and made quite a mess. They were lucky to get her off. She was up there for a month I got transferred to another ship down here on Howe Sound while they were getting her off. She was in drydock for quite a long time.

"The Union Company abandoned her to the insurance company. They got her off. They blasted rocks out from underneath her. They fixed her up and as the Union Company was desperate for a boat, they bought her back." [86]

Front view of *Catala* aground on Sparrowhawk Reef *(M. Dean)*

Now, McCombe's story:

"Old man Dickson, Captain Dickson, had a certain routine. He was quite an old man. Everyday he came on the bridge, he looked over, I don't think he saw anything, and then he went and watered his flowers, his wee garden. He had pots and wee bits of flowers at the back [of the wheelhouse]. He nursed them along. The next thing we knew, the *Catala*'s belted Sparrowhawk Ledge. The man that was on the bridge was a man by the name of Sheppard. He said he saw Captain Dickson on the bridge and he thought he was taking over. The man never took over before. And you never forget old man Dickson at the inquiry. Well, Captain Dickson said, 'Captain Sheppard thinks I took over. I guess I must have taken over.' That was all he said. He took the rub. The old man come up and he looked over. He wouldn't say boo to you, nor anybody else. He had done his niceties before. He had been down for his lunch then. This was on his way back up. I was then put on the *Cardena* and the *Cardena* and the *Catala* switched places. She was sitting up on Sparrowhawk." [87]

Efforts were made to pull the *Catala* off the rock but she held fast and by Nov. 14, 1927 she was abandoned to the underwriters. However, Harold Brown, the Company president, said that if she could be refloated the Company would buy her back, and later they did.

Tex Lyon, longtime wharfinger and Company agent at Port Hardy, gave me the following story about how the *Catala* was saved: "An old hard rock miner was brought out to the *Catala* and he took one look at the situation and said, 'Heck, there's nothing to this. Get me a rock drill, a little powder and some steam on the ship's winches. We'll unload the bugger. We'll blast the rock in her hull, hoist the debris up with the winch and dump it over the ship's side.' They did just that, patched her up and floated her off."

The *Catala* was successfully refloated on

Dec. 5, 1925 and taken into a sheltered spot nearby so more repairs could be made before taking her into Prince Rupert and then on to Vancouver. The Prince Rupert Drydock and the Burrard Drydock in Vancouver both put in bids for the repair job but the Burrard bid was much lower. The *Catala* was towed there with much difficulty but without incident by the *Salvage King*. She was repaired at a cost of $175,000 and went back into service on March 30, 1928.

An insight into the business climate in those days can be seen from the intense rivalry between the two drydocks to get the *Catala* job, which led the Prince Rupert *Daily News* to make this editorial comment: "If the steamer *Catala* did not sink last night it was not because the people of Prince Rupert wished otherwise. In fact, dozens of Prince Rupert people were praying earnestly that she would go to the bottom and remain there. The vessel is clearly unfit to make the trip to Vancouver and it is doubtful if she should be allowed to go. In any event, she goes with the hearty curses of Prince Rupert following her. It looks as if a deliberate attempt has been made to take business away from this port." [88]

When the *Catala* returned to service, Captain Dickson was again her Master but Ernest Sheppard was replaced by W.E. Mounce as Chief Officer. Andrew Beattie went out on her as Chief Engineer and he stayed aboard the *Catala* for the rest of his career, a total of 20 years straight; in fact he died aboard the *Catala* while she was docked at Prince Rupert in 1945. Over those years Beattie had become one of the Company's best goodwill ambassadors.

Playing shuffleboard on the *Catala's* spacious main deck (B.C. Archives)

Some time in the 1930s, the *Catala* developed a serious crack in her boiler and had to be put into dry dock and faced a permanent lay up. As a new boiler was out of the question, the Company decided to try to patch the old one even though steamship inspectors doubted it could be done and still pass the necessary tests. W.J. Bain, a machinist at Vancouver Machinery Depot, was given the job to machine up a patch and install it. Even though the crack was in a difficult spot to reach, he succeeded and the boiler passed the test. [89] The *Catala* thus was able to return to service and indeed sailed for another 20 years with no problems in that spot.

The *Catala* and her crew had another first-hand encounter with the hazards of life on the coast one stormy night in 1934 in the open-ocean waters of Queen Charlotte Sound, north of Vancouver Island. Captain Dickson, still master of the *Catala*, noticed that the Egg Island light, one of the largest, most important and most isolated lights on the coast, was not working. Dickson naturally decided the matter was serious enough to need investigating and so carefully maneuvered the *Catala* through the reefs to get close enough to shine the ship's searchlight on the lighthouse buildings, which found no sign of life and confirmed that the light was out. Dickson then sent second mate Eric Suffield and some seamen out in a lifeboat to try to row ashore, but with the high swells a landing was impossible so Suffield stripped, tied a rope around his waist, dove over the stern and swam ashore. He went into the house, saw a table set for two with the putrified remains of a meal on the plates and on the stove found a pan containing a mouldy sponge of bread. After calling out and receiving no reply, he climbed the stairwell to the power, pumped up the vapour tube, lit the lamp, and wound it up. The main clue to the keepers' disappearance was their boat, upside down in the cove, rising and falling in the surf. Suffield retied his lifeline, swam back to the boat, and they returned to the *Catala*. Dickson sent a message to Prince

Rupert about the mysterious happenings at Egg Island light, and resumed his course with a very subdued crew. What happened to the keepers was never discovered, because their bodies were never found, but it appears from evidence like missing fishing tackle that the keepers, like many then, had suffered the privations of their isolation, run low on meat and gone fishing despite the dangerous waters to try to augment their diet, then capsized and drowned. [90]

In the late 1930s the *Catala* replaced the *Camosun I* on the Rivers Inlet-Ocean Falls-Bella Coola run. This route turned out to be very popular with passengers seeking a six-day cruise to the hinterland.

The *Catala* suffered another serious accident in December 1937, while northbound from Ocean Falls to Prince Rupert on a dark night. The deck officers were Ernest Sheppard, master, Harry McLean, chief officer, Alex Mercer, second mate and Angus McNeill, third mate. The quartermaster was Frederick Corneille, who told me this version: "They decided to alter course slightly and Mercer told me to steer very carefully. They saw a light but thought it must have been a passing fish boat, so they altered course. Minutes later we were aground and had ripped open the *Catala*'s double bottom again. As a result we lost a lot of fuel."

The *Catala* was freed three hours later on a high tide and made it to Prince Rupert harbour with lifeboats swung out as a precaution ready for an order to abandon ship. The drydock was full so a diver was sent down to check over her bottom. After getting his report that only the outer hull had been punctured, and finding no water had entered her hold, a Lloyds of London agent cleared the *Catala* to proceed to Vancouver. Chief engineer Beattie had to use all his skill to utilize every bit of fuel left to get them to Vancouver. They made it with only a small reserve left. [91] At Burrard Drydock, 30 of her shell plates were replaced.

S.S. *Catala* at Bella Bella, B. C. *(Mrs. Woodward collection)*

The *Catala* was featured in the *New York Times* in 1938, after participating in the rescue of five American airmen whose U.S. Navy plane had been forced down into the ocean near Bella Bella due to engine trouble, on the morning of Jan. 30. The *Catala* was proceeding north with Captain Findlay as Master when the wireless operator picked up an S.O.S. from the airmen, so Findlay turned his ship around and went back to the area of the downed plane. Fortunately a passing fishing boat had picked up the men, who had taken to a rubber life raft, and they were transferred to the *Catala*, which later passed them on to the U.S.S. *Teal*. Harold Crompton, then assistant purser on the *Catala*, took photos of the rescue, several of which were published along with a story in the *New York Times*. [92]

During the Second World War, all Union ships that travelled to northern ports and crossed open waters were painted battleship gray and had their portholes blacked out, and some had guns mounted astern. When they crossed Queen Charlotte Sound, they had to be escorted by a Canadian Naval vessel. Initially this was exciting but as time passed no one thought much about the danger of enemy attacks. I remember one evening aboard the *Catala* when Captain Sheppard received a message that a floating

... 15, NO. 76. Member Audit Bureau of Circulations

VANCOUVER, B. C., MONDAY, JANUARY 31, 1938

Trinity 2611   3c IN CITY   5c On boats, trains and in country

Catala Rescues Crew Of U.S. Naval Plane In Queens Sound

Aviators Take to Lifeboat as Seas Smash Machine

EN ROUTE NORTH

Union Vessel Arrives In Nick of Time To Save Men

B.C. Vessel Saves Five Flyers

The well-known Vancouver steamer Catala, nosing her way through sleet and mist off Goose Island at noon Sunday, proved in the nick of time in rescuing five United States navy airmen who had been forced to abandon their disabled flying-boat.

Forced down in heavy seas approximately 185 miles south of Prince Rupert, according to British United Press despatches to The News-Herald, the airmen had to abandon their ship when it started to break up. En route from Sand Point naval air base, Seattle, to Sitka, Alaska, the big flying-boat was one of a squadron of six.

Their tiny emergency lifeboat overloaded and threatening to be overwhelmed at any moment by the rising seas, the wet and almost frozen airmen were sighted by the officer of the watch aboard the Union Steamship Co. Ltd. steamer Catala, on her way to Prince Rupert. The ship was speeded to their assistance and they were taken aboard and soon revived.

Motor trouble had forced them to land their ship on the rough seas, Lieut. J. Horton, commander, told Captain J. Findlay of the Catala and shortly afterward the machine started to break up.

They hurriedly inflated their emergency lifeboat and had only scrambled into it when the flying-boat started to sink. Within a short time, however, the Catala appeared on the scene.

Later, the Catala handed the airmen over to the U.S.S. Teal, which took them northward in continuation of their interrupted flight.

Meanwhile, the remaining five flying-boats rested at Prince Rupert. It was not until the Catala was heard from that the crews of these flying-boats knew anything of the plight of the five in the disabled ship. They had believed them safe in some sheltered part of the coastline.

The airmen with Lieut. Horton were: Aviation Cadet L. E. Matgraw, Aviation Machinist's Mates H. W. Robinson and G. V. West, and Radioman D. P. Reighard.

RESCUES FIVE U. S. AIRMEN

Above is shown the United Steamship Company's well-known coastal steamer Catala, which saved five United States Navy airmen from drowning off Goose Island, 185 miles south of Prince Rupert, on Sunday. The five airmen were in one of a squadron of six big flying-boats en route from Seattle to Sitka, Alaska. Their machine was forced down and when it began to break up in heavy seas they took to a small, emergency lifeboat. Shortly afterward they were sighted by the Catala and picked up.

mine was possibly in our path. Word spreadquickly through the ship. As a result, Sheppard ran the ship at half speed. No mine was ever encountered. I often wondered, why half speed? What good would that have done if we had hit a mine?

Wartime meant the Union ships were nearly always filled to capacity with both passengers and freight. The ships were extended to their limits and crews seldom had time to repair equipment. By the end of the war, the Company's fleet was in dire circumstances because their ships had been run ragged.

The *Camosun II* was sold, the old *Venture* was retired and then sold. The old *Cassiar II* had long since seen better days, leaving only the *Chelohsin*, *Cardena* and *Catala* to carry on. The Company at last embarked on a replacement program and as part of it bought three war-surplus corvettes for conversion to passenger/freight boats. Though they cost only $75,000 each, they soon turned out to be a financial disaster because their engines were designed for military speed rather than commercial efficiency. Since they came out painted all white they were called the White Boats, but soon became known as white elephants, though their hulls were soon painted the familiar black.

Even after the arrival of these new ships, I think most of the Company's personnel still regarded the *Catala* as flag ship of the fleet. The upstart impractical corvettes were just not in her class. The old girl was still a big favourite.

The new *Camosun III* sailed into Prince Rupert on her maiden voyage on Dec. 11, 1946, and it happened that the *Catala* and *Cassiar II* were docked there. The two old workhorses greeted the new ship with their whistles blowing and flags flying, suggesting the beginning of a new era for the Company, but it turned out to be not as grand as it had been in the past.

After the war-time boom, business for Union Steamships began to fall off. The three new corvettes were not economical to operate and so were laid up over the winter, leaving the *Cardena* and *Catala* to service the whole northern coast. (The *Chelohsin* had been lost when she grounded near Stanley Park's Siwash Rock on Nov. 6, 1949, see pp.29-30)

In 1956 the *Catala* had a new boiler installed at Burrard Drydock. It was one of their biggest jobs that year. They took a boiler out of the *Lady Cynthia* and installed it in the *Catala* as the two ships lay side by side. [93]

In the fall of 1957 the Company applied to the federal government for an increased operating subsidy, but was turned down. Company officials responded by announcing that all passenger service to northern ports would be withdrawn effective Jan. 2, 1958.

On Jan. 8, 1958 Captain Harry Roach nosed the *Catala* into the Union dock on what appeared to be her final voyage. All the Union passenger ships servicing upcoast settlements were withdrawn. "There's a lot of sad faces in the settlements along Johnstone Strait," Roach said as he gathered belongings from his cabin. [94] Freight services however were continued and Captain Macdonell, the Company president, announced that the Company was still in the passenger business but needed time to regroup. Meanwhile the *Catala* was put in drydock for reconditioning.

Times were changing though, and with business falling the Company had looked for ways to cut costs, one of which in 1958 was to change the *Catala*'s dining room to - horror of horrors - a cafeteria. What a comedown for the flagship, which amongst the crews had become known as the best feeder in the fleet, and which for passengers had become renowned for excellent cuisine. Who could ever forget the rich eclairs every Sunday, or the delicious clam chowder?

The *Catala* was returned to service in April 1958, much to the delight of all upcoast residents, who greeted her with joy at every port, but the subsidy battle continued. Meanwhile, Captain Harry Terry of Northland Navigation offered to take over Union's routes with or without a subsidy, and Northland ships began

Photo on opposite page:
S.S. *Catala*
(Betz Collection)

Catala sunk at Gray's Harbour, Wash. U.S.A. 1965 *(Betz Collection)*

competing directly with the *Catala* for upcoast freight and passenger business. The competition proved to be too much for Union to take and on Jan. 14, 1959 an announcement was made that Northland had bought Union Steamships, including its fleet and all assets except its Bowen Island properties.

As *Province* marine editor Norman Hacking wrote:

"A pall hung over the Union wharf on Wednesday. The freight shed was practically empty. The office staff faced with termination of employment stood around talking in uneasy groups." What a shock! The Union Steamship Co. was no more, it had been sold. After 70 years operating and known as the lifeline of the coast, Union ships with their familiar red and black funnels would be seen no more. It was hard to imagine.

The grande dame of the fleet, the *Catala*, was Union's last passenger ship to dock in Vancouver. Her Master on this last trip was Wee Angus McNeill, who went over to Northland for a few years but soon retired. Bob Hackett visited McNeill in a retirement home and recorded him on tape shortly before he died. During that interview McNeill said, "Oh, I never liked Northland. The Union Steamship was home to me."

The *Cardena* had been laid up before the *Catala* was retired but soon both ships lay rusting away at the Union dock. In December 1959 both were put up for sale for $60,000 apiece, as is where is. The *Cardena* was sold first and eventually her hull was towed up to Kelsey Bay where she sits today as part of the breakwater for a logging operation's booming ground.

The *Catala* was bought in the spring of 1961 by Nelson Bros. Fisheries and was towed to their shipyards in Queensborough where she was stripped of her boilers. In December of that year she was sold to Catala Enterprises of Seattle, headed by D. MacPherson, and converted into a floating hotel for that city's 1962 World's Fair. My friend Bob Logan of Campbell River still has a receipt for one night's lodging aboard the *Catala* while he visited the fair (p.87).

After the fair the *Catala* was sold to Mr. and Mrs. Back of Los Angeles, who planned to turn her into a nightclub and restaurant. They towed her to Long Beach but soon she was moved to Grays Harbour at Ocean Shores, Washington to become part of a resort development. On Jan. 1, 1965 a severe storm capsized her, so the owners sold her for $5,000 to two Washington state men. They removed what fittings they could and planned to convert her to a barge, but never did, so she just sat there in the sand and a group of hippies took up residence aboard her, then somehow the wheelhouse and bridge were set afire and the local fire department had to let her burn because their hoses couldn't reach the ship.

Eventually the hulk became a danger to

tourists so finally she was cut up for scrap. I am told there is a small mall in Grays Harbour called Catala Mall. There are some artifacts from the old ship in the area, such as her anchor chain. At least the once proud *Catala*, flagship of the Union Steamship fleet, has a small shopping mall named after her. What other ship of the old Union fleet can say the same?

Bob Logan's receipt for lodging while at the Seattle World's Fair in 1962 *(R.A. Logan)*

S.S. Lady Cecilia

The origin of the name Lady Cecilia is unknown but the use of "Lady" had become a practise of the Company at the time, and "Cecilia" may be derived from a relative of the controlling shareholders.

In Union service: 1925-51
Official No.: 152718
Type: Steel twin-screw passenger-freighter.
Dimensions: Length 235.0' (BP 219.5'), breadth 28.6', depth 16.3'. Gross tons 944
Engines: Triple-expansion, NHP 250, IHP 1,600; Yarrow boilers. Speed 15.5 knots maximum, 13.5 average
Services: Employed on Georgia Strait and Howe Sound routes, and excursions
Capacities: Passenger licence summer 800 (excursions 900), winter 500; 3 staterooms. Cargo 75 tons

S.S. *Lady Cecilia*
(Vancouver Maritime Museum)

The Union Steamship Co. purchased two minesweepers from the British Admiralty in 1925, HMS *Swinton*, which became the *Lady Cecilia*, and HMS *Barnstaple*, which became the *Lady Cynthia*.

The *Swinton*, which had been built in 1919, was taken to the Coaster Construction Yards in Montrose, Scotland for conversion to civilian use. An upper deck was added along with sponsons (lateral flotation aids) for better stability. Two funnels were built but the aft one was a dummy. She was designed to be used primarily as an excursion vessel and had a day license to carry 900 passengers, plus a cargo of 75 tons. Her triple expansion engines with Yarrow water tube boilers gave her a maximum speed of 15.5 knots.

The *Lady Cecilia* was the first of the two converted minesweepers to arrive in Vancouver, coming via the Panama Canal under the command of Charles B. Smith and docking on April 12, 1925. Her sister ship, the *Lady Cynthia*, arrived soon after on Aug. 22.

It was difficult to tell the two vessels apart, but people familiar with them could spot one small difference. Looking at both ships head on, the doorway on the forward main deck of the *Lady Cecilia* was on the port side, and on the *Cynthia* it was starboard. Later, in 1944, the *Cynthia*'s second funnel was removed, making the two ships easily identifiable.

When the *Lady Cecilia* went into service she was put on the East Howe Sound daily route under Captain Neil Gray, who retained command of her until 1937. [95] She was usually referred to by her full name, though insiders sometimes called her "the *Cec*."

The *Lady Cecilia* soon was involved in her first accident, on Dec. 27, 1925, though only peripherally. She was northbound to Powell River, returning a full load of mill workers on a Christmas excursion. The weather was foggy as another Union ship, the southbound *Cowichan*, passed the *Cecilia* just off Sechelt, but the Master of the *Cowichan* didn't realize the *Cecilia* was being followed by the *Cynthia* with an overload of passengers, and so the *Cynthia* and *Cowichan* collided (see details under the *Cowichan*, p. 15). Passengers and crew from the *Cowichan* were all safely transferred to the *Lady Cynthia* but when that ship withdrew her bow, the *Cowichan* sank within about 10 minutes of impact. [96]

The *Lady Cecilia* went aground at the mouth of Chapman Creek on the Sunshine Coast some time in the late 1920s. Though details of that accident are not available, I was able to obtain a photo from the Elphinstone Museum showing the *Lady Cecilia* high and dry on a sand bar.

In the late 1920s and mid 1930s the excursion trade boomed, and the *Lady Cecilia* was in the forefront of that trade all along the Sunshine Coast. Early in the 1930s she was used on a day cruise to Jervis Inlet, north of Sechelt, then in 1933 the Company inaugurated the famous Powell River-Savary Island day trip. This scenic full-day round trip initially cost only $2, and later at $3.50 was still a bargain. [97] The deck crew and officers loved the Savary Island cruises because there wasn't much to do other than unload passenger baggage at Westview, so they were able to go swimming and loaf a little while docked at Savary Island.

Norrie Wood, who served as purser aboard the *Lady Cecilia*, recalls the clouds of thick black smoke that streamed from her stack. Because of these long day trips, the engineers had to get all the speed they could get out of her so they lit more burners. If the oil was cold this would cause the black smoke initially.

The *Lady Cecilia*, like other Union ships, had to fuel up at the oil dock in Coal Harbour. John Allan, a former deckhand, recalls one refuelling when the engine crew forgot to turn off the feeder valve and the oil spouted all over the deck. Allan and the other hands had to clean up the mess, but they complained that the engine crew should do it because they were to blame, and eventually they were pressured into helping.

Allan described the crew's mess room on the *Cec* as very hot because it was right over the engine room fiddley. As well, the galley was a deck below so the mess boy had to carry the food up a narrow stairway ladder - a tough job for anyone.

Allan also recalls the time when the *Lady*

S.S. *Cecilia* aground at Chapman Beach in the early 1930s
(Elphinstone Museum)

Cecilia got hung up on the wharf in Vancouver. After the ship docked for the night and tied up, the night watchman forgot to slacken the lines as the tide fell and the ship hung up on the pilings on her starboard side. A shipyard crew had to be called in during the night to get her off and make some repairs so she could sail in the morning.

On July 29, 1940, the *Lady Cecilia*, under the command of Captain Lorne Godfrey, was one of several Union ships participating in "Win the War Cruises" around Vancouver harbour.

Lady Cecilia aground at Pender Harbour Dec. 24, 1940 *(Spilsbury Collection, Vancouver Maritime Museum)*

On Christmas Eve 1940, the *Lady Cecilia* went hard aground on Indian Island while backing away from Pender Harbour wharf. The deck officers aboard at the time were Captain Robert Naughty, Chief Officer Harry McLean, Second Mate Dennis Farina and Third Mate Bob Williamson, and Farina described to me what happened: "Harry McLean was on watch and he backed her out giving the full astern order. Then he rang for stop engines. The engineer on watch was J. Baldry but instead of stopping the engines he gave them full astern. McLean realized what was happening and rattled the telegraph for full ahead again and evidently Baldry thought he wanted more power and gave her all the power he could. She climbed up on that island and almost knocked the Indians' outhouse over. Her stern was up on that rock, right out of the water.

"We had to get down and seal all the side doors so the water wouldn't come in. The tide was falling and there she sat.

"So we took all the mail and important things off in the lifeboats and took them ashore at Irvine's Landing. Some of the crew as well as the passengers stayed in the hotel overnight. Other crew went back to the ship and stayed aboard her all night. Next morning we got all the fish boats we could gather from Pender Harbour and tried to pull her off, but she wouldn't budge. The *Venture* was southbound and she was called in. She hooked a line onto the *Cecilia* but still she wouldn't move. The *Venture* then took our stranded passengers on to Vancouver.

"The *Salvage Queen* came up on Christmas Day. She was a powerful tug and at high tide they put a line on us. She gave us a pull, zig-zagged us, and by God she got us off, but you know, the *Cecilia*'s rudder was jammed hard over so she wouldn't tow straight at all. They had a tough time getting her back to Vancouver. (see adjacent photograph)

"The engineer admitted his mistake and left the company and went over to the CNR."

Another eyewitness to the whole affair was Jim Spilsbury. He was there in his boat because his wife was in Garden Bay Hospital waiting to have a baby. They called him over and asked him to take a line and try pulling but Jim could see it was hopeless for his little boat to try and pull her off. Jim took the now-famous picture (which accompanies this story) and sold it to *The Vancouver Sun* for $5.

The *Lady Cecilia* seemed to have a lot of bad luck, for every few years she seemed to be involved in some sort of mishap. In the late 1940s, for example, there was an incident when she was being docked by Jimmy Galbraith and he had forgotten to have the crew wing in the ship's derricks, so one of the derricks hit a derrick on an adjacent ship and knocked down a boom, which crashed onto the wheelhouse and caused much havoc and damage.

One of the *Cecilia*'s most serious accidents happened on Sept. 18, 1944, when she collided with a freighter off of Point Atkinson. I was aboard as a freight clerk and I remember the accident vividly because I saw it coming only moments before it happened and narrowly escaped injury myself. Afterwards I was assigned to make a list of all the injured passengers and describe their injuries.

Dennis Farina, who was Second Mate on watch with Captain Lawrey when the freighter hit, gave me this account of how it happened: "We didn't have radar in those days. We were proceeding into Vancouver in a very thick fog, sounding our whistle and listening for other ships' whistles. We thought we heard the *Princess Elaine*. We listened carefully and she was getting closer. Captain Lawrey thought he had better stop, so we stopped dead in the water. All of a sudden, coming out of the fog, this huge bow was heading right at us. Captain Lawrey quickly went full ahead on one engine and full astern on the other. His quick action saved the ship for he had been able to swing the *Cecilia* around enough so that the freighter hit us with a glancing blow, but crumpled our starboard side from mid ship to the stern."

My recollection is that I had gone down to our room to change out of my uniform and into street clothes. I felt the ship stop and then heard the telegraph signals down to the engine room. I wondered what was going on and so looked out the porthole. I saw this huge huge bow of the freighter coming right at us and knew it would hit just about where I was. I knew I had to get out of there fast. Somehow I got into my uniform pants, grabbed my uniform jacket and ran out of the room in my bare feet. I remember thinking I'd better head for my lifeboat station. I ran up the dining room salon stairs and at the same time was trying to get my jacket on. By the time I reached the main deck we had been hit and the *Cecilia* was resting, dead still in the water. However there was pandemonium in the starboard

Top: S.S. *Cecilia's* damage from collision with freighter off Point Atkinson, Sept. 1944 (15 people injured)
Left: Passenger lounge damage shown by Fireman John Barnett

passenger lounge where many passengers had been injured. Newspaper reports later said 11 people were injured, but my list, of which I still have a copy, had 15 people listed with injuries. Nine people were taken to hospital but none had serious injuries and soon all were released.

Norrie Wood, Assistant Purser, had been in the office with Purser Les Smith counting the trip's cash. When the ship stopped, Wood went forward to the observation lounge and saw the freighter coming. He ran back to the office yelling to Smith, "We're going to crash!" Smith ignored the remark, and without looking up said "Keep quiet or I'll make a mistake in my cash count."

There was a marine inquiry into the accident but because of the very bad weather no blame was placed on anyone. Other deck officers aboard at the time were chief officer Jack Summerfield and third mate Don Campbell.

Less than three months later, on Dec. 15, 1944, the *Cecilia* had another collision off

Point Atkinson, only this time it was with a much smaller vessel, the 33-ton fish tender *Great Northern 9*, and apparently there were no injuries or serious damage. She hit another fishing vessel, this one unidentified, on Oct. 8, 1945, again in fog off of Lions Gate Bridge and again apparently without major damage. On Christmas Eve 1946 she had yet another minor collision in fog in the area, this time with the Union fleet's own *Chilliwack*. [98]

Lady Cecilia landing at Savary Island (I. Kennedy)

Though there were no fatalities in any of those accidents, I vividly recall one trip on the *Cecilia* in the early 1940s when a fellow crewman was lost overboard. We had just left Roberts Creek on a clear and sunny but windy day. I was on the freight deck ready to check the freight for the next stop but with the ship rolling and wallowing the Mate decided the shell freight doors should be closed. A member of the crew on his first trip was instructed to get a crow bar, insert it in a groove in the open door and yank it closed. He managed to close the door half way but then the ship rolled and the door swung back. Instead of letting go the fellow hung on to the crow bar and disappeared into the waves before our startled eyes.

"Man overboard!" we cried. The ship stopped immediately and we searched for an hour but never found a trace of the poor fellow.

Ken Moir, a frequent passenger on the *Cecilia* in the 1940s, recalls a near-grounding off the Sunshine Coast. The *Cecilia* left Gibsons Landing for Vancouver with a full load of passengers. If the tide was high enough they would proceed through a gap but if not they had to go around the east end of Keats Island. On this day they decided to go through the gap but they misjudged the tide. When the *Cecilia* was halfway through she started churning up mud, starfish and shells. The passengers saw this and someone ran up to the bridge to tell the captain. He stopped the ship, and the mate came back to see it all. The *Cecilia* then proceeded forward very slowly and finally made it through. The only damage was to the pride of the officers on the bridge.

John Allan was aboard the *Cecilia* when one of her propeller shafts broke. "It made a terrible racket, banging away on the ship's steel hull," he says. Neil Campbell, the Captain, thought at first they'd struck a submerged wreck. The engines were stopped and the break was discovered. They proceeded with only one engine, and took six hours to reach Vancouver. Allan recalls the precise length of time because it was his wheel watch, and because it was late at night he was stuck at the wheel for all six hours while everyone else slept.

A grounding on Dec. 23, 1947 almost finished off the *Cecilia*. She was taking a small load of passengers up to Powell River and was due to bring back a full load to Vancouver for the holidays, but she ran aground at 4 p.m. on Tattenham Ledge near Buccaneer Bay. It was a hastily-arranged sort of charter trip and the crew had been hurriedly assembled. The Master was Wally Walsh and the Chief Officer was Jimmy Galbraith, who was on watch when the accident occurred.

Alan Smith, a winchman aboard at the time, gave this eyewitness account: "It was a clear, calm sunny day, though there had been a southeaster blowing for the previous three days. We were enroute from Halfmoon Bay to Buccaneer Bay and were attempting to go through the gap in Tattenham Reef, inside the buoy. I was sitting on the hatch cover splicing a springline and I looked up to see the trees going by like leaves in the wind. I looked over the side and saw bottom, then looked up at the wheelhouse but didn't see anybody. At that moment we hit and bounced with a hell of a crash, then there was dead silence.

"The excuse for going aground was that the helmsman turned too quickly.

"Because the *Lady Cecilia* and the *Lady Cynthia* . . . had their bows filled with concrete, when we hit the reef we bounced like one stone hitting another and landed a third of the way down the outer hull, which was about under the wheelhouse."

were only six passengers aboard when she grounded and they were taken to Secret Cove where they continued their journey. The *Lady Cecilia* resisted the efforts of three Straits Towing tugs to pull her free during the next two days then on Dec. 26 four tugs grappled with the ship for 45 minutes and did finally pull her off. They beached her in the sandy bay rather than abandon her, and began making temporary repairs. Smith recalls taking all the mattresses they could find on the ship and stuffing them into the bow, which they boarded up with lumber that had been aboard. Once the holes were patched and the

Lady Cecilia aground on Tattenham Reef, Dec. 23, 1947 *(Puget Sound Maritime Historical Society)*

The accident badly damaged the *Cecilia*'s bow and ripped open about 75 feet of steel plates, so her bulkheads were sealed to prevent her taking on more water. There

sea water was pumped out, the *Cecilia* was towed stern-first back to Vancouver for repairs, arriving at 10 p.m. on Dec. 27.

About this time Gulf Lines entered the

coastal shipping business with ships that were smaller and faster than the Union ships, and the *Lady Cecilia*, being relatively expensive to run, could not compete with them on the Sunshine Coast. The Union Steamships Company had waited too long to put new ships on its routes and soon began paying a heavy price.

At the end of 1949, the *Lady Cecilia* was laid up. Apparently the Company had considered retiring her for some time, and when the federal government announced tougher fire regulations requiring that expensive sprinkler systems be installed on all coastal ships, her fate was sealed. Before she was laid up, I was fortunate to serve aboard her as Purser in August 1949, and I saved a dinner menu to mark that event.

The *Lady Cecilia* was sold to O.H. New of Coast Ferries in October 1951 and was broken up on Gambier Island, where she formed part of a breakwater.

Two mementos of the *Lady Cecilia* can still be found today. One is her original brass Builders Plate, which is on display at the Hastings Mill Museum in Vancouver, and the other is her brass bell, which Sparky New donated in 1952 to the Canadian Merchant Service Guild, which still uses it to mark special events at certain meetings.

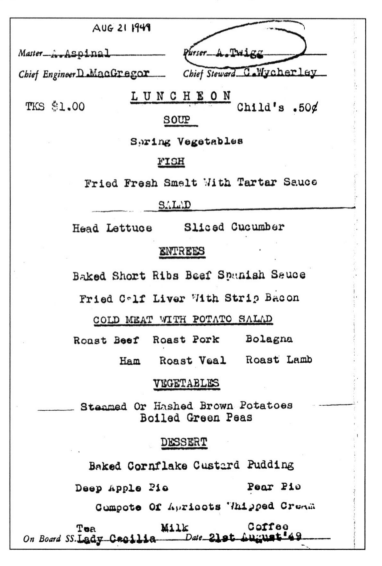

Luncheon menu on *Lady Cecilia* Aug. 21, 1949 *(Twigg Collection)*

S.S. Lady Cynthia

The origin of the name Lady Cynthia is unknown but the use of "Lady" had become a practise of the Company at the time, and "Cynthia" may be derived from a relative of the controlling shareholders.

In Union service: 1925-57
Official No.: 152899
Type: Steel twin-screw passenger-freighter.
Dimensions: Length 235.0' (BP 219.3'), breadth 28.6', depth 16.3'. Gross tons 950
Engines: Triple-expansion, NHP 250, IHP 1,600; Yarrow boilers. Speed 15.5 maximum, 13.5 average
Services: Mainly on Bowen Island-Squamish route and excursions
Capacities: Passenger licence summer 800 (excursions 900); winter 500, 3 staterooms. Cargo 75 tons

S.S. *Lady Cynthia* with two funnels
(McAllister Collection)

The HMS *Barnstaple* was purchased from the British Admiralty in 1925 and renamed the *Lady Cynthia*. Like her sister ship the *Lady Cecilia* she was christened by Lady Rushton at the Coaster Construction Yards in Scotland on the same day as the *Catala* was launched.

Sponsons had been added to her hull for better stability and also, like the *Lady Cecilia*, she had two stacks but one was a dummy. She was brought across the Atlantic by Captain James Findlay and her Chief Engineer was Bob Logan. They arrived in Vancouver on Aug. 22, 1925.

Though the records indicate that the *Lady Cynthia* had fewer accidents than her sister ship, the ones she did have were quite serious, and they began happening only a few months into her new service.

On Dec. 28, 1925, the *Cynthia*, under Captain Jack Boden's command, left Vancouver northbound for Powell River with a post-holiday overflow of passengers from the *Lady Cecilia*, but in a heavy fog off of Sechelt she collided with the Union Steamship Company's venerable *Cowichan*, which sank only minutes later, fortunately without any loss of life.

There are several different versions of this event, which are given in the section on the *Cowichan* (see page 15), but for the purpose here of telling the *Lady Cynthia*'s story we can use the following version by noted marine writer Fred Rogers excerpted from his book Shipwrecks of British Columbia:

"On Monday evening, December 28, 1925, the Gulf of Georgia and lower coastal waters were locked under a thick blanket of foul-smelling fog. Off the Sechelt Peninsula, several vessels were blindly groping their way. Two of them, the Union Steamship's *Cowichan* and the steamer *Lady Cynthia*, were drawing closer. The *Cowichan* was southbound for Vancouver, the *Cynthia* northbound for Powell River.

"On the *Cynthia*, Capt. J. Boden heard what he thought was the whistle of a tug and altered course to pass. Then, to his surprise, another whistle sounded dead ahead. It was from the *Cowichan*. Realizing that she was very close, he ordered slower speed and sounded his whistle. The other ship did likewise. At about 100 yards, the ghostly image of the *Cowichan*'s lights loomed in the fog. When the *Cynthia* first sighted the *Cowichan* at 9:30 p.m. she was making about five knots. Captain Boden ordered the starboard engine ahead and the port engine astern to effect a glancing blow, but the *Cynthia*'s steel bow sliced into the *Cowichan*'s portside, rolling her and knocking passengers off their feet.

"The vessels collided about four miles southeast of Sechelt light. Fortunately, there was a light wind and a calm sea. As water began filling the *Cowichan*'s engine room, the ships were kept locked together to help plug the hole. Capt. R. Wilson then calmly ordered his passengers and crew to transfer to the *Cynthia* by climbing over the forepeak railing. They had already gathered their baggage in preparation for arrival in Vancouver, so there was no panicky rush to save belongings. The *Cynthia* then reversed to free herself and the *Cowichan* sank in 60 fathoms - only 11 minutes after the collision.

"The *Cowichan* carried 15 passengers and a crew of 31, none of whom were seriously injured. After the *Cowichan* went down, the *Lady Cynthia* turned about for Vancouver." [99]

In 1931, as an economy measure in the midst of the depression, passengers destined for West Howe Sound points were dropped off on Bowen Island by the *Cynthia* and transferred to the M.V. *Comox*, which took them to their destinations. The same arrangement took place for passengers going to Vancouver. [100]

In 1933, in order to drum up new business, the Company began day cruises up to Jervis Inlet, between Sechelt and Powell River, and then added what turned out to be a popular day run to Savary Island, north of Powell River. Because of the distance of those destinations from Vancouver, the Company put the relatively fast *Lady Cynthia* and *Lady Cecilia* on those runs even though it was costly to keep them steaming at top speed.

The *Lady Cynthia* had a touch of glory in May 1939 when she, the *Lady Alexandra* and the *Lady Cecilia* participated in the visit to Vancouver of King George VI and Queen Elizabeth. On May 25, 1939, the three Union ships brought thousands of settlers and students from around Howe Sound to Vancouver to help welcome the Royal couple, and on the afternoon of May 29 when their majesties left for Victoria aboard the CPR's *Princess Marguerite*, the *Lady Cynthia* was among six Union ships that closely watched the departure and then followed out of the harbour as far as Point Atkinson, carrying some 2,500 passengers. It was a fitting highlight of the Company's fiftieth year in business. [101]

The outbreak of the Second World War in September 1939 brought many changes to the Company and to their ships, and just before the *Lady Cynthia* was to go in for a refit she experienced perhaps her proudest moment: on the evening of July 29, 1940 she led a parade of six Union ships out into the harbour carrying about 3,000 people who had been given free tickets by the Company for purchasing War Savings Stamps. They were later joined by two other Union ships, making an impressive parade of eight. [102]

The *Cynthia*'s refit was extensive; her dummy stack was removed and the forward lounge was extended to the full width of the ship. Now with only one stack people could quite easily tell her apart from the *Cecilia*.

The war years brought some tough times to the *Lady Cynthia* and to the many people who sailed aboard her, often especially for those travelling on military-related purposes.

Ken Moir, a frequent passenger on the Union ships, recalls sailing into Vancouver in May 1941 when it was announced that the great British battleship *Hood* had been sunk with a heavy loss of lives. Moir said the passengers were shocked to learn of the demise of one of England's mightiest warships, which had visited Vancouver in 1924. He told me that every time he travelled on the *Cynthia* after that, he was reminded of that shocking episode of the war.

Wharfinger Tex Lyon of Port Hardy remembers the *Lady Cynthia* making a special trip bringing military people up to the base at Coal Harbour via Port Hardy. Before loading these men in Vancouver they installed two-tier bunks along with a mattress in any available space such as lounges and companionways. She ran into a southeast gale near Sointula on her way to Port Hardy and began to roll violently, so everyone became seasick, including the skipper. With only limited toilet facilities, the companionways were awash and sloshing with vomit. On her arrival in Port Hardy the crew had to flush the ship out with fire hoses.

The *Lady Cynthia* was pressed into service on a rescue mission of a different sort in December 1943. Torrential rains had washed out the Capilano River Bridge, isolating West Vancouver from the rest of the Lower Mainland, and the *Lady Cynthia*, under Captain Bob Naughty, was one of several ships that ferried passengers from Dundarave Pier to Vancouver and back until a temporary bridge was built.

Just before Christmas 1945, the *Cynthia* made a special run to Port Hardy to bring

Lady Cynthia after refit with only one funnel 1940
(Betz Collection)

Wartime passengers on the *Lady Cynthia*
(Ashmore Collection)

army personnel down to Vancouver for the holidays. As she cleared Cape Mudge she ran into a violent storm and sea. The *Cardena* under Captain Boden was following, and he slowed down in case the *Cynthia* got into trouble. The *Cynthia* came through unscathed but the *Cardena* was damaged, though repairs were made quickly and she sailed the next day.

The war years however still had happy moments, and I particularly remember some in 1943 while I was a young Assistant Purser on the *Lady Cynthia* when she was doing the Cortes-Stuart Island route. It was a very demanding run because it had so many stops going and coming, but every Sunday morning we would be southbound off the south end of Cortes Island and about 11 a.m. a lady would row out in her little boat to meet the *Cynthia* in mid stream. The *Cynthia* would stop and the lady would hand up a bouquet of flowers for the Captain. It was a touching gesture of gratitude from someone who appreciated the Union ships and their service.

At some time in this period, Paddy Farina joined the *Lady Cynthia* as Chief Engineer after an amazing 30 years or so as Chief Engineer of his beloved *Capilano*. To help him feel more at home, he took the whistle off of the *Capilano* and installed it on the *Cynthia*.

In September 1948 the *Lady Cynthia* was pressed into action when the Company's ship *Chilcotin* broke down as she was returning from a cruise to Alaska with a load of American Shriners. A bearing gave out on the main engine as the ship was off Texada Island, so it had to be towed into Gillies Bay and anchored. The *Cynthia* was sent up from Vancouver to take aboard the *Chilcotin*'s 102 passengers and bring them back to Vancouver, which was done in time for their plane and train connections. [103] Bob Ashmore was Chief Officer aboard the *Chilcotin* at the time and said the passengers found it romantic and even quite thrilling to transfer from one ship to another on the high seas.

The *Lady Cynthia* was directly involved in a much more serious event on the afternoon of Oct. 3, 1950 when she collided with the M.V. *A.L. Bryant*, a B.C. Forest Service cruiser, killing three of the *Bryant*'s crew. The collision happened off of Bowen Island while the *Bryant* was under the command of John W. MacDonald, a log scaler who did not possess a certificate of competency to operate a ship. The *Cynthia*, with Chief Officer Al Strang on the bridge, was heading for Snug Cove and the *Bryant* was proceeding across the channel to Whytecliff Point. In an article on the subsequent marine inquiry, Vancouver *Province* reporter Jim Fairley outlined the positions of the different parties:

"Inquiry into the fatal collision between coastal passenger vessel S.S. *Lady Cynthia* and the B.C. Forest Service cruiser M.V. *A.L. Bryant* has been put over until next Tuesday while Mr. Justice Smith and his two sea captain assistants consider four different opinions as to what caused the crash.

"The opinions were offered by the four parties involved - officers of the *Cynthia*, crew of the *Bryant*, the B.C. Forest Service department of transport, and Union Steamship Ltd. - following testimony of more than a dozen witnesses.

"John Farris, speaking for the *Bryant*'s crew, submitted that the *Cynthia* was an 'overtaking vessel' and therefore was required under shipping regulations to give way to the *Bryant*, that the *Cynthia* gave no warning signal, that there was no obligation on the part of those in charge of the small vessel to maintain an aft lookout, and that by maintaining sharp lookout ahead 'they were doing what they were supposed to do.'

"They were entitled to assume that the rules of the road would be observed,' he said.

"J.I. Bird, representing Union Steamships Co. and the *Cynthia* generally, submitted that 'it is up to any vessel to keep a lookout aft, knowing that it is going to be overtaken.' He offered that the *Bryant* 'swung off its course and carried itself across the path of the *Cynthia*.'

Lady Cynthia at Keats Island Baptist Camp *(E. Lashbrook)*

"Glen McDonald, representing the officers of the *Cynthia*, said that First Mate Alan Strang, on watch at the time, was a man of more than 18 years' experience on the coast and had no marks against him. He maintained that when Strang first sighted the *Bryant* it had settled to a course running parallel to the *Cynthia* and was entitled to assume that it would maintain that course 'as is mandatory under shipping regulations.'

"He cited a former inquiry in which it was held that a ship in danger because of being overtaken by another ship should take the appropriate action to prevent a collision.

"R.M. Howard, counsel for department of transport, submitted that First Mate Strang aboard the *Cynthia* 'failed to maintain a proper lookout' between the time he first sighted the *Bryant* and sized up its course, and the actual time when a collision was about to take place. He said there was 'plenty of time' to avoid a collision. He also maintained that the *Bryant* 'should have had a lookout astern.' " [104]

The judgment in the case was handed down by Justice Sidney Smith in Admiralty Court. Al Strang, the officer on the bridge of the *Cynthia*, lost his ticket for nine months and John MacDonald, the log scaler in command of the *A.L. Bryant*, drew severe censure. No costs were allowed either parties.

Three years later, on Oct. 23, 1953, the *Lady Cynthia* was in the headlines again for its involvement in another sinking off of Whytecliff Park, this time on a foggy day but without the loss of life. At 5:45 p.m. the *Lady Cynthia* crashed hard into the big old steam tug *Dola* which was proceeding to Squamish with a barge full of train cars in tow, and the *Dola* quickly went to the bottom as a complete loss. Apparently the *Cynthia* had entered a fog bank, its officers had felt they were on the wrong side of the shipping lane and in turning sharply to try to get into the proper lane they instead turned into the tug.

As in the earlier collision with the *Cowichan*, the *Cynthia*'s sharp bow was kept into the *Dola* while its nine crewmen were transferred over and then when the *Cynthia* slipped free the *Dola* sank in only a minute or so. As tug owner Ted Wilson noted in his book *Full Line, Full Away*, the subsequent marine inquiry apportioned no blame to the *Dola*. [105]

That black mark on the *Cynthia*'s record seemed in keeping with the steadily-declining fortunes of the Union Steamships Company in general. It was losing business, its senior personnel were retiring and dying off, and its ships were having more and more problems.

In 1955 the Union Steamship Co. was hit by a seamen's strike that lasted until September and reportedly cost the Company more than $1 million. And even when the strike was over the Company was faced with operating costs higher than its revenues could support. That September the Company withdrew the last of its day steamers still in service, which was the *Lady Cynthia*. It was moored at B.C. Marine and later was sold to Coast Ferries.

On Oct. 5, 1957, the *Lady Cynthia*, along with the freighter *Southolm*, was towed out of the harbour to be scrapped by Sternoff Metal in Seattle.

M.V. Lady Rose

The ship was built for Union Steamships and launched in 1937 as the *Lady Sylvia*, but because of a registry duplication her name was changed after she arrived in Vancouver, with Rose reportedly chosen in honour of a member of the family of Company general manager Major Harold Brown.

In Union service: 1937-51
Official No.: 170429
Type: Steel passenger and cargo motor vessel
Dimensions: Length 104.8', breadth 21.2', depth 14.3'. Gross tons 199
Engines: Diesel. One 220 BHP propelling unit and one 28 BHP auxiliary, supplied by National Gas & Oil Engine Co., England. Speed 11.5 knots
Services: On West Howe Sound route.
Capacities: Passenger licence 130, winter 70. Cargo 25 tons

S.S. *Lady Rose* launched as *Lady Sylvia* (Marks Collection)

The *Lady Rose* was the last ship built for the Union Steamship Company, and though the plucky little ship continues in service to this day, her arrival sort of marks the beginning of the end for the Company as a going concern because she was a relatively tiny addition to the fleet at a time when they needed much more tonnage. As well, her arrival in Vancouver coincided with a major shift in ownership of the Company from England back to British Columbia.

Noted marine writer Norman Hacking described the *Lady Rose* as a "saucy little lady," and that describes quite well a small ship that survived very rough seas on her voyage out from Scotland and then went on to survive many ups and downs in the commercial fortunes of shipping on the B.C.

coast.

The Company had her built to specifications at the A. & J. Inglis Shipyards of Glasgow for $100,000 and she was launched on March 17, 1937. The christening (originally under the name *Lady Sylvia*) was by Mrs. J.F. Jupp, a daughter of the late J.H. Welsford [106], whose family trust had held onto control of Union Steamships through the depression years but also had failed to add the new capacity needed for the war years and for the post-war boom.

The *Lady Rose* was only 105 feet long, 21 feet wide, 14 feet deep and 199 gross tons but that was still twice the size of the ship, the 53-foot *Comox*, that she was intended to replace on winter service to West Howe Sound. She could handle about 20 tons of general freight forward on the main deck but she was designed mainly for passenger use on short day runs, since she did not have any passenger sleeping rooms. The enclosed cabin aft contained a lounge and coffee bar licenced to carry up to 70 passengers, which Company traffic manager Gerald Rushton described as "disappointing and restrictive." In summer the open upper deck boosted her capacity to 130 passengers.

One of the most interesting features on the *Lady Rose* was that she was equipped with only a single propeller powered by a 220 BHP six-cylinder National diesel motor driven through an oil-operated reverse-reduction gearbox producing a maximum speed of 11.5 knots. Story has it that the motor was designed as a stationary class motor which worked in reverse to a marine class motor. This caused many headaches for the Masters and Mates operating and docking her for many years. It had to be handled in a non conventional way to a normal single screw vessel. Her steering and winches were driven by air. This novel method made it harder to keep constant pressure than with steam. The problem was not rectified until the *Rose* was sold many years later to Harbour Navigation Co. [107]

The relatively small size of the ship and its dependence on a single engine for power made an especially daunting prospect of the crossing of the Atlantic and the voyage up the West Coast from the Panama Canal, and indeed it's generally believed that she became the first single-screw vessel to do so.

There have been very many articles written about the *Lady Rose*, probably because she has continued in prominent service (at time of writing she's still on a sort of romantic seasonal run between Port Alberni, Bamfield and Ucluelet) and because her heroic voyage out to British Columbia and her subsequent reliable service evoke the gritty pioneer spirit of the province.

Many of the articles making reference to her harrowing ocean voyages are based on a first-person account by Eric Oates, the Guarantee Engineer on the voyage, which was published with the assistance of *London Yachting* editor A.M. Kennersley, but while that account indeed portrays accurately the epic nature of the voyage, which took more than two months to cover 9,800 nautical miles through several raging storms with only three stops for fuel and supplies, it is in some instances exaggerated, according to Captain W.S. Smales, who commanded the *Lady Sylvia* on the voyage.

In my research I obtained a copy of Oates' original article that had been read and edited by Captain Smales, and on which he had written several comments. While some of his notes are minor corrections, such as on his proper initials and on the time it took to sail south from Scotland to Las Palmas, other corrections are more significant, such as his notation that their cook was a good baker and so the crew had fresh bread throughout, which is contrary to Oates' version, and his scoffing of Oates' report that a hurricane had crossed their path only 100 miles astern as "news to me."

Perhaps the real truth is somewhere in the middle, since it's clear from Smales' acceptance of the bulk of the Oates' story that the gist is true, namely that the little ship was bouncing wildly through heavy seas for days on end, and in such conditions one can't imagine there being much cooking done, and nor would it be comfortable for the nine-member crew, who had only temporary quarters in the lounge.

Indeed we can draw much from Smales' accepting Oates' attribution of his nickname as "Make it or bust" and from Oates' comment that Smales "steered his ship relentlessly for her destination" rather than alter course to find shelter in a lee, to which Smale added "in spite of a scared Guarantee Engineer."

One of the better summaries of the voyage was written by Eric Jamieson and published in the Fall 1989 issue of *Canadian West Magazine*, from which the following edited excerpt is drawn:

"Undaunted by the cloud and drizzle of a sombre Glasgow day, the *Lady Sylvia* left her berth at 12:30 p.m., Friday, May 7, 1937, bound for Vancouver. Under the command of Captain W.S. Smales of Leeds was a nervous crew of nine. This was an historic undertaking for such a small motor-driven craft - the *Lady Sylvia* was the first single propulsion vessel to cross the Atlantic - so, as a precaution, the vessel's saloon windows and railings were planked against anticipated rough seas.

"The *Lady Sylvia* was only two hours into her voyage when she made a fuel stop at Old Kilpatrick. While there, one of her crew decided the voyage had already held enough promise for him, and abandoned ship. The following morning, at 8:15 a.m., she slipped from her berth and motored down the Clyde River, passing the great Canadian Pacific liner *Duchess of York* en route. The liner's passengers pressed the railings, in awe of the diminutive *Lady Sylvia*'s ambitious task ahead. Each vessel gave the other the customary nautical salute of the day . . . the voyage had begun in earnest.

"Eric Oates, Guarantee Engineer, reminiscing to *London Yachting* editor A.M. Kennersley, recalled that 'A falling glass [barometer] and a fast rising swell met them on arrival in [open water], and it was soon apparent the *Lady Sylvia* was a lively ship with a movement which made it difficult and often impossible to do more than hold on grimly.'

"The vessel fought gamely forward through mountainous seas which threatened to swallow it, but old "Make it or Bust," as the Captain came to be known, held fast to his course, and six days later *Lady Sylvia* pulled alongside the quay at Los Palmas, having completed the first leg of her momentous journey.

"A few days later she was sweating through the 'Trades' and on June 7 Colon was sighted. Entering the Pacific, 'this ill-named ocean commenced to show its teeth and reduced *Lady Sylvia* in a few hours to a quivering screaming thing again. For seven whole days *Lady Sylvia* crashed and pounded slowly ahead until nerves and bodies were reduced to utter exhaustion.'

"A month later the tiny vessel was still working its way north, but at 6 a.m. on July 10, Cape Flattery was sighted and shortly afterwards Vancouver Island came into sight through the mist. . . . At 4:30 the pilot signal was hoisted and the Canadian Pacific liner *Empress of Japan*, her great white hull making a lovely picture against the wooded background, greeted the *Lady Sylvia* at the end of her journey as her sister had done at the beginning.

"The final entry in the log is terse and expressive: 'Sunday, 11th July, 5:30 a.m., Vancouver: Thank God.'

"After having logged an amazing 9,800 miles with only three stops for fuel and food, the little *Lady Sylvia* had reached the protective waters of her new home." [108]

Alan Thomas, the Company's accounting supervisor at the time, recalls going down to the Union dock to see her and finding her quite bedraggled from her epic voyage, but he also had the honour of taking Captain Smales out to dinner on behalf of the Company. One of the reasons Smales took the dangerous assignment was because he wanted to meet up with an old friend, Neil Gray, whom he had not seen in 40 years. It happened that Gray was then a Captain with

Union Steamships and the two did have their rendezvous, but Smales declined to stay on with the Company in Vancouver. [109]

Soon after the arrival of the *Lady Sylvia* in Vancouver, her name was changed to *Lady Rose* because of a duplication in the Ships Registry files, and about the same time it was announced that control of the Company had been acquired by a group of senior Vancouver-based business executives, reportedly for about $1 million, which as Gerald Rushton noted was only about a third of what the Company had been worth in 1928. "It was certainly a bottom price for the historic Company, but the equipment was old, necessitating frequent repairs, and there was much to be done to bring the fleet up to date," he wrote. [110]

The *Lady Rose* was refitted under the direction of Major Harold Brown, who stayed on as President, and she was quickly put into summer service. At the time she carried a crew of 10, consisting of the Captain, First Officer, Chief Engineer, two deck hands, an oiler, a combined Purser/Chief Steward, a cook, a steward and a dishwasher.

Though the *Rose* was quite manoeuverable, she soon proved to be too small to be of much help as a utility backup on the heavy runs, and even in local waters she sometimes got bounced around roughly.

Former Purser Denis Shaw, who joined the *Rose* in 1937 as a waiter at $23.50 a month, remembers rounding Point Atkinson on the *Rose* one day with a strong westerly blowing, creating quite a sea. Not many passengers came up for lunch that day. They were heading up Howe Sound when a wave tossed a huge log right through the stern windows. The crew couldn't dislodge the log in the heavy sea but Captain Jock Malcolmson and Mate Buster Brown knew their situation was precarious and so struggled to steer the ship to the shelter of

Lady Sylvia in Vancouver, her windows still boarded over for her Atlantic crossing
(City of Vancouver Archives)

nearby Fisherman's Cove, where they eventually did manage to dislodge the log.

"The precaution taken by the builders [boarding up the windows] when she came out from Scotland was a wise one," Shaw said. The windows were replaced by conventional portholes when the *Rose* went into service on the West Coast.

Among the crew Shaw recalls working with were Captain E. Sheppard, Chief Engineer Bob Travis, Purser/Chief Steward Pat Wyllie, deck hand Jimmy Arnett, cook Roy Jewit, and Alex Switzer, another waiter in a neat white jacket, and mess boy Cecil Skinner.

The *Lady Rose* was the second diesel ship to operate in coastal waters, following the M.V. *Comox*. She was also wheelhouse controlled - the engines were directly controlled by the Captain in the wheelhouse. This proved unsatisfactory and at the urging of Chief Engineer Bob Travis they reverted to the standard telegraph system.

A sad story is told about Travis. On one trip after docking at Britannia Beach late one night, Captain Malcolmson prepared to depart and signalled down for standby. There was no response. He sent a deckhand down to the engine room. The man found Travis hanging by his neck. He had committed suicide. The death predictably gave rise to a rumour that the *Lady Rose* had a ghost aboard. Former seaman Ed Roach recalls one recurring event. "She had a door in the aft end of the wheelhouse bulkhead, right in the back side. When you opened the door there was a ladder going directly down to the engine room. That door used to fly open on its own every now and then, so whoever was on watch would say, 'Oh, there's Bobby coming up!' "

The compressed air winches were also controlled from the bridge. Alan Thomas recalls the time he had to go down to the *Rose* on business while she lay alongside the dock in Vancouver. She was due to sail that evening with a layover at Squamish and to make calls at Woodfibre and Britannia next morning. Everything was being made ready for sailing. Captain John Halcrow secured the booms by putting the hook of the winch line in the eye of the bow, thereby taking up the slack. Leaning out of the wheelhouse he kept the pressure on too long, and the next thing he knew one of the booms crashed down onto the wheelhouse. Embarrassed but unhurt, the Captain could only secure the downed boom and set sail, and figure out by the next day what to tell management.

The *Lady Rose* was busy at the beginning of the Second World War ferrying military personnel, such as to the fort on Yorke Island, and on July 29, 1940 she took part in the "Win the War" parade of Union ships, then later in 1940 she was requisitioned by the Canadian government for naval and air force transport on the west coast of Vancouver Island. She was returned to the Company in 1946 and resumed her West Howe Sound services. [111]

On July 23, 1949 I sailed on the *Lady Rose* as Purser. The Captain was Vic Hayman, Jimmy Main was Chief Engineer and Charlie Lanches Chief Steward. The dinner menu for that day follows this story. I remember that the Purser's safe was screwed into the deck of the room shared by the Purser and the Chief Engineer. There was no Purser's Office aboard her as such. The Purser and Freight Clerk took over one of the four dining room tables and used it as their desk. At meal times you had to pick up all your papers and the typewriter, then get out of the way while meals were being served.

Though the *Lady Rose*'s record is relatively free of accidents, she did have one close call in March, 1950, when she blew a cylinder off of Merry Island while on her way to Stillwater. John Smith, Quartermaster on that voyage, told me she drifted for many hours in a snowstorm, almost over to Nanaimo. She took a bad beating and many people aboard were sick. Finally, an engineer whose last name was Watson (who was relieving Jimmy Main) was able to jam the cylinder tight and allow the ship to make its way slowly back to Vancouver. Unfortunately that was the last voyage for Captain Vic Hayman because it was discovered that he had a cataract problem which brought his sea-going career to an end.

In 1951 the *Lady Rose* was sold to Harbour Navigation Co. and was put on a run servicing Port Mellon then in February 1954 she was chartered to Coast Ferries on a Steveston-Gulf Islands run. A labour dispute resulted in the vessel being returned to Harbour Navigation and she was then put on the Kelsey Bay-Alert Bay run in Johnstone Strait. [112]

In 1960 the *Lady Rose* was purchased by Captain Dick McMinn and Captain John Monrufet, who put her on a combined freight and passenger service in Barkley Sound from a base in Port Alberni. In 1982 she was sold to Captain Brooke George and partners Larry Barclay and Ken Toby, who kept her on the same run.

In 1990 the Vancouver Maritime Museum opened a major exhibition on the Union Steamship Co. under the guidance of curator Leonard McCann. This marked the 100th anniversary of the founding of the revered old Company in 1889, and one of the features of the show was to see the last of the original ships in the Union fleet that is still operating, the *Lady Rose*. (One other Union ship is still afloat, the *Comox II*, but it is not operating and instead is being used as a floating home by its owner, Keith Thorpe.)

With the co-operation of the owners of the *Lady Rose*, the Vancouver Maritime Museum arranged on to bring her down from Port Alberni on April 14, 1990 to a stop at Victoria, where she picked up 53 passengers and took them to Vancouver, where she tied up at the Vancouver Maritime Museum wharf. The majority of the passengers were ex-Union Steamship personnel. It was a great experience to be aboard her again. I was able to get a recording of her whistle sounding the old Union Steamship signal, one long, two shorts and a long. Captain Johnny Horne, an ex Union Steamship hand, was her acting Captain for most of the trip over to Vancouver.

She was opened to the public on April 15, 1990, and the next day ran a couple of tours, one over to Bowen Island, site of the Union Company's extensive real estate development, and the other around Vancouver harbour from where the Company was born.

At time of writing, the *Lady Rose* continues to operate year-round out of Port Alberni in much the same fashion as she did with the Union Steamship Co.

M.V. *Lady Rose* at the Vancouver Maritime Museum
April 14, 1990
(W.M. Laren)

106 Union Steamships Remembered

Model of the
Lady Rose by
Douglas Dyer

Dinner menu on board
Lady Rose July 20, 1949
(Twigg Collection)

```
          DINNER MENU  --  M.V. Lady Rose

  Master   V. Hayman          Purser        A. Twigg
  Chief Engineer  J. Main     Chief Steward C. Lanches

                        Dinner

                Cream Of Asparagus Soup

                          •

        Steamed Finnan Haddie, Drawn Butter.....$1.00

                          •

        Beef Stew & Vegetables..................$1.00
        Grilled Liberty Steak & Onions..........$1.00
        Fried Sausage, Mashed Potatoes..........$1.00
        Plain Or Cheese Omelette................$1.00

                          •

        Roast Leg Veal, Dressing................$1.25

                          •

                    Mashed Potatoes
                         Corn

                          •

        Sliced Bananas.          Assorted Pies
              Ice Cream.         Ala Mode 5¢ extra

        TEA            COFFEE            MILK


  On Board SS  M. V. Lady Rose   Date July 20th 1949.
```

S.S. Camosun II

Camosun was taken from the Native name for the bay where Victoria stands. The original settlement was called Camosack or Camosun, meaning "a deep narrow gorge" or "swift-running water." Three Union ships carried this name.

In Union service: 1940-45
Official No.: 124202
Type: Steel passenger-freight vessel
Dimensions: Length 241.7', breadth 33.1', depth 11.1'. Gross tons 1,344
Engines: Single, triple-expansion, 257 NHP. Speed 13 knots.
Services: In continuous wartime operation between Vancouver, the Queen Charlottes and Prince Rupert.
Capacities: Passenger licence on Queen Charlottes route, 150, otherwise 178; cabin berth 87. Cargo 150 tons

S.S. *Camosun II* (Vancouver Maritime Museum)

This ship was built in the Troon Yards of Ailsa Shipbuilding Co. for the David MacBrayne Fleet and was launched May 11, 1907 with the name *Chieftain*. She commenced running on the Glasgow-Stornoway route in the north of Scotland. She had a graceful yacht-like appearance, with a beautiful clipper bow. At the time she was one of the largest ships in the MacBrayne fleet.

Before long it was found that she was costly to operate and that her cargo handling facilities were unsuitable. In 1919 she was sold to the Orkney and Shetland Steam Navigation Co. and renamed the *St. Margaret*. This company ran into similar problems, and in 1925 sold her to Canadian National Steamships. She arrived on the west coast of B.C. in 1926 and was registered in Prince Rupert. Her name was changed to the *Prince Charles*.

In 1926 she was put into the Prince Rupert drydock for a major refit and when she left in 1927 she was a quite different ship. Her passenger facilities had been altered and now 95 cabin berths could accommodate 240 first class passengers. Her gross tonnage was increased from 1,081 to 1,344. However, her beautiful clipper bow was replaced with a more standard style. She resumed service on northern routes and to the Queen Charlotte Islands on March 3, 1927.

In June 1940 the *Prince Charles* was sold along with the *Prince John* to the Union Steamship Co., which was desperate to add tonnage. Their names were changed to *Camosun II* and *Cassiar II* respectively. Union also took over the CNR's route to the Queen Charlotte Islands and both ships stayed on this run throughout their career with Union.

On Oct. 15, 1940 the *Camosun II* collided with an Italian ship, *Lido*, in the First Narrows. Photos accompanying this story show the damage the *Camosun II* sustained. A Marine Inquiry cleared the *Camosun II* of blame.

In 1942 there was an interesting mix-up between the names of the *Camosun* and the freighter *Fort Camosun*, a freighter built locally for the war effort but whose name was never made public due to wartime security. The freighter was sailing from Victoria on her maiden voyage on June 19, 1942, carrying a full load - mostly plywood - and riding low in the water. That night she was spotted off Cape Flattery by a Japanese submarine, the *I-25*, and in the early morning hours of June 20 the sub fired a torpedo which ripped into the *Camosun*'s bow right below the bridge.

Word of the attack made headlines but the only *Camosun* anyone knew of at the time was the Union Steamship's *Camosun*. Naturally everyone thought it was the *Camosun II* that had been torpedoed but much to their surprise, she came sailing into the Union wharf right after the attack. Dockworkers and office staff were amazed and all crowded down on the dock to greet her arrival. They hollered and shouted, "We thought you had been sunk! We thought you had had it!"

Oddly enough, the *Camosun II* was the first B.C. coast passenger vessel to be armed and classed as a defensively-armed merchant ship. Colin Park was quartermaster on her at the time and related an amusing story about this. The gun was

S.S. *Camosun II* showing damage after collision with Italian steamer *Lido* 1940 *(Vancouver Maritime Museum)*

mounted aft and on the day for her first trial shot she was crammed full of Navy brass "mostly with gold braid up to their elbows," as Colin noted. They sailed out into the gulf and prepared to fire off the first round but when they did the old *Camosun* shook and rattled so violently that all the light fixtures in the dining room came crashing down. The old ship had to limp back into the shipyards for further modifications and reinforcing. To add insult to injury, on the way back into Vancouver harbour in all the excitement they forgot to fly the proper wartime flag signal identification so the defence installation underneath the Lions Gate Bridge thus fired a warning shot across the *Camosun*'s bow and a navy launch came out to intercept her. As the launch came alongside the *Camosun*, all the Navy brass lined the rail and hurriedly assured the launch crew that they were not an enemy ship.

The Master aboard the *Camosun II* was Captain James Watt, who had transferred over to Union from the CNR. One day in 1942 he was due to go on watch and when he didn't arrive on the bridge, the Chief Officer, Buster Brown, sent a man down to his room to rouse him. The man found Captain Watt lying on the floor of his cabin, dead, with his hair brush clutched in his hand. Watt was the first of four captains who collapsed and died aboard their ships in the Union Steamship fleet.

During the war, the *Camosun II* and *Cassiar II* carried thousands of Army and Air Force personnel to the Queen Charlotte Islands, particularly to the Air Force Base at Alliford Bay. When Germany surrendered in May 1945 and Japan that September, business declined rapidly and the *Camosun* was taken out of service at the end of the summer. She was badly in need of repairs and an overhaul after exhausting years of non-stop service to aid the war effort.

In August 1945 the *Camosun* was sold to the Oriental Navigation Co. Ltd. of Tel Aviv, Palestine, for approximately $77,000. The *Vancouver Province* ran a story on the sale on Aug. 24, 1945 but they illustrated it with a photograph of the first *Camosun*, which had been taken out of service in 1935.

When the *Camosun II* sailed out of Vancouver for the Mediterranean she carried Greek officers and crew. Her name was changed to *Cairo*, registered in Tel Aviv. She began service for her new owners carrying illegal immigrants to the Holy Land. In 1946 she was caught in a blockade preventing these immigrants from Marseilles and Italian ports from entering the country.

In 1947 she was sold to the Zarati Steamship Co. registered in Panama but continued to run in the Mediterranean. She was finally laid up in May 1950 at Marseilles and sold the next year for scrap. She was finally broken up in 1952 after 45 years of steady service.

Camosun II showing damage to outer deck and dining lounge after collision with *Lido* in First Narrows
(Vancouver Maritime Museum)

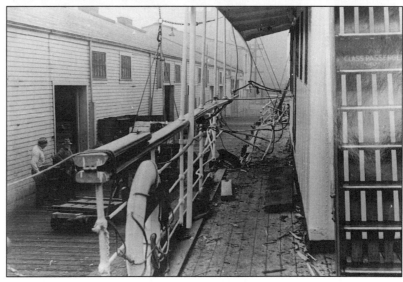

S.S. Cassiar II

Cassiar originated with the Caska Indians, a division of the Nahane People, and is said to have been corrupted from Caska by the French-Canadian explorer Thibert. The original word, caska or casha, meant "a creek." The district from which it is taken contains many streams and extends between the Coast Range and the Rocky Mountains, along and north of the Stikine River.

In Union service: 1940-49
Official No.: 127472
Type: Steel passenger-freight vessel.
Dimensions: Length 185.3', breadth 29.6', depth 11.9'. Gross tons 905
Engines: Triple-expansion, 136 NHP, 850 IHP. Speed 11 knots
Services: Queen Charlotte Islands direct and via Prince Rupert in 1940-41; continued in cargo and general northern service
Capacities: Passenger licence 85, cabin berths 38. Cargo 400 tons

S.S. *Cassiar II*
(C. Park)

This ship was built in Scotland in 1910 and named *Amethyst*. Grand Trunk Pacific purchased her, renamed her *Prince John*, and sailed her to British Columbia where she arrived July 26, 1911. The Grand Trunk Pacific went into receivership in 1916, in August 1920 the federal government took it over and in 1923 the *Prince John* and all other Grand Trunk assets were put into Canadian National Railways.

On April 1, 1920 the *Prince John* collided with the *Prince Albert* during a blinding snowstorm in Skidegate Channel. This was the *Prince John*'s most serious accident. Her stern on the starboard side received a serious gash. Fortunately the Captain of the *Prince Albert* realized the seriousness of the other ship's plight and pushed her into shallow water. All the passengers and crew were removed safely. When the two ships separated the *Prince John* sank, with only her upper boat deck showing above water. She was later salvaged by the Pacific Salvage Co. and put back into service. [113]

The Union Steamship Co. purchased the *Prince John* and *Prince Charles* from the CNR in 1940. They changed the *Charles*'s name to *Camosun II* and the *John*'s to *Cassiar II*, thus keeping the names of former famous Union ships alive.

The *Cassiar*, although slow, had the reputation of being a good sea boat. The CNR had operated her on the Queen Charlotte Island run and the Union company did the same. She had good cargo space and a second refrigerator capable of handling 40 tons of frozen fish.

I served aboard the *Cassiar II* as Assistant Purser under Purser/Wireless Operator Joe Barrowclough, who came over from the CNR when Union bought the ship. We were on the Queen Charlotte Islands run, doing the north island one week and the south island the next, always going and coming from Prince Rupert before heading south to Vancouver. Crossing the open waters of Hecate Strait and Milbank Sound could be pretty rough at times but the *Cassiar* handled the seas there quite well.

During the war period the *Cassiar* was a real work horse and served the Company well, particularly for the building and expansion of the military establishments at Sandspit and Alliford Bay on the Queen Charlotte Islands, and the Shearwater base near Bella Bella.

I recall one morning around 7 we were heading into Shearwater and I was down in the hold checking freight and mail to be unloaded at the base. Suddenly I heard a very low boom and the old *Cassiar* shook like a bowl of jelly. It seems the Officer on the bridge had not flown the proper signal flag establishing our identity, so the commanding officer of the base ordered that a warning shot be fired across our bow. The old ship shuddered violently and came to a sudden stop. All this precaution seemed a little silly to us because we sailed in and out of Shearwater base every week and those at the base knew the ship well, especially in daylight.

I also was aboard her one season when we did the Rivers Inlet-Bella Coola run. On one trip we had finished discharging passengers, freight and mail at Goose Bay and were backing away from the wharf when we hit a deadhead and lost our propeller. We were pulled back into the cannery wharf by a fish boat and waited there for a tug to come up from Vancouver to tow us back to drydock. As I recall it, the *Cardena* came alongside and took off passengers heading north, as well as perishables and mail. Those of us aboard had a nice holiday waiting for the tug to arrive but when it did the weather in the sound turned nasty so we had to sit idle some more. One day at the mess table we were having coffee with the tug boat skipper and someone asked our Captain, "Rajah Big Mac" McLellan, when we were likely to get going. He replied, "Don't ask me, ask him (the towboat Master). He's the man in charge now, I've got no say in the matter, he's the guy with the brass nuts now."

On Sept. 23, 1947, Lorne Godfrey, Master of the *Cassiar* for the previous two years, died aboard ship. Tom Lucas was Mate at the time and they were leaving Prince Rupert. He had called for Captain

S.S. *Prince Albert*, later S.S. *Cassiar*, sunk in Skidigate Channel April 1920
(Mrs. Roy Field)

Godfrey to come to the bridge and when there was no reply, he went back to his cabin, just behind the bridge, and found him lying dead on the floor, apparently from a heart attack.

The *Cassiar* was retired from service in 1949 and sold a year later to a scrap dealer in San Francisco. The *Cassiar*, along with the *Chelohsin*, was rusting away at the B.C. Marine Yards. They were made ready for the long and difficult tow down to San Francisco and thus left Vancouver stern first in tow by their anchor chains, in April 1951. It was a sad departure for these two colourful veterans that had served the B.C. coast for many years.

Prince John at the Vancouver C.N. dock
(J. Smith Collection, Vancouver Maritime Museum)

The White Boats Era

S.S. *Coquitlam* and S.S. *Camosun,* two of the three white ships at the Union Steamship docks
(J. Turner)

When the Second World War came to an end in 1945, the Union Steamship Co. was in bad need of new tonnage to augment or replace their aging and overworked northern vessels, namely the *Venture*, the *Chelohsin*, the *Cardena*, and their flagship the *Catala*.

The *Catala* was the youngest of that group and she had started her service back in 1925, so clearly the ships were really getting old. Company managing director Harold Brown in the mid-1930s did propose an addition to the fleet, a larger ship to be modelled after the *Cardena*, but shareholders turned down the idea [114] and after that little was done to increase capacity other than adding the small *Lady Rose* in 1937. Though control of the Company shifted from England back to British Columbia-based investors in 1937, the new owners initially seemed more interested in acquiring and developing the Company's extensive real estate assets than in rebuilding the historic shipping service, and only after the war broke out did they finally move to expand capacity, first by buying the Frank Waterhouse Company, a Vancouver-based freight-oriented shipping company that had a modest fleet of old tramp ships that had been giving Union Steamships some tough competition over the years [115], and second by buying two old steamships from Canadian National in June 1940, which had been losing money with them on a service to the Queen Charlotte Island despite having a subsidy from government. [116]

Control of the Union Steamships Company changed again in 1941, with Canadian Pacific Railway having acquired the shareholdings of several of the B.C.-based investors through its Consolidated Mining & Smelting subsidiary. However, there was little change in the Company's personnel or style of operations. [117]

During the war years it was virtually impossible to build new ships, but in 1944 the Company, through its Waterhouse division, did buy the 165-foot cargo-oriented motor vessel *Island King*, which was renamed *Chilliwack III* and for a time did a thriving business on a weekly run to bring back pulp from Port Alice. Then in 1945 the Company acquired a 1,336-ton freighter then under construction in Victoria, which it named the *Chilkoot II* and put into service in 1946 on the weekly run to Port Alice. [118]

The extraordinary demands on all of the ships in the war years also brought into focus the Company's need for more passenger capacity, especially for more modern on-board accomodations on the northern routes, and especially after several of the older ships had been sold off. Finally in late 1945, with an annual profit of $461,000 on the books and a new management team in place, the Company at last made a move, buying three castle-class corvettes from the War Assets Corporation for what looked like a bargain price of $75,000 each. Though the ships had been designed to defend convoys in the North Atlantic, the Company's plan was to convert them in local shipyards to combined passenger-freight vessels at a total cost of $1.25 million. [119]

When the converted corvettes came into service, their hulls and superstructure were painted white from stem to stern, and soon they were nicknamed the White Boats. Their actual names were, *Coquitlam II*, *Camosun III*, and *Chilcotin*. However, after they had been in service for a while, they became known as white elephants, because they proved to be costly to operate and inappropriate to the needs of the market.

The various problems with the White Boats are described in uncharacteristic detail by long-time Company staffer Gerald Rushton in his book *Whistle Up The Inlet* [120], and one senses from reading between the lines that Rushton felt some antipathy for the new management team, particularly for Carl Halterman and Gerald McBean, who had joined the Company in 1938 and 1941 respectively and quickly risen to top management. By 1945 Rushton was about the last vestige in the Company of the Welsford family that had built it up in the 1920s, and he was stuck at a middle rank. Nonetheless it's clear that the new management's decision to buy and convert the corvettes, which Rushton attributed mainly to Halterman, was a grave mistake that sealed the Company's fate.

Furthermore, the mistake was compounded because the directors and new managers went ahead without consulting the Company's personnel either ashore or afloat. As Rushton wrote, "The haste with which this decision was made stands out in sharp contrast to the hesitation in laying down any passenger ship replacements for the northern services since the *Catala* was built in 1925. The operating officials received only the sketchiest outline of the corvette plan upon which to project any meaningful forecast of trading results. To my knowledge, no conversion plan in detail was examined by either the marine or engineering staffs in advance of the purchase." [121]

Rushton notes that the Company knew the need was for a diesel-powered ship of about 250 feet and a service speed of 16 knots that could accomodate 150 first-class passengers and handle up to 400 tons of general cargo, but the ships it got were somewhat smaller than that and had quite a bit less capacity for cargo, and while almost that fast they burned too much fuel. As well, the conversions came in $500,000 over budget. He described it as "trying to make Union's trade fit the ships instead of vice versa." [122]

A more detailed and hands-on view of what was right and wrong about the White Boats can be seen in an essay titled "In Defence of the White Boats" that was submitted to me by Ben F. Smith, a former engineer with Union Steamships who had worked on these same corvettes in wartime and aboard them after their conversion. He wrote this article after consulting with John Smith and John MacAulay, both of whom also served aboard these corvettes after their conversion:

"No one can tell me why these vessels were originally allowed to set sail painted all white. Surely it was not for Purity. Perhaps instead it was an ego trip by the shipyards, or by the boys in the front office who wished them to present the image of The Queen of The North. In any event it was found, after a few nudges up against dirty and rotten pilings, that being painted white was not so practical. However, the nickname White Boats stuck. After awhile many considered them to be disasters, and they were soon labelled White Elephants.

"After consulting with fellow mariners, both upper deck and engine room, between us we did come up with some shortcomings, but in truth the vessels themselves were not totally to blame. A number of problems were built into them, and it would seem that the shipyards sold a bad bill of goods to the Board of Directors and to the Boys in the Front Office. These in turn foisted the blame onto the vessels in order to hide their own shortcomings. The old adage which goes like this, "It is a poor workman who blames his tools," is apt in this case.

"This was the start of phase one of the post-war rebuilding of the Union fleet. I was also told that there had been horrendous over-runs in the conversions of these three White Boats. Also it should be noted there was little or no input asked for by management from the hardened old skippers of the fleet, as to what they thought was needed when converting these vessels. Unfortunately, these were the hapless fellows who had to account for any of these renovations for the remainder of their careers.

"There were indeed some shortcomings associated with these White Boats, such as lack of enough cargo and freezer space, cargo handling and hold workability, all of which were decided by the limited or fixed boundary of the existing hull, and operating costs were soon found to be high.

"Regarding the lack of cargo space, one has to compare these new ships with the *Catala* and the *Cardena*, which were custom-built for the coastal trade. The *Cardena* was able to take 350 tons of freight, and the *Catala* 300 tons, whereas the White Boats were only able to handle 150 tons, which wasn't a profitable payload.

"The three corvettes had fixed hull dimensions and the existing space allocations of engine room and boiler rooms occupied two-thirds of the hull length, leaving minimal room for freight and mail bags, etc. Another thing, their hatch conning or opening wasn't long enough to load automobiles down into the hold. Shipping automobiles from Prince Rupert was starting to be a lucrative trade so the Company lost out on this business which they had counted on getting. One wonders how these things were overlooked when the idea of renovating these ships for service on the coast was first brought up and looked into.

"Looking at their operating costs, they were certainly higher than was anticipated. The main reason for this was in the blunder of removing the Pressure Stokehold. This in effect was like removing the carburetor from an automobile. Right away, the efficiency of combustion was removed and most of the heat losses went up the stack or into the atmosphere. This problem was never corrected and so they steamed on, wasting barrels and barrels of costly fuel oil.

"When the White Boats first came out they all had very streamlined-looking funnels. They looked nice but in the end proved to be another very costly mistake. One only has to look at pictures of the *Coquitlam* on her trial run to see the black smoke screen that was laid down, not to mention the soot accumulation on the deck, which kept the deck hands busy with mop and bucket. The funnel had to be lengthened by six feet to solve the problem.

"The first two of the corvettes came out with bow rudders in place. The maneuvering capabilities of these ships was already well-known. These ships readily answered their helm. Who ever thought that installing bow rudders would be a good idea and was necessary? These bow rudders proved ineffective and were sealed up on both ships on their first dry-docking. Before the third corvette was renovated they cancelled the bow rudder beforehand. This was another costly mistake that could have been avoided, more than likely, if management had consulted with their skippers beforehand.

"Another innovation that didn't turn out well was the deepening of the stern and providing a bottom skeg and pintle for the rudder. Besides reducing the speed with all of this conglomeration of metal, this also disturbed the flow of the propeller, equating in a propulsive inefficiency and adding to the fuel costs. This added framework on the

S.S. *Chilcotin*, one of the White Boats, off Prince Rupert *(J.J. Claxton Collection, Vancouver Maritime Museum)*

Chilcotin set up such a horrendous vibration in the stern that the whole thing broke away from hull. Another costly innovation.

"Conversely, there were some refinements in place in the engine room which the engineers welcomed with open arms. First, there were the Manzell Lubricators mounted on the main engine, which provided a steady and ample supply of oil to all bearings. These operated when the vessel was moving and shut off when stopped. Consequently, there was not a steady drip or waste of oil to the bilges. Secondly, there were Co Recorders, a pen and ink graphic instrument that recorded the gas and fuel wasteage up the funnel, boiler pressure and stack heat, and revolutions. This also served as a monitoring device to make sure the fireman was doing his job. There also were devices on the boiler known as Eye-Highs that provided a ready reading of water levels and were a boon to the engineers. These features were in place when the ships were in military use and none were removed or tampered with during the conversions, for which the engineers were thankful.

"One thing that the front office seemed to think was a necessity was speed. These three converted corvettes were capable of doing 15 knots. They were to replace the *Catala* and the *Cardena*, whose maximum speed was 12 knots, so the extra speed wasn't all that important.

"The *Coquitlam II* was the first of these White Boats put into service. In 1946 she was put on the Queen Charlotte route. There were a number of calls for her northbound before she reached Prince Rupert, then a run over to the Islands, a few short stops over there, then back to Prince Rupert, then some more calls southbound to Vancouver. Not much chance for speed nor fuel efficiency there.

"One good thing about these White Boats was their seaworthiness. Built for use in the North Atlantic, they could easily handle the open seas on the Pacific Coast. Another thing, the passengers loved them for their comfortable cabins and other passenger amenities aboard.

"The crews' quarters were great. I remember my first voyage on the *Venture*. There were six of us cooped up in the forepeak, head to toes, breathing in foul air and no port hole. Then I was transferred to the *Coquitlam II*. There were two men to a cabin, with foot lockers, stand-up lockers, two-tiered bunks and a port hole in every cabin. This helped make for a happy crew and as well, they were almost always on time, which meant one always had some time off in Vancouver. With the older ships sometimes you never even got home, which was a downer. This was the cause of a lot of turnover in the crew and was inefficient.

"For my money, these three converted corvettes gave yeoman service to the best of their built-in capabilities. They were on time, comfortable and seaworthy. If there were inadequacies, the blame should be put on the shoulders of the Company's top management and the builders, all the so-called experts, who themselves should be blamed. The defence rests."

In 1956, the White Boats suffered an ignominious fate. The Company hired an efficiency expert and one of his first brainstorms was to paint over the traditional black and red colours of these ships and colour them in fancy streamlined streaks and angles, using colours of copper, cream and turquoise. One of the locals at Masset, upon seeing this for the first time, asked the Captain, "Where did you get the war canoe?"

(This chapter was written by Ben Smith)

S.S. Coquitlam II

Coquitlam means "a small red salmon" - a fish that once teemed in the Coquitlam River but is now extinct. It was also the name of a Salish tribe from the north arm of the Fraser who spoke the Cowichan dialect. It is one of the few native names in the lower Fraser Valley still used as place names: Coquitlam and Port Coquitlam municipalities, the Coquitlam River and Mt. Coquitlam (1,766 m.).

In Union service: 1946-58
Official No.: 176902
Type: Steel passenger-freight vessel (former Castle-class corvette).
Dimensions: Length 235.6', breadth 36.6', depth 22.2'. Gross tons 1,835
Engines: Triple-expansion, IHP 2,800. Speed 15 knots maximum
Services: Queen Charlotte Islands and northern B.C. routes, also Alaskan cruise service
Capacities: Passenger licence 200, berths 114, deck 24. Cargo 250 tons

S.S. *Coquitlam*, formerly the HMCS *Leaside, K 432*

The *Coquitlam* was the first of three castle-class corvettes to be converted over to passenger/freight ships for the Union Steamship Co. She was the prototype and test vessel for the next two corvettes to be converted. She was originally built in England in 1944 and was named the HMS *Walmer Castle*. She then was transferred to Canada and renamed HMCS *Leaside, K 432*. The *Coquitlam II* was converted at West Coast Shipbuilders.

Her sea trials were disappointing and it wasn't long before problems and difficulties were discovered. These ships and their conversion to coastal passenger/freight vessels proved to be a costly mistake for Union, and hastened the company's demise.

The *Coquitlam II* sailed out of Vancouver on her maiden voyage on Nov. 8, 1946, headed for Prince Rupert and Stewart with a full load of Shriners aboard. The Master was Jack Boden Sr., Chief Officer Wally Walsh, Second Mate Al Strang, Third Mate Geoff Hosken, Chief Engineer Freddie Smith, Purser Reg Stover and Chief Steward Bert Attewell.

A report on the four-day voyage in the Nov. 12 *The Vancouver Sun* by reporter Bill Fletcher tried to paint a positive picture of the event, suggesting the *Coquitlam* would be successful in her new service, but the report also mentioned some unidentified problems adjusting to a civilian role:

"Bright and jaunty in a shiny white coat with Nile green trimmings, she is the toast of the north.

"She is the S.S. *Coquitlam*, formerly His Majesty's Canadian Ship *Leaside*, latest addition to the Union Steamships Ltd. coastal fleet.

"At the helm of this trim ex-corvette when she steamed proudly into Prince Rupert harbour on her maiden voyage Sunday afternoon was Captain Jack Boden, a plump, pink-cheeked laughing man who guided the original S.S. *Coquitlam* through these same waters 41 years ago to the day.

"His chief engineer is Fred Smith, who served for years as second engineer on the first *Coquitlam*, now toiling in coastal waters as a cargo carrier under the name SS *Bervin*.

"Like other veterans of the Second Great War, the ex-*Leaside* had to go through the pains of rehabilitation. Captain and crew admit she is not yet completely readjusted to her role in civilian life, but it won't take long to straighten out the gallant little vessel in her new role.

"There's nothing wrong with the *Coquitlam* that a few twists of a monkey wrench and a little loosening up won't cure."

"Union Steamship representatives who came north on the ship were Gerald McBean, general manager, Al Newman, wharf freight agent, Harold Crompton, assistant traffic manager, and J.H. Gilligan, assistant superintendent engineer. Frank J. Skinner is the Union's Prince Rupert representative."[123]

S.S. *Coquitlam* as HMCS *Leaside K432* 1944
(McPherson Collection)

Some of the problems on the *Coquitlam II* soon became apparent to passengers too, as indicated to me by Ivor Jones, one of three quartermasters on the maiden voyage (the others were John Smith, who went on to be a Master with B.C. Ferries, and Pete Patton). Jones said this about her steering. "She still had the Navy steering gear on her and it took us a while to get used to it. It was new to us and we tended to over-steer. It had telemotor steering and a barn-door-size rudder. Every time we hit some tide it flopped and rolled along like a gaffed salmon. If you put her hard over at full speed you would clear the dining room tables of dishes!"

That problem was echoed by John Smith, who recalled an incident when they were approaching Butedale to make a landing. The *Coquitlam* got into a tide rip off Work Island and would have gone aground had not the order "hard over" been given. She responded immediately and Smith said, "Yeah, on that one we cleared all the dishes off the table and in the galley as well alright, but her smart response saved her that day."

A recollection that tells something more of the difficult transitions involves Captain Boden, who at the time was senior Master in the fleet and thus slated to be Master of the *Coquitlam* when she came out. He asked the Company to put his favourite quartermaster, John Smith, aboard her just to keep an eye on things while she was being converted in the West Coast Shipyards. The corvettes were all equipped with the latest gyro compasses, but nonetheless went into service for Union with the old magnetic compasses instead, at Boden's insistence. As Smith explained, "One day I was in the wheelhouse tidying up, when Captain Jock Muir, the Company's Marine Superintendent, and Captain Jack Boden came aboard to see how the conversion was coming along. They looked into the wheelhouse where I was working and when Captain Boden saw the gyro compass he said 'What the hell is that?' I replied, 'It's a gyro compass, Captain.' Being of the old school and used to the old magnetic compasses, Captain Boden shot back at me, 'Get that damn thing out of here. I won't have that aboard my ship.' He was adamant, so these new ships came out with the old-style magnetic compasses."

The *Cardena* and the *Catala* were both twin screw ships and were easy to maneuvre in tight bays and inlets up the coast. The castle-class corvettes however were single screw, so the company installed bow rudders to make them more maneuverable when backing out of tight spots. The *Coquitlam II* and *Camosun III* thus were delivered to the company with bow rudders. However they were very ineffective as they were manually operated and slow to activate and disengage. On their first drydocking these bow rudders were sealed up and their machinery removed. They cancelled the bow rudder on the *Chilcotin* before it was delivered.

Another problem evident from the outset had to do with the funnels being too short. Ben Smith, who served on the *Coquitlam* as an oiler and later became a Third Engineer, described it this way: "When these White Boats were first commissioned their funnels were short, squat, streamlined and pleasing to the eye but not too practical. When steaming full out, there was a tendency for these funnels to leave vast quantities of soot all over the aft deck and as well continually burned the lifeboat covers. One of the chores of the midnight to 4 a.m. watch was to administer vast quantities of steam up the funnel to get rid of any unnecessary soot and grime. This work usually took place at about 1 a.m. Later in the morning the deck crew would wash down the decks and boat covers before any passengers began to stir. The funnel problem was later corrected with the addition of about six feet of metal to the top of the funnel. At the same time the hull was painted black to conform to the rest of the USS fleet."

An added feature of this funnel was that it was merely a dummy around a much smaller funnel inside. The enclosure held some additional auxiliary equipment, as well as the oil pipe and valves for refuelling. There was also a full grating, and an access ladder down to the boiler room below. On the port side there was a door off of the boat deck. Passengers never ceased to be startled by the sight of an oiler walking along the deck, stopping to adjust the engine room ventilators, then disappearing inside of the stack, never to be seen again.

Still other problems were of a more serious commercial nature, such as the hatch conning opening being too small to load automobiles into the hold, and the cargo capacity being only about 150 tons of general cargo--too little to be profitable.

The converted corvettes also proved to

S.S. *Coquitlam*, from White Boat to U.S.S. Co. colours
(J. Smith Collection)

be very costly to operate. Many people thought they should have been converted to diesel engines before going into service but the Company had resisted this idea for years, mainly because its old engineers were steamboat men and were very reluctant to learn late in their lives about the operation of diesel engines.

An unusual feature of the *Coquitlam II* was that it had a mast house forward. It was originally designed to accommodate prisoners or mental patients in transit. They were seldom used and eventually became quarters for the winchman and the dayman, but these quarters were never insulated and thus very cold.

Nearly all of the Union ships at the time had Chinese cooks aboard, but for some reason the Company decided the *Coquitlam II* would have white cooks, so a whole new crew of white cooks was hired. It was a disaster. On the ship's maiden voyage they got drunk, and when the ship crossed Queen Charlotte Sound they all were terribly seasick. As well, according to crew members the food they served was terrible. Bert Attewell, the Chief Steward, had a terrible time with them too and after the third or fourth trip they all were fired and a Chinese crew was brought in.

One of the *Coquitlam*'s early mishaps took place when she was southbound for Butedale. They were to take on loads of frozen fish and canned fish. Landing at Butedale was tricky because of a waterfall discharging into the ocean just before the ship reaches the dock. If the ship is not going fast enough her stern would swing out before reaching the dock, but on this occasion Captain Boden brought her smoothly alongside the dock, as he usually did. However, it was necessary to move the ship ahead to load the frozen fish. John Smith was the quartermaster at the time and he described what happened:

"Captain Boden was on the bridge and rang down for slow ahead, and instead got slow astern, then he rang for full ahead and went backwards even faster. Something was wrong!

"Fred Smith, the Chief Engineer who should have been down below at the throttle, was up on deck watching the move. Captain Boden saw him and yelled at him to get below, but by now it was too late. We did get an "ahead" motion from someone below and the ship went flying ahead. It crashed into the ice shed and the ship's lines broke, which were all cable and were whipping every which way. The ice chute was broken and timbers were landing up on the bridge. A big hole was gouged in the wharf. When the ship was able to back away, one of the shed's windows was stuck over the bow of the *Coquitlam*. In short, it was a terrible mess."

What had happened was this: the engineer on watch had had a nervous breakdown at that instant and in his confused state he responded incorrectly. He had spent time as an engine room artificer (military apprentice) aboard the *Lady Alexandra* and when he came back from wartime service he was a sick man emotionally. He managed to stand watch for the rest of the voyage and sailed out again the following week but he had another breakdown and had to be put ashore at Campbell River and admitted to hospital.

In 1949 the Company switched the *Coquitlam* over to the Queen Charlotte Island route. She sailed to the North Island one week and the South Island the next. Because of the old and shaky wharves on the islands, the officers had to be very careful when making landings to not damage the wharves and thus avoid claims against the Company by the government.

On July 10, 1949, the *Coquitlam* under Captain W. McCombe was backing away from the wharf at Masset when she reportedly hit a rock and damaged her rudder and tail shaft. I was aboard her as Assistant Purser and recall that her bow was aground on a sand bar and the stern was low the water. Two lifeboats were slung out over the side and immediately filled with passengers, all wearing life jackets. For reasons I'll never know, Captain McCombe put me in charge and ordered me into a lifeboat that was full of women, including the cruise director whose last name I believe was Wallace. It was nighttime and dark. The ship's lights cast eerie shadows on the water below and as I stood there waiting for the lifeboat to be lowered into the water, I wondered to myself how in hell I would get a lifeboat full of women to manage oars, let alone row?

As it turned out, Captain McCombe had served on corvettes during the war and had experience with the water ballast on these ships, so he was able to pump out ballast and the *Coquitlam* eventually floated free, so the lifeboats never had to be launched, thank goodness.

I don't recall how we got safely back to the wharf at Masset, but we did and waited for a tow boat to come up from Vancouver to tow us back. All the crew aboard enjoyed a nice holiday on the way back to town.

Coastal shipping received a boost from the Aluminum Co. of Canada's announcement they intended to build a smelter at Kitimat. The *Coquitlam* was often under charter taking crews up to the project in addition to its regular scheduled trips. According to Gerald Rushton, the ship grossed $3,000 a day for charter service. [124]

Coastwise passenger revenues however began to decline in this period, due to the combined effects of air travel for passengers and barges for freight.

Management of the Union Company was changing too, and in 1956 an efficiency expert was hired to reverse the Company's falling fortunes. One of the expert's first innovations was to paint the converted corvettes with gaudy circus colours. Abandoning the old colour scheme of black hulls, white superstructure with black and red funnels, the company opted for a rainbow of colours which moved one citizen of Sandspit to quip to Captain Angus McNeill, "Where did you get this war canoe?" [125]

"It was a good advertising stunt," said Captain Billy McCombe. "They said they would get everybody talking about Union Steamships, and they sure did!" But in marine circles the ships in the new dress became a laughing stock all over the waterfront.

In 1957 the *Coquitlam II* was placed in the hands of Charles West Alaska Cruises and operated with Union Steamship crews. At the same time this company repainted her to their own colour scheme, which was a dark blue hull with a yellow band or stripe around the funnel. In 1958 she was sold outright to Alaska Cruise Lines and renamed the *Glacier Queen*, though she remained under Union Steamship management until the end of the year.

Alaska Cruise Lines operated her successfully for another 10 years, but as the tourist trade continued to grow, she and her sister ship the *Yukon Star* (formerly the *Camosun III*) proved to be too small and too expensive to operate and were sold. A Mr. Ernie Warner took options on the two ships and planned to operate them as floating hotels at Granite Falls, but he died before his plans could be carried out. [126]

The *Glacier Queen* was sold to American buyers in 1970 and towed to Seattle. They planned to convert her into a barracks ship by the Lake Washington Shipyards at Houghton. Some time later she was taken up to Alaska again and used as a floating restaurant. She sank at her moorings and was raised by the coast guard and towed to Kachemak Bay at Cook Inlet and scuttled in January 1978. [127]

Advertising Alaska Cruises from Vancouver on *Glacier Queen* (formerly *Coquitlam*) and *Yukon Star,* (formerly *Camosun*)

The *Glacier Queen*, formerly the *Coquitlam* cruising the Inside Passage between Vancouver, B. C. and Skagway, Alaska *(Humphreys Collection)*

S.S. Camosun III

Camosun was taken from the Native name for the bay where Victoria stands. The original settlement was called Camosack or Camosun, meaning "a deep narrow gorge" or "swift running water". Three Union ships carried this name.

In Union service: 1946-58
Official No.: 176903
Type: Steel passenger-freight vessel (former Castle-class corvette).
Dimensions: Length 235.7', breadth 36.6', depth 22.2'. Gross tons 1,835
Engines: Triple-expansion, IHP 2,800. Speed 15 knots maximum
Services: Northern B.C. and Queen Charlotte Islands routes, and later several seasons in Alaskan cruise service
Capacities: Passenger licence 200, berths 114, deck 16. Cargo 250 tons

S.S. *Camosun III*
(Twigg Collection)

This was the third Union Steamships vessel to carry the name *Camosun* and the second of three war surplus castle-class corvettes converted to passenger/freight vessels for the Company. She was built in 1943 by Smith's Drydock Co. of Southbank, Middleborough and was named the HMS *Sandgate Castle*. She was transferred over to the Canadian Navy in June 1944 and named HMCS *St. Thomas*, K 488. On Dec. 17, 1944 she was credited with sinking a German submarine, U 877, in the North Atlantic. She was transferred to Pacific duty in 1945.

Her conversion to a passenger ship was carried out by Burrard Drydock Co. in North Vancouver in 1946. She sailed out of Vancouver on her maiden v+oyage on Dec. 11, 1946. Her Master was Captain E. Sheppard, Chief Officer was Jack

S.S. *Camosun* as HMCS *St. Thomas* (MacPherson Collection)

S.S. *Camosun III* as a White Boat (Ashmore Collection)

Summerfield and Chief Engineer Fred Matheson.

This voyage inaugurated a new service run directly to Ocean Falls, then to Prince Rupert and Ketchikan. It had been 40 years since Union Steamships had made a call into Ketchikan. The Jones Act had been passed by the United States Government and it prohibited any freight being carried into Alaska by foreign ships. This being the case, the *Camosun* was only allowed to carry passengers into this port. [128]

During the 1947 summer season the *Camosun* carried capacity loads of tourists, but looking ahead, the Company was concerned with the falling off of the passenger trade in the fall and winter season, so they decided to extend the schedule and take in Petersburgh and Wrangell. This was to be a fast service to northern ports. She would leave Vancouver at 9 p.m. on Wednesday and proceed directly to Prince Rupert, a 36-hour trip. She would then continue to Petersburgh and Wrangell. This run began in late October but was a failure so it was cancelled and the *Camosun* was laid up. [129] During this season Captain Harry McLean was her Master, Fred Matheson Chief Engineer, Amos Robinson was Purser and Harry Keen Chief Steward.

The *Camosun III* seemed to have a relatively quiet life compared with her sister ships in the Union fleet. There were no marine mishaps that put her name in the news.

One of the few incidents in her career was off Bowen Island in 1949 when, according to Irene Howard in her history of the island, the *Camosun* got pranged in the fog off Cape Roger Curtis and damaged her steering gear.

In the winter of 1949, thick ice at the head of Portland Canal prevented the *Camosun* from getting to the wharf at Stewart, so Captain Boden pushed in as far as possible and then had the freight unloaded off the ship into lifeboats and then onto sleighs waiting on the ice, which were then pushed ashore. The deed earned a letter of thanks published in *The Province* (Vancouver). [130]

Ed Roach served as quartermaster on the *Camosun III* in 1950 and recalls an incident at Alice Arm when they were loading bars of silver ingots. One sling load broke and the ingots fell into the ocean between the ship and the wharf. There was no way to recover them on that trip. It was judged they were in a safe place, and the following week a diver was brought up and retrieved every bar. (pp.404-5 in the Deck Crews Chapter)

Chad Chadwick served as a fourth engineer on the *Camosun* and recalls one southbound trip when the ship slowed inexplicably while going through a channel. The officers on the bridge wondered why they were making so little headway and accused the engineers of cutting back the revs to save fuel, but the engineers insisted they were doing no such thing. A verbal battle ensued and even some spying into each others' departments went on until the real source of the problem was finally discovered. A floating tree had somehow tangled in the bow and the ship had been pushing it through the water for quite some time. There were red faces on the bridge and the engineers really heckled the officers over this.

One of the greats in the annals of the Union Steamship Co. was Captain Jack Boden Sr., and after 48 years with the Company he made his last trip on Oct. 1, 1953, bringing the *Camosun III* into Vancouver from Stewart. Interestingly, he had served as a Mate on the *Camosun I* early in his career.

Although the *Camosun III* carried full passenger loads in the summer of 1957, the Company's fortunes were still slipping and in the winter she lay idle.

In February 1958, Union sold the *Camosun III* to Alaska Cruise Lines and at the same time one of her sister ships, the *Chilcotin*, was sold to the Sun Line of

Camosun III at Alice Arm, June 1955 *(Betz Collection)*

Passengers relaxing on *Camosun* en route to Alice Arm, June 1955 Fred Matheson, Chief Engineer, right *(Betz Collection)*

Monrovia. The Alaska Cruise Lines changed the *Camosun*'s name to *Chilcotin* because cruise tickets had been sold and booked aboard the *Chilcotin*. This caused much confusion.

Once the season was over, the former *Camosun III*, now *Chilcotin*, had her name changed again, to the *Yukon Star*, and she operated under the Alaska Cruise Line flag for another 10 years.

Like her sister ship, the *Camosun III* was found to be too small to handle the growing tourist trade, and too expensive to operate, so she was sold to Phil Gadison, a Vancouver machinery dealer, who planned to break her up. Both she and the *Glacier Queen* were tied up side by side at the Lynn terminal in North Vancouver awaiting their eventual end. A night watchman was retained but still the ships were plundered by vandals. They broke her windows and looted her furnishings. Lying idle without maintenance, her wooden deck rotted and her steel hull rusted. [131] She was eventually towed to Tacoma and broken up for scrap in 1974.

Camosun operating as the *Yukon Star* for Alaska Cruise Lines *(McCormick Collection)*

S.S. Chilcotin

Chilcotin is said to mean "the people of the Chil (or Cinl) waterway." The Chilcotin country, which lies east-west between the Fraser River and the Coast Range, is an undefined maze of mountains and valleys in central British Columbia traversed by the Chilcotin River, a tributary of the Fraser. To many old-timers, the name is "Chilly-cootin."

In Union service: 1947-58
Official No.: 178070
Type: Steel passenger-freight vessel (former Castle-class corvette).
Dimensions: Length 235.7', breadth 36.6', depth 22.2'. Gross tons 1,837
Engines: Triple-expansion IHP 2,800. Speed 15 knots
Services: Completed specifically for Alaskan summer cruises, with extra features for tourist entertainment. Used for winter relief service only on Union's northern routes
Capacities: Passenger licence 200, first-class berths 106; deck none. Cargo 250 tons

S.S. *Chilcotin* as a White Boat
(D. Foote)

The *Chilcotin* was the last of the three wartime corvettes converted to coastal passenger ships by Union Steamships. It was said she was the most costly of the three due to delays and the increased costs for labour and materials.

She was built by Henry Robb Ltd. of Leith, England and launched in 1943 as the HMS *Guilford Castle*. She was transferred over to the Canadian Navy and renamed HMCS *Hespeler*, K 489. On Sept. 9, 1944 she sank a German submarine, *U 484*, south

S.S. *Chilcotin* as HMCS *Hespeler* (McPherson Collection)

of the Hebrides. In July 1945, after the Japanese surrendered, she was transferred over to Pacific Command and patrolled the straits of Juan de Fuca watching for wayward and diehard Japanese submarines. In November 1945 she was decommissioned, and was sold to Union Steamships in 1946.

West Coast Shipbuilders converted her to a passenger ship in their False Creek yards. She was designed specifically for the Alaska cruise service and carried 106 passengers. As well the company used her in the off-season as a relief vessel on northern routes.

Marine writer Norman Hacking was aboard the *Chilcotin* when she was on naval patrol duty and he was also invited to be aboard her when she left the West Coast yard after her refit. As he described it:

"The queen of Canada's Atlantic corvettes put to sea again in Burrard Inlet Sunday morning, but even her best friends wouldn't recognize her.

"The streamlined, white-hulled *Chilcotin*, latest addition to the coastwise passenger fleet of the Union Steamships Ltd., has little resemblance to original self, HMCS *Hespeler*.

"I was a passenger on the bridge of the *Chilcotin* as she slipped down False Creek from the yards of West Coast Shipbuilders Ltd., but it was far different than the last time I stood on her bridge when she berthed at Esquimalt to lay up after two notable years of war service.

"Then she was strictly a warship, grey-green hulled, with towering tripod radar mast, equipped with the latest in death-dealing anti-submarine weapons.

"Now she is white-hulled, streamlined and yacht-like, fitted with luxury accommodation for the Alaska tourist trade. There was nothing that I could find aboard her to remind me of old times, except the sharp flaring lines of her hull, and her sturdy reciprocating engines, still capable of nearly 17 knots."[132]

The *Chilcotin* sailed on her maiden voyage May 21, 1947. Her Master was Captain A.C. McLennan, the Chief Officer was Wally Walsh, Second Mate Robert Ashmore and Third Mate was Geoff Hosken. The Chief Engineer was George Craigen. This first voyage was in company with the CPR *Princess Norah*, jointly taking a convention of Shriners to Prince Rupert. [133]

On June 7, 1947 the *Chilcotin* began her outstanding 10-day cruises to Alaska, which Company traffic manager and historian Gerald Rushton described as the most successful cruise venture ever developed by the Company, for which he gave full credit to longtime Company executive Harold Crompton. Such things as nightly movies and a bar aboard ship helped entertain the passengers. She also carried a cruise director and hostess. The cruises traversed the scenic Gardner Canal in daylight, made sightseeing stops in Prince Rupert, Ketchikan and Juneau, and offered a side-trip on the White Pass and Yukon Railway to the gold-rush capital of Carcross.[134]

On one cruise, a ship's officer was entertaining some ladies in his cabin when one of them said she was surprised he didn't have any pictures of girls pinned up in his room, and after some discussion she offered to draw one on the ceiling of his cabin. The officer told her to go ahead. This drawing became famous throughout the fleet, especially after the officer's wife came aboard a few trips later and discovered it!

Fortunately someone took a photograph of this painting and this priceless piece of art has been saved and recorded for posterity. (See adjacent photo)

When Captain McLennan retired, Captain Harry McLean took over the ship on her Alaska Cruise run and made a name for himself as a most genial host. He loved entertaining but had a penchant for playing practical jokes on passengers and crew alike. These jokes often left hard feelings toward him. Interestingly, after Captain McLean's first wife died he married a woman he had met on board his ship during a cruise. They spent their honeymoon aboard his ship, the *Chilcotin*, on one of its regular cruises.

In 1948 the Company finally began to see that the converted corvettes were too expensive to operate on regular routes. They were seaworthy but had too little cargo capacity and were slow to load and unload. The *Chilcotin* was the only one of the three former corvettes to pay her way because of the successful Alaska cruises, but they were made only 11 or 12 times a year.

The *Chilcotin* did relieve other ships on northern runs at times in the off-season, and one winter she became blocked in by thick ice and was unable to get into the dock at Stewart. The adjacent photo shows crew member Earnie Gibson standing on ice in front of the ship's bow while she was in Cumshewa Inlet in the Queen Charlotte Islands.

Like her sister ships, the *Chilcotin* operated relatively free of accidents in her time with Union Steamships, though in September 1948 she did have a problem when she was disabled by a hot bearing while southbound in the vicinity of Powell River. A tug was called and towed her into Gillies Bay, while the *Lady Cynthia* was dispatched from Vancouver, came alongside and took off all 102 passengers, mostly a group of American Shriners. Second Mate Bob Ashmore recalls that "This high-seas drama was really fun and exciting for the passengers and no one was in danger at any time. They all arrived back in Vancouver in time to make their train and plane connections." A picture of this event, supplied by Ashmore, is on page 137.

In 1951 the huge construction project at Kemano provided a boost for the Company's revenues. Both the *Coquitlam* and the *Chilcotin* were engaged in charter services transporting workers up and down the coast for this project.

The cruise business continued to prosper for the next seven years, but overall the Company's fortunes declined. The Company's problems were exacerbated by several factors in this period, such as the increasing competition from airplanes and the politcal-related loss of a federal government mail subsidy, but not the least of these problems was that the increasingly-frustrated employees of the Company had finally rebelled against their long-parsimonious employer and formed a union. The employees, who long had suffered from low wages, lack of benefits and tough working conditions, went on strike along with other marine workers in the mid-1950s and emerged with a settlement that in retrospect the Company could not afford. The Company may have provided an

The famous painting on the Chief Officer's cabin ceiling
(Ashmore Collection)

Left: Earnie Gibson standing on the ice in front of the ship's bow circa 1949
(Gibson Collection)

S.S. *Chilcotin* in her U.S.S. Co. colours *(Betz Collection)*

excellent service, but it was not a good employer.

The *Chilcotin* was the last ship acquired by the Company, and it was one of the last to be operated. As the *Prince Rupert Daily News* reported on Jan. 4, 1958, "After 69 years of service by the Union Steamship Company, the *Chilcotin* sailed out of port marking the end of its service to this port."

Union Steamships was finished. The company that had become a legend and was known as the "lifeline of the coast" was permanently out of business. As Captain Harry Roach said as be brought the *Catala* into the Union dock for the last time, "There are a lot of sad faces on people all over this coast right now. They are filled with disbelief that the Union Steamships' remarkable service has come to an end and is no more."

On Feb. 7, 1958, the *Chilcotin* was sold to the Sun Line of Monrovia and was renamed the *Capri*. She was taken back to the East Coast and for the next two years cruised out of Montreal, down the St. Lawrence and to the Great Lakes ports. She was then sold to Greek interests and renamed the *Stella Maris*. She operated out of Piracus, Greece, cruising the Greek islands and to Istanbul, Turkey. Three other vessels from B.C. were also cruising the area: the former *Princess Alice*, former *Princess Adelaide* and former *Princess Charlotte*.

The Alaska Cruise Lines were doing a booming business with the ex-Union

Chilcotin operating for Alaska Cruise Lines *(M. Dean painting)*

Steamships' converted corvettes and they decided to buy back the *Stella Maris* from her Greek owners and put her back on the West Coast.

Harold Humphreys, who had served as Chief Steward on the *Chilcotin* when she was operated by the Union Steamship Co., was now Assistant General Manager of the Alaska Cruise Lines. The company sent him over to Greece along with Ray Kesler, one of the company's principals, to check over the ship. They spent a week cruising the Greek islands and reported back that the ship seemed to be in good shape. They then arranged for her to be drydocked in Sardinia for a final inspection and then Harold flew back to Vancouver. A crew was sent over to bring her back. They got as far as Sardinia and were bunkering for her long trip home. While they were fuelling up, there was trouble with the pipeline, and the problem was compounded by language difficulties. A flange broke and hot diesel fuel poured onto the stoke hold. An explosion followed and the ship burned completely, killing two crew. The rest escaped unharmed.

The former *Chilcotin* was a total loss, but Humphreys says the insurance claim and settlement was very favourable to the company. He added that Kesler was a real smart man and had told him that they received twice the value of the ship from the insurance claim after that accident.

Instructions at muster stations on Union Steamships

PART II

SEAGOING PERSONNEL OF THE UNION STEAMSHIP FLEET
1920-1958

stories and anecdotes about the
Company personnel

Chapter 1   MASTERS AND MATES 134
Chapter 2   ENGINEERS 273
Chapter 3   PURSERS, ASSISTANT PURSERS & FREIGHT CLERKS 305
Chapter 4   CHIEF STEWARDS, WAITER/STEWARDS & COOKS 353
Chapter 5   DECK CREWS 373

"Do you mean to say," the Captain was asked,
"that you know where every reef, rock and sandbar is in these waters?"
"No," he replied, "but I know where they ain't."
(Anonymous)

Chapter 1
MASTERS AND MATES

Dining room officers' mess table on U.S.S. *Coquitlam II*
Front (L-R): Hugh Tozer, Slim Holdgate, Freddie Smith
Back (L-R): Art Twigg, Tom Lucas, Reg Stover

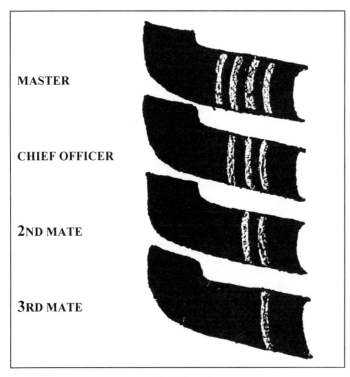

Gold braid
BUTTONS - GOLD

Originally in the U.S.S. Co., the Deck Officers' arm braid was:

Captain: 3 Broad Stripes

Pilot (Chief Officer): 3 Narrow Gold Stripes

Mate (2nd Mate): 2 Broad Gold Stripes

2nd Mate (3rd Mate): 2 Narrow Gold Stripes

This was changed sometime in the 1930s. See the attached sketch of the later and final braid for Deck Officers in the fleet.

Alphabetical List of Masters, Chief Officers and Mates 1920-1958

This list has been compiled from various sources, including ship registry files and personal acquaintances. While efforts have been made to be accurate, it is not to be taken as comprehensively complete and may have some errors, especially of omission.

Ashmore, Robert "The Black Prince"
Aspinall, Alfred "Uncle Alfie"

Biles, Harry "Hurricane Harry"
Boden, Jack Sr. "Handsome Jack"
Browne, John H. Sr.
Browne, John R. "Buster"

Calderwood, James McMillan "Flannel Foot"
Campbell, Donald P.
Campbell, Neil
Charters, Tom
Coles, H. George
Connelly, Connal
Corneille, F.E. "Cornie"
Crowles, Byron F.

Dickson, Alfred E.

Farina, Dennis
Findlay, James
Freisen, Irving J.

Gaisford, George
Galbraith, Jimmy
Georgeson, Edward "Eddie"
Gilbert, F.W.
Godfrey, Lorne A.
Gray, Neil
Green, Stanley
Guthrie, Stew

Hackett, Joe "Mouldy Joe"
Halcrow, John J. "The Viking"
Hamer, C.A. "Charles"
Hannigan, M.J. "Paddy"
Hayman, V.D. "Vic"
Horne, John "Johnny"
Hosken, Geoff
Hunter, James "Jimmy"

Johnstone, Andrew "Andy"

Kelly, Harvey
Kennett, Bill
King, Leonard, C.

Lamacraft, Harry
Lang, R.C.
Lawrey, Howard E.
Lewis, Charles "Charlie"
Lucas, Thomas M. "Tom"

Malcolmson, John I. "Jock"
Marette, Billy Jan
McAskill, J.A.
McBeath, Robert P. "Bob"
McCombe, William Jr.
McCombe, William Sr. "Billy"
McIntosh, Dave
McKillop, James
McKinnon, A.J.
McLean, Henry Edward "Harry"
McLennan, A. Jr.
McLennan, A.C. Sr. "The Rajah" or "Big Mac"
McLeod, Jack
McLeod, John M. "Pop"
McNeill, Angus. "Wee Angus" or "Holy Saints"
McPhee, J.D.
Mercer, John
Morrison, Don
Morrison, Iain
Mounce, William W.
Muir, John "Jack"

Naughty, R.T. Sr. "Bob"
Naughty, Robert Jr.
Nicholson, William "Nick"
Noel, James E.

Owen-Jones, Bertram G.K. "Curley" or "Alphabet Jones"

Park, John
Parker, Fred "Searchlight"
Perry, Ray W.

Reid, Alex
Roach, Henry "Harry"
Robinson, Miles "Robbie" or "Gigli"

Scanlon, "Paddy"
Seymore, R.

Sheppard, Ernest M. "Ernie"
Sims, "Paddy"
Smales, W.S.
Smart, Bill
Smith, Bob
Smith, C.B.
Spry, Bill
Stacy, R.
Stewart, Jim
Strang, A. "Al"
Suffield, Eric W. "The Sea Beast"
Summerfield, J.E. "Slim" or "Anxious Moments"

Thompson, Bob

Walker, Joe
Walsh, A.E. "Wally" or "The Baron"
Warden, Bill
Warren, Gordon
Watt, James
Whalen, George
Whitehurst, George
Williams, J.W. "Chips"
Williamson, Robert "Bob"
Wills, Ralph
Wilson, Angus
Wilson, Robert "Bob"
Winstanley, T.

Yates, W.I. "Billy"

(J. Horne)

Robert "Bob" Ashmore

Bob working a winch aboard the *Chilliwack* (Ashmore Collection)

Bob started his sea career in 1938 working as a deckhand aboard the *Chilliwack*. She was owned by the Union Steamship Co. but was chartered out to the Frank Waterhouse Co. The Captain on her at that time was Fred Talbot and he plays a part in Bob's career later in 1954.

While working on the *Chilliwack*, Bob severely injured his foot. They were making a landing at Ketchikan and Bob was handling the aft capstan. Somehow his foot slipped and it got caught by the drive shaft of the capstan. He was taken to the hospital in Ketchikan for treatment, but x-rays of his foot suggested nothing had been broken. He rejoined the ship and the Master wanted him to run winches as he felt Bob could sit on a chair and do the job. The crew came to his rescue and protested on his behalf. When they arrived back in Vancouver he went to the hospital again and this time it was found all of his toes were broken. They put his foot in a cast, but after three months they had to remove the cast as the pain had become unbearable. It was then discovered a nerve had been damaged and as a result his foot shrank in the years ahead. Ever after he walked with a slight limp, and sometimes around the ships he was nicknamed Hop Along Cassidy.

Later when the *Chilliwack* went into dry dock for her refit, the shore mate from the Union Steamship Co. was sent over to keep an eye on the job. It happened to be "Wee" Angus McNeill and he came to know Bob quite well and told him any time he wanted a job with the Union Steamship Co. to come over and see him. Working conditions on the Waterhouse Ships compared to the Union Ships were poles apart at that time, so one day Bob did walk off the *Chilliwack* and the next day he was hired aboard a Union ship. He started as a deckhand but soon was running winches. In the beginning he spent a good deal of his time on the *Cassiar II* and *Camosun II*.

Bob's favourite ship was the *Venture*. When he was aboard her, the Master often was A. C. McLennan, Jimmy McKillop was Chief Officer, Paddy Hannigan was Second Mate and Bob was 3rd. "We all worked hard and it was like a big happy family. Big Mac

Chilcotin and *Lady Cynthia* at Gillies Bay August 1950 (Ashmore Collection)

the skipper was stern but had a heart of gold," Bob said.

He especially recalls an incident on June 24, 1946, when he was Second Mate on the *Venture*. It was a beautiful Sunday morning, the ship had just cleared Cape Mudge southbound for Vancouver and the Captain that day, Eric Suffield, had gone below to join the chief engineer for a morning coffee. Bob was out on the wing of the bridge keeping watch when all of a sudden the ship

Bob on the bridge as a second officer (*Skinner Collection, Vancouver Maritime Museum*)

shuddered. Bob looked down into the water and he saw millions of little bubbles coming up all around the ship. He knew they hadn't hit a big log because he'd been keeping a careful watch. He couldn't understand what had happened and as the ship proceeded, it shuddered again. Once more he looked all around and then he saw Captain Suffield rushing to the stern of the ship and peering over the side. Again more bubbles appeared in the water. Captain Suffield came up to the bridge, questioned and accused Bob of hitting a log. Bob said, "I didn't hit anything." Captain Suffield said, "I saw a big log back there." Bob replied, "You didn't see any log back there. If I was the type that reads books while on watch you might be able to say that, but you know damn well I don't do that." With that Suffield told him to go down and have his coffee, and no more was said, but when Bob went back up to the bridge he noticed Captain Suffield had written something about it into the log book.

After the *Venture* docked in Vancouver, Bob went down to his cabin and started to pack his bags. Just then Captain Suffield came into his room and said to him, "I understand the *Chelohsin* hit the same log that we did." Bob replied, "So you're still insisting we hit a log, eh. If you don't trust me, I ain't going to sail with you anymore."

Captain Suffield said, "Forget it. It was an earthquake." And it was! It was the famous quake in 1946 that shook the Campbell River and Powell River areas and caused considerable damage to the pulp mill at Powell River. After that, Bob could do no wrong as far as Captain Suffield was concerned.

Bob studied and sat for his Coastal Mate's ticket, which he obtained in 1943. He says that the famous skipper who loved to play the bagpipes aboard ship, James Watt, was a great help to him in this endeavour. Later in 1948 he obtained his Coastal Master's ticket, which enabled him to sail as a Chief Officer.

While serving as Chief Officer on the cruise ship *Chilcotin*, Bob earned a mention in the company newsletter by organizing a baseball team from among the ship's crew to play against local teams in Skagway, Alaska. There are no records of who won any of those games.

The only marine mishap Bob could recall in which he participated took place in September, 1948. The *Chilcotin* was southbound to Vancouver, and they were near Powell River when a bearing gave out on the main engine. The ship was dead in the water. A tug had to be called from Powell River and it towed the *Chilcotin* into nearby Gillies Bay. There were over 100 American Shriners aboard. The company sent the *Lady Cynthia* up to take the passengers off the *Chilcotin* and bring them on to Vancouver. It was calm weather and the *Cynthia* was able to come right along side the *Chilcotin*. A gang plank was put across between the two ships. The passengers happily changed ships on the high seas! Actually this was quite a thrill for them.

Captain Harry McLean was Captain of the *Chilcotin* when Bob was aboard her. In general, throughout the fleet, Captain McLean was not well liked. Bob says he was a strange man, and in his opinion, jealousy played a large part in this dislike. He was the ideal Master to have on a cruise ship, as he was a comic and had everybody laughing with him. Captain McLean was also a great practical joker, which on many occasions made him disliked even amongst the crew, but as Master of the ship he could pull off all the stunts he wanted. Nevertheless, Bob credits Captain McLean for getting Bob on his ship as his Chief Officer. Captain McLean went to Eric Suffield, who was then Marine Superintendent, and he insisted that Bob be given the Chief Officer's job on the Chilcotin with him over others in the company who had more seniority. Captain McLean had a great deal of confidence in Bob and he would say to him, "Remember, if I'm not here, you are in charge."

Times were changing and the fortunes of the Union Steamship Co. were not looking too good, so in 1954 Bob decided to make a change in his life. He went up to Captain Suffield and told him he was quitting, and that he was going to take a course in television repair and maintenance. Captain Suffield said, "You don't have to quit, I'll give you a leave of absence." Bob took the course and finished second in his class. He soon realized however he was going to starve to death in the business, so a year later he went down to the Union Steamships looking for work. He was in for a big surprise, for who was sitting in the Marine Superintendent's chair but Captain Fred Talbot, the same man who was Captain of the *Chilliwack* way back in 1938 when Bob had walked off his ship! Bob realized right away he was out of luck.

Bob went over and applied at the Black Ball Line and was hired right away. When the Black Ball was taken over by B.C. Ferries, Bob stayed with them for 20 years. He was employed in various capacities, including Master on several of their ships. He retired from the sea in 1980.

Alfred "Uncle Alfie" Aspinall

Capt. Alfred Aspinall
(Ashmore Collection)

When Alfred Aspinall came to B.C. to work for the B.C. Electric Co., it was likely that he had been hired to bolster the company's soccer team. Aspinall had been a star footballer in the old country for Liverpool, but in his first season he broke a collar bone and next season he did the same, thus ending his playing career. He then went to work for the Union Steamship Co. in 1924.

Geoff Hosken believes Aspinall started in the stewards department, like so many

Union people did. As is quite often the case, he transferred over to the deck crew and worked his way up the ranks to become a Captain. Reports have it that his brother John was a mate aboard the *Cheslakee* when she sank at Van Anda in 1917.

Ben Smith, an engineer in the fleet, tells the story about being aboard the *Coquitlam II* in the Queen Charlotte Islands, and Aspinall was Master at the time. They were off Rose Spit and a big sea was running. Tom Lucas, who was Chief Officer, had asked Ben to come up to the wheelhouse after his lunch, to replace some faulty fuses. Ben got to wheelhouse just as they rounded Rose Spit. Ben had been on corvettes in the North Atlantic during the Second World War but says he had never seen a sea so bad as it was on this occasion off Rose Spit. Also in the wheelhouse were Chief Officer Tom Lucas, Third Mate Ralph Wills, and quartermaster Kenny Hines, a young fellow from North Vancouver.

As soon as the seas started to pound the ship, Captain Aspinall came back up to the bridge. "What the hell is going on?" he asked, as the ship was being buffeted. Massive waves were breaking over the bow, hitting the screen. You couldn't see a thing. Captain Aspinall let it be known that he didn't like these damn White Boats one bit. He felt they'd capsize at any given moment!

There was no way Ben could leave the wheelhouse to get down below to the engine room. He realized he was stuck there for the whole watch and just settled himself in a corner of the wheelhouse. As the seas were pounding away, it seemed every third wave was a giant! Captain Aspinall was stomping around with his cap jammed down on his head and was getting exasperated. As every third wave hit, the ship seemed to go right under it. Captain Aspinall turned to young Hines at the wheel and said, "For Christ sakes, you're missing all the little ones and only hitting the big ones!"

Ben says he thought Tom Lucas would die laughing. This showed the lighter side of Captain Aspinall, as he did have the reputation of being a very unpopular man up and down the coast, because he was so sarcastic with everyone.

Captain Aspinall's seagoing career came to an unfortunate end when he ran the *Chelohsin* aground close to Siwash Rock in Stanley Park around 8 p.m. on Nov. 6, 1949. Captain Aspinall had been on the bridge steady for many hours because of a dense fog all the way down from Lund. As he neared the Lions Gate entrance to the harbour, whistles were heard from two different ships, one unencumbered and the other with a tow. His radar had broken down after they had left Lund. It was one of the old type, a number 268, which according to others I have interviewed was always breaking down and in any event would have been next to useless at the harbour entrance. Another factor was that the *Chelohsin*'s radio telephone was in the Captain's cabin away from the bridge, so contact with the First Narrows Bridge lookout was awkward at times, to say the least. Apparently, Paddy Hannigan, Chief Officer at the time who was off watch, came up to the bridge to see if he could be of any help. He asked Captain Aspinall if he would like him to go back and call the bridge to see if they were on their radar screen. Captain Aspinall thought for a moment, then said, "Oh no, we're almost there now." Too late! The *Chelohsin* hit rocks at low tide, a rock punched a hole in her, and the engine room was flooded in no time at all. Shortly after, the lights went out, so getting passengers into lifeboats was difficult, but all were put ashore safely in Stanley Park.

Captain Harry Roach was the regular Captain of the *Chelohsin* and he was off on holiday leave when this accident took place. His son Ed Roach took Harry down to see the *Chelohsin* on the rocks. Harry shook his head and felt sad. He said, "None of us has clean hands."

Captain Aspinall never returned to sea after this grounding, which also ended the seagoing days of the *Chelohsin*. She was dismantled in 1951, towed backwards out of the harbour and on to San Francisco, where a scrap dealer had paid $25,000 for her.

Harold Cecil "Harry" Biles

Harry was born in Jersey, Channel Islands, on Oct. 22, 1904, and started his seagoing career, ostensibly with a 1902 birthdate, by signing aboard the HMCS *Rainbow* on Sept. 17, 1919. It was the first Canadian warship on the B.C. coast. He was demobilized on March 31, 1920, but on Jan. 22, 1919 he had applied to join the Marine Firemen and Oilers' Union and on his application form had stated he had been working on the tug *Fearless* and was 17 years old, suggesting that he, like many men then, had lied about his age to get into the service.

What Biles did after his demobilization is not known, but records show he joined Union Steamships in 1928, starting as a watchman on the *Catala*. He worked his way up and eventually obtained his Coastal Mate's ticket, and though no records are to be found which would tell us whether or not he obtained his Coastal Master's ticket, yet he has been frequently referred to as Captain Biles. The Vancouver Maritime Museum for example has a photo of the *Capilano II* docking at Granthams Landing and underneath there is a write-up about Biles which says he had been in command of several Union vessels, but one ex-Union man who is quite an authority on such matters is doubtful that he obtained a Coastal Master's ticket.

During these years, Biles was given a nickname by his contemporaries and that was "Hurricane Harry." I sailed with Harry on the *Cassiar II* in the 1940s and particularly remember one trip when we had pulled into Butedale to take on a load of frozen halibut. It was in the winter and was cold! cold! cold! I was on the dock watching the loading with my big Hudson's Bay Company winter coat on, yet I was still shivering. Harry came along and said, "You're cold, aren't you son?" "I sure am," I said. "Come along with me, then," he said, and I followed him up the gangway to his room up behind the bridge where he poured me a lovely drink of brandy! It is one drink that has stayed in my mind and to this day I always have had fond memories of Harry Biles.

Harry had a serious accident in the late 1920s when he was aboard the *Catala* in Ocean Falls loading bales of pulp. He was down in the hold when somehow after getting one roll in place, a second one slipped and Harry's head was caught in between! This was reported to me by Frank Skinner, who was Freight Clerk at the time. The accident put Harry in the hospital, of course, but his long career with the company indicates he did recover satisfactorily and continued to work aboard ship as a deck officer.

Over the years, Harry was an active member of the Canadian Merchant Service Guild. He was their treasurer for six years, from 1946 to 1952. He was shore mate on the Vancouver dock during the war years but in 1956 this position was eliminated. The following is the text of a letter dated June 29, 1956, which is a telling commentary on the state of affairs existing on the Union dock at that time.

Capt. H. C. Biles
(from a photocopy of a studio portrait by C. West)

Mr. H. Biles:

As of the 1st of July 1956 the position of Shore Mate will cease to exist, you will thereafter be employed as rigger at an hourly rate of $2.00 and will report to the Machine Shop Foreman for orders. You will punch the time clock and fill in time sheets. The other six shore gang and three watchmen will fill in time sheets as at present done by the regular Machine Shop crew. The work will be carried out on a job number basis.

Kindly instruct your crew accordingly.

(Signed) Thos. W. Morgan,
Supt. Engineer.

After 28 years with the Company starting as a deckhand and becoming a Deck Officer, he was handed the above notice! A sad state of affairs. Harry left the Company and his son tells me he worked at doing odd jobs. He died on April 14, 1975.

John "Jack" Boden, Sr.

Capt. Jack Boden
(A. Hemion)

Jack Boden was born in Glasgow in 1882. He came out to B.C. and started his seagoing career on the Fraser River aboard such old sternwheelers as the *Transfer*, *Ramona* and *Hamlin*. He then joined the Union Steamship Co. in 1905 on the freighter *Coquitlam*.

Captain Boden is perhaps better remembered than any other person that one associates with the Union Ships over the years. One of his endearing trademarks was the way of wearing his cap. It was always set at a jaunty and peculiar side angle on his head. Frank Lawrence, a Union Purser, says that you could tell whether or not Captain Boden was going to make a port or starboard landing by the direction the peak of his cap was pointing. Others however dispute this story and Iain Morrison, a deck officer who sailed with Captain Boden, says it just wasn't true.

Norman Hacking, the well-known marine writer, said there was not a navigable nook or cranny as far north as Alaska that Captain Boden had not entered. [135] Boden told Hacking he recalled rowing the first surveyors ashore at Ocean Falls and took the first supplies into the site of Prince Rupert. He remembered it being a town of tents.

Captain Boden served on practically every ship in the Union fleet over his 48 years of service. At some time in his career he was tagged with the nickname, "Handsome Jack." Another nickname he received in later years was "Slack." He was Senior Captain of the fleet when he retired on Sept. 30, 1953. The *Camosun III* was his last command. He joined the Canadian Merchant Service Guild on Feb. 11, 1921.

Mike Benson, former Purser and later Assistant Traffic Manager for the company, called Captain Boden a great man and as well a great skipper. He related the following story about him.

"I had gone up to the bridge during a dense fog and observed Captain Boden giving orders, calling out course alterations, all the time working off the echoes of his whistle blasts. Once during a course alteration, Mike asked, "How did you know to change course that time? What told you to alter course?"

"Well, didn't you hear that bloody dog barking over there!" Captain Boden replied.

Ed Roach recalls being quartermaster with Captain Boden and said "Even though the ship had radar, Boden would rarely look at it. One time they went from Seymour Narrows right up Johnstone Strait in a dense fog and Captain Boden stayed out on the bridge all the way, navigating by whistle and echo. He never looked at the radar once."

In the early 1920s, Jack Boden became Captain Jack Boden. He was given the Master's position on the *Lady Cynthia* soon after she had arrived in Vancouver from England. He was Master on her when she was in collision with the *Cowichan* off Roberts Creek on Dec. 27, 1925. His ship sliced into the *Cowichan* commanded by the venerable Captain "Bob" Wilson, in a dense fog. No lives were lost, all passengers and crew from the *Cowichan* were safely transferred to the *Lady Cynthia*. Once they were transferred and the *Cynthia* backed off, the *Cowichan* went to the bottom within 10 minutes.

It is interesting to note that Gerald Rushton in his book *Whistle Up The Inlet* said, "Captain Boden shouted from his bridge that he was going to hold the Cynthia pinned into the Cowichan." [136]. I have read and have also been told by the wife of a quartermaster who was on board the *Cowichan* at the time, it was the other way around, that in fact Captain Wilson had to plead with Captain Boden to keep the *Lady Cynthia*'s engines going slow ahead and keep her pinned into the *Cowichan* while Captain Wilson transferred his passengers to the other ship.

Here we have two different viewpoints relating to this incident and the demeanor of both skippers, but Rushton says further, "The subsequent inquiry praised the seamanship of both masters involved in this regrettable episode." [137]

Captain Boden took command of the *Cardena* from Captain Andy Johnstone in 1934. Soon after taking this command, Captain Boden arranged a most unusual holiday for himself - to join with some friends who were going to ride horses from Bella Coola all the way to Anahim Lake in the Interior, which was quite a journey for a seafaring man to consider, but all went well.

After reaching their destination, they took the P.G.E. train down to Squamish and boarded the *Alex* to sail to Vancouver. Captain Boden received a warm welcome aboard from all of the ship's officers, who were very surprised to see him coming aboard there and then to hear of his adventure. Who would have thought that gruff old "Captain Jack" would be so adventurous and ride a horse for so long.

Another marine incident, involving the *Cardena* and Captain Boden about which next to nothing has been recorded, took place one evening in October 1942 in the Shushartie Bay area. The *Cardena* was rammed on her starboard side by the tug *La Pointe*. Two staterooms were heavily damaged, as well as the top deck, and a hole was punched in the *Cardena* below its water line. One passenger, a Mrs. Cross, had been lying down in one of the staterooms and miraculously escaped being killed. The passengers were taken off and according to Mike Benson, who was Assistant Purser at the time, Captain Boden ran the *Cardena* aground on a rising tide. Repairs to the puncture were made by the second engineer, the ship was refloated and it returned to Vancouver under its own power.

In 1944, again in the Shushartie Bay area, the *Venture*, with Captain Boden on the bridge, rescued four people just before daylight in rough seas. They had attempted to row to a float in the bay to meet the *Venture*, when their rowboat capsized. Captain Boden while coming in to make a landing at the float turned on his searchlight in order to see the float and in doing so saw them clinging to their overturned boat. He quickly maneuvered his ship into position so they could be picked out of the icy water.

The year 1946 saw renovations going ahead on the three corvettes. I did an interview with John Smith, who had started in the U.S.S. Co. as an AB seaman and worked his way up to being a first class quartermaster. Captain Boden held him in high regard. John related the following information to me about Captain Boden and the compasses aboard these converted corvettes.

John had been sent down to the shipyards to watch the rebuilding job and one day while he was in the wheelhouse doing some tidying up, Captain Jock Muir, Marine Superintendent, came down along with Captain Boden to look over the ship.

Captain Boden in his younger days on the S.S. *Cassiar* (Halliday Collection, Campbell River Museum)

They looked into the wheelhouse and when Captain Boden saw the gyro-type compass, he said "What the hell is that?"

According to Smith, these corvettes had come equipped with the latest-style compasses known as Gyro's. But Captain Boden, being of the old school, was adamant and had the Gyro compass removed and an old-style magnetic compass installed in its place. Through his influence, all three of the "white boats" as they were known, came out with the old-style magnetic compasses.

The *Coquitlam III* went into service in 1946 with Captain Boden as her Master. Ben Smith was fourth engineer on her at the time. He recalled one trip when they were going through Seymour Narrows, bucking a 15-knot tide. The top speed of the *Coquitlam*, according to Ben, would be about 15 knots. She was now the fastest ship in the fleet. Freddie Smith was Chief Engineer and he came down to the engine room and said to Ben, "For God's sakes Benny, pile on the coal, Boden's going to take her through and we're going to buck this 15-knot tide." Ben went to the fireman and said, "Look, fire this thing up and keep her right up to a full head of steam because I'm going back to the engine room and open her up as far as she can go." The engine was dancing in its bearings, she was rattling and shaking. The Chief was standing there and he was pretty concerned.

After this had been going on for a half an hour, the Chief said to Ben, "Go up and see where we are." Ben came back and said, "By God Chief we're right abaft of Maude Island Light." The Chief said, "Jesus Christ, we were there half an hour ago." However, they got her through, but it took about two hours, because Boden was determined he was going to take her through, and he did. "He was one of the more daring of the Union skippers," says Ben.

One time Captain Boden came down to the officers' table in the dining room and said, "This damned rheumatism in my left arm is driving me crazy. Do you happen to have a bit of copper I could make a bracelet out of?" Ben said, "Leave it to me Captain, I'll find something." He found a piece of tubing, flattened it out, filed and polished it, and presented it to Captain Boden that evening at dinner time. Chief Engineer Smith looked on approvingly, but next morning when he saw where Ben had got the tubing from, he was very upset, because Ben had cut off a piece of exhaust tubing from a circulating pump. The pump ran just as well, but didn't sound so good!

A new silver mine named Torbit Silver went into operation up at Alice Arm, and the *Coquitlam*, with Captain Boden on the bridge, was the first ship to make a landing there. They were to take on a load of silver ingots for the Eastman Kodak Co. This was something new and Johnny Horne, who was second mate, proceeded to load these ingots in the usual manner, using a pallet board wheeled out to the ship's side to be hoisted aboard by the winches. An official from the mine was up on the bridge visiting Captain Boden and when he saw this he let out a yell. As a result, more precautions and security measures were adopted for loading this type of valuable cargo, though later one load of ingots was lost overboard while loading at the same wharf. (see story about quartermaster Ed Roach, pp.404-5)

Captain Boden, being the senior Captain in the fleet, would get the idea every once awhile, towards the end of his career, to leave the northern runs for the summer and take out one of the day boats, particularly the graceful *Lady Alexandra*. People on Howe Sound were used to seeing Captain Yates on the bridge of the *Alex* and they often asked who that new skipper was. I was told that Captain Boden used to dive off of the ship himself and go for a swim in the bay when the Alex was laying over in Snug Cove.

Captain Jack no doubt was a great seaman and navigator and as such his reputation lives on to this day. He was of the old school and was a hard taskmaster. One mate, who later became a Captain, said he did not fraternize much with his officers and ate Third Mates for breakfast, though he had to tolerate Second Mates because they stood watch with him.

He retired on Sept. 30, 1953 and was granted a lifetime honourary membership in the Canadian Merchant Service Guild on Oct. 3, 1953. He died at age 85 in 1967. His son Jack Jr. also started his seagoing career with Union Steamships.

John H. Browne Sr.

Capt. John Browne Sr. on *Camosun I* (J. Smith Collection)

Information on this early Union skipper is scanty, but fortunately his grandson John Smith, a Union Steamships man himself for quite a few years, was able to provide me with the following details.

He was born in Belfast, Ireland, and was a master of sail and steam. To have a combination sail and steam ticket in those days was quite remarkable. He served as Master for the City Elerman Lines in the Old Country on the Baltic, East India, Australia and New Zealand trade.

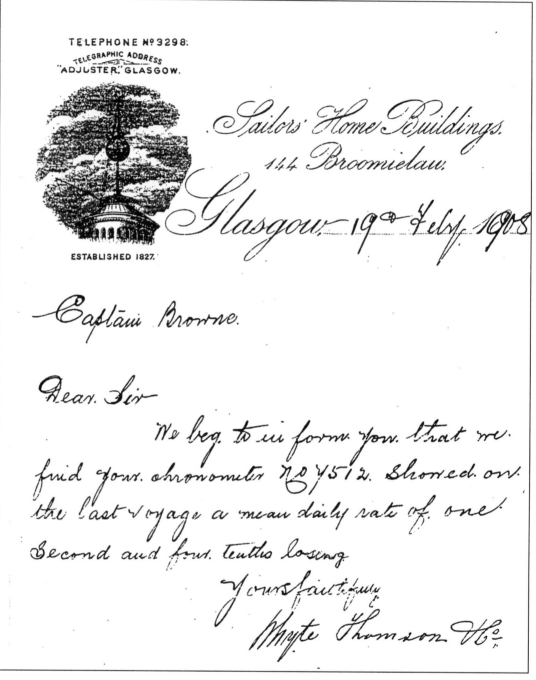

A very interesting letter to Capt. Browne regarding his chronometer, written in 1908

For some reason he signed aboard the *Cariboo* as Pilot under Captain Polkinghorn, to bring her over from England to the Union Steamship Co. in Vancouver. She coaled up at Barry and left on April 23, 1908 and arrived in Vancouver on July 21, 1908. Upon her arrival it was discovered there was another steamer operating on the Great Lakes with the name *Cariboo*, so her name was quickly changed to *Cowichan*. Captain Browne obviously liked what he saw here in B.C. and forthwith sent for his family, then living in the town of Rothsay on the Isle of Bute, Scotland. The family settled on Cambridge Street in the Hastings East area of Vancouver.

Captain Browne and his wife had two children, a girl and boy. The boy was later to become a skipper in the Union fleet, the well-known John R. "Buster" Browne. The girl of course was the mother of John Smith, who gave me all this information and who himself later became a Union employee in the 1940s and eventually a Master on B.C. Ferries. Obviously going to sea was a family tradition with the Brownes.

In his early years with Union Steamships, Captain Browne was Pilot and Master of several notable ships including *Camosun I*, *Cassiar I*, *Chelohsin*, *Capilano*, and latterly the M.V. *Comox* operating out of Porpoise Bay and Sechelt Inlet.

While he was Pilot on the *Chelohsin* in the 1920s, there was a mail robbery aboard ship which is seldom mentioned in company lore. It is quite a bizarre story because the thief, who worked aboard ship, did not get found out for along time and indeed was caught only after an undercover RCMP officer was put aboard ship as a member of the deck crew. It soon was learned that the mail sack had been stolen and stashed in the lower hold of the *Chelohsin*, where, from time to time, the culprit was able to get money from it whenever he wanted. In due course the suspect was convicted, but for some unknown reason Captain Browne was suspended for a time too. Meanwhile, the undercover agent also had become romantically involved with Captain Browne's daughter and eventually they married in 1924.

But what an unusual situation: here we have an English undercover RCMP man, wooing the daughter - a Scot - whose father was Irish and somehow implicated in the robbery! There was a terrible clash of personalities and loyalties within the family, and old Captain Browne took all of the upheaval very hard. The family ties and relationships were strained to the limit and apparently were never mended.

Captain Browne eventually was reinstated and ended his sailing days as Master of the M.V. *Comox*. Curiously enough his son, "Buster" Browne later became master of the *Comox* himself, running between Whytecliff Park and Bowen Island.

Old Captain Browne was forced to retire in 1932 because of serious cataracts on both eyes. He had one of the first cataract operations performed in B.C. He passed away in 1935.

John R. "Buster" Browne

"Buster" Browne, 2nd Mate
(J. Smith Collection)

Buster took to a sailor's life naturally as his father was Captain John H. Browne, who had first gone to sea on sailing vessels and came to hold a Master's ticket for both sail and steam, a remarkable achievement at the turn of the century.

Buster was born in Rothsay, Scotland in 1903 but soon was relocated to Vancouver after his father had piloted a new ship out to the Union Steamship Co. in Vancouver and once there decided to stay on with the Company and so sent for his family to join him.

Buster followed in his father's footsteps in 1921 and joined the Union Steamship Co.

as a deckhand. He obtained his coastal Mate's ticket in 1925 and in 1927 was sent over to Scotland with Captain Findlay and Wee Angus McNeill to bring back the *Chilliwack II*. Buster sailed out on her as Third Mate, and served aboard many of the Union ships before he left to join the pilotage in 1945.

His nephew John Smith, who also worked on the Union ships, said Buster had the reputation of being an excellent ship handler. "Few could match him," John said. Buster was well-liked and had a fast rise in the Company. In 1930 he had a run-in with Captain Boden. Buster had made a complaint to head office over Captain Boden's behaviour and as a result they never sailed together or spoke to each other after that.

About 1931, Buster was on the bridge of the *Lady Cecilia* when she went aground during a dense fog at the mouth of the Chapman Creek, logged as Mission Point near the Wilson Creek wharf. The *Cecilia* wasn't damaged at all but passengers had to be put ashore and Bob Hackett, a resident of Sechelt who was aboard at the time, recalls Buster busily getting passengers into lifeboats and shouting "Women and children first" as though it was the Titanic sinking, yet they were only about 200 feet from dry land.

Buster made news in May 1933 when as Captain on the M.V. *Comox*, running between Whytecliff Park and Bowen Island, he sighted a capsized sailboat. He came to the rescue of five people who had been clinging to their craft for over an hour.

Buster left Union Steamships in 1945 and afterwards moved back and forth between a number of jobs. He joined the Pilotage operating out of Victoria and bought a home in nearby Oak Bay. In 1954 he joined up with Gulf Islands Ferries operating out of Ganges as Master of the *Motor Princess*. He then joined up with Sparky New's new company, Coastal Ferries, and for a while was Captain on the *Lady Rose* then Master on their new ship, the *Island Princess*. In 1960 he made another move, over to the B.C. Ferries as Master on the M.V. *Tsawwassen*. In 1965 he left B.C. Ferries and went back to Coastal Ferries to again be Master of the *Island Princess* operating out of Kelsey Bay, but when B.C. Ferries took over this operation, Buster left and became Master on the M.V. *Malibu Princess*. From here he had a short spell on the Church of England Mission Boat and then went back again to Coast Ferries. He was Master of the *Seymour Princess* (formerly the *Teco*) but was off watch when the ship went aground on Drury Island in the Alert Bay area on July 14, 1978. The ship was considered a total loss.

Johnny Smith says that to his knowledge Buster never went to sea after this accident. Buster died in North Vancouver on Feb. 22, 1991 in his 88th year.

James McMillan "Flannelfoot" Calderwood

Jim Calderwood, it is said, did wear flannel underwear, which partly accounts for his nickname, but it came about more from the fact he was a very big man with big feet and they say he walked like a duck. He was also known as Jungle Jim.

He was born in Campbelltown, Scotland and joined Union Steamships in the 1920s. The 1924 *Canadian Merchant Service Guild Annual* lists him as obtaining his Mate's Coastwise Passenger Steamers Competency ticket at examinations held in Victoria.

John Horne says of him, "He was a fascinating man. He was frequently Chief Officer on the *Catala*. When Mercer wasn't, Calderwood was."

Fred Corneille remembered him well and said, "He used to drive Captain Suffield nuts. Suffield thought Calderwood was too easy-going in the way he did things aboard ship. Suffield used to shriek down orders to him from the bridge, "Mr. do this, Mr. do that," but Jim Calderwood paid no attention to him whatsoever. He would just go on with what he was doing, and old Suffield would be dancing with rage up on the bridge. The last time I saw him he was Master of the ferry that ran between Powell River and Texada Island. He looked like a grizzly bear out for a walk."

Donald P. Campbell

Don did not stay aboard the Union Ships too long. He served as Second Mate on various ships in the fleet in the 1940s but he decided to leave the sea life and go into longshoring, where he could make more money and be at home every night. However he did play a part in one dramatic event while he was serving as Mate on the *Capilano* on Feb. 5, 1947.

The *Capilano* was just leaving New Brighton when the steering mechanism jammed. Captain Malcolmson quickly gave orders to Don to get a crowbar in order to free it. When Don returned, Captain Malcolmson had collapsed and was lying unconscious. Don took over command of the ship, radioed head office and asked them to have a doctor meet the *Capilano* at Gibsons Landing, where he headed to at full speed. The doctor immediately examined the Captain but pronounced him dead on arrival. The rest of the ship's schedule was abandoned for that day and Don took the Capilano straight back to Vancouver.

Neil Campbell

Neil was born on the Isle of Skye in 1905. A Campbell who comes from Skye, whether or not he is of the Campbell ilk, is often referred to as a "Black Campbell." In the Union fleet therefore he was generally known as the Black Campbell.

Fred Corneille, a former deck officer with the company, related the following story about Angus McNeill and Neil Campbell, who never got along well together although both were born on the Isle

Capt. Neil Campbell (*N. Krischuk)*

of Skye. One time Angus had forgotten to turn in his overtime slip to the pay office, so he asked Neil to take it up for him and Neil refused. This made Angus real mad, and he said, "That damned Black Campbell. Those Black Campbells are not to be trusted, they are not to be trusted you know."

Neil joined the Union Steamships in 1935 and by the time the Company ceased operating in 1958 he was serving as Chief Officer and Master. I have two dinner menus off of the *Cardena* dated Aug. 17 and 21, 1953, both of which show Neil Campbell as Master. The Chief Engineer was Tom Dick, the Purser was R. Van der Werf and the Chief Steward was Jack Minnes.

John Allan, a deckhand with the Company, recalls Neil as being a quiet and efficient officer who went about his job with no flamboyance or harsh words. John said, "Being a new hand, on one occasion, I had tied a rope around a cleat but hadn't put enough turns around it and Neil came along, put a couple more turns on it just to show me what was needed. I also remember Neil

Capt. Tom Charters on the *Camosun* 1945 (T. Charters)

had a habit of quietly coming into the wheelhouse on a dark night, then letting out a loud whoosh behind me. It would scare the daylights out of me."

I also sailed with Neil. He was a Second Mate at the time and I was always happy to see him aboard because he handled the deck crew well. As he was responsible for loading and unloading freight, things usually went along smoothly.

There is next to nothing recorded about Neil, except one mention of him in Gerald Rushton's book *Whistle up the Inlet* as follows, "The *Cardena* had a narrow escape on her logging route early in 1953. The circumstances were quite unusual when, just after midnight, entering Patrick Passage en route to Sullivan Bay with Chief Officer Neil Campbell on the bridge, she struck a rock off a small island in the channel. Although badly holed in the forepeak, Captain Harry Roach managed to keep the flooding under control with the pumps until reaching Sullivan Bay. The vessel was close to the end of her run with 22 passengers on board and her crew of 54. Later, with the aid of tugs, she returned to Vancouver under her own steam. The curious fact is that the high mountain peaks caused shadows in the narrow channel and obscured outlines. Immediately after this grounding, the department of transport installed a light on the island." [138]

Neil Campbell died in Vancouver at age 87 on July 14, 1992.

First passenger off the *Camosun* at Butedale 1954 (T. Dougan)

Tom Charters

Tom was born in Burnaby in 1921. His family settled in the area in 1898. He first went to sea in 1939 aboard an Imperial Oil tanker, the *Albertalite*, running down the coast. Then he joined Union Steamships in 1942, starting on the *Camosun II* as a deckhand. In 1943 he sat for and obtained his Coastal Mate's ticket. His first Mate's job also was aboard the *Camosun II*, under Captain Harry McLean.

Tom spent a lot of time on the Queen Charlotte Islands run and he recalled a story about Alfred Aspinall who was Chief Officer at the time. "It was a terrible night and if you've been over there you know how foul the weather can be. The landfall on the Charlottes is different. There is a low sandy spit that stretches out and it's called Sandspit. There is a narrow channel down to Queen Charlotte City. We were heading down this channel and we couldn't see anything, we had no radar, it was a beggar of a night. Alfie was pacing up and down on the bridge, blowing the whistle trying to get an echo but there was nothing to echo from. Anyway, we finally reached Queen Charlotte City. The skipper comes up and asked, 'Well, Alfie how are you doing?' and Alfie says, 'Look at my uniform, I've torn my coat!' He had caught his coat in the binnacle. It was incredible. Here he had completed this amazing feat of getting the ship into Queen Charlotte City and all he could think about was having torn his uniform."

Tom then talked about Purser Pat Pattison. "When the ship was loading canned salmon, Pat would come out and stroll around where they were loading the cases. Invariably a case would be dropped and break open. Pat would rush over and fill his pockets with cans!"

Angus McNeill, later a Captain, became a good friend of Tom's, but Tom says Angus was very, very superstitious. "One thing he would tell me, 'If you ever see something moving on the shoreline such as a deer or a bear, you must never mention it or point it out as it would be a bad omen.' If there was a corpse on board, Angus would be at his wits end until it was unloaded.

"The *Catala* had sort of an upper and lower bridge. We had a corpse on board on this particular trip. Bob Hackett the Mate got a sheet, draped it over himself, and went up to the upper bridge and then leaped down to the lower bridge right beside Wee Angus, who just about jumped overboard.

"Poor Wee Angus was the butt of so many pranks, but all in all he was a fine man."

Tom also brings up the famous Chief Steward, Bogey Knight. Tom and his wife had gone down to Reno for a holiday. Reno was one of Bogey's haunts as he always went down there on his holidays. He was a great gambler and told everyone he had a system and always came back a winner. Tom and his wife were waiting to board a plane for home and there was Bogey in the line as well. Tom could hear Bogey talking and telling everyone that he was a captain aboard a passenger ship back in Canada. Bogey could spin quite a yarn if he wanted, so Tom thought he would sidle over and say hello, but this never stopped Bogey, he just continued right on telling his tale to anyone who would listen.

I asked Tom if he had a favourite skipper and he said, "I guess it would have been Captain Sheppard, but he was a strange one." He went on, "If we were in a bad storm and I was on watch with Angus, he would send me down to Captain Sheppard's room to get him to come up to the bridge. Invariably I would go in and find him down on his knees praying. Then he would say, 'Yeah, yeah, I'll be up.' "

Tom couldn't make up his mind which was his favourite ship, but it was either the *Lady Pam* or the *Camosun II*. "The *Camosun* wasn't built for rough weather. From the bridge you could look down into her hatch in a rough sea. The hatches would be square one minute and triangular the next. I can still see her twisting and wrenching when we were crossing Hecate Strait. That could be a terrible piece of water."

In 1946, Tom decided to quit the sea, for the simple reason he was bored. Captain Muir, the Marine Superintendent, thought he was crazy, but Tom had decided he wanted to go into sales. So he went into sales, first selling lumber, then life insurance. Then he went into heavy construction, such as road building and estimating, and that's what he is doing today. He is still working and lives with his wife on a wonderful piece of wooded land up behind Haney.

Frederick E. Corneille

Fred Corneille, 2nd Mate 1928
(F. Corneille)

I interviewed Mr. Corneille at his home in Victoria in 1990 and at that time he was a spry 84 years old. He was born in Port Arthur, Ont., on Sept. 6, 1908.

Fred, or "Cornie" as he says he was often called, was one of the many Officers in the Union Steamship Co. that one doesn't hear or read much about even though he was with the Company for 22 years. Whenever his name is mentioned it is invariably pronounced wrong, usually as "cor-nelly", though he says the proper pronunciation is "cor-neel."

Fred started as a deckhand on April 1, 1926, aboard the *Cheakamus*. He remembers two well-known deck officers in the Company's history that were aboard her at the time, "Chips" Williams and Fred "Searchlight" Parker. Promotion in the Company was slow for junior officers, and as Fred said, "In the winter, particularly in the early days, the Company tied up quite a few of their ships, so men were laid off. The ships that were running were operated by a skeleton crew. If you were Third Mate in the summer, you went back to being a quartermaster in the winter. You would know when it was spring because you would go back up to being a Third Mate."

Fred obtained his coastal Mate's ticket in 1928 and his Master's ticket in 1939. Although he never served as Master on the Union Ships, he did serve as Chief Officer. He left the Company in 1948. The last ship he was aboard was the *Coquitlam III*. He recalled sailing with Captain Bob Wilson, Captain E. Georgeson, Captain A. C. McLellan, Captain W. McCombe, and Captain E. Sheppard.

Fred recalls being on the *Venture* on the logging camp route with Captain Bob Wilson. Fred said, "He was always as cool as a cucumber. Most ships have two telegraphs, one on each side of the bridge, but the *Venture* had only one and it was right in the middle of the bridge. Captain Wilson would often make a landing, sitting on the bridge rail, legs over the forward side, and operate the telegraph with his hands behind his back. That took a great deal of skill and confidence.

"Captain Georgeson was a very short man, so short in fact that he couldn't see over the dodger on the bridge. He would have to run to the side of the bridge or around the corner to see where he was going, but he was a very, very efficient Captain."

Sailing with "Big Mac" McLellan on the *Cassiar II* was difficult because of his pipe smoking. "He used to close the wheelhouse up tight and light up his pipe with that Irish Twist tobacco, and damned near killed us."

One trip that Fred recalled was a charter direct to Menzies Bay. A logging Company had chartered the ship to take the whole crew up to camp, all at one time. The Company put a policeman aboard to keep order amongst the drunks. When a fellow started to make trouble he was put in jail aboard the ship. Of course it wasn't a very big jail and the policeman left the door open. Even with the door open they all stayed in the jail. When the jail became full he would look around to find a fellow who had sobered up and he would push him out and replace him with his latest catch. They all sat there quietly waiting their turn to be released.

I asked Mr. Corneille if he was in any marine mishaps. There was only one that he could recall and it wasn't serious, but it does illustrate some of the difficult landings that the skippers encountered. He was Chief Officer on *Lady Cynthia* and was making a landing at Stuart Island. He said, "Just as I headed up to land, the tide shoved the wharf in front of me, and I had to quickly go full speed astern or I would have cut the wharf float in half. The tide took another surge and took the ship right up against the beach, broadside, but it suffered no damage. I found out later that Jimmy Hunter, reputed to be an excellent ship handler, had had the same problem. The Captain at the time was Bob Naughty and I told him 'Next time, you had better take her in,' which he did, and also hit the wharf."

Delivery of the mail was an important function of the Union ships, and of particular importance was the Lock Sack which contained all of the registered letters, money payrolls for the logging camps, etc. On one trip on the Cortes-Stuart Island route, with Mr. Corneille as Chief Officer, the freight clerk came up to the bridge and reported they had lost a mail sack. The ship had just left one stop and was proceeding to the next port. "Which one?" he asked. The freight clerk said it was the Lock Sack. "Well, you couldn't have picked a better one! So we put the ship about and went back and looked for it. We couldn't find it. It had obviously sunk. I had the whole crew up, one by one, and made them write out what had happened and sign it, and when I came back into town I turned this all over to the proper authorities. When they came back after their investigation they said that there were no valuables or registered mail in the bag so the matter was forgotten."

Mr. Corneille still takes a keen interest in shipping affairs. In the March 1990 issue of the *Westcoast Mariner* magazine, he wrote a most interesting Letter to the Editor. In it, amongst other things, were more comments about jails aboard the Union ships and he talked about the jail on the *Catala* in particular. "As for the jail on the *Catala*, it was used for the police when taking prisoners to jail, all right, but I remember on one occasion they had two men bound for Oakalla but their escort allowed them free run of the ship. Little did some of the round-trip passengers realize who their shuffleboard partners were!"

"The only other use of the jail was once when we had a lot of new chicks on board going for the full distance. We let them out in the jail so they would get a little air and exercise," Fred said.

Mr. Corneille left the Union company in 1948 and went over to Imperial Oil to work aboard the Imperial Namu and Imperial Nanaimo. He also served for 15 years as Assistant Superintendent of HMCS Chart and Chronometer Depot, and also worked for the Fisheries Protection Service.

After a period of poor health, he passed away at his home in Victoria on Dec. 31, 1994.

Native families aboard the S.S. *Venture* for seasonal cannery work 1923 (*Sound Heritage*)

Alfred E. Dickson

Capt. Alfred Dickson
(Vancouver Maritime Museum)

When one person I interviewed was asked about Captain Dickson, he said, "Ah yes, that incredible old Captain of the *Catala*." Incredible is the right word to use when talking about this fine old skipper. He was born in Antigonish, Nova Scotia, and started with the Union Steamship Co. in 1895. Rushton says of him, "This taciturn Nova Scotian mariner - who had served on Union ships since the days of the *Senator*, had no peers as a navigator. His contemporaries said he was in a league by himself!" [139]

For many years, Dickson was the Senior Master or Commodore of the Union Fleet, having been with the Company since its earliest days. He retired in 1935 after 40 years service. His first command was the *Camosun I*.

During the First World War he served overseas in the Water Transport Division. For 18 months he was towing ammunition barges across the mine-filled English Channel. [140] When he came back from his war service he rejoined the *Camosun I*. 1918 saw him as Master on the *Venture* going to the aid of a U.S. ship, the *Ravalli*, which was on fire in Lowe Inlet. He took the *Venture* alongside the *Ravalli* and began pumping water into her, but after four hours of trying to put out the fire, the valiant struggle to save her was abandoned.

Captain Dickson was sent over to Scotland in 1923 to bring back the newly-built *Cardena* to Vancouver. He left Napier and Miller's yard on the Clyde on May 3, 1923, arrived in Vancouver on June 11, 1923 and was Master on her maiden voyage to northern waters on June 20, 1923. Also on the inaugural run were Chief Officer Bill Mounce, Second Mate Ernest Sheppard, Third Mate William Mercer and Chief Engineer G.H. Foster.

As senior Master in the fleet, Captain Dickson also had the honour of taking out the *Lady Cynthia* for her maiden voyage to Powell River in August 1925.

1927 saw Captain Dickson as Master of the *Catala*, now the Company's flagship. On Nov. 8, 1927, at 1 p.m. in broad daylight, with Chief Officer Ernest Sheppard on watch, the *Catala* went hard aground on Sparrowhawk Reef. The reef was named after a British naval vessel that had also gone aground there in 1874. There are some very spectacular pictures of this grounding, some of which are shown under the *Catala* in the Ships section of this book. The details as to how this grounding happened have never been fully explained, and Rushton for example does not tell us in either of his books. But in researching for this book, I was told the following explanation by Ernie Plant, a Union employee who was aboard the *Catala* at the time but was off watch: "Captain Dickson had a fondness for flowers and at the time of the grounding, being off watch, he was tending and watering some plants he had set up in boxes aboard ship, behind the wheelhouse. The *Catala* was southbound and on the approach to the reef there was a marker buoy set far to the starboard side of the reef, so ships would stay close to this buoy in open water, to avoid the reef. Apparently the night before there had been a terrific storm and the buoy had been dislodged from its anchor and had floated across the channel, catching onto the reef." The rest is history, but one can't help but wonder why the Chief Officer in broad daylight didn't notice something amiss.

William "Billy" McCombe was a mate board the *Catala* when she went aground on Sparrowhawk and he had this to say about the accident: "Captain Dickson had a certain routine. He was quite an old man. Everyday he came on the bridge, he looked over, I don't think he ever saw anything, and then he went back and watered his flowers, his wee garden. He had pots and wee bits of flowers at the back of the wheelhouse. He nursed them along. The next thing we knew, the *Catala* belted Sparrowhawk Ledge. The man that was on the bridge was a man by the name of Sheppard. He said he saw Captain Dickson on the bridge and he thought he was taking over. The man never took over before. And you never forget old man Dickson at the inquiry. Captain Dickson said: 'Captain Sheppard thinks I took over, I guess I must have taken over.' That was all he said. He took the rub." [141].

This Sparrowhawk grounding of the *Catala* rates as one of the most notable and newsworthy marine mishaps in the Company's history. She was aground for about a month before they got her off. The salvage of the flagship of the fleet was a remarkable job itself, and the story is told under the *Catala* in the ships section of this book. The cost to put her back in service was $175,000. She resumed her sailings under Captain Dickson on March 30, 1928.

There is an excellent commentary about Captain Dickson, which throws a very personal light as to the gentleman he was, in a lovely book, *A Pour of Rain*, by Helen Meilleur, published by Sono Nis Press in 1980. In brief, she says this about Captain Dickson, "We could not picture him without white hair, a moustache, and dignity. We never heard his mirth in guffaws, we saw it in his eyes, which were mariner's eyes, protected by lines and creases and were of compelling blueness." And of the Union Steamships she says, "Captain Dickson and the Union Steamships became an extension of our lives." [142]

Dennis Patrick Farina

Dennis Farina circa 1944
(Farina Collection)

Dennis was born June 5, 1915 in Vancouver, B.C. His father was "Paddy" Farina, who was a Chief Engineer with the Union Steamship Co. for 47 years and is one of the best-known names in the Company's history. Dennis followed in his father's footsteps and started with Union Steamships as a deckhand in May, 1932.

However, before joining the Company he often took trips with his dad on the day boats, so he became very familiar with the ships at an early age. When the *Lady Alexandra* first came out, the news agent on her was a Bob Wilson, who used to hire Dennis to help sell his wares. He would have Dennis circulate around the ship with a basket filled with newspapers, magazines, and ice cream to sell to the passengers. Dennis did this for two or three summers when he was in his early teens. Then at age 16, Dennis sailed out on the *Empress of Russia* as a bridge messenger.

When Dennis joined the Union Steamship Co., the first ship he worked on was the *Cardena*. The Master was Captain Georgeson, Buster Brown was Second Mate and Joe Hackett was Third Mate. This was in the Depression years and often you would be laid off, then taken on again in the spring. Eventually he was working steadily and served as deckhand, dayman, winchman and quartermaster while studying to obtain his Coastal Mate's ticket.

Dennis recalls being on the *Lady Pam* one summer when she had a crew of about six fellows on board, every one of whom had their Mate's ticket. Fellows like Wally Walsh, Harry Biles, Owen-Jones and Al Strang - all were working as deckhands even though they had a Mate's ticket.

Dennis got his first break when they brought out the *Cheakamus* again in 1937. He was given the Third Mate's job on her, and he said, "At the same time Owen Jones went out as Third Mate on the *Chelohsin*. But these jobs only lasted for a month and then the Company tied up six or seven ships, I went quartermaster on the *Catala* and Owen Jones went quartermaster on the *Venture*."

In the 1930s, the fellows were always going up and down in positions but by about 1940 Dennis was working steady as Third Mate and at times as a Second Mate.

Dennis recalled the strike of 1935. "They brought fellows in from all over, even from the Prairies. After a couple of months or so, they were operating as well as they ever did before the strike. Six months later the strike more or less drifted away," he said.

Promotion was very slow in the Company, because at the time none of the senior Officers would or could afford to leave because there was no pension set up within the Company. The old skippers and engineers worked until they dropped. Some even died aboard their ships!

After his first job as mate in 1937, Dennis slowly made his way up the ladder.

Dennis Farina and Bobby Wilson, news agent
(*Farina Collection*)

When he left the Company in 1945 he was working as 1st Mate on the *Lady Cynthia*, but went over to the Union Oil Co. as Mate on the *Unacana*. He stayed there about a year and then went over to the Vancouver fireboat as Master, where he stayed for about 30 years until 1975, when he became 60 years old. He didn't waste any time obtaining another position, though, for he went to work the very next day as Master of the *Malibu Princess*, which runs up to the heads of Jervis Inlet and Princess Louisa Inlet two days a week in the summer months to a lodge operated by Young Life of America. They also service the church camps in the Howe Sound area. Dennis retired from this position in 1995 after 63 years at sea.

When Dennis and I began reminiscing about past days and fellows who were with the Union company over the years, the first person he thought about was an old Chief

Steward named Willie Gardiner. He said, "Willie was Chief Steward there when I first started and he was still there when I left. He must have been 80 years old. They were going to lay him off but he just refused to go. They practically had to carry him off the ships."

Then there was "Major" Watts. His name was Ernie Watts, a real Old Country type, and he always claimed he had been a Major in the British Army in India. He was a Chief Steward in the Company for many years. Fred Corneille remembers him being on the *Lady Cynthia* in 1926-30. He and the Company had a disagreement and Ernie left the Company and became a doorman at the Beacon Theatre on Hastings St. in Vancouver. Dennis said he would go down to the Beacon and "Major" Watts would slip Dennis in the door without having to buy a ticket.

I asked Dennis if he had been in any marine mishaps. Yes he had, and the first one he recalled was aboard the *Lady Pam* with "Big Mac" McLennan as the Master and Dennis decking. "We came around Point Atkinson on a real dark night and just off the Great Northern Cannery we suddenly saw a bloody sailboat on our starboard side. There were no running lights on her or anything. Big Mac hollered "hard a port." The *Pam* was hand gear steering and you had to get over the other side to pull her over. We hit that boat right amidships, half of her went down one side of the *Pam* and half went down the other side. She was a big boat but she sank quickly. We stopped and lowered a lifeboat. There were several people aboard her, both men and women. We could hear them hollering, but by God we picked them all up in short order." There was a court hearing on that one, Admiralty Court, Judge Sidney Smith. He held a Master's ticket himself so he understood navigation very well. Because the sailboat had no running lights they were found to be at fault.

The second accident that Dennis told about was when he was on the *Lady Cecilia* and she backed onto Indian Island at Pender Harbour on the day before Christmas, 1940. Pictures of this accident are often seen in various magazines even today. One of the coast's well-known pioneers, Jim Spilsbury was on his boat tied up to the wharf at Pender Harbour when the incident took place and he saw the whole thing.

The Captain of the *Lady Cecilia* at the time was Bob Naughty, but he was off watch and it was the Chief Officer Harry McLean who was on the Bridge when she grounded. However, he was not to blame as he had received the wrong response from the engineer below, to one of his orders telegraphed down to him. The Engineer on watch was Robert Baldry. Dennis described it all as follows: "Leaving the wharf, we backed out and Captain McLean rang down for full astern. We were swinging around and backing towards Indian Island. We would then move ahead towards the Gap at the harbour entrance. Captain McLean rang down for stop and the engines were stopped. He then rang down for full ahead but instead he got full astern. Captain McLean quickly signalled for full ahead again but the Engineer figured he wanted more power so he gave her all she had but still going astern. The *Cecilia* hit Indian Rock and her stern climbed right out of the water almost knocking over an outhouse sitting on the island."

The stewards' quarters were aft right above the propellors and when she hit, Cecil Skinner, one of the stewards, was sleeping there. He awoke with a fear that the propellors were going to come right through the deck. He jumped right out of bed and ran up on deck still in his pajamas.

Spilsbury immediately started his boat and went over to the *Cecilia* but there wasn't much he could do to help. "Somebody threw me a line and wanted me to pull, but there was no way I could pull that size of a ship off the rock," he told me.

Dennis continued: "The *Venture* was on her way down the coast so we called her in and she put a line aboard the *Lady Cecilia* but she wouldn't budge. So we took all the mail and important things off in the lifeboats and took it all over to Irvings Landing. The passengers were put aboard the *Venture* and taken on to Vancouver. We went back to the *Cecilia* and we called all the fishboats in Pender Harbour together and they all hooked on to the *Cecilia* but they couldn't move her. The *Salvage Queen* came up and at high tide they pulled and zigzagged and were able to pull her off. They started to tow her but had a great deal of difficulty because the rudder on the *Cecilia* was jammed over to one side. They had to tow her back to Vancouver almost side by side because there was no way she would tow in a straight line." (Pictures of the jammed propellor can be seen under *Lady Cecilia* in the Ships section of this book, p.90.)

According to Dennis, engineer Robert Baldry admitted it was his error and left the Company shortly afterwards, joining the CNR ships.

The third and last marine mishap Dennis recalled was when he was Second Mate aboard *Lady Cecilia* on Sept., 27, 1944, when it collided in a fog near Port Atkinson with a 10,000-ton "Park" ship out of Burrard dry dock (a merchant-type ship built by the government for war service, all named after parks). The Captain was H.E. Lawrey. I recalled this accident very well because I happened to be aboard her as Assistant Purser. Dennis described the crash as follows: "We didn't have radar in those days, and we got to know the whistles of other ships. We thought is was the *Princess Elaine*. We listened and could tell she was getting close. Captain Lawrey said, 'I'd better stop.' So we were stopped, dead in the water. I can remember all of a sudden this huge bow coming out of the fog, so Captain Lawrey very quickly put one propeller full ahead and the other full astern. This swung the *Cecilia* around so the freighter hit us a glancing blow. Our starboard side was stove in. The big freighter stopped and we signalled back and forth to each other. Fortunately the *Cecilia* was not holed and we were able to proceed into Vancouver under our own power."

Several people were injured in the crash, though, and nine people were taken to hospital, but all recovered shortly after. It was a miracle that the *Lady Cecilia* wasn't cut in two and everyone agrees it was the quick action by Captain Lawrey that saved the day.

Dennis Farina (left), deckhand on *Lady Evelyn,* posing on lifeboat
(Farina Collection)

James Findlay

Here is a man who served aboard Union Steamships for 30 years yet very few stories or personal anecdotes about his career with the Company were known, but I was able to make contact with his daughter, Mrs. Cora Tosh, and she gave me some marvelous details about this great Captain of the Union fleet. The picture on page 161 is from Mrs. Tosh's collection.

Mr. Frank Skinner, former Purser and later Agent for the Union Steamship Company at Prince Rupert, sailed with Captain Findlay on the *Camosun I* in 1928. This was the cannery run, to Rivers Inlet, Smiths Inlet, Namu, Ocean Falls and Bella Coola. The ship left at 2 p.m. Thursdays and returned either Monday or Tuesday depending on how many cases of canned salmon they picked up southbound. Frank says that Captain Findlay was a very fine man, a competent Master, and he was like a second father to all of the crew.

Captain Findlay was what one could call a real sailor for he gained his seagoing experience and obtained his Master's ticket aboard clipper ships sailing around the Horn. Mrs. Tosh wrote out the following details about her father's early career:

"My father was born Jan. 18, 1873 in Baffshire, Scotland. He went to sea at the age of 14 on the beautiful clipper ship *Glenmorag*, where he served for seven years. From there he went to other sailing ships, the last being the *Falls of Foyer*. At the age of 26 he obtained his Master's certificate and then went into steam. Two steamships he was Master of were the *Elleric* and *Orteric*. My mother sailed with him for three years all over the world, aboard the *Elleric*.

"The certificate my father had was called a square rig certificate and with it he could command any size ship anywhere in the world. I still have this certificate. Having this certificate is why he never needed a coastal master's ticket and this was the reason he was sent to Britain to bring out so many ships for the Union Company. There was only one other skipper in the Union Company who had this same certificate, namely Captain Dickson. [Actually there were two, including John H. Browne Sr.]

"He had decided that he wanted to settle in British Columbia. He himself was sailing out to B.C. on the *Orteric*, so he sent his wife and family out by another ship to Canada. They travelled across Canada by train, arriving in Vancouver before the Captain did. They put up in a hotel to await his arrival. In the meantime their son came down with scarlet fever and the health officer at the time had to move them out of the hotel. He found them a little cottage to live in out in the Grandview area as a quarantine precaution for the boy and his scarlet fever. The health officer was very good to them, realizing their predicament. He rustled around and found some pots, pans, and bedding for them as their own belongings were coming out with the Captain on the *Orteric*. When the *Orteric* arrived, he was there to meet her and

Capt. James Findlay
(Skinner Collection)

explained to the Captain what had happened. As the Captain had previously planned, he signed off the *Orteric* after she arrived in Vancouver, with the intention of starting a chicken farm.

"After six months on dry land, sea fever began to catch up with him and he began to go down to the waterfront to watch the ships coming and going. He decided to give up the chicken farm idea and he applied for a job on the coastal steamers. He applied to the CPR, the CNR and the Union line all at the same time. He was offered jobs with all three right away but chose Union Steamships because he felt they were the up-and-coming company.

"So he joined the Union Steamship Company in 1911 and one of the first commands my father had was to take the old ship *Lonsdale* to Japan for scrap. This was on Nov. 28, 1912. After being checked out for seaworthiness, they loaded coal and wheat, then sailed on Dec. 2, 1912. They ran into bad weather and heavy fog off the Columbia River and this lasted for the whole voyage. Every day they had terrible gales and mountainous seas. At one point the ship nearly floundered. They were shipping heavy seas, water in the bilges, water in the forepeak, the steering chain broke, plates broke, the stove broke etc. I have all this from the log book of that voyage. What a terrible voyage it was, but they arrived safely in Yokkicchi on Jan. 18, 1913."

Upon his return to a seagoing life and looking at our B.C. coastline, even though he had a Master's certificate good anywhere in the world, he requested a Third Mate's job on the Union ships to start with, so he could familiarize himself with the B.C. coast. He signed on the *Chelohsin* as Third Mate, as he realized he had a lot to learn about the coast and so, more or less, he started at the bottom again. A story is told about Captain Findlay launching a lifeboat, with a deckhand to row him about, to take his own soundings with a lead line at various places for his own use and guidance. He then recorded these soundings on his own personal charts.

On March 6, 1916 he was Second Mate aboard the *Camosun I* when she grounded during a snow storm at Lima Point, near Digby Island. Due to poor tides, the *Camosun* was not refloated until March 22. There was a marine inquiry but no blame was laid upon any of the deck officers. Damages to the ship were heavy and the tendered price for repairs was $18,669.

Captain Findlay joined the Guild in 1917 and became the President in 1928-1929.

The Union Steamship Company had a new freighter built in the Wallace Shipyards. She was named the *Chilkoot* and was launched Feb. 26, 1920. Her maiden voyage was made on June 20, 1920 under the command of Captain Findlay. The *Chilkoot* along with the *Coquitlam I* were charted out to the Kingsley Navigation Company and they ran between Vancouver and San Francisco. Captain Findlay was Master on both of them at one time or another. They carried gold ore to Tacoma. From Blubber Bay they carried lime, cement and lumber. From Sidney on Vancouver Island they carried canned oysters and clams to San Francisco. On return trips they carried canned fruit and vegetables, lumber, rough salt, coal and blasting powder, and fuel oil. Captain Findlay stated in his journal that they had some terrible trips weather-wise.

With the Master's certificate Findlay had, the Union company sent him over to Scotland to bring the Company's new flagship, the *Catala*, out to B.C. in 1925. He followed this up by bringing the *Lady Cynthia* over in the same year, arriving in Vancouver with her on Aug. 20, 1925.

The Company called on him again to bring out another well-known ship in B.C. waters, the *Chilliwack II*, formerly the *Ardgarvel*. Captain Findlay docked her in Vancouver on May 5, 1927.

Several Union ships were under his command at various stages in his career, including the *Coquitlam I*, the *Cassiar I*, the *Camosun I*, the *Chilkoot*, the *Cardena*, the *Lady Cecilia*, and his last command was the

Catala.

"While captain on the *Cardena* on Nov. 22, 1929, operating in poor weather the *Cardena* grounded on a Skeena River gravel bar, near the North Pacific Cannery. The tide was falling and the ship was unable to back off. Unfortunately the next day's tide did not rise high enough to enable her to back off, so all the passengers, along with a load of canned salmon had to be taken off her before she could be refloated. Damage was not extensive and she was back in service within three weeks." [143]

Shortly before he retired, Captain Findlay and his ship the *Catala* made headlines in rescuing a crew of five from a U.S. Navy flying boat which was forced down in the sea near Bella Bella on Jan. 30, 1938.

The *Catala* picked up their S.O.S. call and Captain Findlay turned his ship around and proceeded to the area through heavy sleet and mist. The airmen had abandoned their airplane and had taken to a small emergency lifeboat which was overloaded and was in danger of being overturned at any moment by the heavy seas. The plane was one of six in a flight from Sand Point airbase, near Seattle, to Sitka, Alaska. The *Catala* arrived on the scene and took the airmen aboard not long after they had abandoned their airplane. The men were soon revived, and later were turned over to a U.S. Navy vessel, the USS *Teal*, which proceeded north and took the men to their original destination. A report of this event was carried in U.S. newspapers, a clipping of which was loaned to me by Mrs. Harold Crompton, whose husband was Assistant Purser aboard the *Catala* at the time. He was able to take several pictures, some of which were subsequently published in the *New York Times*.

Captain Findlay was now Commodore of the Union fleet, and retirement was near. After sailing all over the world, he had decided to settle and build his retirement home at Whaletown on Cortes Island. He started to build his home in 1936, retired in 1941 and was granted a life membership in the Guild. His wife had died before he retired. He also had built a little cabin on the property and his brother moved into it prior to the Captain's arrival. His daughter's family spent all their holidays there for the next 12 years.

As the Captain was a very popular man up and down the coast, he received many gifts from the coastal people he had so faithfully served over the years. One man gave him a horse and a promise to follow this up with a wagon. When the wagon came, it was brought up on a Union ship. The Captain at the time was Harry McLean. When he found out who was to receive this wagon he saw to it that it arrived with a flair. He had the ship's crew deck the wagon out so it looked like a small boat complete with a mast, flags, and with red and green running lights. No doubt Captain Findlay was very pleased and amused at all this fuss.

Shortly after Captain Findlay took up residence on Cortes Island he was appointed by the then Lieutenant Governor Robert Maitland as a Justice of the Peace and a Stipendiary Magistrate for the Whaletown-Cortes area.

Capt. Findlay
(Mrs. C. Tosh)

In 1943 he came out of retirement. The Union Steamship Company sent him back to Halifax to take command of a Liberty ship, the *Kensington Park*, and bring her back to

George F. Gaisford

Captain George Gaisford (Vancouver Maritime Museum)

B.C. He sailed in a convoy and was lead ship. This was all new to him, through the submarine zones etc., then up through the Panama Canal to Vancouver. He arrived in the Port of Vancouver on Jan. 7, 1944, which also was the date of his 71st birthday. Having completed this job he retired again to his home at Whaletown.

The Captain was diabetic and finally he was unable to look after himself. Gangrene had set in on one of his toes, so he left his home and went to live with his daughter in Vancouver in 1953. He died on March 15, 1954.

The well-known Rev. Rollo Boas purchased Captain Findlay's property. The Captain had left behind some of his belongings which he no longer wanted and amongst them were his personal charts and a "Compactum" which Captain Findlay had obtained from the Union Company when he retired. This is a unit of furniture that has a fold-away washbasin, mirror, etc. found on board many early steamships. Rev. Boas kindly donated these items to the Campbell River Museum.

Captain Findlay's Compactum on display at the Campbell River Museum (Campbell River Museum)

The picture accompanying this story was given to the Vancouver Maritime Museum recently by his granddaughter, Mrs. Patricia Veldhuisen. He was very short in stature but he stands high in the early history of the Union Steamships.

He was born in Westbury, Wiltshire, on Aug. 15, 1865. As a boy he received his education in the British Navy and came out to the B.C. coast on the British naval ship *Nymph*. He received his discharge in September 1892, at age 26, then joined the Union Steamship Co. and served with distinction for 41 years. He was still actively employed by the Company being Master of the *Chelohsin* before he died at home on June 23, 1933 at age 67 after an illness of two months.

When he died, Mr. Harold Brown, Managing Director of the Union Steamship Company, paid tribute to him with these words: "During the years I have known him I had the highest confidence in his ability. He was one of the most valued Captains of our Company and was most conscientious and careful in the care of his ship."

Rushton in *Whistle Up The Inlet* mentions that Gaisford was Pilot aboard the *Comox I* then was moved to Pilot on the new *Cassiar* in 1901. The term Pilot was changed in later years to Chief Officer, but both titles meant he was second in command of the ship. In 1908 he was promoted to Captain of the *Cassiar*, which became known along the coast as the loggers' palace.

Later when he was Captain of the *Cowichan*, his expertise in guiding his ship safely along the difficult B.C. coastline is again told by Rushton: "The Chief Officer sounded his whistle to summon Captain Gaisford from his cabin to check bearings. Pulling on his jacket, the Captain hurried from his cabin under the bridge, halted briefly before ascending the ladder, took one sniff of the breeze and yelled 'Hard a port.' His sense of bearing too close to the land and his reaction were instantaneous." [144]

When the British warship HMS *Hood* visited Vancouver in 1924, Captain Gaisford had the honour of taking command of the Union Steamship's newly-arrived *Lady Alexandra* to take her out on her maiden voyage to greet the *Hood* in the Strait of Georgia with 800 people aboard.

Frederick Corneille, who sailed with Captain Gaisford, said of him: "He was a clever man, especially on the logging run. He had a lot of eccentricities, similar to old Captain Dickson. Like, if Captain Dickson wanted to make a starboard landing and the winds were against him, he'd make the landing anyway, not wait until the weather changed first."

"Another thing," Mr. Corneille continued, "Captain Gaisford hated to see or have the ship's officers receive mail addressed and delivered to them aboard ship. Buster Brown and a Freight Clerk liked to play jokes and they started to get Captain Gaisford's goat. This one time they arranged with Gibb Rennie, Purser at the time on the *Chelohsin*, to have the freight clerk deliver this letter up to Buster Brown, who was on the bridge with Captain Gaisford. Buster was handed this letter and of course Buster looked at the Captain who quickly said, 'It's all right Mister, go ahead and open it.' Buster opened it and it was filled with toilet paper. All Captain Gaisford said was, 'Well I see somebody knows what you are, Mister.' "

In a booklet put out by the Provincial Archives of B.C., Captain Robert Naughty Jr. related the following story about Captain Gaisford: "I joined the *Chelohsin* under Captain Gaisford. He could see in the dark. No radar. Captain Gaisford liked to keep one quartermaster. He did six and six. One quartermaster was with the Chief Officer. The Chief Officer made his own landings from midnight until six in the morning with his own quartermaster. I was on the six to twelve with Captain Gaisford. If you were quartermaster with Captain Gaisford and he liked you and you got to know what he wanted docking, he didn't want to let you go. And as I was a fair-haired boy, I got his magazines. He didn't read them for a week and I'd get them. The crew didn't get fruit, of course. The steward would bring up his fruit and that was all handed to me. He didn't eat fruit. I spoiled all that one day by telling him about the weather.

"It had been boiling hot, oh boy. We had six weeks without rain and it was sweltering. The old *Chelohsin* had her steering engine in the wheelhouse. It was steam and you stood with the wheel at your hand and a little seat if you wanted to rest. You know, six hours is a long time, but it was only a tiny thing that you got your rear end up on and kind of leaned against. This engine would go 'brrrr' every time you turned the wheel, and the steam came out of this engine. It was sweating in the wheelhouse.

"Captain Gaisford's room was behind and on one side of the wheelhouse and the other side was the Chief Officer's room. I was kind of young and brash. He had a window that looked out onto the passengers' deck. He had a wooden venetian blind that he used to put down so passengers wouldn't look in on him. It was quite dark. He had to put the light on all the time.

"I had to call him at five o'clock to get ready for supper. That was my job. I walked in. God it was hot! He said 'Okay sonny, how's the weather?' and I said 'Pouring cats and dogs' as a joke, you know, but he came out in 15 minutes had his sou'wester on, his gumboots and his jacket and there's the sun blazing down. Well, did he ever light into me! I lost my magazines and fruit for two weeks. I thought I was being funny, but he figured you've got to have some respect for the Master." [145]

James "Jimmy" Galbraith

Captain James Galbraith at Halfmoon Bay
(Roach Collection)

Jimmy was a popular man aboard ship but his career with Union Steamships was up and down. He would rise in the ranks of deck officers and then he would be demoted due to a drinking problem. However, he did attain the rank of Chief Officer on the day boats.

In an interview, one deckhand who sailed aboard ship with Jimmy as Mate said he was a good officer and treated the crew well, but he did drink a lot and was a womanizer.

On one occasion when he was Mate aboard the *Cecilia* he had brought a lady friend out for the day trip and so entertained her in his cabin, but once she was there she refused to leave the ship for two or three days. Jimmy had a terrible time hiding this fact from the Captain. At times when quite a few passengers were aboard she would leave the cabin and mingle with them but when the ship returned to Vancouver she refused to leave.

Another time when Jimmy was docking he had forgotten to wing in the ship's derricks. The Union ships were docked in a line and sort of overlapped each other and it was a tight fit. This time the *Cecilia*'s derricks caught the derrick of another ship and it came crashing down, knocking the corner off the *Cecilia*'s bridge.

John Allan was a crew member on the *Lady Cecilia* when Jimmy was Chief Officer and recalls entering First Narrows with an inexperienced hand at the wheel. With the combination of very strong tidal currents and a green man trying to steer the ship, the *Cecilia* came through the narrows sideways. Jimmy of course was humiliated and bawled the crew out and told them never to send that fellow up to the wheel again.

On another occasion, Ivor Jones was at the wheel of the *Capilano* with Vic Hayman as Master. Ivor had brought a lady friend out for the day. She was in the wheelhouse and Captain Hayman offered to take her down to lunch and left Jimmy to make the landing at the next stop.

Captain Hayman ordered a bowl of chicken noodle soup and was about to put a spoonful in his mouth when the ship hit the dock with a reverberating bump. The soup and noodles went all over his clean uniform. Needless to say he was not amused at Jimmy's expertise in ship handling.

Jimmy was Chief Officer and was on the bridge of the *Lady Cecilia* heading into Buccaneer Bay when she grounded on Tattenham Ledge. This happened on Dec. 23, 1947 at about 4 p.m. She was en route to Powell River to pick up a load of millworkers going to Vancouver for Christmas. There were only six passengers aboard at the time. None of the passengers or crew were injured. The six passengers were then taken off the ship and continued their journey by other means. The ship's bow was badly damaged and it took three days to get the *Cecilia* off the rocks and beached in nearby Buccaneer Bay in order to make temporary repairs so she could be refloated and towed back to dry dock in Vancouver.

Sometime after this accident, Jimmy was sailing as Second Mate on the *Coquitlam* under Captain Jack Boden. Jimmy got himself involved in an altercation with Captain Boden and as a result Jimmy was banished from the bridge for the rest of the trip. When the *Coquitlam* docked in Vancouver, Jimmy was suspended.

Jimmy left the Union Steamships and went to work for Northland Navigation as a barge master. He travelled with the barge and on one occasion it had been towed to Klemtu. While coming across the sound, the derricks were down, so Jimmy was raising the derricks and was putting a runner or cable on the drum. Being by himself, he put the handle of the winch down so the drum would run free and he was feeding the cable into the drum. Apparently either his sleeve or his glove got tangled with the line and his arm was pulled off his shoulder - a terrible accident. The people at Klemtu tried to get him to the hospital at Bella Bella but he bled to death before he reached there.

Edward "Eddie" Georgeson

Capt. Edward "Eddie" Georgeson
(Mrs. Helen Neale)

Edward Georgeson's grandparents, Henry and Sofie Georgeson, settled on Galiano Island in 1863 on a little bay which now is called Georgeson Bay. From such early beginnings, the Georgeson family became synonymous with history and progress in and around the Gulf Islands. Edward's parents were John and Elizabeth Georgeson and he was one of 10 children, 7 boys and 3 girls. Edward was born in 1886. Edward learned to play the violin and his grandfather, whose nickname was Scottie, taught Edward and his brothers Scottish dancing. The Georgeson boys were always in great demand to perform their dancing and play their music at dances on the Islands, according to *Memories of Our Father*, a family history by Helen Neale and Joan Carolan. [146]

Edward was bright and was encouraged to leave the Island in order to better himself in his life ahead. He went to Vancouver at age 16 and though he had only an

Cars parked at the Vancouver docks
(C. Woods)

elementary school education, he also had determination, ambition and was a hard worker. He did become a success, for in time he was recognized as one of the best seamen and navigators on the B.C. Coast. He joined the Union Steamship Co. in 1910, sailing as a Mate on the *Camosun I*. With more studying and determination, he obtained his Coastal Master's ticket in 1912.

He served as Master of several Union Steamship vessels over the years, including the *Chasina*, *Camosun*, *Chilkoot*, *Catala*, and *Cardena*. In 1929 Captain Georgeson was on the Board of the Canadian Merchant Service Guild representing passenger ship Masters, and a dinner menu from the *Cardena* dated 1934 shows Edward Georgeson as the Master.

After 25 years of outstanding service, Captain Georgeson left the Union Steamship Co. in 1935 to join the B.C. Pilotage service. It is interesting to note that Captain Georgeson helped his younger brother Arthur obtain his Coastal Master's ticket in 1937, letting him study charts in the Georgeson house in Kitsilano. In 1944, Arthur also went into the Pilotage but lost his life on May 13, 1950, while working in Nootka Sound on the west coast of Vancouver Island. His was the first and still only life lost in the Pilotage service.

Captain Edward Georgeson was one of the great Union Steamship Captains, and cuts quite a swath in the history of B.C. coast steamboating. "He was respected by his Officers and crew alike. He was always immaculate in his dress. When Helen, one of his daughters, was allowed by her mother to iron and fold carefully the Captain's linen handkerchiefs, she felt very honoured and proud. At Christmas time she also recalled the many gifts the Captain received from people up and down the coast, even including a pair of long-johns one year. When his ship was laying over in Prince Rupert, Captain Georgeson would organize a baseball game with the crew. Mrs. Georgeson was very proud when the Canadian Navy asked to copy some of his marine maps he had drawn up himself, as they planned to sail into uncharted waters and knew of his reputation as an excellent navigator and seaman. He also did chartwork for the British Admiralty," his daughters wrote. [147]

Rushton describes one marvellous feat of navigating by Captain Georgeson when he was Master on the *Camosun I* in 1923. "The *Camosun I* was returning from Bella Coola which is 340 miles from Vancouver and he

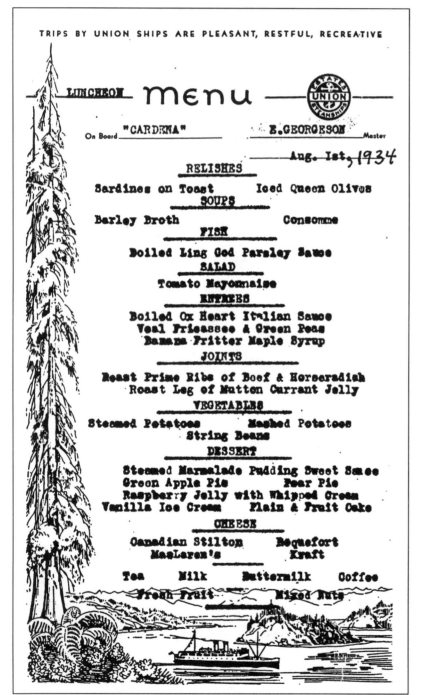

Luncheon menu on *Cardena* Aug. 1, 1934

had come all the way down the coast, being constantly on the bridge in a dense fog for over 40 hours, and on entering the harbour, still in a dense fog, the *Camosun I* went briefly ashore near Brockton Point. It was decided to take the passengers off the ship and it was done in a most unusual way. The Vancouver Fire Department was summoned to bring their ladder truck into Stanley Park and the passengers were disembarked over it." [148]

While in command of the *Cardena* in 1934 when she was servicing the canneries on the Skeena River, he also was instrumental in saving a cannery from fire, according to Jessie Van der Burg's company history: "Captain Georgeson and his ship were approaching the B.C. Packers cannery at Claxton, and he noticed flames and smoke rising from the cannery. He ordered full speed ahead and the *Cardena* was soon alongside the dock. Hoses were connected with the ship's pumps. Cannery men manned the hoses, and for three hours the *Cardena* pumped water into the fire. The blaze was confined and the cannery was saved from total destruction by Captain Georgeson and his crew." [149]

Another story of Captain Georgeson's determination and expert seamanship was written up in the *Vancouver Sun* in February, 1935. In brief, here is that story: "The *Cardena* arrived back into her home port of Vancouver 12 hours late after encountering freezing weather and tempestuous waves. Three of the crew suffered frostbite, seas were breaking over her, leaving deposits of polished ice all over the ship. As the *Cardena* was moving southward to cross the Queen Charlotte Sound, the ship ran into a howling blizzard whose grim music sang overpoweringly of the trouble ahead for her. Captain Georgeson made a decision to drop both anchors to ride out the storm. There was no rest for the officers and crew. The situation demanded the greatest watchfulness and the highest seamanship. For 12 hours the Captain and crew were peering through a raging snowstorm watching for a break in the weather, which came at last, and the *Cardena* was able to proceed to Vancouver, arriving well behind her schedule." [150] The reporter had to drag the story out of Captain Georgeson, as he was not one to seek publicity.

His fellow Officers held "Captain Eddie" in high esteem, with Fred Corneille describing him as "a very, very efficient Officer" despite being so short a man as to need to stand on a stool to see over the dodger on the bridge. Fred Smith, the famous Chief Engineer of the Company, said "I think Captain Georgeson was the smartest seaman - the smartest skipper - the Union Steamship Company ever had." Freddy knew and sailed with them all so his statement is a very powerful endorsement for Captain Georgeson, as a man and as a seaman.

Captain Georgeson was of mainly Scottish descent but did have some Indian blood in his system and as a result was sometimes referred to as "the Indian Skipper." Fred Smith the Chief Engineer however took great offence at anyone using that description, and in a taped conversation with Bob Hackett in 1970, explains why: "I liked him well. Some ape who had been a deckhand wrote a letter to Charlie Defieux which he printed in his "Ship and Shore" column in a Vancouver newspaper. I knew Charlie very well and was a good friend of his. I was so incensed over it, I wrote a letter to Charlie and he published it. I told him in my letter that the man who had called Captain Georgeson "the Indian Skipper" no matter what nationality, was wrong to say this. (Captain Georgeson) was an excellent seaman and a well respected gentleman. I received a letter from Captain Georgeson's widow thanking me for coming to his defence. She said it is very gratifying for his two daughters to read that."

Captain Georgeson died after only about five years with the B.C. Pilotage service, on Dec. 23, 1940 at age 54.

F. W. Gilbert

Capt. F. Gilbert
(D. Jones)

The Union Steamship Co. purchased the Terminal Steam Navigation Co. from Captain J.A. Cates in 1920 and two ships were included in the sale, the *Ballena* and the *Bowena*. Captain Gilbert, who was with Terminal Steam Navigation, transferred over to Union Steamships at the same time.

Prior to going into service for the Union Company, these two ships were tied up at the Union dock. The *Ballena* caught fire and was a total loss, and though the *Bowena* also caught fire it was rescued before too much damage was sustained. The Company repaired her at a cost of $15,000 and renamed her the *Cheam*.

The *Cheam* went into service for the Union Steamship Co. in 1921, and Captain Gilbert went out as her Master. Ship registry records show Captain Gilbert as being Master of the *Capilano* and signing off her on Sept. 10, 1929, so his period of service with the Company was approximately nine years.

Gilbert "Gibb" Jones, who in later years was a well-known and well-liked winchman and quartermaster with the Company, was Captain Gilbert's nephew.

The adjacent pictures were taken aboard the *Capilano* in 1928. One shows Captain Gilbert standing by himself at the stern of the *Capilano* and the other, which is a very rare picture from the Farina collection, shows Captain Gilbert seated with some of his Officers. Standing, left to right are, unidentified, Mate Harry Roach, 3rd Engineer J. Miller (who held the No. 1 Steam Ticket in Canada), and Purser Harvey Anthony. Seated, Captain Gilbert and Chief Engineer Paddy Farina.

Officers of the *Capilano* 1928: standing (centre), Mate Harry Roach, 3rd Engineer George Miller; seated, Capt. Gilbert, Chief Engineer Paddy Farina
(Farina Collection)

Lorne A. Godfrey

Lorne Godfrey was born in Manitoba and came to Vancouver at an early age. His death notice said he spent 35 years with the Union Steamship Company, which suggests he started with them in 1912. Very early in his career he was serving aboard the *Cassiar I* as Second Mate when she hit a reef off Privett Island, on Aug. 26, 1917 at 2:30 a.m. He was not on watch, but it's interesting to note he died 30 years later aboard another *Cassiar*, the *Cassiar II*, while serving as her Master on Sept. 23, 1947.

In 1919 Godfrey was 1st Mate on the *Chilliwack* and was in charge of loading 700 tons of ore, bound for Tacoma. Before she sailed, the ore had frozen in the ship's hold and as she proceeded south, it thawed and became an unstable fluid mass, giving the *Chilliwack* a 30 degree list. She encountered heavy seas and had to be beached. Eventually, after three days of backbreaking work restowing and barricading the ore, the ship was again seaworthy and completed her trip to Tacoma.

Captain Godfrey and Captain Aspinall frequently sailed together, with Godfrey the senior of the two. Word has it that they didn't like each other and when one came into the wheelhouse, the other went out. However, they did have one thing in common and that was their love of sports. If the ship they were on was in Prince Rupert unloading freight, the two of them would rush up town together to the local soccer field and watch a game being played. After the game, arriving back at the ship, the two would be volubly arguing over the game they had just watched.

During his career, Captain Godfrey served aboard many of the Union ships as Master. It is on record he was Master of the *Lady Cecilia* when she participated in the Win the War cruises on July 24, 1940.

Captain Godfrey died "with his boots on" aboard the *Cassiar II*, and Tom Lucas, the well-known Mate and later Master of the fleet, was aboard when Captain Godfrey died. Tom related the following story to his nephew, Ed Roach, who was also with the Company but not aboard at the time. "The *Cassiar* was outward bound from Prince Rupert and Tom Lucas was on the bridge. It was a dark, rainy and windy night. Visibility was very poor. Tom was having trouble picking up the Tripple Island light, so he went back and knocked on Captain Godfrey's cabin door and said loudly, 'Come out here, I'm having a bit of trouble and I need a hand.' He then went back to the bridge expecting him to be right up. Several minutes went by and the Captain still hadn't showed up so Tom went back again, this time opened the door and said, 'Come on, Christ, you're getting paid for this, I need help!' But still getting no response, Tom went into the cabin and found the Captain - dead. He had had a heart attack and died in his cabin. He had been Captain on the *Cassiar* for the last four years."

The pall bearers at his funeral were all Union Captains: A.C. MacLennan, A.E. Walsh, J.J. Halcrow, N. Campbell, John Boden and J.J. Hunter.

Capt. L.A. Godfrey
(Vancouver newspaper clipping on his death, Sept. 1947)

Neil Gray

Capt. Neil Gray, Master of *Lady Cecilia* 1939 *(Hackett Collection)*

Neil Gray was described by Gerald Rushton as being a quiet Argyllshire seaman. He started with the Union Company in 1906 at the age of 26. In 1910 he was serving as Second Mate on the *Capilano I*, a freighter passenger type vessel, one of the three pre-fab ships assembled in Coal Harbour for the Company.

April 1917 finds Neil Gray as Captain of the *Coquitlam I*, taking supplies to Drumlumon mine located in a small inlet off Douglas Channel. The tides in the inlet run very strong. Freddie Smith described them as being just like Seymour Narrows. Upon entering this inlet the strong tides took the ship into the rocks and her hull was punctured. She started taking on considerable water. Captain Gray decided to try and make a run for Lowe Inlet where there was a good place to beach her. It was about a three hour run but they made it. Unfortunately Captain Gray ran her straight onto the beach which left her stern in the water where the holes were that had to be patched.

A temporary patch was put in place by Chief Engineer Fred Smith and 2nd Engineer John Hogan. The patch held well enough so that the ship was able to continue and finish her run before returning to Vancouver where she went into drydock, with the patch still there and holding.

Next year, with Captain Gray still her master, The *Coquitlam* hit a deadhead in the Queen Charlotte Sound and lost her propeller. As there was no wireless in those days, the *Coquitlam* just had to wallow in the swells and wait for a passing ship to come by and help them. As it happened, the Union Steamship *Venture* came by and took her in tow to Alert Bay, where they beached her again. A replacement propeller was brought up from Vancouver and installed, again under the direction of Chief Engineer Fred Smith.

The *Lady Cecilia* arrived in 1925 and Captain Gray served on her as Master almost continually until 1937. On Dec. 27, 1925 the *Lady Cecilia* was proceeding to Powell River on a charter run returning people to Powell River after the Christmas holidays. It was a foggy day and Captain Gray was on the bridge. His ship was loaded to capacity. The *Lady Cynthia* under Captain Jack Boden was called into service to take the overload. The *Cowichan* was southbound and off of Sechelt. With both ships sounding their whistles in the fog, they passed each other safely, but Captain Wilson on the *Cowichan* was not aware that the *Lady Cynthia* was following and the two ships collided in the dense fog. The *Lady Cynthia*, with her sharp bow slashed into the *Cowichan* and she sank in 10 minutes, but no lives were lost, thanks to the quick thinking of Captain Wilson of the *Cowichan* and Captain Boden of the *Lady Cynthia*.

Alex Reid tells the following story about Captain Gray. It took place on the *Lady Cynthia* when she was doing the West Howe Sound run. Being a day run, she only carried one quartermaster and the deckhands took turns relieving him during the day. George Corson was the quartermaster and Alex went up to relieve him. Alex was then at the wheel, Captain Gray was at the little table to the right where the log book was kept. He was reading the latest company bulletin on next week's schedule for the ship. George Corson stopped on his way out and peered over the Captain's shoulder to read it as well. Alex also leaned over to try and see what it said. He happened to look up and see where the ship was heading and there, dead ahead, was a monstrous log. They were heading right for it with no chance to miss it at all. He hollered, "Oh my God, we're going to hit a log!" Captain Gray quickly signalled Stop Engines. The log rolled under the ship and fortunately didn't damage the propeller. George Corson quickly took over the wheel and said to Alex, "You better get the hell out of here, fast." Alex did just that, but he went out the wrong door and ran right into Captain Gray. "He kicked me so hard in the bum as I passed, I can still feel it," Alex said.

Later he was supposed to go up again and relieve the quartermaster and he tried to get someone, anyone, to take his place. They all said, "No, you've got to go." Reluctantly he went up. These guys knew Captain Gray better than Alex. The next landing was at Bowen Island, so Alex sneaked into the wheelhouse on the quick stop and turn around. When the Captain came into the wheelhouse, Alex thought he was going to get a tongue lashing, but he didn't. "You know, he never said a word about our earlier meeting, all he said was 'Well we didn't lose any time there did we boy?'"

Captain Gray died in 1939 but just before he died he had ordered a new bridge coat for himself. This is a heavy, long coat or great coat as they were often called. Unfortunately he died before he had a chance to wear it. His widow gave the coat to Captain Harry Roach and he wore it for years, according to his son, Ed Roach.

There is an interesting story about Wee Angus McNeill and this coat. Angus was a very superstitious fellow and there is a saying amongst seamen that "You don't wear a dead man's clothes." Angus was serving as Mate under Captain Roach, who of course would be wearing the bridge coat at times. If Captain Roach happened to leave it hanging in the wheelhouse, Wee Angus would not go in or stay there until it was removed. Captain Gray was dead but his ghost haunted poor Angus!

Stanley Birchell "Stan" Green

3rd Mate Stan Green
(S. Green)

Stan was a deep sea man and served in the Canadian Navy during the Second World War. He joined the Union Steamship Company and signed aboard the Frank Waterhouse ship *Southholm* as Third Mate. During his career, he alternated between the two fleets, being on the Waterhouse ships during the winter, and summers on the Union ships. The Union Steamship skippers he remembers sailing with were, Captains Boden, Roach, McLean, Yates, Hunter and Findlay.

The first Union ship he joined was the *Chelohsin* and her skipper was Harry Roach. He sailed as Third Mate.

The picture accompanying this story shows him in uniform but it can be seen it was his navy uniform with the Canada emblem on the shoulder. Stan said, "I just tore off two navy stripes and kept one in place when I joined the Union Steamships."

On Stan's first trip there was a full load of loggers aboard. They had been partying in town for a week or so and they were still partying when they came aboard. After the ship sailed, they got out of hand and Stan had to gather up the crew, who were given night sticks to help in quieting the loggers. It was a rough start for his first trip.

Sailing with Captain Findlay came about in an unusual way. Stan had come from India off a deep sea vessel and was going to write for his Mate's foreign-going ticket. The Union Steamship Co. wanted to bring a large ship, the *Kensington Park*, from eastern Canada to Vancouver. Captain Findlay came out of retirement to serve as Master. Even though Stan was not a Union Steamship employee he was approached because they needed a mate to go with Captain Findlay. Stan signed on. It was 1943 and the war was on, so they had to sail in convoy down the East Coast. The *Kensington Park* was the lead ship in the convoy and this was all new to Captain Findlay. She carried a full load of paper which was unloaded in Tampa, Florida. Stan said that Captain Findlay was one of the finest seamen he had ever sailed with. Four years later Stan joined the Union Steamship Co. himself.

In 1950, the Company wanted to bring another ship around from the East Coast named the *Blue Peter II*. She was formerly named the *City of Belleville*. A new man in the Company, Jim Stewart, was to be the Captain. Ralph Wills was to be Chief Officer, Stan Green was Second Mate and Johnny Horne was Third Mate. They loaded a full load of nitrates in Hopewell, Virginia. They stopped in Los Angeles and picked up a deck load of winches. The nitrates were discharged at James Island. After arriving in Vancouver, the ship's name was changed to the *Cassiar III*.

Early in Stan's career with the Union Steamship Co. he was posted to the *Cardena* under Captain Boden. Captain Boden was of the old school and he did not particularly like young deep water officers. Captain Boden started to criticize everything Stan did. Finally Stan had had enough and told Captain Boden when they next arrived in Vancouver he was going right up to Captain Suffield, the Marine Superintendent and lay a complaint. Captain Suffield realized the situation and transferred Stan to another ship. Other young officers had experienced the same treatment from Captain Boden and had refused to sail with him.

Other young officers I have interviewed said that Captain Suffield liked the younger men with their new ideas and they got along fine with him. Some of the senior Deck Officers in the fleet did not get along with Captain Suffield at all.

Stan served for a while on the *Lady Alexandra* under Captain Yates, and he well recalls the Moonlight Cruises. I asked him to tell me about some of the goings on during the cruises and he said, "I'd rather not commit myself."

He spent a lot of time on the Alaska Cruises under Captain Harry McLean. He felt that Captain McLean was the ideal Captain for that cruise ship. He loved parties and entertaining the passengers, yet at the same time he was a very capable seaman, Stan said. Captain McLean had a masquerade party every trip for the passengers and he made sure all of his officers participated. Harold Humphreys, the Chief Steward, said "Stan would always dress up as a woman for these parties and was a big hit."

Stan sailed on the *Cardena* as Second Mate under Captain Harry Roach. One trip he remembers well, for they went aground twice in 24 hours!

The first time was at Savary Island on Nov. 13, 1950. The tide was low but Captain Roach misjudged it and headed in for a landing but the ship grounded in the sand. With the falling tide, the sand just sucked in and held her fast. Stan tried rocking the ship to break her loose, using the winches to swing a load of boom chains, side to side, but she wouldn't budge. They sat there for three or four hours before she floated free.

Later in the same day in trying to make a landing at Surge Narrows, coming around a point, the strong tidal current took the *Cardena* ashore, a short distance from the dock. Stan says that he ran wire lines from the two masts to large trees on the point. This was a safety measure to make sure that on a falling tide the ship would be held upright. The passengers were taken off and over to the dock in lifeboats for safety reasons, but again the *Cardena* floated off on the rising tide and she was able to proceed on her run.

On the morning of Oct. 23, 1953 the *Cardena* collided with the outward-bound CPR *Princess Elizabeth* almost under the Lions Gate Bridge. The *Cardena* under Captain Roach was proceeding into Vancouver and there was a dense fog. Stan was on watch with Captain Roach and he had called in to the bridge lookout from Cape Roger Curtis and was told it was all clear. He called in to the bridge again at Point Atkinson and again was told it was all clear, so the *Cardena*, with its whistle sounding, kept coming in. Stan said, "Captain Roach and I were on the bridge sounding our whistle, peering through the fog and as we were just approaching the Lions Gate Bridge, all of a sudden this ship came right through and hit us in the bow. She drove about 10 to 15 feet into the *Cardena*'s port side. When they hit us I yelled to them, "Keep going ahead, to hold us together, and push us over into English Bay."

The two ships were locked together and did maneuver themselves over into English Bay, away from other ship traffic. Both ships were damaged above the waterline so there was no worry about either ship taking on water. Stan said that the *Cardena*'s passengers were taken ashore to Stanley Park by lifeboats. Both ships were so tightly locked together that they had to get a cutting torch to cut them apart.

According to Stan, the collision should never have happened because when the CPR ship was leaving Vancouver they were supposed to phone the Lions Gate Bridge lookout and report that they were coming out of the harbour but they had forgotten to do so. In the subsequent inquiry, the attendant on the Lions Gate Bridge lookout swore on the stand that he had never been called by the CPR ship.

The *Cardena*, once she was separated from the *Elizabeth*, was able to proceed under her own power into the Vancouver dock. Stan recalls putting a collision mat over the hole, but as it was above the waterline there wasn't much worry about the ship taking on water.

Stan Green enjoying deck shuffleboard (*Ashmore Collection*)

Stan was with Company for another year after this accident but he could see the Company's fortunes were slipping and he left the Company in March, 1954. He joined the RCMP patrol boat serving up and down the West Coast of Vancouver Island. He was with them for 22 years. He left them and went to work on the Department of Highways ship running between Powell

River and Little River at Comox. Then he was on the Port McNeill-Sointula-Alert Bay route. He retired from active sea life in 1985 and is living in Comox with his wife Betty.

Stan has always been an avid and accomplished musician. He played trumpet in a high school orchestra. He still plays regularly for the Comox Concert Orchestra but now plays the saxophone because he doesn't have to practice it as much as the trumpet.

Joseph Kennidy "Joe" Hackett

Joseph "Joe" Hackett
(Mrs. Tosh Collection)

Very little has been recorded about this man. He is remembered more by his nickname of "Mouldy Joe" than anything else. I was also told that he had another nickname which was "Key Hole."

In one of the Guild Annuals, I discovered he was born in Dumarton, Scotland and he received his Coasting Competency ticket in examinations held in Vancouver in 1924. He is mentioned once in Rushton's *Whistle Up the Inlet* as having served as a Mate in the Union Steamship Co. for over a decade since 1928.

I vaguely recall seeing him at Butedale when I was aboard the old *Cassiar*. He had come aboard to see his old shipmates while we were unloading freight and he was the subject of much conversation at the mess table after we had sailed and were on our way to Prince Rupert. I remember him more for his unusual nickname than anything else, and when I asked others about Joe Hackett the usual answer was, "Oh yeah, Mouldy Joe," but that's about all they remembered as well.

It seems he never had his uniform cleaned and always was unkempt. Johnny Horne said, "He lived in his sea boots, never cleaned his clothes, his room or his bunk, so the nickname 'Mouldy Joe' was pinned on him. According to Johnny, later in life he became very religious.

Johnny Smith, an ex Union hand and later a Master on B.C. Ferries, recalled that when the *Cheakamus* was sold to the U.S. Department of Transport Service in 1942 and converted into a tow boat, Joe Hackett went to work for them during the war, running to Alaska. He was also on call to the Union Steamships. He made big money while working for the Americans and supposedly never paid any Canadian income tax on it. It is reported that he was in big trouble when it was discovered.

He didn't return to the Union Steamship Co. when the war was over but went to work for Canfisco as a Master/Mate on one of their fish packers. He lost a packer which was overloaded with herring off the Sandheads. After this incident he more or less disappeared from the coastwise shipping scene.

John Johnston Halcrow

John Halcrow was often referred to as "The Viking." He was born in Sandwich on the Shetland Islands and his thick Scottish brogue never left him.

On one occasion when he was Second Mate and being in charge of unloading freight, he came to the hatch and yelled some instructions down to the crew on the freight deck, What he said and what they thought he said were two different things. The load of freight came up the same as before. Once more he came and yelled down the same order, and still the freight came out of the hold the same way. Seeing this, Halcrow quickly scampered down to the freight deck and in his explosive manner started to berate the crew. When there was a pause in his tirade one of the crew members looked at him and said, "For Christ sake man, speak English."

John Halcrow came to Canada in 1916 and worked for a short time for the Griffiths Shipping Co. He went back to Scotland to marry his wife Jessie and brought her to Canada. She became an expert seamstress, working in an exclusive ladies wear shop on South Granville. He went overseas in 1917 with the Canadian Army and served in France. He started with the Union Steamships on August 5, 1919 as a deckhand on the *Chilco* and received his coastal Mate's ticket in 1924. When he retired he was the 12th senior Company employee.

John was a big strong man and often was referred to as "Big John." John's movements were always somewhat boisterous. Every door he opened aboard ship was never just closed, it was slammed shut. Many a pointer of a ship's telegraph was broken by his violent action in giving signals.

Alan Thomas, an executive with the Union Steamship Co., recalled the following incident. "I had occasion to go down to the *Lady Rose* one evening. She was sailing to East Howe Sound. She would lay over at Squamish and do the return trip next morning, arriving back about 11 a.m. Everything was being made ready for sailing. The winches were run by compressed air and operated by two handles in the wheelhouse. Halcrow was operating them and taking up the slack by putting the hook of the line in the eye of the bow. He applied too much pressure. The next thing, one of the booms came down with a resounding crash on top the wheelhouse. As he was about to sail he had to make the best of the situation and figure out what to tell management next day."

"The Viking" liked his fish. Norrie Wood, an ex-Purser with the Company said, "Every time Captain Halcrow sat down to dinner and if halibut was on the menu, he would say, 'Ah, beef of the sea.'"

Dennis Shaw, another well-known Purser with the Company, recalls a feed of shiners aboard the *Lady Rose*. "We were putting into Seaside Park, about 7:30 p.m. and Halcrow, who was the Mate at the time, came running down to the galley and said, "Hey Danny, throw some butter in the big skillet." A couple minutes later he came

Capt. John Halcrow
(Ashmore Collection)

Jack Halcrow "The Viking" as 3rd Mate in 1928
(H. Ives)

Charles Hamer as a naval officer in Victoria 1951
(C. Hamer)

Captain Halcrow's life had a very sad ending. The Union Steamship Company did not set up a pension plan for its employees until its latter years, and when he retired he had a pension of only $100 a month. He supplemented this by checking freight on the Packers dock and doing night watching work on deep sea ships arriving in port. He also worked as a patrol man at the PNE, it has been said.

His wife Jessie had a stroke and was incompetent for over a year before she died. Captain Halcrow had turned all of his earnings over to her and she had invested it. Reports say that she gave him $1.50 a week for tobacco. He had never paid any attention to where she was investing the money and when she died he had no idea where all the money was. A thorough search was made of all the financial houses and banks. He searched for two years and never found a trace of the money. He gave up and went back to the Shetland Islands a broken man. He died while walking by himself along a lonely stretch of beach. His body was found the next day above the high tide mark.

back with a bucket full of shiners, which had been swimming around the dock at Seaside. They drained the water off and there must have been a half bucket of live shiners. He just dumped the whole works of live shiners into this big frying pan. They cooked them up, and Captain Malcolmson joined them and they had had kippers for breakfast, for lunch and they had Alaska Black Cod, and of course the shiners for dinner. In the evening they all sat down to play a game of bridge and before going to bed they had a 'mug up.' I asked them what they would like and do you know what they said? Sardine sandwiches!"

Towards the end of John's career his hearing began to fail him. He spent most of his latter days as Master of the *Camosun*. He retired in 1955. He was well-known for two hobbies, photography and model boat building. Often he could be seen at Trout Lake racing his model boats.

Charles Hamer

The name Charles Hamer is relatively unknown in the annals of Union Steamship events, mainly because he was only with the Company for a little over a year, but during that short time he was a participant in the fateful grounding of the *Chelohsin* at Stanley Park on Nov. 6, 1949. Mr. Hamer was Third Mate at the time.

The grounding and loss of the *Chelohsin* was a blow to the Company. The weather was foggy and it took place almost at the entrance to the First Narrows. When the fog cleared, the ship could be plainly seen from Lions Gate Bridge and areas of the North Shore. Newspapers reported a traffic nightmare ensued because of all the sightseers.

The Deck Officers at the time were Captain Alfred Aspinall (who had 25 years service with the company), Chief Officer Paddy Hannigan, Second Mate William Nicholson, and Charles Hamer, Third Mate.

There has always been some controversy about this accident. The newspaper stories at the time never came to grips with the "down to earth" details as to what actually happened. In the following edited excerpts from his own written statement, Charles Hamer for the first time recounts exactly how he saw the grounding unfold, and he expresses his opinions about the Company's part in the dramatic accident.

"Sunday, November 6, 1949 found *Chelohsin* southbound on Route 5A, calling at Lund in decreasing visibility. On leaving Lund, the Type 268 radar was started up but no picture could be obtained on the scan (cathode ray tube). While calling at Savary Island and en route to Westview (Powell River), I as Third Mate (with operational but not maintenance experience of radar) inspected and changed fuses and visually checked what electric connections I could, but was unable to right the problem. *Chelohsin* made the Westview landing in decreasing visibility.

"It was known that a radar technician resided in Powell River, and the Master delayed departure while awaiting an answer to a telephone request he had made to the Company for authority to employ this individual to repair the set. This request was denied.

The last days of S.S. *Chelohsin* aground off Stanley Park
(F. Rogers Collection)

"The immediate approaches to Pender Harbour saw a slight improvement in visibility and the landing was made without difficulty. Leaving Pender Harbour the fog clamped right down and the Sechelt landing was made with difficulty.

"The call at Wilson Creek I believe was omitted and the landing at Roberts Creek was made only with the assistance of automobile horns and lights at either end of the dock. Thus from Powell River south, most of the run had been by dead reckoning, wheelhouse log, and whistle echo.

"It should be noted at this point, it being a Sunday, a goodly number of passengers, many of them weekend commuters from the city, had been embarked at each stop, so that the *Chelohsin* had a very full load. One of the passengers, a lady, had one or two crates of valuable fur-bearing animals. [The *Vancouver Sun* newspaper report of the day says they were chinchillas worth $2,000.]

"At 3 p.m., with *Chelohsin* abeam of Point Atkinson, the Chief Officer and Third Mate were relieved by the Master and Second Mate. Through a brief thinning of the fog, we all saw and heard Point Atkinson lighthouse and all concurred the vessel was in her correct position. The fog immediately closed in again, thicker than ever, and the Master voiced his doubt about the wisdom of entering First Narrows under the prevailing conditions of thick fog and a strong ebb tide. He stated his intention of lying in English Bay until there was some improvement.

"At this point, the Chief Officer and Third Mate left the bridge, while the Master proceeded to his quarters on the starboard side, abaft the wheelhouse and below the bridge, to use the radio telephone which was installed there and not within hearing of the bridge. He must have received a reply in short order, as much later, during the inquiry into the grounding, it became known that the signalmen on the Lions Gate Bridge, who were watching the *Chelohsin* on their radar, had been trying to contact the vessel by radio telephone from shortly after the time she had passed Point Atkinson.

"That *Chelohsin* proceeded on toward First Narrows, is fact. However, what is not clear is what took place in the Master's cabin. That he changed his mind and did not phone the Company with his intentions, is a possibility, though extremely unlikely, as he was <u>most</u> emphatic about his intentions when he left the bridge. That leaves the question, if he did make the call, who answered it, and what was said to a Master showing prudence with respect to the safety of a vessel committed to his charge?

"As First Narrows was approached, speed was reduced on hearing the sound signals of two vessels, one unencumbered and the other with a tow.

"At this point, I was below and contemplated returning to the bridge, but knowing the Chief Officer had already gone up, I decided 'too many cooks' etcetera and therefore remained handy in my cabin below and just abaft the bridge on the port side, where a call would bring me out if needed.

"When *Chelohsin* struck, there was some grinding noise and a 'jumping' motion at the forward end of the vessel that caused many to believe that we had fouled a log boom - the tow we had heard.

"It soon became apparent that this was not the case but that we were aground as proved by a quick inspection, and that we were held fast.

"There appeared to be no immediate danger except that the tide was ebbing and still had some way to go. As the water dropped, there was no certainty that the vessel would remain upright or heel steeply. The Master therefore decided to put all the passengers ashore immediately. Boat stations were called and boats swung out and manned. Not as easy as it sounds, as there was a slight starboard list, making it an uphill swing for the port radial davits.

"With the number of passengers aboard, orders were issued that no baggage was to be allowed in the boats. This gave rise to some hassle and frayed tempers, strangely enough on the part of male passengers, while the females seemed to accept it all calmly. (Perhaps this is what gave rise to the insinuation in the local press that the officers appeared to 'have taken drink' - which was definitely not so.) The only lady who did raise an objection regarding baggage was the owner of the fur-bearing animals, and perhaps understandably. On being assured that as soon as the passengers were landed, the boat would return for the animals (which it did), she was reasonably content. Of course, the lifeboats grounded before reaching dry land, so some passengers were carried ashore by the boat's crew. It is understood that buses were quickly on the scene to take the people to town.

"The boats returned to the ship, where further and fruitless attempts to free her were made. While this was going on, a tug was standing by but could not come alongside due to there being insufficient water. One of the Freight Clerks, Mr. J. Pattison and myself were instructed to remove the mail sacks from the ship to tug and thence ashore. [The ship's registry shows the freight clerk as a Mr. H. Pattison.]

"By this time, the ship's lighting had failed, so it would have been impossible to check the mail against the manifest. There seemed to be an unusually large amount of mail, including lock sacks. Accordingly, with the aid of weakening flashlights, we each made our own tallies as the mail was transferred to a lifeboat, repeated this on transferring to the tug, and again to the dock. In every case, our count of mail sacks and lock sacks came out the same and we both agreed upon our individual tallies. Though I don't recall which dock was used, I do recall a dock policeman there, and he also making a count.

"Mr. Pattison and I returned to the ship in the tug, only to be joined by other crew members and put ashore again with instructions to go home. By this time it was daylight.

"By noon it was discovered that a lock sack was missing and Mr. Pattison and I were called back in to account for it, and were checked again and again during the ensuing days by the RCMP.

"Three years later, on July 27, 1952, having served with the RCN in Korea, I was walking down Granville Street with my lovely bride, on the first day of our honeymoon, when we met up with Mr. Pattison coming from the direction of the Post Office. He had some astounding news! He reported that the postal authorities were having renovations and painting done in the Post Office and had, that very morning, found the missing lock sack intact behind a bin! What a wedding gift! Incidentally, to this very day, the Post Office has never contacted me, nor said a word to me in any way about this matter."

The reader can see from Hamer's account of this event that many questions arise and make one wonder more than ever that perhaps the Company was more at fault in the overall picture than is generally thought. Mr. Hamer felt that way, as you can see in the following conclusion to his written statement:

"Evidence at the inquiry following the grounding showed that the Lions Gate signalmen could not only see the movement of other traffic on their radar, but also that as *Chelohsin* approached she was veering more and more towards Stanley Park. Was this brought about by the strong ebb currents or by the Master tending to steer away from the West Vancouver shore for safety because of the notoriously inaccurate whistle echoes, or was he obeying the rule of the road and keeping to the starboard side of the channel in the presence of other shipping whose fog signals he could hear or was it a combination of all three?

"It must have been frustrating to say the least for Lions Gate staff to see an accident about to take place and be so impotent because their radio transmissions were being (apparently) ignored.

"It is my primary and strong belief that little blame for the grounding lies at the feet of the Master or those on the bridge with him - in fact, one could say he was blameless because:

1. No echo sounder was fitted in the vessel;
2. The repair and maintenance clause in the lease agreement should have been unacceptable to the underwriter, let alone the owner;
3. No formal radar training had been provided the ship's officers;
4. The siting of the radio telephone should have been unacceptable to the Steamship Inspector, the underwriter and the owner.
5. What really transpired in the Master's call to the owner (or his representative) from the area of Point Atkinson?

"It is my belief that the owners, underwriters and Steamship Inspection Services were criminally negligent with respect to a passenger-carrying vessel. The Master's only fault lies in his sailing in such an ill-found vessel."

Charles Hamer started with the Union Steamship Company in the fall of 1948, as Third Mate on the *Chelohsin*, with Harry Roach as the Master. He had come from England and had been serving on deep sea ships since the age of 13.

Coming to the coastal shipping trade was frightening and somewhat bewildering for him because of the constant proximity of land to the ship compared with deep sea, where one might not see land for several

Capt. M.J. "Paddy" Hannigan
(Ashmore Collection)

days. As well, he was amazed at the great deal of local knowledge required by the Deck Officers, to be able to navigate so well under the great difficulty of the B.C. coast. Here's how Mr. Hamer describes his initiation to coastal navigating:

"We left Cracroft to enter Chatham Channel, and I came on watch at midnight to find Captain Roach and Chief Officer Owen Jones peering down at the water with a flash light from the port side of the bridge. Being nosey, I asked what they were looking for.

" 'Here son,' said Captain Roach, giving me the flashlight, 'Let us know when rocks are abeam.' To a deep water man yet! My hair went straight up. Pretty soon the rocks appeared, close, very close indeed, as a matter of fact. I realized why they were so named, as it was plain to see they were much-loved by all bird life in the area. These rocks were so named by the Union Steamship deck officers and marked on charts as White Rocks, but this was purely only a Company name. In time I learned there were many others, such as Lonesome Pine, Dead Fir, The Beeches etc. However I still can't make up my mind about our proximity to white rocks that night. Was it a Harry Roach leg pull, was it getting a greenhorn familiar to the West Coast - or what?"

M. J. "Paddy" Hannigan

Paddy, without a doubt, was one of "the" characters to appear on the scene of the Union Steamships. He was as Irish as the Blarney Stone itself. I was fortunate to have known and sailed with him as he was one of a kind. I believe he knew his trade well, was a no-nonsense handler of his seamen and had their grudging respect. However, when he became Master he did not have the reputation of being a good ship handler. In fact, one of his contemporaries said of him, "He couldn't dock a kiddie car!"

Records show that Paddy came to Vancouver on a Blue Funnel Line ship and he jumped ship, then joined the Union Steamship Co. as a seaman in 1930. His first ship was the *Chilliwack*, and a story is told about Paddy having his first run-in with Eric Suffield, who was Mate on the *Chilliwack* at the time and who later became Marine Superintendent of the Union Steamships. They were unloading coal at Prince Rupert and Paddy was in the hold shovelling coal, and had been for hours. At 6 a.m. Suffield, who had had a good night's sleep, came on watch, looked down into the hold and hollered, "Do you fellows want anything?" This really got to Paddy, for in short time that he had known Suffield, he never knew of him doing anybody a favour. So Paddy hollered back, "Yeah, send down a bucket of ice to cool my shovel, it's red hot." From that day on, Paddy and Eric were at loggerheads with each other.

Paddy then went on to become a winchman, and ran winches for many years.

During a period when I was on the *Cassiar*, Paddy was Second Mate and we used to play chess together. Always, he fiercely wanted to win, and as I recall, he usually did. He also was a great horse player. Every year on his holidays, he and his wife would go south, along with Alex MacDonald and his wife, to play the horses. Alex MacDonald was well-known to Union people as he was a partner with Fred Wastell in the mill at Telegraph Cove. Paddy also loved the ladies. I don't think you could say he was handsome but I guess his thick Irish brogue was very captivating.

There is one very fascinating story in Paddy's life. He was one of a group of men who set out on Feb. 21, 1932, under the lead of Col. J. Leckie, C.M.G., C.B.E., D.S.O., F.R.B.S., who sailed from Vancouver on the Silver Wave to search for the supposedly buried treasure on Cocos Island.

Paddy wrote up a complete and detailed story about this expedition which he had copyrighted in 1937. I have a copy of the first part of this story which was published in the 1937 edition of the *Canadian Merchant Service Guild Annual*. It's interesting reading and shows full well Paddy's love of detail. This first part ends with a sentence that reads, "We did considerable work on the place but the only things we found were old picks and shovels."

One of the stories I collected about Paddy's Union Steamship days was when he was Mate on the *Lady Pam* plying the west Howe Sound route. Going from New Brighton to Gambier, there was a shortcut one could take if the tide was right, between Twin Islands. The wheel on the *Pam* was enormous; when one stood on the deck, the spoke would be about the height of your neck. Often two men were needed to turn it, one pulling, the other lifting, and once you were on course you jammed a stool under it, where the pressure was. Then when you wanted to come amidships, the Officer would say, "O.K., let her run."

On this trip, they had taken on an old man, as a favour to someone. He was an alcoholic and was living on skid row. He was sick and really wasn't capable of doing the job. It so happened he was at the wheel when Paddy decided to take the shortcut. This required some strong pulling on the wheel which the old man couldn't handle. Paddy himself was on one side of the wheel and could see this. Suddenly he blew the *Pam*'s whistle and the crew popped out of the fo'c'sle and Paddy hollered, "One of you guys come up here, this old bastard couldn't pull the skin off a banana!"

Like I said, Paddy was "a no-nonsense guy."

Paddy was with the Union until the end, 1958. He then went over to the Black Ball Ferries running out of Horseshoe Bay. He went from there to become Master for the B.C. Ferries. He was Master of the *Tsawwassen* on her maiden voyage. During his time with the Ferries he gained the nickname of "Hard Over Hannigan." Learning his trade on the Union Steamships, he was used to running a ship from point to point and changing course abruptly at the point. The B.C. Ferries operation was a little different, one could run a ship a little easier and not have to change courses so often. But Paddy never changed his way. Paddy still ran to a point and then swung the ship over quickly. As a result, dishes and cutlery and whatever was loose would come clattering to the deck, so it was natural the "Hard Over Hannigan" nickname stuck to him.

Left: "Paddy" Hannigan on the bridge
(J.Smith Collection)

Below: M.J. "Paddy" Hannigan
(Skinner Collection, Vancouver Maritime Museum)

When the Blackball Line came into B.C. and was later taken over by B.C. Ferries, a number of Union Steamship fellows left and joined this new company. Some fellows who were lower in the seniority list at the U.S.S. Co. ended up being senior to others who came over later. This created hard feelings and friction developed. Paddy Hannigan was one fellow who was caught up in this situation, although I'm told he handled it better than others. This circumstance came to be known and was referred to as the Union Steamship Circus.

Another story about Paddy is when Monty Aldous was head of B.C. Ferries, he called Paddy into his office. For some reason he was anxious for the ships' officers to wear their uniforms around town when they were on shore whenever possible. Paddy's laconic answer was, "Mr. Aldous, wearing a uniform ashore is like seeing a seagull in Saskatchewan!"

Paddy developed heart trouble and had a pacer put in his chest. He died at home a few years before the retirement age of 65.

Victor D. "Vic" Hayman

Capt. Vic Hayman
S.S. *Cassiar* 1945
(Twigg Collection)

Vic was born in Nova Scotia in 1896. He came to B.C. and joined Union Steamships in 1922, signing aboard the *Cheakamus* as a deckhand. Frank Skinner, former Freight Clerk and later Agent for the Company at Prince Rupert, recalled sailing with Vic when he was quartermaster aboard the *Lady Alex* in 1925/26.

Like others, Vic worked his way up the ladder and served as Mate and then Master on several ships including the *Capilano II* and the *Lady Rose*. I sailed with Vic when he was Chief Officer aboard the *Cassiar* on the Queen Charlotte Islands run. The accompanying picture shows Vic on the bridge on the *Cassiar*, the former *Prince John*. Billy McCombe was the Master at that time.

During his career Vic served aboard every ship in the fleet. He was quartermaster on the *Cowichan* and had just gone off watch when she was rammed and sunk by the *Lady Cynthia* on a foggy winter night, Dec. 27, 1925. Vic was able to dash down to his cabin, which by then was knee deep in water, to save a new suit of clothes he had just bought. Vic of course told his wife all about this sinking and his version of the affair differs in one particular aspect over the one that is usually told. Vic told his wife that Captain Wilson was the real hero, not Captain Boden, as is commonly reported. Vic said that Captain Wilson had to plead with Captain Boden to keep his ship pushing into the gaping hole in the *Cowichan*'s side, to enable the passengers and crew of the *Cowichan* to pass over to the *Cynthia* before she sank. Captain Boden apparently had other ideas, but it was really Captain Wilson's coolness and quick thinking that night that saved everyone aboard his ship and when the Cynthia did back away, the *Cowichan* sank, without a trace, in 10 minutes.

Tex Lyon, the wharfinger at Port Hardy for years, tells the story about taking Vic on a fishing trip in Port Hardy while his ship was unloading. Vic had never caught a fish nor had he been fishing before. So Tex took Vic out in the bay and they hadn't gone very far away from the wharf when he hooked into a big one. As Tex says, Vic had no experience at all in fishing and he just hauled the line in hand over hand until he had brought the fish right alongside the boat. It was too big to bring aboard so he just bent the line over the side of the boat and the fish waggled its head, until it tore itself off the hook!

After that disappointing experience Vic never wanted to go fishing again. Tex didn't say whether or not they were fishing his favorite fishing spots, "Hook Ass Bay" near his home, or over in "Bass Hole."

Vic's career at sea was cut short by serious eye trouble. His eyesight began to fail him so he came ashore to work on the Union dock as a checker in the late 1940s. He retired from the Union Steamships in 1954 and at that time he was the 20th senior employee in the Company. Vic had joined the Checkers Union and he began to work on call at various docks in the harbour. Soon he was working steady. Word has it that he eventually was in charge of the Royal Mail and baggage claims at Ballantyne Pier.

His health was beginning to fail him. He suffered from emphysema and his eyesight was getting worse, so he had to retire. He was over 70 when he retired, and he died in 1984.

John "Johnny" Ian Audley Horne

John, or Johnny as he is better known, joined the Union Steamship Co. in June, 1942 as a deckhand on the good ship *Venture*, at the age of 16. He had worked the previous summer aboard the *Eastholm*, but found humping 100-pound sacks of lime was pretty heavy work for a 15-year-old.

I interviewed Johnny on two different occasions. He was a wealth of information and was very exuberant when telling his stories.

When he joined the *Venture*, the Captain was R. T. Naughty, the Chief Officer Jimmy

Capt. John Horne
(J. Horne)

McKillop and the Chief Engineer was G. Craigen. After a short period of time as deckhand he was made a quartermaster. At age 17, when he was on the *Venture*, the Second Mate, Al Strang, and Third Mate, Bob Ashmore, went on holidays. The Company didn't have enough men to fill up these positions, so John was sent out as Third Mate without a ticket. Both Captain Naughty and Chief Officer McKillop said this was okay with them, so Johnny sailed as Third Mate at age 17, an exciting time for a young man, and he never looked back.

While on the logging camp run he met his wife, Patricia Dorman, as her father, Jack Dorman, was Manager at Bones Bay, for Canfisco.

John stayed with the Union Company until 1952. During the 10 years he was with the Company he sailed on every ship in the fleet except three, the *Capilano II*, *Cassiar II*, and *Camosun II*. He was on the *Venture* all through the war, 1939 to 1945. In time he obtained his Home Trade Masters Ticket, being Number 18289.

He recalls Captain Bob Naughty as being

THE VANCOUVER SUN: Thurs., Feb. 3, 1955 ★★★7

Ship's Mate Tells How He Saved Man

Courageous Young Officer Dives Into Narrows to Rescue Fisherman

A courageous young ship's officer told today how he saved the life of a Vancouver fisherman by diving into the black cold waters of Seymour narrows Wednesday.

The dramatic rescue was revealed when the B.C. Packers' freighter Teco put in to Steveston at 2:15 a.m. with two survivors from the seiner East Bay No. 1 after the vessels collided with the loss of one life.

TWO SURVIVE

Skipper Ivan Radijov, 50, of 2928 West Broadway and engineer Peter Mihovilich, 52, of 2282 Adanac, survived the collision.

Nick Valkovic, cook, of 616 Prior was apparently trapped in his cabin and drowned when the vessel plunged to the bottom.

Radijov managed to jump from the bridge of his boat to the deck of the Teco, but Mihovilich was only saved by the prompt action of the freighter's mate.

MATE ON BRIDGE

The mate, John Horne, 28, of 3658 Marine drive, North Vancouver, was on the bridge when the vessels collided.

"It was about 5 a.m. when it happened," he said.

"Our ship struck the seiner in the stern.

"We saw the engineer in the water and he was yelling as loud as he could.

"I threw him a life line and we all started to pull him out.

"But the line got fouled up in the sinking boat and started to pull him down.

"I threw him another line, but in his desperation, he didn't see it."

Horne said he then jumped overboard and swam to the drowning man.

He managed to keep Mihovilich's head above water until other crew members could pull them both to the Teco's deck.

---

the best-dressed skipper in the fleet. His uniforms were always of the finest material. (Perhaps it was the fact he had a son in the clothing business.) He was a gentleman and loved his drink, which in the end was his undoing. He was known for his bumpy landings. The last docking he made was a beautiful, smooth, and gentle landing. The only thing wrong with it was, he landed at the wrong dock! He had landed at Pier H, instead of the Union Wharf. He was relieved of his command on the spot by Captain Eric Suffield, the Marine Superintendent.

Another story of John's was about Wee Angus McNeill, who wasn't known to be the best at docking a ship. On this occasion, Angus was on the *Lady Cecilia* making a landing at Roberts Creek. In all fairness this could be a very difficult place to land at times, because of strong winds and tides. Anyway, after having a difficult time of it, he finally did get the *Cecilia* alongside. The engineer on watch at the time, Jack (Broken Nose) McLeod (whose nose had been smashed by a German rifle butt in the war), came up topside and said, "Angus, I'm 22 moves behind, do you want 'em or shall I ring off?"

John said that Captain Harry Roach was the main source of Irish Sweepstake tickets along the coast and one of his regular customers was the Catholic priest at Churchhouse. John asked the priest about this one day and he said, "My son, this is a pretty lonely and isolated parish and buying a ticket allows me to dream of all the good things I could do if I won. It keeps me going."

He recalls his days with Captain Alex McLennan, "Big Mac" as he was affectionately known, who John says was an outstanding ship handler, and a great Captain. In his old age his hands were not very good and he used to come out on the bridge, hand John his straight razor, and say, "John, shave the back of my neck." He also says, despite his size and reputation, he was a kind, gentle man.

Two other very fine ship handlers in his opinion were Al Strang and Jimmy Hunter.

In discussing the Masters with whom Johnny had sailed, he felt that Captain Harry Roach was the most beloved of all, with Captain Alex McLennan close behind. In his opinion, Captain Naughty was quiet but pompous, Captain Jack Boden Sr. rarely had anything to do with his officers, Captain Harry McLean was the least liked of all, with Captain Aspinall close behind in this respect. He was also very fond of Capt. E. W. Suffield, who was liked by most of the younger officers. They felt he was a tough but fair Marine Superintendent.

The Vancouver Maritime Museum put on a major exhibit starting in April 1990, to mark the 100th Anniversary of the Union Steamship Company. The *Lady Rose*, the last of the original fleet still running, was brought down from Port Alberni, stopping at Victoria to take on a group of Union Steamship fans, and then came across the Gulf to take part in the opening of the exhibit. On this occasion Johnny Horne piloted her over to the Museum's dock in Vancouver. I had him blow the old Union whistle which I recorded for posterity, the familiar one long, two shorts and a long. It was a nostalgic trip and wonderful to be aboard the last of the Union Ships still operating, with Captain John Horne on the bridge.

Shortly after this trip, in doing research I discovered a news story which tells about John diving into the waters of Seymour Narrows to save a man from drowning. It's one story that John never mentioned to me in any of our interviews at all. It's a fine tribute to John and a fitting end to this story. (See clipping on previous page.)

Geoffrey Hosken

Geoff's first job at sea was aboard the Silver Wave which left Vancouver on Feb. 21, 1932 to search for buried treasure on Cocas Island. He was only 15, going on 16 years old and was hired as a mess boy.

Geoff started with Union Steamships in 1946, shortly after the end of the war, coming from the marine arm of the R.C.A.F. His first ship was the *Lady Cecilia*. After a few days on her he was transferred to the *Coquitlam II*, on her maiden voyage under Captain Jack Boden, as Third Mate.

In May 1947, Geoff was aboard the *Chilcotin*, also making her maiden voyage under Captain A.C. McLennan, again as Third Mate. The unusual thing about her first voyage, the *Chilcotin* sailed out of Vancouver, not from the Union dock, but the CPR dock, along with the CPR *Princess Norah*, both with a capacity load of Shriners going to Prince Rupert for a convention.

Geoff related the following story to me about himself, when he was on one of the Corvettes, under Captain Harry McLean, as Second Mate. They were on their way to Ketchikan and Geoff was on the bridge with the Captain, working the 6 to 12 watch. This day they came on watch at 6 a.m. and while the Captain was down having breakfast, Geoff was in charge of navigating the ship. He had not been in Ketchikan before, so he checked the course as laid out in the log book, and gave it to the quartermaster. This course would have taken them around the outside of an Island at the entrance to Ketchikan harbour. He soon realized this would make no sense, as going around this island was a much longer route than going in direct. So he plotted a new course, and as they were approaching the city, Captain McLean came up for breakfast and immediately said to Geoff, "Oh, you're going in the wrong way." Geoff replied, "No, I just laid the course and it is correct."

Captain McLean suddenly realized what was happening and he said, "Oh, I forgot, you've never been here before have you? You see, I always take the long way around the island to show our passengers the wreck of the old CNR ship, *Prince George*. This creates a lot of interest for our passengers and at the same time gets a dig in at our opposition." Also, Captain McLean loved to get the Purser to broadcast over the ship's loudspeaker system telling the passengers to look at the shipwreck on the port side as they were going into port.

For a while after this, Al Strang, who was Chief Officer at the time, in jest nicknamed Geoff "Wrong Way Corrigan" after the aviator who flew his plane in the wrong direction.

All in all, Geoff spent nearly 12 years with the Union Company and sailed aboard every ship in the fleet, except the *Lady Rose* and the *Cassiar II*. He made his last trip for the Company aboard the *Chilliwack*, in April 1958. Later he joined B.C. Ferries. He was Master on the Ferries and after 20 years service with them he retired and now lives in Nanaimo.

Capt. Geoffrey Hosken

James John "Jimmy" Hunter

Capt. Jimmy Hunter
(Ashmore Collection)

Jimmy was born in Weisdale, Shetland Islands, Scotland, in 1890. He joined the Union Steamship Co. on Dec. 1, 1920, starting as a deckhand and worked his way up the ranks. Four years later in 1924 he sat for his examination to obtain his Coastwise Competency Ticket in Vancouver and was successful.

Jimmy looked like what one would think an old sea Captain should, rough features, stout, in later years, rumpled uniform, taciturn, a hearty laugh, and always smoking a pipe. Once you got to know him you learned he was a great shipmate and a wonderful man. Behind the scene, his was not an easy life, for he cared for a mongoloid son throughout his career. When he retired in 1955 he moved to Manson's Landing on Cortes Island, where he felt his son would be able to live a better life. I am happy to say I knew and sailed with Jimmy Hunter.

He was with the Union Steamships Co. for 35 years. In his later years he was Master on many of the Union ships, including the *Cardena* and *Coquitlam II*. He gained the reputation of being one of the very best ship handlers in the Company's history.

One of the best ways to judge how well a man handles a ship is to ask an engineer. They are the fellows down below who must obey the commands the Captain sends down from the bridge by telegraph, to change the speed or thrust of the engines, particularly when docking the ship. A good ship handler will only give few commands, but others will rattle the bells in mad confusion. Ben Smith a well-known engineer with the Company, rated Jimmy Hunter in the top three of Deck Officers for ship handling, the other two being Al Strang and Tom Lucas. He said, "They were just amazing, two or three signals and you were alongside."

Although he had a very long period of service with the Company, very little is known or said about him. Stew Hale, a former Purser in the fleet, recalled one story, which is typical of Jimmy. "He was on the bridge approaching Seymour Narrows. There were some tourists on the bridge and at the time there were many dolphins cavorting around the ship, darting across the bow, back and forth. One gentleman asked, 'What are they doing?' 'Waiting for slack tide in the narrows,' was his laconic answer."

Jimmy Hunter died in Nanaimo, March 17, 1985, at age 85.

Lifeboat drill for a Union Steamship
(Ashmore Collection)

Andrew "Andy" Johnstone

Andrew Johnstone was born in Scotland in 1897. He came to B.C. with his parents in 1890. They were en route to New Zealand, but got no further.

When he was 11 years old, Andy Johnstone used to go down to the Union Steamship dock and watch the *Coquitlam I* load freight of every description, including horses and oxen. There were usually so many passengers that some had to sleep on top of their belongings piled upon the deck. The excitement of all this stayed with him, and at an early age he decided to go to sea himself. He signed aboard as an apprentice cabin boy on a government survey ship named the *Kestrel* in 1903. He was aboard her in Prince Rupert harbour in 1906 when the Union Steamship passenger vessel *Camosun* called into this new harbour. She was the first ship to arrive in this new northern port. Andy was 19 years old at the time. [151]

According to a write-up by Charles Defieux, Johnstone then joined the Blue Funnel's *Oanfa*, in Vancouver, for a couple of Orient voyages as quartermaster. He signed off in Liverpool and he joined the Cunard's *Umbria* and at this time he was the line's youngest quartermaster. Then it was a voyage on the old Allan Line's *Corsican* as an AB and thus spent most of his time below moving coal bunkers. In 1908 he signed on the CPR's new *Princess Charlotte* for the maiden voyage from Glasgow to Vancouver. Now he was a junior officer. The voyage was 58 days around the Horn and they arrived in Vancouver Dec. 31, 1908. Within months he started with the Union Steamship Company, on the old *Camosun* as Second Mate under Captain Saunders. He moved up fast for on May 19, 1912 he obtained his Master's ticket. [152]

At the beginning of the first world war in 1914 Andy was serving as First Mate on the S.S. *Venture* under Captain John Park. He joined the Royal Canadian Artillery and was overseas for nearly four years. Upon his return he became Master of the *Venture* and made a name for himself as the "Cannery Skipper."

The Union Steamship Company was building the *Catala* in Scotland and Andy was sent over to act as advisor during her construction. Although Captain Findlay brought her out to B.C., Captain Johnstone took her out on her maiden voyage, July 28, 1925.

Captain Johnstone really enhanced his reputation while serving as Master of the *Cardena*. On August 22, 1927, he and his ship came to the rescue of the CNR steamer *Prince Rupert*, which had hit and become stranded on Ripple Rock in Seymour Narrows. The *Rupert* was completely immobilized with one propeller going around in mid air. She could easily have foundered or been taken by the tide into nearby cliffs. She had a full load of passengers, with mail aboard and was in a very hazardous position. Captain Johnstone maneuvered the *Cardena* close to the

Capt. Andy Johnstone *(Vancouver Maritime Museum)*

stranded ship and was able to get a steel towing cable onto the *Rupert*'s stern. The *Cardena* pulled the *Rupert* off and they towed her into a nearby cove where she could be safely anchored. As many of the *Rupert*'s passengers as the *Cardena* could handle were transferred to the *Cardena*, as well as the mail and valuables. Just then the CPR *Princess Beatrice* was passing and she was signalled to stop and was able to take aboard the remainder of the *Rupert*'s passengers. Captain Johnstone's great seamanship and quick thinking saved the *Rupert*, her passengers and crew, from what could have been a total disaster. [153]

In December 1929, the *Cardena* had just come out of drydock after going aground in the Skeena River the previous month under the command of Captain Findlay. Captain Johnstone was on the bridge this time when she went aground again, on Village Island in the Skeena River. She was in no danger but the passengers were taken off. The next day she was refloated and returned to Vancouver where she underwent more repairs. [154] Photographs of these two groundings are almost identical and can be seen under *Cardena* in the Ships section, pp.59,60.

There often was rivalry on the coast between Union Steamships and the CPR and CNR, and Captain Johnstone was always happy to tell the story of how he was able to outwit and out-maneuver the CPR's *Princess Joan*. Both ships were racing to Bella Bella where a big load of cases of canned salmon was waiting for the first ship to arrive. The *Joan* was the faster ship but was only able to load 500 cases an hour, whereas the *Cardena* could load 1,500 cases an hour. If the *Joan* arrived at Bella Bella first, the *Cardena* would have to wait her turn and in doing so would miss a vital tide in the Skeena River. Both ships were in Ocean Falls at the time and the *Joan* got away first with a 15-minute head start. It was getting dark and the *Joan* took a safe, circuitous route, but Captain Johnstone took a route through Gunboat Passage which was dangerous even in daytime, especially for a large ship, but Captain Johnstone had used this passage many times and had no hesitation in taking the *Cardena* through. In order not to give his game away he had all the *Cardena*'s lights turned off so the CPR ship wouldn't see what he was doing. He won the race to Bella Bella and had already loaded 1,000 cases of salmon before the *Joan* came in sight. [155]

Captain Bob Naughty Jr., in an interview appearing in the booklet titled *Sound Heritage: Navigating the Coast*, described Captain Johnstone as follows: "Andy Johnstone was a very gruff skipper, especially with Third Mates, and I was Third Mate on the *Cardena*. Captain Godfrey was Chief Officer. The Second Mate went with the skipper, although the skipper didn't stand (much of) a watch. Andy would go down and talk to the passengers. He always made sure he had a good Second Mate on the bridge. That was the style those days. If you wanted the skipper, all you did was buzz or send the quartermaster down. You buzzed a little button in the wheelhouse and the watchman came running up. "Coffee?" "No, no coffee. Get the skipper up here on the double, I've got a problem." Most of the time when the Mate buzzed, it was for coffee.

"The Skeena River had 12 canneries and you couldn't waste any time there because when the tide dropped you were on the mud. We had to try and do the 12 in one stop and then another place was the Skeena River slough. You had to be on the ball. Captain Andy Johnstone says, 'When I come alongside you only got two slings of freight. When I come alongside I'll stop the derricks on this corner and get freight off and I'll slide up and expect you to be at the other end with the empties. Just leave the boards there. Just get the empties out of the other corner.' Whew! He told me, 'You got to sharpen up.' Boy, I thought I was running as hard as I could!

"And then he called me up on the bridge. And he says to me, 'Now there's a rule on this ship. I want them lifeboats inspected every night.' And I says, 'Oh.' 'I want you to get the winchman and the watchman up.

Get them covers off and check all the gear and report to me.' We had to do that every night, even though all the rockets were still there, the oars were still there, and you'd think, nothing's changed. He was very disciplinary." [156]

Ernie Plant was a deckhand on the *Cardena*. He recalled one trip when Captain Johnstone got married and a relief skipper was put aboard. Andy had decided on a busman's holiday and came aboard with his bride for their honeymoon. The new skipper called Ernie up to the bridge. They were approaching Bella Coola where he knew Andy had a lot of friends. He wanted Ernie to string a message from mast to mast using the signal flags. Having had no experience in such things he asked another deckhand, Jim Watson, who had been in the navy, to help him. They made up the message and when the ship arrived at Bella Coola all Andy's friends were waiting to greet him and his bride. Everyone had a great laugh when they were told what the signal flags said. It read, "I am in dire need of assistance. My stem is badly bent!" Ernie says the crew of the *Cardena* took up a collection and bought the Captain and his bride a silver tray set.

Often in the fog the Captain would station a man up on the bow. Ernie was called upon to do this and Captain Johnstone would call out to whoever was out on watch, "Are you still awake out there?" One time when Ernie was out there they were proceeding through Seymour Narrows in a thick fog and all of a sudden a low flying plane loomed out of the fog. Ernie hollered and Captain Johnstone reacted quickly, blew the ship's whistle and the plane just veered away in time.

When the *Cardena* went to the rescue of the *Prince Rupert* the time she grounded on Ripple Rock, Ernie was working aboard the *Cardena* and recalls that Jock Muir, who was Chief Officer, was on watch when word was received of the *Rupert*'s grounding. He said to Ernie, "We're just going to go right on by, because the CNR has never done anything for us." However, he told Ernie to stay around, for there was fun ahead. Captain Johnstone, Master of the *Cardena*, did go to the aid of the Rupert and the rest is history. There is a famous picture of the *Cardena* alongside the *Rupert* and Ernie can be seen in the picture standing and holding onto the forward mast guy line. (p.59)

On another trip, Ernie was given a big halibut. He put a label on it and stored it in the cook's locker. Captain Johnstone had also been given a halibut, only his was smaller than Ernie's. Ernie had to keep checking the fish because the Captain was continually putting his name tag on the biggest fish!

Helen Meilleur's excellent book, *A Pour Of Rain*, said this about Captain Johnstone: "Captain Andy Johnstone, hero of a hundred coastal legends, commanded the *Cardena*. His ship was like a dancing partner as he docked her; slide, pivot, swing, glide, reverse and stop. The stop was always on her toes, dramatic, to a generous applause. If he had ever decided to command a barrel going over Niagara Falls any north coaster would have accompanied him without a second thought. It was Andy Johnstone who taught us with much hilarity, how to splice rope and make Turks' heads for our oars. He taught us such assorted essentials as where to watch for blackfish, etiquette of the bridge, and coast history - he seemed to know a good story for every rock and point along the Inside Passage. He also taught us where to place our shuffleboard shots and never to pass up the Union Steamships' crab cocktails at dinner. Andy Johnstone still had a boyish look and laugh when he went out of our lives to join the Pilotage service after 23 years with the Company."[157]

Captain Johnstone went to the pilotage in 1934 and served with them until 1967. He retired to his home in North Vancouver and tended his beautiful flower garden. Captain E. Georgeson succeeded him as Master of the *Cardena*.

Leonard C. King

Second Mate
Leonard King
(Mrs. Tosh Collection)

Harry Lamacraft (left)
and Neil Campbell
(H. Lamacraft)

Leonard served as a mate in the Union Steamships for nearly a decade. He was Second Mate on the *Chelohsin* in 1938 and on the *Venture* in 1942 under Captain MacLennan, and Chief Officer Jimmy McKillop.

Jimmy McKillop and Len King used to have many verbal battles aboard ship, for McKillop was teetotal and Catholic, and King was a drinker and a Presbyterian.

Leonard left the Company in the 1940s to become skipper on the J. H. Todd, the newest fish packer in the Todd fleet at the time.

Harry Lionel Lamacraft

Harry was born in Yorkton, Sask., Jan. 18, 1928 and he came out to B.C. with his parents to Summerland in 1939. He came out to the coast in 1944 with the idea of joining the navy. The navy had so many recruits at the time they weren't interested in signing up a 16-year-old, so Harry went back to Summerland where he obtained work in a box factory.

In 1946 with the war over, Harry came back out to the coast with the idea of getting a job aboard a ship. As luck would have it, he ran into an agent for the Seafarers' Union who signed him up and Harry was sent down to the Union Steamship Co. He signed aboard the *Catala* as a deckhand on Sept. 28, 1946. Harry McLean was the Master, Miles Robinson was Second Mate, and Johnny Horne was Third Mate.

He stayed on the *Catala* for five months and then he decided he wanted to go deepsea. While he was on the *Catala* he recalled on two different occasions they picked up crews from two different ships that had come to grief in B.C. waters. The first was the *North Sea* which had gone aground on a reef near Bella Bella. The second ship as near as he could remember was named the *General Ludinback*. She was a big ship and had run too close to the side of Grenville Channel and had torn out her bottom. The crew had to abandon ship in such a hurry that they had no time to save any of their belongings. They picked the crew up at Butedale and took them to Prince Rupert. Harry recalls giving one of the fellows a heavy shirt to wear because all he had on was a light T-shirt. The strange thing about this last incident, Harry says, is that he's never seen anything written up about the sinking.

Harry said the *Catala* was a hard-working ship. If you weren't loading or unloading freight, the Mates had you washing paint or scrubbing the decks or cleaning the life boats. Like nearly everyone who has worked aboard the Union ships, Harry said the food was great.

He came back from his deep sea job at the end of 1953 and wrote for his Coastal Mate's Ticket in April 1954. By this time he was married and he didn't want to go back deep-sea, so he joined the CPR, first as a quartermaster, then served as Third Mate until the summer of 1958. He then went back to the Union Steamship Co. Again he was on the *Catala*, but this time as Third Mate. The Master this time was Ray Perry.

One amusing incident came to his mind during this second time around on the Union ships. They had taken aboard a rather big and friendly dog which was being sent to Vancouver. The dog was tied up between decks. Harry was on the 12 to 6 watch. It was dark, but a pleasant evening so one of the wheelhouse windows was open. All of a sudden two big paws are placed on the window ledge followed by this huge, furry head of this big dog. It immediately started to bark. Harry and the quartermaster were almost scared to death when this hairy creature appeared out of nowhere. What had happened, the dog had chewed his rope lead apart and he went around the ship looking for company. At that time of night there was no one around and somehow he had made his way up to the bridge to find the only sign of life aboard ship in the wee small hours of the morning.

When the Union Steamships ceased to exist at the end of 1958, Harry was out of work. He joined a Shell Oil tanker early in 1959 and he was with them for ten and a half years. During this period he obtained his Master's Certificate. The tanker was sent back east, so Harry decided he would try his hand at selling real estate but he found that the sea life was more to his liking. He then obtained work with Westward Shipping for two years. Then he joined up with the Aqua Transportation Co. In 1973 this company became part of Seaspan. He served aboard various Seaspan vessels including the Seaspan *Greg* and Seaspan *Doris* and became Master of the *Doris* running between Vancouver and Nanaimo.

Harry retired from the sea on Jan. 23, 1993 and now lives in Powell River.

Howard Ernest Lawrey

Capt. H. Lawrey
(Farina Collection)

Captain Lawrey was a Cornishman born at sea and had sailed in schooners when he was 15 years old, sailing to Labrador and Iceland. He commanded railway steamers in the English Channel before coming to Vancouver. In the spring of 1911 he joined the All Red Line, and served as Mate on the *Selma*. He came over to the Union Steamships in 1917 when they took over the All Red Line. On July 26, 1917 he joined the Canadian Merchant Service Guild, which had come into being that year. He served with the Union Steamship Co. for 28 years before retiring. He was particularly well-known as Captain on the excursion vessels. [158]

The picture of Captain Lawrey below shows him wading at Savary Island, with his ship the *Lady Cecilia* in the background. I've been told that he had a nickname of "Bimbo" but I never heard him called this by anyone.

Roberts Creek was a difficult landing at times because of the tides and strong winds. Fred Corneille, a former Deck Officer with the Company, recalls being on the *Lady Cynthia* with Captain Lawrey. One trip northbound at Roberts Creek, the Chief Officer was making the landing and he sliced off the front of the wharf. (The *Lady Cynthia* had two feet of reinforced concrete in her bow, so she didn't suffer any damage.) On the southbound call, Captain Lawrey was making the landing and he took out some more pilings.

The wharfinger was livid because it was springtime and the start of the season. His dock would be out of service all summer. He hollered up to Captain Lawrey, "What the hell did you bother coming back for?" Captain Lawrey replied, "Just to cover up the damage we did on the way up!"

Mr. Corneille remembers Captain Lawrey on the *Lady Evelyn*. When he was off watch he used to take off his starched collar and wander the deck with his vest and arm bands in place, open collar, and pipe in his mouth (see picture) trying to drum up a game of bridge.

Captain Lawrey's ship, the *Lady Cynthia*, with Captain Muir, the Marine Superintendent aboard, led the parade of Union Ships in the "Win the War Cruises" around the harbour in July 1940.

On Sept. 24, 1944 the *Lady Cecilia*, with Captain Lawrey on the bridge, was in collision in a dense fog with a 10,000-ton Liberty ship off of Point Atkinson. I was aboard her as Assistant Purser and Les Smith the Purser gave me the job of interviewing all the passengers who were hurt in the crash. Fortunately no one was seriously injured or killed, although five people were taken to hospital when the ship made port. The hospital reported that their condition was not serious.

I recall the accident vividly and I think the fact that the *Lady Cecilia* was not either cut in two and sunk or damaged seriously, was due to the expertise in handling the ship by Captain Lawrey, who was on the bridge. He was able to reverse his engines immediately and back away moments before the freighter hit. Norrie Wood, who was Freight Clerk at the time, also felt the same way, that Captain Lawrey saved the day. (For more details see the story in the Ships section under *Lady Cecilia*, p. 91.)

Captain Lawrey apparently had retired in 1939 but returned temporarily to the Company because of the shortages of Deck Officers in wartime. He did retire permanently in 1946. One of his pastimes when not aboard ship was lawn bowling and

Capt. Lawrey
(Spilsbury Collection)

he was an active member of Vancouver Lawn Bowling Club.

He died at home of a heart attack, Aug. 10, 1949.

Charles "Charlie" Edward Lewis

Charlie was born June 16 1926 in Calgary. He joined the Union Steamships as a seaman on July 2, 1942 aboard the *Camosun II*. He obtained his Home Trade Mate's ticket No. 16895 in November 1945 and at age 19 was the youngest certified officer in the Company. He immediately went out on the *Chelohsin* as Third Mate, standing watch with Alfred Aspinall who was Chief Officer at the time.

Charlie recalls he and Aspinall were constantly arguing. "We argued every watch, every hour, every day, and I became used to his nature and I think in the end he rather liked me," Charlie said.

Over the 12 years he was with the Union Steamships, he built up many fond memories. He had a very high regard for Captain Robert Wilson and especially for Harry Roach, as he gave Charlie a great deal of help along the way. He had much respect for Captain Jack Boden and Captain Billy McCombe, whom he sailed with on the Stewart and Queen Charlotte Island routes, respectively. He recalled, as have many others, what good ship handlers Jimmy Hunter and Al Strang were. Jimmy Hunter was in fact, one of Charlie's favourite people. He also has fond memories of the following Chief Officers he was happy to have sailed with: B. Owen-Jones, Paddy Hannigan, Jack Summerfield, Wally Walsh, and Angus McNeill.

One funny incident Charlie remembers was when they were transporting four elk up to Queen Charlotte City. Evidently they were going to attempt to establish an elk herd on the Islands. There were three calves and one bull in the shipment. The calves were unloaded onto the dock without incident, but when the bull was set down on the wharf in the cattle box, someone opened the box door too soon and the bull bolted out, jumped over everything in its way, galloped down the dock and was last seen running down the main street of Queen Charlotte City and was never seen again.

Another not so funny but amusing-in-the-end story was when Charlie was Second Mate on the *Coquitlam* under Captain John Halcrow; they sailed away from the Union dock and left behind a pallet board containing all the Mail Lock sacks for the whole trip! This was discovered by the stevedore as the ship was just going under the Lions Gate Bridge! The ship had to turn around and go back into Vancouver to pick up these essential mail bags. Charlie thought Captain Halcrow would give him hell, but later he came over to him, put his hand on his shoulder and said, "Every once in awhile we do stupid things." In Charlie's opinion, Captain Halcrow was "a real gentleman."

On another occasion when Charlie was sailing as Second Mate on one of the

Charlie Lewis 2nd Mate, U.S.S. Co. *(Roach Collection)*

Captain Charlie Lewis on the B.C. Ferries' M.V. *Queen of Esquimalt* 1990 (C. Lewis)

corvettes, he was on watch with Captain Jimmy Hunter. They were proceeding out of Prince Rupert down to Butedale. Jimmy was down having dinner so Charlie was navigating on the bridge. They were overtaking a small motor vessel and suddenly it changed course and was cutting across the channel in front of the Union ship. It was a well-known fact that the converted corvettes where quite touchy to handle, and if given too much helm they would just about roll over. Charlie had no alternative but to quickly change course, and in so doing the ship just about laid right over on her side. As it was supper time, all the dishes and food on the dining room tables crashed to the floor! Jimmy Hunter was less than pleased. He rushed up to the bridge to see what was happening, and when he saw the situation, he understood, but there was one helluva mess in the dining room to clean up that day.

Late in December 1950, Charlie was serving as Third Mate on the *Catala* and was at sea when his wife Helen went into the New Westminster Hospital and gave birth to twin boys. The first was born just 20 seconds after midnight, January 1st, followed 16 minutes later by a second boy. These were the first babies born in the New Year and as a result they received a multitude of gifts from local merchants, which had to be doubled for these twin boys. The *Columbian Newspaper* at the time reported that their father was away at sea on his ship. Upon his arrival back in port it was reported he was "still at sea" over this surprising turn of events.

Charlie left the Union Co. in 1954 because he wanted to be able to spend more time with his family than he was able to being away at sea so much. As well, looking ahead, the future of the Company didn't look so bright. He went to Alberta and managed a truck business. He was there for 14 years. He returned to B.C. in 1971, joined the B.C. Ferries fleet as Second Mate in 1972, and obtained his Master's Ticket in 1973. In 1975 he became a relieving Captain and became a permanent Captain in 1989. Charlie retired on May 6, 1991 after 49 years at sea on the B.C. coast.

Tom Lucas

Capt. Tom Lucas S.S. *Coquitlam* 1950s (Roach Collection)

Tom Lucas joined the Union Steamship Co. in July 1921, signing aboard the *Camosun I* as a deckhand. Later he became a winchman. He was winchman on the

Cardena in 1938 along with his brother Ernie.

He worked his way up and became Chief Officer aboard several ships. From 1941 on, most of his time was spent on the Queen Charlotte Islands route. He then served as relief Master on many runs. In January 1955, he was promoted to Assistant Marine Superintendent. In 1957 he played a large role in building the Company's new containerized freight boxes, which proved very successful in boosting freight volume for the Company.

With the sale of the Union Steamship Co. to Northland Navigation Co. in January 1958, Tom moved over to Northland along with several other Union employees. His position with this new company was wharf freight manager.

Gerald Rushton, in his book *Whistle Up the Inlet*, tells about when Tom was quartermaster on the *Cardena*, and how he formed an orchestra from members of the crew. The orchestra consisted of his brother Ernie, Ted Tite from Prince Rupert, Johnnie Walker, and Tom. There was a trumpet, saxophone, accordion and drums. When the *Cardena* was in her home port of Vancouver the group rehearsed under Al Lexington, a former member of the Boston Symphony. [159] They played aboard ship to entertain passengers en route. At times these "Musical Mariners" played for dances in Port Hardy providing the *Cardena* was ahead of schedule and was able to lay over for a while.

Colin Park, a former Union employee on the *Camosun II* (ex *Prince Charles*) speaks about Tom Lucas when he was Second Mate aboard her, coming down in the hold, along with Al Strang, who was Third Mate, helping the crew load and stow cases of canned salmon. Colin tells of Tom and Al, both husky fellows, being able to throw a case of salmon up to the top of a pile.

Tex Lyon, the longtime wharfinger at Port Hardy, tells about one of the local people asking Captain Billy McCombe, who was up on the bridge watching the freight being unloaded, why Lucas wasn't on the run anymore. Captain McCombe answered, "Well, because his language was so foul." Captain McCombe was one to talk about bad language!

Ben Smith, an engineer with the Union Co., said this about Tom: "When we were sailing together, he was Chief Officer and I was 3rd Engineer. We got our movements down pat. Tom could bring a ship in with about three movements. It would be, stop, full astern, slow ahead, and you were there. Then stop, finished with engines. He was a fantastic man to work with, as he was a wonderful ship handler."

U.S.S. Personnel aboard the S.S. *Coquitlam*: Walter Farley (Q.M.) Charlie Lewis (3/O) Tom Lucas (CH/O) *(C. Lewis)*

James Alfred McAskill

Capt. James McAskill
(J. McAskill)

Jim McAskill was born in New Westminster, June 16, 1914 and started his sea career at age 21, sailing deep-sea out of New Westminster in 1935.

During the war years he sailed deep-sea on British ships and obtained his Second Mate's and First Mate's foreign going certificates in Glasgow. With repatriation at war's end, he returned home and sailed deep-sea as First Mate on the *S.S. Tahsis*, formerly the *Selkirk Park*.

In the summer of 1947 he signed up with the Union Steamship Co., sailing out on the *Chelohsin* as Third Mate. He recalls that Harry Roach was the Master, Vic Hayman the Chief Officer and Second Mate was Bob Smith. From the *Chelohsin* he went over to the *Cardena* whose Master was Jack Boden Sr. After the *Cardena*, Jim went to the *Lady Cynthia* and as he says, "All that string of day boats."

The *Cardena* and Captain Billy McCombe were to play a major role in Jim's life, for it was aboard her he met his wife Pegeen. She had come aboard the *Cardena* as a passenger taking a cruise up to Rivers Inlet in the summer of 1948. She encountered this handsome Third Mate quite often during the trip. She heard that passengers were allowed to visit the bridge, so one day she went up and after a while Captain McCombe said "Jim, take this lady down for tea." Pegeen was a very persistent lady and liked this Third Mate but he was a little hard to get to know. The day they were to dock back in Vancouver she had to think of some way of meeting him again. Then she got the bright idea of obtaining a ship's dinner menu and getting the autographs of the ship's officers. She approached him for his autograph and managed to get a date with him after the ship docked in Vancouver. The romance was started and they were married a year later, Oct. 22, 1949.

In 1947 Jim and I sailed together on the *Cardena* although neither of us recalled one another. We were aboard her when she ran aground July 17, 1948 at False Bay. Angus McNeill was on the bridge at the time, along with Jim. There were no injuries, but the ship had to be taken into drydock. The passengers were taken off in lifeboats to the wharf at False Bay. They were later picked up by the *Chelohsin* and taken back to Vancouver. The cargo was transferred to a scow and Jim came back to Vancouver aboard the tug boat.

Jim was in another grounding, this time aboard the *Chelohsin* under Captain Harry Roach, when she struck a rock in Chatham Channel. Paddy Hannigan and Jim had just come off watch and as they were about to enter their cabins Paddy said to Jim, "Well Jim, it's been an odd sort of watch, hasn't it?" They had run into a bit of fog and other problems. At that moment the *Chelohsin* hit the rock. Paddy turned around and said, "It looks like Captain Roach is going to have a strange watch too!"

They managed to get the *Chelohsin* into the Minstrel Island wharf. Jim said, "I thought I would get a bit of a holiday as a result of this accident, but it wasn't to be. The *Catala* was sent up and took our passengers, etc. on board. She had come up without a Third Mate so I stepped off the *Chelohsin* onto the *Catala* to another tour of duty on her."

We talked about Captain Billy McCombe. Jim said, "He was a real Glaswegan and his language at times was rough and ready to say the least."

Jim recalled being in Glasgow on one occasion looking for a ship to sign on. Someone told him there was a ship at a wharf nearby looking for a crew to take her to Vancouver. Jim scurried around, found the wharf but couldn't see any ship. Upon enquiring he was told, "Oh yeah, she's there, over the edge of the wharf." Jim went over and looked down and saw this tiny ship and said, "That's going to Vancouver?" It was, and her name at the time was the *Lady Sylvia*. This would have been in 1937. After sailing deep sea for two years Jim didn't want to take a chance sailing half way around the world on her. She did arrive in Vancouver alright but her name was changed to the *Lady Rose*!

Jim left the Union Steamship Co. in the fall of 1948 and went to navigation school where he obtained his Home Trade Master's Certificate. In 1949 he spent a season in the Arctic as First Mate with Cecil Roberts on the *Snowbird II*.

On leaving the Arctic, Jim worked on tugs in the Fraser River for about two years. He then rejoined Captain Roberts on the *Gulf Mariner*, with Al Strang as Mate. Captain Roberts eventually shifted to the *Chelan* and was lost with that ship and crew in Alaskan waters. Jim heard the sad news as he was sitting at home rocking his baby son.

Prior to "swallowing the hook" in 1954, Jim worked on several tugs towing to Vancouver Island. He then went to work on the waterfront and retired in 1977.

Robert "Bob" McBeath

Bob was born in Glasgow, Scotland in 1902, came out to Canada and started work as a deckhand with the Union Steamship Co. when he was 24 years old in 1926. It is on record that he did serve as Third Mate on the *Venture* and then relieved Angus McNeill as Shore Mate, before leaving the ships entirely to work as a longshoreman in 1944. When I was a Freight Clerk in the 1940s I remember Bob. He was the foreman in charge of loading all the Day Boats at the time. He was a short man with a strong voice and obviously you could tell, he was in charge. He died in 1976.

Little is known about Bob's career with the Union Steamships, but fortunately in *Sound Heritage: Navigating the Coast*, one in the series published by the Provincial Archives, it does give us some details about his career with the Company from personal recorded interviews with Bob. The following are all excerpts from that book:

"You unloaded freight at every stop. The deckhand had no watches. They slept between stops. Naturally, there was a lot of places where you'd go for two or three hours, some down below and some on the dock, working. You did that all the way up the coast. They had what they called the Skeena Run. You'd go from Vancouver to Campbell River, Inglewood, Alert Bay, Sointula, Port McNeill, Port Hardy, then you'd cut across Queen Charlotte Sound from there. Smiths Inlet, Rivers Inlet, Namu, Bella Coola. These places were several stops each. You had a stop at Tallyho, Anvil Island, Ocean Falls, then you'd go into Walker Lake. You had about three or four stops in Bella Bella. From Bella Bella to Klemtu to Butedale. Sometimes from Butedale you went to Kitimat. You might stop at Hartley Bay. There was an Indian village there and in the early days you might run into Lowe Inlet."

Bob next talks about working conditions in earlier days: "In the wintertime, some boats tied up. They doubled up on runs and these crews were laid off. During the Depression they tried to divide the work. Married men got six weeks on and two weeks off. Single men for a month on, a month off. It was tough going but it was better than nothing. I've got to admit that the Union Company was pretty good. Them days it was hand-to-mouth. They always tied up their boats in the wintertime, anyway. The day boats, a lot of them tied up and the other runs, some of them were doubled up. Some of these boats that tied up went in for dry dock, and then the guys that were laid off got work fixing them up. I wouldn't say that anybody starved on the Union Company. It was tough going, but you got by. Wages for deckhands were $65 a month and your board, and if you were a watchkeeper you got $70, and a quartermaster, $75. The stewards were paid very low wages."

Example of foredeck cargo aboard a Union Steamship vessel

Bob next talks about the hard and long working hours aboard the freight boat *Chilliwack II*: "I was working on the *Chilliwack*. We were loading spruce for the Mosquito bombers in a place called Seal Cove up in Prince Rupert and we'd been working on the Skeena River. When we got to Rupert, we started loading bloody logs, lumber it was, lumber. Comin' up to midnight. We'd been working all day and the mate, Suffield, wanted to knock off at midnight, start again at 6 o'clock in the morning, both watches. But the skipper wanted to catch a tide and he says we'll work right through. The skipper's got the final say, but then he goes away to his bed. But not the mate. I was working in two - that was the big hatch. The winchman and I were waiting for them to move a barge. I was down below and hollering to him, 'Have they moved that barge?' and I got no answer, so I come up on deck and here, he fell asleep. He was sleeping on the deck. The Mate had been working with me down below so I told him, 'Boyles is asleep, Eric, what are you going to do?' He said 'That's it!' and he knocked everybody off. He never went near the skipper."

Bob then describes the hiring practices for the ship's crew, before a Personnel Office came into being on the dock: "In them days you were always hired off the dock. Actually, you went on board the boat and looked for the Mate. It was usually the second mate that hired the crew. But that changed. The shore mate took charge of finding men. Angus McNeill was shore mate and then I went shore mate. I was third mate on the *Venture*. I came ashore to relieve Angus. That was after Harold Brown had died (in 1945) and Halterman was Superintendent. I used to keep a list of guys looking for a job."

There was a longshoremen's strike in 1935. Strikes had a profound affect on the ships' personnel and the Company alike. Bob McBeath became very active in organizing waterfront workers in his later years and perhaps this strike in '35 had given him some ideas. In the last of his interviews in the *Sound Heritage* series, Bob had this to say: "It started in Powell River and ships that got loaded at Powell River were said to be carrying 'scab paper.' Deep water ships were struck first. Then they called in other locals. Two weeks after being struck they called out the coastwise boats. It cost a lot of good men their jobs for life. They never got back. I was a young fella then and I eventually got back on the boats. A lot of mates and skippers sympathized with the sailors and then had no compunction about replacing these men who broke strike with the old crew. It was dangerous in the boats for the men working underneath the winches."

William "Billy" McCombe Sr.

Captain Billy McCombe was a prominent personality in the Union Fleet for over 30 years.

He was born in Glasgow in 1893, and came out to B.C. as a junior officer aboard the newly-launched *Cardena*, which was to be brought over to B.C. by Captain A.E. Dickson. Billy McCombe said that he was actually heading for Australia to work for the North Coast Shipping Co. of Australia with whom he had worked previously. Getting to Vancouver was part way but when he contacted the Company in Australia after arriving in Vancouver he was told they had no job for him, so he stayed in Vancouver and went to work for the Union Steamship Co. He obtained a job as Third Mate on the *Cowichan* and never looked back.

At that time the *Cowichan* was on the logging-camps run. "In those days navigating was by guess and by God as there were no navigational aids to speak of, and you made note of your own landmarks and if you missed one, you were lost. Loggers would hang up lights but authorities would make them remove it because it was not officially put in place," Billy told *Sound Heritage*. [160]

Billy had a hard time getting used to navigating on the B.C. coast because he was a deep water man to start with, where you always had lots of water and room. Navigating on the B.C. coast at night used to terrify him but he adapted quickly. He said that navigating at night by the whistle on a diesel ship wasn't easy as you had the continual chug, chug, chug. With steam there was no noise, so it was quiet enough to hear the echoes.

In 1937 he served as the Freight Officers' representative with the Canadian Merchant Service Guild.

When the Second World War was declared, he joined the Canadian Navy and in 1942 was a Lieutenant Commander on a corvette in the North Atlantic Convoy Service. He wrote a description of this job which appeared in the *Canadian Merchant Service Guild Annual* of 1946. In the previous war he had been in the army.

Stories about Billy McCombe's career are numerous. Over the years there were several babies born aboard the Union ships. He describes one of these births in *Sound Heritage: Navigating the Coast*, though in the story he says Norm Pattison was the Chief Steward who was involved but I think he meant to say Norm Davidson as Pattison was a Purser:

"We gave birth to a baby aboard ship! There was an experience for you! Norm Pattison [or Davidson] the Chief Steward was there. If it hadn't been for Norm, I think that baby would have died. The Freight Clerks were sleeping down in the cabin ahead of this young fellow and his wife. She

Capt. William "Billy" McCombe
(Ashmore Collection)

would be about 19, I think. He wasn't much older. When the pain started, she started to scream like bloody murder and the two freight clerks took off. The Chief Steward come up to me and said, 'We've got a birth coming.' I said, 'Oh no, Christ no. Don't say that, Norman. She can't last out, eh?'

" 'No.'

" 'Oh, Jesus,' I said. 'We'd better get the book out I guess.'

"We got the book out, trying to read all about it, you know. You ever try to read a book with the sweat coming down your face and the woman screaming her bloody head off? However, we brought it around, by God. We wanted the husband to do something. We turned around and he had fainted right there. He was a big help.

" 'We'll have to get lots of hot water, Captain. Hot water. I think you'd better get some more men out,' Norman said.

"I said, 'Turn the whole bloody crew out, Norman, we got an emergency. Who knows, one of these bloody clowns may have done this before.' Nobody wanted any part of it.

"However, we got her to Rupert all right. None of us were quite sure of the cord. It just said cut the cord. It didn't say, cut it here or anywhere. It just said cut it. Where the hell do you cut it? Where? Anyhow, we cut it pretty well close to the body and we got her into Rupert. The baby was doing fine, but you only want once like that in your life if you're not a doctor. That was out of my line completely. That was a frightening experience - a baby."

Captain Harry Roach's son Ed sailed with Captain McCombe and he felt for some reason Captain McCombe didn't like having him aboard, perhaps because he was the son of another Captain in the fleet, although one cold and foggy day when Ed was lookout, Captain McCombe came down from the bridge and loaned him his bridge coat while he was out on the bow on watch.

Tex Lyon, the wharfinger at Port Hardy, tells about Captain McCombe on one occasion when his ship was tied up at Port Hardy unloading freight. Three or four fellows who were drunk had fallen into the water between the dock and the ship. Freight unloading had to stop while the crew rescued these fellows and pulled them up onto the wharf again. After the fourth one fell in, Captain McCombe had the crew put a rope ladder down and said, "The next one will have to rescue himself!"

I was Assistant Purser aboard the *Coquitlam II* one time when we were backing away from the dock at Masset with Captain McCombe on the bridge and the ship stranded on a sand bar and damaged her propellor. This happened July 10, 1949, in the evening, with a very strong tide running. Captain McCombe had two life boats slung over the side, loaded with passengers ready to launch and of all things, I was put in charge of one of these boats! I recall that the boat was filled with women and I thought to myself, how in hell will I get these women to man the oars? It turned out that the life boats didn't have to be lowered. Captain McCombe, having been on the corvettes during the war, was familiar with the water ballasting on these ships and he had the engineer set to work pumping out this water ballast. The ship soon slid off the bar on a rising tide and we were able to get back to the Masset wharf.

The passengers were taken back to Vancouver by plane and we crew stayed aboard. The ship was then towed to Vancouver. What a wonderful holiday trip that was, no work to do, no passengers aboard, nothing but good food and relaxation. We were tourists on our own ship!

Billy McCombe also put the *Cardena* aground up in the Masset inlet. This would have been prior to the accident related above and Billy was the Chief Officer This incident was told to me by Johnny Horne who was Third Mate aboard at the time. The Captain was Alex "Big Mac" McLennan, so Johnny was on watch with Bill McCombe when the grounding took place:

"Billy McCombe had just returned from the war, back about three months. We were going up to Juskatla and Port Clements and were in the middle of Masset Inlet. John

Martinson, who was the winchman, looked up to the bridge and hollered, 'McCombe you're aground.'

"We were bucking an ebb tide and only making about 4 or 5 knots. Lo and behold we were aground, we were hard aground! The tide was going out and soon the *Cardena* was absolutely high and dry. I walked completely around her myself. Two fish packers were in the inlet prior to the tide going out and they tried to pull us off. One was the *Arrandale M*, but I can't remember the name of the other one. We put one of our wire headlines onto the stern of the *Arrandale M* to see if she could pull us off. She pulled so hard she broke the drum off the starboard windlass of the *Cardena*. I nearly lost my head as the end of the runner actually knocked the cap off my head when it went out the hause pipe.

"We didn't have many passengers on board.

"When we finally got off, Mr. Arthur was the Chief Engineer and he was able to pump the tanks to such an extent (I rather think personally that he pumped out a helluva lot of oil to lighten her, which would be frowned on today) that on the next high tide she floated off. We went across to Prince Rupert and we discharged all our cargo and passengers before we could return to Vancouver, so we went down empty. That was my first time sailing with Bill McCombe Sr.

"Over the years I sailed with him quite often. I liked him; he was harsh and loud, but his bark was worse than his bite. He was beloved amongst his sailors in the Navy. He was a real seaman. He and Captain Suffield, the Marine Superintendent, hated each other. For a time before the war Billy McCombe was shore mate on the Union dock and he and Captain Suffield had a terrible row. They never spoke to each other."

John Allan, a deckhand with the Company, recalls McCombe being Master on the *Lady Cecilia* on the West Howe Sound run. His Chief Officer was B.G.K. Owen-Jones. John said that Captain McCombe did not like Owen-Jones because he had a tendency to maneuver boldly and fast. According to John, Captain McCombe would not let him make certain landings.

Gerry Jones, a former Purser with the Company, had a high regard for Captain McCombe. When Gerry was married he and his bride were to honeymoon at New Brighton. Getting there was a bit of a problem but Captain McCombe solved that. They were married on a Saturday night and Captain McCombe was taking the *Lady Rose* up to Bowen Island Sunday morning and was to lay over for three or four hours, so he told Gerry to buy tickets to Bowen Island, which he did, and Captain McCombe, instead of laying over at Bowen, took the newly-weds up to New Brighton without getting authority from anyone. A real nice thing for him to do for a newly-married couple. Typical U.S.S. Co. service! This trip never appeared in the ship's Log Book!

Billy McCombe was a popular man amongst crew and passengers alike. He was always a jovial, hale-fellow-well-met type, but under the surface there were contradictions in his demeanor.

Ben Smith, an Engineer in the fleet, told about sitting at the mess table one day with "Big Mac" McLennan, a well-known Union Steamship skipper. He had been ill and was just returning from sick leave. Billy McCombe had relieved him. When Big Mac returned and was sitting at the mess table with Ben, he said, "Well Ben, how did you get along with McCombe while I was away?"

Ben replied, "Oh, okay Cap."

Big Mac said, "Yeah, he's 90 per cent, you know."

"Eh, what's that Cap?" Ben asked, "What do you mean?"

"He's 90 per cent bullshit!" Captain McLennan observed.

This sort of insight into Captain McCombe's character was quite illuminating. The following story provides another side of Captain McCombe's personality.

When the Union Steamships' three corvettes were sold, two were taken over by the Alaska Cruise Lines. Captain McCombe assumed command of one, the former *Coquitlam* which was renamed the *Glacier Queen*, and Captain Sheppard assumed command of the former *Camosun*, which was renamed the *Yukon Star*. Several other Officers from Union Steamships transferred over to this new company as well. One young Officer in the group was Bob Williamson, who was serving as Chief Officer and was the next in line to be given a Captain's job in this new fleet.

When Captain McCombe decided to retire in 1965, he went to the management of the Alaska Steamship Line. With his influence and standing, he persuaded them to promote his son Billy McCombe, serving as Second Mate, to Captain over Bob Williamson, who, as has been pointed out, was senior to Captain McCombe's son.

It turns out that away back in 1935 there was a big seamen's strike and Bob Williamson, who was a young deckhand at the time, had crossed the picket line in order to work and earn his living. Billy McCombe saw this and remarked to him one day that he shouldn't do that. Bob paid no heed. So, approximately 25 years later, Captain McCombe helped his son obtain a job which Bob Williamson felt was rightly his. Captain McCombe carried this grudge for 25 years and later had his way.

Harold Humphreys, a former Chief Steward in the Union Steamship Co., went over to the Alaska Cruise Lines. He eventually was appointed Assistant General Manager and was in turn to become Captain McCombe's boss. He says that Captain McCombe refused to talk to him and would not acknowledge the fact that a former steward, much lower in rank, could end up being his boss and be in charge of the whole operation.

Starting with Captain McLennan's remark about Captain McCombe at a mess table aboard ship, his grudge against Bob Williamson and observing Captain McCombe's behaviour towards Harold Humphreys who became his boss, one can only wonder about his real character. He always appeared affable and genial but under the surface his demeanor showed him to be a very complex man.

William "Bill" McCombe Jr.

Capt. William "Bill" McCombe Jr. (Humphreys Collection)

Bill McCombe Jr. started as a deckhand with the Union Steamships. Ship Registry records show he signed aboard the *Cardena* as a deckhand on March 4, 1938. He worked his way up to being a Third Mate and was serving aboard the *Venture* when war was declared on Sept. 1, 1939. He joined up along with many others in the Company, at the time, with the rank of Lieutenant. Although he did not obtain the rank of Captain, he did have command of four different naval vessels in 1945.

He returned to the Union Steamships after the war and eventually attained a Second Mate's position and relief Chief

Officer on the Day Boats.

Ed Roach recalled an interesting bit of family history that took place between the Roach and McCombe families. Ed Roach said he was serving as quartermaster under Captain Bill McCombe Sr. while Bill McCombe Jr. was serving as Second Mate under Ed's father, Captain Harry Roach. Bill was aboard the *Coquitlam II* when he began to suffer a very severe cough. He went to the doctor for a checkup and it was discovered he had tuberculosis, so he had to leave the ships and he spent two years in Tranquille. He returned to the Union Steamships and joined the *Coquitlam II* sailing under Captain Jack Boden, Sr.

On Oct. 29, 1953, Bill was serving as First Mate aboard the *Lady Cynthia* when she collided with the big steam tug *Dola* off Whytecliff. The Master at this time was Captain "Billy" Yates.

He stayed with the Company until its demise in December 1958. Along with his father, they went over to the Alaska Cruise Lines. Bill Jr. first served as relief Chief Officer and then was promoted to Captain when his father retired in 1965. On one trip he was on the bridge of his ship southbound from Prince Rupert when they collided with a Japanese freighter off Oona River, Porcher Island. His ship was able to continue under her own power to Vancouver, but before finishing the trip he had more misfortune. Attempting to land at the CN wharf, his ship rammed the Campbell St. fish dock.

When the Alaska Cruise Lines ceased operation he went over to B.C. Ferries. He was serving as relief Master on the *Queen of Prince Rupert* in August 1977 when he was called upon to perform a service of scattering the ashes of a former shipmate at sea. These were the ashes of the former Master and later Marine Superintendent Captain James Muir of the Union Steamship Co. They were consigned to sea in Queen Charlotte Sound off of Cape Caution, between Rivers Inlet and Smith Inlet.

James "Jimmy" McKillop

Capt. Jimmy McKillop
(Ashmore Collection)

Jimmy worked as a labourer at the Claxton Cannery on the Skeena River and it is thought he started with the Union Steamships about 1917. I asked Fred Corneille, a former deck officer, about Jimmy and he said, "When he started with the Company he could neither read nor write."

He did learn and was able to obtain his Mate's and then his Master's ticket, but like so many of the Union Steamship Officers he was many years sailing as Third and Second Mate trying to accumulate the required 24 months as a Second Mate in order to write for his Master's ticket. Alex Reid, a former ABS and winchman in the Company, made the following comment to me: "Yeah, he went up so many times they gave it to him for good attendance!"

Johnny Horne sailed with Jimmy and had this to say about him: "He was so Irish, so Catholic, and so uneducated. He was a big

Capt. "Harry" McLean
(McLean Collection)

craggy man, very strong but very gentle. He could coax his crew to work very hard and he would join in pushing dollies and changing slings. Making the southbound tide in Chatham Channel was one of his great challenges. I did Jimmy's income tax return for him when we were on the *Venture*, from 1942 until he died. He and I used to take the street car from Kerrisdale together when we were going down to the ship. It was Jimmy who agreed to let Bobby Ashmore have his vacation in the summer of 1944 and then myself, at age 17, was promoted from quartermaster to Third Mate."

Johnny also described the word battles between Jimmy McKillop, who was Chief Officer, and Len King, who was Second Mate. This was on the *Venture*. Jimmy, who never drank and was a devout Roman Catholic, and Len King, who was a heavy drinker and staunch Presbyterian, used to have some terrible rows. A classic example after one of their verbal battles, Len King said to Jimmy, "Fuck the Pope." Jimmy staggered and was quite taken aback, but recovered and then shot back to Len "And fuck Harry Lauder too!"

In July 1945, Jimmy was sailing as Master on the *Venture* and Johnny Horne was Third Mate. Johnny recalls going down to the Union dock on the street car along with Reggie Emms, second engineer, to stand the noon watch for the Tuesday evening sailing and when they arrived at the dock everyone was talking about Jimmy McKillop. He had died overnight at his home, on his day off!

Henry Edward "Harry" McLean

Harry McLean was born in Melbourne, Australia on Jan. 22, 1895. The family then moved over to Christchurch, New Zealand. When Harry was eight years old the family returned to Melbourne where Harry completed his schooling.

Harry went to sea at an early age, sailing on Australian coastal ships then graduating to deep sea sailing ships. One trip his ship was sailing from Australia to Victoria, B.C. with a load of coking coal. Half way between Hawaii and B.C. the ship caught fire, the crew had to abandon ship and take to their lifeboats. They were adrift for two weeks before they were spotted and picked up by a passing German sailing ship, which took them to Astoria in Washington State.

Harry then made his way to Victoria. It was here he met his first wife.

He obtained a job on a small survey vessel operating out of Victoria and as he had obtained his Foreign-going Mate's ticket by this time he had no trouble finding a job. Next he went to work on a tug boat hauling garbage out of Victoria which was dumped out in the straits.

The war broke out and Harry joined the Navy in Victoria where he became a crew member aboard one of two small submarines that had been given to Canada. The well-known Captain Barney Johnson was Captain on one of these submarines. However, the submarines never left the harbour and Harry could see he wasn't going to get anywhere here so he transferred over to the Army and was sent overseas right away. He was severely gassed in France and in fact was blind for nearly two years. He eventually regained his sight and was sent back to Shaughnessy Hospital in B.C. They started a series of operations on his nose, which had been badly damaged by the mustard gas. Over the years he had 42 operations on his nose but he never regained his sense of smell.

After being released from hospital Harry joined the Union Steamship Co. It is recorded that he was Second Mate on the *Cowichan* in May 1920 and Guild records show that he joined this organization on May 10, 1920.

Frank Skinner, former Purser and Company Agent at Prince Rupert, recalls being Purser on the company's new freight boat, the *Chilkoot*, in 1930. The Captain was Bill Mounce and the Chief Officer was Harry McLean. He was Chief Officer under Captain Gaisford on the *Chelohsin* in 1932 and he was Chief Officer on the *Catala* in 1937 under Captain E. Sheppard.

The first record of him being a Captain was in July 11, 1940 on the *Lady Rose*. He also was Captain on the *Lady Pam* when she participated in the "Win the War Cruises" in Vancouver Harbour.

John Allan, a former deckhand in the company, tells an interesting story from the late 1940s about Harry McLean liking a challenge. "One day when he was skipper on the *Lady Alexandra*, he decided he would turn the *Alex* around in Snug Cove instead of backing her out, as was the usual way of departure. It was just my luck to be at the wheel during this act of daring and skill. I don't know how many wheel commands and engine commands there were but we did it! He just wanted to prove it could be done," John said.

McLean's son Bob, who later went to sea himself, recalled his father used to take him out on trips aboard ship quite often in his younger days. When we were going into a stop his father would say, "Blow the whistle and count to five and let it go." Bob said, "I would do this, counting very carefully to five and then let go of the whistle cord, but the whistle would still be blowing. Unbeknown to me he was standing on the other wing of the bridge holding the other whistle cord down after I had let go of mine." And there we have an early example of the jokester for which Harry McLean soon became famous.

In the latter years of his time with the Union Steamship Co., Harry made quite a name for himself as the Master aboard the company's cruise ship, where he was in his element. He loved to dance, he loved the ladies and loved cocktail parties and entertaining. He was always organizing something for the entertainment of his passengers. One interesting thing he had going was a contest whereby the passengers would have to guess the number of revolutions the propellor turned perhaps in eight hours or one day. Passengers would write their guess down on a slip of paper along with a donation to the cancer fund. Of course there would be a prize, but Captain McLean was able to turn over the proceeds to a very worthy cause. One wonders if Harry had an inkling at this point about cancer, for he died of stomach cancer a few years after he retired from the ships.

He always had a masquerade party aboard his ship when she was running summer cruises. Geoff Hosken recalled they would leave Prince Rupert and anchor off Port Simpson on the day of the party. Every Officer on board had to participate, there was no doubt about that. Stan Green, a Mate under Captain McLean said, "We worked six hours on and six hours off. One could catch up on their sleep after one of these parties when the ship would lay over either at Prince Rupert or Ketchikan." Captain McLean didn't spend a lot of time on the bridge during these cruises, but Stan said he was a very competent skipper.

Captain McLean married a second time. He met his second wife aboard the *Chilcotin* and after the wedding they sailed aboard his ship on their honeymoon. As the ship pulled away from Vancouver his bride was on the bridge in her bridal dress. [161]

Geoff Hosken recalls his first trip aboard one of these cruise ships and being on watch with Captain McLean. They were going into Ketchikan port, for which there were two ways of entering. One was short and direct and the other was a long way around. Geoff plotted his course and was going in the short way. Captain McLean who was not on the bridge saw this and came rushing up to the bridge but it was too late to change course. Captain McLean always took the long way around into Ketchikan because the former CNR ship *Prince George* had wrecked and burned at the harbour's entrance and was a sight to see and Captain McLean loved to point it out to his passengers. He would always get the Purser to announce this over the ship's public address system, gleefully pointing out that this was a ship of a competing line that had come to grief.

Although Captain McLean was a popular skipper with the cruise passengers, he was not all that popular amongst the crew, partly because he was an inveterate practical joker. Here is an example of why he was unpopular with some crew members: there was a casket between decks and one of the quartermasters was known to be frightened when coffins were aboard ship. Harry knew this so he had another deckhand put a rope around this casket and when this quartermaster was walking to his quarters he had the man pull on the rope and groan at the same time. The poor fellow was terrified. That was Harry McLean.

When he was Master on the cruise ship he became well-known for his practical jokes, such as buying little plastic worms and slipping them into passengers' salads. Not very nice, and further it would infuriate whoever was the Chief Steward.

Frank Skinner, the Company Agent at Prince Rupert, often dined aboard any Union ship, often with his wife Martha, and one time they were the butt of one of these worm tricks. His wife didn't know what to do or say when she found what she thought was a worm in her salad!

Harold Humphreys, the Chief Steward, was livid over such antics but with McLean being the Captain he could pull off all the stunts that he wanted and get away with it. Another one of his tricks was to put boot black on the rim of the bridge binoculars, then hand them to a passenger telling the person to look at something in the distance. Of course when they put the glasses down they had two black rings around their eyes!

Another trick he used to play on the passengers was that he would unravel the graph paper in the echo sounder and draw little fish and sea life on the graph, rewind it and then when passengers were in the wheelhouse he would show them how the echo sounder worked. As it came rolling out he would say, "Oh look, see here, we're passing through a school of fish!"

Captain McLean and his first wife had a home at Soames Point which is half way between Granthams and Hopkins Landing. They had two sons, Bob who worked on the Union Ships in 1942 and eventually became Captain on the City of Vancouver's Fireboat, a position he held for 31 years, and Neil who worked on the Union Ships for four years before the war.

Harry McLean retired from the Union Steamship Co. on April 10, 1953. His last ship was the *Catala*. He was granted Life Membership in the Guild on April 1, 1953. He then moved down to California into a town named Monrovia where his second wife lived. They travelled extensively. In the winter season they used to collect clothing, etc., and drive down into Mexico and distribute these items to the poor. They became friends with many Mexican families. Harry developed stomach cancer and on one of these trips he had to be hospitalized in Mexico. His son rushed down to see him and he died soon after in Mexico. He was cremated and his ashes were sent back up to Vancouver in January, 1973.

The family obtained a small boat and took the ashes out to Burnaby Shoal where they cast them into the sea. The thought was, as he had been around Burnaby Shoal so many times in his life, it was like he was coming home.

John McKillop "Pop" MacLeod

"Pop" McLeod
(Twigg Collection))

"Pop" was a Highlander born on the Isle of Harris in the Hebrides in 1874. Prior to joining the Union Steamships in the early 1930s he was working on a river boat for the Hudson's Bay Company on the Peace River. He obtained his Master's Ticket for River Boats during this period. However, during the Depression years he was bumped and he just knocked about until he had a chance to join the Union Steamship Company. He started as an A. B. seaman and eventually obtained his Coastal Mate's Ticket.

He worked on the wooden hulled *Capilano* for years and often took his son Rod along and let him sleep in his bunk and work aboard ship, for fun. When the new White Boats came into service, Pop was aboard them as 2nd Mate.

Rod recalls his father taking his mother aboard one of the White Boats for a trip up to Stewart. Everybody aboard ship fussed over her and she had a wonderful time.

When Pop was on the cannery route, they always had plenty of canned salmon in the house. Usually there was a Scot working in some capacity at these canneries and they would ask Pop how his stock of canned salmon was holding up. "Well, it's getting low," he would say. He would promptly be given another case. Christmas trees were another thing. At every port of call, a fellow would bring him down a Christmas tree until the foredeck was full of trees. When they arrived in Vancouver there would be enough trees for everyone aboard ship.

Pop did a lot of relieving and filling in. The office would phone him up and say, "We want you to go out on the *Chelohsin*." When he arrived down at the dock, they'd suddenly need him on another ship and he couldn't even get time to phone home, so his wife often never knew where he was.

He was a very popular person and often when he would step out of his cabin to go on watch there would frequently be a fellow on deck who knew him and insist that he have a drink. Pop would go into his cabin and get a tumbler, pour a drink then take it back to his room. Later when he came off watch he would get out a bottle and pour the drink into it. Rod said, "God, he could bring home some awful mixtures! His wife would often make a party punch and Pop would pour his mixture into the punch bowl when she wasn't looking. Guests would wonder what hit them."

He ended his service with the Union Steamship Company working aboard the *Lady Alexandra* with Captain Yates, until she was laid up in September 1952. His son said, "He was turfed out without a pension at age 78." However, he did get some work as a night watchman aboard two wooden minesweepers tied up at B C. Marine for a time. He died at age 88, in February 1962.

A. C. "Big Mac" McLennan

Capt. A.C. "Big Mac" McLennan
(Belveal Collection)

Of all the Captains in the Union fleet whom I sailed with, and there were many, "Big Mac" was my favourite. Paul St. Pierre, writing in the *Vancouver Sun*, said of Captain McLennan, "He was a quiet and resourceful mariner with an enviable safety record. He was a short, jolly man who'd look well in a Santa Claus suit." Gerald Rushton meanwhile described him as a "consummate mariner." [162]

For some reason Alex McLennan seemed to fit my idea of what an old, experienced sea captain should be like. First of all, though he was not tall he was still a big man, with a ruddy complexion and a deep voice. He just seemed to have an air of authority and confidence about him. Obviously he was very competent, judging from the statements above. His crew were respectful and were a happy bunch while he was aboard. He had a hearty laugh and a twinkle in his eyes. He knew his job.

Only one report of a marine collision involving Captain McLennan came to light in my research. He was Master on the *Lady Pam* in the early 1930s. Dennis Farina was decking aboard her when the accident took place. The *Pam* came around Point Atkinson on a very dark night and they ran into a large sailboat that had no running lights going. The *Lady Pam* hit the sailboat amidships, cutting her in two. Several people were thrown into water but all were picked up by a lifeboat launched by the *Lady Pam*. In the court hearing that followed, Judge Sidney Smith, who held a Master's Ticket himself, ruled that as the sailboat had no running lights going its operators were found to be at fault.

I recall one time aboard the old *Cassiar II*. We had just discharged a big load of freight at the Goose Bay cannery and we were backing away from the wharf when we hit a submerged deadhead and lost the propeller. A fish packer had to pull us back to the wharf. We couldn't go anywhere so we just sat at the wharf waiting for a tow boat to come up from Vancouver to tow us back to town. The *Cardena* came alongside while we were waiting and took aboard our passengers, the perishable cargo and other important freight, all except the mail sacks for the Rivers Inlet stops. I was delegated to go up Rivers Inlet in a fish boat, along with Dr. Darby's son, to deliver the mail sacks to all the canneries in the Inlet.

The towboat arrived, but all of a sudden the weather changed and turned nasty. We just had to sit there waiting for it to change so the towboat could move us safely. One lunch hour the towboat captain was aboard our ship for lunch. The Chief Steward asked Captain McLennan when we might be moving. Big Mac, also known as the Rajah, replied, "I don't know, ask him (the towboat captain), he's the man with the brass nuts now, he's in charge, I've nothing to do with moving her now!" No pretentiousness with Big Mac!

McLennan was born in Kyle, Rosshire, Scotland in 1887 and first went to sea at age 15 in trawlers dragging between the Hebrides and Greenland. He then sailed deep-sea aboard a tramp steamer which took him to New York, Halifax and Montreal. On another voyage he ended up in Seattle, where he signed off his ship and came up to Vancouver. He signed aboard a ship of the CPR's B.C. Coastal Service, serving as 2nd and 3rd Mate. In 1914 he joined the RCN and served aboard minesweepers in European waters. He returned to B.C., signed up with the Union Steamship Co. in 1921 and served with them for the next 29 years.

Starting as a junior officer in the Company, McLennan learned about the B.C. coast from some very fine Masters along the way, such as Captains Wilson, Findlay and Dickson. In looking through ship registry records I noted that Big Mac also served as 1st Mate in 1924 aboard the *Cheam* under Captain Billy Yates.

Big Mac wasn't a flamboyant fellow so he didn't catch the public eye and didn't get the press from the marine writers of the day like his contemporaries Captain Boden and Captain Sheppard. However, through my interviews with many fellows who served under him, I was able to collect many fine anecdotes about this great Union Steamship skipper. Following are some of the best.

Geoff Hoskens told me of the time he was 2nd Mate on the *Cassiar* under Captain McLennan doing the Queen Charlotte Island run. Watches were six hours on and six hours off. On one occasion they ran into some terrible and typical foul weather going over from Prince Rupert to the Islands. After six hours on the bridge battling the elements, they were exhausted. As the watch changed, Big Mac said to Geoff, "Come with me for a moment," and he took Geoff into his room and poured him a wonderful nightcap of good Scotch whisky. A typical gesture of thanks by the Rajah to his officers.

Captain McLennan also was a no-nonsense man. An Assistant Purser by the name of Harry Braddick, who at times could be a bit of a smart aleck, once said to him, "Well Cap, if you ever need any help up on the bridge, just call me!" The Captain said nothing but waited and on one particular foul night he sent for Harry to come up to the bridge and had him stand out on the bridge in the cold and rainy dark night for a couple of hours, supposedly helping to spot landmarks and lights. That, cooled Harry off!

Fred Corneille recalls sailing with Big Mac and the awful pipe tobacco he loved to smoke. It was a terrible Irish Twist and in bad weather with the wheel house windows and doors closed the smoke and fumes would almost kill a person. "Oh, it was foul smelling stuff," Fred said.

One beautiful summer evening as we approached Campbell River I went up to the bridge to view the large forest fires burning at the time. Captain McLennan was on the bridge and I started to chat with him. I asked him, "In all your years at sea you must have seen some strange things. Did you ever see the likes of sea serpents that people are supposed to be seeing today?" "Bah," he said, "I've been at sea for many, many years, all over the world and I've never seen anything like that. It's nonsense." That was the end of that conversation.

Ben Smith was a 4th Engineer aboard the *Coquitlam II* when McLennan was the Captain but he took sick and had to be relieved by Captain McCombe for two or three weeks. One day afterwards Big Mac was sitting at the mess table with Ben and asked him, "How did you get along with Wee Willie McCombe while I was away?" Ben replied, "Oh pretty well, Captain." Big Mac, a slow talker, then said "He's 90 per cent, you know." Ben looked up and said, "Aye, what's that Cap?" Mac answered: "90 per cent bullshit!"

Abe McCormick related a story about the deck crew aboard one of the ships that started to raise a fuss about the food being served to them, particularly some soup. They were raising hell with the Chief Steward and the cooks. The fellows stuck to their complaint and further said they were not going to work and wouldn't get the ship going. The chief steward called the Captain who that day was McLennan. The Rajah came down to the crew's mess and said, "What's the matter boys?" They repeated their complaints, so Mac said to the Chief Steward that he wanted to taste the soup. He stood there and tasted several spoonfuls, then turned to the crew and said, "Tastes damn good to me boys, just as good as I would get home." With that he turned and walked out. The crew knew that was the last word and if they wanted to keep their jobs they'd better get back to work, and they did.

Another story involves a shipment of pigs stored on the foredeck in crates. During some bad weather one or two of the crates were broken and the pigs escaped and were running around the deck. Captain McLennan was watching the crew trying to round up these pigs. With a hearty laugh he hollered down to the crew, "Take them into the Purser's Office, they're the fellows who are supposed to keep track of the freight."

Capt. Alex C. McLennan on the bridge
(Vancouver Maritime Museum)

Captain McLennan also could be firm and strict, as seen in the following story related by Charlie Lewis, who served as 3rd Mate aboard ship with him. The event took place at Masset as the ship was southbound. There was a pile of empty oil drums on the wharf along with a considerable pile of empty gasoline drums. Charlie was on watch and told the wharfinger that they could take the oil drums but the gasoline drums would have to wait for a freight boat, because being a passenger ship the gasoline drums were not allowed aboard. The crew started to load the oil drums on to the foredeck. Just at that time the watch changed and Charlie went to his room. The other mate came on watch (Charlie wouldn't give me his name) and proceeded to load all the drums including the empty gasoline drums. Not only that, he was storing them down in the hold! Captain McLennan happened to come out and saw what was going on. He raised hell with the Mate who had loaded the gasoline drums and fired him on the spot, then banished him to his room. With that he called Charlie back on deck and promoted him to 2nd Mate, then and there. Charlie had to go work and unload all the gasoline drums. This of course took up a lot of time and the ship was running pretty late by now. When the ship reached Prince Rupert Big Mac put the offending mate ashore and made arrangements for him to get passage back to Vancouver on another Union vessel.

Little Joe Kelly was Assistant Purser aboard the *Cardena* on the Rivers Inlet run and Captain McLennan was on the bridge. Joe was at the gang plank and a few minutes before the ship was about to sail a fellow came running down to the ship pushing a hand truck loaded with one of those big boxes similar to what frozen fish was shipped in. He said it was full of groceries for his crew up at Margaret Bay. He was going aboard the *Cardena* and he wanted to get this box on board as well. A big hassle took place between the wharf police, Joe, and this fellow, about getting this box aboard the ship. There were no freight bills and the hatches had been battened down. Just then a freight checker came along and said he would make out some freight bills. Captain McLennan was impatient to cast off and hollered down, "Come on, what's going on down there?" It was decided to take this box aboard, so they took off the hatch covers and lowered it down into the hold, rather hastily, in a rope sling. The box was bumped on the way down and was damaged. After getting away, the stevedore came up to the Purser's Office and said to Joe, "You know, that's not groceries in that box, it's booze!"

When they arrived at Margaret Bay, Joe was off watch and was asleep in his room. Charlie Guy, the Purser, knocked on his door and woke him up. He said, "Joe, that box you took aboard at the last minute in Vancouver wasn't groceries, it was full of booze and it's been pilfered by the crew. The owner is furious." The owner started screaming at Captain McLennan up on the bridge about his box being damaged and the contents pilfered. The Captain came rushing down from the bridge like a bull moose and confronted the fellow himself and said, "Look, you told us it was full of groceries and we went to a great deal of trouble to put it aboard for you. Now we find you are a liar as it wasn't groceries in that box, it was liquor. You know damn well it's illegal for any booze to be shipped by anyone other than the Liquor Board. Don't you tell me what to do aboard my ship. If you want we'll put you aboard the ship and take you to the first RCMP detachment on our route and let them charge you."

The fellow realized he was in a tight spot so he said, "Okay, we'll forget the whole thing, Captain." This was good example of Big Mac's common-sense approach to things. He got to the heart of a problem and settled it with very little fuss. He was a great one.

Captain McLennan had one son, Alastair, who also served in the Union Steamship Co. He obtained his Coastal Mate's Ticket and was a 2nd and 3rd Mate with the Union Steamships until its end and then he transferred over to the Alaska Cruise Lines.

Captain McLennan died in Vancouver General Hospital after a short illness on April 28, 1950, just two weeks after he had had to give up his command of the *Cardena*. He was buried in the Mountain View Cemetery.

Alastair Fraser "Alec" McLennan, Jr.

Capt. "Alec" McLennan, Jr. on the *Coquitlam* circa 1955 *(Belveal Collection)*

Alec was born in Vancouver, April 26, 1925. His father was Captain A.C. McLennan, one of the senior skippers in the Union fleet, so Alec took to the sea and ships quite naturally.

Records show that at age 17, Alec joined the *Chelohsin* on August 18, 1942 as a deckhand, then went on to become quartermaster on the *Cassiar II*, in 1943. He then obtained his Mate's Ticket and in 1945 he was aboard the *Chelohsin* as 3rd Mate. His next move was to the *Lady Alexandra* where he served as 2nd Mate in 1946. Seldom did father and son serve on the same ship but on one occasion, for two weeks in 1949, he and his father were together on the *Cardena*.

Alec was a shy and quiet fellow and I have been told his shipmates began calling him Silent Sam. Many felt that some of his shyness was because he felt so overshadowed by his illustrious father. As well, Alec apparently had a slight hearing problem in his left ear. Iain Morrison, a deck officer who sailed with Alec,

Alec McLennan, Jr. in the wheelhouse of the *Yukon Star* circa 1967 *(Belveal Collection)*

Right: "Wee" Angus McNeill *(D. Shaw)*

confirmed that this was so.

One story that has been passed along to me about Alec was that he was a pretty fair baseball player. At times, a Union Ship on the West Howe Sound run would lay over at Hopkins Landing for a few hours before resuming its schedule, so the crew would go up to the local ball park and play baseball. It was said that Alec could hit the ball a mile.

When the Union Steamships ceased operation in 1958, Alec continued to sail in the summer seasons with the Alaska Cruise Lines as Mate. In the off season he lived on Bowen Island, in a cottage he had bought on Miller's Landing Road. When the Alaska Cruise Lines ceased operating, he retired from an active sea career and reports say he became a partner in the BoMart Store on Bowen Island.

As time went by, Alec began to drink heavily, which no doubt hastened his death. He died in about August, 1986 and one of his friends on Bowen Island, Carl O'Day, took care of the funeral arrangements. Alec was cremated and his ashes were consigned to the sea between Horseshoe Bay and Bowen Island in a ceremony held aboard the B.C. Ferry on that run. Carl also gave the eulogy as the Minister who was supposed to perform the ceremony missed the boat! There are conflicting reports that Alec's sister died the same day as Alec or that she died two days later.

Carl O'Day has an extensive collection of Union Steamship Company memorabilia and amongst the items is a brass wall clock which Alec had removed from the *Lady Alexandra* after she had been taken out of service for good. Alec had given this clock to his friend and it is still in use to this day.

"Wee" Angus McNeill

"Wee Angus" or the "Skye Man" as he was affectionately known in his Union Steamship days, was born at Waternish, Isle of Skye, in 1887.

In 1926, Gerald Rushton was over in England looking for another freight vessel for the company and he purchased the *Ardgarvel*. She was fitted out in Glasgow and Captain Findlay was brought over to bring her out to Vancouver. Angus McNeill was one of her officers on this trip. She was renamed the *Chilliwack II* and arrived in Vancouver May 5, 1927. Angus's career with the Union Steamships started with this trip and ended 31 years later, when Northland Navigation took over the Union

Steamship operation.

In an interview taped by Bob Hackett shortly before McNeill died, he said he never liked working for Northland and that the Union Steamship Co. had really been his home.

I had the pleasure of sailing with Angus. He was very well-liked by both crew and passengers. He was a jovial person and always very dapper in his appearance.

My most vivid memory of Angus is a sad one. I was serving as Assistant Purser on the *Cardena*, July 16, 1948, when he put her hard aground at False Bay on Lasqueti Island. As I recall, the grounding took place around 1 or 2 a.m. I was in my cabin preparing to go to bed. My room was port side and right at the water line. As I was removing my jacket, I heard a scraping noise along the hull. Instinct told me this wasn't right and as I hurriedly left my cabin - crash! - we hit the reef!

More details of this grounding will be found under *Cardena* in the Ships section, p.63-64. The morning after all the passengers had beeen put ashore, the *Cardena* was sitting high and dry. The miracle was she seemed to have wedged herself between two rock formations and was sitting there as though she was in a vise. Next morning, with the ship still high and dry, I was walking around the deck to look over the scene and who do I see coming in the opposite direction but Wee Angus, his head down and hands behind his back - a picture of utter dejeaction. What do you say to a man in that situation? His career could be in jeopardy, a lifelong dedication to seamanship and he runs a big ship aground fully loaded with freight and passengers. We just nodded to each other as we passed and went on with our walk, going in opposite directions. Truly, he was a lonely soul at that moment on the deck of the *Cardena*.

The following story was told to me by Geoff Hosken and in it Angus ends up a hero, of sorts. A horse was being loaded onto one of the day boats and Angus was 2nd mate. He was in charge of the loading operation. It was summertime and the dock and other nearby ships were all crowded with passengers who were watching all the proceedings with great interest. Livestock such as horses and cows were put in a heavy reinforced wooden box with doors that opened at each end. An animal was gently coaxed into the box with one door already secured. On this occasion the horse was nearly into the box when it was frightened by a noise and reared up on its hind legs and when it came down its front legs came down outside of the box. What a panic, what excitement. What to do about this? The horse would be the last thing to be put aboard before sailing, and it was time for the ship to leave, but the horse couldn't be loaded in this situation. Everyone was laughing and hollering. The longshoremen were scratching their heads, deckhands stood around helpless, and poor Angus was frantic, for in front of all the people he was looking a little foolish. He tried this and he tried that, but to no avail. Angus was at his wit's end when, out of frustration and without thinking, he swung his clenched fist at the horse and hit it square on the snout. With that the horse reared up and, miracle of miracles, when it came down both of its front legs were inside the box! The crowd let out a huge cry and hurrah. Angus was an immediate hero!

Angus had another run-in with livestock, when a cow was being loaded aboard ship from the float landing at Shushartie Bay. This animal had been brought out, with great difficulty no doubt, to the small float in the bay. When the Union ship arrived it was late at night, a ramp was put out from the ship to the float, with the idea of walking the cow up this ramp to the freight deck. Don McLeod was the Freight Clerk and he grabbed the halter and began pulling the cow up the ramp, while Angus drew up to the rear, to push. It should be said at this point that Angus was wearing a brand new uniform. As the two of them were pulling and pushing this cow, it let go a big cow plop, which went all over Angus and his new uniform. Mercy!

They finally did get the cow aboard but when Don went to wake up Reg Stover, the Purser, to tell him about this cow, Reg said, "You can't take that cow into Vancouver without special papers and documents from the Department of Health." So the poor cow had to be led off of the ship and back onto the float, much to the dissatisfaction of its owner. There is no reference as to what Angus did with his uniform.

Ben Smith talked to me about Angus and said he was a great fellow to sail with, but felt he was quite nervous. He told me the following story about Angus which wouldn't have helped his nerves one bit. Angus was Chief Officer on the *Coquitlam II* and the ship was proceeding south in a very thick fog. The 3rd Mate on board was a chap by the name of Stan Green. He had come down from the bridge for a mug up, and at the same time Ben had come up from the engine room to have a coffee himself. As they sat there chatting, they could hear Angus blowing the ship's whistle continuously and as the ship had radar everything was fine. All of a sudden Stan said, "I'm going to give Angus the scare of his life." Stan played the trumpet, so he went to his cabin, opened the port hole and as soon as Angus blew the whistle, Stan blew a blast on his trumpet, out the port hole. Then Angus would pull the whistle cord, and Stan would blast off his trumpet again. Later, when Ben asked Stan how Angus had handled all this, Stan's reply was, "God, when I came back up to the bridge, Angus's face was green and he said, 'There was a bloody fish packer right alongside us, and now I don't know where it's gone.'"

It was well-known in the fleet that Angus was a little nervous and as well a little superstitious. For instance, he would never steer a course that was say N 13 W or N 13 E, he would always call for N 12 or N 14. Another thing, he was terribly upset if he saw a priest or a minister come aboard. I am told that he didn't like to go into a darkened room without someone with him. When I discussed such superstitions with an old seaman, he said, "Oh yes, quite true and another thing, this is why you'll never see a room 13 on a ship!"

Whenever dead bodies were being transported Angus was uneasy, and the crew knew this, although he always instructed the crew to handle a coffin with care, remove their hats, and company policy was to always drape the coffin with a Canadian flag. As a result of his uneasiness, a crew on the *Catala* made him the butt of a nasty practical joke. He was 2nd Mate and the ship was carrying a coffin to Vancouver which was stowed in the lower hold. Knowing how terrified Angus was of dead bodies, a pretext was set up for him to come down into the lower hold to examine some damaged freight before the ship docked since as 2nd mate freight was his responsibility. The crew arranged to have one of their members lie down beside and behind the coffin. They sprinkled flour over him and pasted his face white. The coffin, was stowed in behind this damaged freight and when Angus was looking over the damaged goods, the fellow lying behind the coffin, first let out a groan and then this white apparition rose up! Angus took off in a flash and was up the ladder from the lower hold and was gone before any of the crew hardly had time to move. He was terrified for sure, indicative of his nervous nature, although such a joke would scare the best of people. This story was told to me by Denis Shaw, who was Purser aboard the *Catala* at the time.

Ed Roach related another story about Angus along the same lines regarding a dead man's coat. When Captain Gray died, his widow gave Captain Harry Roach a brand new bridge coat that had been made for Captain Gray but he never had worn it. Harry was very pleased with the coat, because in those days the Masters spent a lot of time out on the bridge, especially in foul weather. Anyway, when Angus joined the *Lady Cynthia* under Captain Roach and learned about Captain Gray's coat, he would not enter the wheelhouse if it was just hanging there, because of the seaman's superstition of "not wearing a dead man's coat." Ed said it was a brand new coat and his father wore it for years.

Angus's sea career on the B.C. coast lasted over 50 years, 31 years with the Union Steamship Co., then with the Northland Navigation Co. and ending with Harbour Navigation Co. Finally, at age 82, he dropped anchor and retired. He died in Vancouver at a ripe old age of 92 and it truly could be said, "He was an Officer and a Gentleman, through and through."

John "Jock" Leask Malcolmson

Captain John Malcolmson like so many of the Union Steamship skippers hails from the Shetland Islands. He was born at Hoswick, the Parish of Sandwick, on Sept. 14, 1892.

I interviewed his daughter, Dr. Anna Welbourn, and she recalled her father as having a great sense of humour which she explained was a common trait of the Shetlanders, as well as their love of children and family. She said, "He was a big man," which indeed he was, being well over 6 ft. tall and weighing over 200 pounds. She remembered him as being very good-natured and being a firm but fair disciplinarian.

His father owned a fishing vessel and John used to sail with him on school holidays as a junior member of the crew, or "boy" as they were called aboard ship in those days. He had started to train as a grocery apprentice but the urge to go to sea like his father took over and at the age of 15 he signed aboard a fishing vessel the *Native Queen* as a cook and coiler. That was in 1907.

John came to Canada with plenty of sea time under his belt. He joined the Union Steamship Co. on March 26, 1913, signing aboard the *Camosun I* as a quartermaster. The Master aboard her at that time was the famous Captain Wilson. In 1916 John was then transferred over to the S.S. *British Columbia* (the name was later changed to the *Chilliwack*) as quartermaster. At this time he obtained his Coastal Mate's Ticket, being number 8279, and later that year he was sailing as 2nd Mate aboard the *Chilliwack*. Then in 1917 he sailed as 2nd Mate aboard the *Cowichan*, then later as the Chief Officer, under Captain Georgeson. In 1919 he took a brief period of time off to visit his family in the Shetlands.

On March 23, 1921, at 29 years of age, he obtained his Coastal Master's Ticket being number 9606. Promotions in the Company were slow. He sailed on the *Venture* as Pilot for almost three years under Captain Noel and then on the *Chilliwack* until Sept. 30, 1924. From Sept. 1924 to March 1929 there is a blank in his records. During this period he returned again to the Shetlands in 1925 to marry his childhood sweetheart. Their daughter Anna was born on Christmas eve 1927.

Although "Big Jock" Malcolmson, as he was affectionately called aboard ship, spent most of his career on the northern and

Capt. "Jock" Malcolmson
(Anna Welbourn)

logging camp routes, it was on the West and East Howe Sound runs that he left his mark. His first sailing as Master was on the *Lady Pam* in the summer of 1936. He soon became very well-known and liked throughout the whole area. During this period he suffered a heart attack but soon was able to resume his command.

Captain Malcolmson was an active member of the Canadian Merchant Service Guild for years. In 1941 he sat on the board as a representative for the Freight Masters on the B.C. coast.

Denis Shaw, the well-known Purser in the Union Co., sailed frequently with Captain Malcolmson and he had many anecdotes to relate about Big Jock.

Captain Malcolmson owned a long leather coat which he would wear on the bridge during poor weather and Denis said, "He reminded you of a First World War German general. The coat went right down to his ankles. Sometimes he even wore the coat to bed in cold weather," Denis said.

In the early days, the Union ships used to load and carry on the foredeck plain timber or logs. According to Denis, and this he says was told to him by Captain Malcolmson himself, "The crews were issued caulk boots to wear while loading these logs. As 2nd Mate, Jock Malcolmson would be in charge of the loading. On one occasion he felt the loading wasn't going fast enough and he donned caulk boots himself to go to work and try to get things moving faster. He jumped down from the shell door opening between deck onto the logs floating in the water alongside the ship. Being a big man, when he landed his caulks stuck fast into the log and he couldn't extract himself, the log rolled and Big Jock went right into the saltchuck and very nearly drowned!"

Another story Denis tells indicates that the crew were aware of his good nature. The *Lady Pam* did not have hot running water in any of its quarters, the captain's cabin being no exception, so Captain Malcolmson used to send down for a jug of hot water so he could have a shave. The stewards got used to this and one day they got the bright idea of playing a joke on Captain Malcolmson so they heated up some salt water and sent it up to him. Try as he might he could not get any lather, so he sent down for another jug of water and the same thing happened. He finally realized that someone was playing a trick on him so he stormed down to the galley, shouting as he came, and everyone disappeared, fast. With that he started to laugh, proving to one and all, he could take a joke.

Captain Malcolmson's daughter told me they always had plenty of fish in their house and that the cats in the neighbourhood were the best-fed cats in Vancouver, for the Captain was always bringing home fish, either fresh or canned. For her, in those days, having fish of any kind wasn't a treat.

On one occasion when Captain Malcolmson was boarding the streetcar on his way home, he had a bag of fresh herring with him. As he made his way up the aisle of the streetcar to a seat, he soon began to hear people laughing behind him. Turning around to see what it was all about, he saw instantly. Fish had been falling out of his bag as he walked to his seat. Without hesitating he calmly went back and picked them all up. He brought them home, washed them off and had them up for his supper that same night. He loved his fish!

The first day I started to work as a Freight Clerk on the Union Steamships, the Master was Jock Malcolmson. In those days you went out without any training at all. As long as you could type you got the job. At the first stop with all the freight being unloaded I was standing on the dock thoroughly confused. Then the whistle blew, indicating we were about to leave for the next port. I turned around and hollered up to the Captain, "Hey, wait a minute!" I sure received a very cold stare from him and as soon as I went aboard, Neil Morlock, the Purser, grabbed me and said, "Son, don't you ever, ever call the Captain 'Hey' again. If you want to hold your job, remember that."

On the afternoon of Feb. 5, 1947 the *Capilano* had just left New Brighton in

West Howe Sound and was making for its next stop, Hopkins Landing. Captain Malcolmson was on the bridge. A passenger came rushing up to the Captain and said that the steering chain had come off of quadrant, which meant the helm would jam and the ship couldn't be steered. Captain Malcolmson exclaimed, "Oh my God!" and sent his Mate Don Campbell to fetch a crow bar so the chain could be put back in place. When the Mate returned he found Captain Malcolmson lying unconscious at the door of the wheelhouse. Don immediately took charge and brought the ship to a stop. He phoned head office to advise them what had happened and at the same time asked them to phone Gibsons Landing to have a doctor and the police meet the ship. The *Capilano* then proceeded full speed for Gibsons Landing.

Dr. Hugh Inglis went aboard immediately when the ship docked, examined Captain Malcolmson and pronounced him dead. Wally Graham, the town's undertaker, also attended. He closed the Captain's eyes, and with that the ship departed and proceeded direct to Vancouver, abandoning its schedule for that day. Norrie Wood, who was Purser aboard that day, recalls that Captain Malcolmson was such a big and heavy man, it took three men to lift and carry him to his room.

After 27 years of service with the Union Steamship Co., this popular skipper died aboard his ship at the relatively early age of 55 years, with his boots on as I'm sure he would have liked.

Union Steamship Co. docks in Vancouver, B. C.

Billy Jan Marette

Billy Jan Marette

Bill Marette served with the Union Steamship Co. for only three months, Aug. 8 to Nov. 6, 1953. He was 3rd Mate on the *Catala* and the *Camosun III*, first under Captain Sheppard and then briefly under Captain Halcrow when it relieved the *Catala* for two weeks in October. During that short period of time he could see for himself that there was not much of a future for the coastal passenger ship operations in B.C.

Bill was born in Nottingham, England on April 30, 1931, and went to sea as an apprentice with the Clan Line, sailing briefly with Canadian Pacific on the Empress ships before passing his 2nd Mate's Ticket. He eventually came out to the B.C. coast on the *Tacoma Star*. He liked what he saw in Vancouver and was determined to come back to B.C. He returned to the U.K. and obtained his 1st Mate's Ticket. He arrived back in B.C. on a Sunday morning in 1953, went down to the Merchant Service Guild office on Monday morning and was hired that afternoon by the Union Steamship Co. He sailed out the following day on the *Catala*, under Captain Sheppard, as 3rd Mate.

On one trip aboard the *Catala*, Bill said he came the closest he had ever come to being sunk aboard any ship he had ever sailed on.

The *Catala* was proceeding south and was abeam of Campbell River in a dense fog, with himself and Iain Morrison the Chief Officer on the bridge. All of a sudden this huge American freighter, high out of the water, loomed out of the fog ahead travelling on the wrong side of the channel. Iain quickly put the *Catala* full astern and they missed a collision by inches. Geoff Hosken, who was 2nd Mate and off watch, heard all the whistles and signals rattling, came up onto the bridge in his pajamas to see what was happening.

Bill also recalls going up Johnstone Strait on the *Catala* during the fishing season with the fish nets strung out all over the channel. It was impossible to miss them, try as you might. The *Catala* being a relatively flat-bottomed ship you could hear the nets with their weights clinking along her bottom.

Many of the deck officers on the Union Ships spoke the Gaelic language fluently. Bill recalls the manager at Powell River for one and an executive at Ocean Falls for another, would come aboard ship, go up to the bridge and converse in Gaelic, just for the pleasure of it.

He also recalled Iain Morrison, the Chief Officer who hailed from Oben, arriving late and somewhat tipsy on sailing night. He received a real dressing down by the Master and then he sent Iain below.

Bill Marette's tour with the Company was short, but one he enjoyed. He said the *Catala* was a happy ship and the meals were wonderful. However he was very perceptive to observe in the short period he was with the Company, that the Company's coastal shipping business was losing out to the airplane. He noted that a person could fly to Vancouver from Port Hardy in under two hours for perhaps only one dollar more than the boat fare, which would take a day, plus the cost of meals adding to the expense. The ships could not compete. Bill saw the future and decided to leave the sea and go to air. He went to flying school, took flying lessons and became a pilot with CP Air (now part of Canadian Airlines) in February 1955.

After flying all over the world for 36 years, Bill retired in June 1991 to a beautiful home in West Vancouver. He could have been a Captain aboard a ship but he saw the future and decided on being a Captain aboard an airplane. A very astute career choice!

Isaac French "John" Mercer

Capt. John Mercer (Ashmore Collection)

Born in Bay Roberts, Newfoundland, John Mercer signed on aboard the *Venture* in early 1923. He wasn't long on the *Venture* for he was moved over to the Company's brand new ship, the beautiful *Cardena*, on her maiden voyage, June 20, 1923, as 3rd Mate. Captain Dickson was her Master, Bill Mounce was the Chief Officer, and E. Sheppard was 2nd Mate.

John was aboard the *Cardena* when she

came to the rescue of the CNR ship *Prince Rupert* which had grounded on the treacherous Ripple Rock in Seymour Narrows, Aug. 22, 1927. Captain Andy Johnstone brought the *Cardena* close enough to the hapless *Prince Rupert* and gave great praise to Mercer at the time for his marvellous ability throwing a heaving line from the *Cardena* to the stranded ship. This is what he is reported to have said: "It was a superb feat of heaving line throwing by big John Mercer, who was an old time halibut schooner man with huge hands." [163]

Ship Registry records show John Mercer serving on the *Catala* as 2nd Mate, then as Chief Officer on the *Cardena*, and later he was Master of the *Lady Cynthia*.

Though information and records about John Mercer are practically non-existent, Johnny Horne was able to give me one story about him which is rather sad: If Jim Calderwood wasn't Chief Officer on the *Cardena*, John Mercer was. In later years John suffered terribly with very bad varicose veins. He could not stand for the whole six-hour watch so he used to bring a stool into the wheelhouse to sit on during his watch. On one occasion, according to John, Jack Boden was the Captain and he did not like to see a stool in the wheelhouse. One time after his finishing watch, John forgot to take his stool out of the wheelhouse, so Captain Boden took the stool and cut the legs off unevenly. A pretty cruel joke for Captain Boden to perpetrate on his suffering Chief Officer.

John Mercer died during the war years, having worked 20 years for the Union Steamship Co.

John Iain Morrison

Iain was born in 1909 at Oban, a town that he described as being "The Gateway to the Highlands." He joined the Union Steamships in the late 1930s as a quartermaster aboard the *Catala*. When he signed aboard her the Master was Ernest Sheppard, John Mercer was Chief Officer, and the two mates were Neil Campbell and Bob Naughty Jr. As the years went by, Iain always felt the *Catala* was his favourite ship.

Capt. Iain Morrison (left) with Robert Smith
(McAllister Collection)

I interviewed Iain at his home in October 1990. He was in his eighties then and unfortunately he wasn't able to recall too much about his times on the Union ships.

When Iain married, he and his wife Winnie took their honeymoon aboard a Union ship. His wife remembered calling into all the little ports, especially the Skeena River canneries.

During the war years, competent deck officers were scarce and getting time off was very difficult. He recalled one occasion when he had come in to Vancouver on the *Chelohsin* and as he was leaving her to go home, the Shore Mate, Harry Biles, stopped him and said, "Sorry but we want you to go out tonight on the *Cardena*." For days you never received any time off. The lay day system was in place, but it didn't help much because there was nobody else available to relieve you. Later in his career, Iain used to relieve Harry Biles as the Shore Mate.

Iain was one of Captain Boden's favourites, and he was always trying to get Iain aboard his ship. He would say to Iain, "Come on, when are you coming home?" Obviously Captain Boden thought highly of Iain. He said himself, "I never had any trouble navigating and handling ships and I was never in a serious accident other than maybe hitting a log."

I asked him if he ever got the wrong response from the engine room and he said it did happen. He recalled taking the *Lady Cynthia* out of Garden Bay and he rang for slow astern and he received slow ahead. They bumped the float, but he quickly rang again for slow astern and was able to clear away alright. However, he and the engineer were called into the office and the engineer admitted the error was his.

Iain also recalled that docking in Heriot Bay was sometimes an adventure. He said if you went in there at night you couldn't see a thing but you always docked without too much trouble but during the daylight it would scare the wits out of you because you could see there were rocks everywhere.

He also related a story about the ship's engines breaking down while they were coming through treacherous Seymour Narrows. He couldn't remember what ship it was but they navigated safely just using the tide and ended up drifting safely off of Cape Mudge. Another of his memorable trips was aboard the *Venture* on her last run for the Company.

We started to discuss the day boats and without fail the *Lady Alexandra* and her Moonlight Cruises came to the fore. Iain recalled many of the passengers coming aboard sober, but on the return trip that night some of them would be so drunk they couldn't stand up so the crew would load them on the freight dollies and wheel them out to the taxi stand on the wharf. His wife recalled going along on some of those "booze cruises" and she said she was scared to death. Iain said: "It was perfectly obvious the ship was often overloaded as to her passenger limits."

During our conversation Iain also offered his opinion that most of the news agents aboard the ships were bootlegging whisky to people at the various stops, a suspicion that is shared by the crews in general. Most ships had news stands staffed by members of the news agents' association, and people at the stops, some of which would last for hours, would come aboard to buy newspapers, magazines, cigarettes, chocolate bars and soda pop, and probably some of that pop had been spiked and recapped. News agents carried a lot of merchandise in their tiny stands, such as souveniers, but they also did a lot of commerce on the side, even in some cases buying wedding rings for crew and casual customers alike. They used to say they could get you anything you wanted.

Iain also recalls playing a lot of poker aboard the ships. He told me in one poker game after he was married he made enough money to buy all the furniture they needed for their house. After he retired he ran into Don Campbell, a former deck officer he hadn't seen for 30 years, and he said, "I remember you and the first thing that comes to my mind is that you were always playing poker."

Iain was on the *Camosun III* when the Union Steamship Co. tied up all their ships. They never had any warning or notice that such a thing would happen. Iain then went over to the Alaska Cruise Line when they took over the corvettes. He was with them for five years and sailed as Master. The pictures of Iain accompanying this story show him as Chief Officer aboard a Union Steamship and as Master aboard the *Yukon Star*. She eventually went down to the Caribbean and Iain was supposed to take the ship down. He was going to take his wife Winnie along. They both had all their shots and had obtained their passports, but it never came to pass. Iain then went over to the CNR and served aboard the *Prince George II* for another five years as 2nd Mate and Chief Officer before retiring. He died at age 82 on Jan. 24, 1991.

William "Bill" Mounce

William "Bill" Mounce served with the Union Steamship Co. from 1917 to 1937, and then he went into the pilotage. Bill was born in Blaine, Wash.

Jesse Van der Berg in her book *History of the Union Steamships* states that Bill commanded a minesweeper on the Atlantic in the First World War. [164] Mr. Rushton in his book *Whistle up the Inlet* says that Bill Mounce was the first Captain of the *Chilco* when she was taken over from the All Red Line. His First Mate was Harry Roach. The first sailing of the *Chilco* under the Union flag was on July 17, 1917. [165]

Bill Mounce was Chief Officer under Captain Dickson aboard the *Cardena* on her maiden voyage to Prince Rupert, June 20, 1923. He went on to serve as Captain aboard the *Lady Pam*, *Capilano II*, *Lady Cynthia*, *Cardena*, and the freight boats *Chilkoot* and *Chilliwack*, before going to the pilotage in 1937.

Frank Skinner, former Purser and later Prince Rupert Agent for the Union Steamship Co., first met Bill Mounce aboard the *Catala*. Bill was Chief Officer and Frank was Freight Clerk. Frank said, "Bill used to chew tobacco all the time, and everyone thought that it was terrible, because he really was quite a chewer." Bill then became Master on the *Chilkoot* in 1930 and Frank was Purser. It was unusual, but at that time the Purser also had to look after the victualling aboard the ship. The *Chilkoot* was mainly a freight boat but she had limited passenger accommodation. Harry McLean was the Chief Officer. A fellow from Powell River by the name of Jack McKay was the Mate.

Fred Smith, longtime Chief Engineer with the Union Steamships, who had sailed with Bill Mounce and was a lifelong friend, said, "Later in life Bill was afflicted with Parkinson's Disease and didn't get around too well."

Capt. William "Bill" Mounce
(Dorothy Audley)

John "Jock" Muir

Capt. "Jock" Muir
(Meredith Collection)

John Muir was born in Campbelltown, Argyleshire, Scotland, on May 23, 1885. He was the eldest of 14 children and became an excellent scholar. He won a scholarship and attended first-year university but after that he had to go to work to help support the family, though his scholarly pursuits continued throughout his life. He later learned to read and write shorthand and in fact some of the entries in his personal diaries are interspersed with shorthand almost like it's a code being used to hide certain things he is saying. He also could speak and write French.

Muir's father owned a fleet of fishing boat's so "Jock" worked with him, following in his father's footsteps. He then joined a company whose ships were sailing from Scotland to the north of France and into the Mediterranean. While working for this line he obtained his first ticket, a British Home Trade Mate's Certificate. In June 1912 he joined the *Orantas*, a fishing vessel, in a little town named Bowling, on the river Clyde. They sailed from Bowling, going around the horn to Vancouver, a voyage that took 110 days. At last they anchored off North Vancouver. The *Orantas* had been purchased by Wallace Brothers and was to be operated as a fish packer. When the season closed Jock packed his bags, signed off the *Orantas* on Oct. 16, 1912 and moved into a boarding house near the harbour. He quickly obtained work shovelling coal for 50 cents an hour, bunkering the Empress ships. He was now 28 years old and he left this job and joined the Union Steamships in September 1913 and sailed out as quartermaster on the *Cassiar I*, whose Master was Captain Gaisford. [166]

Before Jock left home on this voyage he promised his father he would never take a drink while he was in command of a ship. In his early days aboard Union Steamships one of the crew referred to him as "John the Good."

The *Cassiar I* became famous along the coast and was known as the "loggers' palace." Jock had started his career with the Union Steamships aboard the *Cassiar* in 1913 and on her last year of service in the Company Jock was aboard her as Chief Officer in 1923. [167]

Muir soon was serving aboard the *Coquitlam I* (which later became the *Bervin*) and it was here he said he learned everything about the coast and freighting. In April 1912 the *Coquitlam*, under Captain Neil Gray, was travelling south to a new mine operation in Douglas Channel when she came into difficulties. "Jock" described it this way: "Our freighter, half loaded with coal, was lined up for the landing when it was suddenly caught and swung by a strong current towards the cliffs and bumped heavily several times against the rocks. I was assigned, with the chief engineer, to investigate the damage below deck, and a hurried check disclosed she was taking in some water. The hull was clearly punctured where some rivets had been knocked out. With his vessel in grave danger and with the pumps set to work, Captain Gray decided to make a three hour run for it up Grenville Channel to Lowe Inlet, where there was a shelving beach. During these critical hours I had to keep a constant watch on everything down below where the engineers were striving to control the water. If this condition had worsened we could well have sunk outside in the channel. But we made it into Lowe Inlet, and the Captain ran the *Coquitlam* straight up ashore at the head of the bay, alongside the old cannery. He had implicit faith in the skill and resource of our engineers to tackle the job of making the vessel seaworthy again in these unusual surroundings." [168]

Fred Smith, the Chief Engineer, tells what happened next: "The deck crew then dug through the coal before Second Engineer John Hogan and I could get working on the repairs. One of the deckhands had been a logger and, although we only had a blunt axe on board, he chopped through wood sheathing which enabled us to put a patch inside and tighten the seams of the careened hull with iron bolts. We just had to makeshift with no means of communication on board or ashore, and get home the best way we could." [169]

That accident took place in April, 1917. In August of that same year Jock Muir sat for his Master's Ticket and was successful.

He obtained his Certificate, being #8548.

Again we find Jock aboard the *Coquitlam* and being involved in another near disaster. Fred Smith says it took place right after the accident described above when the *Coquitlam* was southbound heading back to Vancouver in Queen Charlotte Sound, while Rushton says it happened in 1918. Whenever, Captain Muir was there and took part in the drama and he described it this way:

"The *Coquitlam* hit a deadhead in the middle of Queen Charlotte Sound and 'lost her wheel,' slipping off the propeller and lying helpless with no means of propulsion. We just had to wait, without any ship-to-shore telephone, until it happened that the *Venture* came steaming by southbound, a most welcome sight. She took us in tow and some said the *Coquitlam*, which was only making over eight knots loaded, had never travelled so fast before! But the work of repair had only just started. While still in Johnstone Strait, Chief Officer Charles B. Smith slipped overside the *Coquitlam* in his bathing suit to check the propeller shaft. As a result of this inspection it was decided to strand the *Coquitlam* on the beach at Alert Bay below the school. The *Camosun* brought up a new propellor - spares were always kept in Vancouver. When the tide was low enough and with the help of chain blocks Chief Engineer Fred Smith safely put on a new propeller as she lay. The vessel was refloated and continued right on her way north, as the bulk of her cargo was non-perishable." [170]

Fred Smith meanwhile says in another interview that it was no easy job, first because they sent up the wrong propeller, the one for her sister ship, so they had to do a lot of filing to make it fit, and then because the working conditions at low tide were very unpleasant, since being next to a cannery meant there were fish heads and guts everywhere.

Over the years and working together often, Jock and Freddy Smith became close friends and their families used to visit together frequently.

Muir's daughter recalled her father telling her about an incident that took place when he probably was Master on the *Chilliwack*. She thought he had said the ship had unloaded supplies at Bella Coola. There were several families of Indians that were going back to their homes in Kitimat and they were preparing to leave in their canoes. It was a terrible day, strong winds and blowing rain. Captain Muir looked at their plight and phoned down to head office and got permission to take them all aboard his ship as they were going up in that direction. This was granted, so Captain Muir put them all down in the hold. There was a load of coal down there. Before they knew it, the squaws had started to make dinner or something, down there, and the coal caught fire! Captain Muir said they had quite a time getting them all back up on deck and putting the fire out. Captain Muir said, "It was quite a scary night!"

The lighthouse keepers along the coast had quite a lonely life. Captain Muir tells about Mary Pike on the Pine Island light. He marveled at her courage and strength. "She would run that light and she would row her boat into Shushartie Bay and get anything she wanted," he recalled. "I used to roll up newspapers and when it was a fine day, I'd blow the whistle and they would know us anyway, coming along. You can go right in close to Pine Island and throw the bundle of papers over to her. Whether they were wet or dry, she didn't care. That was the Pikes." [171]

Captain Muir said: "I used to marvel at some of the elderly men that were Masters and the places they would go through in daylight in clear weather. It was the same in the dark.

"There was one minister at Van Anda. This minister used to put his lamp outside just the same as if he was a government light. Mrs. Thompson, in Whaletown, had the job of putting a light on certain rocks if you were going from Whaletown to Manson's Landing. You could go through that way if this light was on. Sometimes you'd be so close to the beach the ship's lights would shine on the beach.

"Going into some places in the wintertime, there'd just be a watchman and maybe his wife looking after the cannery. If he slept in, the ship's whistle would usually waken him up. The dog was a great friend. As soon as it heard the whistle, the dog started barking and the watchman would know the ship was coming.

"Some people don't understand navigating with the echoes. If you were going along a narrow channel and you heard a fellow blowing his whistle, you knew it was a ship's whistle 'cause there was nothing else there. You made sure you were on your side of the channel. Toot your whistle. You got maybe three seconds on that side and only one second back here. Well, you knew you were closer here and on side of the channel, so you tell the man at the wheel starboard so many degrees. You get back onto your own side on a foggy night." [172]

One of the biggest nightmares for the skippers navigating along the coast occurred during the fishing season, trying to get through all the fish nets particularly at night. The fishermen would string their nets every which way all across the inlets. The skippers would do their best to miss them but many a net was cut in two. Fred Smith in an interview with Bob Hackett told about an event involving his friend Captain Muir. Fred said, "At times Jock used to get very excited. One time the Japanese fishermen were at odds with the white fishermen around Rivers Inlet and they started shooting at each other. Jock was on the bridge of his ship at the time and a couple of shots hit the bridge. He was so mad he took off his cap and started to stamp on it in a rage. He was dancing around and threatened them all with all kind of mayhem if he ever got a hold of them." Freddy chuckled and said, "They weren't shooting at Jock, it was some shot that went astray." Freddy laughed again and said, "Jock was a Prince." [173]

On March 20, 1929 Captain Muir and his crew on the *Chilliwack* rescued five people from an American airplane that had been forced down into the waters of Grenville Channel.

Jock Muir was Chief Officer aboard the *Cardena* when on August 22, 1927 she went to the aid of the CNR *Prince Rupert* which had caught fast on Ripple Rock. The *Cardena*, after leaving Rock Bay, was headed for Seymour Narrows southbound. Muir had just come off night watch when he heard the sharp blasts of a distress signal. Muir told it this way: "There had been persistent fog in patches, and at this moment, shortly after 6 a.m., visibility was limited to within a hundred yards. Captain Johnstone immediately proceeded through the mist to render aid, and soon perceived the shape of the Canadian National's crack *Prince Rupert* caught fast on Ripple Rock, the bogey of the Narrows. Maneuvering with superb seamanship, Captain Johnstone brought the *Cardena* in close and, as he approached the scene, saw that the vessel was completely immobilized with one of her propellers going around in mid-air. The *Prince Rupert* could easily have foundered or been flung against the cliffs." [174] The *Cardena* was able to pull the *Prince Rupert* off and tow her into a safe anchorage nearby in Deep Cove.

In 1930 Captain Muir was Master of the *Chilliwack*. Two officers serving with him at the time were William McCombe and Lorne Godfrey. On one of his trips to Prince Rupert he took along his son Jack and his friend Bob Hackett, whose father was the Company Agent at Sechelt. Bob has a picture album recording this trip.

By 1936 Muir was Captain of the *Venture*, when Pinky Hughes was the Purser and J. Ackers was Chief Steward.

Two major personnel changes took place in the Union Steamship Co. in 1938 when two key men had to be replaced. Marine Superintendent Sandy Walker retired in June after 31 years with the Company, and Superintendent Engineer George H. Foster died.

Captain Muir, at age 53 with 25 years service behind him, succeeded Captain Walker, and Robert Logan took over for

Call Ripple Rock After Gerry

DECEMBER 27, 1947

LOOKING TOWARDS THE SOUTHERN END OF MAUD ISLAND ACROSS THE RIPPLES THAT HIDE RIPPLE ROCK, A MENACE TO NAVIGATION. PHOTO TAKEN FROM THE VANCOUVER ISLAND SIDE. THE 225-FT. UNION BOAT CARDENA IS SEEN HOMEWARD BOUND FROM THE NORTH

By CAPT. JOHN MUIR

Recently many varied and splendid views were expressed in The Sun by a cross-section of the public as to a suitable memorial to the late Mayor-Senator G. G. McGeer.

Having noted how the Dominion Government hydrographers have been changing conspicuous place names and occasionally duplicating them on their unexcelled new charts of British Columbia coastal waters, the thought occurred to me that the resounding burr in McGeer could quite logically be added to all the other "Macs" familiar to navigators between Puget Sound and Alaska.

We have, for instance, McNab Creek, McKay Passage, McKenzie Sound, McNeil Island, Port McNeill and others.

Frederick Seymour, former Governor of British Columbia, supplied the sobriquet for Seymour Inlet, where rushing currents attain the highest velocity of all B.C. tidal waters, a factor which could be emblematic of the marvelous aggressiveness and driving force displayed by our late mayor; but this indenture is in the hinterland, and comparatively speaking is very little known or traversed by navigators so that it would be most inappropriate for our purpose.

However Seymour Narrows is named after Admiral Sir George Francis Seymour, whose memory would not in the least be slighted if this well-known artery was renamed "McGeer Narrows," as no geographical name in B.C. could be more repeated than Seymour. It is emblazoned on Seymour Street intersections in the business area of Vancouver City, and further protected for posterity by Seymour Mountain and Seymour Creek, so well known to hikers and sports fishermen. Moresby Island has Seymour Point. On the latest chart of Howe Sound we have Seymour Cove, formerly officially Cowans Point, on the southeast shore of Bowen Island.

Again, many rocks, shoals, points and bluffs on this coast have the repetitive "Ripple" for a cognomen, so that the internationally known and highly respected Ripple Rock in the middle of Seymour Narrows could be rechristened "Gerry Rock"—not Gerald, as there already exist a Gerald Cove and a Gerald Point.

The Dominion government had offered to subsidize contractors to blast this same Ripple Rock to make the narrows safe for shipping, but it still apparently stymies and baffles our engineers, just as Senator McGeer withstood and bested his opponents in political debate.

The writer has known Seymour Narrows in all its moods. In the middle of a big ebb its waters rush very smooth but irresistibly up to Ripple Rock, over which they break vociferously into seething cauldrons, whirling and sweeping all flotsam and jetsam hither and thither. This characteristic is surely emblematic of how the late mayor at the last moment ebulliently and turbulently threw his "Donegal" into the electoral ring and topped the poll.

The peaceful scene that reigns when negotiating the narrows during high or low slack is reminiscent of the somnolent and restful surroundings enjoyed in the Senate, as once portrayed by the ever-alert Gerry.

... Maud Island were changed to Gratton Island, with its white day-beacon and red occulting light, those fortunate enough to experience the homeward-bound elated feeling, as they glide swiftly southward on the glassy track during the third hour of a long-range incoming tide, would certainly be cheered by the remembrance of Gerald Gratton McGeer's success in life through his catching that tide in the affairs of men which, taken at the flood, leads to fortune.

Being fully cognizant of the effort put forth by Senator McGeer to stir up the authorities in Ottawa and interested sources in the United States to take proper action to eliminate the danger menace to most of the ships that plies to and from northern B.C. and Alaskan ports, I am sure, had he been spared, would have been swept away in due course.

So, to honor a great Canadian it is respectfully suggested when the list of geographic names comes up for revision by the Hydrographic and Map Ice Surveys at Ottawa, Maud Island and Ripple Rock in Seymour Narrows should be changed to Gratton Island and Gerry in McGeer Narrows.

George Foster. These two men were a perfect match. Both were real gentlemen and had a way with the officers and crew alike. They were able to get the best out of everyone and in return they gained respect from their crews. When he was appointed to this new position, Captain Muir resigned from the Canadian Merchant Service Guild. His resignation was accepted with a great deal of regret.

One of Captain Muir's first pieces of business was to see that all ships in the fleet were equipped with radar, which took until 1946. The old timers didn't like it and some refused to even look at it. This was the beginning of a new era. Another thing Muir did was to put a stop to the Union ships going through Gunboat channel, a very narrow passage with rocks on each side that was used on occasion to save time.

After the start of the Second World War, the Union Steamship Co. aided the war effort with "Win the War Cruises," so on July 29, 1940 Captain Muir as Marine Superintendent had the honour of leading a parade of ships around the harbour from aboard the *Lady Cecilia*, then Captained by H. E. Lawrey.

It is on record that Captain Muir was appointed to a special committee which was set up in 1943 to discuss and come up with proposals for safer navigation rules for ships going through Seymour Narrows because of the increased wartime traffic. Muir later wrote an article about Seymour Narrows and Ripple Rock suggesting that they be renamed McGeer Narrows and Gerry Rock in honour of the former Senator and Mayor of Vancouver Gerry McGeer. It was published in *The Vancouver Sun* on Dec. 27, 1947, but the names stayed the same and it wasn't until April 5, 1958 that the terribly hazardous Ripple Rock was removed by a massive internal detonation. (see p.225)

Wartime brought many extra difficulties for Muir and Union Steamships, including shortages of qualified personnel, ships having to be armed and having to run blackened out, tremendous increases in freight and passenger movements, and troops being transported up and down the coast. The *Cardena* moved a whole Air Force squadron from Sidney on Vancouver Island to Annette Island in Alaska. Passenger and cargo space was at a premium. Captain Muir was continually juggling ships and men. For relaxation Captain Muir participated in soccer activities. He was an avid fan and as well served on the executive of the St. Saviour's senior team. At the same time he worked for the Vancouver Boys Club and was on their executive for 18 years.

With the war on, one of the favorite boat trips was the Moonlight Cruise to Bowen Island. It soon became widely known as the "booze cruise." Captain Muir was well aware of what went on during these trips. He used to come home and tell his family about all the damage that the revelers had done aboard the *Lady Alex*. His daughter recalled that her father absolutely forbade her to go on one of those cruises. However, her graduation class was to have their graduation and dinner party celebration at the Bowen Island Inn and she managed to sneak aboard without her father seeing her. As she said, "He often was down on the dock watching the ship leave, but this time he was nowhere to be seen." One wonders if he had an inkling and deliberately didn't appear on the scene.

In 1946 the work load of the war years caught up with Muir and he was hospitalized. Their were complications, including a bout of hiccups that lasted four months. During this extended period of ill health he was succeeded by Captain Eric Suffield. When Captain Muir recovered and was able to come back to work in April 1947, he came back to a newly-created position carrying the title of General Superintendent. He retired the following year in April, 1948.

Captain Muir had been one of the organizers of the Canadian Merchant Service Guild and served for years on their executive, serving in various offices including one term as president. The Company wasn't overly fond of this organization, as Muir indicates in the following *Sound Heritage* excerpt:

"Mr. Goodlad, a Shetlander, was the first secretary we had in the Guild. He wasn't a seaman, he was in business here in office work. He came from the Shetland Islands and naturally, seamen, shipping, and all that was in his line. One morning, Captain Walker, the Marine Superintendent, was on the dock seeing the picnic boats going out and I took Andrew Goodlad along to talk. Walker just didn't like it. They didn't want opposition because they knew that there would be a call for increased wages and time off and this kind of business. (But) the money wasn't in it for me. When you had a wife and family and a home in Vancouver, the wages were small for what you did. I'm not speaking for myself, but for the Guild. We didn't get what we were worth, for what we were doing for British Columbia." [175]

Captain Jock Muir was an extremely well-liked man, not only in the Company but all over the coast. Perhaps because he went ashore in the middle of his career with the Company he never attained the legendary status of such as Billy Yates or Jack Boden but it can readily be seen Muir still played a large part in Company lore as a whole. After he retired he was still called upon for various activities, such as being asked in 1952 to be Honourary Examiner for that year's examinations of pilot candidates.

In 1960 he and his daughter made a trip back to his old home town, Campbelltown in Scotland. Over the years when he was with the Union Steamship Co. he used to contribute regular letters and news reports to the Campbelltown Courier newspaper informing them of news of the Scottish people out in B.C. and other newsworthy events. Upon his return he was given the key to the City. As he walked down the street people would stop him and say, "Aren't you Captain Muir from Canada?" He was a celebrity and somewhat of a hero in his home town.

In May 1975 Captain Muir was celebrating his 90th birthday. Norman Hacking wrote about this event in his newspaper column: "For his 90th birthday party he entertained many of his old friends from the Union days, some of whom had been his shipmates 60 years ago. Some who were there were Captain John Park, Captain Alf Booker, Captain Bill McCombe, Captain Angus McNeill, Captain George Coles, Chief Engineer Fred Smith, Purser Don McLeod, Ben Swinhoe from Frank Waterhouse & Co., Gerald Rushton, and Bob Hackett who had been his guest aboard

Lady Alexandra approaching Bowen Island dock
(Newspaper clipping)

An orderly queue of picknickers line up at Bowen Island to board *Lady Alexandra* for return trip to Vancouver at the end of the day.
(Ashmore Collection)

the *Chilliwack* away back in 1930. His son Jack came out from Montreal for the party."

Captain Muir died later that year, Dec. 22, 1975 in Vancouver. He was cremated and it was his wish that his ashes be buried at sea in a location off the mouth of Rivers Inlet. The Guild made arrangements for this to take place with the help of B.C. Ferry Corporation. His daughter Mrs. Betty Meridith, her son Muir Meridith, his wife Karen, and their son Paul were aboard the ferry *Queen of Prince Rupert* on August 10, 1977. A short ceremony was conducted aboard ship by Acting Captain Bill McCombe Jr.

The ship's log book reads:
At 20.10. ship stopped
Lat. 51° - 27' N
Long. 127° - 51' W
Deposited the ashes of one
  Captain James Muir
Resumed speed at 20.15

Robert Taylor "Bob" Naughty

Capt. Bob Naughty circa 1940
(Mrs. Helen Kerr)

Naughty was his name and towards the end of his long career with the Union Steamship Company, naughty was his behaviour. It did him in.

He was born in Aberdeen, Scotland in 1891, and started his sea career working on fish trawlers. At times they used to go to ports in Portugal and he would often tell his family, what a beautiful country it was. He also learned the trade of "rigger" in the old country, which in general can be described as splicing wire cables and rope etc. aboard ship. This trade was to become a very important asset for him near the end of his life.

He left Scotland in 1913, leaving his wife and family behind, and came to B.C. with the idea that he would send for them when he made his stake. Oddly enough when he arrived in B.C. he started work for the B.C. Telephone Company. Then in 1916 he decided to go back to sea and took a job as deckhand for the Union Steamship Company aboard the *Cheakamus*.

The family joined him in 1918 and settled in a home in New Westminster which he had purchased. The children were still very young and when they arrived they really didn't know "who this man was." After the long arduous boat trip from England and the train ride across Canada, with only hard benches to sleep on, their arrival in their new home, where each child had their own bed, soon dispelled their bewilderment and fears of this strange man in the house.

Captain Naughty's daughter, Mrs. Helen Kerr, says that as near as she can recall he obtained his Coastwise Master's Ticket sometime between 1918 and 1923. She recalls her brother, Bob Naughty Junior, helping and working with his dad to prepare for the examination.

Records indicate his first Master's job was aboard the *Chilco*. She was in service from 1917-1935. Her name was changed to the *Lady Pam* in 1935 and records show that Captain Naughty became her Master, taking over command from Captain Harry Roach. He then went on to be Master of *Capilano II*, the *Lady Cecilia*, the *Lady Cynthia*, the *Venture* and the *Chelohsin*. Most of his time was spent on the Sunshine Coast and Howe

Sound runs so he was better known in this area than up north.

Captain Naughty was well-liked by the passengers even though he was not known for being one of the best ship handlers in the fleet. He was a very capable seaman, and I have never come across anyy records of him being in a marine accident, but he was sometimes nonchalant about his landings, as Kelsey McLeod wrote in the *West Coast Mariner*: "Residents along the coast came to know what Captain was in command by his landing skills - or lack of skills - displayed. Ruddy-faced Captain Naughty was not renowned for precision landings, not that it ever seemed to bother him. He would gaze impassively down from the bridge after his ship had slammed into the wharf." [176]

Nothing to do with ship handling but he was also known aboard ship as a poor poker player. Denis Shaw, a well-known Purser in the Fleet, tells about having to refuse the "Cap" any more draws in a game, as he was so far in debt already. Gerry Jones, another Purser recalls he had to leave a game when he was $40 ahead, so Captain Naughty played with his winnings and lost it all. I myself remember a game in which he borrowed $10 from me and soon lost it. The fellows said, "Art, you'll never get your money back." But I did!

One story I was told indicates why Captain Naughty was so well thought of by the coastal residents. A young lady by the name of Mary McIntyre, who lived at Gibsons but went to private school in Vancouver, used to take sail every Sunday to Vancouver. Captain Naughty would always bring her up to the bridge or to his cabin and generally looked after her and made her feel secure and special. She recalls the Union Ships with a great deal of fondness.

Captain Naughty also became known as the best-dressed Captain in the fleet. He was always immaculately tailored in the finest material. His son Eddie, being in the clothing business, probably accounted for this fact.

Shaw remarked on the fact that the Captain had very small feet and had a dainty, quick step. His daughter added that he was an excellent dancer and just loved to dance.

Naughty's first wife died in 1923, five years after she came to Canada, at age 39. He told his daughter, Mrs. Helen Kerr, that he would not remarry until she herself married, which she did in 1937. He then married for a second time to Mrs. Finneghan who had three daughters by a previous marriage. One of these daughters married Mr. Brennan, the well-known manager at Woodfibre.

About this time it was noticed that the Captain had started to drink excessively. I can recall being on the *Lady Cynthia* and we were making a call into Lund. Word got around the ship that Captain Naughty wasn't well and that Denny Farina, the 2nd Mate, was going to dock the ship, and those of us aboard wondered what would be worse, having Denny do the job or the Captain, no matter what his condition. We all lined up at the rail to watch what was going to take place, but Denny did a fine job, I'm happy to say.

Geoff Hosken, a former deck officer in the Company, said in later years that the Captain started to rely more and more on his Mates.

There is another story about Jimmy Hunter, who was Chief Officer under Captain Naughty and due on the bridge at midnight. The next stop was to be Heriot Bay which at night was a very difficult landing to make. Jimmy, who had the reputation of being a very fine ship handler, arrived on the bridge a little early and could see that Captain Naughty was dilly-dallying with the ship and didn't want to take her in, so Jimmy, puffing away on his pipe, snorted and said, "Here, for God's sake go below, I'll take her in."

Captain Naughty's downfall with the Union Ships cane in June 1948. He was Master of the *Lady Cecilia* and was returning from a day cruise up to Savary Island. It was late in the evening. Strangely enough it came when he was about to make a perfect landing for a change, the only trouble was that he had gone into the wrong dock! He had gone into the Evans Coleman dock instead of the Union dock. He suddenly realized his mistake as no one was around to take his lines. He quickly had to reverse engines, back out and go over to the Union dock. Captain Naughty was relieved of his command the next day by the Marine Superintendent, Eric Suffield - a very ignominious end after three decades of service to what had been a fine career for this well-known and popular skipper with the Union Steamship Company.

Naughty family reunion: son Ed Naughty (bus boy and waiter, 1920s), brother Lewie Naughty, daughter Harriet Gray, Captain Bob Naughty, daughter Helen Kerr, son Captain Bob Naughty, Jr. *(Mrs. Helen Kerr)*

However, much to their credit the Company offered him another job, which was as a "rigger" - his old trade - in the net loft on the Union dock, though it must have been quite a come down for him. John Allan, a deckhand with the Company at the time, recalls seeing Naughty walking around the wharf in blue overalls. He was a proud man but at his age he still needed a job because there were no pension plans to speak of at the time. It is interesting to note that he never let on to his family what had happened. He merely went down to the Union dock as usual every day and they apparently didn't know the difference.

How long he worked in the net loft at the Union dock is uncertain but Captain Terry of Northland Navigation later offered Naughty a job as 2nd Mate on one of Northland's ships which he accepted.

Captain Naughty was now in his sixties and the 2nd Mate's job was a pretty strenuous role for him at his age. He took the job but on one trip they ran into some very rough weather and he had a bad fall, injuring his leg. It so happened he had had a toenail removed from one of his toes in this same leg and it wasn't healing properly. The leg injury added to the deterioration, so the doctor decided the leg would have to be amputated and that put an end to his seagoing career.

His daughter tells of visiting him in the hospital and as he was coming out of the anesthetic he was a little delirious. He knew his daughter was there with him but he was raving about being back in Portugal and how beautiful it was. He had slipped away back in his mind to his teenage years. He recovered and had to walk using crutches, but what could he do, with no job there was no income? Captain Terry came to the rescue again. He set Bob up with a workshop in his basement so he could resume working from his home as a rigger. Northland delivered all of their work to him.

His daughter tells the following amusing story of how he adapted to his new job. He could not go down the steep basement stairs to his workshop so he would go out the front door carrying his lunch and jokingly say, "Well I'm going to my office now." He would go down the front walk to the street, walk a short distance to the corner and walk around the back lane and enter into his workshop from this level. His pant leg was pinned up and there were some little children along the route who would speak to him on his way. He would stop and talk to them and tell them that his leg would grow back. They were in awe. Gradually he would lower the fold in the empty pant leg and the children could tell it was getting longer. He would say, "See I told you it would grow back didn't I?" They would clap their hands and laugh with him about the whole thing.

It can't quite be said that Captain Naughty died with his boots on, but he worked away at his trade to the very end.

His daughter, Mrs. Kerr, said that he was half way through repairing a big cargo net when he died. She said that his son Bob Naughty Jr., her brother, finished the job for him.

The Captain died Dec. 17, 1961. His ashes were carried out to sea on the *Alaska Prince* and scattered at Manson's Deep by Captain John Eveliegh.

Robert "Bob" Naughty Jr.

Robert Naughty Jr. was born in Scotland in 1906. His father, Bob Naughty Sr., had come out to B.C. in 1913, leaving his wife and family behind until he got himself settled and employed (see previous profile). Bob Jr. was 12 years old when the family first lived in New Westminster.

Bob made a few trips with his father during his summer holidays, usually on the Powell River run aboard the old ships, the *Chilco* and the *Chasina*. [177] Bob followed in his father's footsteps and joined Union Steamships himself in 1923 as a deckhand. He eventually obtained his B.C. Coastal Mate's Ticket and the first entry in his Seaman's Discharge Book shows him signing aboard the *Lady Cecilia* as 3rd Mate on May 27, 1930.

From 1930 to 1942 he served on many ships in the Union Fleet, including the *Lady Evelyn*, *Lady Cecilia*, *Chelohsin*, *Catala*, *Venture*, *Camosun II*, *Lady Rose*, and *Lady Pam*. The *Lady Pam* was the last ship he sailed on with the Union Company and he was 1st Mate on her when he signed off on March 12, 1942.

A good many of his experiences while he was with the Union Steamships are chronicled in the booklet *Sound Heritage: Navigating the Coast* from which the following three excerpts are taken:

"When the Union Steamship Co. took over two of the CNR ships I was sent over to join the *Prince Charles* which had been renamed the *Camosun*. They were so old that every time she'd take a sea I wondered if the bottom was going to fall out. Captain (Buster) Browne was the skipper. I was 2nd Mate, and God, to go across Hecate Strait in the wintertime, you had no radar. You had to pick these navigation lights up. We used to go right up to Masset, into all the logging camps and I thought, gee, this time of year, I hope the fog doesn't come down and Buster Browne says: "Well, we've got two good anchors, anyhow." [178]

"The *Lady Cecilia* and the *Lady Cynthia* had sponsons on the sides. We never filled them with water. You could walk along them. They were wide enough that I could walk along them because one night we were on a moonlight cruise to Bowen Island and the skipper said: "Look?" I looked over the side and there's this drunk out there staggering up - these sponsons are about two feet wide. 'God,' he says, 'We'll have to get him off there.' And it happened the general manager was aboard up on the bridge at the time so I knew I had to do something. So I said: 'I can get along there.' I'd walked

Capt. Bob Naughty Jr. *(Bill Naughty Collection)*

them quite a few times, but not when the ship was running full speed. Not chasing a drunk anyhow. He saw me come out the freight door and I started up the sponson and I wasn't running neither. He spotted me. The sponson tapers off into nothing, into a point, by the saloon portholes aft. They're big enough to get a man through. They were the biggest portholes on the ship. I was watching my feet and going along and then I looked up and I couldn't see him. He'd gone. I got up as far as the saloon part and I went in there and I couldn't find him cause it was getting dusk and I didn't know how he was dressed. They had an orchestra taking the dance cruise up. I couldn't pick him up anyhow. I went up to the bridge and I said to the skipper, 'Gee, I don't know if he went in through the porthole.' I didn't want to do that again, I'll tell you." [179]

"When Christmas came, they had a Christmas party. We used to sail Christmas Eve. There wasn't a day off, but they used to have a Christmas supper on for the crew about 6 o'clock. She didn't sail until 9 and it was the tradition that the officers waited on the crew. All the crew were in the saloon in our seats and we waited on them. That was another tradition that's passed away, but anyhow, I remember I was coming out with two plates of turkey and stuffing. I bumped into Captain Andy Johnstone and I thought, holy mackerel, no! He can't bawl me out. He's only a waiter like me, anyhow. He didn't say a word."[180]

Iain Morrison, a former deck officer with the Company, said Bob was always singing "Waltzing Matilda" and "Blow the Man Down." Also he recalled that Bob always had to phone his wife from any port with a telephone, like Alert Bay.

Bob left the Union Steamship Co. in 1942 and went to work on B.C. coastal tankers, first the *Unacana* as 2nd Mate, from March 8, 1941 to June 3, 1946, then the *Britamerican*, which he was sailing on as a 1st Mate when he signed off her on May 16, 1951. He then joined Captain Macdonell's firm, General Transportation Co., and sailed as Master on the *Northern Express*. Later this firm became known as the Tidewater Express Co., which later merged with the Union Steamship Co.

There is a blank in his discharge book which is explained by the fact he had become a Captain and thus couldn't sign his own discharge book. After a lapse in time we find Bob signing aboard another tanker, the M.V. *Standard Service*, as a 2nd Mate, Dec. 4, 1966. He signed off her July 3, 1967. By this time he was 61 years old. However he continued his sea career with Coast Ferries Ltd. sailing on the *Lady Rose* and the *Island Princess*. I could find no records as to when Bob last worked for Coast Ferries but he could have worked with them until he was 65 and then retired, which would have been 1971. His son Bill told me after he retired he did go out as Master on the United Church Mission ship, the *Thomas Crosby*. Again, for how long we don't know.

Unfortunately Bob found out he had throat cancer, probably in the middle or late 1970s, and finally he had to have an operation which left him with a hole in his throat and unable to talk. For some reason he couldn't have a voice box so he had to communicate by holding a speaker up to this hole in his throat and sort of grunt into it. Naturally this was terribly embarrassing for him and he soon adopted an attitude of not wanting to see anybody. His sister, Mrs. Helen Kerr, said he suffered terribly in the last three years of his life. He died on Dec. 4, 1986 at age 80.

Mrs. Kerr said Bob was a wonderful fellow who would have given anyone the shirt off his back.

William "Nick" Nicholson

It is not known just when Nick joined the Union Steamship Co., but he was sailing on the Union Ships in the 1940s.

It was reported to me that he came to the West Coast aboard the Duke of Sutherland's yacht, the *Sandpiper*. Nick was his official photographer. Photography was in his blood for when he sailed in the Union Steamship Co. he was forever taking photographs. This was his legacy. Many of his photos have survived and were made into post cards and Christmas cards during his stay with the Company.

Charles Hamer, a deck officer who sailed with Nick, told me about one time when G.B. Owen-Jones was Chief Officer on the *Chelohsin* and they were about to leave a certain port but 2nd Mate Nick Nicholson wasn't aboard. Looking around, the Chief Officer spotted Nick away up on a rocky bluff busily engaged in taking photos of the ship. Anyone who had sailed with the demanding Owen-Jones can imagine his ire over this, holding up the ship while he takes pictures!

One time when Nick had newly joined the company he was sailing aboard the *Chelohsin* and was on watch with Chief Officer Paddy Hannigan. Paddy was going down for breakfast and gave Nick meticulous instructions about some course changes to make while he was down eating. Nick had just come off deep sea ships and he ignored Paddy's instructions which for him at the time, didn't make sense. When Paddy returned to the bridge he could see they were away off course. In his slow, deliberate way, Paddy questioned Nick. Nick's answers were not at all suitable to Paddy and he very tersely told Nick, "You are not sailing deep sea now. Do as I tell you from now on or get off the ship!"

Nick also was 2nd Mate and on watch with Captain Aspinall when the *Chelohsin* went aground at Stanley Park on Nov. 6, 1949.

Henry Dutka, an Assistant Purser, recalls Nick having an argument with a drunken logger on the float at Dawson's Landing. A fight broke out and Nick, who wasn't a big man, was flattened in no time. He just picked himself up, brushed off his uniform, shrugged, and went back to doing his job. All in all he was a popular fellow and a good ship mate.

That Nick was a good photographer is evidenced by the fact many of his photos survived him and are in the private collections of fellows who had worked with him in the Union Steamship Co. One photo that is most frequently seen is seen on the back book leaf. I think it is one of his best, as it shows the type of places that the Union Ships called at. This is at Morgan's Camp on the Queen Charlotte Islands. Note two of the ship's officers feeding a deer in the foreground. They are Assistant Purser Tom Hatchen and Freight Clerk Hugh Tozer.

In 1959 "Nick" assumed command of the Mission Ship *Columbia*. He left this ship in 1964 and went over to B.C. Ferries.

Capt. William "Nick" Nicholson *(Roach Collection)*

James E. Noel

Clockwise: Captains James Noel, Andrew Johnstone, Sandy Dawe, John Park, Andrew Sinclair (seated)
(J. Horne)

James Noel was born in Newfoundland, came out to B.C. and served with the Boscowitz line. The well-known Captain John Park said, "When I was Master of the *Venture*, James Noel was Master of the *Vadso* under the Boscowitz flag in 1911." [181]

When the Union Steamship Co. purchased the Boscowitz line in 1911, Captain Park and Captain Noel transferred over to the Union Steamship Co. Captain Park stayed as Master of the *Venture* and James Noel was his Chief Officer. In 1916 Captain Noel succeeded Captain Park as Master of the *Venture*. Captain Noel had as his Chief Officer Andy Johnstone, while the 2nd Mate was Andy Sinclair.

In 1966 Captain W. J. Main wrote a letter to *The Vancouver Sun* telling about being quartermaster on the *Venture* in 1918, when Captain Noel and his ship went to the aid of the S.S. *Ravalli* bound for Alaska which had caught fire in Grenville Channel. The fire had got out of control and the ship turned into Lowe Inlet where the passengers and crew got off her safely. The *Venture*, under Captain Noel, came along and discovered the burning ship. The *Venture* got her hoses going even before they came alongside, but it was too late. Captain Noel decided to beach the *Ravalli*, so the *Venture* pushed her across the bay and she burned down to the waterline. Deck officers aboard the *Venture* at the time were Pilot Eddie Georgeston and Mate Jock Malcolmson. [182]

In 1922 Captain Noel left the Union Steamship Co. and joined the pilotage. *The Province* (Vancouver) newspaper on Jan. 30, 1922 wrote about his last trip as Captain of the *Venture* and about a surprise party held aboard the *Venture* in the ship's saloon before her departure. Captain Noel was presented with a pair of binoculars suitably inscribed. In attendance along with the ship's crew were many well-known figures from the north. Universal regret was expressed by all who attended the gathering that Captain Noel was leaving the Company.

Captain Park, Captain Noel, Captain Johnstone, and Captain Sinclair all joined the Pilotage and ended their sea careers with this organization. The picture accompanying this story shows them all together at a reunion party held in Captain Park's home in December, 1955.

G. Bertram K. Owen-Jones

With such a long name, G. B. K. Owen-Jones, people were unsure what to call him. Most of the time he is referred to as Owen Jones as though Owen was a first name. Also, he often was referred to as "Alphabet Jones." He also had two nicknames, "Curly" and "Sonny," but it was worth your life to use these nicknames when talking to him. He was a very complex person and a difficult man to befriend but, without a doubt, most fellows who sailed with him acknowledge he was an excellent ship handler.

Bertram followed in his father's foot steps. His father Bertie Owen-Jones was a sea captain and retired from the sea in 1949.

I came across a very interesting write-up in the *Canadian Merchant Service Guild Annual* of 1936 about Bertram when he was a deckhand aboard the *Lady Pam*. Here is a slightly condensed version of that story:

"A junior member of the Canadian Merchant Service Guild, Bertram Owen-Jones displayed proper seaman qualities early in August of this year when a moment arose calling for quick decision and a prompt display of courage. Working aboard the *Lady Pam* one day and standing on deck while the *Pam* was proceeding to Sechelt, there was a good wind and a strong sea running. He was looking idly out to sea when he was galvanized into action, for he saw a young woman feebly swimming in the rough water and waving her arms. Bertram yelled to the officer on watch, kicked off his shoes and dived overboard. Swimming strongly he drew up to her. She was barely keeping herself afloat in the hysteria of the moment she grabbed onto him. He broke her hold and dived under her, then turned and told her what to do to make the rescue easier for him. Bertram then stripped of his outer clothing and supported her to await aid from his ship. She had been with two other girls in a canoe that had overturned. They clung to the canoe while she bravely attempted to swim ashore for help.

"In the meantime the *Lady Pam* had turned around and had sighted the girls clinging to the canoe. A lifeboat was launched and the girls were brought aboard safely. Then the *Lady Pam* proceeded to Bertram and his maid and soon they were brought aboard safely as well.

"Mr. Owen-Jones was presented with a bronze medal for this brave rescue on October, 1936."

The article goes on to tell about Bertram rescuing another young man on the Fraser River when he was only 14 years old. Both these rescues show great heroism by Owen-Jones but he never spoke of the events himself. One of his shipmates recalled that Bertram occasionally wore that medal but never drew anyone's attention to it.

Dennis Farina told me that he and Bertram were deckhands together on the *Lady Cecilia* in 1937 and they both had certificates. Later in that year, both he and Bertram moved up in rank for a month or two and served a spell as 3rd Mates. Bertram went out on the *Venture*. When the summer season was over they both went

Capt. Bertram Owen-Jones
(Naughty Collection)

back to being deckhands and according to Dennis, Bertram was very unhappy over this backward step and wouldn't eat his meals anymore with the crew, but ate by himself.

When the war started Bertram joined the Navy along with many others from the Company. After the war he returned briefly to the Union Steamship Co., then obtained a leave of absence and went deep sea. In this period of time he obtained his Foreign Going Mate's Ticket and his Coastwise Master's Ticket.

Owen-Jones served on many of the Union ships, gradually going up the ladder in rank. He was serving on the *Lady Alexandra* in 1947 as Chief Officer when he put her aground at Brunswick Point, July 15, 1947 at 11:12 p.m. She struck a rock on the east shore of Howe Sound in a blinding rain and electrical storm. There were only eight passengers aboard at the time. Captain Yates, who was off watch and was sleeping in his room, was awakened by the crash and quickly took charge. As the tide was rising the *Alexandra* floated free and was able to get over to Snug Cove in Bowen Island under her own power. The passengers were put ashore and managed to get to Vancouver via Horseshoe Bay.

Charles Hamer was a Mate in the Company for a little over a year. He had come off deep sea ships directly to the U.S.S. Co. and said, "Bertram was a great help in familiarizing me with the B.C. coast and navigation."

One amusing incident Charles related about Bertram took place on the *Chelohsin*. The ship was unloading at a small logging camp and Bertram had given orders to keep all the drunken loggers off the ship. He even posted a deckhand named Red at the freight doors. Red did his job zealously, even to the extent of throwing the camp superintendent into the salt chuck!

Bertram left the Union Steamship Co. in the early 1950s and joined the Black Ball line. Records show he was Master on the *Kahloke* in 1954. He then joined B.C. Ferries and was their Senior Master when they commenced their service. It is said that he carried employee card #1. He took early retirement in 1979 and is presently living in Vancouver's Dunbar area.

John Park

Capt. John Park S.S. *Venture* (*Vancouver Maritime Museum*)

Captain Park was born at Killy Keira, Lonmay, Aberdeenshire in 1880. He went to sea in December 1897, working on sailing ships. By 1906 he had obtained his Master's Ticket for Square Rigged-Foreign Going ships. In December 1906 he joined the Blue Funnel line and left them in 1909 to come to British Columbia. He then joined the Union Steamship Co. as second mate on the *Coquitlam I*, one of the three Union Ships built in sections, shipped over from the old country and reassembled in Coal Harbour.

In May of 1910 he went over to the *Capilano I* as First Mate or Chief Officer, as this position was referred to in later years.

He took over as Master on the *Venture* in September 1911, a month after the Union Co. bought her from the Boscowitz line. His Chief Officer at the time was Jack Boden

Sr. Ernie Sheppard, who later became a Master in the Company, served as his quartermaster.

On his first trip north after taking command of the *Venture*, he and his ship rescued the passengers from the CPR's *Princess Beatrice*, which had gone aground in Christie Passage. The *Venture* had just left Port Hardy when Chief Officer Boden received a message of the *Beatrice* going aground. The *Venture* proceeded immediately to the stricken vessel and took aboard her 200 or so passengers. She then took them back to Alert Bay so they could be picked up by another ship.

In Gerald Rushton's book *Whistle Up The Inlet*, he tells the story about Capt. Park and a new Chief Officer who had come over to Union Steamships from the CPR. The new man was supremely confident but didn't know anything about the smaller port landings. When the vessel arrived off Salmon River (now known as Kelsey Bay), Captain Park told the new skipper it was "always a starboard landing" on account of the strong current. The newcomer assured him he could manage a port landing alright and promptly crashed the vessel against the wharf, shaking every timber. "He shook up a good deal more than timbers. There were 21 tons of dynamite in the bow of the *Capilano* and I was petrified, a miracle the whole place with all of us, wasn't blown up!" Soon afterwards, Park was given command of the *Capilano*. [183]

In 1921, Captain Park joined the B.C. Pilotage District, which was how it was named in 1921. In March 1942 he was asked by the Royal Canadian Navy to take the S.S. *Ocean Venus* from Portland to Los Angeles and then on to Halifax but it was torpedoed and sunk off Cape Canaveral on May 3, 1942. Five men in the engine room were killed but Park survived and later was commended for bravery, receiving a citation in the King's name signed by Winston Churchill. [184]

Park retired from the Pilotage in September 1948 at age 68 but even then still kept his hand in. For a number of years he took new B.C. Ferries, which were built at Burrard Drydock, out on sea trials. Johnny Horne recalls Captain Park was Yard Master when John took command of the *City of Vancouver*, later renamed the *Queen of Vancouver*.

In 1955 Captain Park held a party at his home for the officers who had served with him on the *Venture*. Those attending included Captains James Noel, Andy Johnstone, Sam Dawe, and Andy Sinclair. All had commanded the *Venture* at one time in their careers and all became B.C. Coast Pilots. [185]

In 1981 another party was held for Captain Park, this time to celebrate his 100th birthday. It was mostly B.C. Coast Pilots who were in attendance including the McNeills, Docherty and Coles. Also attending were members of his Masonic Lodge and the Scottish Societies. On this occasion Captain John Horne had the honour of presenting Captain Park with a clock, in the form of a ship's wheel to honour Canada's oldest living Pilot.

Captain Park died shortly after his 101st birthday.

Capt. John Park, Canada's oldest living pilot, receiving a clock on his 100th birthday from Captain John Horne 1981 *(J. Horne)*

Fred H. "Searchlight" Parker

Henry "Harry" Roach

Left: Chief Officer Fred Parker on board S.S. *Venture* circa 1928 *(Skinner Collection)*

Right: Capt. Harry Roach *(Roach Collection)*

In my research I was able to uncover only a little information about this man, but he must have been a very interesting person judging by his nicknames "Searchlight" and "Daredevil." Frank Skinner was able to supply me with a very good picture of him sitting in a deck chair aboard ship, smoking an unusual pipe.

"Searchlight" Parker came to the Union Steamship Co. from the All Red Line in 1917. He served aboard several ships, mainly on the logging camp routes. He was Pilot on the *Chelohsin* in 1922 and later Master of the *Cheakamus*. He was elected President of the Canadian Merchant Service Guild in 1921. He served with the Company until 1930 and died in 1931.

Harry was a Cornishman, born in Wales, Oct. 4, 1898. His father died when Harry was six years old. Harry was put into the Royal Merchant Seamen's Orphanage for the children of seamen, and when he was 16 he automatically had to leave. He was then apprenticed to sea for two years, sailing out of London on the S.S. *Rachel* for Thomas Stephens & Sons Co. During this period his mother had come to Canada and eventually came out to the west coast, to Vancouver.

Harry was aboard a ship at the time that had to go into the Brooklyn Naval Yard. A Welsh barman got to know Harry because the Mate on his ship was sending Harry up to the bar every day for beer. Being Welsh, he recognized Harry's accent. Somehow he knew Harry's mother was out in Vancouver Through the auspices of the Salvation Army and the Masonic Lodge, the bartender arranged to obtain funds and sent Harry across Canada by train so he could be united with his mother. This was in 1916 and Harry would have been 18 years old.

His mother was a good friend of Captain Sam Mortimer, who owned the Vancouver-based All Red Line, which had two ships, the *Santa Maria* and *Santa Cecilia*. Harry joined up as deckhand with this All Red Line and was aboard the *Santa Maria* when the Union Steamships bought the company on Aug. 17, 1917 and took over the ships, renaming the *Santa Maria* the *Chilco* (later the *Lady Pam*). Harry was 18 at the time.

As a result of this move, there was always a seniority question with Harry. Did his seniority start when he joined the All Red Line or when he started with the Union Steamships Co.? In later years this became a very meaningful thing to him because it affected whether he was going to become Master of the *Cardena* or the *Chelohsin*, there being a fair difference in salary for the Masters between the two ships.

Harry stayed with the Union Steamship Co. and obtained his Masters ticket when he was 28, in 1926. His son Ed says that his father had very good mentors, especially Captain Robert Wilson whom Harry reportedly held in awe.

One of the toughest runs in those days was the logging camp run and Captain Wilson was on it for a long time. When he left, Harry Roach took over his command, which says a great deal for his seamanship. Harry was Quartermaster on the old *Cheakamus* and the *Cowichan* when they were servicing the area. He started learning the coast well, in this position, aboard these two ships.

During the war he served aboard the *Chelohsin* as Chief Officer under Captain Wilson. Harry spent a lot of time on the *Chelohsin* and became very fond of her. He said, "She handled like a little tea kettle, and when she came out from the Old Country she did 11½ knots and when she ended her days, she still did 11½ knots." However, his favourite ship was the *Cardena;* he thought she was the ultimate. He had the misfortune to run her aground on the sand bar at the mouth of the Capilano River on March 24, 1952 at 7 a.m. The *Cardena* was inbound to Vancouver with 86 passengers aboard. The passengers were put off and taken to Vancouver by tugs. The *Cardena* suffered no damage and was pulled off the sand bar later in the day by tugs at high tide.

Harry's first job as Master on a Union ship was on the *Lady Pam*, where Harry had started as a deckhand. Promotions in the Union Company for deck officers were very slow, as nobody retired. There were no pensions so everybody just kept working, but by 1943 Harry was a relieving skipper and by 1950 held a permanent job as a Master.

Harry was very active in the Canadian Merchant Service Guild. He became President in 1955 and at this time was the ninth senior employee in the Company.

He was nominated in 1953 for an executive position in the Guild by Captain Stewart McGillivray of the CPR ship *Princess Elizabeth*. He signed his nomination papers under very unusual circumstances on the morning of Oct. 23, 1953, under the Lions Gate Bridge! His son Edward tells the following story:

"The *Princess Elizabeth* under Captain McGillivray was outbound from Vancouver and the *Cardena*, under Captain Roach was proceeding into Vancouver. It was foggy and the two vessels collided in the channel, below the Lions Gate Bridge. Damage to the two vessels was well above the water line so there was no danger of either ship taking on

Capt. Harry Roach and 2nd Mate Al McLennan on a dark stormy night on the upper bridge of the *Chelohsin*

water, but the two vessels were locked together by bent plates and the *Cardena*'s anchor. So the two ships stayed that way, and aided by a little power from the *Elizabeth*, they got out of the channel and drifted over to the English Bay area. With the two ships held firmly together, their bridges were so close that Captain McGillivray was able to pass over the papers he had in his hands for nominating Harry Roach for office in the Canadian Merchant Service Guild, for him to sign."

Patrick Hind, who was Assistant Purser on the *Elizabeth* at the time was on his way to the bridge with the passenger report for the Captain, when he saw the *Cardena* looming out of the fog. He reports they had to get a cutting torch to cut the ships apart. Even so, the *Cardena*'s anchor was left embedded in the *Elizabeth*'s bow. Once separated, both ships then proceeded slowly into their respective docks, discharged their passengers, and then went over to Burrard Drydock for repairs.

One of Harry's accomplishments while an officer of the Guild was establishing the lay day system for crew members of the Union Steamships. For every seven days worked without a day off you earned a lay day. Some fellows built up quite an accumulation of lay days and were able to take long periods of paid holidays. As well, Harry convinced the Guild Officers that they should buy their own office building.

The Union Steamship Co. began to suffer several setbacks in the middle 1950s and Harry Roach had the dubious honour of bringing the *Catala* down the coast on Jan. 8, 1958 and docking her in Vancouver, to join five other Union ships which were tied up and out of service.

A Vancouver newspaper reported this with headlines reading, "*Catala* Blows Her Engines to End Famed Ship Service." The first three sentences of this report read as follow:

"Vancouver coastal skipper Harry Roach hesitated a moment before he rang down 'Finished with Engines.' This time, for Union Steamship passenger service, that signal might mean 'forever.' It would be the end of an era of 67 years of carrying passengers along the B.C. coast." [186]

An attempt to revive the service was made in April of 1958 so the *Catala* resumed a coastal run which was enthusiastically supported by coastal communities, but by the end of 1958 the Union Steamships, due to competition from Northland Navigation and other factors, had ceased to exist.

With the Union Steamships finished Harry went to work for Sparky New, who owned Coastal Ferries and Towing. He had to sign on as 2nd Mate and had to work freight. At his age and being asthmatic, the job was to much for him. He worked for Harbour Ferries for awhile, then came ashore to work for Woodward's Stores sea supply outlet down in Coal Harbour, and after that he operated a little paddle boats rental service in False Creek.

By then he was 75 years old and one night his son Ed, who had come down to pick him up and give him a ride home, said "Don't you think it's time to swallow the anchor?" His answer was "I think that would be a good idea."

Many times, up and down the coast, people would come up and ask me if I was Harry Roach's son. People obviously thought we looked alike at the time. Harry also was well-known as source of Irish Sweepstakes tickets but whether he ever sold a winner isn't known.

Harry passed away in November 1975 at age 77. Norman Hacking reported his passing in his column and said this about him: "A soft-spoken Welshman, who was one of the real gentlemen of the sea." What better reputation to leave behind than that! Of all the Masters in the Union Fleet, he is generally spoken of as being the most beloved of all.

Captain Roach's ashes were consigned to the sea at Mansons Deep.

The President's Message

Many projects of considerable magnitude have been undertaken in Canada during the past few years. I wish to stress the importance of these undertakings and the effect they will have on the economic future of our country.

I firmly believe that there is none more important to the seafaring fraternity or marine industry as a whole than the St. Lawrence Seaway.

When completed this gigantic construction project will open the Great Lakes system to larger ships of all nations for the carriage of raw materials and manufactured products both in and out of Canada and the United States.

We sincerely trust that our Canadian Government, aided by all branches of the maritime industry from the building to the sailing of Canadian ships, will take the necessary steps to see that Canadian cargoes are carried in Canadian ships manned by Canadian Seamen.

CAPTAIN H. ROACH
President — 1955

Board of Management

PRESIDENT..CAPTAIN H. ROACH
TREASURER..Capt. G. J. McInnes
IMMEDIATE PAST PRESIDENT..................Capt. A. R. Phelps

Vice-Presidents:

Captains S. C. McGillivray, G. A. Thomson, B. B. Larsen, Alfred Lucking, J. M. Wakefield, R. E. S. Armstrong & Mr. H. D. Adlem

Representatives:

Pilotage Service..Capt. R. W. McNeill
Ocean-going..Mr. R. Montgomery
Passenger Vessels..................Capt. R. Barry & Mr. A. McKinnon
Freight Vessels..................Capt. F. R. Davies & Mr. C. F. Martin
Tug Boats..................Captains Eldon L. Tisdale, John Balatti, C. W. Rystedt, A. Bachan, A. W. Teesdale
Fast Water Tug Boats..Capt. F. R. Cottell
Fire Boats..Capt. Ian Milne

Government Ships..................Capt. H. Hill & Mr. R. D. McLellan
Coastal Tankers..Mr. Angus Galbraith

Eastern Advisory Board:

CHAIRMAN..Capt. R. Barrett
Great Lakes..................Captains H. Dodd, H. W. Curtis, G. Gendron, Mr. S. Larosse
Pilots..................Capt. Oscar Fleury & Capt. M. Bouille
Foreign Going..Capt. G. Clermont
Sailing Master..Capt. P. Tetrault

Trustees:

Captains D. A. Connell, C. C. Sainty, W. A. Gosse
GENERAL SECRETARY..Mr. George F. Bullock
Montreal Secretary..Capt. Noel J. Maw
Representative..Capt. J. J. Deslauriers
VANCOUVER REPRESENTATIVES..................Capt. E. W. Meadows
Capt. J. G. Leonard

Two

Harry Roach as President of the Canadian Merchant Service Guild for the year 1955

Miles Robinson

Capt. Miles Robinson
(*Roach Collection*)

Miles Robinson had two nicknames; the natural one was "Robbie" but the other one was also quite natural and was pinned on him by Captain Harry Roach, who was talking in the wheelhouse one day and said "Yeah, that nervous giggle of Robinson's" and it stuck. From that point on he was known as "Giggly" Robinson.

He had a short career with the company. Before the war broke out he was serving aboard the *Chelohsin*, under Captain Roach as 3rd Mate. Like others, he went into the services and naturally chose the navy. Ivor Jones, who knew Robbie from being shipmates on the *Chelohsin*, related the following story to me:

"Captain Suffield, who also joined the navy in wartime, had designed a 'boom defence' for the harbour of Prince Rupert. It was to protect the harbour against Japanese submarines. Miles Robinson happened to see the plans passing through some Navy department. He looked them over, added a few things of his own to the plans and sent them on, under his name. Top brass must have liked the whole idea for they did put in place this so-called boom defence at the entrance to Prince Rupert harbour. At the same time Miles received a big promotion and was put in command of this defence system. When the war was over and the fellows came back to work for the Union Steamships, Captain Suffield became Marine Superintendent. He was pretty upset at Miles for stealing his idea. Promotion for Miles under this circumstance would be difficult."

At this point, a brief description of this submarine net or boom defence is in order: Every time a ship was cleared to enter or leave the harbour these booms with nets suspended from them had to be pulled open by a Naval launch or tug. (I had a friend, Mack Minions, who worked on this launch and we got together in Rupert on one of my trips to that port aboard the *Cassiar*. We sure had a party lacing our usual fare with tots of Navy rum!) Whether or not this set up would have worked as a defence against a submarine was open to question. It took a lot of time to open and close this thing and created lots of red tape and many angry words between ship captains and Navy brass.

Apparently Miles was not a good sailor for he was chronically seasick. One trip while serving on the *Cardena* under Captain Boden, going across Queen Charlotte Sound, he was seasick out on the wing of the bridge. Captain Boden was disgusted. He just left him there and he got soaking wet.

Going away to the services, Miles maintained his seniority position in the Union Co. Before he went he was a relatively new 3rd Mate with very little experience. When he returned he had risen in the seniority ranks so as to be a Chief Officer. Having never sailed in the Union fleet in this capacity the old established Captains refused to have him aboard their ships. The Company finally put him aboard the *Lady Cynthia* as Chief Officer on a day run.

Whatever happened to Miles is uncertain, but Ivor Jones said he ran into him upcoast on a smaller boat after the Union Steamship Co. had ceased to exist.

Ernest M. "Ernie" Sheppard

In 1958 when the Union Steamship Co. ceased operations, Captain Sheppard was the Commodore or senior skipper in the fleet, since other Captains who had been ahead of him in seniority, such as Captains Wilson, Lawrey, Boden, Yates and Naughty, had already retired before then.

Ernie was born in Grace Harbour, Newfoundland in 1894. His brother Captain Bert Sheppard said that he recalls fishing off the Labrador Coast in a 35 foot open boat along with his brother Ernie. Both were sailors at a very young age. Veteran Union Steamships Captain John Park, who had joined the Company in 1911 as Master on the *Venture*, said that Ernie Sheppard was his quartermaster. [187]

Captain Sheppard was with the Union Steamship Co. for 47 years, which included his service time in the First World War from 1916 to 1919 as a pilot in the Royal Airforce. He was injured in a forced landing and as a result of this accident required surgery, after which he carried a metal plate in his head, but it didn't prevent him from having a productive career.

Gerald Rushton says that Ernie Sheppard had obtained his Coastal Mates Ticket prior to joining the Airforce in 1916. At this time he was 3rd Mate on the *Chilliwack I*. Prior to rejoining the Union Steamships in 1919, and while still in his Airforce Lieutenant's uniform, he was married. [188]

In 1923 Sheppard was 2nd Mate aboard the *Cardena* on her maiden voyage. Deck officers aboard were Captain Dickson, Chief Officer Bill Mounce, Ernie as 2nd Mate and 3rd Mate was L. Mercer. Ships Registry records show he was Chief Officer on the *Camosun I* under Captain Findlay in 1925.

Just when he obtained his Coastal Master's Ticket is uncertain. Defieux says it was either in 1928 or 1934 while Rushton says he served on the *Camosun I* as master before she was sold in 1935, so 1928 would probably be the likely date he obtained his Master's Certificate. News reports say Captain Sheppard served for a time as Master on the *Chilliwack II*, the former *Ardgarvel*.

Captain Sheppard became best known up and down the coast as Master on the *Catala*, which for many years was the flagship of the Union fleet. However, along with such recognition, the *Catala* also was his nemesis because he twice was on watch on the bridge when she went aground. The first time was at Sparrowhawk Reef on Nov. 8, 1927 at 1 p.m. in broad daylight, and the second time was late one night in December 1937 on Herbert Reef. The grounding at Sparrowhawk has been documented by some very dramatic photos and thus rates as one of the most famous in the Company's history, though how she got there has been a constant topic of discussion through the years.

Ernest Sheppard, Air Force Pilot in W.W. I *(Skinner Collection)*

The Fall 1958 edition of a magazine named *Ship and Shore* reported that the reason for the ship going aground was poor atmospheric conditions, but Captain William McCombe Sr. described the grounding differently in the booklet *Sound Heritage: Navigating the Coast*, which tells what really happened and how Sheppard sidestepped the issue and avoided being fully blamed: "Old man Dickson had a certain routine. He was quite an old man. Every day he came on the bridge, he looked over, I don't think he saw anything, and then we went back and he watered his flowers, his wee garden. He had pots and wee bits of flowers at the back (of the wheelhouse). He nursed them along. The next thing we knew, the *Catala*'s belted Sparrowhawk Ledge. The man that was on the bridge was a man by the name of Sheppard. He said he saw Captain Dickson on the bridge and he thought he was taking over. The man never took over before. And you never forget old man Dickson at the inquiry. Well, Captain Dickson said: 'Captain Sheppard thinks I took over. I guess I must have taken over.' That was all he said. He took the rub! The old man come up and he looked over. He wouldn't say boo to you, nor anybody else. He had done his niceties (many times) before. He had been down for his lunch then. This was on his way back up." [189]

The Herbert Reef grounding took place in December 1937 during the usual Christmas trek of travellers. The *Catala* had an amazing escape from disaster. The ship grounded heavily on Herbert Reef, losing fuel in the main tanks after ripping open her double bottom. Fred Corneille was quartermaster at the time and he remembers he was told to "steer very carefully." Captain Sheppard was on the bridge. Fred said, "The usual light on the rock was out but you could see the cement block and the light standard. It was decided to alter course to the left and a moment later we hit. We had gone too far over."

Angus McNeill was the 3rd Mate and had this to say: "She was held fast on it for three hours but freed herself at high tide and we were able to reach Prince Rupert harbour, with life boats swung out, using the fuel oil left in her settling tanks." [190]

Captain Sheppard also was on the bridge of the *Cardena* when she went aground at Duval Point shortly after leaving Port Hardy, on Nov. 30, 1956. Tex Lyon, the wharfinger at Port Hardy, watched her leave and recalls, "It was a dark night but you could see the blinker light a mile away, but I noticed she was on a odd course. Half an hour later I received a call from D.O.T. telling me she had gone aground at Duval Point."

The curious thing I find about these groundings is that Captain Sheppard was on the bridge in each case but little or nothing has ever been said or written about his part in these accidents.

Over the years Captain Sheppard received great press and praise from the marine writers of the day in the Vancouver papers, yet here we have three serious groundings where Captain Sheppard was in charge and it seems they didn't report anything about his participation in these accidents. One ex-Union hand, later a Master on coastal vessels himself, said: "Captain Sheppard seemed to always manage to pin the blame on someone else in any of the accidents he was involved with." Iain Morrison, a former deck officer in the Union Steamships, said Captain Sheppard "would accuse anybody of anything just so he wouldn't get the blame."

It was a fact and well-known that Captain Sheppard became a very pious man. He was constantly reading the Bible and praying but in doing so, according to one Union deck officer who sailed with him, he became a problem. Fred Corneille, who was quartermaster under Captain Sheppard when the *Catala* grounded on Herbert Reef, said: "He had the habit of leaving the bridge. Suddenly you would find yourself all alone. You would look around and no one was there, then you would see Captain Sheppard down on his knees praying. This kind of thing spoils your sense of security you know."

Another story that Captain Billy McCombe told went like this: "We were coming out of the Narrows in a heavy fog. I'm blowing the whistle every few seconds and I look around and no Captain Sheppard. As soon as I was able I went down to his room and there he was down on his knees praying. I said, 'You get the hell up on the bridge, I need you more than God does!'"

In a Company newsletter dated October 1954, there was a write-up about Captain Sheppard. Amongst other things it states Captain Sheppard had sailed on all Company routes and had made nearly 50,000 landings in his career.

From my research it appears he had more marine mishaps than anyone in the fleet. Three of the more serious mishaps are described above but there are more, perhaps not as dramatic but serious enough. These accidents have never been written up but were told to me by other officers in the fleet who were either there when they happened or had been told of them by others who were there.

1. The *Cardena* grounds on Merry Island.
2. The *Catala* rams the wharf at Klemtu.
3. The *Lady Pam* runs down a yacht in Howe Sound.
4. Almost loses one of the new Corvettes off the Skeena.
5. *Catala* rams head-on into the end of the U.S.S. wharf.

With Sheppard having had such a long period of service with Union Steamships, there was bound to be many anecdotal stories about him. One of the earliest of these takes place up at Port Hardy and was told to me by Tex Lyon. The *Catala* would spend many hours unloading freight at this port. There were some tame geese that used to swim around the bay. The Chinese cooks aboard the *Catala* who used to fish off the stern noticed these geese and started to feed them. They began to come around the ship regularly and were coming closer and closer all the time. On one occasion all of a sudden there was the greatest noise and squawking at the rear of the ship and Captain Sheppard went running back to see what this noise was all about. When he got there he found one of the cooks had put a nice bit of fish on a large hook and had caught one of the geese. He was about to strangle it when Captain Sheppard arrived on the scene and saved the day, or to be more exact, the goose. As a result, the cooks were banned from doing any more fishing in that port.

One of the famous characters of Hardy Bay was Nel Dumas. She ran the Hotel at Port Hardy for years. She finally had decided to retire, sold her hotel and was moving up to Prince Rupert. She was boarding the *Catala* along with all her furniture and belongings for the trip north. Needless to say the whole town, along with people from miles around, came down to the wharf to give her a big send off. It was one huge party down on the wharf. Finally it was time for the ship to leave and Captain Sheppard came down to the gang plank to welcome this famous lady aboard. I was at the plank as well, checking the people who were coming back aboard and Captain Sheppard was standing right beside me. Now Nel as the saying goes "was no lady."

Capt. Ernest Sheppard on the bridge of a Union Steamship
(Ashmore Collection)

She could swear like a trooper and could drink with the best of them. The send-off was pretty wild with plenty of drinking and swearing, which of course Captain Sheppard wasn't at all fond of. As Nel stepped on the gang plank, she turned to the crowd and started to swear at them all. It was really something to hear. As she made her way up the gang plank, swearing all the way, Captain Sheppard turned to me and quietly said, "My boy, now you have heard everything!" And I think he was right.

Stew Hale a former Purser with the Company, remembers Captain Sheppard giving him a lecture one day about avoiding evil but also avoiding the appearance of evil.

There was a deckhand aboard the *Catala* whom Captain Sheppard had taken under his wing. He was known as Springline McGuiness and had been on the *Catala* for years. He could neither read nor write but was a very willing worker and after a time he handled the springline and no one else could touch it. However he was a bit of a hindrance when it came to unloading freight as he couldn't read the names on the boxes and cartons. If the stevedore wasn't careful, Springline would load anybody's freight on the pallet board. The crew would complain to the mate that Springline wasn't pulling his weight and the Mate would speak to the Captain, but to no avail because Springline was under the Captain's wing and nobody could touch him. When a new Mate came aboard he was told by Captain Sheppard, "Whatever you do don't you dare think of firing Springline."

Frank Lawrence, a former Purser in the Company who had sailed on the *Catala* for a long time with Captain Sheppard, said he was called "Daddy." Frank said: "He could never seem to make up his mind, he was always dithering." Which is to say, he would act nervously and indecisively. One has to wonder if the accident he suffered in the airplane crash in 1919 didn't play a part in his lack of decisiveness in his later years.

Captain Sheppard also had some family tragedies in his later years. His son was a Second World War flying ace but he was killed in action, which people say broke Captain Sheppard's heart. As well, I was told that a while later his daughter was killed in a traffic accident while she was on her way to pick him up at the Union dock.

In 1957 the Union Steamship Co. assigned the *Coquitlam* to the Alaska Cruise Lines. Captain Sheppard was her Master for the season, which was fully booked . [191]

Early in 1958 Captain Sheppard was back on the newly-reconditioned *Catala*, but things had changed. The ship's once-beautiful dining room had been turned into a cafeteria. Horrors! The Company was desperately trying to recoup its coastal trade but by the end of the year their ships were tied up for good. In the summer of 1958 Captain Sheppard and Captain McCombe went over to the Alaska Cruise Lines of Seattle, never to return to the Union Steamship Co. which had been their home for many, many years. Captain Sheppard took over command of the *Glacier Queen*, the former USS *Coquitlam II*. He was their senior skipper.

Later Captain Sheppard took command of the *Polar Star* for the same Company. He retired from an active sea life in 1969 at age 75. He had sailed 47 years with the Union Steamships where he had participated in the growth and development of the coastal communities. He had made friends with thousands of coastal people and tourists alike. He spent 11 years with the Alaska Cruise Lines, later known as West Tours. Captain Sheppard had a total of 58 years sailing on the B.C. coast.

When he retired it was announced that although he was retiring from an active sea life he was going to be retained as a consultant by West Tours.

Captain Sheppard was a respected member of Master Mariners of Canada and was one of the pioneers of the Canadian Merchant Service Guild. One of his greatest tributes came in 1953 when the President of the United States presented him with citizenship to the State of Texas for his services while Master of the *Catala*. [192]

Captain Sheppard died in Vancouver in March 1972 at the age of 78. Charlie Defieux in one of his columns said of Captain Sheppard when he died: "He was a quiet, unassuming gentleman of the sea."

Robert Smith

Robert Smith *(Ashmore Collection)*

Robert Smith was born in Banffshire, Scotland in 1896 and came over to B.C. in 1928. He had gained sea-going experience working aboard seiners in the North Sea. When he came to B.C. he went to sea again working on tug boats along the B.C. coast.

He joined the Union Steamship Co. in 1937 and Canadian Merchant Service Guild records show he became a member of that organization on Feb. 2, 1944, likely having received his Coastal Mate's Ticket at this time. Johnny Horne remembers him as being a real Scot and a man dedicated to his task.

The family purchased property on Cortes Island and his wife would spend the summer months there. Bob would always try and get on this Cortes Island route. The ship would usually arrive at Cortes Island late in the evening and Bob would dash home for a quick visit. Naturally, when he returned to the ship, he usually took quite a ribbing from the crew about such a short, nocturnal visit.

Captain Harry Roach often used to take his son Ed out with him when he was on the day boats. On one occasion Captain Roach was aboard the *Lady Cecilia* and Robert Smith was with him as 2nd Mate. Ed, Captain Roach's son, also was aboard and as he loved to steer the ship he spent a lot of time that day steering. They were about to go in to Hopkins Landing and Captain Roach said to Bob Smith, "You may as well take her in Bob for practice." Bob said, "Alright, but I'd like to have young Ed at the wheel." Harry said, "Oh no, you can take the ship in but you can't make the landing with him at the wheel."

Robert Smith was 2nd Mate on the *Lady Cynthia* on Oct. 3, 1950 when it rammed into the port side of the M.V. *A.L. Bryant*. This tragedy took place abreast of Snug Cove on Bowen Island and the *Bryant* was cut in two. He and Captain Yates were down having dinner when this accident occurred. They immediately returned to the bridge and in two minutes a life boat was launched with Bob Smith in charge. He was credited with saving two of the four survivors.

On Jan. 15, 1954 he was again 2nd Mate on the *Lady Cynthia*. They were docking at Britannia Beach. He was helping to move the heavy gangplank in place when he suffered a heart attack and dropped dead on the spot - a very sad and sudden end to the career of this popular officer. Relatives acting on his behalf argued successfully with the Workers Compensation Board that his heart attack was brought about by the strain of helping to move the gangplank and thereby obtaining a pension for his widow.

James "Jimmy" Stewart

James Stewart, who had his Deep Water Ticket, was hired by Captain Suffield and one of his first jobs for the Company was to bring back the *Blue Peter II* from Eastern Canada in 1950. The deck officers who went back with him were all from the Union Steamship Co.: Chief Officer Ralph Wills, 2nd Mate Stan Green, and 3rd Mate Johnny Horne. When this ship was put into service for the Company in 1951, she was renamed the *Cassiar III.*.

In 1952 Jimmy Stewart was again sent back east, along with Stan Green and Angus Wilson, to bring back another ship, the *City of Belleville*. On their way out to the west coast they picked up a load of nitrates in Virginia. According to Stan Green, the potential volatility of this cargo created quite a stir on their way through the Panama Canal, but they got through alright and discharged it at the dynamite factory at James Island off of Sidney before going on to Vancouver.

Jimmy then went to work aboard the Union passenger ships. Although he had his Deep Sea Master's Ticket there was no way he could beat the seniority system within the Company and he had to start as a 3rd Mate. This did not sit well with him and he didn't stay very long with the Company. I was told he obtained a Master's job on the Albion ferry running across the Fraser River.

The accompanying photo shows Jimmy Stewart sitting to the right of Captain Harry Roach at the Officers' Mess Table on the *Cardena*. The other two men on the left are B.K. Owen-Jones and Jack Summerfield.

Left to right: B.K. Owen-Jones, Jack Summerfield, Capt. Roach, J. Stewart on the *Cardena* (Ashmore Collection)

Alan Gosse "Al" Strang

Capt. Al Strang on board the *Chelohsin* (Roach Collection)

Word has it that Al started as a deckhand with the Frank Waterhouse Co. around about 1923 and sometime along the way switched over to Union Steamships. Ship Registry records show he was quartermaster on the *Cardena* on March 15, 1938. He stayed with the Union Steamship Co. until 1950.

Al was a very popular officer aboard ship and was well-liked by other officers and crew alike.

Colin Park, a former deckhand in the Company, told me that Al was a pretty strong fellow. He used to come down into the hold when the crew were loading canned salmon and help out just for the exercise. He said Strang and Tom Lucas could actually throw the cases up to the top row of the pile, and that the crew had a lot of fun working with them.

During my research and interviews with many of Al's shipmates, they all reported he was an excellent ship handler, in fact one of the best in the fleet.

Ben Smith, a former engineer with the Company, said: "We soon learned who were good ship handlers just by observing how many signals they sent down to us when they were docking a ship. You soon began to anticipate what they wanted, they were amazing. Fellows like Tom Lucas, Al Strang, and Jimmy Hunter were three of the best."

I was up on the bridge of the *Cardena* one beautiful sunny day and we were just coming out of Heriot Bay. Al Strang was Chief Officer and as we approached a buoy channel marker Al said, "Let's see how close we can come to that damn thing." He rang down for full speed, the *Cardena* raced ahead, and as Al barked orders to the quartermaster from the bridge, we skimmed by that buoy, not five feet away from it!

Mike Benson, a former Purser with the Company, related the following story to me about Al docking the *Cardena* at the cannery dock in Bella Bella: "The dock juts out into the bay and right at the very end, past the dock, are huge rocks. Al was coming in, lining up the landing, with the engines stopped. He rang down for full astern in order to stop the ship alongside the wharf, but the engineer gave him full ahead! The ship started to move ahead instead of back, and Al, quick as a wink, rang down for full ahead. He got full astern! He didn't have much room to spare, but his split second thinking saved the ship, and no doubt his career at that point. What a chance he took! Whew!"

Austen Hemion of Seattle, a frequent traveller on the Union ships, wrote me a little story about meeting Al Strang for the first time and a fun time they had. It was on the *Venture* in 1944. The skipper was Big Mac McLennan, Al Strang was 2nd Mate and Don McLeod was the Purser: "We were clearing Smith's Inlet around midnight. My friend and I were walking back to our stateroom and we ran into Al and Don. They asked where we had been as they had made themselves at home in our room waiting for us to return. They had a case of beer, so we went back and had a little party. Don went down to the galley and brought back a plate of sandwiches and coffee. Our room was directly under Captain McLennan's room. Next morning, Al was out on the dock assisting the crew in loading some barrels and in hooking some up, he went head over heels. Big Mac was looking down from the bridge and seeing this he hollered out, 'That will teach you to party all night.'"

Al was soon sailing as a Chief Officer but Oct. 3, 1950 proved to be a fateful day for him. He was Chief Officer on the *Lady Cynthia* as she was proceeding down Howe Sound from Britannia Beach to her next stop at Snug Cove, Bowen Island. A B.C. Forestry vessel, the M.V. *A.L. Bryant*, was proceeding from Gambier Island to Whytecliff Point and the *Lady Cynthia* overtook it. A collision occurred, the launch was cut in two and three lives were lost. A newspaper report of the Admiralty findings of this disaster appears adjacent.

As a result of that accident, Al lost his ticket for nine months and so left Union Steamships, never to return.

He went up to the Great Slave Lakes and ran tugs up there for several years during the open season of navigation on the lakes and rivers. He then came back to B.C. and worked for Seaspan towing a rail barge between Squamish, North Vancouver and Seattle. This was in the 1960s on the tug Lillooet.

Al died from cancer of the prostate in 1985.

Ship's Officer Loses Ticket For 9 Months

Probe Here Raps Mate of Cynthia, Launch Operator

Master's certificate of Alen G. Strang, former chief officer of SS. Lady Cynthia, was suspended today for nine months for his part in the ship collision off Bowen Island, October 3, in which three men died.

The judgment was handed down in Admiralty Court by Mr. Justice Sidney Smith, sitting as commissioner of a three-man board at an inquiry ordered by the Federal Department of Transport.

Government log scaler John W. McDonald, who was in command of the provincial forestry launch A. L. Bryant at the time of the crash, drew "severe censure" for his default.

NO COSTS ALLOWED

No costs were allowed against any of the parties concerned in the accident.

In the collision the wooden launch was sliced in two by the steel prow of the steamship. Three log scalers perished, while four were saved.

The judgment said the collision and loss of life "was caused or contributed to" by both Strang and McDonald.

SEVERE CENSURE

While suspending the certificate of the chief officer, the court notes that the forestry man "is not the possessor of a certificate of competency, and, therefore, we can only severely censure him for his default and this we do."

Mr. Justice Smith was assisted in the inquiry by Capt. Samuel Robinson and Capt. James Patrick, nautical assessors.

Their joint findings state they can find no excuse for the failure of the Lady Cynthia to keep clear of the motor vessel she was overtaking, and that the Bryant was to blame, but in lesser degree, for failing to keep a lookout astern.

They found nothing wrong with the steering gear on the Union Steamship vessel.

Left to right: Lorne Godfrey, Eric Suffield and Bob Naughty, Jr. *(Naughty Collection)*

Eric W. Suffield

Capt. Eric Suffield
(Ashmore Collection)

Whenever I brought up the name Eric Suffield with ex Union Steamship hands it always brought forth exclamatory remarks. One of the first things they would say was, "Oh, you mean the Sea Beast," or "You mean Eric Von Suffield." Gerald Rushton refers to him as "something of a martinet." [193] He was either liked or disliked, there was no in between. After researching about him I would certainly say he was an enigma.

Captain Suffield had a long career with the Union Steamship Co., nearly 26 years. He distinguished himself early in this career, but in the end he was given the "bum's rush" when new shareholders took control of the Company.

He served in the navy in World War I and joined the Union Steamship Co. in 1921.

In 1934 he was 2nd Mate aboard the *Catala* and the Master at the time was Captain Dickson. One trip they noticed the Egg Island light was not functioning so Captain Dickson took the *Catala* in closer to investigate. Following is a description of what took place narrated by Robert Naughty Jr. in the booklet *Sound Heritage: Navigating the Coast*:

"He went in as close as he could in order to get his searchlight on and there was no light in the lighthouse. So he said, 'Something's wrong. We better get ashore.' So they launched this lifeboat and Eric took four deckhands with him to row and when they got in close to the beach the breakers started surfing up on them. They can't make it in 'cause it's all rocks. They had a rope aboard so Eric put it around his waist and dove in. He's a strong swimmer. He swam ashore with these guys holding onto the other end in case he didn't make it. He got in there and he started the light. I don't know how he knew how to do it. There was nobody there and nobody ever came back. They found a boat wrecked at the other end of the island. The two lighthouse keepers (I guess) went out fishing and they got swamped. That was Eric Suffield. He was a good swimmer." [194] No bodies were ever found and the disappearance of the two lightkeepers remains a mystery.

When war broke out in 1939 Eric Suffield soon joined up, naturally in the Navy, serving on three different ships. The longest stint was on a minesweeper named the *Kelowna* or *J 261*, from August 1943 to 1945. Before he joined up, the Union Steamship Co. sponsored "Win the War Cruises" in which the public was urged to purchase War saving stamps and then they received a ticket for the cruise. On the first cruise July 19, 1940, Eric Suffield was Captain of the *Lady Alexandra*. [195]

When Captain Suffield returned to the Union Steamships after the war his first command was Master of the *Venture*. Bob Ashmore recalls being 2nd Mate along with Captain Suffield for nearly two years. In 1946 he was appointed "Acting Marine Superintendent" and was given the job and responsibility of overseeing the installation of radar on the Union Steamship vessels. This was the latest tool for navigation but most of the old-time skippers, like Captains Wilson and Boden, didn't like it. They had been navigating by the whistle echo all their lives and they didn't trust this new gadget. The younger officers, having used and experienced it during the war, adapted to it readily. This new innovation caused friction between some of the Old Masters and Mates and their new Marine Superintendent, whereas the younger officers were all for this new radar.

In 1947, with the wartime boom over, the Union Steamship Co. was looking for new business opportunities along the coast. The *Camosun III* was sent to investigate the possibility of extending their service to the Alaska ports of Ketchikan, Wrangell and Petersburg. Captain Suffield was aboard, along with other Company officers.

The Company suffered a blow on Nov. 6, 1949 when the *Chelohsin* grounded in a dense fog near Siwash Rock in Stanley Park. No lives were lost but the ship was given up by the underwriters. Captain Suffield took a standby crew aboard but nothing could be done to save her.

Captain Suffield was somewhat implicated in that grounding because the radar set had broken down at Lund when the *Chelohsin* was southbound. The *Chelohsin* made it into Powell River and Captain Aspinall knew there was a radar technician in Powell River, so he phoned to head office and presumably talked to Captain Suffield, as he was the Marine Superintendent. Captain Aspinall asked for permission to get this radar man down to the *Chelohsin* and check out the radar but the request apparently was refused. Subsequently the *Chelohsin* had to come all the way down to Vancouver from Powell River in a thick fog, making several stops along the way, all without radar because of head office's decision. (see the report on Charles Hamer, 3rd Mate on the *Chelohsin* at the time, for further details of the grounding, pp.177-79)

In 1955 Captain Suffield was relieved of his position as Marine Superintendent when he had a personality clash with the new owners. He was succeeded by Captain Fred Talbot who had been in charge of the cargo side of the Union Waterhouse operation.

John "Jack" Ellis, formerly with B.C. Packers, was appointed General Manager of the Union Steamships on Jan. l, 1955. I was told that one of the conditions he made was that when he took over, Captain Suffield, who had been Marine Superintendent since 1947, was to be fired, and he was!

Geoff Hosken, a former deck officer with Union Steamships, told me that when Captain Suffield was let go, he went to work as a mate on a towboat operation on the Fraser River. He also was Master of the Rosedale ferry in the late 1950s. At this point he was approached from an unusual source. Captain Billy Yates, a well-known Union Steamships skipper, had a son who had been decking on the CPR ships who had become an entrepreneur and had formed his own shipping company. It was known as Pacific Tanker Ltd. They operated an old tanker which they named the *Pacific Wind*. She was a sister ship to the *Imperial Vancouver*. They also had some towboats and barges. Later they bought the *Unicana*. So Captain Yates, who had been a constant target of Captain Suffield when he was Superintendent at Union Steamships, went to his son and asked him to give Captain Suffield a job as Superintendent of this new Company!

Captain Suffield suffered with varicose veins and shortly after making this move he had to go into Shaughnessy Hospital to have these veins operated on. He had not informed the doctors that he was a diabetic and two days later he had to go back up to the operating room and the doctors removed his leg. Gangrene had set in which necessitated removal of his leg.

Geoff, along with a young Scotch lad by the name of Ken Fletcher, a deckhand on the Union boats, went up to visit Captain Suffield while he was in hospital after he had had his leg removed. Captain Suffield was glad to see them of course and said, "Oh I can hardly wait to get back to sea again, I can feel it in my toes!" Obviously he wasn't aware that he had lost his leg!

Geoff and Ken didn't know what to say, for they knew he had lost his leg. Even so, Captain Suffield did go back to work at Pacific Tankers and was to be seen hobbling around on crutches.

Once when Geoff was between jobs he went down to see Captain Suffield to see if he had any work for a short period. Captain Suffield said, "Geoff, you wouldn't want to work on that old tanker, she's a cranky ship, but I've got a towboat here that has to go through inspection, how'd you like to look after that for me?" So Geoff took on this job, getting the tug ready for inspection.

Geoff said, "It was an amazing set up. Here was old Cappy Yates helping out a man who was always watching him with an eagle eye, determined to have his job if he ever caught him, shall we say, over imbibing. Then to see the once proud and belligerent Captain Suffield hobbling around on one leg, Marine Superintendent of a little company with an old tanker, some towboats and barges, operating probably on a shoe string." Geoff concluded, "Poor old Suffield, I sure felt sorry for him because I got along well with him and I thought he was a darned good Superintendent."

Many anecdotes about Captain Suffield and his career in the Union Steamships were related to me by his contemporaries, some of which are as follow:

Johnny Horne said, "Ah yes, the Sea Beast. The younger Officers generally liked him. For instance you knew where you stood with him. There was a big difference between him and Captain Muir, who was Marine Superintendent before Captain Suffield. With Captain Muir you could never find out when your days off were coming, but with Captain Suffield he had it all figured out and could tell you immediately."

Captain Boden, who was the senior skipper in the fleet when Captain Suffield was in charge of things, never got along with Captain Suffield. Captain Boden was always complaining about the younger 2nd and 3rd mates who were put aboard his ship. Indeed, some of these younger officers simply refused to sail with Boden. Captain Suffield finally had to tell Captain Boden, "Look, anytime you want to fire someone, write to me first."

One thing that Captain Suffield wanted to do was rid the Company of the many family relatives who were working in the fleet at the same time. One example was Captain Harry McLean's son, Robert. Captain Suffield made it hard for these young fellows to obtain berths and get promotions. In Robert McLean's case he eventually left the Company and became a Captain on Vancouver's fire boat, a position he held for 31 years.

Denis Shaw, a former Purser, had this to say about Captain Suffield: "He was a very tough and demanding man. He had a belligerent nature and would be quite happy to settle an argument with a fist fight down at the end of the wharf." Denis once told him, "You know Cap, if you were to die tomorrow nobody from here would come to your funeral." Captain Suffield's answer was, "They hate me that much, do they?"

Frank Lawrence told me a story about Captain Suffield that illustrates how ready and willing he was to do battle. This story took place on the *Venture* and a fellow by the name of Pat Wylie was the night steward. Captain Suffield was the Chief Officer and was on the 12 to 6 watch. Pat was a well-known jokester. On this particular trip they were taking loggers back to work and there was a lot of partying going on. Pat joined one of these parties and told the night porter that he was going up to this particular room and that if he didn't return in 10 minutes he was to go on up to the bridge and tell the Chief Officer, Suffield, that he was in trouble and needed to be rescued. Pat left and didn't return, so the porter went up to the bridge and summoned Eric Suffield for help. As Eric neared the room he could hear all sorts of banging, thuds, and crashes, so he banged on the door. The door partly opened and he could see Pat being held in a strangle-hold. The door was then almost closed so Captain Suffield took one step back and went crashing through the door. In that same moment, before Captain Suffield had burst in, Pat had stepped behind the door, and as Eric went crashing across the room, Pat stepped out the door and ran down the alleyway. It wasn't long before Eric was in hot pursuit for he realized he had been fooled. Eric chased Pat round and round the ship. Pat wound up in the rigging of the after mast. That's where he spent the night because down below him was Eric Suffield shaking his fist and uttering all the Anglo-Saxon profanities in the book and as well as telling Pat, "When you come down, I'll kill you."

It can be seen that Captain Suffield was a tough customer and was in his glory bossing people and ordering them around. The two stories following offer a comic relief about this hard-driving man:

Frank Skinner, a former Purser, recalls working on the *Capilano II* and Eric Suffield was Mate. Frank said, "Eric was very positive about things and great at giving orders, you do this, you do that, put that over there, move this here, etc. He ran an efficient ship. He did all the talking. He and Captain McCombe had great conversations at the Mess table, but one day Captain Suffield brought his wife out for a trip and SHE did all the talking, Captain Suffield hardly said a word."

Ben Smith, a former Engineer, tells a similar story. This event took place on one of the northern route ships and Eric Suffield was the Master. Again, he had brought his wife aboard for a trip and this time she had brought along their pet macaw bird. Everyone wanted to hear the bird talk and after some urging it complied. One can imagine Captain Suffield's embarrassment when the macaw squawked out these words: "Do the dishes Eric, do the dishes Eric!"

John E. "Jack" Summerfield

Capt. Jack Summerfield
(McCue Collection)

Jack, or Slim as he was sometimes called, served with the Union Steamship Co. for nearly 27 years. He left the Company in 1950 and went aboard the CNR train barge as 3rd Mate.

His contemporaries and crew called him Anxious Moments for when he was docking a ship he would always be muttering to himself "She'll never make it, she'll never make it." He was somewhat of a worrywart. Jack and Captain Suffield, the Marine Superintendent, never hit it off for some reason. There was a clash of personalities. Jack never obtained a Master's position on the northern routes as long as Captain Suffield was in charge although he did serve as Chief Officer on all of them and did sail as Master on the *Lady Rose* on Howe Sound runs.

Records show he served as Chief Officer aboard the new *Camosun III* when the

U.S.S. Co. inaugurated a new service running to Ketchikan in December 1946. The Master at the time was Captain Ernest Sheppard. Summerfield also was serving as Chief Officer on the *Cardena* under Captain Bob Wilson on Dec. 21, 1947 when Captain Wilson collapsed on the bridge. The ship was bringing a full load of loggers to Vancouver for Christmas and as Chief Officer Jack had to take over. He ran the ship full speed for Campbell River and made it in time for Captain Wilson to be rushed to the hospital there, but he later died while being treated there.

Fred Corneille tells of meeting Jack Summerfield at the coffee stand on the Union dock one day after he had left the Union Steamship Co. He was complaining to Fred about the fact the CNR wanted to promote him from 3rd Mate to 2nd Mate and he said, "All I want to be is 3rd Mate." The company finally gave him an ultimatum, either move up to 2nd Mate or be let out. He did move up to 2nd Mate and ended his career aboard the *Canora*.

A.E. "Wally" Walsh

Capt. Wally Walsh
(Ashmore Collection)

Wally was one of the better-known characters in the Union fleet during his 31 years with the Company. He also was known by the nickname "the Baron."

Prior to joining the Union Steamship Co. he sailed as a cadet on one of the Empress ships, the *Mount Eagle*, under Captain A.J. Hoskens, who was the father of Geoff Hoskens, a Union Steamships deck officer. Captain Hoskens and his ship went to the aid of a French vessel which was in trouble as a result of the severe earthquake in Japan in 1922. All of the crew, including Wally Walsh, thus received a medal from the French Government. By coincidence, Geoff's first trip on a Union ship was on the *Lady Cecilia* and Wally Walsh was the Captain. Geoff and Wally had never met. On being introduced, Wally said: "I sailed with a Captain Hoskens on the *Mount Royal*." "Yes," Geoff said, "that was my father!" Then Wally said, "As a matter of fact I have a discharge paper signed by your father right here in my pocket!"

Wally joined the Union Steamships in 1927 and worked his way up to Captain. Most fellows called him Wally but I asked John Smith, a fellow Union hand who knew and worked with him, how the Baron nickname came about. "It was the way he wore his cap and his general demeanor. At times he reminded us of a German Baron," John said. "If you were right he would back you to the hilt but God help you if you were wrong. He was tough, and if it came to a battle between the Sea Beast (Captain Suffield) and the Baron, I'd bet on the Baron!" Another nickname he had which wasn't as well-known was "Clark Gable" because he apparently was quite a ladies' man.

It is said that Wally was an expert ship handler. Johnny Horne said Wally used to love skimming around Point Atkinson, 50 feet from the shore line. However, perhaps his career as a seaman was jeopardized a little because he suffered terribly with migraine headaches. John Smith said he had often seen Wally sit in the corner of the wheelhouse holding his head in great pain.

Colin Park, who sailed with Wally, told me that Wally was a great joker. On the *Camosun II* on the Queen Charlotte Island run they would often be transporting corpses over to Prince Rupert. They stored these bodies in the ship's lifeboats because this was the coolest place available. One lunch hour Wally came down to the Officers' Mess and with a big smile announced to his fellow officers, already eating, "I've finally got something I've wanted for years, I just have to show you fellows!" With that he brought out a little box from his pocket, took the lid off and carefully showed some cotton batten spattered with blood along with a human finger laying in there. There was a gasp from those at the table. Wally went on to say, "Yeah, I cut this off the stiff we've got up there!" One of the engineers who had been eating suddenly got up and rushed out, for he just about threw up his lunch right there and then. Of course it was an old trick that Wally played but he knew how this poor fellow would react.

Denis Shaw, a former Purser, tells a story about sharing a cabin aboard the *Lady Pam* with Wally. Denis had the top bunk. One day after snoozing, Denis quickly jumped out of the bunk and instead of landing on a solid floor, he went right through the floor boards. Recovering his composure, Denis knelt down to examine what had happened and looking down into the hole he could see that something had been stored down there, wrapped in burlap. He called Wally down and they went to work and were able to retrieve this bundle. Upon closer examination they found it was a ship's bell inscribed *Santa Maria,* one of the names of the *Lady Pam* before the Union Steamship Co. had acquired her. Wally immediately said, "By God, this is mine, I'm taking it home." According to Denis he did. When the Vancouver Maritime Museum held a Union Steamship Exhibition in 1990, Denis went to the trouble of advertising to see if he could locate any of the Walsh family and thus learn the whereabouts of this bell with the idea of having it on display in the show, but nobody came forward.

Another story from Johnny Horne was about the time Wally had been entertaining a couple of young lady passengers in his room aboard the *Chilcotin*. They were sitting around in Wally's cabin having a wee nip when one of the girls asked why he didn't have any pin-up girls in his room. Wally just shrugged and the young lady said, "I'll draw you one, I'm am artist." Wally laughed and said. "Okay, go to it." She proceeded to draw a naked girl on the ceiling above Wally's bunk! This drawing became famous throughout the fleet. (Thanks to Bob Ashmore's photo collection I have a copy of it - see p.129.) When Wally was transferred to another ship he couldn't take the painting with him. His replacement was Wee Angus McNeill and when he saw this painting he had a fit and wanted to have it painted out, but fellow officers prevailed upon him and they had a sheet pinned up to cover it over. This satisfied Angus, because he didn't want his wife to come aboard and find this sort of thing in his quarters.

Austen Hemion of Seattle, a frequent traveller aboard the Union ships, often met Wally and they became good friends. Austen told this story about Wally. He was making the round trip on the *Chilcotin* in 1947 when she was on the Ketchikan run. The Captain was Big Mac McLennan and Wally was Chief Officer. They had tied up at Ketchikan and Austen had invited an old friend of his, Joe Williamson, to come aboard for a cocktail. Joe had his own boat moored nearby and Wally came down and joined them. Joe was admiring the small scatter rug with the Union Estates symbol on it and Wally said to Joe, "Don't take Austen's, he'll get billed for it. I'll get you one." It seems that the Chief Engineer, George Craigen, for some reason owed Wally one of these rugs and had never returned it. So Wally went down to the Chief's room, knocked on the door and getting no answer, opened the door, went in and picked up the rug from the Chief's room, then came back with it to Austen's room. They found some paper and wrapped it up. As the three of them were leaving the ship with this parcel, they ran into Captain McLennan. Wally said to Big Mac with a straight face, "I'm just giving Joe here some of our old charts." "Joe wore that rug out in his wheelhouse long before he sold his boat," Austen said.

Wally served on the Union wharf for quite a few years as Shore Captain. In the summer season the day boats oftten were jammed full with day trippers and excursion groups and no doubt they sometimes were overloaded, especially the *Lady Alexandra*. On one occasion the *Alexandra* was coming in with a huge load of passengers and Wally caught sight of two Customs officers who were inside the shed and were ready to take a count of the passengers coming off the *Alex*. Seeing this, Wally sprang into action and ordered the Mate aboard the *Alex* to put out four gang planks in order to get the passengers off in a hurry. There was no way that the two Customs Officers could count four gang planks and they gave up in disgust! Wally's quick action saved the day. [196]

On Dec. 23, 1947, Wally was Captain on the *Lady Cecilia* making a special Christmas run to pick up mill workers at Powell River, but he was not on watch when the ship went aground on Tattenham Ledge in Buccaneer Bay. The officer on watch was James Galbraith. [197]

Wally must have been getting tired of life at sea for one of his shipmates asked him one day, "When you retire where do you think you will go?" His reply was, "I'll get an old oar, walk up into the Interior and when somebody stops me and asks me what it is, that's where I'll retire."

Wally Walsh left the Union Steamship Co. around 1949 to accept an appointment with the Canadian Merchant Service Guild as a Guild Agent. He then left this job to accept a position as Marine Superintendent for the Crown Zellerbach Co. The date of his death is uncertain but it was believed to be in the late 1950s.

Capt. James Watt (Ashmore Collection)

James W. Watt

Captain Watt was one of the CNR men who came over to the Union Steamships in 1940 when the *Prince Charles* and the *Prince John* were taken over by the Union Co. He served two years in the Company as Master of the *Camosun II*, formerly the *Prince Charles*, but died aboard his ship while it was over in the Queen Charlotte Islands in 1942. He was the first of four Captains in the Union fleet to die aboard their ships. The others were Captains Malcolmson, Godfrey and Wilson, in that order.

Details of Captain Watt's death were given to me by Captain John Smith, whose uncle Buster Brown was the Chief Officer aboard the *Camosun* at the time. Captain Watt died before he was due to come on watch at 6 a.m. The *Camosun* was in Cumshewa Inlet. Buster Brown had sent his 3rd Mate down to wake up Captain Watt. He knocked on his cabin door and Captain Watt answered, "Yes, okay, I'll be up shortly." The first thing Buster knew he was making the landing at Cumshewa and still no Captain Watt. This was not unusual because he was never on time. After the landing was made, in checking on Captain Watt, they found him, in his uniform, lying dead on the floor of his cabin with a hair brush in his hand!

Union hands who worked under Captain Watt and the passengers aboard his ship will always remember him as the Captain who played the bagpipes. This was his gift to crew and passengers. He would get out his pipes when the mood struck him and stride back and forth on the bridge of his ship squeezing and blowing out a Scottish ballad.

I understand he had a son who worked for awhile on the Union ships and who also played the bagpipes. Apparently he ran a piping school up at Squamish and was also very active in the Caledonian Games.

Bob Ashmore, a former deck officer with Union Steamships, recalls that when he sat for his first ticket, Captain Watt wrote out a recommendation letter for him.

Captain Watt was an active supporter of the Canadian Merchant Service Guild in B.C. and was president for one term. He was well-liked by his crew, but he did have a problem: he liked the "Jolly Juice" a little too much.

An ex deck officer who sailed with Captain Watt recalled a trip when the *Camosun* was in Alliford Bay. They were to be there for quite awhile unloading supplies for the base. The commanding officer of the base invited Captain Watt up to the Officers' Mess for a wee tot but Captain Watt not only had a wee tot, he had a full load, and had to be helped back to his ship!

Colin Park, who was a quartermaster on the *Camosun*, tells a very amusing story about Captain Watt and his ship being challenged by the military at Yorke Island. This was a military post on an island passed just before a ship proceeded into the open waters of Queen Charlotte Sound or before a ship proceeded south into Johnstone Strait. A military launch would come out and any passing ship would be hailed, stopped and asked for identification. On this occasion, which was at night, the officer in charge called out, "What is the name of your ship?" Captain Watt answered, "The S.S. *Camosun*, out of Vancouver." Then, "What is the Master's name?" "Watt," was the answer. Repeat, "What is the name of your Master?" "Watt." This time there were signs that the military was getting annoyed, so he repeated the question in a more forceful voice, "What is the name of your Master?" "I'm telling you," the Captain answered, "Watt, Captain James Watt." Silence for a moment, then "Okay, proceed." The crew on watch at the time got a great kick out of "Watt" was going on and the Captain's fun with the military.

J.W. "Chips" Williams

Information on this man is very scanty. His nickname Chips makes one wonder if he was an avid poker player.

He served aboard Union Steamship vessels from 1911 to 1928, which included service in the First World War. He went overseas as a member of the 29th battalion who were called Tobin's Tigers. He was Pilot on the *Chilkoot* when she first went into service in 1920. Captain Findlay was the Master.

Johnny Horne, a former deck officer with the Union Steamships, related the following story about him to me: "He was a tough old character. One trip he had been up on the bridge all night in a thick fog, and was standing out on the bridge wing. One of the crew brought him a mug of coffee. Standing there with the cup in his hand, a seagull flew over and crapped right into his cup of coffee. Chips looked up and hollered, 'To hell with you, God Damn it,' and drank the coffee mixture, in one gulp, as is!"

Robert Thomas "Bob" Williamson

Capt. Bob Williamson on the *Cassiar II*

The accompanying photo of Bob was taken on the *Cassiar II* (ex *Prince John*) in the early 1940s. He was 3rd Mate. I was also aboard in the Pursers Department and found Bob to be a good shipmate. He had the respect of the crew and was a conscientious officer.

Tex Lyon, the wharfinger at Port Hardy, recalls Bob being a dapper young officer. Bob was a heavy smoker but he always smoked his cigarettes using a fancy cigarette holder. When he held this holder at a jaunty angle it always reminded me of the pictures of President Roosevelt.

Bob started work in the Union Company as a deckhand in 1934. During the dock strike in 1936, Bob crossed the picket lines and went to work. One of the well-known and senior masters in the fleet never forgave him for this and in later years refused to have him on his ship.

Williamson worked his way up the ladder and obtained his Coastal Mate's Ticket in 1941. He then sailed as 3rd Mate on the *Catala*. He sat for his Master's Ticket on Dec. 9, 1946 and was successful, receiving his Home Trade Master's Certificate number 17224. In the summer of 1947 he was 2nd Mate aboard the *Lady Alexandra* and therefore stood watch with the Captain who at the time was the well-known Billy Yates. The ship and its crew participated in a celebration of the opening of a new wharf at Gibsons Landing. Captain Yates celebrated a little too much and on the return trip to Vancouver Bob was called upon to dock the ship.

During the summer of 1956 Bob was Captain on the *Lady Rose*. April 1958 found him as Chief Officer aboard the *Catala* when she resumed service on the Bella Coola route. The Company had cancelled its Northern Routes because of lack support from the Federal Government. The resumption of boat service by the Union Company was welcomed by the coastal communities, however by the end of the year the Union Steamships came to their end. All their ships were tied up and in January 1959 all the Company's assets were taken over by Northland Navigation Company.

In 1959 the Alaska Steamship Line took over two of the new corvettes, being the *Camosun* and the *Coquitlam*, from the Union Steamship Co. The *Camosun* was renamed the *Yukon Star* and Bob sailed aboard her as Chief Officer for the next five years. He was scheduled to become Captain on her the next season but by a cruel twist of fate this promotion eluded him. Captain William McCombe Sr., who was a Captain in the Alaska Cruise Line, was retiring, and this was the vacancy that Bob was to step into. When Captain McCombe learned of this, he went to top management in the Company and persuaded them to promote his son, William McCombe Jr., who also was a Mate in the Company but junior to Bob. It is hard to imagine that a man could carry a grudge against another man over an event that took place almost 27 years ago and which had no effect on him personally, but he did so, and with a vengeance!

Bob resigned immediately, badly broken over this terrible event, and never sailed again. He took sick and died July 15, 1977 at age 61.

Ralph Wills

Ralph was a slightly-built young man and always impeccably groomed. He was a Conway Boy who had a great career in the British Navy before coming to British Columbia and joining the Union Steamship Co. His ability and qualifications as a seaman and navigator were second to none.

Most of his shipmates thought he was born in England but in fact he was born in Ottawa, on Sept. 2, 1918. He received his education in Canada and in the mid 1930s he went over to England. He attended and trained aboard the square-rigged school ship H.M.S. *Conway* based in the River Mersey off Rock Ferry pier. After two years of training he joined the CPR as a cadet, sailing aboard their ships running from London to Montreal and back. When war was declared he was drafted into the Royal Naval Reserve. He served aboard various warships including the H.M.S. *Witch*, which Ralph said was the luckiest ship on the seven seas, the H.M.S. *Freesia* and the H.M.S. *Loch Dunvegan*, among others. At one time he served aboard the same warship as Prince Philip. Two of Ralph's shipmates with the Union Steamships state that Ralph was one of the youngest Lt. Commanders in the British Navy. He saw action at Narvik, Dunkirk, and made a run to Murmansk.

When the war was over he went back to the CPR but found there were very few jobs available because the company had lost so many of its ships during the war.

He had met his wife, Susette, in Londonderry in 1945. They were married in June of 1946 and came to Canada later that year. However, before coming over to Canada, Ralph sat for and received, all at one time, his 2nd and 1st Mate's Tickets as well as his Foreign-Going Master's Ticket.

When they arrived in B.C. Ralph obtained a job with the Western Canada Steamships, sailing deep sea all over the world. He was away more than eight months. Upon his return he took a temporary job ashore, but decided to go to sea again and joined the Union Steamship Co. as a 3rd Mate in 1948. Despite his excellent qualifications he had to start out as 3rd Mate, for sailing on the B.C. coast was another story and as well, of course, the seniority system was in effect. He was with the Union Steamship Co. for six years and he always marvelled at the seamanship of the Masters and Mates, especially working under the harsh weather conditions and the many navigational hazards here on the B.C. coast.

In 1950 the Union Steamship Co. purchased a ship back east named the *Blue Peter II*, which they wanted to bring back to B.C. To bring her around, a new man in the Company, Jimmy Stewart, was the Captain. Ralph, because of his navigational skills, was the Chief Officer, while the 2nd Mate was Stan Green and the 3rd Mate was Johnny Horne. Upon her arrival in B.C. her name was changed to *Cassiar III*. Once the ship was delivered, Ralph went back to the Union ships but now he had moved up in seniority and sailed as 2nd Mate. He sailed on several Union ships including the *Catala*,

Capt. Ralph Wills
(Ashmore Collection)

Cardena, Chelohsin, Cassiar and his last ship was *Chilcotin*.

Ralph left the Union Steamship Co. in 1954 and joined the Canadian Hydrographic Service. He sailed aboard the *William J. Stewart*. Then they needed a liaison officer to join the American Coast Guard ship, the *Storis*, which was circumnavigating the continent, and Ralph was given this prestigious posting. Upon the completion of this voyage Ralph was put in charge of hydrographic survey aboard the *William J. Stewart* operating on the B.C. coast. They surveyed the coast from April until October. Then the surveyors worked ashore until the following April, supplying the data to make up the navigational charts. After several years Ralph came ashore and served as Regional Field Superintendent until his retirement in 1979.

His health was failing and finally it was determined that he was suffering from Non Hodgkins Lymphoma. After a valiant fight he died in 1989 at age 71, in Victoria.

Robert "Bob" Wilson

Capt. Robert Wilson
(Twigg Collection)

Robert Wilson was born in 1882. Some records say on the Shetland Islands, others the Orkneys. He went to sea in 1899 at age 17, and joined Union Steamships in 1910.

Captain Bob, as he was affectionately called all over the coast, elicits praise whenever his name is mentioned. Mr. Rushton, in his book *Whistle Up The Inlet*, said of him, "Such a man helped create the Union Legend." John Horne a former deck officer said, "He was an outstanding seaman. If ever there was a person who was synonymous with the Company and everything it stood for, it was him."

It is reported that when he came on watch, he would take one look at the charts and never have to look at them again during his watch. As John Smith, who served under him as quartermaster, told me: "He never got excited. If there was a possibility they might miss a tide, he would say, 'Well that's alright, there's lots more tides in the book.' He was a thorough gentleman, he seemed to radiate something to people around him with his way of doing things. As a navigator he was the best there was; some were like him, but not many. He was in a class by himself."

He was Chief Officer, or as the position was called in the early days, Pilot, on the *Cheslakee*, when she sank at Van Anda, Jan. 6, 1913. He was on watch when the *Cheslakee*, after leaving Van Anda, heading for Powell River, heeled over in a sudden squall and he made the decision to turn her around and head back to Van Anda before calling the Captain. She sank at the wharf. Most of the passengers were taken off safely, but seven were drowned. Hearings went on for weeks after this tragedy, but in the end the Coroners Jury had this to say of Bob Wilson: "We desire to express our admiration of the good judgment displayed by Pilot Robert Wilson (prior to calling the Captain) in turning the ship back to Van Anda."

Wilson also was Master on the *Cowichan*, southbound into Vancouver on Dec. 27, 1925, with a full load of Christmas passengers, when she was in collision just off Roberts Creek in a heavy fog, with the *Lady Cynthia*, under Captain Jack Boden Sr. The *Cynthia* had a very sharp bow and I'm told it was filled with concrete as well. The coolness displayed by both Captains prevented any lives being lost, but there is an on-going controversy about which Captain said what after their ships collided. Gerald Rushton has reported it was Boden who said, "I'll keep my engines going slow ahead and keep my ship pinned into the hole, while you transfer your passengers on to the *Cynthia*." [198] However, other sources suggest Wilson had to plead with Boden to keep his ship jammed into the *Cowichan*, so his passengers could cross over to the *Cynthia*. Vic Hayman, a quartermaster on the *Cowichan* at the time, who was off watch when the ships collided, told his wife, whom I interviewed, that it was Captain Wilson who was the real hero, and that he did indeed have to plead with Captain Boden to keep the Cynthia pushed in to the gaping hole in the *Cowichan*'s side. Harry Ives, an assistant Purser at the time, also told me Rushton's version is definitely wrong, based on conversations Ives heard between Eric Suffield, Jack Halcrow and Harry Roach, who were deck officers at the time. "It was Captain Wilson who had to tell Captain Boden what to do. Captain Wilson was very, very cool. He was the last person to cross over to the *Cynthia*. He watched the *Cowichan* sink then turned away saying, 'Well I guess I'll go down for coffee.' "

In his later years Captain Wilson was the senior captain in the fleet, and spent most of his last four years as Master of the *Chelohsin*. However, he died aboard the *Cardena* on a Christmas run on Dec. 21, 1947. He was the last of four captains in the fleet who died aboard their ships, all in the 1940s.

On Dec. 21, 1947, the *Cardena* was engaged in picking up a load of loggers and bringing them home for Christmas when Captain Wilson collapsed on the bridge of the *Cardena* at the ship's telegraph. The *Coquitlam II*, under the command of Captain Boden, was northbound at the time and saw the *Cardena* laying off Quathiaski Cove. Those aboard the *Cardena* saw the *Coquitlam* and contacted her by radio telephone, informed them of Captain Wilson's collapse, told them they were proceeding to Campbell River where there was a hospital and asked them to stand by.

The Purser aboard the *Cardena* at the time was Don McLeod. He gives the following report in the book *Navigating the Coast*: "I radioed the office of the Marine Superintendent to ask permission to have the Chief Officer (Jack Summerfield) turn the ship around and they wouldn't grant it and so I asked for a doctor and they gave me a doctor and I told the doctor what the symptoms were and the doctor told me it was heart. They figured he would survive to Campbell River. (Jack Summerfield then ran the ship full steam ahead for Campbell River.) Once he got to Campbell River (and was taken to the hospital) they didn't have the modern equipment they have today, so he died there." [199]

In the meantime, Captain Suffield, the Marine Superintendent, had contacted Captain Boden on the *Coquitlam II* and instructed him to take Captain Jimmy Hunter, who was the Chief Officer aboard the *Coquitlam*, over to the *Cardena* and have him go aboard her as her Master for the rest of the voyage.

Bad feelings between Captain Suffield and Jack Summerfield were a factor that always prevented Jack Summerfield from being promoted to Captain on any Union Ship sailing up north. The above incident illustrates the point quite well and it wasn't long before Jack Summerfield left the Company and went over to the CNR.

Left to right: Don McLeod and Capt. Wilson circa 1945

William Lawrence "Billy" Yates

Capt. "Billy" Yates on *Lady Alexandra* 1945 *(J. Smith Collection)*

"Billy" Yates was born in the town of Llanfairfechan, Bangor County, North Wales on May 23, 1889. He began his sea career at age 11 when he was indentured by his mother to train to become a ship's officer. She agreed to pay 50 pounds a year to the captain of the *Indefatigable* for the Royal Navy to teach him the profession of seamanship. Young master Yates thus trained aboard the *Indefatigable* for 2½ years, signing off her on Oct. 26, 1903.

He wasted no time in going to sea again for he signed aboard the *Lake Manitoba* as deck boy sailing to Montreal the very next day, Oct. 27, 1903. From this day on he was continuously serving aboard ships until 1957. After the *Manitoba* he served on six more deep sea ships, the last one being the *Cyclops* sailing to Japan and the West Coast of North America. While the *Cyclops* was docked in Vancouver in March, 1907, Billy jumped ship and signed aboard the Union Steamships' *Camosun I* as an A.B. seaman and winchman on Jan. 1, 1908, but his ship-jumping couldn't have been too serious because he later received a positive letter of reference from the chief officer of the *Cyclops*.

Thus began Billy Yates' long and distinguished career on the West Coast of British Columbia, mainly with the Union Steamship Co. Over the years his name became a fixture with the Union Steamships, particularly on the East and West Howe Sound routes, and as the Captain on one particular ship, the *Lady Alexandra*.

However, early in his career he did change employers quite often, moving from company to company before he finally settled down with Union Steamships. In later years, that moving around prevented him from making it to the top of the Company's seniority list.

Yates' discharge book shows that after little more than a year with Union Steamships he left them, on Feb. 2, 1909. He apparently spent some time with the CPR, signing aboard the *Princess Beatrice* on Sept. 1, 1909 as winchman, but he signed off there only one month later, on Oct. 1, 1909. Although it isn't recorded in his discharge book, a news clipping from that time tells of Billy also doing a stint as Master of the steam passenger/freight tug *Tartar*.

The next entry in his discharge book shows Billy signing aboard the Grand Trunk Pacific's ship *Prince Rupert* as quartermaster under Captain B.L. Johnson, on June 7, 1910. There is a gap of approximately eight months between leaving and signing aboard another ship. It seems likely that during this time off, he sat for and obtained his Coastwise Mate's Ticket.

Yates moved again, leaving the Grand Trunk Line and going back to Union Steamships, signing aboard the *Cowichan* as

> S.S. "Cyclops"
>
> Tacoma, Wash. U.S.A.
>
> To whom it may concern:
>
> This is to certify that although the bearer, W.L. Yates, deserted this ship at Vancouver, in March '07, his good conduct during service prior to that date, viz 14/7/06 till the end of March '07 was such, that I sincerely hope that the fact of his desertion will not interfere with his application for examination being accepted. During his service on board the Cyclops, he proved himself sober, and attentive to his duties, and I can recommend him to anyone requiring his services.
>
> Signed *G. Fiddes*
> Chief Officer
>
> Date 20th Feb 1909

(Photocopy of original letter)

quartermaster on July 5, 1910 but again staying only until Nov. 17, 1910. Although it is not written in Yates' discharge book, there is a written statement on U.S.S. Co. letterhead, signed by Captain Gaisford, that Yates had sailed aboard his ship, the *Cassiar*, as 2nd Mate from Nov. 20, 1910 to June 4, 1913, which indicates that Yates did obtain his Mate's Ticket in that time gap mentioned above.

Another gap appears in his records around this time. There is a period of five months between signing off and onto his next ship. Again it is possible that during this time off he wrote for and obtained his Coastwise Passenger Master's Ticket. A newspaper article states he did obtain his Master's Certificate #7128 in 1913, for he next signed up with a new company, the Marine Navigation Co., as Master of the *Marine Express*, on Oct. 26, 1913. He was aboard her for six years.

During this period Yates married his wife Marjorie, who came out to Vancouver directly from Bolton, Lancashire in 1913. They were married in Christ Church Cathedral on Dec. 8, 1914.

Captain Yates signed off the *Marine Express* on May 19, 1919 and went aboard the *Britannia* as Master. Captain Yates took the *Britannia* out on her final voyage in Vancouver harbour, with a full load of passengers aboard, to see the giant U.S. battleship *New Mexico*. When he gave the order to back away or go astern, the ship jumped forward and rammed into the big battleship but bounced off. As they were backing away one American sailor yelled to Captain Yates, "Try again Captain and we'll see if Britannia rules the waves." The American sailors were highly amused over this little ship charging into their Goliath of the sea, so much so that they all began to sing "Rule Britannia." As soon as Captain Yates got clear of the *New Mexico* he was amazed to see some sailors being lowered over her side to touch up the paintwork.

Captain Yates, still with the same company, signed off the *Britannia* on May 17, 1921 and then signed on as Master aboard their new ship, the *Lady Evelyn*, on May 18, 1921. He was still aboard her in October 1923, when she was acquired by the Union Steamship Co. Captain Yates thus found himself back in the employ of Union Steamships but this time he stayed on for the next 33 years, becoming a legend on the coast.

Captain Yates and crew on the *Lady Evelyn* 1921

The next entry shows that Captain Yates signed aboard the *Cheam* May 10, 1924. At this point, on becoming a Master, no more entries were made in his discharge book but we know from here he sailed as Master aboard the *Capilano*, *Cheakamus*, *Comox II*, *Lady Pam*, *Lady Cynthia*, *Lady Cecilia*, and of course his favorite ship, the *Lady Alexandra*.

Frank Skinner, who served aboard the Union ships in the Pursers Department and later became the company's Agent in Prince Rupert, states in a letter that to the best of his knowledge Captain Yates served as Shore Captain on the Union Wharf during the summer season, May 24 to Labour Day, 1925. He was still acting as Shore Captain in 1939 when Frank went to Prince Rupert. He wore his Captain's uniform and was on duty from 4 p.m. to midnight. In the winter months he would go back on the ships as Master, according to Skinner.

In 1941, the seniority of various Masters within the Union Steamship Co. needed to be settled. The then-managing director, Carl Halterman, sought help from the Canadian Merchant Service Guild. A seniority list had to be established as many men left to join different military services. Those who left to join up were to maintain their seniority positions, so it was necessary to have this on record. On April 24, 1941, the Guild made up a list and the first three in order were Captain Robert Wilson, Captain Jack Boden, and Captain Yates. The fact that Captain Yates had moved back and forth between various companies early in his career put him in the third spot, but if he had stayed with Union Steamships after he signed aboard the *Camosun* in 1908 he would have been the senior skipper by two years. However this list had to be based on continuous service. This created friction between Captain Yates and Captain Boden. Every once in a while, Captain Boden would decide that he wanted to be home more during the summer months so he would bump Captain Yates off the *Lady Alexandra*. He did this for seven summers running. People along the Howe Sound route found it hard to get used to seeing this big rumpled man on the bridge of the *Lady Alexandra* compared with their slight and dapper "Captain Billy."

In 1940, on July 29, the Union Steamship Co. sponsored a parade of ships to help the war effort. Free cruise tickets were given to anyone who purchased war saving stamps. That evening six ships sailed around the harbour carrying over 3,000 passengers, and on this occasion Captain Yates was in command of the *Capilano*.

Captain Yates was a founding member of the Canadian Merchant Service Guild. In 1927 he was elected treasurer and when he retired in 1952 he was the longest-standing member. The Guild then granted him Honourary Life Membership. Marine writers in the newspapers of the day, often referred to him as the Commodore-Skipper of the Union Fleet but this was unofficial because of the seniority listing established by the Guild in 1941.

There are many anecdotes about Captain Yates. Following are a few that survive among ex Union hands still around to reminisce about the good old days.

John Allan, who was one of Captain Yates' favorite quartermasters in the late 1940s, relates the following story which shows why Captain Yates was so well-liked in the Howe Sound area:

"One afternoon as we were about to leave the dock at Bowen Island, I blew the five-minute warning whistle for our departure to Vancouver. A child on the boat deck began to howl because a gust of wind had blown his hat off into the water of Snug Cove where it floated some yards away from the ship.

"Captain Yates turned to me and said, 'Allan, go and get that kiddies' hat.' You do not argue with the Captain, so I ran down to the dock and over to the boat float where I was fortunate to meet Howard Hines just tying up his 14-foot clinker-built putter. Since he knew me, I asked to borrow his boat and I putted out into Snug Cove in front of an audience of hundreds who had lined the rails of the *Alex* to watch the Great Hat Rescue. Fortunately, I was familiar with Mr. Hines' boat and scooped up the hat on the first pass. A great cheer went up from the crowd on the *Alex*. I returned to the float, ran back to the ship, returned the child's hat, and went back up to the wheelhouse. We left Bowen a little later than usual, because of having performed another unique service for the customers of the Union Steamships."

When the then newly-built wharf at Gibsons was officially opened, Aug. 16, 1947, the Union Steamship Co. was invited to take part in the opening ceremony, since its ships called there every day. Captain Yates brought the *Lady Cecilia* into the new wharf at 4:30 p.m.

The opening address was given by Mr. J. Sinclair, MP for Coast Capilano. Then the ribbon was cut and a presentation was made to Captain Yates by C. P. Smith, the harbour master. Yates thus had to say a few words and even though he hadn't prepared a speech for the occasion, his wit and informal nature soon put the guests at ease. There was quite a party after the ceremony and when Captain Yates returned to the ship he was somewhat the worse for over-imbibing, so the 2nd Mate who was on watch with him, Bob Williamson, took over. When the ship approached the Union dock in Vancouver this created a little problem, as it was possible some of the Company officials might be down to watch the *Cecilia* dock.

Capt. W. Yates elected treasurer of the C.M.S.G. 1927 *(C.M.S.G. News)*

Captain Yates turned to Bob and said, "Bob, you had better take her in." It was decided Captain Yates would stand out on the wing of the bridge, in full view, right by the telegraph and act as though he was docking the ship, whereas standing in the background was Bob, who was actually giving the orders and sending the telegraph signals down to the engine room.

This next story takes place at Hopkins Landing with Captain Yates bringing the *Capilano* into a landing in a thick fog, and was told to Charlie Defieux by Eric Thompson:

"We heard the *Capilano* make her way slowly around Soames Point, bound for the Hopkins wharf. When she got in front of our house she stopped and there ensued long hoots from the *Capilano*. I came to the conclusion that Captain Yates was trying to get an echo from the freight shed on the wharf. Then to my surprise, I saw the top of *Capilano*'s mast showing above the fog and saw that, as she was on the diagonal to the wharf shed, the echo went off at an angle. I got out my bagpipes and sent forth a few notes of Westering Home towards the troubled steamer, and this was followed by a series of short toots on the whistle indicating that the impromptu aid to navigation had been understood by Captain Yates. Where else but on the B.C. coast would you find a ship taking directions from the bagpipes?" [200]

Records indicate that Captain Yates was involved in four marine mishaps.

The first was aboard the *Lady Pam* when she grounded at Gambier in the early 1930s. Joe Hackett was on the bridge at the time. There was no damage, but as the tide was falling there was fear that she might keel over, so the crew propped her up steady, using a cargo of lumber that was on deck. She was easily refloated at high tide.

The second mishap was a more serious grounding which took place in a very bad weather, on Jan. 15, 1947, when the *Lady Alexandra*, with Chief Officer G.B.K. Owen-Jones on watch, went hard aground at Brunswick Point.

The third accident took place on Oct. 3, 1950 involving the *Lady Cynthia* and the forestry vessel *A.L. Bryant*. Captain Yates was down in the dining room having his dinner when the collision occurred and Al Strang was the officer on the bridge. Unfortunately two crewmen on the *Bryant* lost their lives in this disaster.

The fourth accident again took place aboard the *Lady Cynthia*, Oct. 29, 1953. The *Lady Cynthia* collided with the big steam tug *Dola* off Whytecliffe at 5:45 P.M. Fortunately there was no loss of life in this collision but the *Dola* sank quickly and was a total loss. From all the records that I reviewed of this accident, not one indicates who was on the bridge when the collision occurred but as it happened at 5:45 p.m. Captain Yates would not be due on duty until 6 p.m.

No one can establish for sure when Captain Yates really did retire permanently. In fact his daughter, Mrs. Ray Tayner, said, "He always wanted to keep busy." When the *Lady Alex* ended her days, and tied up for good in 1952, that was the end of Captain Yates' career with the Union Steamship Co. He would have been 63 years old then, but he didn't stop working.

With the Alexandra gone from the scene and East Howe Sound needing transportation, what was to be done? It so happened that the West Vancouver Ferries was offering three of its ships for sale, the *Hollyburn*, the *Bonnabelle*, and the *No. 6*. The Union Steamship Co. wanted to buy all three of them but was successful in making a deal for only the *No. 6*. It was operated on East Howe Sound and Vic Haymen was her skipper. Ed Roach, Captain Harry Roach's son, served aboard her as quartermaster. Les Gore, a former cook with the Union ships, ran a coffee bar on her.

Harbour Ferries obtained the *Hollyburn* and leased it to the Union Steamship Co. and Captain Yates was hired as her skipper. He ran her for two years until 1960.

Mr. Ken Moir of North Vancouver provided me with some details of these two years that Captain Yates had with Harbour

Navigation as Captain of the *Hollyburn*. He related one episode when the *Hollyburn* encountered a heavy gale when proceeding to Britannia Beach. The weather office had advised there would likely be some strong westerly winds but when the ship went through the narrows later it was blowing a gale. With all of Captain Yates' experience he realized he could not risk turning the Hollyburn around so he had to proceed out into the gale in the Gulf of Georgia. With great skill he finally rounded Point Atkinson and made it into Snug Cove, at Bowen Island. The waves had smashed the wire glass windows in the forward cabin where the mail sacks were stored and they were all soaked and sloshing about. While at Bowen, the ship was made shipshape before proceeding up the sound to Britannia. Ken says there was a picture in one of the Vancouver daily papers showing the Hollyburn totally suspended on a huge wave as she headed out into the Strait. "It took a good skipper and a good sea boat to survive that trip," Ken said. According to Ken, a framed copy of this picture is on the cabin wall of the *Hollyburn* to this day.

Ken, who was working at the Royal Bank in Britannia Beach at the time, also recalled the day after Labour Day 1956, when he noticed many people were walking down to the wharf. Upon enquiring he learned they were all going down to say good-bye to Captain Yates and the last passenger ship to service their town, so Ken joined them. They were going down to give thanks to Captain Yates, his crew and his ship, for the many many years of service to their town. This was the end of an era and many no doubt remembered past ships and their crews, particularly the Union Steamships, for they had been their only link with the outside world for years. They stood and watched as the *Hollyburn* sailed away into the distance, sad with the knowledge that Captain Yates and the ships would never return to Britannia Beach with that dependable daily service from Vancouver.

Shortly before the end of Captain Yates' stint with Harbour Navigation on Aug. 27, 1956 the Pacific Great Eastern Railway, now B.C. Rail, celebrated the extension of its railway from Squamish to North Vancouver. Captain Yates received an official invitation to be aboard this run from Premier W.A.C. Bennett. Story has it that Billy Yates got off the train just as soon as he could, saying he preferred ships to trains.

When the *Lady Alexandra* was turned into a floating restaurant in 1959 and moored next to the Bayshore Inn, Captain Yates was the guest of honour on its opening night. Charlie Defieux wrote the following piece about Captain Yates and his continued interest in his old ship:

"When the *Lady Alexandra* became a restaurant, Captain Yates was living in White Rock and he would journey in to town once a month, for a morning visit to her. He had to see how they were treating his old ship. I was told down at the ship that he always refused invitations to be their guest at lunch." [201]

On Dec. 6, 1964, Captain and Mrs. Yates celebrated their 50th wedding anniversary. They held open house for their many friends in a private suite at the Hotel Vancouver and that evening they celebrated with a family dinner in the Panorama Roof.

Even at Yates' advanced age, his daughter said he couldn't stand to be idle so he obtained work as a signalman on top of the Lions Gate Bridge during 1964/65.

Two years later he was hospitalized with a collapsed lung. His health was failing. His death came suddenly on Feb. 14, 1966. He was visiting his son's home in White Rock and was endeavouring to clean the swimming pool. The pool had been drained but there was water in the deep end. It had the usual log floating in it in case the water ever froze. Captain Yates must have slipped on the slope, fallen into the water, hit his head, become unconscious and drowned. Cremation followed and then his ashes were cast to the deep six over Mansons Deep. In his marine column in the *Vancouver Sun* on Feb. 24, 1966, Charlie Defieux wrote about his passing:

"Private funeral services were held at White Rock for this fine mariner. His final voyage was aboard Captain Harry Terry's *Northern Princess*.

"Ships moored at Vancouver Wharves dipped their flags in respect as the *Northern Princess* moved through the Narrows and out into the Bay. The funeral notice for Captain Billy asked that no flowers be sent to the service. The operators of the *Lady Alexandra* Restaurant wanted to pay some tribute to him from his old command. I suggested they phone Mrs. Yates and that wonderful lady, even in her grief, sensed their feelings and acquiesced."

The only floral decoration at the funeral apart from the family's observance was one simply marked "From *Lady Alexandra*." [202]

They Also Served

Top Left:
Jack "Pop" Freisen,
2nd Mate

Top Right:
Harvey Kelly
(Ashmore Collection)

Bottom Left:
Dave McIntosh
(Ashmore Collection)

Bottom Right:
Jack McLeod,
Mate on board the
Cardena 1933
(K. McLeod)

Left:
Angus McKinnon
(R. Finlayson)

Right:
Paddy Scanlon,
2nd Mate on S.S. *Venture* 1928
(Skinner Collection)

Left:
George Whitehurst,
2nd Mate 1946

Right: Angus Wilson,
3rd Mate, S.S. *Catala* 1949
(Belveal Collection)

Below: S.S. *Chelohsin*
(J. Smith Collection)

Top: Transferring cargo from the *Venture* to the *Catala* after the *Venture* had been fogbound for two days *(N.E. Woodward Collection)*

Bottom: *Comox* standing off Trail Bay while guests from Whitaker's Sechelt Hotel are brought aboard from the beach *(Helen Dawe's Sechelt)*

Union Steamship dock in 1919 with most of the fleet alongside (left, closest): *Coquitlam, Chelohsin, Cheakamus;* (end of dock): *Cowichan;* (right, farthest): *Camosun;* close in on right are believed to be two of Captain Cates' ships; (foreground left): wharf machine shops and Supt. Engineer's office
(James Crookall)

On the bridge of the *Lady Alexandra* for the Union Steamships Co. 60th Jubilee picnic:
(left to right) E.G. Eakins, personnel manager; John Gilligan, assistant engineer;
Captain Billy Yates; Captain E.W. Suffield, marine superintendent; Gerald Rushton, assistant manager
(Vancouver Maritime Museum)

Chapter 2
ENGINEERS

PORTHOLE NAVIGATION
or
HOW A BLACK GANG KNOWS WHERE THE SHIP IS WHEN SHE AINT

With callipers and a twelve inch rule,
The Chief climbed up on his cabin stool.
He glanced from his port at a piece of land,
And shifted six pencils from hand to hand.

A two finger bearing of God-knows-what,
As he greedily swilled his morning tot.
Then down below the revs to take,
And see what knots he'd have to make.

He glanced at the clock. He yelled for steam.
He wrote in the log: "Diamond Head's abeam."
"Right Ho, Chief," as the Aussies say;
Abeam twelve hundred miles away!

On an ancient chart of Old Cathay,
He ruled his course with a corset stay.
His callipers slipped with the vessel's roll,
But his marked his fix with a piece of coal.

He added, deducted, divided by three;
And yelled to the mate: "Cape Flattereee!"
To him navigation is but child's play;
Flattery's a thousand miles away.

He took bilge soundings; he added the log;
Deducted the draft; made allowance for fog,
Divided the tonnage by pressure of steam,
And added her length to her maximum beam.

The temperature by her speed multiplied,
Then threw all his calculus over the side,
Three blasts on the whistle, his watch back an hour,
His safety valves down with a half sack of flour.

"Another three days," he said to the Mate,
"Will bring her in sight of the Golden Gate."
"Better grab something Chief, and take a round turn.
We're inside the Bay, and the Gate's far astern!"

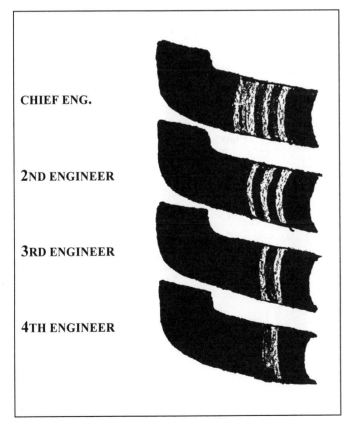

Gold and Purple Braid
Buttons - Gold

Capt. Aspinall, Paddy Farina, George Miller who had #1
Steam Ticket in Canada *(Farina Collection)*

Alphabetical List of Engineers
1920-1958

This list has been compiled from various sources, including ship registry files and personal acquaintances. While efforts have been made to be accurate, it is not to be taken as comprehensively complete and may have some errors, especially of omission.

Annan, Tom
Armour, James
Arthur, Clarence

Bain, Iain
Baldry, Robert
Beattie, Andrew "Andy"

Cahill, Al
Calbeck, Fred
Capewell, Tommy
Carpenter, Jack
Catchpole, C.
Chadwick, C.T. "Chad"
Charlton, John
Chester, (?)
Craigen, George
Croucher, George

DeGrouchy, A.
Dick, Thomas M. "Tom"
Douglas, J.

Emms, Ernie
Emms, Reg

Farina, Patrick J.V. "Paddy"
Fisher, Johnny
Fletcher, Alex
Foster, George H.
Francis, James "Jimmy"

Gilligan, John
Goddard, George
Goodall, John
Granquist, Edward
Green, Jimmy
Gregory, Robert "Bob"
Grieves, James "Jimmy"

Halliday, Sam
Hill, Jack
Hogan, John
Hunt, John C.I.
Hunter, John

Jefferson, Lancelot James Foss

Kando, Bob

Liston, Walter
Logan, Robert
Lyall, Jimmy

MacAulay, John
MacDonald, Hugh
MacKenzie, R.G.
Mackie, William
Main, Boston "Jimmy"
Marrs, George
Matheson, Fred
Mattock, Edwin A.
McCormick, Clarence "Abe"
MacGregor, Duncan
McLean, Don
McLean, James "Jimmy"
McLelland, Davie
McLeod, Angus "Jock"
McQuarrie, E.
Miller, J.
Millier, Cecil E.
Munro, Jack
Murchant, Michael
Muskett, Larry

New, Oswald J. "Sparky"

Paterson, Bill
Pope, William

Scott, Ned
Shugg, Gordon
Smith, Ben "Benny"
Smith, Fred Edward "Freddie"
Spencer, Tommy
Spring, C.
Steele, Andrew "Andy"
Stein, Robert A.
Strand, Bob

Tatlow, Jim
Thompson, Don
Travis, Bob
Turnbull, W.
Tweedie, Napier

Vince, Gordon

Watson, (?)
Whitelaw, Robert "Bob"
Whiteman, Bill
Widdess, Jack
Williamson, W.
Wishart, William

Clarence Arthur

Clarence Arthur was born April 2, 1877 in Nova Scotia, but little else is known about his early days. His daughter, Isabela Becket, recalled that he worked on a ship on the Fraser River in the early 1900s then went over to Victoria to work for the Boscowitz Line. He was engineer on the first wooden-hulled *Venture* and was aboard her when she caught fire and burned at Inverness cannery in the Skeena.

The Boscowitz Co. then sent Clarence over to Glasgow to supervise the installation of the engines in the new *Venture* in 1911. He was Chief Engineer on her when she was brought out to B.C. As the Panama Canal had not been built yet, she had to sail through the Straits of Magellan and up the Pacific Coast of South and North America to Vancouver.

When the Union Steamship Co. took over the Boscowitz Company in 1911, Clarence Arthur stayed with the *Venture* and thus became an employee of Union Steamships. He had nearly 40 years of service when he retired in 1950. He died one year later, Sept. 11, 1951, at age 74.

Records show Clarence was Chief Engineer on the *Venture* in 1912, and on the *Lady Alexandra* in 1928 and '29. He also was Chief Engineer on the *Lady Cecilia* for a short time. In later years his name was closely associated with the *Cardena*. In fact, when he was on the *Cardena* he was the only Chief Engineer in the company who had a deck cabin - his home away from home.

In 1912 the *Venture* had been changed over from a coal burner to oil. Shortly after this changeover she had a narrow escape: the oil stopped flowing to the engines so her engines stopped. Captain Park wisely dropped her anchor to prevent the ship from drifting into danger. Clarence, who was Chief Engineer, went below and drilled a hole in one of her extra tanks in order to get the oil flowing so the engines could turn over again. [203]

Stew Hale, who was in the Pursers Department and had sailed with Clarence, said, "In my opinion, Clarence was like a square peg in a round hole. Here was this gruff old engineer working on the *Lady Alexandra*, amongst all the young people on moonlight cruises etc. He was just so out of place with that group." Even so, Mr. Rushton reported that he was a great asset to the Company on the Northern Cruises due to the fact he did a wonderful job of hosting the tourists aboard the *Cardena*. [204]

Gordon Vince, who was 2nd Engineer with Clarence Arthur on the *Cardena*, reports that he was a great ladies man, for he was often to be found in the passenger saloon when he was supposed to be on watch in the engine room.

Obviously he was an enigma, for having sailed with him and sitting at the Officers' table aboard ship, it was readily noticed that Clarence would only talk to the Captain and just grunt to anyone else. Chief Arthur certainly had a long service record with the Company, and as Stew Hale said, "He never failed to impress this fact on everyone, that he was one of the originals in the Company." He probably got tired of seeing all the new hands come and go and he didn't

Chief Engineer Clarence Arthur *(Arthur Collection)*

want to bother to be friendly, as they were here today and gone tomorrow.

He was human like the rest of us. His daughter told me this amusing story about his family life. There were three children in the family and it was decided they all had to learn to play a musical instrument. Two of the children chose the violin and the other chose the trombone. Clarence was said to have made this comment. "Greater love has no other father than he who allows his children to take up the violin and the trombone all at the same time!"

Andrew Beattie

Chief Engineer
Andrew Beattie
(Mrs. Tosh Collection)

Andrew Beattie came out on the *Camosun I*, in 1905, from Scotland and stayed on with the Union Steamship Company until the day he died.

He served as Chief Engineer on the *Lady Alexandra* in 1926. He was also Chief Engineer on the *Cardena*, and then he went to the *Catala* in March 1930. When she came back into service again after her Sparrowhawk grounding Andrew Beattie again was her Chief Engineer and the rest of his career was spent aboard the *Catala*.

As a matter of fact, Andrew Beattie died aboard the *Catala* when she was dockside at Prince Rupert. The Chief Steward at the time was Bert Attewell. He went to call Chief Beattie for his lunch and getting no response, stepped into his cabin and saw the Chief sitting in his chair. Bert spoke to him, but he didn't get an answer. A further check revealed that Andrew Beattie was dead. He had died right there in his room, while sitting in his chair! This was in 1945.

A conference was held between Captain Sheppard, Frank Skinner, the Company's Agent in Prince Rupert, and the other three engineers aboard the *Catala* at the time. First it was decided, the three engineers could rotate their shifts and would be able to get the ship back to Vancouver without any difficulty. Seeing Chief Beattie's family were all in Vancouver, it was agreed his body should be taken back to Vancouver. It was wrapped in a shroud and put into the freezer hold aboard ship.

Frank Skinner says that Andrew Beattie was well-known up and down the coast and was a very popular man. He was an excellent bridge player and often would organize bridge games with the passengers aboard ship. He and Captain Findlay were very close friends and they enjoyed entertaining the tourists aboard their ship. Mrs. Tosh, Captain Findlay's daughter, told me about one of their little jokes they often played on the passengers. The two of them would be talking to a group of passengers and Captain Findlay would mention there had been a slight accident down in the engine room that day and turn to his chief engineer to tell them about it. Chief Beattie would go into detail about how one of men down there got a little careless and lost one of his fingers in the works. Then he would bring this little box from his pocket and say, "Yes, as a matter of fact I have saved his finger as a souvenir!" He would open the box carefully and sure enough there was a finger inside, with a little blood spattered in the box. It was an old trick, and the passengers loved it.

Mr. Dave Tosh, Captain Findlay's son-in-law, would often go down to the Union dock to pick up Captain Findlay and drive him home. On one occasion the *Catala* had to go over to the oil dock and refuel, so Captain Findlay said, "Come on aboard and come over with us." While they were waiting Chief Beattie came up and said, "How about coming down to the mess and I'll make us some scrambled eggs." Dave said that Chief Beattie loved to make scrambled eggs but he did them differently than anyone else, he wouldn't add milk, but Dave said "They were sure good."

Mrs. Tosh recalls taking a trip aboard the *Catala* with her father when she was a little girl. She remembers at the time Andrew Beattie was trying to lose weight and he would go up to the boat deck with a skipping rope and start skipping. She would join in and they had great fun.

There is an excellent story about Andrew Beattie in Helen Meilleur's book *A Pour of Rain* which she tells as follows:

"Tall stories were a specialty of the officers, and one chief engineer, Andrew Beattie, was famous the entire length of British Columbia for his. He told them in such an honest Scottish accent and with such earnestness that even old-timers were sometimes caught by them, though tourists were his favourite game. Once when the *Catala* was loading salmon at Alert Bay, a group of officers and passengers went ashore to explore the town and converged on the store. The door bore a notice, 'Seal noses bought here.' At that time there was a bounty on hair seals, the salmon's natural enemy, and it was collectible when a seal's nose was produced. Only the larger centres had bounty depots so storekeepers all over the coast paid the Indians the bounty, salted down the grisly proof in casks, and shipped them once or twice a season.

" 'Seal noses,' said a female tourist. "Why do they buy seal noses?'

" 'There's a great demand for seal noses,' said Andrew Beattie. 'They're shipped straight to New York. Restaurant trade, you know. Of course they give them a French name and no one knows they are eating seal noses. Delicious sautéed.'

" 'Well, fancy that. But the poor little seals - it must be hard for them to manage without noses.' "

Andrew Beattie died aboard his ship, the *Catala*, in 1945 and as they say, "with his boots on." With his passing, the Union Steamship Co. lost one of its finest ambassadors.

George Craigen

Chief Engineer George Craigen
(Skinner Collection)

I could find little information about Chief Craigen. During the course of my interviews with other Union Steamship men I was only able to pick up three stories about him.

This first story was related to me by Johnny Horne, who was a deck officer with the Union Company. The following story John had obtained from Mr. Craigen himself: "Chief Craigen was missing two fingers off of one hand. This had happened before he joined the Union Steamship Co., and it came about when he was checking the heat at the bottom ends of a triple expansion steam engine."

Gordie Vince, an engineer with the Union Steamship Co., related the following event in Mr. Craigen's career to me: "The *Lady Cynthia* was in for an annual checkover and the government boiler inspector was coming down to inspect her boilers. Mr. Craigen decided he would do the test before he arrived to make sure everything was in order. There were three boilers on the *Cynthia*, all the same diameter. He was pumping them up and had just about reached the desired 600 lbs. pressure, when the top drum, the steam drum, burst in half spewing cold water all over the place. In order to repair the steam drum they had to remove the top deck of the *Cynthia* and what they did, they removed the boiler from the *Cynthia*'s sister ship, the *Cecilia*. The top deck of the *Cecilia* had to be removed as well. One can imagine what this must have cost the Company. According to Gordie this happened about 1946. Mr. Craigen was pretty shaken up and worried about this turn of events."

Bob Ashmore, also a deck officer with the Company, remarked, "When George Craigen became Chief Engineer aboard one of the new converted corvettes he turned a new leaf. Up until this time he had been a typical grease monkey and he was more often to be seen in his dirty overalls rather than in his officer's uniform. Once aboard the new ships he spruced himself up and began to spend more time entertaining passengers."

Mr. Craigen was Chief Engineer aboard the *Chilcotin* on her maiden voyage, May 21, 1947. The Master was Captain A. McLellan. They sailed from Vancouver with a full load of Shriners going up to Prince Rupert to attend a convention in that city. [205]

Chief Engineer Patrick Farina
(Skinner Collection)

Patrick James Victor "Paddy" Farina

"Paddy" Farina became a legend in his own time with the Union Steamship Co. He probably was with the Company for a longer period of time than any other employee, 47 years all told with this one company! He had started in 1910 and retired in 1957.

Paddy was born in Newcastle on the Tyne, Sept. 10, 1887. He married his wife Margaret in Sunderland, Durham, England in 1908. They came to Canada in 1910 and Paddy obtained work with the Union Steamship Co. the same year. Before coming to Canada Paddy had served with the British Merchant Marine.

He started as 2nd engineer on the *Camosun I*. Then he was moved over to the *Comox I* as Chief Engineer. Later he joined the *Cassiar I* in the same capacity. After being on the *Cassiar* he joined the newly-commissioned *Capilano* in 1920 and stayed with her for the next 30 years. When the

Capilano was taken out of service, he went over to the *Lady Cynthia*. He took the *Capilano*'s whistle with him and installed it on the *Lady Cynthia* and finished his long career aboard her, retiring in 1957, at age 70.

Paddy is well remembered today for his 30 years on the *Capilano* and the legend he built up while aboard her. She became his pride and joy. Gerald Rushton said Paddy kept the *Capilano*'s engine room the best polished in the fleet. [206] The ship was his baby. Abe McCormick related a story that Ed Mattock, an engineer, told him about working on the *Capilano* with Paddy: "The *Capilano* had a terribly hot engine room. Ed would open all the doors down below that he could, in order to cool things down. Paddy would come along and close them, as he figured this would put up his fuel consumption!"

The *Capilano* was Paddy's baby alright and over the years when she was on the Howe Sound run his name became a legend, for word soon spread around that it became good luck to have Paddy carry new-born babies ashore. He would escort the pregnant mothers aboard the *Capilano* and carry their babies off the ship for them when they came back home. This became a routine and Paddy became a legend in his own time, especially at Woodfibre and on East Howe Sound. Whenever Paddy's name comes up today in conversation this story gets told over and over again.

Early in his career he had a narrow escape with his life. He was Chief Engineer on the *Cassiar I*, known in those days The Loggers Palace. On one trip she ran aground on Privett Island in Simoom Sound at 2:30 a.m., August 26, 1917. The Master at the time was Bob Wilson. The Pilot was a fellow by the name of Jock Robertson and he was on watch when she went aground. Lorne Godfrey was the 2nd Mate. According to Dennis Farina, Jack Robertson had a habit of falling asleep and perhaps this is what happened in this accident.

"Privett Island is shaped like a half moon and he ran her into the bay at full speed. When she hit, Jock put her in full speed astern and backed her up on the other side of the bay. She was ripped open and sank very quickly," Dennis said.

The *Cassiar* was salvaged and patched up at the sight of her sinking, then 10 days later she was towed back to Vancouver. Paddy stayed aboard her during this tow back to Vancouver, keeping the pumps going. At the time Paddy told Dennis, "For awhile during the tow, I had to walk over dozens of drowned rats that were aboard her when she sank." After she was repaired Paddy stayed with her as Chief Engineer until the *Capilano* came into service in 1920.

Paddy joined the *Capilano II* as Chief Engineer and was with her for 30 years, which must be some sort of a record for a man to stay aboard one ship.

The *Capilano* was launched at 3 p.m. Dec. 20, 1919 from the B.C. Marine Shipyards, having been built to order for the Company. In a brochure given out at the time of the launching, this is how the ship was described when she was launched: "The *Capilano* is built of seasoned Douglas fir, is 145 feet in length, with a beam of 27 feet, and 10 feet moulded depth. She will accommodate 320 passengers, and is destined for the Selma Park and Buccaneer Bay Run."

Paddy was aboard her until she was decommissioned in 1949. Her hull with some of her superstructure still intact, was towed up to Lang Bay and sunk there as part of a breakwater.

It seems the *Capilano* wasn't involved in any accidents of a serious nature. The only one accident that I came across was that she went aground at McNab Creek on the mud flats there. As it was a sandy bottom there was no damage and she floated free on the next high tide. However this accident did not escape being noticed by one of the famous newspaper columnists of the day, Jimmy Butterfield of the Vancouver *Province*. It bears repeating as both Paddy and the *Capilano* were discussed by this very talented humourist.

"An awful thing has been only narrowly avoided. The S.S. *Capilano* ran aground but by the grace of that luck that sometimes looks after ships she escaped permanent hurt, I would hate anything to happen to her because she was once very nearly my own downfall and I thereby made a good friend.

"Twelve years ago I went to Squamish on her and I came back and wrote an article called The Path To Squamish, wherein I described this good ship as a pot-bellied and fussy little boat that put in at every sawmill dump in Howe Sound. That was a tactical error. Because there is a man called Pat Farina - who is a perfectly good Irishman, believe it or not - and who is chief engineer on that ship.

"If you have ever seen Pat in action you will understand the grave peril in which I stood. For I went on the ship again a year later and I saw a man with a prognathous jaw glaring at me. He said, 'Are you called Butterfield?' I said I was afraid so. He said, 'Come here, I'm going to kill you. I have a dull axe I have been keeping it for, since you called this packet a pot-bellied something or other.' He seemed to mean it. It took me two hours and most of the Scotch I had, to correct his bad impressions of me.

"You can't tell just how touchy these fellows are about their ships until you speak disrespectfully of them. It is almost as bad as Sydney Smith's man who spoke disrespectfully of the equator. What would have happened to Pat if they hadn't refloated the good *Capilano* is hideous to think about."

From the *Capilano* Paddy went over to the *Lady Cynthia*. I served on her and feel fortunate to have sailed with, and to have known Paddy Farina. He was famous for carrying new babies ashore and at the Officers' Mess he held court and never failed tell to you his secret for his long life and good health. Everyday for lunch he would sit down to a plate of sliced tomatoes and olive oil. Not everyone's cup of tea but he swore by it.

He retired in 1957 at age 70. His son Dennis said after all those years of service with the Union Steamship Co. he never received even one cent, or five cents, or a watch, or even a handshake on the day he left the wharf. Paddy was very bitter over this lack of acknowledgment by head office for his long years of faithful service to the Company. Dennis said, "He put the curse of Cromwell on the Company and was amused to see them go down hill."

In 1968 he and his wife celebrated their 60th Wedding Anniversary. Paddy died suddenly and peacefully, one week short of celebrating his 70th wedding anniversary in 1978. His son Dennis was also with the Union Steamship Co. and also was a long-time active mariner, being Master of the M.V. *Malibu Princess* running regularly to Princess Louisa Inlet from Vancouver until he retired in 1994 at age 79.

George H. Foster

Chief Engineer George Foster on trial run of *Cardena* May 5, 1923 *(Vancouver Maritime Museum)*

George Foster started with the Union Steamship Co. in 1900 and soon was appointed to the famous *Cassiar*, as her Chief Engineer. This ship became known as the Loggers Palace.

In 1908 he was sent over to Scotland along with Captain Polkinghorne to bring out the newest addition to the Union Steamship fleet, the Cariboo. She travelled around the Horn and arrived in Vancouver, July 21, 1908. Due to a duplication of names, her name had to be changed to the *Cowichan*.

1912 finds George Foster as Chief Engineer on the *Chelohsin*, making her maiden voyage up north to service the Skeena River area and Prince Rupert on Feb. 24, 1912.

Mr. Foster was again sent over to Scotland and stood by the *Cardena* as she was being built and having her engines fitted. She sailed for B.C. on May 3, 1923 under the command of Captain A.E. Dickson and George Foster was her Chief Engineer. The *Cardena* arrived in Vancouver June 11, 1923. Not too long after her arrival on the Coast, George Foster became the Superintendent Engineer for the Company, succeeding Mr. De Gruchy.

1924 finds Mr. Foster back in Scotland supervising the construction of the *Lady Alexandra*. This new ship left Scotland for B.C. under the command of Captain C.B. Smith, and again with George Foster being the Chief Engineer. The ship arrived in Vancouver June 21, 1924.

George Foster died in January in 1938 having served the Union Steamship Co. efficiently and faithfully since 1900. According to Mr. Rushton, he was well-liked by everyone and always had time to listen to anyone.

John Hogan

John Hogan was one of those legendary Liverpool engineers. He had a long and distinguished career in coastal shipping and was the senior employee of all ranks when he retired from the Union Steamship Co., in July 1957.

He came over to Canada aboard the S. S. *Vadso* of the early Boscowitz Line in 1911. In September of that year, the Union Steamship Co. acquired the Boscowitz Steamship Co. whose head office was in Victoria. John Hogan then became a Union employee from that day on. Some of the ships he served on over the years were the *Coquitlam I*, in 1917 as second engineer, the *Chilkoot I* as Chief Engineer on her maiden voyage on June 20, 1920, the *Venture*, the *Lady Alexandra*, the *Lady Cynthia* and the *Cardena*.

When he was aboard the *Coquitlam I* in 1917, he was 2nd engineer under Chief Freddie Smith when he and Fred were called upon to make some emergency repairs to her hull. The ship had to be beached in Lowe Inlet as she was taking on water. The two of them had the difficult task of installing a temporary patch so the ship could carry on her journey.

In the 1940s he helped train many engineers for the Canadian Navy, as the Union Steamships carried these trainees aboard their ships as part of the war effort.

Denis Shaw, Purser on the Union Steamships, relates the following story about Mr. Hogan when they sailed together on the *Lady Alexandra*.

Mr. Hogan was a devout Catholic and one day he came to Denis and asked him if there was any possible way he could get some nails. The congregation of the church he belonged to were trying to build a new church in South Vancouver, and as

Chief Engineer John Hogan on board *Lady Alexandra* circa 1943 *(D. Shaw)*

everything was in short supply in those war years, it was a difficult task. Denis said he didn't know but would ask Joe Eng, head of the Chinese work crews at Woodfibre, and was able to get four kegs of nails from Joe. John Hogan then made them up into little packages of nails and sold them to everybody he could, and that money went toward building the new church. With that success, Denis then secured three 100 lb. sacks of rice, again from Joe Eng, and four 100 lb. boxes of raisins from the Bowen Island store. These items were all packaged up and sold. The proceeds from the sale of all these items were donated to help build the new church. A fine example of good will and teamwork aboard ship.

Chief Hogan died at his home. It is said he suffered from diabetes. According to Denis Shaw, Mr. Hogan had had his supper, went into the living room and sat down. His wife was in the kitchen and hearing something fall she went to check out what it was. Upon checking, she found Mr. Hogan's big pipe had fallen to the floor. He had slumped over and died at home, sitting in his favourite chair.

Lancelot James Foss Jefferson

Chief Engineer Lancelot James Foss Jefferson

Although Mr. Jefferson served with the Union Steamship Co. for 15 years and was Chief Engineer on such ships as the *Cardena*, *Catala*, *Chelohsin*, *Coquitlam II*, and as well as the Company's freight boats, he is not that well known. Those who worked with him said he was a very quiet, soft spoken and competent engineer. He was a good man to work for and went about his work quietly and with efficiency, never seeking the limelight.

He was born in Laurencekirk, Kincardineshire, Scotland, March 28, 1897 and at age 16 apprenticed to Hall, Russell & Co., Engineers and Shipbuilders. He served with the Royal Field Artillery in World War I and was wounded in action. After the war he went back to Hall, Russell & Co. In 1921 he joined the British Merchant Navy, and in 1940 came to Canada and joined the Union Steamship Co., serving as 2nd Engineer on the *Catala*.

During 1942 he served aboard the *Lady Cynthia* and the *Lady Cecilia*, then in 1943 he was sent back to Pictou, Nova Scotia to be on hand for the fitting out of the S.S. *Manitou Park* for the Union Steamship Co. He was 2nd and then Chief Engineer on her in 1944. In 1945 he was moved over to the *Chelohsin*. He was Chief Engineer on the *Chelohsin* when she grounded at Stanley Park in 1949. He was also aboard the *Cardena* when she was hit in the Narrows by the CPR's *Princess Elizabeth*.

Mr. Jefferson served as Chief Engineer on several vessels from 1949 to 1958, including the *Chelohsin*, *Cardena*, *Catala*, *Coquitlam II* and the freight boats *Chilkoot*, *Chilliwack* and *Redonda*. His last job with the Union Steamship Co. was Chief Engineer on the *Yukon Star*, the former *Camosun*, when she was operated by the Alaska Cruise Lines in the summer of 1958.

With the demise of Union Steamships at the end of 1958, Mr. Jefferson went over to the Black Ball Line and was Chief Engineer on the *Smokwa*, and again when B.C. Ferries took over Black Ball. He was now 64 years old and he went to work for B.C. Marine as a relieving shore engineer. One morning down at B.C. Marine an engineer aboard the *Glacier Queen*, which was up on the ways, investigated why the steam pressure had dropped and he discovered that Mr. Jefferson had collapsed and died during the night on March 26, 1964.

His son, also named Lance, often travelled aboard the *Cardena* with his father. He has happy memories of Captain Harry Roach letting him steer the ship and blow the whistle. Lance himself worked as a steward in the summer aboard the *Camosun* and the *Catala*.

When the *Chelohsin* grounded at Stanley Park, Lance remembers Victor David visited their house often to discuss his plans for buying the *Chelohsin* and converting her over to a floating fish cannery.

Being a quiet and unobtrusive man, stories and anecdotes about Mr. Jefferson are almost non-existent but I did manage to come up with two. Once when he was asked if the ship would make the tide at Seymour Narrows, his reply was. "Well if we don't, there is always another one."

Ben Smith worked with Mr. Jefferson who was then 2nd Engineer, described him as being a quiet-spoken man and not easily rattled, however if there had been a dress code in the Company Mr. Jefferson wouldn't pass inspection, at least down in the engine room, and he explained why. "While all the other Engineers wore white coveralls, Old Jeff always wore a faded blue boiler suit. He also had an old belt around his waist, which hauled the pants up to half-mast. But the real clincher was his cap. It perhaps was the 'saltiest' cap in the Company, covered in oil and the binding on the peak had come loose and always hung down over his left eye. I guess it got to be too much for his oiler, and one day he put the proposition to us that we all chip in and buy Jeff a new cap. So we all put in 50 cents but we found we were a bit short. Ernie Emms, the 3rd Engineer, coughed up another 50 cents. We decided to let our Chief Engineer, Robert Baldry, a rather solemn stoic fellow, in as well. It was my job to approach him. I almost got fired! The end result was that Jeff never did get his new cap. He continued wearing the old faded blues and the battle-scarred cap, probably until the end of his career."

Clarence Leslie "Abe" McCormick

Engineer Clarence "Abe" McCormick

Abe was born on Jan. 27, 1925 in Bracebridge, Ont. The family moved to Toronto and when Abe turned 14 the family moved to B.C.

He started working for Union Steamships aboard the *Camosun II* as a mess boy on Sept. 25, 1942.

The 4th Engineer aboard the *Camosun* was a fellow by the name of Jack Hill. One day he said to Abe, "Why don't you switch over to the engineering department? There is no future in being a steward." Abe thought that made sense, so Jack went to the Chief Engineer who was none other than the now famous Fred Smith, and he was hired on as a fireman on April 15, 1943. Next he became an oiler, then he was promoted to 4th Engineer on the *Camosun*.

Wally Walsh, a deck officer, gave him the nickname Abe and kept telling him he should transfer over to the deck crew because he wouldn't have to get his hands dirty.

During this period he worked on various ships including the *Venture*, the *Cassiar*, and *Lady Cecilia*. He next decided to leave the ships and to go up to Prince Rupert and work in the drydock there as a pipefitter He left there and decided to go deep sea for awhile. One day he had a phone call from John Gilligan who offered him a job as 4th Engineer on the *Cardena*, whose Chief Engineer was Clarence Arthur.

Abe said that he had heard about this Arthur fellow, but also, he had heard more about the 2nd Engineer on the *Cardena*, a fellow by the name of R.G. MacKenzie. The second engineers aboard the Union Ships, according to Abe, were like gods, and the chiefs were just figureheads. The second is really running the show on any vessel. The Chief is running around in a uniform being the glamour boy. Abe had heard Mr. MacKenzie had been firing guys left, right, and centre. He apparently had fired 14 fellows in the last year, so Abe was somewhat reluctant to take the job. Mr. Gilligan said, "Well, if you have any trouble come and see me."

So Abe goes down to the *Cardena* at 7:30 p.m. on sailing night and reports to Mr. MacKenzie. "He was standing there as I come down the stairs, and I put out my hand saying, "I'm the new 4th Engineer." "So what? I've fired 14 of you fellows over the last year." Mr. MacKenzie said. "Well here is one guy you don't fire." "What do you mean?" he said. Abe said, "I quit right now, I'm not going to sail with you." "Oh, you can't do that." Mr. MacKenzie said, "The ships going to sail in another one and a half hours." Abe said, "Well if we start out like that Mr. MacKenzie, there is no use me even coming here." "Oh well," he said, "That's okay, you do your work and you'll be fine." After that he never bothered me too much and Abe stayed with the Union Steamship Co. until they were taken over by Northland in 1959. He then signed on with the Alaska Cruise Lines as third engineer. He left them and went over to the B. C. Ferries on Oct. 22, 1961 and was with them for 29 years.

The Chief Engineer of the *Cardena* was old Clarence Arthur. Abe was one of the few men who got along well with Chief Arthur and he suggested it was because his name was Clarence also. Abe said "Old Arthur would come down to the engine room right on the dot of 10 a.m. every day and say, "Away you go young fellow, take your coffee break." He always called Abe "young fellow." The first time Abe went for his break he didn't know how long he should take and he came back down in about 10 minutes. Chief Arthur said, "You are entitled to half an hour, young fellow, go back up and take it." Another thing that Abe did which endeared him to the Chief was he repaired a steam valve which had been leaking for some time and it could only be fixed when the ship was down and laying alongside the dock. Abe was doing this repair job in the wee small hours of the morning and Chief Arthur had come back to the ship in order to have a little sleep before the morning watch started. He heard the noise of Abe working away and went to see what was going on. He was very surprised and pleased to find what Abe was doing.

One time Abe's mother had come down to see him aboard ship, as she had some papers she needed Abe to sign. Coming aboard ship she ran into the Chief and asked to see Abe. She had no idea who she was talking to at the time. Chief Arthur took her down to the dining saloon and had one of the stewards fix her up with lunch and a pot of tea. He then went down and told Abe his mother was up in the dining saloon waiting to see him. When Abe saw her sitting at the Officers Mess he was surprised. She looked up and said, "What a nice man that was, how kind and thoughtful he had been in getting this lunch for me." Abe could only laugh because he was always telling her about that son of a bitch, the Chief Engineer and how miserable he was.

Chief Arthur did not like deck officers and showed great disdain for most skippers. He told Abe not to get too friendly with them and further don't fraternize with the unlicensed personnel. On most of the Union ships the Captain and the Chief Engineer sat opposite each other at the Officers Mess table, but on the *Cardena*, Chief Arthur had his own table. He and Captain Boden rarely spoke to each other. "There was only one skipper that Chief Arthur liked and that was Captain Bob Wilson." Abe said, "When Captain Wilson came onto the *Cardena*, Old Arthur threw his arms around him. I thought he was going to kiss him, I couldn't believe my eyes."

Abe recalls one incident which illustrates clearly Chief Arthur's feeling as to who was running things aboard the *Cardena*. Abe was on watch and the Skipper called down to him on the speaking tube and asked for more revs as they were just going through the Narrows. The *Cardena* usually ran at 115 revs, so Abe opened her up to the maximum of 120. The Chief came down to relieve Abe and he asked right away, "Who put up the speed of the engines?" "I did," Abe answered. "The skipper phoned me." Chief Arthur shot back, "Don't you ever do that again, young fellow, I'm the Chief Engineer here, if they want more speed, they have to send me a note!" So Chief Arthur cut back the revs. Then the skipper phoned down and said, "What is going on, we're going backwards." Chief Arthur said, "Don't answer them."

Abe was promoted to third engineer on the *Coquitlam* and would be working under Fred Smith. When Chief Arthur learned of this he went to Abe and said "If you will stay with me, I'll give you the third's job but Abe had made up his mind. Old Arthur had tears in his eyes and said, "I'm sure sorry to see you go."

The replacement for Abe was a new fellow by the name of Smith and he asked Abe what were the fellows like that he was going to be working with. Abe told him, "Oh a great bunch of guy's." Later he ran into Smith on the dock, and he said to Abe, "You sure gave me a bunch of bullshit about those guys, didn't you!"

So Abe starts his tour of duty under the well-known Fred Smith. One of the most important events in Abe's life was instigated by Fred. He introduced Abe to his future wife, Florence. She was travelling as a passenger and as usual Fred soon made acquaintance with most of the ladies travelling aboard ship. He told Florence he had a nice young engineer working for him that she should meet, so he brought her down for a tour of the engine room and it could be said, it was love at first sight.

The stories about Freddie are legend and Abe adds another to the list. It seems that Fred had been partying and entertaining a lady passenger in his room most of the night. When he woke up in the morning he had a big head and decided to have another drink to steady himself. He reached for a glass and he noticed there was something in it, but paid no attention, opened the port hole and emptied the glass. It turned out that the lady had put her false teeth in the glass and had left them there by mistake. One can picture the consternation of all parties, the lady having to travel the rest of the trip without any teeth and Freddie's dilemma, as the news raced around the ship.

Freddie had been with the Company for 44 years when, in 1957, Abe says they were tied up at Prince Rupert when Fred received a wire from head office advising him he was to be retired when he returned to Vancouver and would receive a pension of $60 a month. What a callous and unfeeling way of dealing with one of the Company's best-known and faithful employees! Fred had no idea this was coming and was in shock. Further, when the Company closed down in the following year, Fred lost his pension, according to Abe.

Abe was aboard the *Catala* and was up on the bridge with other officers who were listening to an announcement coming over the radio that the Union Steamship Co. was to be taken over by Northland. Ray Perry was the Skipper, Angus McNeill was the Chief Officer and he was never known to swear but on hearing this announcement he let go and said, "God Damn it, all these bloody years I put in and look what happens." Angus was one skipper who went over to Northland, but it is on record that he never liked Northland. He felt that the old Union Steamships were his second home.

A frequent traveller aboard the Union Ships was a chap from Seattle, Austen Hemion. He told me this amusing story about Abe. "The toilet, or head as it is called aboard ship, used by the Captain and the Chief Officer was acting up. I happened to be visiting the engine room when a message came down they needed a wrench to fix the Captain's head. So Abe took a huge spanner which was used to tighten up the main engine connecting rods and had chalk marked on it 'for the Captain's Head.' I lugged that big wrench from the engine room floorplates up to the bridge. I don't think Captain Tom Lucas thought it was funny!" [207]

Chief Engineer David McLelland
(Sharon Edwards)

One of the Company's Pursers, Harry Gill, committed suicide by jumping overboard from the *Camosun II* in the Queen Charlotte Islands. Abe was aboard at the time. The ship was turned around and his body recovered. He recalls they tried to revive him. Mate Al Strang and 4th Engineer Jack Hill gave him artificial respiration. They rubbed his back raw, but without success. Abe was also aboard when Captain Watt dropped dead of a heart attack. Tom Lucas the Chief Officer had to take over and Captain Watt's body was put into the ship's freezer hold and brought back to Vancouver.

When the Union Steamships folded, Abe went over to the Alaska Steamship Line, going aboard the *Yukon Star* as third engineer. While he was with this Company he had the opportunity to go over to Greece and bring back the *Stella Maris*, the former U.S.S. *Chilcotin*, which was a sister ship to the two other ships operated by the Alaska Cruise Line. They were going to add her to their fleet. Fortunately for him he didn't go as the man who went as third engineer was burned alive aboard the *Stella Maris* when it accidentally caught fire while refuelling for the trip back to Vancouver.

Abe retired from the B.C. Ferries on Jan 29, 1990 after 29 years of faithful service with them. He now lives in Vancouver and spends his leisure time fishing. When I visited him and interviewed Abe at his home I must say, "I've never seen such a collection of fishing rods and reels in all my life."

David "Davie" McLelland

Davie had a long career with the Union Steamships. He started with the company in 1920, coming off deep sea ships, and he stayed with them until the very end in 1958, a span of 38 years with one employer. He started as 3rd engineer and worked his way to the top, being a senior engineer when the Company ceased operations.

He was born in Kilmarnock, Scotland on Aug. 10, 1896 and spent his early childhood on the Isle of Skye. At an early age he was brought over to Canada as a foster child by Mr. McNeish, one of the early Mayors of North Vancouver. He enrolled Davie in a Catholic seminary to train for the priesthood. Davie didn't like this and ran away to join the navy at age 14. Mr McNeish found him and, as was a custom at that time, he was able to buy him out, but later he joined the navy again and served on a minesweeper on the east coast in the First World War and according to his daughter he also served aboard the HMCS *Rainbow*, here in B.C. His daughter thought he would be about 18 years old at the time. While still in his teens he joined Burrard Shipyards in North Vancouver to serve an engineering apprenticeship. Then after the war Davie then went deep sea. His daughter Sharon says he was over in China and he returned with many souvenirs from that country, which she still has in her home. He also went to Liverpool, for it was here he met his future wife, Edith Banks.

In 1920 he joined the Union Steamships and in 1921 he married the girl he had met in Liverpool.

Davie was serving aboard the *Chilliwack II* in the early 1930s, as his daughter recalls him taking her on a trip aboard the *Chilliwack*, going from Vancouver and up the Fraser River to New Westminster. She remembers it well, for it was her sixth birthday and he had told her to wear her best party dress. She remembers the wonderful little Chinese cook aboard baked her a birthday cake and presented it to her with a big grin.

His daughter recalled that they always had lots of fresh fruit at home as Davie would always fill up his suitcase with fruit he had saved from his meals aboard ship and bring it home. She would run down the street to meet him and he would let her search his bag for an apple or an orange. She also said that Davie was teetotal which was a bit unusual for anyone working aboard the Union ships. Most fellows like Davie who had such a long career with the Company usually ended up having a nickname and Davie was no exception. I am told his junior officers nicknamed him "the Mouse." On one of his trips he had an attack of appendicitis aboard ship. The nearest hospital was at Powell River so the Captain sailed full steam ahead for that port and Davie was rushed into the hospital.

Another engineer in the Company, Jimmy Grieve, married Davie's wife's sister, Dora. Davie had brought Jimmy home to dinner one evening and introduced the two, who later were married.

During the war the *Catala* was engaged to ferry a group of Canadian airmen up to the American base on Annette Island. One of the airmen aboard happened to pass Chief McLelland's room and as the door was open he noticed a crib board on the table. The airman asked if Davie played crib, which he did, so the two of them played crib together for the whole trip. Some years later his daughter brought a gentleman home for her parents to meet, whom she had met at her place of work. Davie and the man looked at each other and then let out a big cry, for this was the same man that Davie had played crib with on that trip up to Annette Island some years back. Sharon later married this same man. A small world!

Chief Engineer Andrew Beattie died aboard the *Catala* in 1945 while she was alongside the dock in Prince Rupert. When the ship returned to Vancouver, Davie took over as Chief Engineer and the *Catala* became his home. He stayed aboard her until the Union Steamship ended business in 1958.

Davie was 62 years old when the Union Steamship Co. was taken over by the Northland Navigation Co. He did not transfer over and began to look for other work. Most of the jobs available were on diesel engines and Davie could not work with the fumes, for they made him ill. He tried to find a job as a stationary engineer but with no luck. At his age no one wanted to hire you and as the Union Steamship had had no pension scheme it was tough going, for all he had to carry on with was a small pension from the First World War. He died at age 70 in Vancouver.

Frederick Matheson

Chief Engineer Frederick Matheson
(B. Woodside & E. Matheson)

The *Lady Cecilia* and the *Lady Alexandra* at Sechelt circa 1930
(Hackett Collection)

Frederick Matheson was born in Larvik, a little village just outside Oslo, Norway, on Aug. 2, 1886. He came to Canada in 1905 and went to work in the engine rooms of the CPR ships plying the waters of the Kootenay Lakes. He left this Company and signed on with the Union Steamships as second engineer on the *Chasina*, Aug. 3, 1918.

He was appointed Chief Engineer of the *Chilliwack* in 1927. During his career he sailed on various Union ships, namely the *Chelohsin*, *Venture*, *Cardena*, *Catala*, *Lady Cecilia*, *Lady Cynthia*, *Lady Alexandra* and finally became sort of a fixture on the *Camosun III*, which he said was his favourite ship of them all.

In 1955 he was the third most senior engineer in the Company and the 12th senior employee overall.

When the *Camosun III* was converted and refitted in drydock, to a sleek, jazzy B.C. coastal passenger ship, Chief Matheson was there to oversee the work being done. He was Chief Engineer when she sailed on her maiden voyage to Ocean Falls, Prince Rupert and Ketchikan, a new Company route, on Dec. 6, 1946. Chief Matheson stayed aboard her until he retired in July, 1956. He was 70 years old. Prior to retiring he acquired a 40-foot cabin cruiser named the Harla, which he sailed himself down from Prince Rupert to Vancouver.

Bob Ashmore, a former deck officer with the Company, told me that Fred was the most cooperative of all the engineers he ever came across in the Union fleet.

His son Earl had worked for two summers on the Union ships. The first year was 1936 and he scraped boiler tubes for two months. Again in the summer months of 1937 he worked as a deckhand aboard the *Lady Alexandra*. After his second summer Earl decided to pursue his education rather than choose a sea career. Earl told me an amusing story about a crew member who said he had trouble detecting Fred's nationality. "When my father had first come to Canada he spoke very little English but working in engine rooms with predominately Scottish engineers he learned his English with a Scottish accent. By the time he joined the Union Steamships he had a Scottish accent." The crewman said, "After listening carefully to your father I could tell he was of Scottish descent alright!"

Chief Matheson was a favourite with the tourists. A Seattle-based magazine related the following little story about Fred: "As the ship made its way up Observatory Inlet, the sun broke through giving us a fairly clear afternoon. Passengers were out on deck, lounging around enjoying it all. Among them was Chief Engineer Frederick Matheson, who mentioned having problems - the necessity of changing a number of burner nozzles. At the same time he looked up in disgust at the black smoke pouring out of the stack. Indeed, many a jacket and passengers' clothing was ruined by the smoke and soot that poured from the stacks of the three White Boats, as the converted corvettes came to be called."

"Dad had many stories to tell about passengers on the cruise ships," his daughter Bernice said. "One I remember was the *Camosun* was docked at Ocean Falls and one gushy lady came up to him and started chatting to him and asked, 'Chief, how far above sea level are we here?' Dad pointed down to the water and said, 'Oh I'd say about 17 feet.' Her reply was, 'Oh, I'd have thought we would be higher than that, being as we are so far north!' "

For a while Bernice and her family lived in Prince Rupert. She has pleasant memories of going down to the *Camosun* with her whole family to have Sunday dinner aboard ship, with her father. The Chief Steward, Norm Davidson, would invite them all and when they left one of the stewards would make sure she left with a big bag of fresh fruit for the children.

Denis Shaw, a former Purser with the Company, recalled sailing with Chief Matheson aboard the *Catala* and the *Cardena*. Frequently the ship would be carrying crates of chickens consigned for people along the coast. He said that Fred loved fresh eggs and he had the habit of going between deck to where the crates were stored and he would feel around in the crates for freshly laid eggs, often coming back to the galley with three or four fresh eggs which he would then fry up for himself.

On one trip the fellows decided to play a trick on Fred, so they hard-boiled several eggs and planted them in the crates. Fred went up as usual and made quite a haul. He came back to the galley, whistling away to himself, thinking about this windfall of fresh eggs. He got his fry pan ready and then tried to crack his eggs. Everyone was watching this. When Fred realized how he had been tricked he just left the galley without a word and his happy whistle was silent. His search for fresh eggs never resumed after that.

This very popular and efficient engineer took sick not too long after he retired and died Oct. 2, 1958.

Benjamin F. "Ben" Smith

4th Engineer Ben Smith

The word ebullient characterizes Ben completely. Of all the Union fellows I've interviewed and written about, Ben stands out because of this quality that comes through loud and clear when you talk to him. As well he is a wonderful storyteller, chronicler of events and people. Without a doubt he has given me more stories about the Union Steamship Company and the personnel than anyone.

Ben was born on Feb. 16, 1921 in New Westminster. He joined the Union Steamships Jan. 4, 1946. He came straight out of the navy and signed aboard the old *Venture* as an oiler. Ben said, "She was ready to fall apart at that time, as six months later she was sold to the Chinese, and was probably the only 'junk' that sailed from west to east. When I joined her she was probably the senior ship, in numbers of years of service, in the fleet. When I first went down into the engine room and looked around, everything seemed to be leaking and blowing. You felt like you needed an umbrella to walk around the engine room. I thought to myself, 'this is the living end.'

"As well, the crew's quarters were up in the bow and in heavy seas you caught every green one that came along. It wasn't the most comfortable quarters and place to be in a storm."

When the *Venture* was sold and leaving for China, Ben actually tried to sign aboard her for the trip, but a fellow with more seniority, Pat Morrissey, received the nod, which turned out to be fortunate for Ben because the *Venture* caught fire in Hawaii and the crew lost most of their possessions.

Despite Ben's years of service with the navy, he still had to spend a year on Union ships as an Oiler before he could qualify for his 4th Engineer's ticket. However, on one occasion, the Chief Engineer, the famous Freddie Smith, took ill on sailing night. The 2nd Engineer, Ed Mattock, moved up to Chief; the 3rd, Jack Widdess, moved up to Second Engineer; the 4th, Abe McCormick, sailed as 3rd; and Ben, upon agreement from Ed Mattock, sailed as the 4th. Shortly after, he qualified for his Ticket, and from that point in time sailed continuously as 4th Engineer and relieving 3rd Engineer on the *Coquitlam II* for the next two years. The Chief Engineer was his uncle and godfather, Freddie Smith, and Ben was not keen on sailing with a relative as his boss, but the office persuaded him with these words, "You haven't lived until you've sailed with Freddie." Fortunately the Chief chewed Ben out from time to time, so there was never any favoritism shown.

As Ben had been in the navy and had sailed on the corvettes, he was very familiar with their engines, more so than the Chief Engineers in the Union Company. When he went aboard *Coquitlam*, one of the Company's converted corvettes, it was like old home week. He says there were some gadgets on them that some of the Chiefs had never seen before on other Union ships. When he came aboard he started to point them out, the next thing he knew he was standing in a circle of a bunch of engineers telling them all what the gadgets were and what they were required to do.

On the *Coquitlam* they were having trouble with boiler tubes bursting. When this happened they would have to hole up in Prince Rupert, shut the boilers down and replace these tubes with new ones. One day he casually said to the Chief, "When do we oil the sliding feet on these boilers?" The Chief didn't understand what Ben was talking about. They were not familiar with this type of Yarrow boiler, but as Ben had had experience with them in the navy and he knew it was essential, with the expansion and contraction of the metal due to heat and cooling shifting the boilers a degree, you had to oil their 'sliding feet.' However, as these boilers were so close to the bulkheads only the skinniest man in the engine room was able to get there and do the job. So guess who did it? But they never had trouble with the boiler tubes bursting from that time on.

Ben didn't like the day boats, because you never seemed to get a day off. However one did receive what was called Lay Days. If you didn't get 24 hours clear from the ship every week you earned a Lay Day. One could accumulate a lot of time off. A long time after Ben left the Company, in moving to another home, he discovered several Lay Days signed by Tom Dick, which he had never cashed in.

Working in the engine room, as an engineer, you get to know how capable a bridge officer is in handling a ship and making landings. Some would rattle the signals so fast, you would get behind in trying to respond. Three of the best ship handlers in the Union fleet in his opinion were Jimmy Hunter, Tom Lucas and Al Strang.

Ben had high praise for the meals aboard ship. The whole crew ate the same food as the officers and passengers.

After joining Union Steamships, Ben used to regale his mother with stories about how the Union ships used to haul just about anything, to any place, and it was not uncommon to see a cow or a horse or maybe a crate of chickens up on the foredeck when the ship sailed. One day while in port, he brought his mother down to the ship. It was early afternoon and the shore gang were busy loading freight. His mother stood at the edge of the hatch and looking down into the gaping hold, all at once she said, "Where do they keep all the animals?" One of the shore gang looked up from down below and said, "We're all down here, lady, we're all down here."

Stories about his uncle and godfather, Freddie Smith, are legend. Ben says that at times Fred was kind of absent-minded. One day he decided he needed a new pair of black oxford shoes. Off he went to Woodward's, which wasn't very far from the Union dock, and bought himself a new pair of dress oxfords. That evening before the ship sailed a couple of his staff joined him in his room for a little drink. Freddie started to tell them about the new pair of shoes that he had just purchased. He then got them out and was showing them his new shoes. Then he said, "I guess I don't need to keep the old ones." With that he opened the port hole and threw out first one shoe and then another. Trouble was he threw out one old shoe and one new shoe!

Of the many stories Ben related to me, the following I think are two of the best:

The first one could be called the "Beachcombers." This incident occurred aboard the *Camosun*, during a homeward journey from Prince Rupert. Ben says he heard this story second hand. It seems that the Mate phoned the engine room to verify that they were travelling at the specified speed of 150 revs per minute. The engineer, Chad Chadwick, did a count, and assured the mate that they were indeed doing the required speed.

About half an hour later, the mate made the same request again, because they were making such poor time. Once again, Chad made a count of the revolutions, and assured the mate they were actually going 152 revs. Sometime later, Chad chanced to look upwards towards the overhead grating and was surprised to see one of the quartermasters standing there and doing a count as well.

And so they continued to plow along at this speed, when all at once the telegraph rang "Full Stop." Later "Full Astern." Then "Full Stop" again. Chad was somewhat perplexed because they seemed to be in the middle of nowhere. So he sent his oiler topside to see what was going on. The oiler returned, somewhat jubilant with the following report. "You will not believe what is going on up there. There is a great big tree caught on the bow, and we have been pushing it for the last hour."

Some time later, when the watch was over, Chad went up to the dining salon for a coffee and the mate came down from the bridge at about the same time. Chad casually inquired, "Do we get paid extra for that?" and the mate replied, "For what?" Chad said, "For clearing logs and trees out of the channel."

The mate was somewhat enraged and said, "What do you know about it?"

"Well, fair is fair. If you can send a quartermaster down to count revs, I can send an oiler up to see what you guys are doing topside."

Navigators on the B.C. coast have always had to use utmost care and skill to take their ships through the Seymour Narrows safely. When the top was blasted off Ripple Rock in the Narrows in 1958, going through was safer, but the fast-running tides still provided a problem.

The late Captain Boden Sr. decided on one trip going southbound and through the Narrows, to buck a 14-knot tide. Freddie Smith was the Chief Engineer and Ben was on watch with him on this occasion. The ship was the new *Coquitlam* whose top speed was about 15 knots. Here is Ben's version:

"Captain Boden was a pretty daring old captain. We were coming through the Narrows and the top speed of the *Coquitlam* would be about 15 knots. She was the speediest ship in the fleet. The Chief comes down below and says to Ben, 'For God's sake Ben, pile on the coal, Boden's taking her through and we're bucking a 15-knot tide.' So I go to the stoker and I said to him, 'Look, fire this damn thing up and keep her right on the 300 mark because I'm going to wind her up.' I went back to the engine room and cranked her open as far as she could go. The engine is fair dancing in its bearings, she was just rattling and rattling. The Chief was standing there all the time because he was pretty concerned. After this had been going on for half an hour, he said, 'Go up and see where the hell we are?' So I went up and looked around, came back down and said, 'By God Chief, we're right abeam of the Maude Island light.' The Chief replied, 'Jesus Christ, we were there half an hour ago!'

"But we got her through that ruddy narrows, although it took us about two hours. Boden was bound and determined he was going to take her through and he did."

Ben was married on Sept. 9, 1950, and decided that being away at sea a good part of the time was no life for a married man. He left the Company in April, 1951, and went to work for B.C. Telephone Co. in January 1952. He retired in May 1981.

Chief Engineer Fred "Freddie" Smith aboard S.S. *Catala*

Fred Edward "Freddie" Smith

In the 70 years that the Union Steamship Co. was in business serving the coastal communities of B.C. until 1958, many of their officers and crew left their mark on the settlers. Their names, their kindness and friendship were remembered everywhere along the coast. Some fellows were better known on the lower routes or day runs and then others spent nearly all their time on the northern routes. Such names as Yates, Farina, Gaisford, Findlay, Wilson, Georgeson, Muir, Arthur, Beattie, Stover, Robinson, Hughes, Knight among many. However, probably more people will recall one man over all others, and with a smile no doubt: that very colourful Chief Engineer, the great Fred Smith.

In an interview I had with one of the junior engineers whom Freddie had encouraged and brought along, he asked this question, "Is there any end to the stories of this old Chief?" The answer without a doubt is, "There doesn't seem to be." His name gets mentioned whenever the Union Steamships are discussed, whether up north or on the Sunshine Coast. Freddie was one of the greats in the Company and a real character.

Fred was born in 1888 in Somerset, England. His father was a member of the British House of Commons representing Thormbry in Gloucestershire. He had a brewery but got in with a gambling crowd and lost everything. He died at age 33. Fred was the eldest of seven children and he stayed with his mother, but the others were shipped out to relatives. His mother was left with huge debts. She and Fred moved to Bath. Fred had been in a private school and at Bath the public school couldn't teach Fred anything that he hadn't already learned so he looked for a job at 11 years of age. He obtained a job in the Cotswold Hills looking after sheep. At 14 years he was sent to Bristol to learn the engineering trade. He put in a five-years apprenticeship, then he had to go to work and make some money to help his mother.

One of his friends at the school had gone to sea and had written Fred glowing accounts of life at sea, so Fred decided he too would go to sea. He went to Cardiff, in south Wales and wandered around the docks looking for a job. It was a tough town and at 19 years old Fred was alone with no money to speak of. He did find a berth as 4th engineer on an old tramp steamer, 2,800 tons loading coal for the Black Sea. They sailed the same night that Fred had joined her. The glowing picture that his friend had told him about soon faded. Fred said, "If the old ship was pushed and had the tide behind her she would do about five knots. She had no generators, nothing but coal oil lamps and the food consisted of salted meat and hard tack biscuits that were full of maggots. The salted meat I think came from all the horses that had been killed in the Crimean War and had been pickled up, but you had to eat it because there was nothing else."
[208]

When they returned to England they landed at Swansea, Wales and the Captain said to Fred "We're sailing in two days, go up to the shipping master and sign on again." Fred said, "Not me, I'm leaving this ship as soon as I can." So he went home to Gloucestershire where his mother lived and got a job in a factory doing piece work but had to work 12 hours a day. His younger brother Reggie contracted TB and his mother said, "You'll have to take Reggie over to British Columbia, Canada," where one of his brothers had settled. So Fred and his sick brother booked steerage passage to Canada. Getting through immigration with his sick brother and only 15 cents in his pocket took all the ingenuity that Fred could muster, but he was now a man of the world and Fred was able to bluff his way and get them both through. They landed in Vancouver in 1911.

Fred had trouble finding work. Finally he got a job on a tug boat but after one trip it tied up. He then was able to obtain work in a shipyard down in Seattle that was building the first big battleship to be built on the west coast for the U.S. Navy, the West Virginia. They wanted Old Country engineers who could line up shafts. This job lasted six weeks. Fred and one of his buddies then signed aboard a ship in Seattle, the *Kingsly*, which Fred said "was nothing more than a bucket of rust." It was a delivery job to Japan. Fred signed aboard as 4th Engineer for $50 a month. Twenty days out in the Pacific she lost her rudder They drifted for four days, then they sawed up the ship's booms and rigged up a rudder. The sea was terrible and they lost the makeshift rudder on the second night. They had no wireless or light. They were adrift again until a French ship spotted them. He started to tow the *Kingsly* but had to cut them adrift because of a typhoon warning but the captain did send a wire ahead to have a tugboat come out and tow them into port. Fortunately the typhoon missed them or we wouldn't know Freddie at all. The tug did find them and took them into Nagoya. They had finally reached their destination, but the man who had arranged the whole deal had skipped out with all the money so the crew never got paid. The skipper went to the British Consulate and they somehow got the men back home under destitute seaman arrangements. So Fred was able to get back to Vancouver. This would probably be some time in 1912.

Back in Vancouver, Fred obtained a temporary job in Wallace's Shipyards. He was hired to help take the rudder post out of the *Coquitlam I*. He worked alongside another engineer whose last name was Stover. His son Reg Stover later became a Purser with the Union Steamships Co. and worked aboard the same ships with Freddie. In 1917, Fred was Chief Engineer on this same *Coquitlam* that he had done repairs on in the shipyard.

In 1913 Fred joined the Union Steamship Co. and he started as a junior engineer on the *Venture*. Later that year he was transferred to the *Coquitlam I* as 2nd Engineer. Fred said that this was an Irishman's promotion because she only carried two engineers so it wasn't much of a promotion. [209] Fred went on to say, "I was Chief of every ship the Union Steamship ever had in the later years. When I started, the Union Company burned coal, but shortly after that, before the First World War, several of them were turned into oil burners. It was much easier to get firemen then. When they burned coal it was pretty difficult to get firemen because it took quite a bit of energy to keep steam with B.C. coal. It was a hard job steaming with coal. We had a lot of Japanese in the early stages. In the old days when you wanted to get a fireman, you got anybody, but you couldn't run a mixed crew. If you had so many Japanese, you had to get Japanese because they couldn't live with each other. Some boats had all white men. A good many of them carried Japanese below and they were good men. If one was sick and couldn't go to work, he sent someone as good as himself to take his place. The deck crew were all white boys." [210]

In April 1917, Fred was Chief Engineer on the *Coquitlam I* when she bumped heavily against the rock cliff while making a landing at a new mine in Douglas Channel. After leaving port they noticed that the ship wasn't acting properly. The Captain was Neil Gray. Upon investigation it was found that she was taking on water. The pumps were started and with his ship in danger Captain Gray decided to run her up Grenville Channel to Lowe Inlet and beach her there. They made it and Fred describes what happened. "The Captain tried to take her in sidearm but did not strand the ship quite high enough on the beach. It was nearly low tide and the crew shoveled a sandbank around the stern quarters to keep the vessel dry enough for us to get into the hold. The deck crew then dug through the coal before 2nd Engineer John Hogan and I could get working on repairs. One of the deckhands had been a logger and although we only had a blunt axe on board, he chopped through the wood sheathing which enabled us to put a patch inside and tighten the seams of the careened hull with iron bolts. We just had to makeshift with no means of communication on board or ashore, and get home the best way we could." [211]

According to Fred, after the accident mentioned above the *Coquitlam* lost her wheel (propeller) on her way back to Vancouver and had to be beached near Alert

Union Steamships at Quathiaski Cove 1920
Left to right:
Venture
Cowichan
Coquitlam
(Campbell River Museum)

Bay, though Gerald Rushton's book *Whistle Up The Inlet* states this accident took place a year later. Whatever year it was, Fred describes the accident this way: "Coming across Queen Charlotte Sound on the way down she lost her wheel and we had to go into Alert Bay. . . . We beached her (there) and they sent to Vancouver and they got a propeller sent up. They sent a propeller for the sister ship and the key wasn't big enough on that one. It hadn't been cut as big as the key that we had. So we had to file the keyway out. It was quite a job. And hauling that propeller up with chain blocks and trying her on, but we didn't get her right. The tide started to come in. We had to pull out. Every time we'd go astern she'd move a little bit on the tailshaft. We had to wait until we got to the cannery and we put her on the beach again and, of course, you know how they used to throw all the heads and fish guts in the drink. You had to wade through that up to your waist to take the wheel off and file the keyway a bit more so we could get her right. . . . It was quite an experience. We were out about three or four weeks. My wife had a baby, her first, while I was away. I was hoping to be home, but I wasn't." [212]

Fred was Chief Engineer on the *Chilliwack* in December 1919 when she had a very hazardous trip. The Captain at the time was C.B. Smith and Chief Officer Lorne Godfrey. They had loaded 700 tons of wet concentrate bound for Tacoma. They left Surf Inlet mine on Christmas day. The wet concentrate froze solid. Going south, the concentrates thawed and the cargo became a floating mass and was shifting, giving the *Chilliwack* a 30 degree list. Fred described the conditions: "A large amount of water was admitted through the starboard entrance on deck into the engine room and the pumps couldn't keep it down. The situation got steadily worse and the engineers working with the men up to their knees in water were unable to stand up and oil her. It was touch and go and we were reduced to pouring cans of sea water over the bearings to cool them." [213]

Captain Smith was able to beach the ship on a small cove on Price Island. They lay there for three or four days while the water was pumped out and bulkheads, made from logs hauled off the beach, were made to stabilize the concentrate. The engines had to be partly taken down and overhauled. The ship then continued to her destination, Tacoma, Washington. The Captain received commendation from Lloyds of London and he shared his purse with the entire crew. He gave special praise to his namesake and Chief Engineer, Fred Smith.

Fred also recalls a time in 1910 when clearing and blasting was being done at Prince Rupert and his ship was told to leave the dock and go out into the harbour because there was going to be a huge blast to remove rock in order to build wharves. When the blast went off huge rocks were flying everywhere. There was very little dirt around in Prince Rupert then so the Union ships used to haul black loam dirt up from Vancouver so residents could start gardens. [214]

At the beginning of the century, transporting loggers to all the camps along the coast was a big business for the Union Company. One of the famous ships in the fleet at the time was the *Cassiar*. She has been referred to as the Loggers Palace. Fred was aboard her for a little while and he said she was an old American steam schooner. In the *Sound Heritage* book Fred gives a good picture of these loggers at the time: "Loggers were good men when they were sober. They worked in all weather, in a pair of tin pants, they called them. When they bought a new pair, they would take them to a stump and chop the legs off about halfway up the leg with an axe. They'd wear those pants until they were so stiff with gum and pitch they could stand up by themselves. Also, a suit of Stanfield's underwear. The loggers liked the *Cassiar* because they could wear their caulk boots on her. They couldn't on any other ships. They'd even go to bed in their caulk boots. The loggers were always coming and going. They'd come to Vancouver and blow all their money and go right back up to their camps, some even after only one night in town. The loggers had a little poem, 'Vancouver, CPR, Tommy Roberts, *Cassiar*.'" [215]

One episode that is rarely spoken about in Union Steamship history is what is referred to as the Purge. In the late 1930s some Chief Stewards and Pursers were fired for what could be described as short-changing the Company. Fred saw it all and described it this way: "There were some crooked chief stewards in the Union Company. They got their booze by putting food in the laundry bags and the laundry man would carry it up and repay them with bottles of whiskey. The mate's prerequisite was boom chains. They'd accumulate a chain out of a bunch until they had enough and then they'd sell them to these gyppo camps. They'd sell them for about a quarter the price or take booze for them. They did a pretty good business with these boom chains. The pursers had a racket too. They'd sell meal tickets twice over. They'd sell a drunk logger his tickets and he'd usually say he didn't want the tickets, he just wanted to go to bed, so they would sell the tickets to someone else. There was a lot of skullduggery done. You couldn't do any such thing in the engine room." [216]

Fred sailed with the Union Company for 44 years and over the years he sailed with every skipper in the fleet. In a transcript of a tape recording that Freddie made some years ago with his friend Bob Hackett, he said this about Captain Georgeson: "He was the smartest seaman, the smartest skipper, the Union Steamship Co. ever had. He was well respected and liked by all who sailed with him."

Fred also had this to say about the skippers in general: "There were some fine men in the company. There was no radar and very little aids to navigation, such as markers and lighthouses. Many ships had no searchlights. The ships that did have searchlights had the old carbon searchlights, and it would fail just when you needed it. They navigated in thick weather by blowing the whistle and counting the seconds that the echoes came back in. They could navigate in pretty bad weather. Snow was the biggest bugbear because snow deadened the sound coming back. They'd go full speed in fog. They relied quite a bit on the man down below maintaining the revolutions and keeping up the speed so they knew what they were doing. If you started to lose time, then they were lost. It could happen by some defect in the machinery that you couldn't keep the speed up and it could happen by difference in the tidal currents. Of course, that was up to the skipper to make allowance for. They had good navigators in all the companies, but I will say, for the little hazardous holes and corners that the Union Company went into, they had some of the very best. You had to go in because there were people there. You had to maintain service. Up in what we called the jungle in around Kingcome and Knight Inlets, there were some pretty hazardous holes to get in and out of." [217]

Talking about navigation, one of the most spectacular groundings of any Union ship was when the *Catala* grounded on Sparrowhawk Reef, Nov. 7, 1927. It was in broad daylight and Fred said, "I was aboard her when she grounded. The Chief Officer put her aground. He went inside the marker instead of going around it. We had very few passengers aboard. They got them off and took them to Port Simpson. As the tide went out, she took a bad list. She was pretty well over on her side when we left her. The old man called down and told us to abandon ship. The Company abandoned her to the insurance company. The insurance company got her off and as the Union Steamship Co. was desperate for a boat, they bought her back." [218]

Fred's career with the Union Steamships spanned 44 years. Before he joined the Company he had gone through some hard and difficult times. He learned his trade the hard way. Coming to the Union Steamship Co. in 1913 must have been quite a contrast, but still he had some difficult jobs and situations to deal with and overcome. He certainly earned his keep in those days. As time went by, Fred Smith's name became well-known to the people all along the coast and also among the Union hands. He became quite a famous character.

Tex Lyon, the wharfinger and Union Steamship Co. Agent at Port Hardy for years, said laughingly: "Fred was quite a gossip. He picked the brains of every old lady on the coast. I think he knew everything that was going on up and down the coast. He could tell you when anyone had an increase in their family, from Vancouver to Prince Rupert."

In later years, Fred was well-known for his consumption of alcohol. It was said that Fred could hear a bottle being opened anywhere on the ship. If you took a bottle into Fred's room, he would open the port hole, take the cap or cork from the bottle and throw it out, saying, "This stuff won't keep, you know." It was also said that Fred was kept aboard ship more to entertain the passengers than to do any engineering.

Another time, Fred had been invited up to a passenger's cabin. The man was from Texas and apparently he was stingy with the liquor he put in the drinks, it was mostly ice cubes. When Fred was handed his drink, he looked at it and said, "For god's sake man, I'm not Barbara Ann Scott, you've got enough ice in this glass to skate on, come on give me a drink with something in it, not just ice."

On one occasion, before sailing time in Vancouver, Fred had invited some of the crew down to his cabin for a drink. They were all sitting around and Fred said "I bought myself a new pair of black oxfords today. They were laying on his bunk and he showed them to the gang. Then he said, opening the port hole at the same time, "I guess I don't need these old shoes anymore." He picked up one shoe and threw it out the port and then the other. The only trouble was, he had thrown one old shoe and one new shoe!

The following story was given to me by Ben Smith, Freddie's godson. It took place long after Fred had retired: "Fred had taken up residence in White Rock. Captain Billy McCombe had also moved there when he retired and the two became great buddies. It was common knowledge that Freddie made his weekly pilgrimage to the liquor store every Saturday for his weekly supply. It also so happened that his buddy Billy McCombe had gone to California for a vacation. While there he decided to send Freddie a card. Unfortunately, he had forgotten Freddie's address, but Bill McCombe was not without ingenuity. So the next Saturday old Freddie went to the liquor store as always, and after he had made his purchase, the clerk said, 'Oh, by the way Chief, there is some mail here for you,' and with that he handed him a postcard from his friend Billy McCombe. Apparently Freddie was not amused."

This last story is a little touchy. It was said that Fred never wore any pajamas when he went to bed. One morning his crew heard the greatest roar, bellowing, and shouting from his room. Rushing to investigate they found that Fred had got his privates caught in a bed spring and couldn't extract himself. It wasn't funny to see their Chief in such a predicament, but no one could offer immediate help because they were all laughing so hard.

When Fred started with the Union Steamship Co., his first ship was the *Venture*. His favourite ship in the Company apparently was the *Lady Evelyn*, and the last ship he sailed on was the *Coquitlam II*. She was the first of the converted corvettes, the former HMCS *Leaside*, to be put into service. Fred sailed out on her maiden voyage Nov. 8, 1946. Fred pretty well stayed on her until the end of his career.

In the January 1955 issue of the Company's newsletter *Heaving Line*, it was reported that Fred was the eighth senior employee and second in seniority among the engineers. When he was retired in 1957 he was the senior engineer in the fleet. He was 69 years old and had served the Company faithfully for 44 years.

His retirement came as a shock to him, though, as well as everyone else. Abe McCormick, who was working as 2nd

"The Great One"
Fred Smith
in retirement
(Sound Heritage Vol. VI, No. 2)

Engineer Gordon Vince on *Lady Alex* 1952
(Vince Collection)

engineer with Fred at the time, related this story of how Fred's retirement came about: "The *Coquitlam* was tied up at Prince Rupert when Fred received a wire from head office in Vancouver, advising him he was to be retired when the ship returned to Vancouver. Also, that he was to be given a pension of $60 a month! Fred came down to the engine room waving this telegram and shouting, 'Look at this, after all these years, this is the treatment they give me.' Naturally he was furious and in shock. It was certainly a poor way of handling the situation by the office. When the Company ceased operations the next year, Fred lost his $60 a month pension as well."

Fred and his first wife, Christine, made their home in Vancouver, just west of Central Park. They had two children, Douglas, who rose to great heights in the Post Office before passing away in 1991, and a daughter Anne who now lives in Surrey. His wife Christine passed away while Fred was still with the Union Co., and he later married Peggy Elfred, who was the ex-wife of Captain Elfred, former Harbour Master in Prince Rupert. They settled down in White Rock. She too passed on in the mid 1970s.

While in White Rock, Freddie became quite involved in politics, and ran for alderman, but was unsuccessful. He also campaigned for Camille Mather (wife of Barrie Mather) of the New Democratic Party. Freddie spent his declining years in a retirement home in Burnaby. He passed away in 1978 at the ripe old age of 90. He truly was one of the greats in the Union Steamship Co.

Gordon Vince

Gordon started with the Union Steamships in 1942 on the *Cardena* as 4th Engineer. The Chief Engineer was Clarence Arthur and the Captain was Jack Boden. During Gordon's 10 years with the Company, including war services, he never got over being seasick; even if he went to bed he still became seasick.

Gordie was a local boy, born in Vancouver, Oct. 20, 1919, and raised in West Vancouver. His father, Captain Harold Vince, at one time in his career ran winches on the *Venture* and later was manager of the

West Vancouver Ferries for many years.

Gordon left the Company in 1943 for war services on deep sea vessels and returned in 1945. Upon his return to Union Steamships, he served under several Chief Engineers, including George Craigen, Freddie Smith, Davie McLellan, John Hogan and of course Clarence Arthur. He worked on the *Cardena, Catala, Chelohsin, Camosun II, Coquitlam II, Lady Alexandra, Lady Cynthia*, and *Lady Cecilia*.

The first Chief Engineer he worked under was Clarence Arthur, a big man almost as wide as he was tall and not all that liked by his fellow workers. He hardly talked to anyone at the mess table, only grunting answers. Gordie said, "He made us stand our regular watch even when we were dockside in Vancouver."

Gordie had occasion one day, to meet Arthur's son, who asked Gordie, "How in hell do you manage to get along with my cranky old man?" Gordie reports that Clarence nonetheless was a great ladies' man, as he was often found up in the passenger saloon with the ladies during the time he was supposed to be on watch.

Gordie also recalls some circumstances in the death of Alan Mackie, a 2nd Engineer who lived aboard the *Cardena*. He had a sister who lived in Vancouver, and he frequently visited her when he was in port. On one visit he dropped dead at her home. Consequently a steward was delegated to pack up his belongings and clean up his room. In so doing, while turning over the mattress, he discovered 50 pay envelopes, all unopened. Mackie had just stashed them under his mattress! This hiding place was his bank, because the Union Steamship Co. always paid you in cash rather than cheques!

Gordie's favourite ships were the *Catala* and the *Lady Alexandra* - the *Catala* for the wonderful food served aboard her, and the *Lady Alexandra* for her spacious engine room. Even with his well-rounded service with the Company, he realized how the Company was losing ground and decided to leave in 1953. He went to work at the Pacific Drydock Company as a machinist, and later joined B.C. Ferries as Chief Engineer. Now retired, he lives with his wife Trudy at Fanny Bay, on Vancouver Island.

Robert "Bob" Whitelaw

Chief Engineer Robert "Bob" Whitelaw *(Sound Heritage Vol. VI, No. 2, p.20)*

Bob was born in Glasgow and took to a life at sea at an early age, serving on ships in the old country. He decided to come to Canada in September of 1919. He settled in Vancouver and joined the Union Steamship Co. right away.

During his 38 years with the Company, he served on most of the Company's passenger ships. Then he was sent back east in 1950 and was Chief Engineer on the *Blue Peter II* being brought to Vancouver. Though the ship was built by Burrard Drydock, it had been purchased by eastern interests and went back to Newfoundland, where it operated under the name of *Blue Peter*. The Union Steamships bought her, and renamed her *Cassiar III*, and put her in service right away.

On one of his first trips aboard a Union ship, Bob had an experience he never forgot.

He was 3rd Engineer aboard the *Chilliwack* when its cargo of 700 tons of wet concentrate froze solid before she left port and then thawed into an ever-shifting sludge when the *Chilliwack* was proceeding south in heavy seas. The *Chilliwack* began to list badly and the Master, Captain C.B Smith, decided he would have to beach her. She was beached safely and the crew, under Chief Engineer Freddie Smith (no relation), went to work for three days, pumping out water and using logs off the beach to make temporary bulkheads. They stabilized and restowed the ore. The ship was then refloated at high tide and she proceeded to her destination in Tacoma, Washington.

Bob retired in 1957, when he was Chief Engineer aboard the *Chilkoot*. He had been with her almost continually since she was built in 1946. I had the pleasure of sailing with Bob on one of the White Boats in the late 1940s.

They Also Served

Don Thompson

Don Thompson, Oiler, 1942
(D. Thompson)

Don went to work on the *Lady Pam* as a fireman in July 1942 under Chief Engineer Ned Scott. The war was on and there were plenty of jobs. Ned phoned Don's father to see if his son was working and if not, would he want a job aboard the *Lady Pam* and could start right away?

Don was available and he hustled right over via West Van Ferry to the Union dock and joined the *Lady Pam*. They even held the *Pam* up waiting for Don to arrive. Don had never been down in the engine room on a steam ship before in his life. He was given ten minutes of instruction and away sailed the *Pam*.

By the time the *Lady Pam* reached Point Atkinson, Don was in a panic because the dials and gauges seemed to be going crazy, but the Chief Engineer came along to see how he was doing and found all was well, and said, "You're doing fine."

Don recalled that the engine room on the *Lady Pam* was so hot you were paid an extra five dollars per month, but only during the summer. Another thing, the *Pam* wouldn't hold steam, so you had to come down, even on your day off, to fire her up.

Another event he remembers is when the *Pam* rammed into the *Princess Elaine* in the First Narrows. The *Elaine* had to go into drydock but the *Pam* continued on her way. The crew had a good laugh at that.

After a while, Don was transferred to the "good old *Chelohsin*" as he called her. The two Chief Engineers he worked under while he was there were Napier Tweedie and Tom Dick. After one trip as fireman he was promoted to oiler. Promotions came fast during the war years.

Napier Tweedie used to pay his firemen 50 cents a week to wash his white overalls. Don didn't think much of this. On the *Chelohsin* they washed all their rags in a little percolator that they had rigged up, so Don decided, what the heck, I'll throw the Chief's overalls in with the rags. That was the last time the Chief asked Don to wash his overalls.

One trip while the *Chelohsin* was alongside the dock at Port Hardy unloading freight, Don had all his work cleaned up and he went into the stoke hold and sat down with the firemen to have a cigarette. Chief Tweedie came along and with his funny little accent said, "Sitting down, sitting down, when there's work to be done?" He then gave Don a can of brass polish and put him to work polishing the cylinder heads, hot from two days steady steaming, until his watch was over.

Don related the following story to me which illustrates how well Chief Tweedie knew his engines on the *Chelohsin*. When the ships would leave dock on the Northern Routes, sometimes they would race, unofficially of course. The *Chelohsin* would be racing either the *Cardena* or the *Catala*. The *Chelohsin* had beautiful throttles, with very fine adjustments. The fellows would signal from the engine room door that the other ship was gaining, and he would just inch the throttles open a wee bit. Chief Tweedie would be sitting over in the corner on an old truck seat he had in a cool part of the engine room reading his paper. After about 45 minutes, he would pause, put his paper aside, turn his head and listen, then he would come and bring those throttles back exactly to what they were before Don had turned them up.

Another event he recalled was when he was aboard the *Lady Cynthia* after serving in the R.C.N.V.R. during World War II. The *Cynthia* was on the Cortes Island - Stuart Island route. It was a cold, wet, windy night. They were northbound and were approaching the wharf at Van Anda. People were huddled in the freight shed on the dock waiting for the *Lady Cynthia* to arrive. As the ship approached, the Captain called for someone to take her lines. The people just laughed and did nothing. The Captain hollered again for someone to take the lines. They laughed even louder and still didn't move. With that the Captain just backed the ship away. Southbound, coming into this same port, the people practically pulled the ship into the dock because they didn't want to see all their freight and supplies that had been sent up from Vancouver, which were still aboard, go back to Vancouver.

"It was a good life aboard the Union Ships. I have many happy memories of those days, and boy were they good feeders," Don said.

Lady Alex, Lady Cynthia, Lady Cecilia with more than 3,000 W.W.A. picnickers at the Union Dock *(Sound Heritage Vol. VI, No. 2)*

They Also Served

Left: Engineer Tom Annan
(Annan Collection)

Right: Engineer Chad Chadwick (left) with Abe McCormick
(A. McCormick)

Below: Engineer J. Douglas with C. Spring, Wireless Operator
(Belveal Collection)

Right: Chief Engineer Tom Dick with Capt. H. McLean
(Humphreys Collection)

They Also Served

Left: Engineer
Alex Fletcher
(Roach & Fletcher)

Right: Chief Engineer R.M.
"Bob" Logan
(Logan Collection)

Left: Engineer
"Sparky" New
(W. New)

Right: Chief Engineer
Napier Tweedie
(Skinner Collection)

They Also Served

2nd Engineer
Bill Whiteman
(right front)

Camosun II in
heavy seas often
encountered by
Union Steamships
(Ashmore Collection)

Chapter 3
PURSERS, ASSISTANT PURSERS and FREIGHT CLERKS

For more than 300 years, sailors in England's Royal Navy were issued a daily ration of rum by the Purser (which was pronounced "pusser" by the Jack Tars). From 1655 to 1970, Purser's Rum was one of the few daily comforts afforded to the ordinary seaman.

Denis Shaw, who served as a Purser aboard ship in the Union fleet, claimed with tongue in cheek that the white background in the Purser's gold braid symbolized "purity!"

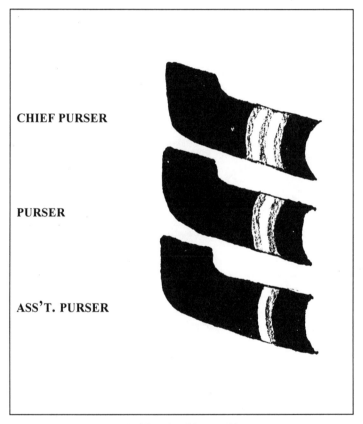

Gold and White Braid
Buttons - Gold

Pat Pattison, probably the best known Purser in the fleet
(J. Smith Collection)

AGREEMENT

Between

UNION STEAMSHIPS LIMITED

and

PURSERS AND CHIEF STEWARDS ASSOCIATION NO. 130 OF B. C.

EFFECTIVE AUGUST 1, 1941

IT IS MUTUALLY AGREED THAT:

1. All Pursers, Assistant Pursers, Chief Stewards and Second Stewards (where employed), employed by the Union Steamships Limited be members of the Pursers and Chief Stewards Association in good standing.

2. The Seniority List compiled by the Company and the Association shall be adhered to as far as possible; it being understood that in case a junior is promoted out of his turn, same shall not constitute seniority, except as provided for in Article 3. A copy of this list to be issued to each member, and to such other members as and when they may be added to the list.

3. All members of the Association must qualify and be suitable for the positions as they occur; and the Company reserves the right to determine such suitability. In the event of a vacant position being filled otherwise than in accordance with the Seniority List the Company agrees to discuss with and give reasons therefor to the Committee of the Association on request before confirming such appointment.

4. All members of the Association shall be given one day of twenty-four hours clear of the ship each week. In cases where members have to work part of their lay-over day, the time used in the Company's business shall be allowed to accumulate and added to their annual leave, in order to prolong employment during the winter months. It is understood that the Pursers shall keep a record of accumulated time and supply the management with this record weekly.

Employees having completed twelve (12) months accumulated service will be granted one week holiday with pay.

Employees having completed twenty-four (24) months accumulated service will be granted two weeks holiday with pay.

Such annual leave to be granted at the convenience of the service.

5. Continuity of employment to be taken care of by disrating the permanent staff, strictly in order of seniority, and by annual holidays to be taken as they can be mutually arranged. It is understood that all members wishing to take extra time off without pay in the winter months may do so at the convenience of the Company.

6. In case a member of the Association is required to join a ship at a distant port, the Company shall pay all travelling expenses and his time shall begin from the date of his departure to join the vessel.

7. It is agreed that a Wartime Cost of Living Bonus shall be paid to each employee at the rate of Seven (7) Dollars per month. Such bonus will be effective from March 1st, 1941 in the case of employees in the service of the Company on that date who are still in the service at the date of this Agreement; in the case of employees who have joined the service since March 1st, 1941, and are still in the service at the date of this Agreement, payment will be made for the time employed during such period.

The amount of Seven (7) Dollars is based on the index figure of 108, as measured by the Cost of Living Index prepared by the Dominion Bureau of Statistics for the Dominion of Canada as a whole.

Should the cost of living as determined by said Cost of Living Index increase by five points, or any multiple thereof, and should three months or more have elapsed from the date of the last determination of the bonus payment, the said bonus shall be increased by Five (5) Dollars per month for each said five point rise, such increase to apply from the first of the month immediately following the date of publication of the said Cost of Living Index showing such increase. In like manner should the cost of living decrease the bonus payable shall be accordingly decreased.

8. Members who are transferred from one vessel to another at the Company's convenience, where such necessitates a layover period awaiting ship, shall be compensated at the rate of pay on the vessel for which they are waiting.

9. Any member who takes a position in the Company's service not covered by this Agreement, shall on application to the Association, retain his seniority, during such special employment.

10. When any vessel relieves another temporarily the personnel of the relieving vessel covered by this Agreement shall assume the rate of pay of the relieved vessel, but when a vessel is replaced by a smaller vessel on account of decrease in traffic the lower rate shall apply.

11. This Agreement shall become effective First (1st) August, 1941.

The Scale of Pay as per attached Scale and Cost of Living Bonus as set out in paragraph seven (7) of this Agreement shall be in effect for the duration of the present War and six (6) months thereafter.

The Leave and Working Conditions embodied in this Agreement may be reopened for consideration at any time by either party giving sixty (60) days notice, such notice to be considered a period for negotiation.

For the Committee:

C. Stewart
A. Knight
R. Storr

For Union Steamships Limited:

_____
General Manager

August 1, 1941.

SCALE OF PAY

	Purser Basic Rate	Monthly Bonus	Chief Steward Basic Rate	Monthly Bonus	Freight Clerk Basic Rate	Monthly Bonus	Second Steward Basic Rate	Monthly Bonus (May 1-Aug.31)
Camosun	$150.00	$5.00	$125.00	$5.00	$115.00*	$5.00	$67.50	$7.50
Cassiar	135.00	5.00	95.00	5.00	---	---	---	---
Catala	150.00	5.00	125.00	5.00	90.00(Sr) 75.00	5.00	67.50	7.50
Cardena	150.00	5.00	125.00	5.00	90.00(Sr) 75.00	5.00	67.50	7.50
Venture	135.00	5.00	110.00	5.00	75.00	5.00 x	67.50 x	7.50
Chelohsin	135.00	5.00	110.00	5.00	75.00	5.00	67.50	7.50
Cynthia	115.00	5.00	100.00	5.00	75.00	5.00		
Cecilia	115.00	5.00	100.00	5.00	75.00	5.00		
Alexandra	115.00	5.00	100.00	5.00	75.00	5.00		
Capilano	105.00	5.00	90.00	5.00	75.00	5.00		
Lady Pam	100.00	5.00	85.00	5.00				
Lady Rose	100.00	5.00						

* Combination Freight Clerk and Wireless Operator.

x Not payable when vessel is on local run.

Alphabetical List of Pursers, Assistant Pursers, and Freight Clerks, 1920 - 1958

This list has been compiled from various sources, including ship registry files and personal acquaintances. While efforts have been made to be accurate, it is not to be taken as comprehensively complete and may have some errors, especially of omission.

Anderson, Clarence Alan
Anfield, Sidney
Anthony, Harvey
Atkinson, Jack

Barrowclough, C.W. "Joe"
Beaton, Raymond
Benson, Michael "Mike"
Berry, William A.
Bigger, Roger
Billingsley, Jim "Bo Bo"
Bergstrom, (?)
Bourne, Herbert A.
Boyd, William M.B.
Braddick, Harry J.
Brynand, Leonard F.
Busby, David

Chapman, Hugh
Charters, David
Coates, E. Darrel
Coldwell, Gordon
Coldwell, Randle
Collier, Ernest J.
Cook, Arthur
Cook, D.J.T. "Des"
Cook, Gordon P.
Crompton, Harold N.

Dean, Morris
Dudley, Leonard A.
Dutka, Henry "Hank"

Enwright, Eddie

Finlayson, Ron
Finnson, John F.
Foote, Gerry
Fordyce, George
    "Lonesome George"

Gerrard, John
Gill, Henry "Harry"
Goody, Fred
Green, Herbert
Greig, George
Guy, Charles "Charlie"

Hale, J.S. "Stew"
Halford, A. Cedric
Halliday, Ian
Hartford, Harold
Hatchen, Anthony Thomas
    "Tom"
Hughes, H.A. "Pinky"
Hunter, Stan

Ives, Harry

Jones, Gerry

Kelly, Joe (Rakowsky)
    "Little Joe"

Lannard, H.B.
Lawrence, Frank
Lawrence, Kenny
Lucas, Michael "Mike"

MacKenzie, Vernon F.
McCue, Philip "Phil"
McElroy, Neil
McLean, Sidney "Neil"
McLeod, Don
Miller, Norm
Moore, James A.
Morlock, Neil

Nelson, Don
Newman, Al
Nogarr, Frank O.

Opko, James Michael

Parsons, Leslie L.
Pattison, J.
Pattison, Norman G. "Pat" or
    "Paddy"
Perrott, Dennis
Pickerill, F.
Price, Lloyd
Procopio, Richard S. "Dick"

Rankin, William "Bill"
Read, George R.J.

Rennie, Gilbert "Gibb"
Richmond, James
Robinson, Amos W. "Robbie"

Shaw, Denis "Danny" or
    "Denny"
Shobridge, H. "Bert"
Showbridge, George W.
Simms, John
Skinner, Frank Jess
Smith, Les
Smith, Russell M.
Spence, G.
Stansfield, Jack
Stewart, Jerry
Stockland, Egolf
Storey, Jack
Stover, Reginald C. "Reg" or
    "Smokey"

Tracy, Steve "Dick"
Tozer, Allan H. "Hugh"
Twigg, A.M. "Art"

Van der Werff, Richard "Dick"
Van Hoove, Danny
Vanantwerp, Stanley
Victor, Bill

Walker, R.W. "Bob"
Waters, Bob
Watts, E.
Wiffen, (?)
Williams, Bob
Williams, Clarence
Williams, J. Wensley
Williams, Ozzie
Wood, Norrie
Wooster, H.J.
Wyllie, Patrick

Youdon, Ivan

Michael A. "Mike" Benson

Vancouver born and raised, Mike started with the Union Steamship Co. as a Freight Clerk on the *Lady Rose* on Sept. 1, 1941. It was a Saturday afternoon sailing and when Mike reported to the ship the only person he could find aboard was the cook, Les Gore. He looked at Mike and said, "You must be the new waiter." Mike said, "I don't think I am but if that's it, okay." Les handed him a white jacket and he went to work in the galley. This was straightened out a short time later out when Chuck McLean, who had hired Mike, came down to the ship for lunch. He looked at Mike and said, "Don't I know you?" Mike replied, "Yes, you hired me." "Well what the hell are you doing with a white jacket on, go and find the Purser, you're working for him," Chuck said. The Purser was Denis Shaw.

The next ship Mike worked on was the *Capilano II*. Working on the *Capilano* was difficult for any freight clerk because you had to stand up to do all your typing. Mike said, "I wasn't the best typist at any time and standing up trying to type made it even worse."

The purser on the *Capilano* wasn't impressed with Mike's work and indicated he didn't want him back, so Mike figured he was fired and never reported for work the next day. Soon the phone rang and it was Chuck McLean asking, "Where the hell are you, why aren't you down here?" Mike replied, "Well I thought I was fired." Chuck said, "I'm the only one who can hire and fire, so catch a cab and get right down here. We will hold the ship for you." Mike came right down and thus began a 16-year career with the Union Steamship Co. He was very successful over the years with the Company, rising from Freight Clerk to Freight Traffic Manager.

Mike next worked under Purser Neil Morlock, of whom Mike said, "He was a great fellow and as for any success I had with the Company I must give him lots of credit."

After getting some experience on the Day Boats, Mike was told to report to the *Cardena* to work under the famous Pat Pattison. Harry Braddick was the Assistant Purser.

Up until then, Mike hadn't had time to get a regulation Company uniform and he was told to get one before he went aboard the *Cardena*. Nobody told you anything about where and how to get a uniform, so Mike went up to Woodward's and purchased a double-breasted blue suit, and had Union Steamships brass buttons sewed on. (I know all about that because I went through the same routine, though I went to Eaton's. You were sent to the Company Store and they handed you some brass buttons and your single gold and white Purser braid for your sleeve and you were on your own from there. Nobody told you that Gordon Campbell Ltd. was the official supplier of uniforms.)

Mike came down to the *Cardena* that evening to find and meet his new boss, Pat Pattison. Pat took one look at him and asked, "Who the hell are you?" Mike said,

Mike Benson, Purser, S.S. *Catala*.

"I'm your new Freight Clerk." "What, dressed like that?" Pat exclaimed, "Oh well, all right, go up to the freight office and get the freight bills."

Mike went up and introduced himself to Harry Braddick, the Assistant Purser, who was already sorting the bills of lading. Harry said, "Get yourself down to the gang plank, and take this ticket punch. Ask the people coming aboard to show you their tickets, but for God's sake don't punch them, just make sure they are getting aboard the right ship." Pattison always insisted that all tickets be punched by himself as he had a special punch which punched out the letter P.

Off to the gang plank he goes and does his job the best he could. At one point, along comes this great big, rather casual and sloppily dressed man with an old, beat-up suitcase. Mike asked him for his ticket. The man said, "I don't need a ticket." "Is that right, why?" Mike asked. The fellow said, "Because I work on this boat." Mike wasn't so sure about this and he asked, "What do you do?" With a big laugh the fellow said, "I'm the Captain, believe it son," and walked on up the gang plank, leaving Mike a little shocked. It was the famous Captain Jack Boden.

The war had started and in October, 1942 Mike made application to join the navy. He started serving in January, 1943 and was discharged in December, 1945 after he had spent two and a half years aboard corvettes on North Atlantic convoy duty.

Upon receiving his discharge, Mike arrived back home at the CPR train station and when he was walking out to catch a taxi cab, unbeknown to him, Harold Crompton, a Union Company official, happened to be driving by and saw him. Mike no sooner got home when the phone rang and it was Harold saying, "Welcome home, when can you go to work? Tomorrow?"

Sure enough Mike went to work next day as Assistant Purser on the *Cardena*. The Company kept the seniority rating for everyone who had joined up. Next summer he was Purser on the day boats. He was on the Day Boats for about a year and then went back on to the *Cardena*, as Purser. He also served as Purser on the *Venture*, the *Chelohsin* and the *Catala*.

Mike recalled one amusing incident that took place on the Stuart Island-Manson Landing route. The incident happened between Lang Bay and Stillwater. There was this funny little man who had a wee farm and he used to come out in his rowboat to meet the Union boat and they would pass out through the ship's shell doors his little bit of freight, along with some mail and papers. This took place on a regular basis. Periodically he would order two bales of hay, which he would somehow take away in his little rowboat. On this occasion he had ordered two bales of hay and as well a bundle of horseshoes. As usual, he came out in his row boat and the ship stopped. He positioned himself alongside and under the ship's booms. The winchman lowered each bale of hay over the side, slowly and carefully. He set one bale of hay on the front of his rowboat and one on the stern, so he could sit in the middle and row back to shore. Once the hay was loaded, he looked up and asked, "Ha' ye got some horseshoes for me as well?" Sure enough, a deckhand found four or five horseshoes wired together in a bundle. He picked them up, leaned over the ship's side and endeavored to drop them onto a bale of hay in his wee boat. He missed! The horseshoes hit the bottom of the rowboat and went right on through. Suddenly, water was gushing up and the poor little fellow realizing his plight, took to his oars. The last Mike saw of him, he was rowing like crazy with this fountain of water coming up between his legs trying to get close to shore and shallow water, before his rowboat sank. No doubt there was a claim made against the Union Steamships on that one!

In 1948 Mike came ashore to work as Assistant Wharf Agent under Al Newman. In 1950 he transferred over to Frank Waterhouse and Co. and went to work in their freight traffic department. Two years later, Sterling Beek resigned and Mike took over his position as Assistant Manager of

Frank Waterhouse and Co. under Rap Solloway. Then a merger took place between the Union Steamship Co. and Frank Waterhouse Co. and Mike was appointed to the position of Freight Traffic Manager.

Mike remembers the horror when the Compnay hired an efficiency expert 1955 as business was not going too well. One of the first things he did was to paint the ships in psychedelic pastel colours, light blues, greens and reds, etc. Mike commented, "God knows how many thousands of dollars this cost!" The ships became a laughing stock up and down the coast. The old familiar black hull, white superstructure, and the black and red funnel disappeared after nearly 70 years. Coastal people didn't recognize the ships in their new circus type dress.

Mike stayed with the Company until early in 1957, and then left to pursue another career because he, along with others, could see the writing on the wall. The Union Steamship Co. was unlikely to survive much longer.

Gordon Coldwell

Gordon's father was Charles V. "Trix" Coldwell, who was a Purser on the *Cassiar I*, prior to the 1920s and later became the well-known Port Steward and Purchasing Agent for the Company. His older brother Randall also did the odd trip as Freight Clerk aboard the Union Ships, but not on a regular basis.

Stew Hale, Purser on the *Chelohsin* in 1939, says that Gordon was sent out with him to be trained as a Freight Clerk. However Stew reports that Gordon must have enlisted with one of the services before he started with the Union Company for he was soon called up. He enlisted in the airforce and became a pilot officer. He had done 21 missions and then was shot down over Denmark.

Phil McCue, a purser with the Company at this time, recalled that Charlie Coldwell had noticed one day that Phil was not

Freight Clerk
Gordon Coldwell

wearing a uniform cap, so he offered to let Phil, who hated to wear a hat of any kind, have his son's cap, but it was a poor fit and Mr. Coldwell's kind gesture had to be rejected, much to Phil's relief.

Harold Norman Crompton

Purser
Harold Crompton
(Mrs. H. Crompton)

Harold was born Dec. 18, 1913 in Vancouver, where he also attended school. He came out of school in the depression years when getting a job was next to impossible, but in 1934 he was sent down to the Union dock by a friend, who had a friend, etc., who was supposed to have some influence. The only job he landed was longshoring, which he did for one day, and then obtained a job aboard the *Venture* as a deckhand.

After one week he transferred departments aboard ship and sailed out as a steward. A week later he moved again and became a Freight Clerk in the Pursers Department. Two years later in 1936 he was Assistant Purser aboard the *Lady Alexandra*. He soon became a Purser, and during his eight years of sea time he served on every ship in the fleet.

Harold was serving as Assistant Purser aboard the *Catala* on Jan. 30, 1938 when she picked up an S.O.S. from a U.S. Navy plane having engine trouble. It was forced down into the ocean near Bella Bella. There were five airmen aboard and they were forced to abandon their plane and take to a rubber liferaft. Captain Findlay was Master of the *Catala* at the time, and he turned his ship around and went back to the area where the plane had gone down. A fishing vessel had picked up the airmen up from their raft and when the *Catala* arrived the men were transferred to the *Catala*. Harold took several photographs of this rescue and these pictures, along with his story, received wide coverage in the New York Times of the day.

In 1942, Crompton went ashore and worked in the Traffic Department of Frank Waterhouse & Co. A short time later he rejoined the Union Steamship Ltd. as Assistant Freight Agent. In 1946 he became Assistant Traffic Manager and in August 1951 was made Passenger Traffic Manager. In 1955 he succeeded Gerald Rushton and became General Traffic Manager.

All this was hard work but he had some good luck in 1959. He had the rare good fortune to win $23,000 in the Irish Sweepstakes!

Harold covered all bases with the Union Steamship Co. and he said, "I feel very fortunate in this regard. I was on every route. I was in the freight end of the business and ended up in the passenger side of the business." He is credited with setting up exclusive cruise ship voyages and Gerald Rushton refers to him in his book, *Whistle Up The Inlet*, as the "Dean of local traffic men in those years."

At that stage in his career Harold was a member of the Passenger Mens Association of B.C. and became President of that group in 1949, presaging his many other outside activities during his very active career. He belonged to the Terminal City Club and in 1962 was elected its President, after which he was a life member. He also was a Director of the B. C. Automobile Club and served as President of it in 1978-80, and was a director of the Vancouver Tourist Association and member of the Board of Trade.

Crompton says the *Catala* was his favourite ship. He felt she was the flagship of the fleet. For one reason, she had the best passenger accommodation, with outside cabins, and a walk-around covered deck. He also recalled the head cook on the *Catala* served beautiful chocolate eclairs every Sunday and a lovely clam chowder soup, southbound, after leaving Prince Rupert.

From his early years when he was Purser aboard the *Lady Rose*, Harold recalls a story about Denis Shaw, who at that time was a steward. Harold recalls him being an enterprising young fellow, for one day he came along and asked Harold if he would mind if he sold a few papers and magazines aboard the ship. Harold thought it would be alright, so Denis began to sell a few papers and magazines. He soon noticed that when passengers left the ship at stops along the way, they very often left the papers and magazines behind, so he would whip around and gather them all up and resell them! All went well until Denis came to Harold one day in his office and said, "I notice you have to spend a lot of time just sitting down at your desk typing etc. so would you mind if I brought up some of the crumpled papers and magazines and put them under your chair cushion to flatten them out so I can sell them again?"

Another favourite story of Harold's is the time a shipment of five steers were to be shipped aboard the *Chelohsin* for a destination up coast. Preparations for shipping these animals were made between decks on the ship. Five stalls were put together to stable these animals. The plan was to walk and lead them aboard, one by one and put them into a stall. They were brought down from the Interior in a truck and of course they were pretty agitated, having to ride in a truck all the way to Vancouver. The truck pulled into the wharf and stopped at the designated loading doors. They were to walk these steers down and off the truck, and then lead them aboard the *Chelohsin* on a plank ramp, through the ships shell doors and into their stalls between decks. So, one at a time, follow the leader, the cattle were coaxed up this ramp. The lead animal going aboard was very nervous, as were the others following, and when it got between decks it saw daylight ahead. The shell doors on the starboard side of the *Chelohsin* had been left open to let fresh air in and offer some daylight for the men working there. Seeing daylight, the lead steer bolted, right across the deck and out the door into the ocean. And then the others followed!

What a panic and commotion that brought about! Now they had five steers in the salt chuck, swimming wildly about in every direction and heading out into the inlet. Quickly the crew, assisted by the longshoremen, lowered the *Chelohsin*'s life boats and chased after them. One doesn't need much imagination to picture this scene: it was pandemonium with lots of yelling and laughter.

Finally the animals were herded back to the Union dock and somehow were retrieved, all except one. It somehow got over to Pier H next to the Union dock and when it was pulled out of the water onto the dock, it escaped again and managed to get itself under a railway car on the dock. It took a lot of time and effort to round up these steers. Needless to say they didn't sail on the *Chelohsin* that trip, but were shipped out on her next run, with a big sigh of relief.

Harold resigned from the Union Steamship Co. in 1956. He felt, and could see, the end for the company was near. In his opinion the owners didn't seem to be interested in the business. There had been no capital expenditures and the equipment was very old. It would be hopeless to try and bring all the facets of the Company back to efficient and profitable levels. Harold felt there was no hope for it to survive. Prospects for the future were very dim.

That same year Harold went over to Coast Ferries as Manager but moved again in 1962 to Island Tug and Barge, one of Seaspan's predecessor companies, as manager of general freight service, while also serving as President of the Terminal City Club.

Harold retired from Seaspan in 1979 after a very long and distinguished career on the Vancouver waterfront.

Henry Thomas "Hank" Dutka

Ass't. Purser Henry "Hank" Dutka, S.S. *Chelohsin* 1947

Henry was born in Fernie, B.C. on July 31, 1923. He came to the coast in 1946 and joined the Union Steamships, starting as Freight Clerk on the *Lady Cecilia*. He was soon moved over to the *Chelohsin* which was on the logging camp run at the time. Don McLeod was the Purser. The logging camp run was one of the most demanding jobs for the Freight Clerks, yet Henry said he liked it better than any other.

Campbell River was usually their second stop and it was a big one. Lots of freight and passengers, mostly loggers who were often very boisterous with drink. Henry commented that they used to take up the payroll for the Elk River Timber Co. and the wharfinger, Reg Masters at the time, would sign for it, then just throw the bag under his little desk while the work of unloading the ship went on.

On this logging camp run the loggers were always coming and going. Most of the time they would be partying and that usually caused problems for the ship's crew. Henry recalls on one trip a riot broke out in the second class area. Rooms were badly damaged, furniture was smashed and plumbing was broken. Captain Roach had to phone ahead to the RCMP in Campbell River to have them come aboard and take the fellows off the ship.

Don McLeod, one of the well-known Company Pursers, made a lot of friends while he was on this run. They would come aboard and ply him with drinks. He couldn't handle it and there were times, it is said, he hardly knew his own name.

Henry recalls being aboard the *Cardena* when she was relieving on this route and when Captain Bob Wilson collapsed on the bridge. There was no doctor aboard and Don McLeod as the Purser radioed to the office who put him in touch over the phone with a doctor. From the symptoms Don gave him, the doctor said it was his heart. The ship rushed full speed to Campbell River where Captain Wilson was taken to the hospital, but he died there. [219] Henry said, "When we pulled away from Campbell River on that trip we were all feeling shocked and saddened over the death of our skipper." Henry felt that Captain Wilson was one of the finest Masters he had sailed under.

Henry reminisced and recalled the following incident which took place at Dawson's Landing: "It was late in the evening. We were busily unloading our freight and two fellows approached Don McLeod the Purser, to see if they could get immediate access to a shipment of liquor consigned to them at a stop further on up the inlet. Don told them this would be difficult because of all the freight that would have to be moved to get their items, but he told them to go and ask the 2nd Mate who was in charge of the unloading. The 2nd Mate was Nick Nicolson. They wanted their liquor right now because they were half sloshed to start with. They went to see Nick and he said 'No, because we would have to move too much other freight to get at your shipment.' They got very mad and started to argue with Nick and soon a fight started. Nick wasn't a very big fellow and he was soon knocked down. He picked himself up, brushed off his uniform, straightened his cap and went on with his job, but the fellows never got their liquor."

Another story Henry told was about a shipment of meat destined for H.O. Sacht at Sayward. It couldn't be found while they were unloading at Sayward. As the *Cardena* was pulling away from Sayward, the deck crew up forward were pulling in the head line and had to move a big canvas tarpaulin out of the way and underneath they found the five boxes of meat. What to do now? They could wire back to Mr. Sacht to see if he would want them to put it off at their next stop so he could pick it up there, or if not, sell it to someone else. On this occasion they managed to sell it to the Port Neville Logging Co. In so doing the Company avoided a loss and Mr. Sacht would be sent a double order next trip. All this would be reported to the Company Office on what was called the O. S. & D. Report, filed by the Pursers Dept. on every trip. O. S. & D. stands for Over, Short and Damaged. This piece of business of selling the meat rather than let it spoil would save the Claims Agent, the dapper Mr. McIllrath, a lot of trouble.

In 1951 Henry was approached by Al Newman, the Freight Agent on the dock, to see if he would like to leave the ships and become a checker on the wharf. Henry jumped at the chance to leave the ships because he was married and had a little daughter. Being away on the ships wasn't the best of situations when there was family to raise. So Henry came ashore and became a member of the Wharf Checkers Union. When the Company went under in 1959, he just switched over to checking deep sea ships.

Though the Company's business had been in decline for several years, its closure still came as a shock to many employees. Henry has given me a graphic description of what happened down on the dock. Here is Henry's story: "In the middle of December 1958 the Company had a survey done, they brought in this efficiency expert and we were told that for the amount of cargo we handled, with the amount of people we had, we were ahead of any other Company on the coast, 2 to 1. Further, at the time I happened to be having a coffee with the accountant for the Company and he told me that we had had a good year and as well, everyone was going to get a raise in the New Year. At Christmas time they threw a special party for a few of us. Ted Eakins, the Personnel Manager, came down onto the dock to tell us about it. That was Dec. 24, 1958. Being the junior man I was the last one to leave work that day and as I was getting into my car, along comes this fellow Chestnut, and he said that everything was going fine and wished me a Merry Christmas. As well he said, 'We are really going to do big things in the New Year.' Comes the New Year and who comes walking down the dock but a fellow by the name of Hargraves who worked for Captain Terry and announced to everyone, 'The Union Steamship Co. no longer exists and that you are now working for Northland Navigation Co.' Just like that! We were stunned."

On Jan. 8, 1959, Captain Roach was docking the *Catala* at the Union dock from her upcoast run and little did he know it would be the last time as a Union ship. The Company was finished and they would now be working for Northland Navigation. Wee Angus McNeill was heart sick with the news.

Captain Billy McCombe also received a shock for he was bringing the *Cassiar* into port with 125 tons of frozen fish and there wasn't anybody around to tell him where to take this load of fish. The only man around was the wharf policeman and he knew nothing. He said to Captain McCombe, "They probably don't even know you are out." [220]

What an ignominious end for this fine old company and how shabbily the employees were handled. As Henry said, in his opinion, "It was a raw deal and politics played a big hand in the whole thing." Henry was asked by Bill Scott, who was in charge of the wharf checkers, if he would stay on to help clear up the leftover freight. He did so and was there until the end of February 1959.

Being a member of the Marine Checkers, Henry just stepped over to doing deep sea work. Then he started doing a lot of their paper work and checking MacMillan Bloedel ships. From there he was "super cargo" for M.B. Again he was away from home a lot so he came back to marine checking, ending up checking and working for the Pad Line. He retired in 1985.

Ron Finlayson

Ass't. Purser
Ron Finlayson
(Finlayson Collection)

Ron started his career with the Union Steamship Co. in 1946 as an office boy at age 17. He was promoted to the Freight Agents Office, but found he liked being on the boats. He had made friends with the News Agent on the *Lady Cynthia* who liked weekends ashore, so Ron would go aboard in his place over the weekends just for the fun of being at sea.

Finlayson applied for a job on the ships and went out on the *Lady Alexandra* as Freight Clerk in August 1947. He soon was on the northern routes under Robbie Robinson aboard the *Camosun III*. At this time Robbie was the senior purser in the fleet. Ron served on nearly all the ships, moving up the ladder to Assistant Purser and then finally he made a couple of trips as Purser on the *Lady Rose*. He left the Union Co. in April, 1950 and went work as a Purser aboard the White Pass Co. ships but returned to Union Steamships in January of 1952.

Ron was married in August of 1952 and at the same time he had just obtained the job of Assistant Agent at Prince Rupert, working under Frank Skinner. Ron came off the *Catala* on a Friday where he had been Assistant Purser under Frank Lawrence, was married on Saturday, and sailed on Monday with his bride to a new job and home in Prince Rupert. He recalls he and his wife had a marvellous honeymoon trip aboard the *Coquitlam*, with three of the most wonderful and colourful Union characters, Captain Billy McCombe, Chief Engineer Fred Smith (the biggest character of all!), and Purser Reg Stover.

Ron and his wife Phylis were at first doubtful about having to live in Prince Rupert, but they ended up loving their stay there. They were there for 11 years and during that time had five children.

After being in Prince Rupert for awhile, he found his relationship with the officers and crew aboard the Union ships changed completely, and he saw them all in a different perspective, usually favourable.

As we were talking about his days on the Union ships, he was reminded about how Wee Angus McNeill was always very strict and careful when a coffin was to be brought aboard ship. The coffin would always be draped with a Canadian flag and the winchman was given strict instruction to run the winches very carefully and not to jerk the line, and as well, all crewmen were required to remove their hats.

Captain McCombe, a favourite of Ron's, really liked his herring. When they were in season and his ship docked somewhere where there were fishing boats tied up, Captain McCombe would send his quartermaster over to a boat with a couple of pails. The fishermen all knew that Captain McCombe was one Captain who always tried to avoid slicing their nets, particularly in Johnstone Straight, and would readily fill his two buckets with fresh herring.

Another favourite McCombe story took place on the *Catala* at Ocean Falls. There was a navy ship tied up to the paper dock and the *Catala* was at the government wharf. The navy ship was scheduled to leave at 8 a.m. and the *Catala* at 9. They were down having breakfast and Captain McCombe said to Ron, "Slim, come up to the bridge and watch this navy vessel try to back out." Between the two docks there was a flow of water from the dam which was referred to as "the tail" race. As the navy ship started to move out it backed into the "tail race" and proceeded to get in one helluva mess. Captain McCombe said, "See that, those silly bastards, all gold braid and no experience!"

Another story Ron told was about Chief Officer B. Owen-Jones or Curly as he was known, and Purser Don McLeod. Curly used to smoke rollings which Don thought was unbecoming of an officer. He should smoke tailor-mades at least! At 3 a.m. one morning on the *Chelohsin*, Ron was down having a coffee and Curly had come down to have his breakfast. He brought down his tin of Player's tobacco, put it on the table, and went into the galley to order his breakfast. At that moment Don McLeod came down, saw the can of tobacco and fired it out the porthole and quickly disappeared. When Curly came back and found his tobacco gone, of course he accused Ron. Ron didn't know what to do but denied doing such a thing. Finally Curly said, "Was Don McLeod down here?" Ron said, "Yes." "I knew it, I knew it, I'll kill him, I'll kill him," he shouted. Needless to say Don McLeod stayed out of Owen-Jones' way for the rest of the trip.

Ron could see in 1957 that the fortunes of Union Steamships were failing and when Northland Navigation offered him a job in Prince Rupert as their Agent, he took it. He stayed another five years in Prince Rupert, then he was transferred to Northland Operations in Vancouver. Ron now lives in Surrey and is Manager of Passenger Licensing, Motor Carrier Branch of B.C.

Gerald Cleland "Gerry" Foote

Purser/ Wireless Operator "Gerry" Foote *(Ashmore Collection)*

Gerry was born in Victoria in 1893 and his career at sea lasted for 47 years. He followed the footsteps of his father, Captain John Calvin Foote, who began his career at sea on sailing ships out of Yarmouth, Nova Scotia. He sailed these vessels to China by way of the Cape of Good Hope. On one occasion his ship, on a return run from China, made a call at Victoria, B.C. After visiting Victoria he decided he would settle in that beautiful city, did so and eventually became a B.C. Coast Pilot operating out of there.

Gerry studied and received his licence as a Marconi radio operator and went to sea at an early age, quickly experiencing a memorable adventure. He was aboard the S.S. *Canadian Importer* when it sailed from Vancouver on Aug. 5, 1921 with a cargo of lumber. She began to list badly and on Aug. 19 was on her side with a 41 degree list.

Gerry's despatching radio went out of order, but they had a small battery auxiliary receiving set which was still working. The ship soon floundered, and not being able to send out distress signals they decided to send a crew out in a whaleboat in an attempt to reach San Francisco 680 miles away.

Several ships searched for the *Importer* and all gave up but one. Captain Cooper on the S.S. *Observer* on Aug. 31 noticed a small light on the horizon. Gerry's receiving set feebly began to click with a message, "I think I see your light, keep it burning." The crew aboard the *Importer* poured gallons of paint onto the lumber they had been burning, enough to shame a volcano. The *Observer* finally caught up to them and came alongside at daybreak.

A San Francisco towboat, the *Sea Lion*, which had put out to sea trying to locate the Importer, spotted a flare on the evening of Sept. 2 from the men in the whaleboat. They were only 100 miles from San Francisco and in another day would have reached their destination!

In the meantime, three other ships including the *Algerine* and the *Canadian Winner* had gathered alongside the Importer to give assistance. A tow line was rigged up and they proceeded towards Victoria. The *Sea Lion* later joined the contingent and they all arrived in Victoria on Sept. 13, 1921 to a huge welcome. Quite an experience for the 28-year-old wireless operator! [221]

Details of Foote's career after that are sketchy but we do know that he worked for both the CPR and the CNR steamship lines. He was working aboard the CNR's *Prince Robert* on a Caribbean run before World War II broke out. When the war started Gerry came over to the Union Steamship Co. when they took over the operation of the *Prince John* and the *Prince Charles*.

About this time Gerry took to writing feature articles for weekend supplements of newspapers, using a pseudonym of Jeremiah Sparks. Unfortunately none of these stories could be found for they likely would have told us a great deal about life aboard our early coastal ships.

Gerry served most of his time aboard Union Steamships in a dual capacity as a Purser and Wireless Officer. During his years with the Company he served aboard the *Camosun II*, the *Cassiar II*, the *Catala* and even one month on the old *Venture*. His last Union ship was the new *Chilcotin*. He was aboard her on its maiden voyage in May 1947. His selection for this position on a new ship and a new venture for the Company was carefully considered by Harold Crompton, who was in charge of setting up this new cruise business. Harold consulted with Frank Skinner, the Company Agent in Prince Rupert, and asked him for his opinion. Frank said, "You've got the best man in Gerry Foote for the job." Another reason for his selection was the fact that Gerry had had plenty of previous experience with American Customs procedures and the *Chilcotin* would be entering U.S. waters and ports in Alaska.

I obtained a copy of Gerry's Seaman's Discharge Book from his son, David. The last entry shows him signing off the U.S.S. *Chilcotin* in September 1953. His son also sent me a copy of a letter he received from his father written when he was Purser aboard the *Catala*, dated Jan. 6, 1956. It is obvious, then, that he worked for the Union ships until they ceased operating in December 1958. He probably didn't bother to have his discharge book filled in. There is a gap of one year and then in May 1960 he joined the Alaska Cruise Lines as Purser/Cruise Director on the *Glacier Queen* for one season. Gerry did not go back to sea after that. He decided to go into real estate and was an agent in West Vancouver until his eyesight failed and he couldn't drive his clients around. He retired in 1967.

I sailed as Assistant Purser to Gerry on the *Cassiar II* in the latter part of 1942. Gerry left you to do your job without bossing you around. One thing I noticed about Gerry at the time was the fact that he always moved very slowly. I learned later that he suffered with an inner ear problem which upset his balance if he moved quickly. This was a temporary disability which he overcame.

Gerry's wife predeceased him in 1970 so he sold his home in West Vancouver and moved to Calgary to live with his daughter. He passed away in Calgary on Oct. 29, 1976 at the age of 83.

J. S. "Stew" Hale

Stew was born 1909 in Portland, Ore., and the family moved to North Vancouver in 1919. He attended school in North Vancouver and graduated in 1925. He went to university in 1926 but found he couldn't afford to continue so in 1927 he joined Union Steamships as a porter. He made one trip aboard the *Catala* under Chief Steward Bert Ebden then transferred over to the *Cardena* to train as a Freight Clerk under Purser N.G. "Pat" Pattison. He recalls a joke going the rounds aboard the *Cardena* at the time and it was that the N.G. initials stood for "No Good" Pattison. Further, some even put a B after the N.G., according to Stew.

On August 22, 1927, the *Cardena* came to the rescue of the CNR ship *Prince Rupert*, which had gone aground on the famous Ripple Rock. The *Cardena* was able to pull the Prince Rupert off the rock and into sheltered waters. Her passengers and mail were then transferred to the *Cardena*. Stew was the Freight Clerk but he was down below in his bunk catching up on his sleep. So he slept through the whole affair. I said to Stew, "My gosh, history was being made and you didn't bother to get up to see it." Stew said, "I had been working for 24 hours straight and I just had to have some rest." I understood what he was saying as Freight Clerks often had to work long stretches without any relief.

In 1928 Stew was on the *Lady Alexandra* as Freight Clerk under Purser Al Newman, who later in his career was the Company Agent at Prince Rupert and then Freight Agent on the Vancouver wharf. Clarence Arthur was the Chief Engineer at the time, which seemed an odd ship for him to be on, for he was like a square peg in a round hole amongst all the young people who were travelling aboard her. Stew spent the next several years working as Freight Clerk aboard various ships.

Stew recalls one trip up north aboard the *Cardena*, the Purser was Harry Gill and the Chief Steward was Harry Audley. It was Christmas time and they had brought their wives along. It was one long party. When the ship tied up at Prince Rupert they decided they all should go and call on the Company Agent in Rupert. Harry Gills' wife didn't want to go because she had heard that he dispensed drinks in a thimble!

1939 was the year of the Great Purge in the Company, and Stew was working on the *Chelohsin* under Purser Gibb Rennie when it all started. Head Office had became suspicious about the trip reports that certain Pursers and Chief Stewards were turning in after every voyage, so they began an investigation and started counting the passengers who disembarked from the various ships. They had a man stationed near the gang plank with a counter and with him was a man who could identify members of the crew. It seems that the number of passengers getting off ship wasn't matching the numbers of passengers the Pursers turned in on their trip reports. Other checks were made to compare the number of meal tickets and the number of meals served. That was only the beginning, as many other forms of cheating the Company began to come to light. As a result several men were discharged almost immediately, amongst them were Purser Gibb Rennie, Purser Pinky Hughes, and Chief Steward Fred Pickerell.

Stew was Freight Clerk on the *Chelohsin* when Rennie was fired, and Stew was called up to the office by the Manager, Carl Halterman, and told: "Stew, we have fired Gibb and I'm sure you know why, so we want to put you on the *Chelohsin* as Purser in his place right away. We're going to put you on her for one solid year because we want to have a complete record of the figures for a year and this job must be done right." So Stew was promoted to Purser and was moved ahead of other fellows who were senior to him. He felt badly and most disturbed about this but this was management's doing and he carried out their wishes to the letter. There were protests but the Company disregarded them as they wanted to stop all the cheating and thievery once and for all. It has been said for instance that the ships' bags of dirty laundry being put off at Prince Rupert for cleaning often contained food of all description from the ships' stores. Payment or some sort of exchange would often be returned in the clean laundry bags brought back.

Stew tells a story he heard about how Bert Ebden, a Chief Steward, was discharged. The CPR had its triangle run, Vancouver, Victoria, and Seattle. Well the Union Steamships had its own triangle run. It was Prince Rupert, Anyox, Stewart. Each one of these towns had its own Red Light district and the girls were travelling steadily between these ports and as well, to have weekly medical check-ups with a doctor. Bert was under suspicion by Company officials and in the course of checking him out they went through his room aboard ship and found a Christmas gifts list that Bert had made out and many of the names on it were of these prostitutes. Alongside the names were the gifts they were to receive from Bert, like a turkey or a ham. It was obvious to company officials where these hams and turkeys were to come from, so Bert was discharged along with many others during this purge.

When Stew was made Purser on the *Chelohsin* his pay was $135 a month, which was still a substantial sum in the Depression. He obtained his Pursers job because of the purge and as he said, "I didn't want any job in this manner, but it was obvious that things were not right. There was no question about it." Stew recalls well how some of the cheating took place, which he described to me this way:

"A system for accounting of the second class meals was this: the deck passengers were expected to go up to the Pursers Office and buy a meal ticket, but this method often proved cumbersome. So the 2nd cook took an empty tin can, a gallon size, around to the table in the 2nd class mess. Each passenger tossed in 50 cents. The 2nd cook turned this in to the Chief Cook, he turned it in to the Chief Steward and he in turn gave it to the Purser, who gave it to the Company. The Company, in due course probably remitted the proceeds to England.

"This had the healthy effect of keeping the Chief Steward economical as he didn't want their meal cost to appear excessive compared to receipts.

"On the logging camp run and on the day boats, the meals were not included in the fare and passengers ate in the saloon. The stewards were very friendly and would inform them they would have to buy a meal ticket from the Purser. The stewards often volunteered to go up and get their tickets for them. On quiet afternoons there would be only one man in the saloon and that's the way he would break the monotony. It was good exercise too.

"There was a coffee counter on some of the day boats. They had cash registers which somehow didn't work very well. Some of the pursers were still on board after everyone else had gone ashore, setting their machines back to zero and ringing up their machines with the proper amount for the day's receipts. They muffled the noise with a blanket so as not to disturb anyone!"

Things began to quieten down and Stew stayed aboard the *Chelohsin* as Purser. On one occasion he had Don McLeod and Ian Halliday with him as freight clerks. They were just learning their jobs and one of them accepted a deer at Menzies Bay to be delivered to Campbell River en route. Due to a change of watch this piece of freight was overcarried. There was no way the Company would pay a claim on such a shipment, so when they arrived in Vancouver Stew phoned back to the person in Campbell River who was supposed to receive this deer, explained what had happened and asked if he would accept a bottle of scotch in settlement. Yes that would be fine, so Stew announced to the fellows, "We've got ourselves a deer." The second cook was brought into the act and he cut up the deer into roasts and chops, etc. Word was spread around on the dock, so the wealth was shared with everyone.

Years later, coming down from Sechelt, Captain Bob Naughty was on the bridge. Don McLeod, who was now a Purser, took Stew up and introduced him to Captain Naughty. Don said to Captain Naughty, "Let me introduce you to Stew Hale, a former Purser on the *Chelohsin*, and let me tell you the kind of Purser he was. Whenever we overcarried freight he made us eat it." This was of course a reference to the over-carried deer some years back.

Often there was trouble with drunken loggers. Following is one incident that Stew related to me: "Late at night I was catching up on my paper work while things were quiet. A passenger with nothing else to do heckled me about something, probably wanted a berth and the ship was full. He was obnoxious and kept coming back. I tried to shoo him away, but it wasn't working, so I tried to goad him into starting something. and if he did the crew would escort him away and he would be hopelessly outnumbered. He was cunning enough to stick to verbal violence, even though I couldn't fight my way out of a paper bag, not even a wet one.

" 'If you didn't have that uniform on, I would sock you,' he said. So I took off my uniform jacket. 'You still have the pants on.' So I slipped them off. 'You're still on the ship's property,' he said. 'Oh, you've too many excuses,' I said, and politely led a weak one with my left. At this moment Harry Carl, one of the waiters, came up the alleyway and was delighted to see me in my shorts and shirt-tails. What the heck, there were no women aboard. We all had a good laugh, and no harm done. It was the day's topic of conversation."

Stew was purser on the *Capilano* in 1940 when she lost her propeller in Howe Sound. A big tug, which he thinks was the Masset, towed the *Capilano* back into Gibsons. The Company had to send another ship up to take all the passengers back to Vancouver.

In 1941 Stew was moved into the Stores Department on the Vancouver wharf as assistant to Charlie Coldwell. Not long after, he was moved again up to Sechelt to work as assistant to Bert Hackett, the Company's Agent there. He was there for the most part of 1942, then he joined the army. When the war was over, Stew did not go back to the Union Company. One day when he was looking for work he ran into Bill Munro who had been a freight clerk on the Union ships and then went ashore to eventually become Paymaster. He steered Stew onto the Marine Checkers and Stew obtained a job as checker on La Pointe Pier. Eventually stew was made Head Checker, a position he held for seven years. When Stew was in his eighties he still was getting calls to do the odd job on the docks. He passed away in April 1994.

Harry Ives

Freight Clerk Harry Ives on the *Lady Cynthia* (M. Clement)

Harry started with the Union Steamships in June 1929. He went aboard the *Lady Alexandra,* with Stew Hale, to train as a

Freight Clerk. The Purser at the time was Al Newman, who later became Wharf Freight Agent. The *Lady Cecilia* was his next ship and he was aboard her for a long time.

In the early days there were only two men in the Pursers Office so the Freight Clerk had to put in some pretty long hours. One occasion he recalled he had had very little sleep and when the ship docked in Vancouver it was early in the morning and he was fast asleep. The next thing he heard was Captain Boden pounding on his door, wanting Harry to get up and unlock the mail room locker door. You don't argue with the Captain and he was a man you wouldn't dare cross, but Harry barked right back at him, "Open it yourself, I've had very little sleep!" Boden thought this was a great joke and roared with laughter over being told what to do by a junior officer.

Harry recalled Paddy Farina, the Chief Engineer, and how he would help all the pregnant wives aboard ship who were going to Vancouver to have their babies. Then, when they were coming back home with their new baby, it was ritual, Paddy carried the little ones up the gangplank.

Harry's favourite ship was the *Lady Evelyn*. He says she was like a yacht. One time while taking tickets at her plank, a lady stopped, looked at the *Evelyn* and said, "I know this ship, where did she come from?" (The *Evelyn*, formerly named the *Deer Hound*, had been brought around from the St. Lawrence River.) When she was told this she exclaimed, "Yes, I was aboard the *Empress of Ireland* and she grounded in the St. Lawrence. This was the ship that came alongside and took all her passengers off! Fancy finding her out here!"

One trip on the *Venture*, coming out of the Skeena River they hit a rock and put a hole in her, but were able to limp into Prince Rupert. However they had picked up all the Chinese cannery crews going out at the season's end. When they heard and felt the *Venture* hit, they grabbed all their belongings, as well as two life jackets each and came crowding up to the forward passenger deck. Harry was in the Pursers Office and said, "If the ship had sunk, there would have been no way for me to get out of the office!"

Harry had made friends with Eric Suffield, who, he says, was a pretty good guy in those days. Eric had many nicknames tacked on him, and Harry refers to him as "Suffering Suffield." According to Harry, Eric never seemed to have any money and was always bumming cigarettes and matches. Also, he would come into the Pursers Office and help himself, if any were lying around. Harry had been given a box of cigars one trip and left them in the office, then he went down into the hold to check freight. Well, Eric came along, saw these cigars and helped himself to nearly all of them.

When Harry saw what had happened to his cigars he decided he had to do something about it, so he went up to a joke shop and bought an exploding cigar. Harry left this on his typewriter one day. When he returned it was gone and he knew who had taken it. The ship was docking at Sayward and Eric was on the bridge. He was in his element, strutting around on the bridge and smoking a cigar. As usual the wharf was crowded with people. Harry was at the gangplank waiting to go ashore with the manifest, with the ship only about five feet from the dock, when the cigar exploded. Eric's cap went flying and for a moment he was scared to death. As well of course, in front of all the people on the dock, he was embarrassed and furious. He came rushing down to the main deck. Harry saw him coming so he jumped ashore before the plank was out. Eric gave chase. Harry was light and could run like a deer and Eric was much heavier. He chased Harry all around the little village of Sayward, in and out of the woods, but he couldn't catch Harry. Captain Suffield soon tired himself out and had to rest, so Harry walked back to the ship. When the dust settled, Harry said they had a good laugh over the incident and their friendship endured.

Harry recalls how Captain Suffield loved to holler orders at people. On one occasion they were docking at Selma Park. It was one of those rough days and about all they could do was to put the ship's nose into the wharf. There were some empty oil drums to load, so the deck crew were just throwing them onto the fore deck. The last one missed and fell into the water and was floating away. Eric started to jump up and down, shouting orders, "Launch a life boat, get after that drum!" This was done as the drum was slowly drifting away. Two seaman got into the boat and started to row after it, with Eric urging them on, "Faster, faster." All of a sudden the fellows in the boat turned and rowed frantically to shore. Eric was beside himself. The row boat gradually was sinking lower and lower into the water. As it came close to shore, the two fellows jumped out and the boat sank! They had forgot to put the plug into the boat's drainage hole. So much for orders!

Harry left the U.S.S. Co. In 1935.

Gerald "Gerry" Jones

In late 1939 Gerry was working at Woodward's and when they offered him a raise of only 50 cents a week he decided to look elsewhere for a job. He went down to the Union Steamship Co. and was asked if he could type. He said he could. "How many fingers can you use?" he was asked. Gerry put up both hands and said, "I've got 10 and I use them all." He was hired right away and went out on the *Catala* as Freight Clerk the next day. This was quite unusual to go out on a northern run before having a week or so training on the Day Boats. He made two trips on the *Catala* with Purser Robbie Robinson then was moved over to the *Camosun* to work under Purser Smokey Stover. He stayed on this route until 1942 when he joined up and went overseas.

Returning to Vancouver when the war was over and before he was discharged, he went down to the Union dock to renew acquaintances and right away was asked if he could go to work tomorrow on the *Catala*. This was a surprise but he decided he would, however his old uniform wouldn't fit anymore so he went up to Regent Tailors to get a new one. They happened to have a uniform that had been hanging there for some time, belonging to Purser Danny Shaw. They gave it to Gerry. Three months later Gerry heard from Danny madder than hell about him having taken his uniform.

Gerry went out on the *Catala* and up until this trip they had been having a terrible time with their O. S. and D. report (Freight Over, Short and Damaged). On his first trip Gerry submitted a report with only one item short, a piece of meat, which was subsequently found in the cook's locker.

Gerry then went to the *Cardena* where "Old Pat" Pattison was the Purser. "Now there was a character," Gerry said. He then related a story about Pat, who was always looking for a deal. One time he went into the cannery store at Wadhams where the storekeeper was a good friend of his. Pat saw that he had some canned peas on sale at 15 cents a tin. He remarked on this to his friend, the storekeeper, who said, "Yeah, or two tins for 45 cents." Pat immediately said, "I'll take six tins at that price." It wasn't until he came back aboard ship that Pat

Purser "Gerry" Jones 1941

realized he had been taken!

Gerry recalled one trip on the *Cardena*. They were southbound on their way to Vancouver just beyond Cape Mudge, where they ran into a terrific storm and tide rip. A huge wave came over her bow and broke all the windows in the Observation Room and water poured into the ship, flooding the Pursers Office and running down both companion ways, six inches deep. Gerry says there was a group of fisherman aboard who went to work stuffing mattresses into the damaged windows. When it was all over, Pat turned to Gerry and said, "Please get my rubbers, I don't want to get my feet wet."

This particular trip of the *Cardena* received a lot of attention in 1989 when a passenger who had been aboard wrote about his experience for the *Westcoast Mariner* magazine and reported that the waves were 80 feet high! This prompted many more letters disputing the fact that waves that high were not possible in that location.

Soon Gerry was promoted to Purser on the day boats. His first stint as Purser was on the *Capilano*. Other ships that he sailed on as Purser were the *Lady Rose*, the *Lady Pam*, the *Lady Cecilia*, the *Lady Cynthia* the *Lady Alexandra* and one trip on the *Cardena*.

One unfortunate incident Gerry was involved in as Purser on the *Lady Pam* was when the Pursers Office was broken into while the *Pam* was tied up overnight at the Union dock.

All the ships in the fleet had a safe aboard and a cash drawer at the wicket. Upon returning to Vancouver at the end of a day trip, after the Purser had made up his trip report along with cash, etc. for the office, the ship's working cash was to be taken out of the cash drawer and deposited in the ship's safe for safekeeping overnight, ready for use next day. On this occasion Gerry had forgotten to put the cash away in the safe and when the thief jimmied the cash drawer they found about $140. Gerry didn't discover this until the *Pam* was out in the Gulf next day. A passenger happened to come along and wanted some money changed. As soon as he reached for the cash drawer Gerry could see it was damaged and upon opening it, found it was empty.

This was reported immediately to head office and at Gibsons Landing, their first stop, Gerry had to run up to the local cafe and borrow $40 in order to have some working cash for the trip. That night, the ship was met by two detectives and the whole crew was detained for questioning, but no suspect was found.

The police did pick up a suspect later in town, who had about the right amount of cash on him, who had been working on the ships and who had just got out of jail before joining the Company, but they couldn't prove anything against him so Gerry ended up having to pay back this money to the Company.

John Allan, who was in the deck crew of the *Pam* when this happened, confirms the incident. He also said a short time after this robbery, his own wallet was stolen aboard the *Pam*. He says there was a suspect but nothing could be proven and a short time later, this particular person departed the ship and was never seen again.

After four years with the Company, Gerry left and went to work for B.C. Pulp and Paper Co. at Port Alice. Gerry worked at various locations for the Company and finally retired in 1982 from their New Westminster sawmill, having attained the position of Mill Accountant. He now lives with his wife Grace at Abbotsford. Recently Gerry has had to have part of his left leg amputated due to circulatory problems, but is very chipper and in good spirits despite this setback.

Joe "Little Joe" Kelly

Joe started with Union Steamships in November 1944, aboard the *Lady Alexandra* as Freight Clerk under Purser Denis Shaw. Joe is only about 5 ft. tall, so it was natural he became known as "Little Joe."

He served on many of the Union ships,

including the *Lady Alexandra*, *Cardena*, *Catala*, and the *Chelohsin*, as well as on the Waterhouse ships. He also made one trip on the CPR *Nootka*, which had been chartered by the Union Steamship Co. He worked his way up the line and eventually served as Purser on the *Chelohsin*.

When the war came along Joe was drafted into the army. When he left the army he worked for awhile switching railway cars for Evans Coleman and Evans, then he came back to the Union Steamship Co. and stayed with them until 1950. He was aboard the *Lady Cynthia* when she ran into and sank the Forestry Launch *A.L. Bryant* off Point Atkinson.

Joe tells an amusing story about the time he was Purser on the *Lady Alex* when they picked up a train load of Indians at Squamish, who were on their way to pick cherries at Chilliwack. Often a ship had to lay over at Squamish waiting for the arrival of the PGE train at the end of its line. At times there might be a two or three hour wait, so nearly everyone in the crew would have a sleep. On one occasion though a steward who was supposed to wake up the Purser and the Chief Steward when the train arrived failed to do so, consequently they were awakened by the noise of a bunch of people who had come aboard without being checked and found that the *Alex* was already on her way to Woodfibre.

Joe quickly ran up to the bridge and explained to the Captain what had happened. He asked the Captain to delay landing at Woodfibre until he had checked out all the passengers. With the help of the Chief Steward and the stewards, they blocked off the ship and started asking all the passengers for their tickets. The Indians all gave the same answer, "Oh, the Chief has got the tickets." So who and where was the chief, was the next problem. With a lot of hemming and hawing, they didn't know. Joe finally located him and asked, "Are you the Chief and how many of your people do you have on board?" "Oh," he said "About 75!"

Joe said, "Like hell, you've got about 150!"

"No," he said, "'I've got a hundred!"

Joe went down and punched out 100 tickets, but he wasn't so sure this was correct. He concluded that if the Chief didn't give the correct figure in the first place, he probably wouldn't do so a second time.

When the ship docked in Vancouver, who should be there waiting for the ship but Gerald Rushton, with a clicker in his hand to take a count of the passengers leaving the ship. Al Strang was on the bridge at the time and knew the predicament that Joe was in, so he pointed to the afterdeck gangplank, Joe nodded, and Al had the after gangplank quickly put out. Though Mr. Rushton was clicking away at one gang plank others were coming off the second plank, so Rushton's count would be useless. As Joe said, "I felt the 100 was a pretty fair count, but with the Chief having tried to mislead me in the first place I couldn't be sure."

When Joe went out on the northern run for the first time, he was astonished to see the casual way ingot bars of silver were loaded and stored aboard ship. They were just loaded onto a regular pallet board and stored between deck. Also, on another northern run aboard the *Cardena*, he was amazed to go down into the steerage section of the ship and witness Chinese crews on their way to the fish canneries openly smoking their opium pipes.

At one time the Union ships were making a regular call at Hyder, a U.S. port in Alaska near Stewart, B.C. In the winter there was always lots of snow and it was cold. Joe said he was surprised at the place, as the whole town seemed to be just pubs and bars. Members of the crew would often go up town and some would attempt to bring back a bottle of American liquor; some succeeded and others got caught.

The American Customs officer had a little shed on the dock. In cold weather he would look at you through a little window and wave you on your way uptown. Coming back he'd open a sort of Dutch door and ask you if you had anything to declare. Joe devised a clever little plan to get liquor back aboard ship. He bought two bottles, tied knots around the neck's of the bottles with a long piece of string and then wrapped the other end around his waist, under his coat. The two bottles would drag along behind him in the snow, about 20 feet back.

"Hi, have you got anything?" the Customs man would ask. Joe would wave his hands and say "No." The fellow would wave him on and shut his little door. Joe would be 20 or 30 feet from the shed as these two bottles were dragging behind in the snow, which of course the Customs man wouldn't see from behind his frosted window.

Little Joe was a well-known and liked personality aboard the Union ships. He had a cheery disposition and was always ready with a quick quip or joke. He left the Company in 1950 and since 1965 has been selling real estate in Vancouver.

Frank Leonard Lawrence

Purser Frank Lawrence

Frank was Purser on the *Lady Pam* when he experienced one of his most anxious moments. There were only a few passengers on board and the ship had just made her last call at Port Mellon before heading to Vancouver. He was in his office typing away at his desk, which was away from the Pursers' wicket and situated under the stairs going to the upper deck. Then he heard this lady's faint little voice at the wicket asking, "Excuse me sir, is there a stateroom on board?"

Frank replied, "No, I'm very sorry, this is a very small ship."

"Well is there a place I could lie down? I'm not feeling very well," she replied.

"No, I'm afraid not, unless you use one of those settees back aft, or one of the benches along the alley way," he replied. By this time Frank was standing at the wicket and could see WHY she needed to lie down. She was very pregnant.

Next she asked "Is there a doctor on board?"

At this point Frank realized he had better act fast, so he quickly went around the ship asking if anyone was a doctor. No luck. Frank had already alerted the Captain, Big Jock Malcolmson, of this looming crisis and he had given the okay to let the lady lie down in the Captain's bunk. As she went in to lie down, she gave a little groan, which prompted Frank to run back down to the passenger area and call out, "Is anyone here a nurse?"

One woman answered that she was a retired nurse and asked why he wanted to know.

"Thank God," Frank answered. "Come with me. We have a lady aboard who is about to give birth. We've got her in the Captain's cabin right now."

"Oh my goodness," she said. "I've been retired for 15 years and never nursed anywhere else but in a veterans hospital." With nothing more than an all-male crew aboard, Frank really began to worry. However the nurse went up to the Captain's cabin and the baby was born between Point Atkinson and the Lions Gate Bridge, with everyone giving a big sigh of relief. In recognition of the unusual delivery, the baby was given the name Jessica Pam.

The Company more often was called upon to make a burial at sea, that is, to sprinkle the ashes of a cremated body into the ocean. Usually such a ceremony was undertaken by one of the day boats off Point Atkinson.

One such burial Frank recalls, was aboard the *Lady Alexandra*. Billy Yates was the Master. He came down to the Pursers Office, signalled to Frank that he would like a word with him then took Frank up to his cabin. Once inside he said, "Would you like one (a drink)?" As Frank puts it, "You just don't say no to the Captain." While he was pouring he said, "See that little box over there on the settee?" The box contained someone's ashes which were to be sprinkled into the sea when they reached Point Atkinson.

They sat round and talked, then all of a sudden Captain Yates dashed out with the little box in his hands, up to the wing of the bridge. He did his duty, and as well, threw in the little box after the ashes. He came back into his cabin saying, "Well that's that, and now I must remember to enter the name into the log book" All of a sudden he said, "Oh my God, what was his name?" Fortunately for Captain Yates, Frank had remembered the name on the box.

Frank worked his way up the ladder, having started as mess boy on the *Lady Cynthia* in 1941. On his own, Frank started practising typing, the hunt and peck system. One day George Read, a Purser, noticed this, came to Frank and said, "Get out of that steward's white jacket. You are going to become a Freight Clerk with me in the Pursers' Office."

Frank continued to work as a Freight Clerk, responsible for seeing that all the freight aboard gets put off at its proper destination. Boom chains were a common freight item and were important to the loggers all along the coast. There was quite an underground trade in stolen boom chains. Frank tells a somewhat different tale of stolen chains at Sechelt. On the way north, 25 chains were unloaded onto the wharf and Frank had obtained a signature on the manifest for them. Several days later the Union Company received a claim for these chains. The owner said he had never received them. Seeing the Company had a signature for the chains, the matter was turned over to the local police. After investigating the disappearance of these chains, it was found the owner's son had stolen them, as he was operating a gyppo logging show of his own on the side.

Frank's first job as Purser was aboard the *Lady Pam*. He is very proud to be able to say he worked on every ship in the fleet between 1941 and 1957, and on every Company route. He purposely liked to relieve other Pursers, in order that he could familiarize himself with all the rates etc. on the various runs. As well, Frank was one of the first Pursers to be put aboard the freight boats when they started to carry general cargo.

When I interviewed Frank he could still remember the names of all the officers who were aboard the *Lady Cynthia* on the day he started work with the Union Steamship Co. 48 years before. The Captain was H.E. Lawrey, Chief Officer Wally Walsh, Chief Engineer Denis Hogan, 2nd Engineer Bob Whitelaw, 3rd Engineer Johnny Fisher, Purser George Read, and Chief Steward Jack Tripp.

Frank died on Nov. 14, 1994, at age 71.

Philip "Phil" McCue

Purser "Phil" McCue
(Twigg Collection)

Phil first started working for the Union Steamship Company up at Bowen Island Estates as a bookkeeper, in April 1940 when he was 18 years old. He obtained the job through a friend of Mr. John Larnie, accountant in the Estate Division of the Company at the time, and stayed until the season ended in September.

In 1941 he went aboard the ships as Freight Clerk and the first Purser he worked under was Denis Shaw. From there he went over to the *Cardena* for one trip under Purser Pat Pattison, then to the *Catala* as Assistant Purser under Purser Robbie Robinson. While Phil was with Robbie, he never saw him take a drink, but he always had the odour of wintergreen about him. Phil suspected he did take a drink, but the wintergreen was sort of a smokescreen to hide the odour of liquor.

Next he was transferred over to the Queen Charlotte Island route working under Purser Reg Stover. This was during the war years. At this time many things were in short supply including men's white shirts. For some reason the store at Skidegate always had a good supply and Phil always remembered having a good supply of uniform shirts. One Christmas Phil was transferred over to the *Chelohsin* to relieve the Purser who was said to be "not well," a euphemism he thought for "too much to drink."

Phil also recalled working on the "killer" Cortez - Stuart Island route. His shift was from midnight to 6 a.m. On this route you were always on the go, for it seemed you were stopping every minute or so. It was hard to stay awake and Phil recalls being so tired he walked out of the ship's shell doors on the wrong side of the ship, two nights in a row, right into the salt chuck. This happened once at Refuge Cove and once at Squirrel Cove. Stunts like this brought forth plenty of laughter from the rest of the ship's crew.

His favourite ship was the *Lady Cecilia*. He was Purser aboard her for the longest time and got to know everybody on the route. People would give him little lists of things to pick up for them, down in Vancouver. Quite often a bottle of liquor would be on the list.

One time during the Christmas season the *Cecilia* went aground near Stillwater. She was holed and had to be patched up, then was pulled free by tugs and towed back to Vancouver. Most of the crew were taken off the ship but Phil had to stay aboard because the money and other valuables aboard were in his charge.

Phil was one officer in the fleet who never wore a uniform cap. One day when he was taking tickets at the gangplank, Charles Coldwell, the Company Purchasing Agent, came down to the ship, noticed Phil wasn't wearing a cap and asked Phil where it was. Phil replied, "Oh I can't wear a cap, I look so funny in a hat of any sort, so I never bought one." Mr. Coldwell said, "I'll bring you down my son's cap, I'd like you to have it." His son had been killed in the war. Phil said, "I'll look very funny, just the same." When Mr. Coldwell presented the cap to him, Phil tried it on and they both started to laugh. Mr. Coldwell could see, wearing a cap didn't suit Phil and he said, "You're right, a cap doesn't look good on you."

Captain Godfrey was a favourite of Phil's. On one trip on the *Lady Cecilia*, Phil was stricken with a terrible toothache. Captain Godfrey could see how bad it was and said he must do something, so he turned the ship around, radioed ahead to Powell River and alerted the dentist in town. Phil was taken up to the dentist, who was waiting for him. He gave Phil a shot of laughing gas, which Phil had never experienced before, and he yarded out the offending molar. It was so pleasant he said he had another tooth removed in the same manner.

He remembers that Captain Yates was always smoking a cigar and Phil swore Captain Yates could hear the cork coming out of a bottle anywhere on the ship. He also recalled Paddy Farina always had to have his hot water with lemon juice before breakfast.

When Dinty McGuiness was Chief Steward on the Queen Charlotte Island route, one day he remarked to Phil, "When I die I want my ashes scattered off Rose Spit, because everything else has been thrown up there anyway." Another Chief Steward Phil talked about was Jack Tripp. He wore a hair piece and he never seemed to get it straight on his head. He would take the palm of his hand and attempt to straighten it. He never quite got it right as the part always seemed to run from ear to ear.

Often when the Purser was taking tickets at the gangplank, departing from Vancouver in the morning, the Captain would come down and ask how many passengers were aboard. Captain Malcolmson was one who did this frequently. This always annoyed Phil. Most of the time you were going as fast as you could, punching and taking tickets and at the same time, using a clicker to get a count of the number of passengers aboard. One day Captain Malcolmson came along and asked in his slow drawl, "How many souls do we have today?" Phil answered, "We have 125 souls and 50 assholes, Captain." The Captain turned away, and they never spoke to each other for a week.

On paydays at the Union Steamships, you lined up in the main floor of the office and waited for the paymaster, Bill Munroe, to open the wicket. When Phil got to the wicket, Bill said there was no envelope for him, and that he would have to get in line with the Chinese cooks, as he was listed under Mah Cue. From that day on Phil's nickname was "Mah Cue."

Phil left the Union Steamship Company in July of 1945 and went up to Port Alice, where he started working in the payroll department. He progressed up the line to assistant accountant in charge of pulp products then in 1976 was transferred to the Vancouver head office as Pulp Production Accountant. He retired late in 1979 and currently lives in North Vancouver.

Donald Alexander "Don" McLeod

Purser Don McLeod ashore at Savary Island 1948
(Lewis Collection)

Don was born in New Westminster on Jan. 3, 1911. He went to sea at age 17, working on tug boats along the Fraser River. In 1935 he left the tug boats and went to work for Union Steamships as a deckhand. He then switched over to the Pursers Department and became a Freight Clerk. By 1940 he was a Purser and his first ship working in this capacity was the *Lady Pam*. He proposed to his wife Dill aboard the *Pam* after becoming Purser.

He was one of the most exuberant Pursers in the fleet. He liked people, and was very well-liked by the passengers and his shipmates. Though he used to kid around with his shipmates and laugh and joke with the passengers, he had very little tolerance for drunken loggers, though he himself over-indulged at times and when he did became very combative, especially towards inebriated loggers. It was a well-known fact that he carried a heavy wire cable billie and cracked more than one logger with it, subduing the poor fellow immediately. It is on record that on one altercation aboard ship with some loggers, Don banged one of the most belligerent fellows over the head with his billie and knocked him cold. The Captain at the time was Billy McCombe, who was soon called to the fracas, and when he saw this, he said, "Jesus man, you've killed him!" Of course he hadn't, but that was Captain McCombe's way of talking.

Nevertheless, Don was very popular along the coast and with tourists. Head office received many letters complimenting the Company for its service and especially mentioning Purser McLeod for his kindness.

Don became good friends with some of the Company's patrons and passengers. His wife Dill told me they spent their holidays one year with the Boardmans, who owned and ran a logging camp up coast. During their stay Don actually did a stint as a whistle punk in the woods with the crew.

Stew Hale, who was a Purser aboard the Union ships in the early 1930s, had Don McLeod with him as a Freight Clerk. Don had accepted a deer at Menzies Bay which was to be delivered to Campbell River. Due to a change in watch this deer was overcarried. There was no way the Company would pay a claim on wildlife meat. So Stew phoned back to the fellow at Campbell River who was to have received this deer, and asked him if he would settle up for a bottle of whiskey. "Sure, that would be fine," he said. Then Stew came out to Don and said, "We've got ourselves a deer." He then went to the ship's cook and asked him to butcher the deer and cut it up for roasts, steaks, etc. They spread the word around the dock and soon all the meat was sold. After taking enough money out of the sale to buy the bottle of whiskey, they made a little profit on the whole deal. Don used to tell people about what a good Purser Stew was and at the same time he would also say, "However when we over-carry freight he makes us eat it!"

In time Don McLeod became good friends with Bertram Owen-Jones, a Deck Officer in the Company. The following story takes place on the *Chelohsin* and Ron Finlayson was the Assistant Purser under Don at the time. At 3 a.m. one morning Ron was sitting at the Officers Mess having a coffee when Owen-Jones came down to have his breakfast. He always rolled his own cigarettes and had brought all the makings with him to roll up more smokes while he had his break. He left them on the mess table and went out to the galley to make his breakfast.

Don McLeod, who had been partying, happened to come down to the dining saloon and when he saw all the makings on the table, he picked up the tobacco, went and opened a port hole and threw it out into the ocean. Ron didn't know just what to do, squeal on Don or stay and bluff it out. He stayed. In a few minutes "Curly," for that was Owen-Jones' nickname, looked around for his tobacco. "Where the hell is my can tobacco?" he hollered. "What tobacco?" Ron asked. "You know damn well what tobacco. Say, was that damn Don McLeod down here?" Curley asked. "Yes," Ron replied. "He threw my tobacco out the port hole, I'll kill him." Needless to say, Don McLeod avoided Curly for the rest of the trip.

Another one of Don's good friends aboard ship was Wee Angus McNeill. Angus was the butt of a lot of jokes. Captain McCombe owned a bearskin coat and one night Don borrowed it. It was a dark night and when Angus went down for his mug up, Don went up to the bridge, wearing this bearskin coat and hid until Angus resumed his watch on the bridge. Don crawled along on his hands and knees and came up behind Angus and brushed him with the fur. Angus was scared stiff. He ran off the bridge in panic, hollering that there was a bear aboard ship!

When Captain Wilson collapsed aboard the *Cardena* it was Don who radioed Head Office asking for permission to turn the ship around but this was refused so he asked them to get a doctor to give directions on first aid until the ship reached Campbell River. According to Don, Captain Wilson was still alive when they took him off the *Cardena* but he died in the Campbell River Hospital. [222]

Don was Purser aboard the *Chelohsin* when she grounded at Stanley Park on Nov. 6, 1949. He realized that this was quite an historical event so he had a post card made up showing the *Chelohsin* aground, sitting submerged in the water near Siwash Rock. As well he stamped these cards with the *Chelohsin*'s official date stamp, giving the date of the old ship's last official day in service. I have one of these cards in my collection.

By 1951 Don was one of the senior Pursers in the fleet, but he could see that the Company was going downhill. He decided to leave the Company and went to work selling paint for Bapco Paint Co. This didn't go so well so he decided to go into to real estate and from all reports he was very successful in this line of work. Don passed away at age 67 in 1978.

Norman G. "Pat" Pattison

Pat was born in Australia in 1880 and emigrated to Canada, but in what year is not known. He obtained a job with the Union Steamship Co. and one of my contacts thought he had served aboard the *Coquitlam I*. This ship ended service in 1923, so in all probability his career with the Company could have spanned 27 years or so. Early ship registry records show him as being Purser on the *Cardena* in 1928.

It was always a point in question as to who was the senior Purser in the fleet, Pat Pattison or Robbie Robinson, and from the above it would seem that Pat would get the nod.

Over the years he became famous up and down the coast. He was generally referred to as Pat or Paddy the Purser. He was one of the real characters in Union Steamship history, as the readers will see for themselves in the following anecdotes about him.

Surprisingly, very little is known about Pat and information about his long service with the Union Steamship Co. is scarce. Norrie Wood, who served under Pat as Assistant Purser, recalled Pat showing him a book giving the history of the Pattison family in Australia, the title of which was *The Rape of the Pattison Estates*.

Pat is only mentioned once in Gerald Rushton's book, *Whistle Up the Inlet*, and that was in a story about Captain Andy Johnstone finding some false teeth left behind by a passenger who had visited in the wheelhouse. Captain Johnstone said about Pat, "Pat was a great talker, and as I was going to play a joke on the fellow who lost his teeth I had to swear Pat to secrecy or else he would give my secret away." [223]

Ernie Plant, who worked aboard the *Cardena* from 1925 to 1929, tells the story about the crew going up to see Pat the Purser in his office aboard ship to draw their pay. Pat would say, "You fellows owe me money, for you've had so many subs already!"

Tex Lyon, longtime wharfinger at Port Hardy, when asked about Pat said, "Yeah, there was a character." Tex went on to tell about when they started fishing prawns at Prince Rupert, Pat brought him back a 10 lb. bag of fresh cooked prawns and asked me if I liked them. "Oh God yes," was his answer, then asking how much they cost. Pat said it was 75 cents a bag and from then on Pat

Purser "Pat" Pattison as a young man
(Mrs. Tosh Collection)

brought him a bag of prawns every trip. Frank Skinner, the Company Agent in Prince Rupert, recalls picking up these bags of prawns and shrimps for Pat. Another deal Pat worked out with Tex was to arrange a shipment of a ton of potatoes every year from Bella Coola to Tex at Port Hardy. Bella Coola potatoes were well-known all over the coast for their high quality.

Frank Skinner worked under Pat as his Assistant on various ships and he remembers Pat had a habit of saying 1,2,3,4, after almost every sentence he spoke, and he could never figure out why. Stew Hale, a former Purser, told me another of Pat's sayings was, "E Pluribus Unam and Dubious Quim."

Gerry Jones, who also served under Pat as Assistant Purser, said, "If we were invited down to a room for a drink, when Pat was asked "how much" he would always say, "Oh just two fingers, the top two!"

Pat liked his jokes. At times, when passengers, probably loggers, would board the ship, they would line up at the Pursers Office waiting to obtain a berth. Pat would emerge from his own room in civilian clothes, get in the line up, and start agitating the fellows to complain about the Purser and his poor service.

Tom Charters, a former deck officer in the Company, tells a story about Pat when the joke was decidedly on him. The *Cardena* pulled into Ocean Falls and one passenger boarded and said he wanted a room. He was shabbily dressed, looked dirty and scruffy. Pat looked at him and said, "I've got no rooms, you will have to go in the steerage area." The man looked at Pat and said, "Do you know who I am?" Pat said, "No I don't and I don't care." The fellow said, "I'm Mr. Zellerbach!" The Pursers Office on the *Cardena* had a blind at the wicket, which, when pulled down would read "Closed." As soon as Pat heard this name, he pulled down the blind, poured himself a stiff drink, opened up the blind and gave Mr. Zellerbach the bridal suite.

Pat turned 64 in 1944 and whether it was by choice or at the Company's urging he left the ships and to everyone's surprise, he came ashore and became a checker on the dock. Just how long he stayed at this job nobody seems to know but it probably wasn't any longer than two years.

However, Pat has gone down in history as the only Purser in the Company to be mentioned in a piece of published poetry. It is in a book of poems by Bob Swanson, titled "Bunkhouse Ballads." Here then, following, is Pat's claim to fame:

He stands on the dock in the darkness till she whistles just ten hours late,
And he bounds up her ancient gang plank, while her winches are juggling freight;
Explains to Paddy the purser, in a world-wise sort o' way,
That he's said good-bye to the jungles. Says Paddy, "The Hell you say!"
In the dining saloon he is puzzled by the spoons with the silvery gleam,
He reaches across for the sugar, upsetting a jugful of cream.
Now he wishes he'd bunked in the bullpen (with an ape he's about on a par),
But he's got 'er made and he's headin' fer town on the southbound Cassiar.

George Read

Purser George Read on board *Lady Cecilia* circa 1927 (R. Hackett)

Here is a man who had more than 30 years of service with the Union Steamship Co. yet very, very little is known about him. If I hadn't worked with him on the East Howe Sound Route I probably wouldn't have known he ever existed. I remember him well because he was the only person who ever called me Arthur instead of the usual Art. He was a crusty fellow to work for but if you did your job he never bothered you.

Before coming to Union Steamships he worked for the All Red Line as a Purser on their ships, the *Selma* and the *Santa Maria*. These two ships were originally built in Scotland as private yachts. The All Red Line brought them over from the Old Country and operated them on the Sunshine Coast up to as far as Powell River. The Union Steamship Co. purchased the All Red Line in October, 1917. They then changed the name of the *Selma* to the *Chasina* and the *Santa Maria* to *Chilco*. The *Chilco* eventually became the *Lady Pam*. Read switched over to the Union Steamship Co. at the same time and served for many years on the logging camp run. During the 1940s he was mostly aboard the day boats operating on East and West Howe Sound. During this period he became a fixture on this route and became well-known by all the local people.

For some reason he decided to leave the ships and ended his days as a checker on the Union dock. This would have been in 1949 or 1950, so at that time he would have had at least 33 years with the Company. That's a long span of faithful service yet amazingly next to nothing is recorded anywhere about him, so I felt with such a record he warranted being mentioned in this history. Thanks to Bob Hackett, a long time resident of Sechelt, we at least have a picture of George for posterity.

Amos W. "Robbie" Robinson

Robbie joined the Union Steamship Co. on June 1, 1912 and except for war service in the army during the First World War, he was with the Company for 42 years, retiring in August 1953. When he retired he was the third senior employee in the Company.

Discussion often took place at the Officers Mess aboard ship as to who was the senior Purser in the fleet, between Robbie and Pat Pattison. Records indicate that Pat didn't start with the Company until around 1923, so Robbie was by far the senior of the two.

Robbie was a very private person, always neat in appearance, and sort of direct and curt in his speech.

It has been recorded that he had an uncanny knack of remembering names and faces, which was a wonderful asset for a Purser and serving the coastal people. He was meticulous in his work and expected his Assistants to be likewise. As long as you did your job properly he didn't interfere. However, Robbie was known as a prankster and he liked to play jokes on other people, but he didn't like it when the joke was on him.

Ron Finlayson, who served as Assistant Purser on the *Camosun III* under Robbie, recalled his ability to add up a column of figures in his head faster than one could do it with an adding machine. He was uncanny in this respect.

Robbie certainly was well-known throughout the Company and all along the B.C. Coast. Surprisingly though, next to nothing has been recorded about him. In fact, I have been unable to find even a picture of him. Mr. Rushton only mentions Robbie once in his book and that only briefly. It mentions the fact that Robbie was Purser on the *Camosun III* on Oct. 22, 1947 when she inaugurated a new route taking in the Alaskan ports of Petersburg and Wrangell. [224]

Purser "Denny" Shaw 1945

Despite his long service record I picked up only two anecdotal stories concerning Robbie.

Stew Hale, one of the earlier Pursers in the fleet, recalled that Robbie and Andrew Beattie, Chief Engineer, served together on the *Catala* and were jokingly referred to as "Amos and Andy" - but you never dared say that to them face to face!

Denis Shaw tells a story about working aboard the *Catala* as Assistant to Robbie. After the *Catala* passed through Seymour Narrows Robbie liked to take a check of the passengers on board. Robbie would take one side of the ship and Denis the other. Some of the stateroom doors opened out on the after lounge area. Robbie had the habit of knocking on a door and walking right in. On one occasion he knocked, walked right in and found a couple naked and making love. Robbie immediately closed the door and beat a hasty retreat. Denis happened to come around the corner and a naked fellow came bursting out of the cabin, really annoyed and tried to grab Denis. One of the passengers in the lounge spoke up and said, "No, no, it wasn't him, it was the other fellow." The fellow then suddenly realized he was stark naked and ran back into his cabin. Denis said the love-making couple never came out of their cabin until the *Catala* arrived in Vancouver.

Denis H. "Danny" Shaw

Denis was born April 3, 1914, at a town called Ennersdale, which is near Escort in the Province of Natal, South Africa.

He was the youngest in the family and was orphaned at the age of five. An aunt sent him to England when he was 12. He was there for three years when he decided to leave England. With the help of the Salvation Army, he emigrated on his own to Canada and came out to Vancouver. He obtained a job on a farm in the Fraser Valley, where his wages were $10 a month for a work schedule from 4:30 a.m. to 10 p.m. 365 days a year. From there he went to

a ranch in the Cariboo and became a cow puncher. He left that job in the summer of 1935 and in 1936 got a job working two days a week as a waiter on the *Lady Cynthia*. Ernie Watts was the Chief Steward and Stan Hunter was the Purser. They sailed every Tuesday and Thursday to Powell River and Savary Island. The ship left at 10 a.m. and arrived back in Vancouver at 10 p.m. The round trip fare was $2.50. His wages were $29.50 per month, and in those days 25 cents was a good tip.

When winter came Denis was laid off until next spring and then was rehired as a waiter/mess boy on the *Lady Pam* in 1937. The Captain was Jock Malcolmson, the Purser was Frank Skinner, Pat Wyllie was in charge of the stewards and Les Gore was the cook.

That also was the year that the *Lady Rose* arrived. Denis recalls her arrival and remembers that all the windows along the stern and sides of the vessel were boarded up for protection against the high seas she might encounter in her long sea voyage from England to the West Coast.

From 1938 to 1940, Denis served as a waiter on various Union ships but also came ashore to relieve the storekeeper, Archie

Arnott, in the wharf stores department.

In the spring of 1941 he was called up to the office by Gerald Rushton and offered the job as Purser on the *Lady Rose*. He was aboard her all summer but was bumped in the fall and went over to the *Catala* as Freight Clerk under Purser Robbie Robinson, from November 1941 to January 1942.

He remembers being aboard the *Catala* when the Japanese bombed Pearl Harbour. Charlie Guy was Assistant Purser and Denis was Freight Clerk. They were in Grenville Channel between Butedale and Prince Rupert when Charlie woke him up and told him about the bombing. Captain Sheppard ordered the ship to be blacked out and when they arrived in Prince Rupert, rumours were about that Vancouver had also been bombed.

From that point on, Union ships that crossed the open water of Queen Charlotte and Millbank Sound were escorted by a Canadian Navy vessel. As well, the Union ships were armed, and Denis recalls the crew had to go up at night and practice loading ammunition in the dark. They would also fire a few rounds for practice. While he was on the *Catala* they made two trips to Annette Island, Alaska with troops and air force personnel.

Denis was then transferred in January 1942 to the *Lady Rose* as Purser/Chief Steward until June, then he went over to the *Lady Alexandra*, where he was Purser from 1942 to 1948. He had started as Purser on the day runs and over the years he served as Purser aboard every ship in the fleet.

Denis recalls one difficult job the Purser had on the day runs. Several different types of tickets were used such as daily tickets, single trips, returns, weekend specials and excursions. At times you had over a thousand people aboard and just sorting out the tickets into different types was difficult enough but head office demanded that the serial numbers on all these tickets had to be typed onto the daily trip report turned into the office accounts department. Denis thought this was ridiculous and one day he rebelled and told Gerald Rushton, "I ain't going to do this anymore," and he didn't.

In 1946 he was transferred to the northern ships as Purser. First on the *Venture*, then the *Chelohsin*, then the *Catala*, and last the *Cardena*.

Being a very friendly fellow, Denis made friends everywhere during his long career aboard the Union ships. He is very voluble and can relate many stories about the ships and the fellows who sailed on them. Following are just a few of these stories.

One of his favourite stories took place aboard the *Lady Rose*. She was pulling into Seaside Park on a Saturday evening and would lay over until next day. Jock Malcolmson was the skipper and the Mate was Jack Halcrow. One day mate Halcrow came running down to Denis and said, "Get the big skillet out, throw some butter in it and we'll have a feed of shiners." A couple of minutes later he came down with a bucket full of shiners that had been swimming around the dock as the ship pulled in. He drained the water off and threw the shiners, still alive, into the skillet. Then Captain Malcolmson, Jack Halcrow and Jimmy Main, the Chief Engineer, sat down to this feed of shiners. These fellows loved their fish and to cap the story, on this particular day they had had kippers for breakfast, Alaska Black cod for lunch and a salmon steak for dinner plus the feed of shiners. That evening, as they were laying over, they sat down to a game of bridge. As usual they had a midnight mug up before going to bed and what did they want? Sardine sandwiches!

New, inexperienced hands were always coming along. Stan "Buddy" Beck started as a green deckhand. He later became an expert winchman and quartermaster. One day on the *Lady Rose* he was told to get a bucket of salt water so the Captain could bathe his feet. He picked up a bucket, tied a rope to it and wrapped the other end around his arm and threw the bucket straight out from the shell door of the *Lady Rose* while she was running. Of course, with the speed of the ship, the bucket filled instantly and pulled Buddy out of the door and into the salt chuck. The ship had to stop, turn around and go back to pick him up. Lucky for him it was a nice sunny day and the water was warm.

New crew members were nearly always given a hard time. The Union ships had regular fire drills. This time a new mess boy was told he'd have to get dressed, ready for the fire drill. They got him dressed in a Sou Wester outfit, being a heavy oilskin pants and jacket, with a bucket of sand in one hand and a fire axe in the other, and as well, a bundle of rope on his shoulder. They sent him down into the engine room and when the whistle blew he was to get up to the bridge, lugging all this equipment, as fast as he could. When he got up there the Captain looked at him and said, "What in hell are you dressed like that for, take it all off and get down to the engineer and bring me back a bucket of revolutions." So the poor kid rushes down to the Chief Engineer and asked for the bucket of revolutions. The Chief said, "I don't have any revolutions, take this iron bar up to him." He runs back up to the Captain with the iron bar and the Captain said "That's no good, take it back and get me the key to the Keelson." Back down he goes and the Chief shook his head and gave him another iron bar, saying "Maybe this will do." Back up he goes. The poor kid never caught on.

Another interesting tale Denis told was about the ship's bell off the *Santa Maria*, which later became the *Chilco* and then the *Lady Pam*. When Denis was Purser aboard the *Lady Pam*, he shared a room with the Mate, Wally Walsh. Denis had the top bunk and one day he jumped out of his bunk and he went right through the wooden deck. Beneath this floor was a concrete bathtub, and all wrapped up in burlap, placed in the tub, they found the *Santa Maria*'s old bell. Wally Walsh said, "I'm taking this bell home." It's never been seen since. Denis even ran an ad in the paper in 1990 to see if he could find anyone who might know the whereabouts of this bell, but there were no replies.

Still with the *Lady Pam*, Denis recalls being on her when she rammed into the Princess Elaine during a thick fog in the First Narrows. The *Pam* had a schooner bow on her and when she pulled herself free, stuck onto the bow nose was a seaman's bag. The bow had penetrated into a seaman's room and his bag was plucked right off his bunk. Lucky for him that he was not lying in his bunk at the time! Don Thompson, who was an oiler on the *Pam* when the accident happened, says the *Pam* continued on her way, but the Elaine had to go into drydock, which is a sort of David and Goliath tale.

Jack Tripp was a Chief Steward who wore a wig. Many a story is told about Jack and this wig. Denis tells this one which again took place aboard the *Lady Pam*. They were on the East Howe Sound route and often a ship on that run would reach Squamish early and have maybe a two or three hour wait for the PGE train to arrive. Usually most of the crew would lay down and take a nap while waiting for the train to arrive. On this trip, after the passengers were aboard at Squamish and the *Pam* was on her way to Woodfibre, Denis noticed that the Chief Steward, Jack Tripp, wasn't around so he sent a young steward to go and wake him up. On the way to Britannia, still no Chief Steward, so Denis asked the young steward again, "Where's the Chief Steward?" The young lad said, "I don't know, he's not in his room, but there is a bald headed man in his bunk." He didn't know that Jack wore a wig so he didn't recognize him without his wig on.

One of the famous Pursers in the fleet was Pat Pattison, who liked to have a cold beer now and again. He devised a way of keeping his beer cool, by tying two or three bottles together and hanging them outside the port hole in his room on the *Cardena*. This worked quite well until on one stop, Denis, who was serving as Assistant Purser, noticed these bottles of beer hanging from Pat's port hole. It was a float landing and quite often the freight would be unloaded out the ship's shell doors. Standing there on the float, Denis could easily reach up to those bottles so he took two bottles, went behind the freight shed, took off the caps, emptied out the beer, urinated in them, put the caps back on and hung the bottles back up along with the others, saying nothing. It was the last time Pat hung his bottles of beer outside to keep cool!

In 1948 Denis was called into the office and offered a shore job, which he accepted. He was appointed Freight Solicitor for the Company, but after three years of that, and nearly 17 with the Company, he quit. "I felt I would never become President of the Company so I decided to leave," he said. He went into selling real estate, joining MacCauley, Nicolls Maitland & Co. in February 1953 and then Newcombe Realty in 1977. He became very successful in the trade.

When I interviewed Denis in 1990 he was 76 years old but still very active and still selling real estate on a part time basis for Newcombe Realty. There is no doubt that Denis Shaw had become one of the best-known and liked Pursers in the Company's history.

Frank Jess Skinner

Born and raised in Vancouver, Frank had a long and varied career with the Union Steamship Co.

His first job on a Union ship was during the summer in 1926, helping the news agent, one Aubrey Jones, on the *Lady Alexandra*. This was the only ship in the fleet on which the news stand was owned and operated by the Union Steamship Co. itself. All other news stands aboard other ships were operated by the Canadian Railway Association. The Master on the *Lady Alexandra* at the time was Captain John Boden, the Chief Engineer was Andrew Beattie, the Purser was Stan Hunter, and the Chief Steward was Ernie Watts.

In those early years, the 1920s and 1930s, Charlie Coldwell was Purchasing Agent for the Company and was also in charge of hiring freight clerks and stewards. Frank says he was just like a father to the young fellows coming along.

Frank started to work full time aboard the Union ships on May 11, 1927, as a Freight Clerk aboard the *Venture* under Purser Gibb Rennie. In those days there was no Assistant Purser. He worked on several ships over the years, the *Venture, Chelohsin, Cardena, Catala, Capilano, Lady Cynthia, Lady Cecilia*, and of course, all the time he was rising up in the seniority scale. He felt that his favourite was the *Catala*.

After Frank started to work in 1927, things started to move pretty fast within the Company. Some fellows who were Freight Clerks, like Harvey Anthony and Al Newman, obtained jobs in the office ashore. As a result Frank moved ahead rapidly himself. In 1930 he went aboard the *Chilkoot* as Purser, although she was mainly a freight boat. It was unusual, but the Purser at the time had to look after the victualing, etc. The Master on her was Bill Mounce, the Chief Officer was Harry McLean, and a chap from Powell River was the Mate. The Chief Engineer was a man by the name of Harley.

Frank had previously sailed on the *Catala* with Bill Mounce and remembers him well because he was the only man in the

Frank Skinner as Freight Clerk on *S.S. Catala* 1936 *(Skinner Collection)*

fleet who chewed tobacco, but Frank says he was pretty good with it. Another man Frank remembers from his days on the *Catala* was the stevedore, Paddy Hilditch. On sailing night he would come aboard ship immaculately dressed. One would think he was a passenger. Then, while he was aboard ship, he wouldn't shave, he was constantly working, sorting out freight and getting ready for the next stop. He knew his job and he knew how to do it.

Bogey Knight was another fellow Frank remembered well. He first met Bogey when he was night steward on the *Chelohsin*. According to Frank, he was another man who was a very fine dresser and could be mistaken for a passenger as he came aboard.

The biggest salmon year in coastal history was 1930 and the *Chilkoot* was kept very busy. The canneries were begging ships to call in and take their canned salmon down to Vancouver. Then the Depression hit, and though it didn't reach the coast until 1931, when it did half of the Union fleet was tied up. Many ports of call were cut off the schedule and one ship did what two did before. Frank recalls the *Chelohsin* used to be five or six hours unloading at Menzies Bay and when the Depression hit, half an hour or so was all the time that was needed. There were only five ships running during that period and Frank was the last of the Freight Clerks to hold a year-round job. He recalls that during winter Eddie Enwright and Harold Crompton had to go back to being stewards.

In fact, in order to keep a nucleus of a work force, men worked three weeks on, then a week off without pay. Gradually things improved and Frank was made Purser on the *Lady Pam* in 1937. He recalls Pat Wyllie was Steward and looked after things as there was no Chief Steward aboard the *Lady Pam* in those days.

In 1939, Frank was Freight Clerk on the *Capilano II* working under Purser George Read, who had come over to the Union Steamship Co. from the All Red Line. Frank was called up to the office by Carl Halterman, the General Manager of the Company and offered the job as Company Agent at Prince Rupert. He and his wife Martha decided this was a good opportunity, so they moved up to Prince Rupert. He took over the office and the Agent's job there on April 15, 1939.

One of Frank's fondest memories while in Prince Rupert was the occasion of a cow arriving in port aboard a Union ship. It was discharged and kept on the wharf for a couple of days, waiting to be transferred to another vessel for shipment further north, up to Stewart. Frank had to confer with the longshoring people as to how this could be handled. They decided to build a coral on the dock. Fortunately one of the fellows was used to animals and he volunteered to look after the cow. Somehow this got into the Prince Rupert paper and as a result the people in Rupert, who hadn't seen cow in years, came down to see the animal.

Some school children had never seen a cow so the school teachers brought their classes down to the wharf to see this marvellous animal and were fascinated when she was milked. It turned out to be a big event in Prince Rupert at the time.

Frank also recalls the sad occasion of

Frank Skinner, Agent at Prince Rupert *(Skinner Collection)*

Chief Engineer Andrew Beattie's death aboard the *Catala* while she was alongside the dock in Prince Rupert. Bert Attewell was Chief Steward at the time and he always used to give Beattie a call for lunch. This time when he knocked and received no response to his call, he opened his stateroom door, and there was Chief Beattie sitting up at his desk, so Bert stepped in and spoke to him and got no response. He had died, just after noon, sitting in his chair! His body was wrapped in a shroud and taken back to Vancouver.

Frank ended his career with the Union Steamship Co. on Dec. 31, 1953, after a most interesting and enjoyable tenure with the Company. He had been 14 years as Company Agent in Prince Rupert. He joined up with Straits Towing in 1953 and was looking after their scow fleet. He left there and went to work for the Canadian Stevedoring Co. as a public relations man for grain handling contracts. He retired in Dec. 31, 1974 and now resides in West Vancouver. His wife Martha died in 1995.

Leslie James England "Les" Smith

Les was born in England in 1893 and came to Canada in 1913. At the outbreak of World War I he joined the Seaforths or Westminster Regiment and rose to the rank of Captain. He was wounded in action. After the war he became involved with hotel management and managed several small hotels in Vancouver.

Prior to World War II he was working in Burrard Drydock and was in charge of their blueprint department. Perhaps at the urging of his older brother, Fred Smith, the well-known Chief Engineer with Union Steamships, Les joined the Company in the Pursers Department. Due to wartime call ups, Les went ahead quickly. Les was Purser of the *Lady Cecilia* when she was rammed by 10,000-ton freighter off Point Atkinson on Sept. 27, 1944. Both Norrie Wood and myself were his Assistants at the time. It could have been a very serious accident, several passengers were injured, but no one was killed. With all the excitement Les stayed in his office busily counting his cash for the trip; the ship could have been sinking but he was oblivious to what was happening around him. He was Purser on the *Catala* in 1950 and on the *Cardena* in 1951. Prior to this he had also relieved the Company Agent in Prince Rupert in 1948/49.

Les was appointed Company Agent in Prince Rupert when Frank Skinner resigned in 1953 to take another job in Vancouver. Les's tenure in Prince Rupert lasted about a year. A fellow by the name of Jim Foster took over from him and then Eddie Enwright, from the Freight Office in Vancouver, took over from him. Les returned to Vancouver where he resumed managing apartments, the last of which was the Marlborough Apartments in Burnaby.

Shipmates remember one of Les's trademarks was continually having a cigarette dangling from his lips. He wouldn't smoke them much, he just let them burn down and always this long ash would be hanging there. It was fascinating to see.

He was a quiet fellow and had a quaint little smile and laugh. He delighted in tall tales and regaling people with his yarns.

Purser "Les" Smith *(B. Smith)*

One of the best was recalled by his nephew, Ben Smith, as follows:

"Les had a swarthy complexion, and could be easily mistaken for an Asiatic, rather than being of English origin. One day, while in the ship's dining room, he and a lady passenger were discussing Chutney sauce. Les had the last word, and exclaimed 'If you want good Chutney, you have to go to India.' The lady replied, 'You seem to be quite an authority on the subject.' Les replied, 'Well after all, I was born in Bombay!'

When Ben got home after that trip, he asked his father, Les's brother, "Was your brother Les born in Bombay?" Ben said his father almost had a fit at hearing this tall tale. Les passed away in August, 1968, at age 75.

Reginald C. "Reg" or "Smokey" Stover

Reg Stover (left) with Don Nelson
(Vancouver Maritime Museum)

When the Union Steamship Co. ceased operations in 1958, Reg was the senior Purser in the Fleet. The nickname of Smokey Stover came about because Reg was a heavy smoker. He never married and when he retired he settled out in White Rock near his good friend, Freddie Smith. Reg spent most of his career on the northern routes, and a good part of this time he was on the Queen Charlotte Island Route, so he was better known up north than on the local runs.

He was quiet and efficient, a good fellow to work for. I served with him for a few months on the Queen Charlotte Island run aboard the *Coquitlam II*, in the late 1940s. I could not find any record as to when Reg joined the Company, but Ship Registry Records show him as being Assistant Purser aboard the *Cardena* in Oct. 20, 1938, so he probably would have started as a Freight Clerk in the early or middle 1930s.

In the early 1940s, Reg was Purser on the *Camosun II* running to the Queen Charlotte Islands. Gerry Jones started as a Freight Clerk with Reg and he recalled that Reg was a whiz of a two finger typist. One beautiful day they were sitting in the forward observation room, with both side doors wide open. All of a sudden there was this terrible odor and Gerry accused Reg of passing wind. Reg just laughed and said, "Hell no, not me, we're just approaching the Rose Harbour whaling station."

Ben Smith, an engineer with Union Steamships, sailed with Reg and said that he was never known as a very humorous man, but once he surprised his shipmates. On one of their days off, four of them went up town, Reg Stover, Fred Smith, Don Nelson and Ben. They wandered into the Arctic Club and later when they all left, they were feeling no pain. They started across an intersection against a red light. They were immediately whistled down by a traffic policeman and he started giving them 'what for.' At that moment Reg came to their rescue. Using a somewhat Scandinavian accent, Reg said, "Ve joost came down from Soine-Toola." "The policeman realizing that they were a bunch of dummies from the sticks, decided right then and there, to give us the low-down on how the traffic lights worked. Stover stood there stoney-faced while he listened to the explicit instructions, while the rest of us could hardly contain ourselves from bursting out laughing," Ben said.

In 1957 the Union Steamship Co. placed the *Coquitlam II* in the hands of Alaska Cruises, Inc. Reg was the senior Purser in the Fleet at the time so he stayed aboard her, sailing out of Seattle to Juneau, Alaska.

Reg stayed with the Union Steamship Co. until they ceased operations in 1958. They were taken over by Northland Navigation Co. and Reg did some relieving work for them but according to his best friend Freddie Smith, Reg's health was failing. Reg had to go into St. Paul's Hospital and he died there at age 52.

Steve Tracy

Steve joined the Union Steamship Co. in Oct. 1944 as a Freight Clerk on the *Lady Alexandra*, working with Purser Denis Shaw. After the usual training period, he was transferred to the *Catala* under Purser Robbie Robinson.

Steve recalled one trip on the *Catala* when Captain Sheppard was trying to get up to the Skeena River canneries and the channel was filled with fish boats. They had their fish nets strung out every which way, blocking the channel so the *Catala* couldn't get through. Captain Sheppard would sound the ship's whistle to warn them of his approach and to get their nets out of his way. Often they refused to heed his warning, so he went right on through their nets and all. "On one trip," Steve said, "He got to his destination but with a price to pay. Some nets got tangled around the *Catala*'s propellor and he had to call for a diver to go down and cut it all away."

In retrospect, he felt the *Catala* was his favourite ship. The *Lady Alexandra* also ranked high with him, mainly because there usually was a lively and fun crowd aboard. Happy people were always coming and going, mainly to picnics and dancing at Bowen Island. With a laugh he said, "The people who came aboard often didn't seem like the same people when they came back, due mostly to the over indulgence of Jolly Juice. At times the crew had to give assistance to many who couldn't walk when the ship docked back in Vancouver, later the same evening. Some had to be laid out on freight dollies and pulled out to waiting taxis!"

Steve left the Union Steamships in March 1946, as he decided there wasn't much future with the Company and he didn't want to spend the rest of his life being away from home and family. He went to work for the Canadian Blue Star Line in their Vancouver Office. He now sells real estate in Vancouver.

Freight Clerk Steve Tracy

A.M. "Art" Twigg

Purser "Art" Twigg, author of *Union Steamships Remembered* (Twigg Collection)

It was in June 1942 that I heard the Union Steamship Co. was looking for young men who were proficient typists to work aboard their ships in the Pursers Office. At the time, with school being out for the summer, I had a job as a swamper on a 7-Up delivery truck operating all over the North Shore. It wasn't much of a job, so when I heard about the openings at Union Steamships I went to see them the very next day and was told I had to see a Mr. Chuck McLean.

McLean was a dapper little fellow, and he was the assistant to Charlie Caldwell the Purchasing Agent for the Company. When I spoke to Mr. McLean, all he asked me was, "Can you type and how many words can you do a minute?" With all the confidence I could muster, I said, "Yes, 60 words a minute." (I couldn't really.) "Okay," Chuck said, "Be down here tomorrow at 8 a.m."

When I arrived next morning, McLean escorted me down to the *Lady Pam* and introduced me to Harold Crompton, who was the Purser aboard the *Pam* at the time. I was told to go up to the freight office and pick up the bills of lading for the day's trip. Even before we sailed I was lost at sea, swamped by bills of lading, strange lingo and over-awed by Masters and Mates. Somehow I got through the day and thereby started my eight-year career with the Union Steamship Co., which covered some of the best years in the Company's history and sparked my life-long love affair with it. I worked my way up in the Pursers Department, from Freight Clerk, Assistant Purser and then to relief Purser on the Day Boats during the summer months. I was fortunate to serve on every route in the Company's schedule and worked aboard every ship in the fleet except the cruise-oriented *Chilcotin*. Also I served aboard the *Island King* and *Chilkoot* in the Frank Waterhouse fleet when they needed to have a Purser aboard.

I left the Company on my own accord in June 1950 to take a job with the Municipality of West Vancouver, where I had been born and was still residing. It meant I could walk to work every day instead of spending two hours travel time back and forth to the Union dock, plus I was getting more money. It turned out to be a lucky move, for eight years later the Union Steamship Co. ceased to exist, while I stayed on with the Municipality and enjoyed a fruitful career as its Purchasing Agent. I became President of the B.C. District of the Purchasing Management Association of Canada and in 1972 was chairman of that group's national conference in Vancouver. For personal reasons I took an early retirement in 1974 and moved to my present residence near Campbell River.

I liked working for the Union Steamship Co., though, and now feel very fortunate to have worked for them for as long as I did. I observed everything that went on and took a great interest in the affairs of this marvellous company and in the many great people who worked for it.

As I said earlier, Harold Crompton was

the first purser I worked under. He was a good teacher and I feel very proud to have had him as a mentor. He himself went on to a very illustrious career with the company. Gerald Rushton in his book *Whistle Up the Inlet* says that Crompton was undoubtedly the dean of local passenger men here on the B.C. coast.

The next purser I recall working with was Neil Morlock, on the *Lady Rose* doing the West Howe Sound route. One trip we were docked at Hopkins Landing and being my first week on the job I was really lost trying to catch up and learn everything. The next thing I heard was Captain Malcolmson giving the warning whistle that we were about to depart. I turned around and hollered at him, "Hey, I'm not finished yet!" He just glared at me. Neil had been standing on board watching me and when he heard this he motioned me to get aboard in a hurry. When I got beside him he said, "Son, if you want to keep your job aboard ship, NEVER ever call the Master 'hey.' " It was good advice. In those days any Master aboard a Union ship ruled supreme. There were no ifs, ands or buts; you didn't argue with the Master.

After the first couple of weeks, I was told to get a uniform. You went up to Chuck McLean's office and got your cap badge, freight clerk's sleeve braid, and uniform buttons. Then you went up town and ordered a uniform. I went up to Eaton's and came back with a double-breasted blue serge suit on which I had them sew the braid and buttons. I hadn't been told that Gordon Campbell Ltd. was the official uniform supplier for the company. Of course it wasn't a standard-style uniform so I faced continued ridicule over it. Mike Benson, another well-known personality with the company, went through the same humiliating experience when he started there.

Because I had a physical disability, I was exempt from military service during the war years, but they were especially hectic for the Company. The ships were full to capacity with both passengers and freight, coming and going. Due to rationing restrictions on all kinds of items, including food, people everywhere were experiencing shortages of every kind. But those working on the ships were able to obtain extra quantities of rationed food items. The small communities along the coast received their quotas of the rationed items but because so many residents had gone off to war they had lots of extra butter, sugar, syrup, chocolate bars, etc. My mother never went short of butter or sugar during the war years!

Sometimes when we would be unloading freight, maybe a 100-pound sack of sugar would accidentally fall off a freight pallet. It was no coincidence that crew members would be standing by waiting with tin cups and paper bags in hand, waiting to scoop up the sugar from this fallen sack! Many other ingenious accidents took place with commodities that were in short supply. It would have been a shame to waste all those goodies!

During my eight years aboard the ships I was a participant in four different ship accidents, three of which could have been serious. They were:

1. The *Lady Cecilia* was rammed near Point Atkinson by a wartime liberty freighter out on sea trials in 1944;

2. The *Cardena* going aground at False Bay in 1948;

3. The *Coquitlam* grounding at Masset in 1949.

Art Twigg at work in the Freight Agent's Office
(Twigg Collection)

Details of all of these accidents can be found in the section on the ships of the fleet.

The fourth accident was aboard the *Cassiar*, which hit a deadhead as it was backing away from the Goose Bay Cannery and lost its propellor. As a result, we had a nice holiday as we waited in Goose Bay for a towboat to come and tow us back to Vancouver.

My favourite ship is quite an unusual choice, but it was the *Cassiar II*, the old CNR *Prince John*. I guess a lot to do with this choice was the fact I was aboard her for the longest time and that the captain was Alex "Big Mac" McLennan, who was described by Gerald Rushton as the consummate mariner, with which I concur. I've always felt it was a great honour to have served aboard his ship. He was one of the best, without question.

I spent my first Christmas away from home aboard the *Cassiar*, anchored off Tow Hill in the Queen Charlotte Islands waiting for a storm to subside. Some of my shipmates in those days were Vic Hayman, Tom Lucas, Bob Williamson, Freddy Smith, Bob Whitelaw, Harry Biles, Joe Barrowcough and Andy Steele.

Probably the most amusing incident that comes to mind from when I was aboard ship was one time when we were docked and unloading freight at Port Clements in the Queen Charlottes. There was a beer parlour there and it was usual for them to receive a large shipment of cases of bottled beer, which when unloaded was usually stacked 100 cases to a pallet board.

At times the deck crew would get very thirsty and they had a crafty way of stacking the beer in the hold on a pallet board, leaving one case out of the middle of the bottom row. The board would be sent up and off and counted 10 cases along in a row and five rows wide, with a second level on top to match, making 100 cases to a board. Liquor was the last thing to be discharged because it had to be watched carefully and then a signature had to be obtained for it all before the ship left port.

That day I happened to come between deck, unbeknown to the deck crew working below. As I stood there watching them load this board of beer, I saw them sneak one case out of the centre row and stash it in the hold under a pile of rope. "Ha ha," I said to myself, "I'll trick you fellows." The pallet went off and was counted as it appeared, 100 cases.

When a ship leaves port, all the deckhands are required up on deck to man lines, etc. So, as the ship started to leave, I dashed down into the hold, purloined their case of beer and put it in my cabin, which was nearby.

Well you should have heard the yelling and shouting going on between the deckhands after they went to get their case of beer, accusing each other of having taken it. I never said a thing and of course neither could they as they had stolen it in the first place! I laughed about this for the whole trip and every time I think about it now it brings a smile to my face. If any of the crew who took part in this escapade reads this, give me a call.

In 1949 I was offered a shore job working under Al Newman and Clair Williams in the freight agents office. By this time I had married and started raising a family, so getting a job where I was home every day was a great stroke of good fortune.

In my later years with the company, I had

Art Twigg on a pallet loaded with liquor destined for Dawson Landing, Rivers Inlet. 2nd Mate "Nick" Nicholson is watching the proceedings. *(Twigg Collection)*

begun to make copious notes about the company's business, their ways of doing things, good and bad, and recording all facets of things concerning the shipping business. I also made notes on how I thought many company practices could be improved. After I gave my notice that I would be leaving, I was talking one day with George B. Ray, the company's accountant at the time, and told him about the notes. He asked if he could borrow them and read them over. Naturally I was flattered and did loan them to him.

One of the things I had written about was an idea I had of making large freight boxes or containers which could be used on the day runs, particularly during the summer season when all the families would be at their summer camps and getting weekly orders sent out from Woodward's, Vancouver Supply Co. and others. It had been my experience that when these supplies were being unloaded there often were one or two parcels missing. Because all the freight was stored loose in the hold, freight for one place could easily get mixed up with freight for another place. I reasoned that if we had large boxes made and all the freight for a particular port put in them, nothing could get mis-stowed and it would be far faster discharging the cargo. In other words, container boxes.

Well it wasn't too long after I left the company that this idea was tried out and put into practise and became quite a success story all along the waterfront. Unfortunately, these particular notes were not returned to me so my claim to fame and to having had the idea in the first place cannot be established for certain. However, I know I thought of the idea in the late 1940s and gave my notes to Mr. Rae in 1950 and it was in 1956-57 that the company adopted a container style of operation.

The idea of writing a book about the Union Steamship Company had occurred to me off and on over the years because I felt nothing was being written or recorded in detail about all the Union ships and their wonderful mariners, who laboured to serve the isolated B.C. coastal communities under the most difficult of navigating conditions, and how the company gained the love and respect of the people in these lonely settlements. It's no wonder that they soon were referred to as "the lifeline of the coast." I hope I have succeeded to some degree in giving them the recognition they so rightly deserve.

SHIP VIA UNION-WATERHOUSE STEAMERS

For Freight Bookings **CALL**

UNION STEAMSHIPS - PAcific 3411 - Local 24

C. WILLIAMS - A. TWIGG

FRANK WATERHOUSE - PAcific 3411 - Local 20 & 46

H. COPLEY - M. BENSON

Robert "Bob" Walker

Bob had a short career with the Union Steamship Co. putting in about two years in total working as a Freight Clerk. His ability to type well landed him a job immediately. He started on April 29, 1950 but he left a year later and went over to CPR, where he worked aboard the famous *Maquinna*. Bob however found the work load there far more demanding than at Union Steamships, where there also was a lot more camaraderie and a relaxed atmosphere, so he returned to the Union Steamships and worked for another year. In 1953 he left again, along with Assistant Purser Don Nelson, to work for CN Telecommunications. While with Union Steamships, Bob worked aboard the *Lady Cynthia*, *Lady Alexandra*, *Cardena*, *Catala*, *Camosun*, *Coquitlam*, and the *Chilcotin*.

Walker recalled working on the famous "Booze Cruise" with hordes of people clamoring to get aboard the *Lady Alexandra* late at night at Bowen Island. When he was checking over the tickets he had taken from the multitude who had boarded, much to his horror he found several people had passed off B.C. Electric street car transfers as boats tickets! This is understandable because with the crush of so many people, pushing and shoving each other to get aboard, those who were taking tickets had no chance to examine each item handed to them.

Another incident he remembers also took place at Bowen Island. Somehow the *Lady Alexandra* with Billy McCombe as Master pulled away from the wharf and was out in the cove before it was discovered Bob was not aboard. Bob had been in the ticket office on the wharf. Captain McCombe brought the ship back alongside the dock and told him to jump aboard. "Like hell I will, put out the gang plank," Bob replied. So with reluctance, the plank was put out and Bob walked aboard, but anyone who knew Captain McCombe would know this wouldn't sit well with him and it didn't! When the ship got cleared away, Captain McCombe came down and in Bob's words, "Boy, did he ever tear a strip off my ass."

Once when Bob was working on the Queen Charlotte run he recalled an exceptionally rough crossing back to Prince Rupert. The sea was so rough one couldn't do anything but lay in your bunk and hold on. Several port holes had been left open and water was sloshing in the companionways. Nearly all the dishes were broken in the galley. One of the cooks fell and broke two ribs, but Bob said, "Rough sea makes me hungry," so he struggled down to the dining room, opened the door and asked Chief Steward Harold Humphreys if he was going to serve dinner? Harold responded by throwing a plate at him, that is, a broken plate.

Robert "Bob" Waters

Bob Waters with his bride, Patricia, 1954. (*Patricia Nixon*)

Bob started working for the Union Steamship Co. in 1953 at age 18, aboard ship as a Freight Clerk in the Pursers Department.

He soon was transferred into the Freight Office on the wharf to work under Charlie Guy. In June 1954 the Company started to put out a monthly newsletter called *The Heaving Line* and Bob became a frequent contributor, writing historical reviews and records about some of the Union ships.

In 1955 he married one of the girls who worked in the office of the Company, Miss Patricia Nixon.

With the Company falling on hard times, he like many others left it in 1958 and went into business for himself out in White Rock. He died unexpectedly a few years later.

Norrie Wood

Purser Norrie Wood

Norrie was "sweet 16" when he started work with the Union Steamships aboard the *Lady Pam*, as a Freight Clerk under Purser Danny Shaw. It was in 1942, the war was on, and rationing of just about everything was in force, including liquor. If you knew someone who didn't drink and had a liquor permit you had struck gold. One day soon after Norrie had started work he was walking up town with Danny Shaw and they were passing the Carrall Street liquor store. Danny suddenly grabbed Norrie's arm and propelled him into the liquor store and had him apply for a liquor permit. They then proceeded up town to a popular watering hole in those days, known as the Arctic Club. Danny signed Norrie up as a member. So here was Norrie at age 16 a member of the Arctic Club and owning a liquor permit, all in one day.

That was fine until one year later when renewal time came due for his membership in the Arctic Club. The club sent the renewal notice to his parents' home! Norrie had to do some fast talking and explain to his parents that the age of innocence had now passed for him, though his legal drinking age was still several years hence!

After Norrie had served on the *Pam* for a few days to learn about being a freight clerk, he was moved onto a northern route. One trip he recalled was on the *Venture*. She was relieving on the logging camp route for the *Cardena*. They were at Sayward and had finished unloading all the freight except they were short one piece which a local logging contractor needed desperately to keep his operation going. The ship was turned inside out in an effort to find this missing piece. The Captain realized the man's problem and kept the search going for an hour, but it couldn't be found. One year later on the same ship, doing the same relief job, they were again at Sayward unloading freight and a deckhand came up to Norrie and asked him, "What do you want done with this?" He had come across this piece of freight that they couldn't find exactly one year ago! He had found it in the rope locker under a pile of rope. Probably a longshoreman had put it in this locker so it wouldn't get lost and then forgot to tell anyone about it. Mr. McIllrath, the Company Claims Agent, must have had nightmares over that.

The *Cardena* used to make a weekly whistle stop into Swanson Bay. At one time there was a thriving pulp mill operating there. It had been closed for years and was abandoned, but a caretaker was living on the site with his family. The weekly visit of the *Cardena* was a big event in their lives. The *Cardena* would come into the bay and blow its whistle to signal the caretaker, who would then launch his little rowboat, go out to the ship to exchange a mail sack, some parcels and get his weekly food supplies, likely ordered the week before from Woodward's in Vancouver. Usually he would bring out his children with him, and for good reason. The Chief Officer of the *Cardena* was Isaac Mercer and he always made it a point of going down to the ship's news stand before they arrived at Swanson Bay to buy some chocolate bars and candy for these children. They would be sitting in the little row boat eagerly awaiting the appearance of Chief Officer Mercer at the open freight door where he would pass out these chocolate bars and candy to them. One can easily imagine, in such an isolated spot, how these children looked forward to the weekly visit of the *Cardena*.

The *Lady Pam* was one of the first ships on which Norrie served as purser. One of her runs was on a late Saturday afternoon she would do West Howe Sound and lay overnight at Seaside Park. There was a hotel and beer parlour there and it was within easy walking distance to the big pulp mill at Port Mellon. Norrie recalls two ladies of the night who boarded the *Pam* in Vancouver every weekend, booked themselves into the hotel overnight and did a thriving business with the workers overnight, then caught the ship back to Vancouver.

Norrie often sailed aboard the *Lady Alex* and smiles when he recalls the famous moonlight dance cruises. Norrie said, "When the *Alex* left Bowen at midnight frequently many couples failed to get back aboard. We saw many forlorn looking couples boarding the *Alex* late next afternoon having spent all night on Bowen Island with no place to go or stay. The bushes around the hotel were the only places they could find to sleep overnight."

On one trip the freight deck of the *Alex* came alive with shouts of "Where's the horse?" They had loaded a horse in Vancouver destined for Squamish. At Bowen Island the crew discovered the horse box was there but no horse. The Mate at the time was Johnny Horne. He came rushing down to the freight deck and sure enough the horse had disappeared. Someone happened to look out the freight doors on the port side that had been left open and there was the horse, swimming for his life across the cove. Quickly a life boat was launched in pursuit, but the horse was soon climbing out of the water on the opposite shore. Johnny then dispatched another crew to go along the shoreline and cut the horse off and capture it. They did manage to get a rope around the horse and lead it back into the horse box and load it aboard again.

When the horse was unloaded at Squamish the owner was quite concerned because the horse seemed so agitated. But no one said a word.

The *Alex* went aground in July 15, 1947 on the east side of Howe Sound south of Brunswick Point in a blinding rain and electrical storm. G.B.K. Owen-Jones was on the bridge at the time. The *Alex* was not equipped with radar.

There were only eight passengers aboard when she hit. Most of the crew were asleep in their bunks, including Norrie. He awoke with a start, hearing and feeling a bump, bumpity bump, bump. "Oh, oh, I know what this is," Norrie said to himself. Getting up, he reached for the light switch but the light didn't work. He groped around for his clothes, dressed and put on some shoes in the dark. His room, along with those of other officers, opened into a little hallway and then another door opened onto the deck. As Norrie stepped on deck, there, staring him in the face, was a telephone pole, right along side the ship. He proceeded down to the deck to see what was going on. Lights had been rigged up and everybody was milling around, then someone spotted Norrie's shoes. He had on one brown shoe and one black shoe. He had a hard time explaining to the crew that he hadn't been the least bit nervous when he dressed in the dark.

Norrie stayed with the Union Company until the very end, December 1958. He had taken a shore job and was working in the Freight Agents Office when Northland acquired the Company's assets and the Union ships were tied up. He stayed with Northland through the Dutch ownership. They in turn leased the operation out to the CPR who ran it for two years. At this point Norrie went over to Riv Tow and was with them a little over 11 years. He retired at the end of April 1991 after working on the Vancouver waterfront for 49 years.

They Also Served

Top Left:
Freight Clerk Bergstrom
(D. Shaw)

Top Right: Ass't. Purser Jim Billingsley on S.S. *Catala* circa 1949 (note medal on right shoulder) *(McLennan Collection)*

Bottom Left:
Harry Braddick
(Ashmore Collection)

Bottom Right: Dave Charters (right) with Dong Chong at port of call (Alert Bay) circa 1949 *(S.S. Catala)* *(McLennan Collection)*

They Also Served

Purser George Fordyce

Freight Clerk Darrel Coates
(*Finlayson Collection*)

Purser "Pinkie" Hughes aboard S.S. *Venture*
April 1928 (*Skinner Collection*)

Freight Clerk
Hal Hartford 1946

Purser Charlie Guy (right)
with Chief Steward "Dinty" McGuiness
(*Twigg Collection*)

Purser Stan Hunter on *Lady Cecilia* 1935
(*H. Ives*)

They Also Served

Purser Al Newman *(Skinner Collection)*

Purser Gibb Rennie *Lady Cecilia* 1934
(H. Ives)

Purser A.B. Lannard
S.S. *Cowichan* circa 1922
(Vancouver Maritime Museum)

Freight Clerk Hugh Tozer
(B. Smith)

Purser Clarence Williams
(J. Smith Collection)

Freight Clerk "Mike"
Lucas *Chelohsin*
circa 1940
(O. Williams)

A typical U.S.S. Co. dining area. Seated are Reg Stover, Tom Lucas, Fred Smith, Slim Holdgate, Art Twigg, Hugh Tozer
(Twigg Collection)

Pictured here are various items of crockery used aboard Union Steamships. Note the changes made to the Company logo over the years. Art Bennett retrieved these items from Rock Bay, Heriot Bay and Menzies Bay.
(A. Bennett)

Chapter 4
CHIEF STEWARDS, WAITER/STEWARDS and COOKS

The second steward was also called the Saloon Man and he was in charge of all the tables and their settings. He wore a starched white jacket with an oval badge marked No. 1. The waiters and porters wore the same white jackets with the oval badge No. 2 and up.

All stewards/waiters were required to pay a per diem cost for meals and bedding.

The stewards' quarters aboard ship were known as the "Glory Hole."

Setting up tables on *Camosun II*
(Mrs. J. Stone)

THE STEWARDS

Perhaps you never noticed this, but the Stewards always carried a small pickle fork in the breast pockets of their tunics. They always used these to dish out small pats of butter onto the passengers' bread and butter plates.

Also, if you looked closely, you would see a short length of string hanging loose from the flies in their pants. One passenger noticed this and inquired what it was for. The Steward was quick to respond. "You see," he said, "during mealtimes, we are always terribly busy, and if perchance we have to go to the bathroom, all we have to do is lower our flies by pulling on the string, and we are all set. In this manner there is no need to touch our parts, so it is not necessary to even wash our hands afterwards."

The passenger gave this some thought, and he finally said, "That is quite ingenious, but tell me, how do you replace your parts back inside your pants?"

"Oh, quite simply," responded the Steward. "We use the pickle fork!"

Silver Braid on Black
Buttons - Silver

Alphabetical List of Chief Stewards 1920 to 1958

This list has been compiled from various sources, including ship registry files and personal acquaintances. While efforts have been made to be accurate, it is not to be taken as comprehensively complete and may have some errors, especially of omission.

Achers, J.
Attewell, Albert
   "Bert"
Audley, Harry

Booth, G.T.

Cummings, "Scotty"

Davidson, Norman
Deschner, G.
Dougan, Terry

Ebden, Bert
Ellis, Bill

Gardiner, William
   "Willie" or
   "Daddy"

Hartley, Jack
Holdgate, Clarence C.
   "Slim"
Holdgate, C.W. "Bud"
Holmes, (?)
Humphreys, Harold

Innes, D.

Jefferson Jr., Lance

Keen, Harry
Knight, Alfred
   "Bogey"

Lanches, C.

Main, Dickie
McDonald, Hugh
   "Little Mac"
McEwan, David
McEwan, William H.
   "Bill"
McGregor, J.
McGuiness, "Dinty"
McPhillips, Wilfred
   "Yorky"
Minnes, John J.

Pickerall, Fred

Scotter, Edwin I.
   "Teddy" or "Red"
Short, Albert
Singleton, David
Skinner, Walter

Townsend, Ralph
Tripp, Jack

Watts, Ernie
Wycherley, C.
Wyllie, Patrick

Albert "Bert" Attewell

Often when a fellow obtained a job aboard one of the Union ships he would be hired for one department and then see for himself that he would rather be working in a different department aboard ship. This was the case with Bert Attewell, who was born in Oldham, England, came out to Canada in 1924 at age 19, and started working on the Union ships as a deckhand, but he switched over to being a steward early in what turned out to be a long career with the Company.

There is record of the fact Bert was the No. 1 Steward under Chief Steward Ernie Watt but unfortunately there is no record of the date or the ship they were on. The picture of Bert accompanying this story shows him as Chief Steward on the *Venture*, which was in service from 1911 to 1946, indicating Bert had moved up quite quickly to become a Chief Steward. Bert's brother Cecil confirms that Bert became a Chief Steward in the early 1940s, and that Bert had worked aboard every ship in the Union fleet during his career. Bert stayed with Union Steamships right to the very end when all the Union ships were tied up. He then went over to the Alaska Steamship Line on the White Boats or corvettes as they are often called. When these ships ceased operating in the 1960s, Bert retired.

The Union Steamship Company was famous all over the coast for its fine food and wonderful meals aboard ship. A favourite item that nearly everybody recalls was a very fine cheese, which apparently was only to be had aboard the Union ships.

When Bert was Chief Steward on the *Venture* he noticed for two trips in a row he had to re-order blocks of this wonderful cheese. In checking into the matter he happened to mention it to a new steward in his crew. "Oh," the fellow said, "I threw those cheeses out the port hole because they looked and smelled so bad!" That's hard on a ship's meal rate!

Tex Lyon, the longtime wharfinger at Port Hardy, used to have to work long hours when a Union ship was in port unloading freight. In the beginning he never was so much as offered a cup of coffee aboard ship. Then word came through from head office that Tex was to be given his meals anytime a Union ship was alongside the Port Hardy dock unloading freight. Tex remarked that Bert Attewell fed him like a king.

One unusual event in Bert's career happened aboard the *Catala*, flag ship of the Union fleet, when it was tied up alongside the wharf at Prince Rupert. Bert, as Chief Steward, always gave a wake-up call to the Chief Engineer, Andrew Beattie. He would knock on his door and relay the time of day to him. On this occasion he knocked and received no response. He knocked again, still no response. This was unusual, so he tried the door and as it was unlocked he looked in and saw Beattie sitting in a chair at his little desk. Bert spoke to him again, still no response, so he walked over to where Beattie was sitting and then realized what had happened: Beattie had died while sitting in his chair! This was quiet a shock to Bert and of course to the whole crew. A conference was held aboard ship and it was

Chief Steward Bert Attewell on S.S. *Venture* (note wind shute) *(C. Attewell)*

decided the remaining three engineers could run the ship alright and the body was taken back to Vancouver.

Attewell retired in 1968 and passed away in Shaughnessy Hospital on Jan, 16, 1969, aged 64.

Harry Audley

Chief Steward Harry Audley
(Dorothy Audley)

The Union Steamship Company was started in 1889 and Harry Audley was born in Liverpool in July 1889. One could say, so to speak, even though they were miles apart, they grew up together.

Before coming to Canada, Harry worked aboard the Cunard ships and was aboard the Carpathia when it received orders to proceed full speed ahead to try and be of some assistance to the sinking *Titanic*, but they arrived too late to be of any help.

There is no record as to when and in what capacity Harry started with Union Steamships, but we do know he was Chief Steward on the *Cardena* in 1928. Having been appointed a Chief Steward, he would serve aboard various ships in that capacity.

On one occasion while Chief Steward on the *Lady Alexandra*, she was making a special charter run, going first to White Rock to pick up a load of passengers and then proceeding to Victoria. Harry had taken his first wife Alyce along for the trip, and John Gilligan, the Chief Engineer, also had taken his wife along. While Harry was out on the dock taking tickets, Alyce decided to visit Mrs. Gilligan in the Chief Engineer's room, which was behind the galley. On her way through the galley, Alyce slipped and fell, seriously injuring herself. She was taken to St. Paul's Hospital in an ambulance, but sad to say, she was in a wheelchair for the rest of her life. I have been told that because she had not purchased a ticket for the trip she was not a bona fide passenger and therefore no claim for financial support for her medical expenses could be made against the Company. She passed away in 1945.

Harry remarried in 1947 and his second wife, Doris, lived in North Vancouver until her death in 1990.

Harry left the Union Steamships in 1944 at age 55 and went to work as chef at Shaughnessy Hospital.

In the early 1950s, the Union Steamship Co. called Harry up and asked him to serve as Chief Steward aboard one of the new White Boats doing Alaska cruises. He made two trips but didn't like it, so he stayed ashore, continuing to work at Shaughnessy Hospital until he retired at age 65. He passed away May 15, 1979.

Bert Ebden

According to Stew Hale, a former Purser with Union Steamships, Bert started with the Company in the 1920s as a porter.

Before coming to Canada, he was thought to have been a butler in England. Stew recalls he had a very imposing stature, which could well have come from such employment. Scuttlebutt had it that he could carry two drinks from a stateroom to his cabin, in his vest pocket, and never spill a drop.

Bert must have been considered a valued employee because he sailed as Chief Steward on the *Cardena* on her maiden voyage, on June 20, 1923, but he was discharged in the great purge of 1937/38. At that time the CPR had their triangle run, Vancouver-Victoria-Seattle, and Union Steamships had a triangle run too: Prince Rupert - Anyox - Stewart, a trip that many ladies of the night made for business reasons. When Company officials checked out Bert's performance, they apparently found a Christmas gift list of his in his room aboard ship. It listed presents such as hams and turkeys that he was going to give to some of these girls. It was obvious to the Company officials that these items were going to come from the ship's stores, so Bert was fired. Others aboard the ship at the time thought it was all very humorous.

Clarence Thomas "Slim" Holdgate

As the nickname "Slim" indicates, Clarence Holdgate was tall and slim. He sported a pencil-thin black 01mustache and slicked-down hair.

One of his shipmates referred to him as the Colgate man, or the toothpaste man, Colgate Holdgate. In later years when he became a Chief Steward he was called Starvation Slim by his shipmates, which of course was in jest because all the Chief Stewards had a responsibility to control their meal rates aboard ship and Slim was no exception. However I was told he kept a round of Roquefort cheese on the galley shelf for the crew alone. Then again, one engineer I interviewed said he loved olives and he would sit down at the mess table and eat all the olives that were put out, then call for more, but Slim soon noticed that and would ration the supply of olives whenever this engineer was aboard.

Slim was born in Vancouver on May 14, 1904, and at age 14 went to sea as a cabin boy on the *Mount Eagle*, a CPR ship sailing to Australia and New Zealand. His last trip was to the Orient and he was in Yokohama the day after the big earthquake in 1923. He came back to Vancouver from that trip with a string of pearls, presented them to his fiancee and proposed to her. They were married on Jan. 14, 1924.

Prior to his marriage, Slim had joined the Fisheries Reserve and had made friends with a fellow who was a commercial fisherman, Red Percival. This man was an influence on Slim in his later years, for Slim surprisingly took up commercial fishing later in life.

Slim started working as an electrician's helper in North Vancouver. The Depression came and work was scarce so he started working part-time as a steward with Union Steamships. The first ship he worked aboard was the *Lady Evelyn* in 1931.

In the early 1930s, the Union Steamship Co. was having difficulty keeping their ships running and their employees working. The Company went to the extent of opening up their Bowen Island cabins during the winter months, letting their married

Chief Steward Clarence "Slim" Holdgate

employees and their families live in the cabins rent free. Slim moved his family to Bowen Island and from 1932 to 1937 he worked aboard the little *Comox* as a steward/deckhand when she was running between Snug Cove to ports in West Howe Sound. Then in September 1937 he got on full time aboard the *Capilano II* as linen man. His next ship was the *Lady Alexandra* in 1938.

In those days wages were low and the stewards on the *Lady Alexandra* augmented their incomes by collecting all the empty beer bottles left aboard from the famous "Booze Cruises." These empties would be stored aboard the Alex and once a month they'd get together and transport these empties down to the Capilano Brewery and get 25 cents a dozen for them. The proceeds would be split amongst the gang. Small as it was, 25 cents went a long way in the Dirty Thirties.

Slim was reluctant to move upwards to the Chief Steward's job, preferring to stay as 2nd Steward because of the tips he could get. With tips he could make far more money than the Chief Steward. He stayed as a 2nd Steward until 1940, then moved up as Chief Steward on the *Lady Pam*.

In 1949, the federal government instituted strict fire regulations for all Canadian vessels because of the disastrous fire aboard the S.S. *Noronic* on the Great Lakes. The Union Steamship Co. was hit hard by these new regulations, which included a requirement that every ship carrying passengers have a qualified First Aid man aboard. The Company decided the Chief Stewards would be that person, so Slim took the course and obtained his Industrial First Aid Ticket. Not long after, he was able to save a man's life because of that training.

It happened this way on one of the northern route ships: as the ship was making a landing, the passengers who were to disembark were told to stay clear. One fellow didn't heed this warning and as the steel cable head line was being tightened by the winches, it snapped and the loose end flew back, severing this man's leg just below the knee. Though there was no doctor about, Slim was called right away and he immediately ran back down to the galley, found an empty five-gallon lard bucket, poured a large quantity of flour in it, and ran back up to the injured man. He shoved the stump of his leg into the flour. The flour coagulated and stopped the bleeding, which saved the man's life. When they got the man to a doctor, he said it was one of the most unique ways he ever saw of stopping bleeding.

Mike Benson, a former Purser with the Company, has fond memories about Slim. Mike was getting married and the Company brought Mike down from a northern route and put him on a day run in order to help him prepare for the big day. He was on the *Capilano* and Slim was the Chief Steward. Three days before the wedding Mike came down with a very bad cold, but Slim came to the rescue, putting Mike on a strict liquid diet that by the wedding day had him as fit as a fiddle.

Every week Slim would have his men scrub down the dining room floor aboard ship and he always scrounged some very strong soap powder from the engineers, which they used in great quantities. On one occasion, Slim sent one of his new stewards down to the engine room to borrow some of their soap powder. Timidly, he went down with his empty tin. The engineer on watch was George Croucher. He sent his oiler, who also was a relatively new man, back to their stores with the order, "Get this man some of that compound." The poor oiler got things a bit mixed up and instead of the yellowish soap compound, he gave the poor chap a tin of whitish boiler compound. When the stewards commenced to wash the lino floor, the whole floor dried a sickly dull whitish colour. God knows how many times they had to go over that floor in order to regain its original lustre.

Needless to say, Slim was as mad as hell and tried to "come down" on the engine room gang, but he couldn't make it stick. It was a disaster, and Slim was a lot more careful next time when he borrowed powdered soap from the engineers.

Over his 29-year career with Union Steamships, Slim sailed on nearly all of the Company's ships in service during the 1930s, 1940s and early 1950s. His last ship was the *Coquitlam II*. He signed off her in May 1954.

In the early 1950s, the Company's fortunes were waning. Slim could see this so in 1953 he obtained a leave of absence and went commercial fishing for a few months. He bought a small troller, moved a camper up to Madeira Park and operated his boat from there. This was a dramatic change of lifestyle for him, influenced no doubt by his friend Red Percival, whom he had met many years ago. He came back to the Company in October 1953 but in 1954 when he again asked for a leave of absence, he was refused, so he left the Company in May 1954.

Slim then moved up to Madeira Park and carried on fishing from that location until 1969. Then he brought his boat down to Vancouver, lived aboard and kept on fishing for a livelihood. He was in good health and had never been in hospital for a day in his life, until three months before he died. He took sick, was admitted to hospital and had three strokes before he died of natural causes at 86 years of age, in 1990.

Harold Humphreys

Harold came to Vancouver in 1934 and got his first taste of sea life in 1936 when he sailed aboard the *Empress of Asia* and *Japan* out of Vancouver, as a probationary deck steward.

When the war came along, Harold was in the auxiliary of the Canadian Airforce so he was automatically accepted for the permanent forces. He was a Flight Sergeant and after the war he served with the United Nations Relief (UNRRA) as Administration Officer in Germany until 1946.

Harold went to work for the Union Steamship Co. on Sept. 20, 1946, sailing on the *Cassiar* as a steward under Chief Steward Norm Davidson. The Captain was Big Mac McLennan and Chief Officer Tom Lucas. Over the years Tom and Harold became the best of friends. Harold felt that Tom Lucas was a typical seafaring man. Within a year, Harold was promoted to Chief Steward and served in this capacity on all of the Company vessels. In 1947 he joined the new *Chilcotin* cruise ship as Saloon Steward for one season and in the next season he was appointed Chief Steward, staying aboard her until January 1955. It is interesting to note that Harold sailed aboard the *Chilcotin* on her maiden voyage and he also sailed on her on her last voyage, which was under the house flag of the Greek Nomikos lines and with the name S.S. *Stella Maris*.

Chief Steward Harold Humphreys
(Humphreys Collection)

Management of the Company was changing, some jobs were eliminated, old hands were leaving, and some simply retired. Harold was taken off the ships and brought into the office, where he took over Purchasing and was made Catering Superintendent, a position he held until the Company's demise in 1958. Gerald Rushton referred to Harold as the Company's "brisk Port Steward."

During his term as Catering Superintendent, orders came down from top management to make every effort to cut costs. One thing that was tried was a portion control for all meals. Harold did take Ted Mah, Norm Davidson, Bert Attewell and Mat Forester to a session of instruction on portion control for meals served aboard the Union ships, but what a turnabout for a Company that had become famous for its meals up and down the coast! They all agreed to try it but it did not work out in practice, so it was abandoned. A cafeteria was set up on the *Catala*. This is hard to imagine, for the *Catala* was the flagship of the Union fleet and was reputed to be the best feeder of all. As a cost-cutting measure it did succeed, because it eliminated three stewards, but it was a terrible turn of events for the grand dining room aboard this great ship. Harold noted though that the cafeteria in no way affected the ship's officers, because they were all served in the dining room as before.

When the Union Steamship Co. was coming to an end, Harold had no idea what he was going to do, but one day Chuck West of the Alaska Cruise Lines came into his office and offered him a job with the title of Shore Representative, which he accepted and so moved into an office on the CN dock. The company had its head office in Seattle so Harold single-handedly looked after everything for it in Vancouver, including food supplies, personnel, ship repairs, drydocking, etc. As a result, in October 1965 his title was changed to Assistant General Manager. He had progressed a great deal in the 19 years since he came to Canada.

Recalling his days with Union Steamships, Harold said he enjoyed every minute he worked for the grand old company. When he came aboard the *Cassiar* in 1946, there was no news stand aboard her and he remembers Norm Davidson the Chief Steward, setting up shop on one of the dining room tables. He would clear the table off and spread out his magazines, newspapers, candy, peanuts and popcorn etc. for display at each stop. The local people and kids would swarm aboard. Harold said that Norm made a killing.

When he was Chief Steward on the *Chilcotin*, the Captain, Harry McLean, who was famous for his practical jokes, gave Harold fits. One of his tricks was to buy little plastic worms and drop them in customers' salad bowls. In fact Martha Skinner, wife of Frank Skinner, Company Agent at Prince Rupert, says she was the butt of one of these so-called jokes. She went on to tell about him lighting fire crackers under the dining room tables. One can just imagine the embarrassment for the Chief Steward.

Two Union captains who went over to Alaska Cruise Lines at the same time as Harold did were Ernie Sheppard and Billy McCombe. Harold said they were poles apart, one was all bluster and gruff and the other quiet and polite. Harold said there were always problems with Captain McCombe's ship, whereas Captain Sheppard's ship would come and go and you would never know she had been in port. Captain McCombe could never acknowledge the fact that Harold, who had served under Captain McCombe in the Union Steamship Co., was now in effect his boss.

The management of Alaska Cruise Lines also decided to buy back the former *Chilcotin* from her Greek owners, who had changed her name to the *Stella Maris*. Harold was sent to look her over and report back to management on her condition, so he spent a lovely week cruising the Greek islands. He gave a favourable report as to her condition and arrangements were made to drydock her for inspection before she was to sail back to B.C. Harold then flew home but the *Westar*, as she was now to be called, never made it. She caught fire while taking on oil in Sardinia and was a total loss. The Company lost the ship, but according to Harold they did very well with the insurance settlement.

Harold talked about the well-known "booze cruises" of the *Lady Alexandra*. He said he always had made a point to go around the deck of the *Lady Alexandra* after they had docked in Vancouver to make sure no one was hiding aboard or had just passed out in some nook and didn't know the ship had docked. Harold just shook his head when he thought back about all the goings on during those moonlight cruises.

Myself, I recall Harold as a very efficient Chief Steward who was instrumental in seeing that there were fresh flowers in the dining room aboard ship on sailing night. His dining rooms were always immaculate, tables set to perfection and draperies cleaned and hung properly. Another one of his trademarks was the fact that he could always be found at the gang plank at every stop ready to assist any passenger coming aboard or leaving the ship.

Alfred "Bogey" Knight

"Bogey" was as Irish as the Blarney Stone itself, having been born in the Emerald Isle on Aug. 28, 1904. Undoubtedly Bogey was one of the great characters in the Union fleet, and he was known up and down the coast for his blarney and hijinks.

One of his most famous escapades took place aboard the *Chelohsin*, or the "Charlie Olsen" as the loggers used to call her. The Master of the ship at the time was Bob Naughty, the Chief Officer was Paddy Hannigan, as Irish as they come, and Bogey was Chief Steward. Shortly before midnight, Bogey and his staff were sitting around the dining room having a coffee. The deck officers would soon be changing watch as their shifts ran from 12 to 6 and 6 to 12. It so happened a logger had stumbled down the stairs to the dining salon and had passed out at the foot of the stairs. Bogey and his staff were debating what they were going to do with the body when suddenly Bogey had an idea. "Quick boys, get me some ketchup and a carving knife from the galley," he cried. Quickly these items were produced and Bogey hastened over to the "body," opened its shirt, poured ketchup on its throat and sprinkled it around to make it look like a corpse. He also covered the carving knife with ketchup and threw it down beside the "body." It looked as though the fellow had committed suicide, right there and then.

Bogey and his staff returned to their seats, sipping their coffee and awaiting the arrival of Paddy Hannigan, who would be coming down for a coffee before he went on watch. Paddy was a very excitable Irishman and when he came down the stairs and saw this "body" with blood all over the place he stopped in his tracks, aghast, and shouted over to Bogey, "My God, what happened?"

Nonchalantly, Bogey explained that this fellow had stumbled down the stairs and had slit his throat right there in front of them. Excitedly, Paddy asked, "Have you told the old man?" "No, not yet," said Bogey, "We're wondering what to do with the body."

With that, Paddy dashed away up to the bridge to report this to the skipper. As soon as he had gone, Bogey and his boys pulled the "body" out of sight, cleaned up the mess, returned to their places and resumed quietly sipping their coffees. Soon Captain Naughty came rushing down, but when he arrived there was nothing to be seen of any body. He looked over to where Bogey and

Chief Steward "Bogey" Knight *(Skinner Collection)*

his crew were sitting and shouted, "Paddy just reported that there was a dead man down here, that he had committed suicide. Where is he?" Bogey and his crew just looked at the Captain in amazement and asked, "What body? What suicide? What are you talking about?"

Captain Naughty hesitated, thought for a minute or so, turned around and went back up to the bridge, more than likely concluding that Paddy must have been playing a joke on him for he was an easy going man. He no doubt had a good laugh over how Paddy had been fooled by a fellow Irishman.

Bogey loved this type of joke, but that one, which was told to me by former Purser Denis Shaw, probably tops the list. It's easy to imagine the laughter that must have ensued aboard the *Chelohsin* that night and the next day, though Paddy Hannigan would not have enjoyed it because the laughter was all at his expense.

Alfred "Bogey" Knight had joined the Union Steamship Co. as a steward in 1926. He soon was promoted to night steward on the *Chelohsin* and progressed to become a Chief Steward. He was a real fancy dresser, and when he came down to the ship on sailing night, he often was mistaken for a passenger. He spoke with a lisp, sported a pencil-thin moustache, and slicked down his hair so he resembled George Raft, a movie actor of the day.

Bogey also loved to gamble, and every holiday he would go down to Reno or Las Vegas. His gambling exploits and his talk about being a winner every time became a legend in the fleet. Supposedly he had a system, but Stew Hale, a contemporary of his and a good friend who often accompanied Bogey on those trips, laughs and says the notion about Bogey always being a winner just wasn't true. In 1954, the Company newsletter reported, "The 'bogeyman' has just returned from Reno and he says the dice table paid off well for him again, believe or not!" (Stew, by the way, wrote a little booklet titled *How to Play Craps, the Odds Fallacy*, and dedicated it to his good friend Bogey. I have a copy of it in my collection.)

Bogey played an active role in the seamen's strike in 1935, but he survived the subsequent purge in 1939 when Head Office began finding big differences between actual passenger counts and ticket sales, and other problems such as in the number of meal tickets sold. A number of Chief Stewards and Pursers were fired as a result, but Bogey's signature can be seen on a union contract agreement signed in 1941 between the Company and its Pursers and Chief Stewards, a copy of which is located on pages 306 and 307 of this book.

After 14 years on the ships, starting as a steward and ending up as a Chief Steward, Bogey decided to come ashore and became a checker on the Union dock. He stayed at that job until the Company folded in 1958 and then went over to Ballantyne Pier, along with Vic Hayman and Bill Munroe. He retired in 1970 and died on Jan. 24, 1988 at the ripe old age of 84.

Following is a tribute from his friend Stew Hale. As "Bogey" was one of the "larger-than-life" characters in the Company, this is meaningful to his story.

DEDICATION

To my old friend Bogey, successful gambler and original thinker.

When I told him I was going to write this, he was a little concerned that I would give away his secrets of gambling, or at least sell them for a price of a minimal bet on the table.

Don't worry, I told him. You can tell the perfect truth and how many will profit by it?

Tell the casinos not to worry, either. No hordes will sweep down and clean them out.

But here and there someone will say "Hey! This is for me! Why didn't I think of that? Of course, they are right!"

To such a one, here are ideas that have been pounded, propounded, accepted, rejected, abandoned, rediscovered and mauled over.

Good luck!

William H. "Bill" McEwan

The photo of Bill accompanying this text is a very rare one, because he was a fellow who shunned publicity of any sort and was reluctant to have his picture taken under any circumstances.

He came to Vancouver in 1898 and one of his classmates, in his school days at Dawson School, was Gerry McGeer, who later became Mayor of Vancouver. In his youth, Bill was a good soccer player, for he played left halfback on the St. Andrews team in the senior city league.

In his early sea-going days he worked aboard the *Empress of China*, then moved over to the Terminal Steam Navigation Co., which at the time was working out of the Union Steamship wharf. Bill probably saw that the Union Steamship Co. was going ahead fast, so he switched over to it in 1917, as a 2nd Steward. He liked that position and pretty well stayed in it for life, though he did act as relieving Chief Steward towards the end of his long career. By 1955 he was 10th on the Company's seniority list.

Bill's courtesy and friendliness to everyone was his trademark, and was a fine example of the Union Company's motto: "Friendly Service."

Edwin L. "Red" or "Teddy" Scotter

In his younger days he was known as "Red." He came to Canada in 1912 and went to work for the CPR but left them and started with Union Steamships on April 4, 1914. He worked his way up the ladder and in May 1935 sailed out for the first time as Chief Steward.

Over the years he served on every ship in the fleet and on every route. By 1954 he was seventh senior employee in the Company. Loggers all over the coast came to know him for he had served them for seven years in a row on their ship, the *Chelohsin*, or, as they had nicknamed her, the "Charlie Olsen." I only made one trip on the *Chelohsin* but I can still see him standing (or holding himself up?) with his hands clasped over the banister at the foot of the

Left: Chief Steward "Bill" McEwan with his son who was also in the Company on the *Lady Alexandra* (J. Smith Collection)

Right: Chief Steward "Teddy" Scotter (*U.S.S. Heaving Line*)

Terry Dougan (right) with Johnny Westegard on the deck of S.S. *Camosun* 1954
(T. Dougan)

dining room stairs, waiting to seat passengers in the dining room.

He had the unusual distinction amongst the Chief Stewards of being sent over to Scotland three times as a crew member to bring to B.C. three ships for the Company, namely the *Lady Alexandra* in 1924, the *Lady Cynthia* in 1925, and the *Lady Cecilia* in 1926. When he was over in Scotland in 1926, he had the good fortune to be on hand to see the new flagship of the Union fleet, the *Catala*, being launched. Later in 1950, he was to serve on her as Chief Steward.

There must have been a fatal connection between Teddy, as he was called in later years, and the *Catala*, for he collapsed and died aboard her as she lay alongside the dock at Prince Rupert. Harold Humphreys, who was the catering manager for the Company in Vancouver at the time, made arrangements for the body to be brought back to Vancouver and he had the unenviable task of informing Teddy's family of his death.

Terry Dougan

Terry worked during the summer seasons of 1953 and 1954, as either a messboy or day or night porter. In 1953 he had short stints on the *Catala* and *Chilcotin*, then the balance of the summer on the *Lady Cynthia*.

In 1954, he spent his whole summer on the *Camosun*.

The two memories foremost in his mind are from his second year while serving on the *Camosun*. He recalled one evening when the *Catala* and the *Camosun* were both scheduled to leave the Union dock at 8 p.m. The *Catala* was first to leave, as the *Camosun* had some more freight to load. They watched the *Catala* sail out of the harbour and past Brockton Point. Much to his surprise he saw the *Catala* coming back into the wharf. Much to the anger of the *Catala*'s Master, he had to bring his ship back because they had left a pallet of passengers' baggage behind on the wharf.

Terry recalled one trip on the *Camosun*.

They left Namu, which was their last call southbound, at a time which would put them into Vancouver around midnight the next day. As they continued south, the big question was, would they arrive at the Vancouver dock before midnight or after, in which case the passengers would be staying aboard until morning. Finally at 11:15 p.m. they passed Point Atkinson and Captain John Halcrow sent word that "officially" they would be in port before midnight. Terry said he had never seen so many stewards go to work so quickly as they did on that occasion. As the ship slid alongside the dock, the clock on the old post office building struck twelve!

Bill Ellis

Bill and I attended West Vancouver High School together, although he was a couple of grades ahead of me. We did not see each other once we left high school but I did know that Bill was a successful business man in Vancouver dealing in art prints and other work of Northwest Coast Indians. We both worked at different times for Union Steamships and neither of us were aware of this until Bill, who was passing through Campbell River on business, looked me up. Bill is now semi-retired and lives on the Queen Charlotte Islands, from where he runs his business, F.W.E. Enterprises Ltd. I asked him to write me about his job on the Union ships, which follows just as he gave it to me:

"My first away-from-home job was on the *Cardena*, washing dishes, cleaning heads, and Mess Boy for the Officers' table. There were no tips at this table!

"This experience is seared in my memory. Ever since, I have been unable to stand wool or prickly cloth next to my skin. You see, for this job I had to obtain a pair of dark wool pants and a pair of black oxfords. This was in 1938 and everyone was broke so this was a hardship to start with. I was able to buy these items on Cordova Street at a good price. Once on board, the Chief Steward checked me out and put me to work. Soon, I was seriously pearl diving in the steaming hot galley sink. The pants became like nettle and the shoes shrunk a couple of sizes. Oh it was hot, standing there at that sink in those wool pants. I remember how sweet it was to get into cool air on deck and unbutton my issue-white-stewards jacket.

"Another great part of the job was cleaning the heads after we'd crossed Queen Charlotte Sound and got into the lee of Calvert Island. I think every Chinese cannery worker on board was sick on that crossing, and only half of them made it to work at Namu and other canneries. It was all very interesting of course to a kid not yet out of school, who wanted adventure and some spending money. Obviously, I had started at the bottom rung.

"Strangely, that hot summer on the *Cardena* gave me a boost when I joined the navy the following year. Someone asked me if I had any experience on ships and I said yes, and lo I was enlisted RCNR, which was a considerable cut above RCNVR. RCNR types were the salty ones, having worked in the merchant marine, knew all about ships and had been everywhere. I had no end of pretending to do for the next five years, but it did help me get promoted fast. It wasn't long before the RCNR thing gave me the opportunity to get a badge on my arm and get out of the sink and bathtub scrubbing for the rest of the war.

"Whenever I was asked about my time on the *Cardena*, I usually forgot to tell them about the galley work and cleaning the heads."

C.W. "Bud" Holdgate

"Bud" Holdgate

Bud Holdgate was the son of the well-known Chief Steward in the Union Steamship Co., Slim Holdgate.

In the early 1930s, the Depression years, the Union Steamship Co. allowed many of their employees and families to live in their cabins at Bowen Island rent free in the winter months, and the Holdgate family was one of these. Bud's father worked aboard the little *Comox* as a combination deckhand/steward in those years. It was natural that Bud also found work aboard a Union ship. He obtained a job on the *Lady Alexandra* as the news agent's helper during the summer months. He would board the *Lady Alexandra* at Bowen Island and would be given a little basket, much like a shopping basket, full of candy bars, popcorn, etc. There was a little song he used that went, "Peanuts, popcorn, a nickel, five." Bud did this for two summers and then got a job as a helper on a lunch counter that was opened on the upper deck and was run by a fellow by the name of Alex Swiston.

"We used to make sandwiches and sold coffee, cold drinks and donuts. It was a real money maker," Bud said. The second year, Bud got the job as mess boy, which paid $45 a month, a big jump from the $35 a month he was paid for helping the newsy.

Bud recalled an amusing story about the sandwich bar. They always had ham sandwiches, and another meat which was whatever was on the previous day's dining room menu, and as well, a cheese sandwich. On one particular day there was a Jewish picnic aboard and the other meat sandwich for the day happened by chance to be pork! Bud said, "A fellow came up and asked for a roast beef sandwich. I'm sorry sir, all we have today is ham, pork or cheese sandwiches." The fellow was insistent, saying, "I want a roast beef sandwich." Bud didn't know what to do so he went behind the counter and asked his boss Alex Swiston what he should do. Alex said, "Make up a pork sandwich and give it to him. He can't ask for pork being Jewish, just take the sandwich to him and say nothing." Sure enough the fellow ate his sandwich without a word.

Then Bud got a big break. One of the dining room stewards left and Bud replaced him. Now he was making $60 a month plus tips. He said, "Can you imagine such a wage for a young fellow? And I did that up until I joined the airforce in 1942." But being a dining room waiter was no easy job. "Those dining room tables had to be spotless and set up just so. When you served a bowl of soup, you didn't dare put the bowl down on the table if there was a spot of soup on the rim of the bowl," he said. The Chief Steward at the time was Teddy Scotter and the second steward was his father, Slim Holdgate.

One of the Chinese cooks on the Alex at the time was Seto Bow. Bud said, "He liked my dad because he had stood up for him when he obtained his Canadian citizenship papers."

Bud only worked aboard one ship in fleet and that was the *Lady Alexandra*. Whenever the Alex is brought up in conversation the famous midnight dance cruises or "booze cruise" becomes a topic for discussion. Bud recalled some events of these cruises that stayed in his mind. He said, "On one trip I remember a fellow taking a swan dive from the top of the stairs leading down onto the dance floor! Miraculously he survived!"

He went on to say, "We would always have a good strong, strong urn of coffee ready for the return trip on those cruises. We would make it and let it sit for three hours and when the revellers came aboard at midnight that's what they wanted."

On another trip, "We were approaching the First Narrows about 1 a.m. One of our passengers went over the side. The fellow had been arguing with his girl friend and became distraught and said he would jump overboard if she didn't see things his way. She was adamant, so he jumped," Bud said.

"Man Overboard" was the cry and the Captain immediately stopped the ship, the search light was turned on and the fellow was spotted right away. At the same time the *Arangi*, bound for Australia, saw us stopped, and turned their searchlight on and eased towards us. A lifeboat was launched from the Alex and the fellow was picked up. When the ship arrived back in Vancouver, the police were called and arrested the fellow.

When Bud returned from the war he joined the Vancouver Fire Department and was with them until 1984 when he retired.

Wilfred "Yorky" McPhillips

"Yorky" McPhillips

As the nickname "Yorky" might indicate, he was from Yorkshire, England, and had been born there in 1927.

He started working on deep sea ships out of England as a steward. The last deep sea ship he worked aboard was the Celtic Monarch in 1947. He settled in Canada and joined the Union Steamship Co. on March 12, 1948, sailing on the *Chelohsin* as a Porter, then later working as a Night Man. Harry Roach was the Master and Harry Keen was the Chief Steward.

Yorky was aboard the *Chelohsin* when she went aground at Stanley Park on Nov. 6, 1949, shortly after 8 p.m. The Chief Steward at this time was Teddy Scotter. He remembers that the Chief Officer, Paddy Hannigan, pretty well took over handling things after the grounding, from Captain Aspinall. He handled it all very efficiently so there was no panic amongst the 50 or so passengers who were aboard. Paddy knew that Yorky had had deep sea experience so he put him in charge of No. 4 lifeboat launched to ferry passengers ashore.

News stories of the day reported that one of the passengers aboard at the time was a lady who raised chinchillas, and she had three crates of these animals aboard with her. Yorky describes what took place with her and the chinchillas: "She used to breed these animals and was shipping them down as freight. I had lifeboat No. 4 and it was ready to leave but this lady had refused to get into the lifeboat and leave the *Chelohsin* without her chinchillas. She just wouldn't get into the lifeboat without them. Paddy came along and wanted to know why I hadn't pushed off. I explained to Paddy that this lady wouldn't leave the ship without her chinchillas, so he went and got two deckhands to load these crates in the back end of the lifeboat. Well, I couldn't work the tiller because these crates were in the way. We had a helluva time but finally managed to get the boat ashore. The passengers disembarked and the crates of chinchillas were unloaded as well onto the beach. Then this lady started to complain and demand we take the chinchillas up to the road in the park. I had to tell her my duty was to get back to the ship and help bring more passengers ashore. Whatever happened after that to those chinchillas I don't know." (A local newspaper reported at the time that the chinchillas were valued at $2,000.)

All the crew left the ship the next morning and were taken to Vancouver by a tug boat.

In recalling Paddy Hannigan, Yorky laughed and said Paddy always felt that Captain Suffield put him aboard the *Chelohsin* for punishment. Frequently when Paddy came down to the dining room he would exclaim, "What son of a bitch didn't I lift my hat to this morning?"

From the *Chelohsin* Yorky was moved to the *Catala* and then he went over to the *Cardena*. He recalled the "Old Chief Engineer, Arthur," on the *Cardena:* "Old Arthur was not a very congenial fellow and the waiter at his table was a little fellow known as Tich. Chief Arthur was giving little Tich a bad time on one occasion and Tich finally got mad and picked up a plate and bounced it on Arthur's head. Both Arthur and Tich survived to battle another day!"

Later Yorky worked aboard the *Chilcotin*, under the command of Captain Harry McLean running to Skagway. He remarked that Captain McLean was a very competent skipper and an excellent ship handler.

Yorky also recalled Captain Owen-Jones. "He was a difficult man to get to know. I understood this and felt I got along with him okay. You had to have everything ready for him at the mess table when he came down at midnight before going on watch. If ever we had some trouble with drunks fighting in staterooms, we always called upon him to come and settle things. I think he would rather fight than eat at times," he said.

There also was the time Yorky had a run-in with the Marine Superintendent, Captain Suffield. Yorky was wheeling a cart full of passengers' luggage down the dock and had difficulty seeing ahead. He bumped into Captain Suffield who was standing watching the ship being loaded. Captain Suffield immediately walked over to the Chief Steward, Teddy Scotter, who was at the gang plank, and said, "Fire that man!" Just like that, but Teddy paid no heed to this order.

Yorky also remarked about what a good feeder the Union Company had been, especially compared with the poor food in his deep sea years. The first day he joined the *Chelohsin* he heard this big row going on in the deck crews' mess. He asked the Chief Steward, Harry Keen, what all the fuss was about and Harry replied, "Oh they're complaining that they are getting too many apple pies!" Yorky said, "I was lucky if I ever saw an apple when I was deep sea."

Yorky left Union Steamships in 1955 and went over to the Black Ball Ferries, which became B.C. Ferries. He ended his career with B.C. Ferries in 1991, where he was Catering Superintendent at the Horseshoe Bay terminal.

Cecil G. Skinner

Cecil Skinner (right) and Alex Duncan 1938

Cecil was the third person with the name Skinner who worked for the Union Steamship Co. The first was the well-known Chief Steward, Walter Skinner, who was Cecil's uncle, and Frank Skinner, former purser and later Union Steamship Agent at Prince Rupert, who was his brother.

Cecil pointedly said he didn't have any pull in getting his first job as a steward on the *Lady Rose* in 1937, and that he obtained it on his own, but Charlie Caldwell had said when he hired him, "If you're as good as the other Skinners in our fleet you'll do alright."

Cecil's favourite ship was the *Lady Cecilia* and it was aboard her he met and later married his wife Edith. She had just decided to take a day cruise on this particular day, aboard the ship he was on.

One event he recalls vividly was when he discovered a dead Chinese man in the steerage section on the *Chelohsin*. He immediately reported this Captain Wilson, who asked him right away, "How do you know he's dead?" "Well," Cecil said, "he's bloated up something terrible." It turned out he had swallowed a water and lye solution!

Another grim story Cecil related took place on the *Chelohsin* as well. A passenger had slit his throat in one of the staterooms and Cecil had to stay aboard after everyone had gone, to help the police in their investigation of this suicide, and then clean up the room after they left. He was working as a night steward on this occasion.

On Dec. 24, 1940, Cecil was again working as night steward aboard the *Lady Cecilia* when she backed aground at Pender Harbour. He was asleep at the time and the stewards' quarters were aft, right above the propeller. When she hit, he thought the propeller was going to come right through the deck. He jumped out of his bunk and ran up on deck in his pajamas. The passengers were quite surprised at his attire, as it was in the afternoon when this all took place. He recalls one blade of the propeller was torn right off and thrown up on the beach.

Cecil remembers Captain Lawrie suffering a heart attack on the bridge of his ship, during a very heavy fog. The Chief Officer had to take over and he brought the ship safely into the Union dock.

When the war came along, Cecil joined the navy and made friends with Gordon Southam of the *Province* newspaper. When the war was over, Cecil went back to the Union boats for a short time but then while visiting his old friend Gordon Southam, he admitted he didn't want to stay at sea any longer, so Gordon gave him a job at the *Province* in the latter part of 1946.

Ralph Townsend

Ralph spent most of his time aboard the *Catala* and left his mark in the Company's history in an unusual way. When he was working he was constantly reciting a little poem that went like this:

Home presents a doleful picture
Dark and dreary as a tomb
Uncle Willie got a stricture
Ma's got falling of the womb
Sister's got her menstruation
Grandma's got the change of life
Father's got a wreath of clappers
Caught from Uncle Percy's wife.
All our home is desolation
No one hardly smiles
And my present occupation is cracking ice
For Granpa's piles.

S.S. *Catala*
Stewart, B.C. 1947
(B. Smith)

They Also Served

Left: Chief Steward
William Gardiner
*(Vancouver
Maritime Museum)*

Right: Chief Steward
Harry Keen 1945/46

Above: Chief Steward Jack Tripp with
Capt. Malcolmson and Paddy Farina
(Farina Collection)

Right: Chief Steward Charlie Lanches
(J. Smith Collection)

They Also Served

Top Left: Henry Newman on *Lady Cynthia* at Squamish 1952
(*Richer Collection*)

Top Right: Chief Steward Harold Humphreys and his crew
(*Humphreys Collection*)

Bottom Left: Bill Richer 1971
(*Richer Collection*)

Bottom Right: Bert Attewell's crew
(*Mrs. J. Stone*)

They Also Served

Stewards on S.S. *Catala* 1935 *(Skinner Collection)*

Stewards aboard *Camosun II*: (left to right) Dave McEwan, Colin Park, Fred Young, Bill Delany (2nd Steward), Jim Bruce *(Park Collection)*

Steward ringing the "Ding Dong" announcing "Dinner is Served" aboard S.S. *Cardena*
(Roach Collection)

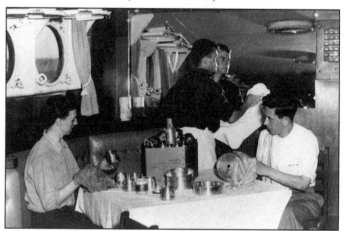

Getting the dining room "ship shape"
(Humphreys Collection)

Stewards and waiters posing on a U.S.S. vessel
(Humphreys Collection)

Chapter 5
DECK CREWS

The deck crew aboard Union Steamship vessels varied from ship to ship. Naturally, the smaller vessels didn't carry as many crew members as the larger northern-service ships. Following are the generally-used job titles in the deck crews:

Basic Seaman	Watchman
Able Bodied Seaman or A.B.	Quartermaster
(earned a certificate and had to have a lifeboat certificate)	
Dayman	Winchman
Stevedore	Bosun (the head seaman)

Some crewmen wore Union Steamship sweaters. These were not regular issue but instead could be purchased by crewmen from Company stores.

In early days, seamen were required to pay for their bed and meals, which included an issue of clean bedding once a week.

Seaman Neil Suffield in Bosun's Chair painting forestays on *Camosun II* 1943
(C. Lewis)

Loading an automobile onto S.S. *Chilcotin*
(Roach Collection)

Alphabetical List of the Deck Crew of the Union Steamships 1920 to 1958

This list has been compiled from various sources, including ship registry files and personal acquaintances. While efforts have been made to be accurate, it is not to be taken as comprehensively complete and may have some errors, especially of omission.

Allan, John
Allin, Clinton
Allen, Doug
Anderson, "Smokey"
Andriani, Frank
Annan, Tom Jr.
Arnett, Jimmy
Auger, George
Aylward, William "Big Bill"

Barron, Stan
Barry, Roy Jr.
Bartlet, Geof
Beck. Stan "Buddy"
Berg, Alfie
Best, Daulfred "Joe" or "Doffie"
Billerby, J. Arthur
Boden, Jack Jr.
Bone, Bill
Borden, Alex
Bridsen, Dick "Dickie"
Brown, Dennis "Brownie"
Brunt, Cliff
Bunker, Bert
Burkmar, George "Barnyard"

Cahill, Tommy
Cambell, Dave
Cambie, Ormand
Campbell, Malcolm
Charleton, Alex
Coles, Bob
Cooper, George
Corson, George
Costigan, Ed
Cushing, Les

Daisely, Neil
Darby, Ken
David, Frank
David, Prosper
Davidoff, Bill "Molotov"
Draper, Len
Dumont, Freddie
Duncan, Laurie
Dwyer, Paddy

Eaton, Dean
English, Dickey
Ericksen, Gus
Estey, Bill
Everly, John

Farley, Walter
Flager, John
Fletcher, Ken
Fletcher, Stan
Foote, Dave
Fraser, Jack
French, Al
French, Wally
Frenchy, "Paper Nose"
Fries, Dick
Frieson, "Squeek"
Fry, Bill

Gammon, Bill "Squeeks"
Geisbury, Billy
Gerbrandt, George
Gibson, Earnie
Gibson, Gib
Gourlay, Henry
Gowdy, Johnny
Greenlaw, D.
Greus, Stan
Grisenthwaite, Dan
Gurley, Henry.

Hacayway, Brothers.
Hadley, Michael J.
Hageman, Norm "Slim"
Haines, Al
Hanke, Kelly
Hansen, Mark
Harper, George "Scotty"
Harris, Bucky
Hart, "Red"
Harwood, Johnny
Hildich, Paddy
Hill, Albert Jr.
Hireen, Bill "Soogie"
Holbrook, Phil
Hornsby, John
Hotra, George

Husband, Gus
Hynes, Kenny

Jamison, Don "Scotty"
Jensen, Magnus
Johansoon, Ole
Johnsen, Ed
Jones, Davie
Jones, Gib
Jones, Gordie
Jones, Ivor
Jones, Len
Jones, Percy "Blighty"
Jorgenson, "Blacky"

Kelly, "Bum Mit"
Kelly, "Suitcase"
Kendall, Adam
Kennel, Bill
Kennett, Fred
Kennett, Ted
Ketchum, Bill
Ketchum, Fred
Krischuk, Nick

Lawson, Bill
Lawson, Ray "Blackie"
Lucas, Ernie
Lyons, Al

MacAulay, Malcolm
MacKenzie, John Angus
Mackie, Scotty
MacLeod, John
MacLeod, Rod
Manning, Ben
Martinson, John
McEwan, Dick
McEwan, William H.
McFadden, Ed
McGuiness, "Springline"
McIntosh, Dave
McLean, Robert "Bob"
McLeod, Jack
McLeod, Scotty
McMeekin, Tom
McMillan, Johnny

McNalley, Jimmy
McNiven, Dan J.
McPherson, Norm
Mercer, Alex
Michael, Percy "Big Mike"
Michaluk, Albert "Red"
Middleton, John
Miller, Jimmy
Mirkly, Red
Morrissey, Pat
Mowat, Doug
Muirhead, Jack
Musgrove, Gil "Squeek"

Nelson, Nels
Nicholson, Danny

O'Donnell, Jimmy
O'Rivers, Penty
Obrecht, Chick
Owens, Johnny

Page, Charlie
Park, Colin
Patton, P.M. "Big Pete"
Peterson, Karl
Plant, Ernie
Prendergast, Al

Rand, John
Rees, Melvin
Reid, Alex
Reid, George "Bucky"

Renwich, Ricky
Richmond, Johnny
Rinder, Don
Rive, C. Elliot
Roach, Edward "Ed"
Roach, Will
Robertson, Scotty
Rosi, Don
Ross, Alan
Russel, Phil

Satchwell, Dave
Scott, Bill
Senvoich, Steve
Seymour, Ralph
Simmons, Arnie "Cowboy"
Smith, Alan
Smith, Boyd T.
Smith, Doug J.
Smith, Joe
Smith, John A.
Smith, Ron
Smith, Stanley A.
Smith, Steele
Solem, Ed
Spence, "Scotty"
Spry, Bill
Stanley, Chuck
Stanley, Ned
Stephens, Charlie
Stephenson, Keith
Stevenson, Johnny
Stevenson, Roy
Stewart, Don

Stewearton, Fred
Storey, Doug
Strachan, Charlie
Suffield, Neil
Swanson, Harry

Taylor, Sid
Thompson, Ken
Thompson, Lorrie
Tite, Ted
Tovash, Johnny "Tiny"
Tufts, Wally
Turner, Al
Turner, Jack

Vanderdike, Johnny
Verge, Rod
Vincent, Carl

Waldon, Jimmy
Walker, Johnny
Watson, Jimmy
Watt, Jimmy
Watt, Wally
White, Jackie
Williams, Al
Wilson, Bud
Wooten, George

Young, Gordon

Capt. Yates and Deck Crew on the S.S. *Cassiar* 1912

John Allan

John Allan (left), Chick Obrecht, Bill Estey on *Lady Pam* 1946

After my letter to the Editor of the *Western Mariner* magazine appeared in the March 1990 issue, requesting people to contact me who had stories to relate about the Union Steamships, John was one of the first persons I heard from, and he had a wealth of information and stories to tell.

John began working on the Union ships in 1945 at age 17, working as a deckhand for the summer months to put himself through university, which he did for six years. He graduated in 1950 and started a teaching career in 1951, and when he retired he was an Area Superintendent in the Vancouver School District.

John and his friend Doug Mowat, the deceased former Social Credit MLA, were in Scouts together and they received a scouting proficiency badge in seamanship, in a course conducted by none other than Captain Wally (The Baron) Walsh, of the U.S.S.Co. No doubt this was a help for them, as they were both hired at the same time by the Union Steamship Co. as deckhands in the summer of 1945. John went aboard the *Lady Pam* and Doug went out on the *Capilano*.

John said, "All I basically knew about ships was that the bow was the front end and the stern was the back end." He was seasick his first trip out, and stepped into the bight of the head line as it was running out, which was very dangerous. He got a quick bawling out from the winchman for being so stupid. However, John soon gained his sea legs and in his last year aboard ship had become a first class quartermaster. Captain Yates was always happy to have John aboard as his number one quartermaster.

John only worked on the day boats, namely the *Lady Pam*, *Lady Cynthia*, *Lady Cecilia* and *Lady Alexandra*. The deck crews changed constantly but here are some names of fellows he sailed with, for the record: Ormond Cambie, Prosper David, Bill Estey, Gibb Jones, Blackie Lawson, Norm McPherson, Jack Muirhead, Gil "Squeak" Musgrove, Chick Obrecht, Elliot "Chuck" Rive, Harry Swanson, Henry Gourlay, and Malcolm MacDonald.

John signed on the *Lady Pam* in the summer of 1945. While he was there, the Purser's safe aboard the ship was broken open. There is no record of what was obtained and the crew were grilled by the police. One crew member was suspected but no proof was found. Soon after, John's wallet was stolen aboard ship, but again, whoever the culprit was, escaped detection. The crew member who was suspected, disappeared soon after John's wallet was stolen.

One time when he was on the *Pam*, the crew discovered the cook was selling the crew's milk to passengers so when they were in port they hung the cook over the side of the ship with his feet just touching the water and made him promise not to do that sort of thing again.

Like everyone else, John said the food aboard ship was great. "We received the same as the passengers and deck officers, but we had no table cloths on our table," he recalls. He made it a point to maintain a good relationship with the Chinese cooks.

He particularly liked sardine salads, so would ask for that and say "hi-yu sardines" - hi-yu being a phrase meaning extra good. On one occasion the mess boy brought his salad along with two cans of sardines, unopened.

The *Pam* made a Sunday night run up to Britannia Beach, Woodfibre, and Squamish to take home workers and people who went to Vancouver for the weekend. Many fellows returning were still celebrating and taking liquor back with them. On one occasion, one man was warned he could not drink on board the ship and finally they threatened to take his beer away from him. With that he said, "If I can't drink it, nobody can!" and threw two cases of beer overboard, much to the consternation of many thirsty passengers. Later, this same passenger became very obstreperous and had to be subdued forcibly. In the ensuing melee he bit the second engineer's ankle and so was trussed up entirely.

On his second year on the *Pam*, the deck crew went up town and decided they would all purchase and wear orange toques aboard ship. In addition, Doug Mowat purchased a long orange scarf. Captain Harry Roach was ecstatic to see such moral aboard his ship.

In speaking about Captain Roach, John recalls when the Captain heard about V. E. Day over the ship's radio and immediately had all of the ship's signal flags run up and sounded the ship's whistle constantly. On approaching the army lookout at the Lions Gate Bridge, even though the war was over, the *Lady Pam* was challenged by the gunners.

From the *Pam*, John went to the *Lady Cecilia*. One run he and the crew liked was the Savary Island day cruise. They only made one stop on the way up, at Westview, with only baggage to handle, and no freight to unload at all. Once at Savary, the crew could relax and have a swim. On the return trip, direct to Vancouver there was very little to do. It was, however, a long day, 9:30 a.m. to 10 p.m.

The *Cecilia* was a twin screw ship and John recalls one trip on her when just off Thormanby Island, one of the propeller shafts broke just forward of the holding bracket. The loose shaft made a terrific racket banging on the hull and the mate, Neil Campbell, who was on the bridge at the time, stopped the ship to try and find out what had happened. Neil thought he had run over a submerged wreck or log. They had to limp back into Vancouver using only one propellor. John was left at the wheel to take over this difficult steering job. He was at the wheel for a gruelling six-hour stretch while all his mates had a long sleep.

He spent a short time on the *Lady Cynthia* in 1946, as he and Doug Mowat had been promised berths on the *Lady Pam*. The *Lady Cynthia* was on the Mansons - Whaletown - Stuart Island run, which was known as a killer. Sometimes you had a stop every 15 minutes or so, starting at Roberts Creek. Jimmy Galbraith was the mate and he did his best to keep John aboard because good men were hard to keep on that route, which had about 32 stops in two days and you worked six hours on and six hours off.

The latter years of John's service on the Union ships were spent aboard the *Lady Alexandra*, where he became a favourite of Captain Billy Yates.

He remembers the "Show Boat Cruises" with such notables as Robert Goulet and Betty Phillips, and all the people coming aboard in costumes. Also some excursions to White Rock and once over to Victoria with a Canadian Legion contingent. One cruise had the Alex loaded with Registered Nurses and one might think this would be a deckhand's dream, but John said it was a nightmare because the girls were so persistent.

John didn't have much to say about the Alex's infamous "booze cruises" except that on one occasion they had a lady aboard who climbed outside the ship's railing and hung on under the ship's bridge. It was decided best not to try and remove her, so they left her there until the ship arrived at the Vancouver dock. Also, he did hear a story from someone else about the crew finding a couple making love in one of lifeboats, so they bolted down the lifeboat covers on them!

Captain Yates became synonymous with the *Lady Alexandra* and two of the best of John's stories about him can be found under Captain Yates in another section of this book. However, following are a couple more stories about this popular Captain as related to me by John.

One time when the *Alex* was departing from Bowen Island with its usual full load of dance cruise passengers, with Captain Yates on the bridge and John at the wheel. The helm was hard a-starboard in order to keep the stern clear of rocks east of the wharf as the ship backed up. Suddenly, just as the *Lady Alex* cleared the end of the wharf, a distraught woman rushed into the wheelhouse, grabbed John and in tears begged him to go back to the island for her husband, who had missed the boat. John pushed her aside and told her she would have to see the captain, who was out on the wing of the bridge, in the dark, watching the stern of the ship. The tearful lady then rushed out to Captain Yates, who had become distracted by her behavior and stopped the engines. He then signalled slow ahead to return to the wharf for the errant husband. His concentration was lost by this interruption and he failed to give the quartermaster the necessary wheel commands. Since the ship was about to go ahead with the helm in the wrong direction, John decided not to add more to the scene and carried out the usual wheel maneuvers on his own, but it was fortunate for Captain Yates that he had an experienced man at the wheel. As John says, your helm is in a different position when you're backing out of Snug Cove, and he could anticipate what might happen. The ship's return to dock is another example of the Union Steamship Company's emphasis on service in days past, but John has always wondered if the husband was really all that pleased to have been rescued.

Captain Yates liked his little drink, but head office and the Marine Superintendent were aware of this and were always watching him. One day Captain Yates noticed John was wearing a windbreaker which was bulky and had inside pockets. Captain Billy thought this was the greatest jacket in the world so he sometimes sent John up to the Carrall Street liquor store, which was not far from the Union dock, to buy a bottle of Scotch. One time the brand that the Captain liked was out of stock, so John brought back a bottle of Queen Anne. Billy thought that Queen Anne was just as great as the wonderful windbreaker that John wore.

William "Big Bill" Aylward

Bill Aylward joined the Union Steamship Co. in October 1917 as a winchman, and worked in that job until September 1950, when he transferred over to one of the new converted corvettes, the *Chilcotin*, to a job that was described at the time as fire control, a job he held until he left the Company in 1954.

Big Bill Aylward and "Little" Dick Bridsen were winchmen together on the *Catala* for years. They were a team. It is often said that they never spoke to each other but Ed Roach said this wasn't the case. He described their relationship this way: "They were actually good friends. They shared the same room together on the *Catala* and worked a 6 and 6 watch. They never spoke because they didn't have to, for each one knew what the other was doing. It was automatic that when one of them left their room he would take everything he might need for the next six hours. Whoever came off watch it was understood between them that it was his room for that six-hour period. The one on watch would never go back to the room and disturb the other fellow."

Bill Aylward was a bachelor and lived at the Patricia Hotel. His friend Dickie was married and had six children. In the strike of 1935, the ships were operated with strike breakers. Dick Bridsen, with his large family to support, could not afford to be on strike so "Big" Bill would escort "Little" Dick through the picket line, warning anyone if they didn't let Dick through the lines they would have to battle with him. Being such a big man nobody dared, so Dickie was able to scab with the sanction of the union so he could feed his family.

Norm Hageman, a former deckhand and quartermaster with Union Steamships, gave me this description of "Big Bill." He called him "Old Bill Aylward" and said he was a huge man, well over six feet tall. He said he was a terrific drinker and could drink a 26-er of the best liquor every day and also, he usually came back aboard slightly "spifficated." When he threw a marlin spike into the deck only he could loosen it. He had sailed on French fishing boats, starting when he was just 13 years old. He told many tales of the Can Can girls and knew the names of all the famous sailing ships, as well as the correct nautical names for all their rigging."

Bill Aylward left the Company in 1954 and passed away on Oct. 9, 1955.

Daulfred "Joe" or "Doffy" Best

The Best of the best Quartermasters, many old Union hands would say of Joe. When his name is brought up in conversation, someone always says, "Oh yeah, the quartermaster on the old *Chelohsin*." He was on her for 27 years and became a fixture aboard her even to her last day of service. He was at her wheel when she grounded at Stanley Park on Nov. 6, 1949. Of course he was in no way responsible but it was an event he would rather have had no part in at all.

Joe was born in the old country on Sept. 1, 1896. He came over to North America with his family and they first settled in Colorado. The family then decided to move up to B.C. At age 26 in 1922, Joe joined

"Joe" Best
(Roach Collection)

Union Steamships, sailing aboard the *Cowichan*, which at the time was still a coal burner. Then he went over to the *Cheakamus* and from there to the *Chelohsin*. The steering engine on the *Chelohsin* was in the wheelhouse and it became Joe's pride and joy. It was immaculate, free from any sign of oil and grease, with all the brass fittings highly polished. It would be a wonderful museum piece today. With the *Chelohsin* gone, Joe went aboard the *Cardena*. He was well-known for looking after the steering gear and linkage aboard any ship he served on, and story has it on one trip the *Cardena* was coming through Seymour Narrows when her steering chain broke and Joe was able to fix it in short order. Quick work on his part avoided what could have resulted in a very dangerous situation.

Johnny Horne tells one amusing story about Joe and a flock of sheep that were to be unloaded off the *Chelohsin* at Westview. The dock at Westview had a ramp and the *Chelohsin* was maneuvered so that the ship's side doors could be opened to allow the sheep to walk or run off the ship and up the ramp. Two crew members were stationed on the ramp, one on each side to make sure no animal stepped over the side. Joe Best was one of them. Somehow in the stampede, Joe was knocked down and the sheep ran over and trampled him. Panic ensued and Joe couldn't get up. By the time all the sheep had run over him, he was covered in sheep manure!

Joe never married. He and his father lived at the Columbia Hotel for years and then when the owners purchased the Anchor Hotel they took up residence there. Joe had a yearly ritual which was to distribute calendars up and down the coast for the Anchor Hotel and the Hub Clothing Store. Ed Roach, who worked with and knew Joe, recalls being in his room aboard the *Chelohsin* and it was full of calendar tubes all marked with the names of the eventual recipients.

Joe was a short fellow. He was well liked by his fellow workers, but he had one trait that bothered people and that was it took him a very long while for him to tell you anything. If you asked him how he was, it would take him an hour to explain to you how he was. He was one of the long-time employees of the Company. Records show in 1956 he was the 19th senior employee. In 1951 he left his residence at the Anchor Hotel and moved into a basement suite of his friend Ernie Gibsons's home. Ernie says that Joe was suffering from anemia and died in that same suite on Nov. 4, 1966.

John A. "Jack" Boden, Jr.

Jack Boden Jr. was born in Vancouver on Jan. 2, 1915. His famous father, Captain Jack Boden, Sr., who was one of the senior skippers in the Union Steamship Co. for years, was instrumental in getting Jack Jr. his first job, as a deckhand in 1932 at age 17.

Jack was brought up in the Union Steamship Company, but there was an unofficial rule in the company that family

Jack Boden Jr. (2nd from right), Denny Farina (3rd from right) at New Brighton
(Farina Collection)

members could not serve on the same ship, so Jack worked with his dad only once, for three months as winchman of the *Cardena*. In 1937 he received his Mates papers. In 1938 and again in 1939 he went to Victoria on training courses with the Royal Canadian Naval Reserve.

As a quartermaster with the Union Steamship Co. he learned many lessons that were of great worth to him later in his career. He stressed in particular the respect he had and how much he had learned from Captain Dickson.

The Union ships always steered the same courses and all was time, tides and the whistle, as it was with all the steamship companies that plied these waters in those days. Captain Boden recalls a run he made as quartermaster on the *Catala*. He was on the 6 to 12 watch. The ship left Stewart, northernmost port on the B.C. coast, after midnight and after a stop or two ran into fog at 8 a.m., at which time Captain Dickson came onto the bridge. He took the ship into Prince Rupert and left at their usual time at 1300, Tuesday afternoon. The fog was very heavy so they passed up three of the smaller ports, which were mainly mail pick-ups, making nine stops en route to Vancouver, where they arrived 12 hours late at 2230 Thursday night. Captain Dickson had been on the bridge continuously for 62½ hours!

The day that Jack arrived back in Vancouver on the old *Venture*, from what was to be his last trip for the Union Steamship Co., World War II was declared. That morning he boarded the midnight ferry to Victoria, drew his kits, and 2 p.m. that afternoon found him aboard the examination ship off Race Rocks, near the southern tip of Vancouver Island. He was immediately posted to a patrol vessel, the S.S. *Malaspina*.

While serving in the Navy, Jack obtained his Masters Ticket in 1943. He was discharged from the Navy in December 1945.

One of my Union Steamships contacts told me a story about when, during the war, the *Cardena* under Captain Jack Boden Sr. had been escorted across the Queen Charlotte Sound by a Canadian Naval Vessel under command of Captain Jack Boden Jr. When both ships were in safe and sheltered waters, Captain Jack Boden Jr. despatched a ship's launch over to the *Cardena*, which picked up his father and brought him back to the naval vessel for a quick visit and no doubt for a quick tot of Navy rum. Jack's father was then returned to the *Cardena* and both ships proceeded on their way, in opposite directions.

He then obtained a job with the B.C. Packers Co. and was Master on the *Teco*. In 1950 he switched over to Frank Waterhouse & Co. With them he served an Mate on the *Chelan*, then Master on the *Eastholm*. He joined the B.C. Pilots in 1953. He retired at age 65 from the Pilots, Dec. 23, 1980. He became very active in the Masonic Order until his death on Dec. 10, 1989.

Dick "Dickie" Bridsen

Dick, or Dickie as he was usually called, was a little fellow who came out to B.C. on the *Catala* in 1925, along with Springline McGuiness. Dickie was a winchman and his partner for many years on the *Catala* was Big Bill Aylward.

It has often been said that even though the two had worked together for years they never talked to each other, but Geoff Hosken, 2nd Mate on the *Catala* for a time, said that wasn't really true but because they had been together for so long working 6 and 6 watches that they just knew what each other was doing. Ed Roach said the same thing. Big Bill did all the rigging on the ship and Dickie took care of the other winchman's chores.

Dickie had a large family to support and during the 1935 waterfront strike his friend Bill Aylward escorted Dickie through the picket lines so he could continue to support his family. No one would dare challenge Big Bill, so Dickie was able to keep going to work, though Aylward himself respected the picket line.

Johnny Horne, a former Mate with Union Steamships, said that when Dick became ill, Bill Aylward looked after his family. Dickie was a diabetic and aboard ship, the Chief Steward would administer his regular insulin injection.

On one occasion when the *Catala* was going into drydock for her annual overhaul, Geoff Hosken was standing beside Dickie and said, "Oh this God Damned old crate." But Dickie turned and replied, "I wouldn't say that about the old girl, many a man has made a good living aboard her!"

"Gus" Ericksen

Old Gus was a well-known character around the dock and on the ships. It seemed to everyone he had been with the company forever, yet nobody could tell you his first name. Nicknames were big in the company and chances are if you asked for a seaman by his real first name they probably wouldn't know who you were talking about. Gus was a friendly fellow but very gruff with everyone and his usual way of greeting

Gus Erickson in the wheelhouse of the *Cardena*, with Capt. H. Roach in background *(Roach Collection)*

Capt. George Gerbrandt standing beside the prawn and crab traps he invented

a fellow seaman was "Hello Sonny." He felt senior to everybody.

Gus was well-known for his liquor consumption. You could usually expect Gus to arrive down to his ship on sailing night smelling of strong liquor and as it has been said, "The truth was not in him." Gus used to tell everybody that he never caught a cold because his system was so full of alcohol a cold germ couldn't get a foothold. Further, he said, being a quartermaster and in the wheelhouse with the skipper, not one of them ever caught a cold either because Gus would be breathing all over them. Gus always felt safer working as quartermaster under Harry Roach because Harry had no sense of smell. The picture along with this story is of Gus and Harry Roach aboard the *Cardena*.

Aboard ship, Gus was a good worker and a competent quartermaster. Another quartermaster related the following story to me about Gus at the wheel on the old *Cassiar* coming across Hecate Strait. The Pilot, Tom Lucas was trying to get a course fix and was watching for the light flashes from Triple Island. The light would flash and Lucas would yell over to Gus at the wheel, "Are you on, Gus?" Gus would reply "Right on" even though he might have been 20 degrees off. This would be repeated and Gus by that time would have corrected a bit but he would still be maybe 10 degrees off the correct course. He would always answer "Right on," but keep correcting until he was.

With a laugh Tom Lucas would say, "Yeah the old ship could be rolling and jumping all around in a heavy sea but Gus was always 'Right On.'"

George Gerbrandt

Born at Herbert, Sask., in 1916, George is a shining example of the saying, "Prairie boys make the best sailors."

George joined the Union Steamships' *Venture* in 1939. A friend had asked him to fill in for him while he went on holidays. His friend never came back, so George stayed aboard. He started as a fireman and soon was promoted to being an oiler. He worked under the Union fleet's famous engineer, Freddy Smith, and recalls standing watch with Freddy and having to record all the movements for him when they were making a landing.

While aboard the *Venture* he had a close call with death. The *Venture* was outbound in the Gulf from Vancouver and it was a very foggy night. George was lying down in his bunk in the focsle, when the *Venture* collided with an inbound tanker ship and the fluke of the tanker's anchor pierced the

Venture's hull and it came in just over George's head as he lay there in his bed! The two ships backed off and fortunately no one was injured. The *Venture* then continued on her voyage, according to George.

George was soon doing relieving work on the Union ships including the *Lady Alexandra*, *Lady Cynthia* and *Lady Cecilia*, but he wanted to switch over to deck crew and the company didn't want to transfer him. So he left the Union Steamships and went over to the Waterhouse ships as a deckhand. While there he learned how to run winches. He served on nearly all of the Waterhouse ships but was off on sick leave and missed being aboard the *Northolm* when it sank off the north end of Vancouver Island.

He left Waterhouse and joined the Packers Shipping Co. which was then run by Jack Ellis, who later became Manager of the Union Steamship Co. While working with Packers, George obtained his Coastal Mate's ticket and then his Master's ticket.

From here he decided to go deep sea. He made a trip over to England and back. Upon arrival back in B.C. he "went off with the heaving line." He hated deep sea sailing and rejoined the Packers Steamships. Later he went over to the B.C. Steamship Co., sailing aboard the *Island Prince*.

One of his most boring jobs as a Master that he could recall was aboard the Shell Oil exploration vessel the *Cedarwood* when they surveyed every square mile of water from the 49th parallel up to Alaska.

He then obtained a contract with the Federal Government to deliver a B.C.-built fish packer named the *Provider* to Trinidad. He gathered a crew together and sailed off. Once they arrived they were supposed to teach the natives how to fish and use the packer. After two weeks of sitting around and getting nowhere with local officials, the crew packed up and came home. George said that to his knowledge that packer did not leave the dock for two years because of local politics and indolence.

George then joined the Tymac operation ferrying men and supplies back and forth to the freighters anchored in the Gulf. Then he was loaned to Canfisco as Master on the *Thorfin* emptying old oil storage tanks from abandoned fish canneries. After this job he did relieving work for the Powell River Co. At this point in his career he obtained his own towboat, the former *Joan Lindsay*, which he renamed the *Maple Wood*.

So George had quite a long and varied career with the Union Steamship Co. and thinking back on it he was most impressed with Union's excellent service to the coastal communities, with its ships continually stopping at little floats where people would get their weekly supply of groceries. He felt the Union Steamship service was far better than what Northland ever provided.

George retired in July, 1990, after 51 years at sea. During his career, he also invented a collapsible crab trap and his Old Age Pension is being supplemented by royalties from this invention.

Earnest "Earnie" Alexander Gibson

"Earnie" Gibson, Quartermaster on the *Cardena* 1949 *(Gibson Collection)*

Earnie was born Nov. 8, 1927, in Trowbridge, Ont. and as a young adult decided to go west and seek his fortune. He landed a job as deckhand aboard the *Lady Pam* in January 1945 and stayed with the Union Steamship Co. for the next six years. He worked first as a deckhand, then stevedore and quartermaster. The accompanying photo shows Earnie when he was quartermaster on the *Cardena*.

In reminiscing over his years on the Union ships, his memories of Captain Suffield came up early. Earnie said he had the reputation of being a tough guy, but Earnie heard him say one day, "I'm afraid of no man and only one woman, my wife!"

I asked Earnie about other Masters he had sailed with, and he mentioned Big Mac McLennan: "He was a good guy. I remember one watch I had with him and we were in fog the whole time. When we went off watch he called me into his cabin and poured me a full glass of good Scotch whisky. Boy was that ever welcome."

He mentioned being on the *Chilcotin* in the winter of 1949 when she was doing the Queen Charlotte Island run and Harry McLean was the skipper: "We couldn't get into the dock at Aero Camp in Cumshewa Inlet because of thick ice on the salt shuck. The ice was so thick we could stand on it so we unloaded our freight onto the ice and then they took it ashore on sleds." (In my collection, I have a photo of this showing Earnie standing on the ice in front of the bow of the *Chilcotin*.)

Earnie also was quartermaster aboard the *Chelohsin* - but off watch - when she grounded at Stanley Park on Nov. 6, 1949. He remembers he was sitting in his room having just showered and dressed, and was listening to the radio when he felt a thud and then the ship's engines stopped. It was such a little thud that he thought they had hit a deadhead, but when he stepped out of his room he ran into quartermaster Joe Best, who said, "We've hit, we're aground!" Earnie next ran into Chief Engineer Lance Jefferson, and across the deck from them was Captain Aspinall peering down into the lower hold. At the time no one realized they were actually aground and the Chief said to Earnie, "What's he going to do, why doesn't he reverse engines?" Earnie's reply was, "Your guess is a good as mine." All the while the tide was dropping and it soon was evident that the *Chelohsin* was hard aground.

Passengers initially were taken ashore in lifeboats but soon Captain Suffield came out in a Cates tug and took over operations.

Earnie recalled talking to Paddy Hannigan, who was Chief Officer but had gone off watch earlier when they were off Point Atkinson. Paddy had told Earnie, "I had suggested the Captain should contact the Lions Gate Bridge signal station to see if they have spotted us on their radar. The Captain replied to Paddy, "I've been coming in here long before there ever was a bridge." History was made shortly after this exchange.

The newspapers at the time reportedly asked why the ship's searchlight wasn't used, but as Earnie pointed out, in a thick fog it would have been useless.

Being off watch, Earnie soon went ashore but was called back to be part of a four-man stand-by crew. There was Captain Halcrow, himself, and two other fellows but he couldn't remember their names. He said they started to remove everything moveable off the *Chelohsin* right down to the pots and pans in the galley. They transferred all this material to a Cates tug, which would take the load into Vancouver and return for more. According to rumour, the last two Union Steamship employees to leave the *Chelohsin* before the underwriters took over were Paddy Hannigan and Yorky McPhillips.

The last ship Earnie worked aboard was the *Cardena*. Captain Harry Roach was the Master, a man for whom Earnie had great respect. Earnie was working as stevedore on her and he says, "Captain Roach knew as long as I was aboard looking after the freight there would be no unnecessary delays, for he loved to get into Vancouver early so he could spend time with his wife, Ivy."

"On my last trip we were doing the Rivers Inlet run and had just finished working almost around the clock. The crew were tired out. William Nicholson was the 2nd Mate. We had just cast off and I had sent the crew to bed when "Nick" noticed some cartons of empty bottles we had loaded which were stowed up on the fore deck. There was a very light drizzle of rain. Nick noticed these empties and turned to me and said, 'Call the crew out, these cartons will get wet so we'll have to cover them.' I was tired and said, 'It's hardly wet at all, the men are tired out, they will be okay.' But Nick insisted. With that I said, 'If you want them covered you cover them yourself. I'm going to bed.'"

Captain Roach realized the situation but didn't want to overrule his Mate. When they came into Vancouver, Earnie quit. Captain Roach tried to talk him out of it but he left and went longshoring. This was in 1951. In 1983 Earnie discovered he had diabetes and had to go on sick leave until 1989. Then he officially retired on full pension. These days Earnie loves to take extended holidays down in Costa Rica.

"Paddy" Hildich

According to Johnny Horne, a former deck officer with the Union Steamship Co., Paddy was a stevedore on the *Venture*. One day he somehow managed to get his hand caught in the drum of the winch. He injured his hand so badly that he was unable to work aboard the ship anymore. In 1944 the Company gave him a job sweeping the dock. He would sweep the dock from one end to the other and he did this until he died.

Bill "Soogie" Hireen

The first ship that Bill sailed aboard was the *Cardena*, but the ship he worked on for the longest time was *Catala*, signing aboard her on Sept. 27, 1946. He started as a deckhand, became a watchman and then a quartermaster.

Like most of the crew, he was known by his nickname, which was "Soogie." The correct spelling of that is uncertain but it was the name for the cleaning compound used for washing down the paint and decks aboard the Union ships.

As a deckhand, Bill often had to throw the heaving line from the ship to the dock at each port. Once when docking at Port Hardy, Tex Lyon was waiting to pull in the line. Tex didn't know Bill's name, and as he had often seen him scrubbing down the ship, he hollered, "Let her go, Soogie." That nickname stuck to Bill from that day on.

Bill told an interesting story about Wee Angus McNeill and his way of giving course changes to the quartermaster while he was on the bridge. He wouldn't say "Port or starboard two degrees," he would say, "Port a bittie" or Starboard a bittie." When he was satisfied with the course the ship was on, he would say, "That's fine laddie, that's fine, leave her there, laddie."

One incident aboard ship that sticks in his mind to this day was when a cow had been shipped and was between decks in a regular cattle box. No one aboard knew anything about cows so everyone was feeding her constantly with anything they could find. After a day or so, the cow became bloated and literally exploded. Ian Morrison who was a mate aboard at the time recalled the incident. Bill was up in the wheelhouse when he saw four hooves rise above the level of the bridge. They had lashed the animal's feet together and were swinging the dead cow over the ship's side to dispose of the carcass at sea.

Bill "Soogie" Hireen on the *Catala*

David "Davie" Jones

Capt. "Davie" Jones in his early U.S.S. days (left to right) Frank Andriani, George Cooper, Dave Jones, John "Scotty" MacLeod on board *Chilcotin* (D. Jones)

Capt. "Davie" Jones as a captain in the B.C. Ferries fleet (D. Jones)

"Davie" Jones started his sea career working as a deckhand and later quartermaster for the Union Steamships in 1952. His father was Gibb Jones, the well-known winchman and quartermaster with the Company.

During his short time with Union Steamships he sailed under such Masters as Jack Boden Sr., Harry McLean, Jack Halcrow, Tom Lucas, Billy McCombe and Angus McNeill.

Commenting on Jack Boden, he said: "He was fearless, for he would run the *Camosun II* full ahead even in a thick fog." On Billy McCombe he said: "Every second word he uttered was a swear word and he'd never use the same word twice!"

One time when he was aboard the *Chilcotin* with Billy McCombe as Master they were having trouble with some leaking boiler tubes so they put into Butedale, which was an unscheduled stop, to take on some more water. Davie and one of the other deckhands decided to wander over to the cannery's commissary and buy a bottle of Coke. We just picked up our Coke and the ship's whistle blew. They went running back to the ship and as they previously had been loading halibut the wharf was very slippery and wet. Captain McCombe was leaning over the bridge and passengers were lined up along the ship's railing.

"My friend's feet slipped from under him and he slid on his back beyond the gang plank. Captain McCombe leaned over and hollered, 'That will teach you fellows to go out clooch hunting.' If there had been a hole in the dock, I'd have crawled into it," said Davie.

Davie said the Union Steamships was a good place to work because there was a lot of camaraderie amongst the employees. He went on to say that Northland wasn't too bad when Captain Terry ran it but that it changed for the worse when he sold out to other interests.

Davie left the Union Steamship Co. in 1955 and transferred over to Northland. While with Northland he obtained his Mate's ticket in May 1958. He was with Northland until 1959 then joined Northern Transportation Ltd. in the Arctic for the 1960 and 1961 seasons. He went from there to a three-day relief job at B.C. Ferries in November 1961 and has been there ever since. He obtained his Coastal Master's ticket in May 1968 and thus became Captain Davie Jones - a great name for a sea captain!

The first ship that he was Captain aboard in the B.C. Ferries fleet was the *Queen of Nanaimo*. I met and interviewed Captain

Jones in February 1991 aboard the *Cowichan* on a trip from Nanaimo to Horseshoe Bay. He retired from B.C. Ferries in 1994.

Gilbert "Gib" Jones

"Gib" was how he was known aboard the Union ships. He was one of the nicest and hardest-working fellows I can recall aboard ship. He would have been in his early fifties when I met him on the *Lady Cynthia*. He was quartermaster and an expert winchman. He ran his winches Siwash fashion.

Ed Roach remembers Gib on the Cortez Island - Stuart Island route and said, "Sometimes there would be only about one board of freight at a stop. Gib would be at the wheel, he'd make the landing and then would slide down the stave, get the winches running, put the board ashore, bring it back, and then run back up to the wheelhouse to take the wheel. Probably there would be another stop in 5 or 10 minutes and this whole scene would be repeated. It was hard work for him."

Gib was born May 23, 1899, at Sandwick, B.C. and the photo along with this story shows Gibby aboard the *Cheam*. She was only in service with the Company from 1920 to 1923, so he would be about 31 years old when the picture was taken. Another picture shows Gib aboard the CNR ship *Prince John*, so Gib must have gone over to the CNR for a while but returned when the *Prince Charles* and *Prince John* were transferred to the Union Steamship Co. in 1940.

Gib was a very popular fellow and was always ready to help anywhere on the foredeck. Unfortunately, it was while helping a fellow seaman, Jack Muirhead, that Gib had a terrible accident and lost his foot. The *Lady Cynthia* under Captain Jack Halcrow was making a landing at Britannia Beach on Dec. 30, 1951, and since the ship was behind schedule they decided the landing would be what was known as "high ball" in order to make up time.

According to Gib's son Davie, who also worked on the Union ships, the Captain had rang down for astern, the telegraph cable broke and the engines just kept going astern. The spring line was still on and Gib jumped over to help Jack Muirhead. As he jumped he landed in the bight or coil of the line. With the ship still moving the line tightened and took Gib's right foot off. He had his sea boots on. His sea boot and his foot were cut off and went out through the fair lead! Doctors later operated and took more off his leg in order that he would have better circulation.

Gilbert Jones (top left) on S.S. *Cheam* (D. Jones)

Gib Jones (D. Jones)

What happened after that is really not certain but the first aid man from the Britannia mine probably was called in to attend to Gib. I was told that Gib never lost consciousness and even gave instructions as to how to put a tourniquet on!

Gib was unable to come back and work actively on the boats but did obtain a pension from the WCB and the Company gave him a job as watchman aboard the *Lady Alexandra* when she was out of service and tied up east of the Northland dock, until she was towed to Coal Harbour in 1959 to become a floating restaurant. Gib then worked as watchman on Max Bell's yacht *Campana*, which was moored in Coal Harbour near the former B.A. Oil dock. When that job came to an end, he retired.

Gib lived at the Royal Arch Masonic home in Vancouver and I visited and chatted with him just two weeks before he died on March 21, 1991, at age 92.

His son Davie also worked for the Union Steamship Co. and retired as a Master from B.C. Ferries in 1994.

Ivor Llewellyn Jones

Ivor Jones, Quartermaster on the *Coquitlam* (J. Turner)

The war was raging in Europe when Ivor at age 17 went looking for work and landed a job as a deckhand aboard the Union ship *Venture* on May 24, 1944. The Captain was Big Mac McLennan.

The *Venture* was carrying huge loads of canned salmon in those days and on Ivor's first trip they had loaded 7,000 cases in six hours. The crew were quite proud of that and asked Mate Paddy Hannigan what he thought of their feat. In Paddy's sardonic way he replied, "Why you guys couldn't stow potatoes in a potato sack." Ivor as a young lad found the job too demanding so went up to the personnel office and asked for a fireman's job. "I saw those guys sitting down on their butts in the engine room and thought to myself that would be a lot easier than humping cases of salmon for six hours," Ivor said.

He did get transferred over to work as a fireman on the *Cardena* under Chief Clarence Arthur but unfortunately that didn't work out too well for Ivor either. "They had three of the most miserable Scotch engineers that I ever set eyes on. I tried to quit after one trip but there was a war on and I was frozen to the job," he said. Three months later the *Cardena* went into drydock and Ivor went absent without leave for two or three days. As soon as he turned up, Chief Arthur fired him, adding: "There's a place for fellows like you. In the army." Chief Arthur even tried to get Phil Lawrey, who was personnel officer at the time, to phone up army headquarters and have them come down and take Ivor away. Phil had to tell Arthur that wouldn't work because Ivor was still too young for military service. Chief Arthur was speechless.

Ivor found jobs were plentiful and as his discharge book shows he jumped around constantly from ship to ship and company to company. He learned how to drive winches and later became a quartermaster. He wasn't one who drove winches Siwash fashion and instead drove them up for up and down for down. He spent two years as winchman on the *Chelohsin*, which he said was the hardest ship of all for a winchman because

of her three decks and narrow hatches. The boards had to come up thwartships or cross ways, he said. However, he felt secure in the job because nobody else wanted to drive winches on her. The S.I.U. would send down two or three fellows to try out but some just about tore the rigging down because of the narrow hatches. Another advantage of being on the *Chelohsin* was that she was supposed carry three winchmen and if only two shipped out, the third man's pay would be divided between the two men aboard. Many times Ivor would be the only winchman aboard, so he would get the pay of three men!

It was Ivor who taught Jimmy Miller, initially a steward, to drive winches. Ivor used to let him practice at Quathiaski Cove where they often unloaded bales of hay. Jimmy subsequently worked his way up to become a Master on B.C. Ferries.

When I mentioned Captain Harry Roach, Ivor said: "Oh he was a fine fellow but he had no sense of smell, you know." Then he recalled a story about himself, Charlie Lewis, and Captain Roach.

Ivor always kept a bottle of Lamb's rum on hand and one trip after a tough watch, Charlie, who was 2nd Mate, turned to Ivor and said, "How about a tot before we turn in?" They had more than a tot so they had a tough time turning out next morning for their 6 a.m. watch. Ivor said they both had a strong odour of alcohol about them but they didn't worry about that because Captain Roach couldn't smell anything. It was a dull, rainy day and Charlie entered the wheelhouse wearing dark glasses in order to hide his bloodshot eyes from the Captain.

As soon as the Captain saw Charlie come into the wheelhouse he looked at him in surprise and immediately asked, "What's with the dark glasses, Charlie?" "Oh," Charlie said, "I've got a violent headache and the light hurts my eyes."

Ivor was aboard the *Coquitlam II* on her maiden voyage under the Union Steamships house flag. He was quartermaster along with John Smith and Pete Patton. He said, "She still had the navy steering gear on her and it took awhile to get used to as it was new and we tended to oversteer. It had telematic steering and a barn-door-sized rudder. Every time we hit some tide it flopped and rolled around like a gaffed salmon. If you put her hard over at full speed you would clear all of the dishes off the tables in the dining room. Another thing, as it was a new ship they decided to put white cooks on her. What a disaster that was! Most of them came aboard half shot and every time the ship rolled they got seasick and headed for their bunks. We never knew if we were going to get a meal or not. I felt sorry for the Chief Steward because he sure had his

Left: Horse being winched aboard a U.S.S.Co. vessel (*Ashmore Collection*)

Below: Horse being unloaded in the hold of a U.S.S.Co. vessel (*Ashmore Collection*)

hands full with that crew. As soon as we hit town they fired the white cooks and they hired Chinese cooks, so things got back to normal."

Our discussion turned around to nicknames. Everyone seemed to have nicknames, especially amongst the deck officers and the crew. Ivor said his nickname was Blackie. Ivor then started to tell a story about his mother, who had come down to the old *Cassiar* one day with some washing she had done for him. She walked up the gangplank and spotted a fellow working on deck and she asked, "Is Ivor around?" The fellow looked up and said, "There's nobody aboard here by that name." "This is the *Cassiar*, isn't it?" she asked. "Yes," was the answer. "Well he's been on the *Cassiar* for three months or so," she said. "Nah, nobody around here by that name," he said. "What does he do?" "He's a quartermaster," she replied. He said, "Well there's me, I'm Red, there's Gus and there's Blackie." She said, "What does Blackie look like?" Red replied, "He's a tall skinny kid." "Well maybe that's him," she said. So Red hollered down between deck, "Hey Blackie, come here." When Blackie appeared he looked at the lady and said, "Oh, hi Mom!" When she left, Red turned to Ivor and said, "I didn't know your name was Ivor!"

Percy joined the Union Steamship Co. in 1910, coming over from Wales to start on the ships as a deckhand. His sea-going career was interrupted by the First World War. He joined up and served overseas with the Canadian Army and was wounded at Ypres in 1918.

After a year in hospital he returned to the Union Co. and in later years he was a night watchman on the dock. Davie Jones tells the story about Blighty helping the crew of the *Camosun II* unload the mail and as well an empty coffin shipping box. The crew decided they would play a trick on him, so one of the fellows got inside this empty box and when they were lifting this box off the freight dolly the fellow inside started to moan. When Blighty heard that he took off like a scared rabbit.

When he retired in 1954, he had been with the Company for nearly 40 years, and at that time was the second senior employee in the Company.

The nickname Blighty was certainly appropriate as his Welsh heritage and accent stayed with him after many years in Canada and it sounded like he had just crossed over from the old country. He was a pleasant and comical man and had a cheery greeting for everyone.

Percy "Blighty" Jones

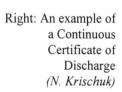

Left: A rare photograph of "Blighty" Jones as a dayman on the *Lady Alexandra* (J. Smith Collection)

Right: An example of a Continuous Certificate of Discharge (N. Krischuk)

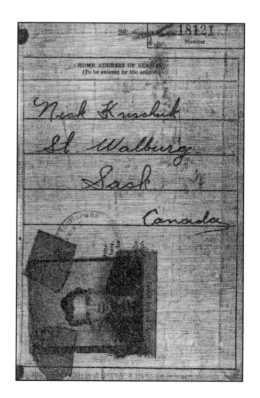

Deck Crews

CANADA SHIPPING ACT, 1934
(Revised 02CR 45)

1. It is the duty of every Master to sign and give to a seaman discharged from his ship either on his discharge or on payment of his wages, a certificate of his discharge in a proper form, specifying the period of his service and the time and place of his discharge, but not containing any statement as to his wages or the quality of his work, unless requested by the seaman. For failure to comply, the Master is liable to a fine not exceeding $50.

2. The Master shall also upon the discharge of every certificated officer whose certificate of competency has been delivered to and retained by him return the certificate to the officer. Failure to comply subjects the Master to a fine not exceeding $100.

Section 188 C.S. Act.—(1) Where a seaman is discharged before a Shipping Master, the Master shall make and sign, in a form approved by the Minister, or any form approved by the proper authority in that part of His Majesty's dominions in which the ship is registered, a report of the conduct, character and qualifications of the seaman discharged or may state in the said form that he declines to give any opinion upon such particulars, or upon any of them, and the Shipping Master before whom the discharge is made shall, if the seaman desires, give to him a copy of such report (in this Act referred to as the report of character).

(2) The Shipping Master shall transmit the reports to the Minister or to such other person as the Minister may direct, to be recorded.

(3) If any person (a) makes a false report of character under this Act knowing the same to be false; or (b) forges or fraudulently alters any certificate of discharge or report of character or copy of a report of character; or (c) assists in committing, or procures to be committed, any of such offences as aforesaid; or (d) fraudulently uses any certificate of discharge or report of character or copy of a report of character which is forged or altered or does not belong to him; he shall in respect of each offence, be guilty of an indictable offence.

Form 1607

NOTICE TO SEAMEN

(1) Seamen are informed that this continuous certificate should be produced and handed to the Shipping Master, Superintendent or Consul when signing Articles of Agreement, so that the engagement columns may be filled in and the certificate given into the safe keeping of the Master.

(2) Should the seaman desert or fail to join, his book will be deposited with the Shipping Master, Superintendent or Consul at the port where he left the ship, who will retain it for a fortnight from the date of the vessel leaving, at the end of which time it will be forwarded to the Director, Marine Services, Department of Transport, Ottawa, Canada.

Krischuk — Surname

Upon the seaman applying for the book it will be returned to him by the officer in whose possession it is, containing an entry in the discharge and character columns that the voyage was not completed. Upon the issue of a new book, consequent on loss, or destruction, a fee of 50 cents will be chargeable.

NOTE.—Should this certificate come into the possession of any person to whom it does not belong, it should be handed to the Shipping Master, or Superintendent of the nearest Mercantile Marine Office, or be transmitted to the Director, Marine Services, Department of Transport, Ottawa, Canada, postage unpaid.

C 18121

Continuous Certificate of Discharge
FOR SEAMEN

DEPARTMENT OF TRANSPORT, CANADA.

Name of Seaman, in full	Year of Birth
Nicholas Krischuk	1929

Place of Birth	Officer's Certificate, if any	
	Grade	Number
Poland.		

Height		Colour of		Complexion
Feet	Inches	(1) Eyes	(2) Hair	
5	6	(1) Blue		Medium
		(2) Brown		

Tattoo or other Distinguishing Marks

Signature of Seaman Nick Krischuk

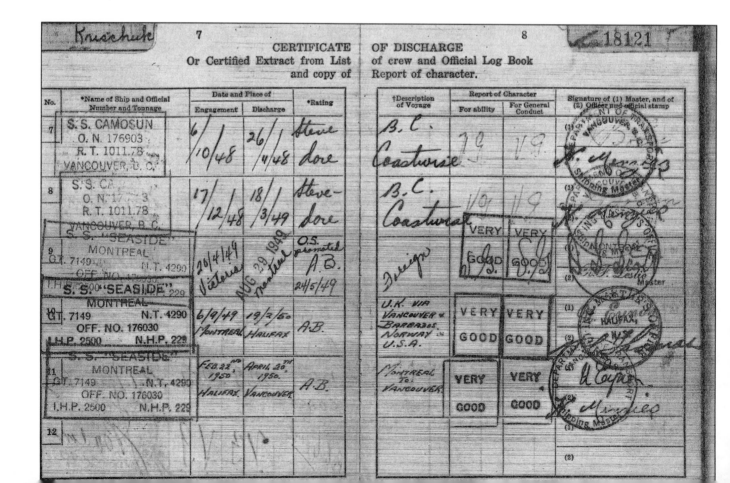

Nick Krischuk

Nick was born and raised on the Prairies and came out to the coast looking for a job in October 1947, when he was 18 years old. He happened to wander down to the Union dock one day and was fascinated with all the hustle and bustle going on around him as he stood there watching a ship being loaded. One of the ship's officers saw him and came over and asked him, "What are you looking for son?"

"I'm looking for a job," Nick replied.

"Well you're in luck, we can use you," the officer said. "Do you know anything about ships?"

"No, I'm just a stubble jumper from the Prairies," Nick replied.

"No problem, they make the best sailors, can you start today?" the officer asked. "We sail today at 4:30 p.m."

"Yes, I only live an hour away from here, I'll get my gear and be right back," he replied.

So Nick hired on as a deckhand and worked for the Union Steamship Co. for the next 2½ years. He started as a deckhand, and after four months was promoted to stevedore. He then was transferred over to a northern boat. At this time he was put in charge of the mail and unloading of the freight aboard ship. In later years he served as helmsman, or quartermaster as the position is more often called. During these years he sailed aboard the *Lady Cynthia*, which was his first ship. Then he was moved over to the *Lady Cecilia*, and then again to the *Camosun III*.

Of interest to readers, Nick was able to produce his Seaman's Discharge Record Book. Copies of the pages in that book are reproduced on pp. 390-92. It shows a complete record of the dates and the ships he worked on, signed by each ship's Master along the way, including a report of the person's character, noted in the appropriate column, usually with the letters V.G., which is short for Very Good.

It can be seen by the entries in Nick's discharge book that he left the Union Steamship Co. on March 18, 1949 and then went deep sea on April 20, 1949.

Nick Krischuk on *Lady Cecilia* tying up at Sechelt *(Humphreys Collection)*

Paddy "Springline" McGuiness

Paddy came over on the *Catala* in 1925 when she came out to B.C. from her builders in Scotland. He stayed aboard the *Catala* for most of his career in the Union Company. He came by his nickname naturally, for he usually handled the springline aboard ship.

When Geoff Hosken went aboard the *Catala* as 2nd Mate under Captain Sheppard, Springline was one of the crew. Geoff gave me the following details about him. Apparently he was gassed in the First World War and as a result had lost his sense of smell. Also, he could neither read nor write and therefore was useless in the hold when they were unloading freight. The deckhands grumbled about him and were always complaining he wasn't carrying his weight. They hoped a new mate would fire him.

Soon after Geoff went aboard, Captain Sheppard said to him, "Now don't get any notions about Springline, he stays aboard this ship as long as I'm the Master." Captain Sheppard stood by him and nobody could fire him.

Geoff said Springline was better than anyone at handling the springline. He lived aboard ship, never spent a nickel and invested half of his pay in B.C. Electric shares and so ended up quite well off.

Robert "Bob" McLean

Bob is the son of Captain Harry McLean, long-time and well-known Master with the Union Steamship Co., and like many other sons of fathers with the Company he decided on a sea life for himself.

Bob was born in Vancouver on April 13, 1925 and at age 15 obtained a summer job working as a deckhand on the *Comox* running between Whytecliff and Bowen Island. The Master at the time was Byron Crowell. In 1941, at age 16, Bob started his sea career as a deckhand on the *Venture*, whose Master at the time was the famous Bob Wilson. The thing that came to his mind about that job was, "We sure threw an awful lot of cases of canned salmon around - it was heavy work!"

When Bob turned 18 in 1943, he joined up in the Marine Section of the Airforce. He was discharged in 1945 and returned to Union Steamships, working as a winchman and quartermaster. He served aboard several ships including the *Capilano*, *Lady Pam*, *Catala*, *Cardena* and finally the *Lady Rose*. During these years he did cross paths with his father within the Company but they tried to avoid this because it could be awkward at times.

In 1949 he left Union Steamships to sit for his Mate's certificate, which he did obtain. His thoughts of resuming his sea career with the Union Steamship Co. were dashed upon receipt of a letter from the Marine Superintendent, Eric Suffield, saying he didn't think it was a good idea to have fathers and sons working at the same time on the Union ships. Bob went to work as a Mate on a Standard Oil Co. tanker.

Bob's career with Union Steamships covered a period of seven years and of course there were many interesting characters and stories that he saw or heard about while aboard Union ships. One of the most amusing was the time aboard the *Venture* when the Captain had received orders to call into one of the logging camps in a lonely inlet that was shut down over the winter months. It was usual to leave a watchman at the camp over the winter. Word had been received by the Company that the watchman had died and a Union ship was despatched to pick up the body. Upon arrival, the Captain sent two deckhands to pick up the body and bring it aboard ship. There was a long board ramp going down to a float over which the two fellows had to carry this body. One of the fellows slipped and in doing so the body sort of doubled up and at the same time, air which was still in the lungs was exhaled and it made a noise as though the body had said something. The deckhands dropped the body and ran, having had the wits scared out of them.

In 1950 Bob went up to Prince Rupert to work on a lighthouse tender, the CGS *Alberni*. He moved his family up to Prince Rupert but after one year they became a little disenchanted with the climate and all the rain so Bob applied for a job with Captain Terry's firm, Northland Navigation. He obtained a position as 2nd Mate on the *Alaska Prince*, so he and the family moved back to Vancouver.

In 1951 he sat for and obtained his Master's certificate. He then became Master on the *Fort Ross*, which was under charter to Northland. He was with Northland Navigation until the end of 1952. In 1953 he applied for the Master's job on the Vancouver City fire boat and was the successful applicant. However there was a delay in this job being available so he took a temporary job with the CPR and sailed on the *Princess Louise* as 3rd Mate. He started the job as Master of the fireboat in September 1953 and stayed for the next 31 years, retiring in 1984. He now lives in Victoria.

I asked Bob if it was a good job on the

"Bob" McLean

fireboat, and his answer was quick, short and succinct: "I wouldn't have stayed for 31 years if it wasn't."

Rod MacLeod

Rod's father was John "Pop" MacLeod, a longtime 2nd Mate with the Union Steamship Co. Rod joined the Company as an A.B. Seaman in the early 1930s. His first ship was the *Lady Cynthia*, but after two weeks he was transferred to the *Venture*. Harry Biles was 2nd Mate and Denis Farina was 3rd Mate.

Rod became a Dayman or Bosun on the *Venture*. The rate of pay in those days for that job was about $40 to $60 a month, plus board. After almost a year on her, he was bumped when another Union ship tied up for the season, so he went over to the CPR for a few a months and then joined the services in 1941.

Recalling Harry Biles, he said: "Harry had a great sense of humour. One story Harry loved to tell was, "Yes, old Captain Boden knows every rock on the coast because he has been on every one of them!"

He said that working in No. 2 hold on the *Venture* was terrible because there was no head room. He remembers the funny looking wind sail aboard her as well. This was a big canvas wind chute, with big ear-like flaps, that faced the wind and was supposed to deliver cool air down to the galley. Also, the *Venture* had no refrigerator hold so sides of beef were stored up on the foredeck. When you were up in the wheelhouse in hot weather you often got this terrible smell from these sides of meat which were getting pretty ripe after a few days at sea.

"The winchman on her in those days was Big Ed Solum, who was a master at running the winches and could really make them hum. The *Venture*'s crew, with Ed running the winches, could load and unload freight faster than the Vancouver longshoreman," Rod said.

John Martinson

John came from Norway in 1912 and joined the Union Steamship Co. almost as soon as he arrived in B.C. He started as a deckhand on the *Capilano I* on Dec. 8, 1912. This ship sank off Savary Island almost three years later, on Oct. 1, 1915. Whether or not John was aboard at the time we do not know.

Records show that in 1954 John had worked with the Company for 42 years and then was the 4th senior employee.

John was winchman on the *Chilliwack I* on Dec. 25, 1919 when a cargo of ore concentrate it had loaded, froze solid before it left the dock. Very soon after the Chilliwack left and was proceeding south, the concentrate thawed and became unstable, causing the ship to list badly. The Captain decided to beach her at Price Island, and the crew including John worked for three days making bulkheads out of timber. They were able to get the cargo balanced, the ship was refloated and made its way to Tacoma where the ore was unloaded. All the crewmen received a $100 bonus from the insurance company for their work in saving the ship and its cargo.

John left the ships in 1951 amd worked under Harry Biles on the "shore gang" until he retired. Charlie Lewis, a deck officer

Loading a boat aboard a U.S.S. Co. vessel
(Ashmore Collection)

with the Company, said John was "the best seaman in the Company."

James Miller

Jimmy is another fellow who started his sea career with the Union Steamship Co. He was born in Camrose, Alberta, Nov. 26, 1929. The family moved to B.C. and at age 17 Jimmy went to work as a mess boy on the *Coquitlam II*, in the fall of 1946. Bert Attewell was the Chief Steward.

After one month as mess boy he transferred over to the deck crew. In time he learned how to drive winches and as well served as a quartermaster. He was with the Union Steamship Co. for about three years and left them in 1949 to go deep sea with Atlantic Shipping Co. sailing out of Vancouver. While with Union Steamships, he worked aboard the *Chelohsin*, *Cardena*, *Catala* and *Coquitlam II* and served under Captains Roach, McLean, Boden, Aspinall, and Officers Strang, Summerfield, Horne, and Morrison.

Jim was at the wheel of the *Chelohsin* when she hit a rock in Chatham Channel, Nov. 13, 1947. She hit at 6.45 a.m. and was holed. She began taking on water but Captain Roach managed to get her into Minstrel Island. The passengers were disembarked and then Captain Roach ran the ship ashore, as far up onto the beach as possible. There were no injuries, but one of the ship's boilers was put out of commission.

The crew stayed aboard and waited for the Salvage Chieftain to arrive on the scene. The hole was patched and she was towed back to Vancouver. (A picture of the beached ship is in the Ships section under S.S. *Chelohsin*, p.28.)

In reminiscing about his time with the Union Steamship Co., Jim recalled an incident with a cow aboard ship: "I remember one time we had a cow aboard going up to a farmer around Lund. It was going to have a calf. One doesn't expect to have to deliver a calf aboard ship, but we were lucky, we had a fireman on board who had been a farmer in Saskatchewan, and he was able to help that cow deliver the calf. When we reached the place where the cow was to be delivered there was no wharf, so we pushed the cow overboard and she had to swim ashore. This was common practice in the old days, and the owner came out in his little rowboat and took the calf ashore himself."

Jim also recalled an incident aboard the *Chelohsin* with Paddy Hannigan on the bridge. They were going into Quathiaski Cove. Paddy was notorious for his poor landings and Jim said, "Up on the bow there was a young, inexperienced fellow by the name of Hinnigan, who was to throw the heaving line ashore. Paddy was still a mile off the dock and yelled to the fellow to 'Throw that heaving line.' The young fellow threw with all his might and as well, threw himself over the ship's railing! However, he had managed to hang on and other crew members leapt to his rescue and helped him back on deck. Meanwhile, up on the bridge Paddy Hannigan was jumping up and down, shouting at Hinnigan, using every Irish invective he could come up with." During all this action and shouting, the rest of the crew were besides themselves with laughter, to hear Hannigan's verbal battle with Hinnigan.

After being deep sea for two years, Jim returned very briefly to the Union Steamship Co. in 1951, but decided to go back deep sea again with the Atlantic Shipping Co. Then he went back to Toronto for a spell where he worked on ships on the Great Lakes, and then ashore, dismantling bell towers. He also got married while he was in Toronto. He then came back to B.C. and joined the Black Ball Line in 1955, working aboard the *Chinook II*. While aboard that ship Jim had a serious fall aboard her, suffering a broken back. He was off work for almost a year.

Jim was able to return to work and in 1959 he obtained his Home Trade Mate's ticket. When B.C. Ferries took over the Black Ball operation in 1961, Jim transferred as well. In 1969 he obtained his Home Trade Master's ticket and in 1970 had his first command and has been sailing as Master aboard the B.C. Ferries ever since. I was able to interview Jim aboard his ship, the M.V. *Queen of Coquitlam*, sailing between Nanaimo and Horseshoe Bay.

Jack Muirhead

Jack joined the Union Steamship Co. as a deckhand and as was usually the case, in time he was sent up to the wheelhouse to relieve the quartermaster, to steer the ship. Having had no previous experience at this, Jack was having a difficult time trying to keep the ship running in a straight line. Bob Williamson was the officer on watch at the time.

The ship was weaving back and forth, leaving a crooked wake behind. If the wake behind the ship wasn't straight, it was said that you were trying to spell your name. Looking back at the ships wake, Bob Williamson asked Jack how he spelled his name? So Jack spelled it out for him, M-u-i-r-h-e-a-d. Bob looked back at the ship's wake and asked him the same question, four more times. Each time Bob asked him to spell his name he would look back at the ship's wake. Jack thought the mate was going crazy, but finally he twigged to what was going on and saw the joke.

On another occasion Jack was on the spring line aboard the *Lady Cynthia* when Gib Jones, a man with many years experience, got his foot caught in the bight of the line and his foot was dragged into the hawse pipe and torn off. This accident took place on Dec. 30, 1951. Fortunately, being winter and the combination of freezing temperatures and manila fibres from the spring line helped to prevent a serious loss of blood. There was no blame on Jack's part as Gib had come over to assist him and in doing so, stepped into the bight and when it tightened up it took his foot off, boot and all. The Captain of the *Lady Cynthia* when this happened was Jack Halcrow but he was not responsible for it in any way.

Later, in the early 1950s, Jack joined the airforce and was killed in a Sabre Jet crash while practising low-level flying in New Brunswick.

Nels "The Mad Swede" Nelson

Nels was described by one of his shipmates as being a real Swede. When asked what being a real Swede meant, he said, "Because he really liked his pickled herring." When the ship docked at Namu, Nels would dash off with a bucket over to where the fish boats were moored to see if he could scrounge any herring. Usually he came back with a bucket full and then would set to work pickling his bounty. Most of the time he had them all to himself because nobody else on board wanted any.

He served as winchman aboard the *Venture* and in 1944 figured prominently in the rescue of four people whose small rowboat floundered in Shushartie Bay, north of Port Hardy. It happened when the postmaster at Shushartie Bay, a Mr. J. Higgins, was attempting to row the wireless operator, Mr. J. Shaw, and his wife and

Loading a car aboard a U.S.S. vessel
(Ashmore Collection)

three-years-old son out to the float landing in the bay to board the *Venture*. It was before daylight and the seas were rough. The little rowboat floundered and the two men clung to the sides of the boat to keep it steady while the woman and child sat inside. By chance they were spotted by Captain Boden when he was using his searchlight to locate the float. He maneuvered the *Venture* as close as possible to the hapless people and a Jacobs ladder was put over the side of the ship, but the people were too exhausted to help themselves, so Nels, the mad Swede, who had been an Olympic diver for Sweden, jumped into the frigid water to help them get up the ladder to the ship's freight deck, where they were immediately taken down to the galley and given dry clothing and warm food. The little boy was so excited he kept telling everybody how he had "swallowed big waves." Without the help of Nels they probably wouldn't have survived for they had been in the water for almost half an hour.

Story also has it that Nels was aboard the *Greenhill Park* when she was racked by an explosion while tied up alongside Pier BC in Vancouver Harbour. He reportedly was blown overboard into the water by the force of the blast. [225]

Jimmy O'Donnell

From the time Jimmy started with the Union Steamship Co. in 1929, he was a strong supporter of Unions and worked continually to strengthen their cause.

Jimmy said there was a seamen's union operating when he joined the Company, called the Federated Seafarers Union. It lasted until 1934. They used to have meetings aboard the ships and each ship would send copies of the minutes of their meetings to other ships.

Jimmy tells of a meeting aboard the *Chelohsin*, and the crew passed a motion to have a shower installed on the *Chelohsin*. Jimmy was delegated to approach the Captain, who at the time was Jack Boden. He went to Captain Boden and said they wanted a shower installed aboard or else the crew would refuse to wash or shave. This was rather humorous, but Captain Boden took their demand to head office and the plumbers were given instructions to install this shower.

Prior to the strike in 1935, deck crews were working very long hours. Here is how Jimmy described it: "You could go for 36 hours without a stop. Two of you'd go up for breakfast while the rest were working. Come back down, two more of you'd go up. Same for lunch and work absolutely steady for 36 hours. Maybe you'd shovel about 150 tons of coal ashore and load salmon after you'd cleaned up the hold. Sometimes they didn't even bother cleaning up the hold. Just on top of coal dust and everything. They didn't care about cargo or anything, just moving."

Before the job of Shore Mate was established, crews were hired usually by the 2nd Mate. Men looking for work would stand around the gangplank waiting to see if there were any openings. The 2nd Mate would come down the gangplank and if there was, he asked to see their discharge books. Naturally if he knew you from somewhere, you probably would be hired over someone else. The Mate hired his friends, that's how it went. Once the Union organized and had a contract, they had a hiring hall and the old system changed, but not for long. The Company created the position of Shore Mate and then he did the hiring on the dock for all the ships. Angus McNeill was one of the first Shore Mates. He was followed by Bob McBeath.

Jimmy left the Union Steamship Co. at the start of the 1935 strike. One of the main demands was a nine-hour day for the deck crew aboard ship. Jimmy was on strike duty at the overhead foot ramp at the foot of Carrall St. which went over the railway tracks to the Union dock. He was in charge of the soup kitchen. Coffee was given out free to those fellows who had been on strike duty and presented a stamped card. Jimmy stayed on the picket lines for five months.

Eventually Jimmy went back to work on the Waterhouse ships, which by then had been amalgamated with the Union fleet. He was there until 1944, then went longshoring. [226]

Colin Park

Colin signed aboard the *Camosun II* on Sept. 4, 1941, as a mess boy, and soon moved up to be a waiter. He then decided to transfer to deck crew and soon became a quartermaster. He only worked with the Union Steamship Co. for three years and he stayed aboard the *Camosun* during these years.

As the war had just started, it was decided that ships that travelled into open waters, like Queen Charlotte Sound, should be able to protect themselves from possible attack by Japanese submarines. Therefore, such ships were to have guns mounted on them, and each ship carried at least one and sometimes two naval ratings aboard to man the weapons. The *Camosun* was the first ship on the coast to have a gun placed aboard and it was mounted aft. On the day it was to be tested, the ship was packed with Navy brass. Colin said, "They had gold braid up to their elbows." The *Camosun* went out into the gulf and they prepared to fire off the first shot. Boom, off it went, and the ship vibrated so much that all the light fixtures in the dining saloon came crashing down! Everything was shaken loose. As a result, modifications and reinforcing had to be done before the gun could be safely used again and the ship made ready for combat.

Heading back into the Vancouver harbour after this rather comical event, the ship was approaching the First Narrows and entrance to the harbour. A Navy signal station and gun emplacement was located just under the bridge. All ships entering the harbour at this point had to fly proper signal flags. Somehow, with all the excitement and having the Navy brass aboard, this was overlooked. The next thing, a warning shot was fired across the *Camosun*'s bow and a Navy launch hurried out to intercept. One can just imagine the excitement and consternation this brought about, having all the Navy officers aboard and being shot at by their own side!

During the war years, shipyards on the West Coast were building freighters generally referred to as Victory ships. When they were launched they were named after bygone forts in the country, and one received the name *Fort Camosun*. According to Colin this ship was torpedoed off Cape Flattery. Due to wartime secrecy nobody had heard of the *Fort Camosun* so when people in Vancouver heard the name *Camosun*, they immediately thought it was the Union fleet's *Camosun* as she was operating regularly out in the open waters of the Pacific. When the *Camosun* arrived back in Vancouver, everybody said, "Oh, we thought you had had it!"

With the war on, logging operations all along the coast were going full out, especially in the Queen Charlotte Island for the Sitka spruce needed for airplane construction. There was always a continual and heavy traffic of loggers leaving camp and coming back again. Colin said, "You would see these fellows come down to Vancouver, arriving one day, spend all their hard-earned pay overnight on wine, women, and song, and board the ship next evening, going back to the woods without a penny in their pockets. This was a typical scene all over the coast at the time."

In the early days of the war, many a logger would get killed while working in the woods. Usually his body would have to be shipped over to Prince Rupert, or down to Vancouver. Since there were no undertakers or the likes on the Queen Charlottes, these bodies would be wrapped in some way and put aboard ship. They were frequently stored in the life boats up on deck, as this was the coolest place to keep them, until they reached either Prince Rupert or Vancouver.

Colin tells the story about Chief Officer Wally Walsh, who was always playing jokes on one of the engineers aboard ship. This fellow used to frequently take a late evening stroll around the deck of the *Camosun*. On one occasion, Wally hid behind one of the life boats where a corpse had been stored and as the engineer walked by, he let out a little groan. The engineer took off like a bolt of lightning!

After being aboard the *Camosun* for three years, working his way up from mess boy to quartermaster, Colin left the company on May 1, 1944 and went deep sea. He eventually obtained his 2nd Mate's deep sea ticket. When he retired he settled in West Vancouver, where he died on Jan. 16, 1994.

Ernie Plant

Ernie Plant
(E. Plant)

Ernie only worked aboard the Union ships for four years, from 1925 to 1929, but as Charlie Defieux wrote in one of his *Vancouver Sun* columns back in the 1960s, Ernie had a sling load of memories, mostly from his being aboard the *Venture* and the *Cardena*. He first sailed on the *Venture*, under Captain J.D. McPhee. He made one trip on the *Catala*, her maiden voyage on July 28, 1925 under Captain Johnstone. During that trip he broke his spring line and Captain Johnstone wasn't too pleased. Ernie decided he didn't like the *Catala* and he transferred back to the *Cardena*.

He was aboard the *Cardena* when she came to the aid of the CNR ship *Prince Rupert* after it had grounded on Ripple Rock, Aug. 22, 1927. Andy Johnstone was the skipper of the *Cardena*. She took the *Rupert* passengers aboard, then pulled her off the rock and took her into Deep Water Bay, where she waited for a tug to come and tow her back to port.

Then in November of 1927, the *Cardena* had to dash up north and come to the aid of the *Catala*, which had gone hard aground in broad daylight on Sparrowhawk Reef on Nov. 7. The *Cardena* took aboard the *Catala*'s passengers and crew and brought them back to Vancouver. There has been very little said and written as to how and why the *Catala* managed to ground on Sparrowhawk Reef in the middle of a bright, sunny day, but Ernie's version of how the *Catala* went aground is as follows:

"There was a buoy on starboard side of the reef, probably a half a mile or so away from the rocks, which you had to go around, keeping the buoy on your port side. But a storm had come in from the ocean overnight and it had blown this buoy over. It had broke its cable and it had drifted up against the reef, so when the old boy (Sheppard) had come up, he was going to go around and pass the buoy, but he plowed into the rocks because the buoy had moved over about a half mile from its usual place. Yes, this was in the afternoon on a bright and sunny day. She went right up there, she ran up and leaned on one side, and one of the officers who had a box camera grabbed it and was about to take a picture when the old mate gave it a kick over the side, saying they didn't allow any cameras or pictures and to get in the boats because she was going to turn over, so we all got off. They finally got

Deck Crews 401

First meeting of former employees of the Union Steamship Co. of B.C. Sept. 15, 1967 on board S.S. *Lady Alexandra* Vancouver, B.C. These are photocopied lists of the people attending that meeting. (E.L. Plant 20422-42A Avenue Langley, B.C. V3A 3B7)

Right:
Les Gore, Cook (on left), with Art Twigg, Purser, at the second gathering of former employees of the Union Steamship Co. of B.C. August 15, 1970 Eatons "Marine Room," Vancouver, B.C.

Below:
Photocopied lists of the people who attended that meeting.
(E. Plant)

her off the reef by blasting rock which had protruded right inside her hold. It was about nine months before she sailed again."

One of his last trips up north ended in disaster. It was on the *Cardena* and the Master again was Andy Johnstone, when she ran aground on Village Island on Dec. 29, 1929. It was very cold, with snow on the ground, and they had to transfer ashore the few passengers who were aboard, along with food, water and blankets. It was so cold that Captain Johnstone ordered the stevedore to take some liquor ashore out of the ship's locker and give it to the stranded passengers to help keep them warm. He and some crew opted to stay aboard the ship, but abandoned her after a few hours as she began to creak and groan and they were afraid she might capsize.

Ernie also spent some time on the day boats, including the *Lady Alex*, under Captain Billy Yates. Ernie then married and decided being away at sea most of the time was no life for a married man, so he left the Company. However, to this day, Ernie has happy memories of his days aboard the Union ships.

After leaving the Union Company, he did many things, including organizing tours and special affairs for groups. One thing he was asked to do was organize a gathering of ex Union Steamship fellows to a dinner aboard the *Lady Alexandra* after she had been converted into a restaurant in Coal Harbour, next to the Bayshore Inn. It was held on Sept. 15, 1967, and was the first gathering ever held for ex Union Steamship employees. Fifty eight people attended.

Then again, on Aug. 15, 1970, Ernie, along with Charlie Defieux, tried to get an ex Union Steamship association launched, by holding a luncheon in Eaton's Marine Room, at the old store on Hastings Street. Nearly 40 people attended. Thanks to Ernie's diligence, he kept the attendance lists of both gatherings.

I attended both of those gatherings and have a copy of the dinner menu for that first get-together on the *Alex*, and a photograph of former ship's cook Les Gore and myself sitting in Eaton's Marine Room (p.402).

Nearing the end of my interview, Ernie chuckled and told me an amusing story about a pie fight on board one of the ships. It seems the cook always made the crew lots of apple pies, and on this occasion the fellows started to throw pies at one another in the crew's mess. Ernie threw a pie at one fellow who ducked in time, but at that moment Mate John Mercer was coming down for a coffee and was hit square in the face with the pie! Although Mercer knew who the pie was supposed to hit, he was not amused, and for sure, there were no more pie fights aboard that ship!

Ernie then remembered another story. In the crew's mess there were two large port holes close together. He had a crew member hold out a hard piece of bread and as a seagull would swoop down and try to get it loose, he would grab it by the legs and haul it in to the boat. Once one got away from him and flew into the galley, then into the main dining room! All the tables were set for the next meal. The second steward, who was as bald as could be, had fallen asleep in a chair and the seagull landed on his head! Well, he just about went crazy. They chased that seagull all around the dining room, dishes and silverware were scattered everywhere. What a mess! When Captain Andy Johnstone received word of this stunt he warned Ernie never to pull a stunt like that again.

With a twinkle in his eye, at 86 years of age, Ernie laughed and said, "Those were fun days aboard those good old ships."

Alex Reid

Alex joined Union Steamships in June, 1937 as an A.B. on the *Venture*. He was transferred over to the *Lady Cynthia* and Paddy Hannigan was driving the winches on her at the time. Paddy was one who drove winches up for up and down for down. Many of the winchmen drove winches in a manner that was called "Siwash" which was up for down and down for up. Alex wanted to learn to drive winches so he asked Paddy if he would teach him. "Yes," he said, "but first you must learn how to splice wire. Alex said he was splicing wire until it was coming out his ears. The *Cynthia* never ran out of snotters after that.

Alex left to join the Navy in 1942 and when he returned from the services he rejoined Union Steamships and of course kept his place in seniority. He went back to the *Cynthia* and wanted to run winches, but Captain Bob Naughty wanted him to take the stevedore's job. There was a lot of stealing going on board the ship and Naughty said to him, "I want it stopped and give you authority to fire anyone you catch stealing. You can fire them on the spot and I'll back you up." Word got around and the stealing soon stopped.

Alex left the Company in 1946 and went over to Frank Waterhouse & Co. He was living in Victoria when he died in 1994.

Edward "Ed" Roach

Ed Roach operating winches on *Chilkoot* (Roach Collection)

Ed Roach is the son of the well-known and very highly regarded Union Steamship Captain Harry Roach.

He followed the footsteps of his father and joined Union Steamships in 1947 as a deckhand, later serving as a winchman and then as a quartermaster. In Ed's younger days his father used to take him along on many of his trips, so it was natural for Ed to take a liking to life at sea.

Ed's grandfather, who was a sea captain himself over in the old country, told Harry, his son, "If I thought for one minute that you would think about going to sea, I'd break your legs." But go to sea Harry did. Then Harry proceeded to tell his son the same thing, and Ed didn't listen either.

As a boy, Ed would sometimes be in the wheelhouse of the Chelohsin getting instruction from his father on steering her. Many a time Harry's wife and son would accompany him on day trips, and he would take them down to the dining room for a mug up and Ed saw the Chinese cooks working away in the galley. On their next visit to the dining room often there would be a big plate of cookies, baked especially for the Captain's son.

When Ed did start to work for the Union Company, it wasn't on a Union ship, it was on the *West Van Ferry No. 6*. It was at the time when the *Lady Alexandra* went aground at Brunswick Point, in Howe Sound. The Union Co. had chartered the *No. 6* to ferry Union passengers back and forth to Squamish for train connections. He recalls Vic Hayman was Master and Don Campbell was Mate. She didn't handle any freight and as Ed said, "She was a poor substitute for the Alex."

The first actual Union ship Ed served on was the wooden-hulled *Capilano*. After her he sailed on the *Lady Rose*, *Lady Cynthia*, *Catala*, *Coquitlam*, *Chilcotin* and *Camosun*, under such masters as Boden, Sheppard, Naughty, McLean, and Hayman, but he never sailed with his father, Harry.

One incident that Ed recalls took place in 1950 while he was on the *Camosun III* on a northern route and they were in Alice Arm loading aboard a shipment of silver ingots destined for Vancouver. While lifting a sling load of ingots aboard, it broke and all the ingots fell into the ocean between the ship and the wharf. There was nothing to be done but leave them there as they were in safe storage, deep down in the salt chuck.

However, on the next trip up, the Company sent up a diver, along with all his equipment, to retrieve the bars. It was in the middle of winter and it was so cold there was ice on the water, which had to be broken before he could begin to work, but he did recover all the ingots, after a cold and strenuous two days. The job was made more difficult because it seemed the town itself used to dump all their junk off the wharf, including two Model T Ford cars!

When I first interviewed Ed for this book, he was Master of the *Fort Langley* operating on the Fraser River. In 1995, he took over the Master's position on the M.V. *Malibu Princess*, running up to Princess Louisa and Jervis Inlets two days a week in the summer.

It's interesting to note that Ed, whose father was a long-time Captain with Union Steamships, took over that latter job from Captain Dennis Farina, whose father had been a chief engineer with Union Steamships.

William "Bill" Scott

Bill was born in Scotland and served in the Canadian Navy on minesweepers from 1914 to 1918. He was in Halifax on Dec. 6, 1917 at the time of the great explosion, an event that was indelibly etched in his memory.

I'm sure many of the Union Steamship employees of later years who knew Bill never realized he had started his career with the Company aboard the *Cheakamus* as a quartermaster on July 2, 1919.

He served aboard many of the ships and was one of the original members of the crew aboard the *Capilano II* when she was launched at B.C. Marine in 1920.

He came ashore and worked in many different jobs on the Union dock, on the shore gang, as a utility man, a freight checker, a baggage man and finally shed foreman. In 1955 he was the 13th most senior employee in the Company.

Joe Smith

Joe Smith
(U.S.S. Heaving Line, Nov. 1954, Vol. I, No. 6)

Joe joined the Union Steamship Co. in 1913, having come over from Scotland the previous year. He worked for a number of years as winchman and quartermaster on the *Camosun I*, *Venture* and *Chilkoot*.

He joined the 22nd Seaforths in 1917 and served with them until 1919. Later he served with the Occupational Army in Germany. He then returned to the Union Steamship Co. In 1924 he came ashore and went to work on the shore gang. In 1954 he was still working on the shore gang under Harry Biles and by this time Joe became the sixth senior employee in the Company.

John A. Smith

John Smith as a seaman on a U.S.S. vessel at Alert Bay
(J. Smith Collection)

John was literally born into the Union Steamship Company, for his grandfather, John H. Browne, came out from the old country as a pilot aboard the *Cowichan* in 1908, and served as master on several Union Ships until he retired in 1932. He was Master of the M.V. *Comox* running out of Porpoise Bay in the Sechelt Inlet and John in his youth spent three exciting summers riding aboard the *Comox* with his grandfather, Captain Browne. Further, his uncle was John R. "Buster" Browne, a well-known skipper in the Union fleet who served in the Company from 1921 to 1945 then went into the B.C. Pilotage.

In 1942, at age 16, John also joined the Union Steamships. He wanted to gain sea-going experience in order to sign aboard one of the freighters or "Park Ships" being built in local shipyards for the war effort. He signed aboard the *Lady Pam* as a seaman. The Master at the time was Jock Malcolmson, and the Mate whom he had to report to was Paddy Hannigan.

Paddy took one look at him and exclaimed, "Jesus Christ, they're robbing the cradle!" Paddy then sent him along to see Captain Malcolmson, who questioned him about his parents. Once Captain Malcolmson learned his mother was from Rothesay, Scotland, John was "in," for being a Scot in the Company meant a great deal; Scots were predominant in the Company over the years, particularly amongst the deck officers.

From the *Pam*, John went on to serve on the *Lady Alexandra*, *Lady Cynthia*, *Capilano II*, *Lady Rose*, *Venture*, *Cassiar*, *Catala*, *Coquitlam II* and *Chilcotin*. He even served on the *West Van Ferry No. 6* when the Union Company had to charter her to replace the *Lady Alexandra*. In 1949, while on the *Coquitlam*, he obtained his Mate's ticket.

Promotion was slow for deck officers in the Company because the old Masters never retired, mainly because there was no old age or company pension plans as we have today. They had to keep working and several actually died aboard their ships.

One day in 1950, coming into Vancouver on the *Coquitlam* and docking at 8 a.m., Harry Biles the Shore Mate stopped John as he was leaving the ship and said, "Look son,

Young John Smith aboard the *Comox* captained by his grandfather, John H. Browne

you're wasting your time in this Company. Get over to the Gulf Lines where you'll have a good chance of promotion."

John took his advice and five hours later, that same day, he sailed out on the Gulf Lines as 2nd Mate. A week later he was Chief Officer. A year later he was a Captain.

His favourite ship in the Union fleet was the *Coquitlam II*, mainly because he was on her the longest. When the *Lady Alexandra* tied up for the winter in 1946 he was sent down to the *Coquitlam II*, at Captain Boden's request, to the Westcoast Shipyards where the new *Coquitlam* was being rebuilt. She was in her final stages of conversion. He was to keep an eye on the job and acquaint himself with the ship, because Boden was to be her Master when she sailed and he wanted John as his quartermaster.

John tells a very interesting and significant story relating to the compasses aboard these new ships:

"I was in the wheel house getting it cleaned up one day when Captain Jock Muir, the Company's Marine Superintendent, and Captain Boden came aboard to look over the new *Coquitlam*. These wartime corvettes were equipped with all the latest in navigational equipment and when they came into the wheelhouse, Captain Boden exclaimed, 'What in hell is that God damn thing?'

"I was taken aback, because for years all we had to work with was the lousy magnetic compasses which were affected by the derricks, or your deck cargo, or some other damn thing. I said, 'That's a gyro compass, Captain.'

" 'Get that damn thing out of here,' he shouted."

As a result, not one of those three new ships came out with the latest compasses aboard them, according to John.

"You see," John said, "half the company did not like anything modern. Boden did not trust electricity, and it was the same with radar. He was very finicky about radar, he believed it to a point, but never trusted it. This was too bad as gyro was the coming thing, and these corvettes were fast steering. The gyro compass was fast and worked with you, whereas the magnetic compass was sluggish, so these brand new ships had old fashioned compasses on them, when put into service in 1946."

John says however that Captain Boden was never a man to be rattled. He recalls once on the *Lady Alexandra* as she was backing out of Squamish, with Chief Officer Jack Summerfield on the bridge, that the telegraph cable between the bridge and the engine room broke. Boden, who was off watch, soon arrived on the bridge when the panic started. John says, "We ended up shouting the bridge commands down to the engine room by the fidley, until we got turned around enough so repairs could be made to the cable."

In 1947, John was on the *Capilano* and close at hand when Captain Malcolmson dropped dead at the wheelhouse door.

John's uncle, Buster Browne, had a fast rise in the Company. He was a likeable fellow and had the reputation of being an excellent ship handler. Because of Buster's excellent reputation, John was at a bit of a disadvantage because if he did anything wrong he would be told, "Buster would never do it that way!"

When John left Union Steamships in 1950, upon the advice of Harry Biles, he had put in almost eight years with the Company. He went over to the Gulf Lines and was with them until late 1951. He then transferred over to the *RCMP Patrol Boat #10*, operating out of Port Alice. He left them in early 1953 to join the CNR Steamships. From here he went over to Black Ball Ferries as Chief Officer. When Black Ball was taken over by the B.C. Ferry Corporation, he became a Captain.

On August 4, 1968, he was Master on the *Queen of New Westminster* running from Nanaimo to Horseshoe Bay, when a young man entered the wheelhouse brandishing a loaded rifle and said he was going to take over the ship. John was able to calm him down and persuaded him to give up his rifle. He then took the youth down to his cabin and talked quietly to him, and upon reaching

Capt. John Smith of the B.C. Ferry Corporation
(J. Smith Collection)

Horseshoe Bay, the police came aboard and took the man into custody.

John received great credit for his cool handling of the incident, including a wonderful letter of commendation from Monty Aldous, general manager of the B.C. Ferry Corporation.

After a long and distinguished career, John retired on sick leave in 1982 and was living in North Vancouver when he died on May 26, 1995. Before he died he made many indispensible contributions to this book project, including loaning and then bequeathing his extensive collection of maritime memorabilia to me, for which I am most grateful.

The accompanying pictures show John as a seaman with Union Steamships and as a captain on B.C. Ferries.

MAILING ADDRESS:
816 WHARF STREET, VICTORIA, B.C.

BRITISH COLUMBIA FERRIES

August 5, 1968

Captain J.A.Smith,
Horseshoe Bay.

Dear Captain Smith:

    I wish to offer the highest commendation on behalf of the Honourable Mr. Black, our Minister, and myself for your very fine handling of the situation last night.

    The situation was most difficult and potentially dangerous, and you could not have handled it in a more efficient manner.

    I immediately advised the Minister as to the circumstances, and he wished to join me in this letter of commendation. Please express our appreciation to the other members of your crew, who obviously also behaved in an excellent manner.

Yours very truly,

M. F. Aldous,
General Manager.

MFA:mp

cc: Hon. Mr. W.Black,
    Mr. W. B. Weston,
    Captain P.J.Reakes.

Goodwill all round as city welcomes Queen

The Royal City entertained a queen Saturday and the 424-foot sovereign dispensed free sandwiches and coffee to several thousand hungry citizens.

The visitor was B.C. Ferries' Queen of New Westminster, the latest of the fleet to undergo an 84-foot "stretch" job.

It was the first visit to New Westminster for the nine-year-old ship — in fact, for any in the B.C. Ferry fleet.

Fresh from sea trials after the rebuilding, she made the visit in government response to an invitation from New Westminster Chamber of Commerce and its Convention and Visitors' Bureau.

New Westminster chamber president Bob Calis estimated there were more than 3,000 visitors to the ferry during the afternoon.

It all began at 11:30 a.m. when the Queen appeared around the bend of the Fraser, surrounded by a flotilla of water-spraying tugs and other craft.

Standout ship in the surrounding crowd was the Edgewater Fortune (better known as Greenpeace II).

It was donated for the day by owners Hank Johansen and Art Proule so Rotary Club members could host 60 senior citizen residents of Rotary Towers in a trip to meet the ferry.

Other participants in the flotilla were the New Westminster Fire Department, Royal City Yacht Club and New Westminster Power Squadron.

The ferry arrived in front of the King Neptune Restaurant on flood tide to the accompaniment of New Westminster secondary school band music and the salutes of the Royal Canadian Sea Cadet Corps Fraser.

Moments later the cloudless sky was dotted with wing-waving small aircraft, piloted by members of the Aero Club of B.C.

The gathering crowd stayed behind high steel fences until the ship's galley opened at 1 p.m., or watched the proceedings from the decks of the Front St. parking garage.

When the Queen arrived the gangplanks sat at 45-degree angles because of the high tide. But the boarding disadvantages were balanced by the view the high-sitting ship afforded people watching from up the hill.

At mid-afternoon Health Minister Dennis Cocke unveiled a plaque commemorating the stretch job and the visit in a brief ceremony.

The day was capped with a reception attended by some 500, including Lieutenant-Governor Walter Owen, Mr. Cocke, Municipal Affairs Minister James Lorimer and Mayor Muni Evers.

Accompanied by the *Edgewater Fortune* (centre) carrying senior citizens, a flotilla of small craft and a few gulls, the *Queen of New Westminster* arrived in the Royal City Saturday. The visit was arranged by New Westminster Chamber of Commerce and its Convention and Visitors' Bureau in cooperation with the B.C. Government.

THE COLUMBIAN, MONDAY, APRIL 30, 1973

Capt. John Smith explains ferry procedure to four of the men responsible for the *Queen of New Westminster's* visit to the Royal City Saturday. From left, New Westminster Chamber of Commerce president Bob Calls, Health Minister and local MLA Dennis Cocke, chamber director Vic Crockford and chamber manager Ray Macdonnell.

Jack Turner

Jack Turner

Jack started with the Union Steamships in 1939 as a seaman aboard the *Venture*. He was soon running winches and he stayed on them for the rest of his career with the company. Jack wasn't one of those who drove his winches Siwash fashion. He drove them the standard way, up for up and down for down. Siwash was the term used for anyone driving the winches the opposite way, that is, down for up and up for down. He said his favourite set of winches was on

Jack Turner working the winches on a U.S.S. Co. vessel
(J. Turner)

the *Lady Alexandra* because they were nice and fast, but one curious thing about being a winchman on the *Alex*, you were called upon to take the wheel when the ship was entering the Vancouver Harbour. It was the only ship in the fleet that had such a system, according to Jack, but he never understood the reason for it.

One time on the *Lady Alexandra* when he was at the wheel, something went wrong. The wheel just wouldn't spin. Quickly he was sent aft where there was another wheel and he steered the ship from there but he had no idea where he was going or what was ahead. Orders were shouted down from the bridge to a crewman on deck who would pass them along to another fellow at the stern, who would then relay them to Jack, but they did manage to dock her safely at the Union pier.

Jack spent much of his time on the *Venture* and recalled that curious round canvas air vent they used on her which was pulled up the main mast with block and tackle. It had two big ears at the top to catch the wind and they were pulled out each side with a halyard. This contraption acted like a wind scoop, and the idea was to get cool, fresh air down to the galley and the crew's mess, but what an odd sight to see on the old *Venture* when she sailed past with this odd looking wind scoop in place.

The summer season on the *Venture* would see her carrying the Chinese crews up to the Rivers Inlet canneries. Jack recalls the steerage area would be filled with Chinese men smoking their long pipes, and the crew had to pass through this blue haze every day to get to their mess room. When the season was in progress the Chinese used to have their own vegetables sent up in open-sided wooden crates, but there was a lot more in these crates than vegetables - booze! The deck crew soon got wise to this and would push long steel rods through the open spaces in the crates and more often than not they would hit glass! The result was that many a bottle of liquor never got to its destination.

Jack retired in August 1952 after 13 years of service. During these years he sailed on the *Venture, Cardena, Catala, Coquitlam II* and *Lady Alexandra*. He now lives with his wife and family at Enderby, B.C. In July 1990, Jack organized a Union Steamships Reunion at his ranch. In spite of the small number attending it was a great success. He reports that one bull session lasted for a full 16 hours, non stop. It was a great show, one he wants to do again, for it demonstrated that the camaraderie of the old Union hands is still very strong.

Jimmy Watson

Jimmy served as a deckhand as well as a winchman aboard Union ships. According to Ernie Plant, he was a good shipmate but he was the kind of fellow who would work for awhile, quit, then come back for awhile, then take off again. He also had been in the Navy, so was familiar with signal flags.

Jimmy and Ernie were working together on the *Cardena*. Andy Johnstone was the *Cardena*'s regular skipper. Captain Johnstone was getting married so a relief Captain took his place, but Andy Johnstone had decided to take a honeymoon cruise aboard his ship. Captain Johnstone had many friends up and down the coast, especially at Bella Coola. When the ship was approaching Bella Coola, the relief skipper called Ernie up to the bridge and asked him to put together a message using the signal flags which he wanted to hoist when the ship docked at Bella Coola. Ernie didn't know anything about this sort of thing so he called on Jimmy to help him. They did the job and the message was flown for all of Captain Johnstone's friends at Bella Coola to see. The wording of this message can be found in the story on Captain Andy Johnstone in the Masters and Mates section of this book, p.189.

Every so often Captain Boden decided he would go over to the *Lady Alexandra* on a day run, and being the senior skipper he would bump Captain Billy Yates off the *Lady Alexandra*.

On one occasion the *Lady Alexandra* was laying over for a few hours in Snug Cove at Bowen Island. Jimmy Watson was working aboard as winchman at the time. There happened to be some Australians in swimming at Snug Cove who were boasting about their swimming prowess. Jimmy Watson was serving as quartermaster and unknown to anybody, he was a pretty fair swimmer himself. Captain Boden urged Jimmy to have a swimming race with these fellows. They were to dive off the *Lady Alexandra*, swim across the cove to a boom of logs anchored there and back to the ship. Over they went and Jimmy won the race.

Captain Boden, who had cheered Jimmy on, said to him after the race, "That was very good, Jimmy. What do you train on?"

Jimmy answered, "Beer, beer, and more beer, Captain!"

Forward deck of *Lady Cecilia* (*Sound Heritage Vol. VI, No. 2*)

They Also Served

Top Left: Doug Allen (left) with Danny Nicholson
(Allen Collection)

Top Right: Buddy Beck
(Twigg Collection)

Bottom Left: Bill Bone
(Ashmore Collection)

Bottom Right: Len Draper on S.S. *Catala*
(Lamacraft Collection)

They Also Served

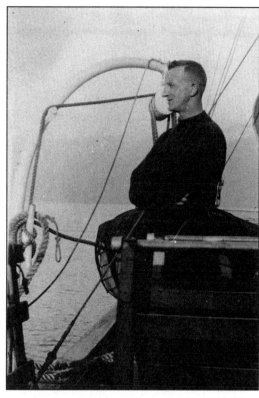

Top Left: Norm Hageman

Top Right: A.B. "Gus" Husband on S.S. *Chilco* *(Skinner Collection)*

Bottom Left: "Blighty" Jones, Dayman on *Lady Alexandra* *(J. Smith Collection)*

Bottom Right: Fred Kennett *(Kennett Collection)*

They Also Served

Top Left: Ted Kennett and Tom Charters on S.S. *Camosun* 1944

Bottom Left: Charlie Strachan *(J. Turner)*

Top Right: Ray Lawson on S.S. *Camosun* circa 1943 *(McLennan Collection)*

Bottom Right: Bill Lawson (right) with Don Rinder (left) on board *Chelohsin* 1943-1944 *(Lawson Collection)*

They Also Served

Top Left:
Lorrie Thompson
(Roach Collection)

Top Right: (left to right)
George Auger
Bill Hireen
Scotty Jamison
on S.S. *Catala*
(Hireen Collection)

Bottom Left: (left to right) Dick Fries
Al McLennan
Neil Suffield
circa 1942
(McLennan Collection)

Bottom Right:
Johnny Smith (left) with Pete Patton, Quartermaster
(J. Turner)

They Also Served

Left: Carl Vincent
(Lamacraft Collection)

Right: Johnny Walker
(Roach Collection)

Above: Deck crew aboard
a U.S.S. Co vessel
(J. Turner)

Right: A deckhand on a
U.S.S. Co. vessel
(J. Turner)

Deck Crews 417

They Also Served

Top Left: S.S. *Catala* crew
(Lamacraft Collection)

Top Right: Alex Mercer and Capt. John Horne on S.S. *Venture*
(J. Turner Collection)

Bottom Left: *S.S. Catala crew*
(Lamacraft Collection)

Bottom Right: *S.S. Chilcotin* crew
(J. Turner Collection)

The End of An Era

The Province

VANCOUVER, B.C., WEDNESDAY, JANUARY 14, 1959

NORTHLAND BUYS OUT UNION STEAMSHIP FLEET

By NORMAN HACKING
Province Marine Editor

The floating assets of Union Steamships Ltd., British Columbia's oldest shipping company, founded in 1899, have been sold to Northland Navigation Co. Ltd., for an undisclosed sum.

Negotiations, which have been on and off for several months, were completed this week. Wharf property and four coastwise ships are involved.

Real estate properties at Bowen Island owned by Union Steamships are not included in the deal.

Northland Navigation which operates a fleet of six freighters and passenger vessels is headed by Capt. H. J. C. Terry.

* * *

IT WAS FOUNDED by Capt. Terry, a native of Australia, in 1943, as British Columbia Steamship Co. Ltd., operating the small coastal freighter Alaska Prince. It adopted its present title in 1954.

The firm has grown rapidly, with the purchase of the freighters Island Prince, Pacific Prince and Northern Prince. Last year the company purchased the CPR passenger ships Queen of the North and Princess of Alberni, which were renamed Canadian Prince and Nootka Prince.

The company operates freight and passenger services to northern B.C. ports, Alaska, and the west coast of Vancouver Island.

* * *

WHARF PROPERTY of Union Steamships at the foot of Carrall is also included in the sale, although the actual waterfrontage is leased from the CPR.

An era ends

THE FAMILIAR red-funnelled fleet of Union steamships is passing from the B.C. scene with its absorption by Northland Navigation Co. Union's wharf property at the foot of Carrall is shown as it was before economic troubles hit the company. Union had operated for 70 years from the Carrall street base.

The End of An Era

Some U.S.S. Co. Personnel who gathered at the Vancouver Maritime Museum Nov. 12, 1989
to celebrate what would have been the 100th anniversary of the U.S.S. Co.
(seated: Art Twigg (left) and Gerald Rushton)

ENDNOTES

1. Gerald A. Rushton, *Whistle Up the Inlet,* pp.34-35, 44.
2. Ibid., p.76.
3. Ibid., p.77.
4. Jessie M. Van der Burg, *A History of the U.S.S. Co. 1889-1943*, pp.44-52
5. Isanor, Stevens, Watson, *Age of Discovery*, p.109.
6. Rushton, p.78.
7. Ibid., p.92.
8. Ibid., p.46
9. Van der Burg, p.68
10. Ibid., p.67.
11. Irene Howard, *A History of Bowen Island*, p.100.
12. Van der Burg, p.67-68.
13. Vancouver *Province,* 1916.
14. Van der Burg, p.68-69.
15. Rushton, p.92.
16. Ibid., p.120.
17. Van der Burg, p.69.
18. *The Province (*Vancouver), July 1908.
19. Rushton, p.83.
20. Peter Murray, *Homesteads and Snug Harbours,* pp.148-49.
21. Rushton, *Echoes of the Whistle*, p.54.
22. Rushton, p.104.
23. Ibid., p.54.
24. Van der Burg, pp.83-84.
25. Ibid., p.84.
26. Rushton, p.54.
27. Ibid., p.55.
28. Fred Rogers, *Shipwrecks of B.C.*, pp.46-47.
29. Rushton, p.68.
30. Ibid., p.69.
31. Ibid., p.69.
32. Frances Duncan and Rene Harding, *Sayward (for Kelsey Bay)*, pp.18-21.
33. Rushton, p.56.
34. Ibid., pp.58, 84.
35. *Progress: Burrard Drydock Co. Ltd. History*, p.46.
36. Rushton, p.64.
37. Ibid., p.58, 60.
38. Ibid., p.69.
39. Vancouver *Province*, April 1, 1914.
40. *Progress: Burrard Drydock*, p.125.
41. Rushton, p.140.
42. Ibid., p.62.
43. *U.S.S. Co. Newsletter*, Vol. 1, No.5.
44. Isener, Stephens & Watson, *Age of Discovery*, p.107.
45. Rushton, pp.64-65.
46. Rushton, p.77.
47. Charles Defieux, *The Vancouver Sun*, Oct. 8, 1966.
48. Rushton, p.89.
49. Ibid., p.139.
50. *Honolulu-Star Bulletin.*
51. Hugh Garling, *Nautical Magazine,* July 1990.
52. Rushton, p.75.
53. Rushton, p.75.
54. Van der Burg, p.98.
55. Rushton, p.81.
56. Ruth Greene Baily, *Harbour Shipping Magazine,* Dec. 1986.
57. Rushton, p.86.
58. *Canadian Merchant Service Guild Annual,* pp.19, 23.
59. Rushton, p.98.
60. Rushton, p.96.
61. Van der Burg, p.100.
62. Rushton, p.102.
63. Rushton, p.109.
64. Van der Burg, p.102.
65. Rushton, p.121.
66. Rushton, p.121.
67. Pat Terry, *The Province* (Vancouver), Van der Burg, p.103.
68. Ibid., p.102.
69. Rushton, pp.172-73.
70. Ibid., pp.184-85.
71. Ibid., p.181.
72. Ibid., pp.190-94.
73. Ibid., p.98.
74. Ruth Greene, *Personality Ships of B.C.,* p.260.
75. Rushton, p.98.
76. Ibid., p.107.
77. Greene, p.261.
78. Rushton, p.144.
79. Rushton, p.126.
80. Rushton, p.140.
81. Rushton, p.154.
82. Abby Day, *The Islander,* May 1990.
83. Ibid.
85. Rushton, p.110.
86. Marine Inquiry.
87. *Sound Heritage,* pp.59-60.
88. Ibid., p.60.
89. *Daily News* (Prince Rupert).
90. Jack Bain, *West Coast Mariner,* Jan. 1991.
91. Graham, Donald. *Lights of the Inside Passage,* p.148.
92. Rushton, p.131.
93. Rushton, p.134.
94. *Progress: Burrard Drydock,* p.375.
95. Vancouver *Province,* Jan. 9, 1958.
96. Rushton, p.102.
97. Rushton, p.104.
98. Rushton, p.127.
99. Mark Paise, *West Coast Mariner,* Aug. 1989.
100. Roger, p.37.
101. Rushton, p.123.
102. Ibid., p.135.
103. Ibid., p.139.
104. Ibid., p.158-59.
105. Ibid., *The Province* (Vancouver).
106. James E. "Ted" Wilson with S.C. Heal, *Full Line Full Away,* p.96.
107. Rushton, p.129.
108. Rushton, p.130.
109. Eric Jamieson, *Canadian West Magazine,* Fall 1989.
110. Ibid.
111. Van der Burg, p.116.
112. Rushton, p.130.
113. Ibid., pp.141,146.
114. Godfrey Castle, *Times Colonist* (Victoria), 1992.
115. Don Stevens, *The Islander.*
116. Rushton, p.123.
117. Ibid., p.136.
118. Ibid., p.137.
119. Ibid., p.141.
120. Ibid., p.146.
121. Ibid., p.147.

122	Ibid., p.147.	176	Kelsey McLeod, *Westcoast Mariner*, March 1990, p.25
123	Ibid., p.147.	177	*Sound Heritage*, p.22.
124	Ibid., p.148.	178	Ibid., p.8.
125	Bill Fletcher, *The Vancouver Sun*, Nov. 12, 1948.	179	Ibid., p.6.
126	Rushton, p.168.	180	Ibid., p.68.
127	Rushton, p.182.	181	*The Vancouver Sun*, Aug. 1971.
128	Norman Hacking.	182	Ibid., Oct., 1966.
130	Rushton, p.150.	183	Ibid., p.56.
131	Rushton, p.155.	184	Alan Daniels, *The Vancouver Sun*, Jan. 1978.
132	Rushton, p.162.	185	*The Province* (Vancouver), Dec. 15, 1955.
133	Norman Hacking.	186	*The Vancouver Sun*, Jan. 1958.
134	Norman Hacking.	187	Charles Defieux, *The Vancouver Sun*, March 1972.
135	Rushton, p.174.	188	*U.S.S.Co. Newsletter*, Vol. 1, No.5.
136	Ibid., p.104	189	*Sound Heritage*, p. 60.
137	Ibid., p.105.	190	Rushton, p.131.
138	Ibid., p.172-73.	191	Ibid., p.187.
139	Ibid., p.64.	192	*U.S.S.Co. Newsletter*, Vol. 1, No.5.
140	Van der Burg, p.86.	193	Rushton, p.153.
141	Provincial Archives of B.C., *Sound Heritage: Navigating the Coast*, p.60.	194	*Sound Heritage*, p.39.
142	H. Meilleur, *A Pour of Rain*, p. 134.	195	Rushton, p.139.
143	Van der Burg, p.102.	196	Rushton, p.144.
144	Rushton, p.93.	197	Ibid., p.154.
145	*Sound Heritage*, p.64.	198	Ibid., p.104.
146	Helen Neale & Joan Carolan, *Memories of our Father*.	199	*Sound Heritage*, p.66.
147	Ibid.	200	Defieux, *The Vancouver Sun*.
148	Rushton, p.92.	201	Ibid.
149	Van der Burg, pp.102-03.	202	Ibid.
150	Ibid.	203	Rushton, p.66.
151	Rushton, .p.46.	204	Ibid., p.120.
152	*The Vancouver Sun*, Aug. 1966.	205	Rushton, p.150.
153	Rushton, pp.108-12.	206	Rushton, p.81.
154	Van der Burg, p.102.	207	Austen Hemion, letter.
155	Rushton, p.121.	208	Bob Hackett, tape.
156	*Sound Heritage*, pp.66-67.	209	*Sound Heritage*, p.22.
157	Meilleur, p.134.	210	Ibid., p.68.
158	Rushton, p.75.	211	Rushton, Gerald. p.77.
159	Ibid., p.121.	212	*Sound Heritage*. p.56.
160	*Sound Heritage*, pp.23, 27, 49, 42.	213	Rushton, Gerald. p.81-82.
161	Rushton, p.151.	214	*Sound Heritage*. p.26.
162	Ibid., p.157.	215	Ibid., p.37.
163	Ibid., p.109.	216	Ibid., p.48.
164	Van der Burg, p.86.	217	Ibid., p.48.
165	Rushton, p.129.	218	Ibid., p.48.
166	*Sound Heritage*, pp.19-20.	219	*Sound Heritage*, p.84.
167	Rushton, p.93.	220	Ibid., p.85.
168	*Sound Heritage*, p.56.	221	L.V Kelly, news report, 1921.
169	Rushton, pp.76-77.	222	*Sound Heritage*, p.66.
170	Ibid., p.77.	223	Rushton, p.112.
171	Graham, p.131.	224	Ibid., p.155.
172	*Sound Heritage*, p.50.	225	Jack Turner, interview.
173	Bob Hackett, interview.	226	*Sound Heritage*, pp.64, 67, 71, 73, 74.
174	Rushton, pp.108-09.		
175	*Sound Heritage*, p.60, 64.		

INDEX of SHIPS

A.L. Bryant, M.V. 98-99, 247, 249, 266
Alaska Prince, M.V. 231, 394
Alberni, CGS 394
Albertalite (tanker) 150
Algerine 318
Amethyst, S.S. 110
Arangi 366
Ardgarvel, S.S. 160, 212, 243
Arrandale M 201

Ballena, S.S. 51, 168
Barnstaple, S.S.) 88, 95
Bervin, S.S. 3-4, 119, 222
Blue Peter, 172, 248, 259, 299
Bonnabelle, M.V. 266
Bowena S.S. 50-51, 168
Britamerican 232
Britannia, S.S. 263-64, 267
British Columbia, S.S. 215

Cairo 109
Camosun I, S.S. 8-12, 20, 27, 59, 71, 83, 145, 147, 154, 159-60, 187, 194, 215, 223, 243, 262, 264, 276, 278, 405
Camosun II, S.S. 85, 107-09, 111, 137, 183, 193, 195, 231, 255, 256-57, 283, 286, 299, 304, 318, 323, 340, 353, 372-73, 386, 390, 399
Camosun III, S.S. 66, 85, 114, 120, 122-26, 142, 150-51, 176, 202, 217, 220, 251, 253, 258, 282, 288-89, 291, 316, 333, 346, 364, 393, 404, 414
Canadian Importer S.S. 317
Canadian Winner 318
Canora 254
Capilano I, S.S. 4, 46, 236, 395
Capilano II, S.S. 46-49, 51, 58, 98, 141, 147, 149, 164, 168, 182, 183, 216, 221, 228, 237, 253, 264-266, 278-280, 309, 321, 324, 337-38, 358, 376, 394, 404-407
Capri, S.S. 130
Cardena, S.S. iii, 12, 29, 33, 57- 67, 79-81, 85-86, 98, 111, 113, 114-15, 117, 120, 143, 149-50, 154, 156, 160-61, 166-67, 172-73, 186-89, 195-96, 199-202, 208, 210-11, 213, 218-19, 221, 224, 226, 239-40, 242-45, 248-49, 254, 260-61, 268, 275-76, 280-85, 288-89, 298-99, 301, 309-10, 314, 319, 323-25, 328, 330-32, 335-40, 343, 346-47, 356-57, 365, 367, 372, 379-85, 388, 394, 396, 400, 403, 411
Cariboo, S.S. 13-14, 146
Cassiar I, S.S. 5-7, 23, 28, 30, 147, 160, 163, 169, 222, 263, 278-80, 295, 311, 332, 375
Cassiar II, S.S. 85, 108-12, 137, 141, 152, 169, 174, 180, 182-83, 185, 208, 209, 211, 242, 258, 284, 318, 344, 360, 382, 390, 406
Cassiar III, M.V. 172, 248, 259, 299, 315
Catala, S.S. 9, 29, 57-58, 63-64, 66-67, 71, 78-87, 95, 113, 115, 117, 120, 130, 141, 148, 151, 153-56, 160-61, 166, 187, 190-91, 194, 197, 205-06, 214, 217-19, 221, 231, 240, 243-46, 250, 258-59, 269, 276-77, 282-83, 285, 287-89, 292, 296, 299, 301, 309-10, 312, 315-16, 318-19, 323, 325, 328, 334-35, 337, 339, 341, 346, 349, 355, 360, 364, 367, 369, 371-72, 378, 380-81, 385, 393-94, 396, 400, 404, 406, 411-12, 415, 417
Cedarwood 383
Charmer, S.S. 31
Chasina, S.S. 37-39, 41-42, 47, 288, 333
Cheakamus, S.S. 17, 21-25, 152, 156, 174, 182, 228, 238, 264, 379, 405
Cheam, S.S. 50-51, 168, 264, 387
Chehalis, S.S. 6
Chelan, M.V. 197, 381
Chelohsin, S.S. 11, 25-31, 58, 64, 85, 112-13, 138, 140, 147, 156, 160, 162-63, 171, 177-79, 190, 193, 196, 205, 207, 211, 219, 228, 231, 233, 236, 238-39, 242, 248, 251, 260-61, 281-83, 288, 299-301, 310-11, 313-14, 317, 319-21, 325, 328, 330-31, 335, 337-38, 351, 361-63, 367-69, 379-80, 384, 388, 396, 398, 404, 414
Cheslakee, S.S. 1, 11, 17-23, 260
Chieftain, S.S. 29, 107
Chilco, S.S. 1, 39-42, 175, 221, 228, 231, 239, 413
Chilcotin, S.S. x, 2, 39, 98, 114, 117, 120, 125-132, 137-39, 185, 205, 255, 260, 278, 286, 318, 342, 346, 359-60, 364, 368, 373, 378, 384, 386, 404, 406, 417
Chilkoot, S.S. 114, 160, 166, 205, 221, 257, 281-82, 300, 337-38, 342, 404-05
Chilliwack, S.S. 92, 137, 139, 148, 160, 169, 180, 185, 198, 212, 215, 221, 223-24, 228, 243, 282, 287-88, 295, 300, 395
Chilliwack III, M.V. 114
Chinook II, S.S. 396
City of Belleville, S.S. 172, 248
City of Nanaimo, S.S. 50
City of Vancouver, S.S. 237
Columbia 233
Commodore, S.S. 11, 75
Comox I, S.S. 6, 163, 278
Comox II, M.V. 1, 55-56, 96, 101, 104-105, 147-148, 264, 394, 406
Coquitlam I, S.S. 3-4, 6, 11, 142, 160, 170, 187, 222-23, 236, 281, 294
Coquitlam II, S.S. 2, 63, 114, 116-22, 129, 140, 185-86, 200, 203, 209, 214, 246, 193-95, 258, 261, 282, 285, 290, 292, 297, 299, 316, 340-41, 343, 359, 388-89, 396, 406-07, 411
Coquitlam III 142, 144-45, 152, 165, 346
Corsican, S.S. 187
Cowichan, S.S. 3, 7, 11, 13-16, 27-28, 53, 89, 96, 99, 143, 146, 163, 170, 182, 199, 205, 215, 260-62, 281, 294, 351, 379, 387, 406
Cutch vii
Cyclops, S.S. 262

Deerhound, S.S. 52-53, 322
Dola 99, 203, 266
Doris (Seaspan) 191
Duchess of York 102

Eastholm, S.S. 183, 381

Index of Ships

Elleric 159
Empress of Asia S.S. 359
Empress of China, S.S. 363
Empress of India, S.S. 10
Empress of Ireland, S.S. 52, 322
Empress of Japan, S.S. 359
Empress of Russia, S.S. 156

Falls of Foyer 159
Fearless 141
Fort Camosun 108
Fort Langley 405
Fort Ross, S.S. 394
Freesia, H.M.S. 259

General Ludinback 191
Glacier Queen, S.S. 122, 126, 202, 246, 283
Glenmorag 159
Grandholm, S.S. 3
Great Northern 9 92
Greenhill Park 398
Greg, Seaspan 191
Guilford Castle, HMS 127
Gulf Mariner, M.V. 197

Hamlin 142
Hespeler, HMCS 127-28
Hollyburn, M.V. 266-67
Hood, HMS 51, 71, 97, 163
Hsin Kong So, S.S. 35-36

Imperial Vancouver 251
Indefatigable, HMS 262
Island King, M.V. 114, 342
Island Prince 383
Island Princess 148, 232

J.R. McDonald, S.S. 5, 7
J 261 250
Joan Lindsay 383

Kahloke 236
Kelowna (*J 261*) 250
Kensington Park, S.S. 161, 172
Kestrel, S.S. 187
Kingsly 293

Lady Alexandra, S.S. 53, 58, 66, 70-77, 96, 104, 121, 143, 145, 155, 163, 170-72, 181-82, 205, 207, 211-12, 220, 226-27, 236, 250, 256, 266, 258, 262, 264-68, 275-76, 281, 288, 298-99, 301, 312, 316, 319, 321, 324-25, 327, 335, 337, 341, 346, 348, 356, 358, 360, 363-64, 366, 376-78, 383, 388, 390, 403-04, 406-07, 410-11, 413

Lady Cecilia, S.S. 53, 58, 88-97, 148, 157-58, 160, 164-65, 169-70, 184-85, 192, 201, 226, 228-29, 231, 235, 247 254, 256, 264-65, 275, 278, 282, 284, 288, 299, 301, 314, 322, 324, 328, 332, 337, 339, 343, 350-51, 364, 368-69, 376-77, 383, 393
Lady Cynthia, S.S. 15-16, 49, 53, 58, 66, 85, 88-89, 93, 95-99, 129, 137, 139, 143, 153-54, 156-57, 160, 170, 182, 192, 196, 203, 214, 219, 220-21, 228-29, 231, 242, 247, 249, 260, 264, 266, 278-82, 288, 299, 301, 316, 321, 324-25, 327, 334, 337, 346, 364, 371, 376-77, 383, 387, 393, 395, 397, 403-04, 406
Lady Evelyn, S.S. 47, 52-54, 58, 158, 192, 231, 264, 297, 322, 357
Lady Pam, S.S. 1, 39-45, 53, 151, 156-57, 181, 205, 208, 216, 221, 228, 231, 235, 239, 245, 255, 264, 266, 300, 324, 326-27, 329, 333-34, 336, 338, 342, 347, 348, 358, 376-77, 383, 394, 406,
Lady Rose, M.V. 1, 53, 62, 100-01, 103-05, 114, 148, 175, 182, 184-85, 197, 201, 205, 231-32, 253, 258, 309, 312, 316, 324, 334-35, 343, 368, 394, 404, 406
Lady Sylvia, M.V. 1, 53, 100-03, 197
Lake Manitoba 262
La Pointe 143
Leaside K432, HMCS 118-19, 297
Lido, S.S. 108-09
Loch Dunvegan, HMS 259
Lonsdale, S.S. 160

Malaspina 381
Malibu Princess 56, 148, 156, 280, 405
Manitou Park, S.S. 282
Maple Wood 383
Maquinna 346
Marine Express, S.S. 263
Mastodon 28
Motor Princess 148
Mount Eagle (Empress) 254
Mount Royal 254
Mounteagle (CPR) 357

Native Queen 215
New Mexico 263

Nootka 325
Noronic, S.S. 358
North Sea 191
Northern Express 232
Northern Princess 268
Northolm S.S. 383
Nymph 162

Observer, S.S. 318
Ocean Venus, S.S. 237
Orantas 222
Orteric 159

Pacific Wind 251
Polar Star 246
Prince Albert, S.S. 110
Prince Charles, S.S. 107-108, 111, 231, 256, 318, 387
Prince George, S.S. 185, 206
Prince George II, S.S. 220
Prince John, S.S. 108, 110-11, 182, 256, 258, 318, 344, 387
Prince Robert, S.S. 318
Prince Rupert, S.S. 58-59, 187, 189, 194-95, 219, 221, 224-, 255, 262, 312, 316-19, 322, 339
Princess Adelaide, S.S. 130
Princess Alice, S.S. 130
Princess Beatrice, S.S. 11, 34, 59, 188, 237, 262
Princess Charlotte, S.S. 28, 130, 187
Princess Elaine, S.S. 43, 91, 158, 300
Princess Elizabeth, S.S. 65, 173, 239, 282
Princess Joan, S.S. 60, 188
Princess Louise, S.S. 76, 394
Princess Louise II, S.S. 76, 77
Princess Marguerite, S.S. 75, 96
Princess May, S.S. 10
Princess Norah, S.S. 128, 185
Provider 383
P.W. 61

Queen, S.S. 34
Queen of Esquimalt, M.V. 194
Queen of Coquitlam, M.V. 397
Queen of Nanaimo, M.V. 386
Queen of New Westminster M.V. 407
Queen of Prince Rupert, M.V. 203, 228
Queen of Vancouver, M.V. 237

Rachel, S.S. 238
Rainbow, HMCS 141, 287
Ramona 142
Ravalli, S.S. 34, 154, 234

RCMP Patrol Boat #10 407
Redonda 282

Salvage Chieftain 29
Salvage King 82
Salvage Princess 59
Salvage Queen 90, 158
Salvor, S.S. 7, 64
Sandgate Castle, HMS 123
Sandpiper 233
Santa Cecilia, S.S. 37-38, 239
Santa Maria, S.S. 1, 39-42, 239, 255, 333, 336
Sea Lion 318
Selkirk Park 196
Selma, S.S. 37-38, 42, 46-47, 323, 333
Senator, S.S. 154
Seymour Princess 148
Smokwa 282
Snowbird II 197
Southholm, S.S. 171
Sparrowhawk, HMS 79
St. Margaret, S.S. 107
St. Thomas, HMCS 123

Standard Service M.V. 232
Stella Maris 130-31, 286, 359, 360
Storis 260
Swinton, HMS 88

Tacoma Star 217
Tahsis, S.S. 196
Tartar 262
Teal, U.S.S. 161
Teco 148, 381
Thomas Crosby 232
Thorfin 383
Titanic 356
Transfer 142
Tsawwassen, M.V. 148

Umbria, S.S. 187
Unacana 156, 232
U 484 127
U 877 123

Vadso, S.S. 33, 234, 281
Venture, S.S. 4, 11, 32-35, 58-59, 63, 85, 90, 113, 117, 137-38, 143, 152-54, 156-57, 170, 183, 187, 190, 197-98, 202, 204, 215, 218, 220, 223-24, 228, 231, 234-38, 243, 249-50, 252, 269, 275, 281, 284, 288, 290, 294, 297, 299, 310, 312, 318, 322, 335, 337, 347, 350, 355, 381-83, 385, 388, 394-95, 397, 400, 403, 405-06, 410-11, 417

Wakena, S.S. 34
Walmer Castle, HMS 118
Washington 47
Westar 360
West Vancouver Ferry No. 6 266, 404, 406
White Boats 2, 85, 113-117, 120
William J. Stewart 260
Witch, HMS 259

Yukon Star 122, 126, 212, 258, 282, 286

INDEX of PERSONNEL

Allan, John 77, 376
Allen, Doug 412
Andriani, Frank 386
Annan, Tom 302
Arthur, Clarence 275
Ashmore, Robert 137
Aspinall, Alfred 139, 271
Attewell, Albert 355, 371
Audley, Harry 356
Auger, George 415
Aylward, William 378

Barnett, John 91
Beattie, Andrew 276
Beck, Stan 412
Benson, Michael 309
Bergstrom, (?) 349
Best, Daulfred 379
Biles, Harry 141
Billingsley, Jim 349
Boden, Jack Jr. 380
Boden, Jack Sr. 142
Bone, Bill 412
Braddick, Harry J. 349
Bridsen, Dick 381
Browne, John H. Sr. 9, 145
Browne, John R. 147
Bruce, Jim 372

Calderwood, James McMillan 148

Campbell, Donald P. 149
Campbell, Neil 149, 190
Chadwick, C.T. 302
Charters, David 349
Charters, Tom 150, 414
Chong, Dong 349
Coates, E. Darrel 350
Coldwell, Gordon 311
Cooper, George 386
Corneille, F.E. 152
Craigen, George 277
Crompton, Harold N. 311

Dawe, Sandy 234
Delany, Bill 372
Dick, Thomas M. 302
Dickson, Alfred E. 154
Dougan, Terry 364
Douglas, J. 302
Draper, Len 412
Duncan, Alex 368
Dutka, Henry 313

Ebden, Bert 356
Ellis, Bill 364
Ericksen, Gus 381
Estey, Bill 376

Farina, Dennis Patrick 155, 380
Farina, Patrick 271, 278, 370
Farley, Walter 195

Findlay, James 159
Finlayson, Ron 316
Fletcher, Alex 303
Foote, Gerald 317
Fordyce, George 350
Foster, George H. 280
Freisen, Jack 268
Fries, Dick 415

Gaisford, George 162
Galbraith, James 164
Gardiner, William 370
Georgeson, Edward 165
Gerbrandt, George 382
Gibson, Earnie 383
Gilbert, F.W. 168
Godfrey, Lorne A. 169, 249
Gore, Les 402
Gray, Neil 170
Green, Stanley 171
Guy, Charles 350

Hackett, Joseph Kennidy 174
Hageman, Norm 413
Halcrow, John J. 175
Hale, J.S. 319
Hamer, Charles A. 176
Hannigan, M.J. 180
Hartford, Harold 350
Hatchen, Tom 233
Hayman, V.D. 182

Index of Personnel

Hildich, Paddy 385
Hireen, Bill 385, 415
Hogan, John 281
Holdgate, C.W. 365
Holdgate, Clarence T. 134, 357
Horne, John 183, 417
Hosken, Geoffrey 185
Hughes, H.A. 350
Humphreys, Harold 359, 371
Hunter, James 186
Hunter, Stan 350
Husband, Gus 413

Ives, Harry 321

Jamison, Don 415
Jefferson, Lancelot James Foss 282
Johnstone, Andrew 187, 234
Jones, Davie 386
Jones, Gerry 323
Jones, Gib 387
Jones, Ivor 388
Jones, Percy 390, 413

Keen, Harry 370
Kelly, Harvey 268
Kelly, Joe 324
Kennett, Fred 413
Kennett, Ted 414
King, Leonard, C. 190
Knight, Alfred 361
Krischuk, Nick 393

Lamacraft, Harry Lionel 190
Lanches, C. 370
Lannard, H.B. 351
Lawrence, Frank 326
Lawrey, Howard E. 191
Lawson, Bill 414
Lawson, Ray 414
Lewis, Charles 193, 195
Logan, Robert 87, 303
Lucas, Michael 351, 352
Lucas, Thomas M. 134, 194

MacLeod, Rod 395
Malcolmson, John L. 215, 370
Marette, Billy Jan 217
Martinson, John 395
Matheson, Frederick 126, 288
McAskill, J.A. 196
McBeath, Robert P. 197
McCombe, William Jr. 202
McCombe, William Sr. 199
McCormick, Clarence 283, 302
McCue, Philip 327
McEwan, David 372
McEwan, William H. 363
McGuiness, "Dinty" 350
McGuiness, "Springline" 393

McIntosh, Dave 268
McKillop, James 203
McKinnon, Angus 269
McLean, Henry Edward 204, 302
McLean, Robert 394
McLelland, Davie 286
McLennan, A. Jr. 211, 239, 415
McLennan, A.C. Sr. 208
McLeod, Don 213, 261, 329
McLeod, Jack 268
McLeod, John M. 207
McLeod, John "Scotty" 386
McNeill, Angus 212
McPhillips, Wilfred 367
Mercer, Alex 417
Mercer, John 218
Miller, George 271
Miller, James 396
Morrison, John Iain 219
Mounce, William W. 221
Mowat, Doug 45
Muir, John 221
Muirhead, Jack 397
Naughty, Ed 230
Naughty, R.T. Sr. 228
Naughty, Robert Jr. 230-31, 249
Nelson, Don 340
Nelson, Nels 397
New, Oswald J. 303
Newman, Al 351
Newman, Henry 371
Nicholson, Danny 412
Nicholson, William 233
Noel, James E. 234

O'Donnell, Jimmy 398
Obrecht, Chick 376
Owen-Jones, G. Bertram K. 235, 248

Park, Colin 372, 399
Park, John 234, 236
Parker, Fred 238
Pattison, J. 178
Pattison, Norman G. 305, 331
Patton, P.M. 415
Plant, Ernie 59, 400

Rennie, Gilbert 351
Read, George R.J. 332
Reid, Alex 403
Richer, Bill 371
Rinder, Don 414
Roach, Edward 404
Roach, Harry 238, 248, 382
Robinson, Amos W. 333
Robinson, Miles 242
Scanlon, Paddy 269
Scott, Bill 405

Scott, Ned 300
Scotter, Edwin L. 363
Shaw, Denis 334
Sheppard, Ernest M. 243
Sinclair, Andrew 234
Skinner, Cecil G. 368
Skinner, Frank Jess 337
Skinner, Walter 368
Smales, W.S. 101
Smith, Ben 117, 289
Smith, C.B. 71
Smith, Fred Edward 134, 292
Smith, Joe 405
Smith, John A. 406, 415
Smith, Les 339, 352
Smith, Robert 219, 247
Spring, C. 302
Stewart, James 248
Stover, Reginald C. 134, 340, 352
Strachan, Charlie 414
Strang, Alan 248
Suffield, Eric W. 249, 250
Suffield, Neil 373, 415
Summerfield, J.E. 248, 253

Thompson, Don 300
Thompson, Lorrie 415
Townsend, Ralph 369
Tozer, Allan Hugh 134, 351, 352
Tracy, Steve 341
Tripp, Jack 370
Turner, Jack 410
Tweedie, Napier 300, 301, 303
Twigg, A.M. 342, 352, 402, 419

Vince, Gordon 298
Vincent, Carl 416

Walker, Johnny 416
Walker, R.W. 346
Walsh, A.E. 254
Waters, Robert 346
Watson, Jimmy 411
Watt, James W. 256
Westegard, Johnny 364
Whitehurst, George 269
Whitelaw, Robert 299
Whiteman, Bill 304
Williams, Clarence 351
Williams, J.W. 257
Williamson, Robert T. 258
Wills, Ralph 259
Wilson, Angus 269
Wilson, Robert 260
Wood, Norrie 347

Yates, W.L. 262, 375
Young, Fred 372

Issue No. 112   VANCOUVER, BRITISH COLUMBIA

SUMMER SCHEDULE
EFFECTIVE FRIDAY, JUNE 25, 1943
UNTIL FURTHER NOTICE

★ SAILING GUIDE ★
TO PORTS OF CALL

Regular Passenger and Freight Service to all Northern B. C. Ports from Vancouver to the Border of Alaska and Queen Charlotte Islands, linking the Coast Communities of British Columbia

●

Information, Reservations and Tickets:

UNION PIER, foot Carrall St., Phone PAcific 3411
CITY TICKET OFFICE, 793 Granville St., Phone MArine 5438
Night calls: Baggage Room and Wharf, PAcific 4608
VANCOUVER, BRITISH COLUMBIA.

●

Victoria Agency: 1 Belmont House, Phone Garden 7822
Prince Rupert Agency: Third Ave., Phone 568

●

Carl Halterman — — — — — — — — Managing Director
G. A. Rushton — — — — — — — — Traffic Manager

PRINTED IN CANADA

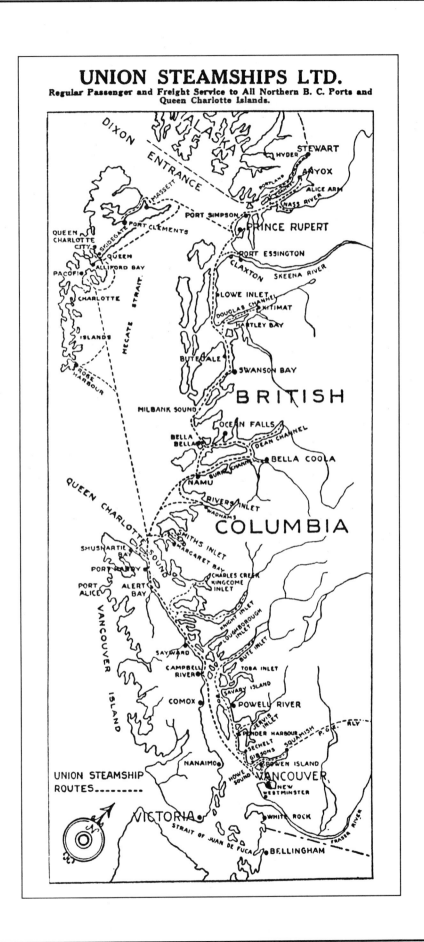

S.S. *Coquitlam* at Morgan's Camp, Queen Charlotte Islands
(William Nicholson)